Strategy for Personal Finance

LARRY R. LANG University of Wisconsin, Oshkosh

FOURTH EDITION

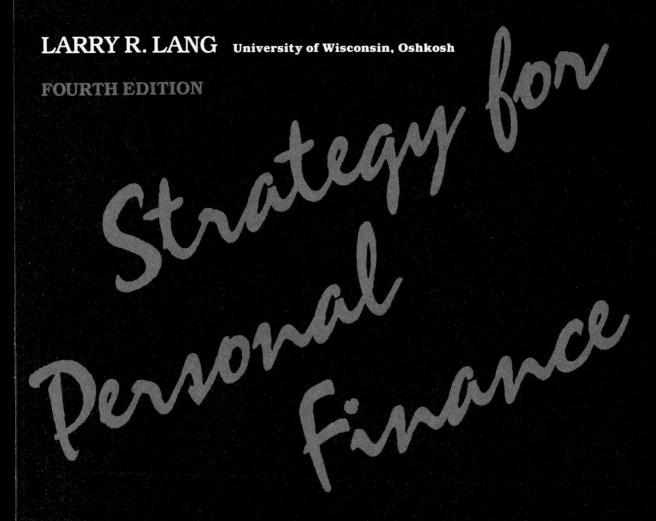

Strategy for Personal Finance

McGRAW-HILL BOOK COMPANY
New York ▪ St. Louis ▪ San Francisco ▪ Auckland ▪ Bogotá ▪ Caracas ▪
Colorado Springs ▪ Hamburg ▪ Lisbon ▪ London ▪ Madrid ▪ Mexico ▪
Milan ▪ Montreal ▪ New Delhi ▪ Oklahoma City ▪ Panama ▪ Paris ▪
San Juan ▪ São Paulo ▪ Singapore ▪ Sydney ▪ Tokyo ▪ Toronto

To **PAMELA, CATHERINA, and LAURENCE**

ABOUT THE AUTHOR

Larry R. Lang is a professor of finance at University of Wisconsin, Oshkosh. He received both his bachelor's degree and his Ph.D. from Michigan State University. Prior to his university teaching career, he was a practicing Certified Public Accountant in an accounting firm that took him throughout Michigan. This is the fourth textbook that he has written. He is currently active in research in the personal finance area. His work has been presented at professional meetings and has appeared in national publications. He has conducted numerous financial planning seminars in both the public and private sectors. Professor Lang is active in numerous professional associations. He lives with his wife and two children in Oshkosh, Wisconsin.

STRATEGY FOR PERSONAL FINANCE

1 2 3 4 5 6 7 8 9 0   DOCDOC   8 9 3 2 1 0 9 8

ISBN 0-07-036317-X

This book was set in ITC Bookman Light by University Graphics, Inc.
The editors were Scott D. Stratford and Larry Goldberg;
the designer was Gayle Jaeger;
the production supervisor was Leroy A. Young.
The drawings were done by J&R Services, Inc.
R. R. Donnelley & Sons Company was printer and binder.

The cartoons were drawn by Phil Frank.

Library of Congress Cataloging-in-Publication Data

Lang, Larry R.
  Strategy for personal finance.

  Includes index
  1. Finance, Personal.   I. Title.
HG179.L26   1988   332.024   87-29338
ISBN 0-07-036317-X

CONTENTS

To the student

Welcome to the study of personal financial planning; you have decided to pursue a rewarding, challenging, and exciting discipline. The principal objective throughout *Strategy for Personal Finance* is to prepare you to be a lifelong personal finance manager.

Each of the book's 19 chapters is specifically tailored to develop and improve your skills as a financial decision maker. Once you have developed and honed those skills, you will be in a much better position to achieve your personal financial goals.

Financial decision-making skills can help you get the greatest benefit from the money you have. Even top-notch planners find available funds are limited, however. Many people earning a six-digit salary still find they do not have enough money to meet their goals. But money management skills, intelligently applied, can help you make each dollar work harder.

Your financial planning skills can also help you avoid the major pitfalls and abuses that challenge consumers. Your study can benefit you in a very measurable dollar-and-cents way throughout your career. You will learn how to develop an insurance plan to safeguard your financial resources and income, for example. Throughout *Strategy for Personal Finance*, we develop decision models that identify the costs and benefits of each financial product or service alternative. The book also examines the qualitative considerations that go along with the dollars and cents of decisions.

Both numerical examples and decision situations are used to illustrate the steps and processes of financial decision making.

During the writing of the text, new products and services continued to be introduced. That does not antiquate the models, guides, and suggestions we give. Though you may have to modify them to account for new developments, they will continue to be valid.

IT IS YOUR DECISION

The objective of the text is to help you develop the personal financial planning skills you need to meet your individual objectives, needs, and goals. The book doesn't offer a standard financial plan that says: Go do this and your personal finances will be well planned. People are so diverse, have so many different needs and circumstances, and have such unique aspirations that a single "super plan" will never work. Instead, you need to use the various financial decisions models to tailor a financial plan for your unique goals, needs, and available resources.

PRACTICING YOUR DECISION-MAKING SKILLS

Developing and improving your financial decision-making skills can best be done by practicing. The numerical examples and sample decision situations used in *Strategy for Personal Finance* give you an opportunity to apply what you have learned. Each chapter contains extensive examples which show how to analyze the costs and benefits associated with different financial products and services. When the example is less involved, the steps are illustrated through one, or two, annotated equations; for more involved, lengthy examples, the associated costs and benefits are developed in a detailed worksheet. Both are integrated into the chapter material, along with a discussion of related points and issues.

You can also practice your new skills on the questions, problems, and case studies that are at the end of each chapter. These exercises will test your understanding and retention of needed concepts. Case studies create situations that call on your analytical and reasoning skills for solutions.

SPECIAL FEATURES OF THIS BOOK

You should find the following features of the book highly useful in your study of personal finance:

First

The chapters cover a broad range of personal finance topics. An informed financial planner understands a wide array of financial topics, ranging from those which require almost daily decisions (individual dollar amounts may be small—they add up to a significant total) to those which are rarely encountered (the dollar amount is large, so the consequences of a poor choice can be *very* costly).

Second

Each chapter opens with a list of the important concepts for that chapter. Read them to get a general guide before you begin the chapter.

Third

Descriptive information has been limited to what is needed to provide you with background in each area.

Fourth

Each chapter provides extensive numerical examples to illustrate the decision model and compares the respective costs and benefits. Actual computations are illustrated through equations and worksheets. You should take time to review these so you thoroughly understand each concept.

Fifth

Whenever a new term or concept is first introduced, it is explained and set off in **boldface** type. Those ideas are listed at the end of the chapter as key terms; use the list to test whether you have mastered the chapter's major points.

Sixth

Practice helps you develop and refine your money management skills. The discussion questions, problems, and case study at the end of each chapter will strengthen your understanding of the chapter's qualitative and quantitative financial concepts.

Seventh

A detailed student workbook accompanies the text to provide further opportunities for practicing money management skills. It includes a crossword puzzle, discussion questions, problems, and a series of sample test questions for each chapter. Many of the problems have a computer-assisted component so you can broaden your skills by using that important tool. A Lotus 1-2-3 template containing useful personal financial planning material is available through your instructor. It is provided to your instructor through McGraw-Hill Book Company. Selected solutions are provided at the end of the workbook to confirm your progress.

START YOUR MONEY MANAGE-MENT CAREER NOW

Now is a good time to begin your money management training. The financial and personal rewards that come from being an astute manager have never been bigger. You face new challenges as the personal finance field continues to evolve and as new products and services are introduced or existing ones are revised.

Expend a reasonable effort and you can develop the skills a good personal finance manager needs. Of course, you need the motivation to begin your money management career. But the very fact you have enrolled in this course suggests you already have that. All that remains is for you to turn to page 1, Part 1 and begin. You will find personal finance to be interesting, stimulating, and best of all, financially rewarding. Good luck on your management career.

Larry R. Lang

To the instructor

Since the third edition of *Strategy for Personal Finance* was published four years ago, the elements of personal finance planning have changed significantly.

The Tax Reform Act of 1986 made revolutionary changes in the tax rules and regulations for individuals. Tax considerations now play a smaller role in many personal financial decisions; choices made primarily for their tax avoidance features are less prevalent. The not-so-good news is that options and choices that seemed prudent under the previous tax rules have to be carefully reevaluated. For example, use of certain types of credit takes on a new aspect as the deductibility of finance charges is phased out. Tax preparation and planning are now very different from what they were under the old tax law.

The experience of the past several years seems to confirm that the double-digit inflation rates of the past are indeed that: past. Inflation, too, plays a smaller role and is less likely to drive financial decisions. For many, purchasing a house returns to its traditional role: a shelter decision.

As inflation has abated, financial assets have returned to their more traditional role. Individuals seem more willing to consider a much wider array of investment options. The rapid growth in mutual funds attests to the fact that traditional savings accounts, CDs, and individual common stocks are not necessarily the principal choice of many consumers. Mutual funds have ranged into new areas, with some concentrating on specialized investment vehicles. Where investment choices were once limited, now there are almost too many opportunities available. Careful analysis and selection have become more demanding yet more essential.

Now that we have had some experience with deregulation, we can better judge how traditional depository financial institutions will be operating in the future. In some cases, deregulation appears to have encouraged them to offer a wider range of service and investment options. While that has expanded consumer choices, it makes a careful analysis of the competing alternatives even more important. As institutions expand to a regional scale (and a national scale seems likely), consumers will face even more choices.

This is hardly a complete list of the changes we have seen in the last four years. Rather, it provides a perspective on just how sweeping change has been. Managing one's personal finances, always a challenge, is now an even greater challenge. A new edition of *Strategy for Personal Finance* was essential so these developments could be incorporated.

LIFELONG FINANCIAL MANAGEMENT

The fourth edition of *Strategy for Personal Finance* continues our objective of preparing students to be lifelong personal finance managers. As the range of alternatives expands, good management becomes increasingly important. A three-step approach to presenting financial concepts is used:

Discuss why a particular finance topic is important to a student.

Show the student how to develop a financial decision model that considers both the costs and benefits associated with choosing a particular financial product or service.

Show students how they can use the decision model they develop to help them make sound personal financial decisions.

In this new edition, financial decision models were developed to assess recently introduced financial products and services. The extensive discussion questions, problems, and case studies of the previous editions have been completely updated. As before, they provide students the opportunity to practice their financial management skills.

CHANGES IN THE FOURTH EDITION

1   The economic data in each chapter have been updated to reflect current conditions in the area of financial products and services.

2   The material on compound rates of return has been moved from Chapter 1 to Chapter 14. The future value interest tables for lump-sum deposits and equal annual deposits have been expanded and now appear as Appendix A.3 and Appendix A.4 at the end of the text.

3   The material on developing short- and long-term financial goals has been moved to the opening sections of Chapter 3. This allows financial goals to be fully integrated into the personal budgeting material presented in the second half of the chapter. Throughout the book, reference is made to Chapter 3 to show the planning role a personal budget has in a financial plan.

4   The material on federal income taxes (Chapter 5) is completely revised to reflect changes resulting from the Tax Reform Act of 1986. Changes are current through mid-1987.

5   Coverage of second mortgages and home equity loans (Chapter 7) is expanded. The continued tax deductibility of the interest on these loans is likely to make them highly popular.

6   The coverage of automobile and appliance purchases has been merged into a single chapter: Chapter 8. Careful editing of descriptive material has shortened the coverage significantly, yet all the material on selection and purchase has been retained.

7   Social Security is no longer covered in a separate chapter. Instead, the topic first appears in Chapter 10, the introductory chapter in the section on insurance. Material on survivor benefits is now fully integrated into the life insurance chapter. Likewise, disability benefits are now part of the section on planning of disability insurance coverage. Last, material on Social Security retirement benefits is included in Chapter 18: Planning Your Retirement Years. Estimating individual survivor, disability, or retirement benefits is greatly simplified through the inclusion of a benefit table in Appendix A.2.

8   Coverage of health maintenance organizations as an alternative to traditional third-party health insurance programs is expanded. Included are guidelines for selecting a suitable HMO.

9   The presentation on risk in the introductory investments chapter (Chapter 14) has been revised to improve the students' comprehension. An expanded discussion of the risk-return trade-off highlights the direct relationship between the two.

10 In Chapter 15—on fixed return investments—the coverage of corporate bonds and municipal notes and bonds has been expanded. People are not likely to purchase individual notes and bonds in large numbers, but they well may consider a mutual fund that invests in such vehicles.

11 To reflect the rapid growth in mutual funds and other professionally managed investments, Chapter 17 is completely revised. New topics include unit investment trusts, limited partnerships, and annuities. The discussion of the latter topic includes a careful review of the claimed tax advantage of this investment vehicle.

12 Chapter 18 on retirement planning has expanded coverage of employer-provided pension plans and detailed coverage of the new limits on individual retirement funding options: IRA, Keogh, and 403(b) and 401(k) plans.

13 The material on estate planning is now separate as Chapter 19: Planning the Transfer of Your Estate. It includes detailed coverage of federal estate taxes. Like the section on income taxes, it stresses the general structure and intent of estate taxes, replete with several diagrams. Numerical examples are included to illustrate the various computations.

14 A Lotus 1-2-3 template is available to you at no cost for use by students. It assists them in developing personal financial information. Many items involving the use of the template can be found in the student workbook that accompanies the text. You may make unlimited copies of the template for your students. To get a copy of the template, contact your McGraw-Hill representative.

PEDAGOGICAL FEATURES

Suitable Courses

This book is designed for use in:

1 Undergraduate personal finance courses at both 4-year and 2-year colleges and universities.

2 Introductory courses in personal financial planning for students who may then take more advanced courses in the personal finance area.

3 Undergraduate consumer economics courses at 2-year and 4-year colleges and universities.

4 Family management courses at 2-year and 4-year colleges and universities.

5 Personal finance courses offered as part of continuing education or adult education programs.

Overall Organization

The 19 chapters are arranged in five major sections. The first section provides background and basic introductory materials to prepare and equip students for their role as lifelong financial decision makers. The second section discusses the key points in managing their income. The third analyzes the benefits and costs of large consumer purchases. Insurance coverage is the central thrust of the fourth section. The fifth discusses building for the future; it includes coverage of currently available investment alternatives. *Strategy for Personal Finance* closes with chapters on retirement planning and estate planning.

Completing the Chapters

While the material has been organized in what we consider a logical sequence, the chapter order can be rearranged to suit a particular instructor's preference. Each chapter is self-contained, so one can generally cover most chapters out of sequence. This also means an instructor can drop one or more chapters, if desired. Instructors who want to emphasize a particular topic or topics will find the book is flexible; time spent emphasizing particular topics in more detail can be recovered by eliminating others, if needed.

Given the broad topical coverage and the extensive end-of-chapter materials, the text should provide sufficient material to fill the available time in single-semester or one-quarter courses.

Organization of Individual Chapters

Each time a new term or concept is introduced in a chapter, it is immediately explained; the term is shown in **boldface** type. Each chapter uses numerical examples extensively to illustrate benefits and costs for different options. When the example is simple, an equation summarizes the computation. On longer, more involved examples, the steps and computations are summarized in a worksheet. In addition, charts, graphs, tables, and cartoons are used throughout the text to illustrate important points and issues. Previous editions have convinced us that good visual displays improve the readability and teachability of the material.

MATERIALS IN EACH CHAPTER

Learning Objectives and Chapter Summaries

Each chapter begins with a short list that outlines the major points the student should learn from that chapter. At the end of the chapter, a summary in outline form reemphasizes the chapter's major points. There is also a list of key words and phrases that were introduced in the chapter.

End-of-Chapter Materials

The fourth edition continues and expands on the extensive end-of-chapter materials introduced with previous editions. Typically, 10 to 20 discussion questions cover the major qualitative points from the chapter. Next, 5 to 8 problems review the major quantitative concepts. Last, a case study provides students with a simulated situation where they can analyze a more complex set of data and develop a solution.

Student Workbook

The student workbook that accompanies *Strategy for Personal Finance* has been extensively revised. New to the workbook is a computer-assisted component that provides several benefits. It minimizes the drudgery of computations and should help reduce possible errors. Because a whole series of computations can be done so rapidly, computer assistance provides the capability to compare competing options by creating several "what if" scenarios. Last, it allows the use of reasonably complex worksheets within the limited class time that is available.

Specific features of the workbook include:

- A larger format so the majority of work can be done in the workbook.
- A crossword based on each chapter's key words and phrases.
- Discussion questions that review a chapter's qualitative points and issues.
- Problems of varying difficulty. Some are intended to be worked by hand, while others rely on the computer-assisted component.
- Test items, both multiple choice and true-false, that are similar to the ones in the test bank.
- Solutions to the crossword puzzles, selected problems, and all sample test items.
- New in this edition is material that shows students how to use the Lotus 1-2-3 template (provided to you for duplication by McGraw-Hill) in personal financial planning. Contact your McGraw-Hill representative for a copy of the disk.

Since materials in the workbook are different from those in the text, the workbook can either supplement items from the text or substitute for them.

The revised workbook can help students with their understanding of the personal finance area. The workbook's self-correcting sections make it suitable for a number of different classroom situations. The amount of class time spent on the workbook can be readily tailored to the time available.

ACKNOWL-EDGMENTS

Many people have participated in the preparation of the fourth edition of *Strategy for Personal Finance.* We would like to express our appreciation to the following reviewers of the manuscript: John Berrigan, Nathaniel Hawthorne College; P. R. Chanoy, North Texas State University; Jerry deFoor, Stanford University; Brenda Hall, Weber State College; Yong H. Kim, University of Cincinnati; Catherine King, Campbell College; Fred J. Kittrell, Middle Tennessee State University; Ross Lowe, Western Illinois University; Jerry Mason, Brigham Young University; Mary Mennis, University of Wisconsin, Madison; David Milton, Bentley College; Lillian Mohr, Florida State University; Richard Peters, Ohlone College; Fred Powers, University of South Florida; Charlotte Cannon Rhines, Essex Community College; Patricia A. Smythe, Wichita State University; Nancy Spillman, Los Angeles Trade-Technical College; Donald E. Sorenson, University of Wisconsin—Whitewater; and Frank Tansey, Baruch College-CUNY.

I would like to thank Larry Goldberg, Senior Editing Supervisor, for the essential services that helped transform a draft to a completed book. Thanks to Tom Herzing for his excellent work on all aspects of the manuscript. Thanks also to our excellent cartoonist, Phil Frank. Reviewing Phil's sketches was positively enjoyable. I also very much appreciated the support and assistance of all the individuals at McGraw-Hill who worked on this book.

Larry R. Lang

Introduction

PART

1

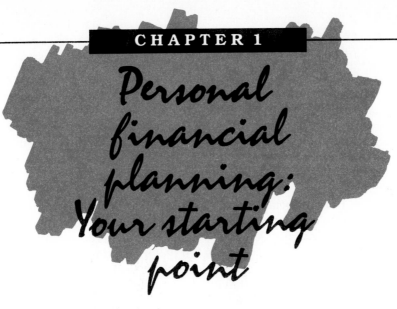

Personal financial planning: Your starting point

AFTER COMPLETING THIS CHAPTER YOU WILL HAVE LEARNED

- The importance of personal financial planning
- How to overcome the hurdles that prevent people from planning their personal finances
- The objectives you can reach through financial planning
- The five stages in developing a personal financial plan
- The relative importance of financial planning areas at different stages of your life
- How income taxes affect your financial plan
- The impact of inflation on the parts of a financial plan
- How cycles of the economy affect a financial plan
- How national markets for financial products and services can affect your financial plan
- Why Social Security benefits need to be built into a financial plan
- How you can help yourself develop a financial plan
- How a specialist can assist you on specific points of your financial plan
- The distinction between commission financial planners and fee planners
- The areas where a personal computer can assist your financial planning

Despite articles, radio and television programs, seminars, and publicity put out by people wanting to be financial advisors, few people spend much time on their personal financial planning. Still, people sense they need to plan. "One of these days I have to get organized," "Boy, I need to control my credit card spending," and "My finances need some work" are common feelings. Others think their finances will "fall into place." How that is to happen is not clear. Often planning is a necessity people neglect.

But financial planning always has been important. Why the recent push? For most of us, income levels have risen, so we have more discretionary income. Deregulation of the financial marketplace has heightened competition for our investment dollars, so we find more financial products and services from which to choose. Look beyond the National Bank of Pigeon Falls (population 338), and we find an increasingly national market for our money. New products are aimed at our special needs. It's harder to choose what to buy, but a good choice is more rewarding.

TAKING CHARGE OF YOUR FINANCES

Of course, you could do without a plan, but that is no more than gambling. You are not in control. Your money ends up wasted or poorly spent. Your decisions become a series of crises. The choice you make today makes tomorrow's harder. Mistakes are repeated.

Will planning "cure" all financial ills? Sorry, but no. Income may still be scarce, decisions complex, changes frequent, choices hard. But developing a financial plan puts you in control of your finances rather than the reverse.

So why do people avoid financial planning? Usually they are scared off by the hurdles they think face them.

Hurdle 1: Background and Training

Many people have not had instruction in personal finance; they feel inadequate to do financial planning. Instead of gaining the skills they need, they rely on tips, fads, or a friend's advice as the basis of their financial plan. Others are impulsive; after a flurry of hasty decisions, they do nothing more. Still others dismiss that "financial stuff" as too complex. This text's goal is to make you a systematic planner who considers options and looks for alternatives. Your intelligence and motivation have let you master much; personal financial management will join your list.

Hurdle 2: Only People with Money Need to Plan

Some believe financial planning is only for people with a million in assets or a six-digit income. But behold Alice Average's potential at college graduation. If her $20,000 starting salary grows modestly each year, she will manage more than a quarter million dollars over the next 10 years, a nice six-digit amount. Over 35 years she will manage $1.5 to $2 million, a nice seven-digit amount. A couple with two incomes could double those amounts. Successful management of your income, no matter what size, increases the likelihood you will achieve your goals and aspirations.

Dismiss the idea that "high" income makes financial planning easy because you have so much income. People who make $20,000 say income is scarce. So do those making $40,000, even $80,000. Claims on your income seem to grow as quickly as income does. Frankly, personal financial planning is a challenge at any income. Postponing financial planning until you have a high income or make a bundle on investments is senseless.

Hurdle 3: Getting Started

Lots of us fall victim to the "When I . . ." excuse. We promise to get serious about financial planning at some mythical point—"When I get that raise," "When I make $50,000 a year," "When my assets reach $100,000." There are numerous aids to help you start now. Articles in *Money, Changing Times, Consumer Reports,* newspapers, and planning newsletters can help. Likewise, there are professionals—accountants, attorneys, insurance representatives—who can answer your technical questions. Tools like the personal computer can assist in your financial planning. Right now is the time to begin your money management career.

OBJECTIVES OF PERSONAL FINANCIAL PLANNING

Let's look at some objectives of financial planning. You may not agree with all of the list. Since your goals and hopes are different from mine, your personal objectives will differ, as will your opinion about which objectives are most important.

Planned Spending and Acquisitions

Planning encourages a systematic, considered approach to spending your income. It lets you allocate that income for expenses and for acquiring assets—the things you own—in advance. When you purchase a major item such as a car, a house, a bank certificate of deposit, or a mutual fund, sound planning lets you consider options, timing, the strengths and weaknesses of a decision. A financial plan lets you "buy" an item rather than be "sold" it. It puts you in control of your finances.

Establish and Implement Your Financial Goals

Planning encourages you to develop financial goals that spell out what you want to achieve and when. It also demands that you develop a strategy for getting to your goals. Long-term financial goals cover the next 15 to 25 years. Short-term goals are those you want to reach in the next 5 years. Both should be part of your financial plan. Building a plan lets you judge what goals are attainable. Once you have set goals, planning can help you reach them.

Financial Peace of Mind

Financial planning allows you the peace of knowing your financial status. It demands you summarize your current financial position. It presses you to find actions to achieve your goals and objectives. Because you have developed the plan, you will know where the flexibility is if change is needed. As the decision maker, you can single out your best options.

Achieving Your Desired Life-Style

What you consider your "ideal" life-style will affect your financial plan. Consumption is high on some people's lists. Others concentrate on accumulating wealth. Still others try to balance the two. Whatever your ideal, financial planning can help achieve it. By revealing your options, a plan can help you decide:

- What you can do
- When you can do it
- What trade-offs must be made

Protecting You and Your Assets

Financial planning encourages you to select the insurance you need to protect yourself and your assets. As you will see, you can "retain" the risk of some losses—by agreeing to pay the first $200 of collision damage on an auto, for example. The prospect of big losses, however, means you must pay some insurance premiums in return for the assurance that your losses will be paid. Reasonable insurance coverage is crucial, but too much wastes premium dollars. A good plan can help you decide what you need and what a fair price is.

Financial Independence

Contrary to what you might imagine, a person who plans may spend less time on financial matters than someone who does no planning. People with no plan often find one financial crisis follows another. Financial planning does not eliminate surprises or adverse developments, but it lets you deal with them better because you know the options you have. This makes managing your personal finances less stressful. It can also be fun.

THE FIVE STAGES OF FINANCIAL PLANNING

Financial planning involves developing a systematic strategy to reach your goals and objectives. A good financial plan requires that you:

1. Determine your current resources and expected income
2. Develop your short- and long-term goals and objectives
3. Design a plan that outlines specific steps to achieve your goals and objectives
4. Make spending and investment decisions based on your needs and the merits of each action
5. Assess progress on your plan and decide what corrective action may be needed

Exhibit 1.1 summarizes the five stages of the **financial planning process.** The process of building a house provides an analogy for these five steps.

Stage 1: Analyze Present Resources and Income

You would not attempt to build a house without examining the proposed underpinnings. *Hoping* the site is not in a swamp or over a seismic fault is not a prudent, reasoned approach. Likewise, to start a financial plan, you need to know what income and resources you have to work with. That is your foundation.

Your present **financial assets** are one resource: savings accounts, shares of stock, certificates of deposit, and mutual fund shares are examples. Financial assets typically provide a return: interest, dividends, or increases in market price. When you need money, the assets can be sold.

Your expected future income is your second major resource. For those beginning their work career, it will likely be *the* resource for reaching desired goals and objectives.

Together, your present assets and projected income are the underpinnings of your financial plan.

Stage 2: Establish Your Financial Goals and Spending Objectives

The second stage in building a house is to decide what you are trying to do. Before addressing the details of construction, you need to decide on the building's design and features: its goals and objectives. Here you answer the question: What do I want to do with the resources I have? It will be impossible to decide whether your plan has worked unless you specify goals in advance. You also need reference points to measure your progress. They will show you whether corrective action is needed.

Developing your **financial goals** entails four steps: (1) Decide what you want to do; (2) decide when you want to do it; (3) estimate each goal's cost; (4) analyze whether you can attain your goals. Chapter 3 expands on these points.

Exhibit 1.1

Total Financial Planning Process

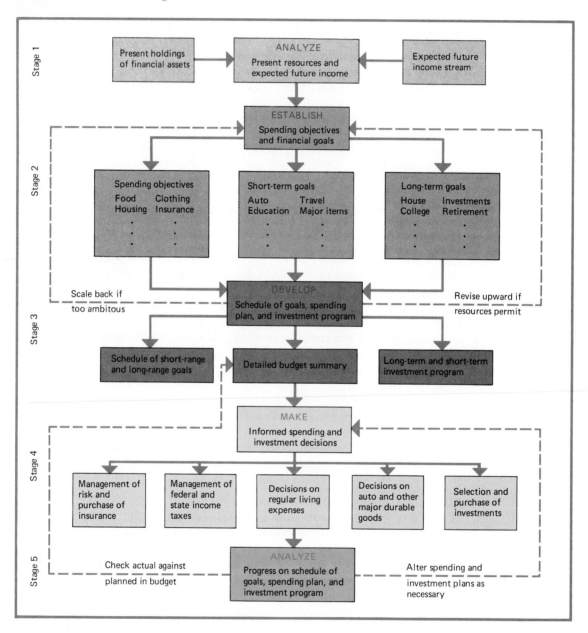

A financial goal generally requires a sizable amount of money. Frequently you will save money for months or years to have enough.

Most spending meets the recurring costs of daily living. You have little latitude on spending for taxes, basic housing, food, utility costs, medical care, and insurance. But with other expenses you have considerable discretion. Still, your ambitions affect spending levels. Backpacking Isle Royale will cost far less than a tour of four-star restaurants in Paris. Chapter 3's budgeting section discusses spending levels in detail.

Stage 3: Design a Plan to Achieve Your Goals and Objectives

Suppose your house plan were for a 5,000-square-foot English Tudor by the lake, with pool, tennis courts, putting green, gardens. Sounds nice. Now comes reality: convert that dream to dollars. In financial planning that means a detailed strategy for reaching your goals and objectives. An early question should be: Can I achieve what I say I want? Little point in having to live with the shell of a half-done house . . . or financial plan. If you compare your resources to what is needed, you can see whether your objectives are feasible and where the pitfalls lurk.

A **budget** is your primary planning document. It summarizes your available resources: the income you project for the planning period. Next, it estimates the costs of your financial goals and your planned expenditures. Resources are highlighted, as are your costs. A budget lets you see whether your plans are too ambitious, too conservative, or on target. Chapter 3 will discuss this important planning document in detail.

Stage 4: Make Informed Spending and Investment Decisions

Now it is time to fit together the pieces to complete the house. Good decisions mean the difference between finishing the house as intended or settling for less. Likewise, informed spending and investment decisions can help ensure the success of your financial plan. A good decision-maker can often increase the satisfaction obtained from an income. Cost control is as important in managing your personal finances as it is in running a business.

Informed spending decisions begin with understanding what you are buying. Betting your salary on the future price of black pepper might turn out to be lucrative, but you had better know the implications. Next, decide whether the purchase meets your needs. If there are competing options, analyze their merits and weaknesses. Buy your products and services rather than have someone sell them to you.

Stage 5: Analyze the Progress of Your Plan and Stand Ready to Take Corrective Action

Even with detailed house plans, changes happen along the way. Similarly, rare is the financial plan that can be set and then forgotten. A revision to the plan might be needed because there is a change in the marketplace, a tax regulation changes, an existing product or service is revised, or a new product is introduced. Changes in your circumstances may require the plan be modified. The original plan might prove overly optimistic or too conservative. All could mean a revision.

LIFE CYCLE OF PERSONAL FINANCIAL PLANNING AND MANAGEMENT

At certain points, your major financial concerns will change. Purchasing major personal assets, such as an auto, clothes for work, or furniture, might be important at one stage in your life. Five years later you may value leisure or travel more highly. Years later, saving for retirement may be your main concern. This series of shifting concerns is the **life cycle of financial planning.**

Exhibit 1.2 highlights the importance of various financial planning areas at different stages in life. The exhibit's left side summarizes the planning areas. Five stages of life are shown at the top, but note that the age range shown is at best "typical." Reggie who leaves the Friends of Love commune at age 30 to be Reginald Jones Smith III, a yuppie, certainly does not enter the "getting started" stage at age 23. He may experience all five stages but in condensed form. The relative importance of each financial concern is rated on a four-point scale. An A rating signifies a priority concern, a D, a low-ranking one.

Getting Started

The "getting started" stage usually is the start of your working career. Your salary is probably several times what you previously earned, but there are heavy demands made on it. Many of you will be purchasing major personal assets: autos, furniture, and recreational items. Developing good money management skills in this stage is important. They can help you stretch your resources to meet a lengthy list of needs. You will use those skills for many years. Finally, they can be used in later stages of your financial life.

Exhibit 1.2

Life Stages in Personal Financial Planning

	Stages of Life for Financial Planning with Typical Age				
Personal financial planning area	*Getting started* 23–32	*Building a foundation* 33–42	*Adding more pieces* 43–52	*Finish the pyramid* 53–62	*Beginning retirement* 62–on
Develop financial records	A	A	B	B	B
Establish financial goals	A	A	B	C	D
Plan through a budget	A	A	B	B	A
Acquire major personal assets	A	A	B	C	D
Develop an insurance plan	B	A	B	C	D
Manage your income taxes	B	B	A	A	C
Select and manage investments	C	C	B	A	A
Plan for your retirement	D	C	B	A	D
Plan your estate's transfer	D	C	C	B	A

Key to letter codes
A Very important
B Important
C Moderately important
D Limited importance

At this stage, investments will not be important because your discretionary income will be limited. Since it is far in the future, retirement planning will likely receive little consideration. For singles and couples with no dependents, transferring what is probably a limited estate will not be a high priority.

Building a Foundation

Your income is likely to increase considerably as you move into the second stage: building a foundation. But that income will still seem "limited." Acquiring major assets will continue to be a concern, especially if a house is in your plan. As personal assets become more valuable, adequate insurance coverage and protection of your earning capacity are crucial. Those with children have new responsibilities.

A higher income means paying a greater percentage as taxes; the IRS will want to relieve you of your awesome income burden. Tax planning will be a concern. Invested funds will permit better financial planning. Discretionary income will rise for those with no dependents or those who limit their purchases of personal assets.

Solid Additions to the Plan

You often enter the highest earning potential of your career in this stage. Expenditures for major personal assets are much smaller, and that frees up income. Retirement, while still distant, will emerge as a concern. Depending on the pension benefits your employer offers, your need to accumulate a retirement fund will range from moderate to very urgent. Investments, integral to any accumulation plan, will be more important. Your higher income level could make higher-risk investments possible: if they falter, you will have time to recover any losses. As you will discover, some investment losses can be shifted to the IRS; the tax collector should share your bad times along with the good.

Finishing the Pyramid

Your income has peaked or will peak during the period "finishing the pyramid." Major purchases completed, you will have considerable discretionary income. Dependents who added responsibility and costs are on their own, or soon will be. High discretionary income gives you funds to invest. The investments you purchased earlier have grown as earnings compounded. Good management will ensure their continued growth.

Fewer exemptions and lower deductible expenses will probably raise taxes. Good management can lessen that added burden. Investments which offer a tax advantage become more attractive.

Begin Retirement

Increasingly, people begin retirement at age 62 instead of the traditional 65. When you retire, income usually drops. Reduced income restores budgeting as a concern. Advisors suggest you need 60 to 70 percent of your working income to maintain your standard of living. People who wait until age 60 to begin saving for retirement have only one choice: continue working if health permits.

At this point, people stop accumulating financial assets: they now count on returns from their earlier investments. Many will begin liquidating their assets. Investments will likely be restructured for lowered risk and a steady income.

A lower income reduces the importance of tax planning. But estate and inheritance taxes may become considerations. Poor planning could expose your hard-earned assets to taxes at the federal and state level.

It is now time to enjoy the rewards of your financial planning. Years of planning have secured your retirement. You can maintain your standard of living. But before we lose you in the sunny sands of retirement, there is the matter of the next 18 chapters.

EXTERNAL ENVIRONMENT FOR PERSONAL FINANCIAL DECISIONS

Central to your personal financial decisions must be the factors in the external environment that affect them. You probably cannot alter those factors. But including them in the decision process can lessen their impact. The following sections discuss some of these factors.

Income Taxes

Federal, state, and city income taxes have been "reformed" countless times, and the process continues. But even the most favorable rules will give you one or more **"tax partners"** to share your money. Depending on income size, source, and where you live, your partners can take 30, 40, or more than 50 percent of each dollar. Even the most patriotic will want to minimize that "take."

Impact on personal financial planning

Planning for income taxes should be a central part of your financial strategy. You can use the tax rules to minimize your payments; that is quite legal. For example, mortgage interest and property taxes reduce income: that lowers taxes. Because these deductions also reduce the cost of home-ownership, taxes should be part of your purchase decision. Taxes should not, however, become the sole basis for decisions; they are one of several. Retaining a reasonable share of your income in "taxland USA" proves a challenge.

This book will not make you a tax "expert." Space is too limited, and the topic too technical. But Chapter 5 will give you the skills you need for intelligent planning.

Inflation

Current inflation rates are down sharply from the double digits of the early 1980s. But goods and services still continue to rise in price. The **"rule of 72"** illustrates inflation's effect: Divide 72 by the expected rate of inflation to estimate how many years it will take for prices to double. At 6 percent inflation, prices will double in 12 years (72/6). Today's $12,000 car would cost $24,000. Another 12 years pushes the cost to $48,000. We assume the car is little changed: only its price is higher. At 9 percent inflation, how long for prices to double? Yes, it is 8 years.

Clearly you need to consider the effects of inflation as you frame your financial plan. The typical financial goal involves a large dollar amount to be spent at some future time. All the while you are saving the money, inflation is pushing up prices. Take Agnes Aspiration. She decides a $154,000

Rolls Royce Corniche convertible would be nice—but that price!! No worry. Her banker suggests she invest $2,000 annually in an IRA (more on this later), making her a millionaire in 40 years. Now grayer, Agnes toddles to the dealer clutching $154,000.

"Nice down payment," announces the salesperson, for inflation has raised the price to $1,580,000. "Want to finance the other $1,426,000?"

Incorporating inflation into your financial plan reduces the prospect of being a dollar short and a day late.

Measuring the change in prices

Let's look at a measure of the impact of inflation over time. One widely used indicator is the **consumer price index (CPI),** which measures the percentage change in the average price of a basket of goods and services a consumer might use. If the CPI rises 5 percent, you pay 5 percent more for the goods and services. Not everyone's cost of living actually rises by 5 percent, though. Your actual "basket" of goods and services may differ. Prices may rise more or less in your area. Improvements in the quality or usefulness of the goods and services may account for part of the price rise. The CPI is not above criticism, but it offers a reasonable approximation of the inflationary trend.

Impact on personal financial planning

The effect of inflation on your financial plan warrants consideration. Suppose your financial goal is to accumulate the money for a child's college education. Planning to save an amount equal to today's college costs almost guarantees you will not have enough money. Planning a savings program that allows for inflation may eliminate that shortfall. Or consider the return on your investments: as inflation does its dirty deeds, part of your earnings are needed to offset the erosion in your purchasing power. Even if the bank promised 10 percent, a 6 percent rise in prices means your real return is 4 percent. An investment's **real return** is what remains after inflation.

Cycles in the Economy

If our economy grew at a predictable rate, developing a financial plan would be easier; employment for economists would plummet, though. The fact is that the economy expands for a time: it can be less than 12 months to more than 5 years. Then it may contract for anywhere from a few months to several years. On average it may all even out. Though financial plans are made at a particular time, they should take into account the impact of future economic changes. Ignore it and you are like a nonswimmer crossing a river posted "Averages 6 Inches Deep." At 3 inches deep, the first part is easy; the 13-foot drop-off in the middle is *trouble!*

Impact on personal financial planning

A few examples illustrate the impact economic cycles can have on a financial plan. Employment and salary opportunities tend to rise and fall with economic cycles. Borrowing money can be costly near the end of an expansion, but much lower in a recession. Inflation often rises near the end of an expansion and drops in a recession. Likewise the attraction of some investments varies with the expected direction of the economy. Your financial plan needs to take as many of these factors as it can into consideration.

Financial Products and Services

You have access to a growing range of financial products and services: payment accounts, investment options, loan alternatives, and insurance options, for example. Once heavily regulated by the government, the financial area is now more open. Providers can now alter and expand their products and services more readily. In the past, you looked to a local financial institution for services. Now firms outside your area seek your business. They use toll-free telephone numbers, advertisements, and price or rate-of-interest competition to attract you. A national market for financial services and products is approaching reality.

Impact on personal financial planning

Opportunities and rewards are greater in the national markets, but the selection effort is also greater. You must learn to find the alternatives and then evaluate their strengths and weaknesses in order to make an informed decision. Careful selection can yield a product or service that meets your needs. Good money management skills can help you use the market for financial products and services to your advantage.

Social Security System

Some people's response to any mention of Social Security is, "With retirement years away, why consider it now?" First, nearly everyone contributes more than 7 percent of each wage, salary, or bonus dollar; so does the employer. That money provides benefits for retirement, payments for disability, and support for your survivors. Pessimists say: "Sure, but nothing will be there when it is my turn." I disagree. Granted, rescue plans that were to fix the system's problems forever failed. But there *were* rescues and they are likely to continue if needed.

Impact on personal financial planning

When you purchase disability insurance coverage, consider your potential Social Security benefit: it may reduce the coverage you need. However, the qualifying rules for Social Security are such that you may want a policy that provides more liberal benefits during the first several years.

Potential Social Security payments to your survivors affect how much life insurance coverage you need. Dependent children in particular qualify for sizable survivor's benefits, as much as $1,000 to $2,000 monthly. So Social Security benefits are an essential part of a well-developed life insurance program. If you ignore them, you may waste your money on excessive insurance.

You also need to consider the timing and amount of your Social Security retirement benefits. The earliest you can qualify for reduced retirement benefits is age 62; that might shape any plans you make to retire at 59. Current retirement benefits of $700 to $800 each month could be a significant part of your retirement income. Two-career couples could receive twice that amount. Building Social Security into your financial plan will improve retirement planning.

ASSISTANCE WITH YOUR PERSONAL FINANCIAL PLAN

You may want assistance in developing your financial plan at different stages of your life. Dealing only with the basics, you may be able to develop your understanding of the planning process enough to complete a sound personal plan. In highly technical areas such as wills, trusts, purchase or sale of a home, complex tax issues, or questions of insurance coverage, you may need the services of an expert. Even the best surgeon does not attempt do-it-yourself brain surgery. Or you may rely on an expert to complete one segment of your financial plan. Perhaps your tax planning is so complex that you need assistance. Finally, you might ask a professional financial planner to prepare a complete financial plan. Your involvement lessens as your reliance on financial planners and other professionals increases. The cost does the opposite.

Self-Help on Your Financial Plan

The goal is for you to develop sufficient expertise so that you can complete your financial plan. Potential information sources include:

- **Periodicals.** *Money, Changing Times, Consumer Reports, Financial Planning,* and others.
- **Newspapers.** The *Wall Street Journal,* the *New York Times,* and many other major metropolitan newspapers.
- **Newsletters.** There is a whole range of newsletters that concentrate on personal finance topics such as taxes, credit and loan options, banking services, mutual funds, and common stocks.
- **Books.** Some books cover a broad topic range, while others concentrate on a few areas. This book typifies the first. *How to Make Millions Speculating on Pork Bellies* represents the second.

These publications can help you throughout the stages of your financial career. Sources that emphasize broader, topical coverage are most helpful to those starting a financial plan. Fred Fretful may find *Financial Independence Through Employer-Granted Stock Options* interesting but of

little use if his employer has no such plan. As Fred—and you—become sophisticated in your financial planning, more-specialized publications will come to the forefront.

If you need more structure to your studies, a course or seminar may be the solution. Many colleges, universities, technical schools, financial institutions, and financial service companies offer these.

A concern

Use care with the so-called **"free" planning seminars** from financial service companies. Some are little more than sales pitches with three goals: *sell, sell, sell.* Even the "free" lunch could prove very expensive chicken if you buy an inappropriate product or service.

Financial Professionals: Assistance on a Specific Problem Area

You could seek help from a professional in a specific area for several reasons. Possibly you lack time or are uncertain in one area. Or the issue may be so complex that a professional is needed. Among these professionals are certified public accountants (CPAs), attorneys, insurance salespersons, and customer representatives of brokerage firms: Columns 2 through 4 of Exhibit 1.3 summarize the major services they offer. Most limit their services to a specific personal finance area. The fee range given is only an approximation. Where you live and the complexity of your situation usually determine the fee. Many professionals will provide a cost estimate.

Strategy

Ask the professionals' hourly rate. Have them estimate what it may cost for the services you need.

A concern

Some insurance salespersons and brokerage representatives call themselves financial consultants, financial analysts, or other creative things. They can be a good source of advice, but remember their primary objective is to sell some product or service. A clever title and a hard sell does not a financial planner make. As the wolf might have said: "All the better to earn commissions, my dear."

Financial Professionals: Developing a Total Financial Plan

An independent financial planner will develop your total financial plan. A good plan will make recommendations covering a range of financial concerns. This distinguishes the services of this professional from the specialists of the previous section. You might request such a plan because you lack time, have complex financial goals and objectives, or see a dramatic change in your circumstances—you finally won the lottery! Financial planners can be separated into those who rely on commissions from the sale of products and services and those who charge a fee based on the time and expertise used in developing the plan. Column 5 of Exhibit 1.3 summarizes the activities of **commission planners.** Column 6 does the same for **fee planners.**

A plan drawn up by a commission planner will recommend specific products and services to achieve the plan's objectives. Most of these are

Exhibit 1.3

Assistance in Developing Your Personal Financial Plan

Description	Certified public accountant	Attorney	Customer representative*	Commission financial planner	Fee financial planner
Compensated by	Hourly fee	Hourly fee	Salary and/or commission	Commission	Hourly fee
Planning services offered	3	3, 10, 11	5, 7, 8, 9, 10	1 through 10	1 through 10
Best when utilized for	Tax issues	Tax and legal issues	Questions on insurance and investments	Complete financial plan	Complete financial plan
Projected cost†	$100 to $500 or more	$200 to $2,000 or more	Buried in price of product or service	Buried in price of product or service	$500 to $5,000 or more
Issues and concerns	a and b	a and b	a, b, c, and d	c and d	e and f

* Includes representatives from insurance, brokerage, and financial service firms.
† Cost figures are an approximation. Actual depends on time spent and expertise.
Key to services offered
  1 Assistance on financial goals   2 Guidance on budget plan
  3 Tax preparation, planning, and shelters   4 Analyze housing alternatives
  5 Develop an insurance plan   6 Analyze employee benefits
  7 Investment options   8 Options for funding retirement
  9 Funding a child's education   10 Estate planning
11 Wills and trusts
Key to issues and concerns
a Range of services offered is limited.
b Service needs to be coordinated with overall financial plan.
c Emphasis on sale of product and service can cause a conflict of interest.
d Product or service offered may not be coordinated with overall financial plan.
e To date, no prescribed education or training required. Qualifications of some planners may be marginal.
f Limited number of planners may mean having to search for one.

sold by the planner or an affiliated company. Planners want you to implement the plan as outlined; their commissions depend on it. The commission is buried in the price and there is no standard: it can range from 2 to more than 15 percent.

Strategy

Ask the financial planner the commissions on each product and service.

A plan from a fee planner will often contain two types of recommendations. Some will be for specific products and services to meet your objectives. Typically, these are items that pay no commission to the seller: they are called "no-load" products. Other recommendations may describe a product or service needed for a goal, but no specific brands. Both types will probably take you more time and effort to implement than would those in a plan from a commission planner. A good fee planner will believe in the plan and want you to implement it, but there is no financial incentive.

Strategy

Ask the planner the hourly rate and the estimated cost for your plan.

Which type of planner?

You may sense a fee planner bias. I believe this arrangement provides greater independence. Commission planners suggest that diligent selection from a range of quality products and services provides choices that meet the client's needs first, and generate commissions second. But when a planner limits himself or herself to the products and services of one or two companies, does that meet this standard? A well-conceived plan using mediocre or poor products and services is hardly "best" for the client.

Strategy

Ask the commission planner how many different companies' products and services will be used to develop a plan.

Any planner who claims to provide a "free" financial plan is deluding you. Either the plan is straight "boilerplate" which fits nearly anyone and is of questionable value, or behind the plan are commissions from the suggested products and services. Ask all planners: Who pays and how?

PERSONAL COMPUTERS IN FINANCIAL PLANNING

The wide availability of personal computers raises the question: Can a computer help you manage personal finances? It depends on your circumstances. Let's look at some of the issues.

Certain features of personal computers make them ideal for your finances. They do such repetitive tasks as weekly, monthly, or quarterly updates very easily. Those who struggled in Miss Higgins's math class will find them a godsend. Dozens of computations can be done in seconds: no errors either. Summaries can glitter with percentages, averages, rates of return, subtotals, totals, graphs, and other measures. With a printer, copies and updates are but a command away. Comparisons between periods or alternatives are quickly produced. A computer can produce high-quality, detailed information for your personal financial plan.

Given that list of pluses, are there drawbacks? Expense: you need access to a computer, a printer, and the software to operate them. You also need the skills to operate the equipment and associated software. Third, available personal finance software may not meet your needs. Modifying a program to meet your needs requires time and expertise. Personal computers will execute incorrect programs as readily as correct ones. Finally, a computer only supports the financial plan *you* develop. You still must gather data, establish goals, identify options, collect statistics, analyze results, and make decisions.

Will It Improve My Financial Plan?

It may assist you in select areas. Providing detailed, accurate supporting records is certainly a computer's forte. To the extent those records make for better decisions, that is an improvement. Using a computer allows a comparative analysis of competing options. That allows more-informed choices, another improvement. Because it can quickly update records, a computer may track your finances in a more timely manner, one more advantage.

But will it produce an improved financial plan? No, at least not yet. Widely available personal finance software does not have the ability to develop an "improved" plan. That is still your responsibility. Nor will the software develop scenarios for a decision. More work for you. Software may develop "what if" analyses, develop alternatives for a situation, and single out the "best" option some day, but right now that is mostly a hope.

Will It Save Me Time on My Financial Plan?

Are you currently familiar with personal computers? Have experience with software? Have moderately complex finances? Answer all three yes and the computer can save you time. Our experience suggests a computer takes more time initially. Reduced time afterward is the payoff. As your finances become more complex, those time savings could multiply. If you answered yes to only one or two of the opening questions, time savings are less certain.

LAUNCH YOUR FINANCIAL PLANNING CAREER TODAY

Congratulations on deciding to pursue your financial planning career with this text. Presumably you will be working through most or all of the chapters to gain the broad understanding you will need for successful planning. Do not be concerned if some terms are not yet "household words." We will explain them in detail. Several chapters from now, you will be more comfortable with the language of finance.

My goal is to help you learn money management skills that you can use to develop plans that meet your needs, goals, and objectives. The emphasis will be on the broad, major topics of personal finance. Special topics receive limited coverage. It is hard to be interested in a topic that has, and likely will have, little relevance to your situation. If you need expert knowledge in some area, numerous books and newsletters cover specialized personal finance topics.

As the text went to press, changes continued to be made to ensure that it would be timely and current. But new products and services, even new federal tax regulations, appear almost weekly; there is always some danger of instant antiquation. As a money manager, keeping current will be a challenge throughout your career. Adopt the view that changes are opportunities to improve your financial plan. Even the best plan needs revision from time to time. As Erma Bombeck might say: "When the financial marketplace gives you lemons, then it is time to make lemonade."

Summary

1 Financial planning can benefit individuals at all income and asset levels.
2 Objectives you might have for personal financial planning include:
   - Planned spending and purchases
   - Financial peace of mind
   - Protect you and your assets
   - Establish and implement financial goals
   - Achieve your desired life-style
   - Financial independence
3 The financial planning process can be summarized in five stages:
   - Determine your present resources and expected income.
   - Develop your short- and long-term goals and objectives.
   - Design a detailed plan outlining specific steps to achieve your goals and objectives.
   - Decide each spending and investment question based on need and merit.
   - Diagnose the progress on your plan and decide what corrective action, if any, is needed.
4 Major resources for implementing your financial plan include accumulated financial assets and your expected future income; the latter is often most important for those starting out.
5 A budget is the primary planning document that summarizes your expected resources and your planned expenditures.
6 People pass through a series of stages in their financial planning careers. The relative importance of various financial concerns changes with each stage.
7 The combination of federal, state, and sometimes local income taxes can take 30 to more than 50 percent of each income dollar; tax planning is a basic part of a financial plan.
8 Your financial plan needs to take into account inflation's upward push on future prices as well as its negative draw on an investment's rate of return.
9 The economic cycle can affect borrowing costs, employment opportunities, investment options, and housing alternatives.
10 The market for many financial products and services is shifting from a local to a national one.
11 As a contributor to the Social Security system, you probably qualify for disability payments, payments to some survivors should you depart the gene pool early, and retirement payments.
12 You can obtain assistance on your financial plan at three levels:
   - *Self-help.* Courses, seminars, periodicals, newspapers, newletters, and books are major sources.
   - *Professional assistance.* Help on a specific point or question would be the next level.
   - *Professional assistance.* Having a planner develop your complete financial plan would be the top level.
13 To date, a personal computer's primary role has been producing high-quality, detailed support information for the financial plan you have developed.

Review your understanding of

Financial planning process	Rule of 72
Financial assets	Consumer price index (CPI)
Financial goals	Real return on investment
Budget	"Free" planning seminars
Life cycle of financial planning	Commission financial planner
"tax partners"	Fee financial planner

Discussion questions

1 At a friend's soiree, Phil Procrastinate was heard to remark: "Financial planning only pays off if you have a big income or extensive assets." Would you agree? Why or why not.
2 Can you give some reasons why you think people neglect financial planning? Do you think that neglect will likely change? Why?
3 What objectives might one set for financial planning? Which ones would be most important to you personally? Why? (*Note:* There is no "correct" list for this part.)
4 What are the five stages of the financial planning process? Briefly describe the purpose of each stage.
5 Describe the steps needed to develop a financial goal. Please choose several goals you can use to show how the steps operate.
6 Glenda Grandiose has completed stages 1 and 2

of the planning process. As she begins stage 3, she wonders if it will help her judge the feasibility of her *very, very* long list of financial goals. Will it help? How?

7   List some financial areas that will likely be important during the "getting started" stage of financial planning. Briefly justify why they might be important. Can you list several of lesser concern? Why might they be on this list?

8   What does it mean to have several "tax partners"? How many partners are there in the area where you live? Why should income taxes be part of your financial plan?

9   Suppose the $1,000 you invested 1 year ago pays its promised $100 return today. During that year prices rose 10 percent. Would that 10 percent inflation be a concern? Why?

10   What impact does the shift to a national market for financial products and services have on your financial plan? How will national providers of financial services and products attempt to attract customers?

11   What features and points distinguish commission financial planners from their fee planning counterparts? Can you name several advantages of each arrangement?

12   What are likely to be the major benefits of using a personal computer in financial planning? What are the limitations and shortcomings of its use?

Problems

1.1   When Rozella Van Wrinkle returned from 6 year's research on a very remote Pacific island, she found that nearly all prices had doubled. What was the average annual inflation during her absence?

1.2   Despite a flashy sales promotion, Fred Bear decides to postpone purchasing a $90,000 unit in Mountain Meadows Condominiums until his retirement in 24 years. The salesperson warns: "If inflation averages the 6 percent a year many expect, the price will be a lot higher then."

   a   At 6 percent what will the approximate price be in 12 years? In 24 years? (*Hint:* The rule of 72 may help.)

   b   Fred presently has the $90,000, which he plans to invest for the intervening 24 years. What annual rate of return will he need just to keep up with inflation? Why?

   c   Will any government agency want to "share" in the investment's return?

Case problem

During the 6 months since his college graduation, Al Weaver has been busy. His new position took him to a much larger city, and it has taken him some time to become oriented. In addition, the firm required that he attend several educational seminars, for which he spent considerable time preparing.

The net effect is that Al has not devoted much time to his finances. Now he wonders if he should do more in that area. Al is not certain how much planning he needs. His income is not large, and he has accumulated few assets. He has not had a personal finance course, so his background is limited.

Al has been pleased with the standard of living his $20,000 annual salary provides. It covers his regular living expenses, and he has accumulated $3,500 in a money market account at the bank. Al continues to make monthly payments on his education loan; the unpaid balance is $6,600. He won't repay that loan early, since the interest rate is low. He uses his credit cards as a convenience rather than carry cash; by paying the entire balance on or before the due date, he avoids the finance charge. Al recently purchased some new furniture for his apartment. But he still drives the car he purchased while at the university. He has made no other major purchases.

Al has not compiled a detailed list of his goals but he has some hopes. Within the next 2 to 3 years he would like to replace his automobile. If possible, he wants to accumulate most of the expected $13,500 cost by that time. Purchasing a house, while not an immediate priority, is something he would like to do in 5 to 7 years. By that time he expects to know whether he will remain in this area. And he hopes his finances will be such that he can handle the costs of a house. Of more immediate concern is replacing more of his present furniture. He would like to change from a decor of "army barracks 1964" to a more "classic" theme over the next year or two.

Al's limited personal finance expertise concerns him. He has considered seeking outside assistance. When he looked in the local telephone directory under "personal financial planning," Al noted a lengthy list of companies and individuals. He is at a loss as to what he would ask if he did call someone on the list. As he prepares to play tennis at eleven o'clock, he thinks he probably should be doing something. Well, maybe next week.

1   Given Al's present situation, do you think he is a candidate for financial planning? Why?
2   Granted, he may need more-detailed information than he presently has. But could he begin work on the early stages of the financial planning process with the information he does have? What should he do?
3   Al's purchase of a house is planned for a considerable time in the future. Should it be part of his financial plan? Why or why not? Which external factor(s) might have a considerable impact on his proposed housing purchase? Briefly outline their potential effect.
4   What guidance would you give Al in the area of assistance on his personal finances? What factors will likely help him decide what level of assistance he might want?
5   What qualifications would you want the financial planner to have? Would you be more comfortable with a ''fee'' or a ''commission'' planner?

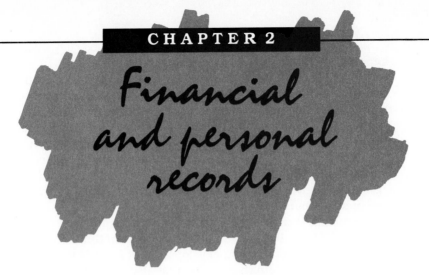

CHAPTER 2

Financial and personal records

AFTER COMPLETING THIS CHAPTER YOU WILL HAVE LEARNED

- The major financial records and personal documents you need for sound financial planning
- How to prepare and analyze your personal income statement
- What a personal balance sheet can show you
- How to inventory your personal assets
- What your income tax file should contain
- How an insurance record can alert you to insurance renewals
- How an investment record can track an investment's performance and show its gain or loss when you sell it
- Where to store your personal records and documents and for how long

*F*rom the day you are born, when a birth certificate officially affirms your existence, to the day you die, when a death certificate officially announces the end, documents and records are a part of your life. When you manage your personal financial affairs, you need a record of what you have done, of what needs to be done, and of what you plan to do.

Keeping records is not the time-consuming drudgery people think. If you keep records in an orderly, deliberate fashion, you can actually *save* time. People who keep good records don't have to hunt for receipts or try to reconstruct barely remembered expenditures.

Starting your record system is the difficult part. Once the system is established, it will take you little time to keep those records up to date.

Our goal is to help you develop a set of records that will help you manage your personal finances. A section also discusses using a personal computer to prepare your records. The chapter closes with points on storing your records.

SETTING UP YOUR RECORDS

If you have a clear idea of the use of financial records, it will be easier to understand why they should be organized in a certain way. In our discussion of each form, we will identify the purpose of the financial record being considered, assess its content, and explain how you can interpret the completed record.

Now let us examine the first financial record: the income statement.

Income Statement

The primary purpose of an **income statement** is to show the relationship between your income and your expenditures. It is a historical statement covering some past period. While most people use a calendar year (January 1 to December 31) for their financial statements, yours can cover whatever time best suits you (for example, if you are a teacher with a contract from July 1 to June 30 of the next year, you might choose that as the span of your record).

The typical income statement has three major sections: income sources, expenditures, and a calculation of your surplus or deficit.

Income

Your first step is to identify all sources of the income you received during the period. For many people, wages or salary and possibly some interest make up their only income. People whose personal finances are a bit more complex may have additional sources of income. Exhibit 2.1 shows some typical sources of income.

Exhibit 2.1

Sources of Income

Wages	Salary	Interest	Bonuses
Dividends	Commissions	Rent	Pensions

24

   While you want your income statement to be complete, don't be concerned about the last few pennies. Some people round all amounts to the
nearest $1 or even the nearest $10. Better to have a statement that identifies major amounts than spend so much time following the last penny
that nothing is completed.

   The sample income statement for Frank and Mary Swanson in Exhibit
2.2 illustrates how to construct the income section of your record. Frank
and Mary could have used their wage and salary statement, federal income
tax Form W-2, for the past year as a source of information. A similar state-

Exhibit 2.2

Personal Income Statement for 19XX,
Frank and Mary Swanson

Income		
Frank's salary	$21,500	
Mary's salary	19,000	
Mary's year-end bonus	2,100	
Dividends and interest	600	
Total income		$43,200
Expenses		
Food		$ 4,250
Housing		
Rent	$ 4,740	
Utilities	1,460	
Homeowners insurance	100	
		$ 6,300
Clothing		$ 1,180
Transportation		
Gas, oil, maintenance	$ 1,630	
Insurance, repairs, license	960	
		$ 2,590
Vacation and entertainment		$ 1,810
Life insurance		$ 310
Medical		
Doctor, dentist, drugs	$ 590	
Health insurance	310	
		$ 900
Personal		$ 1,190
Child care		$ 3,160
Taxes		
Federal income taxes	$ 5,690	
State income taxes	1,790	
Social Security contributions	3,200	
		$10,680
Loan payments		
Auto	$ 3,030	
Applicances	1,200	
		$ 4,230
Total expenses		$36,600
Surplus or (deficit): income − expenses		$ 6,600

Expenditures

ment of interest and dividends, Form 1099, could be the source for information on each of their investments.

The second element of the income statement identifies and summarizes your expenditures for the period. What sort of payments qualify as expenditures? Typically, expenditures are for short-lived items such as clothing and food, or they cover recurring expenses such as dental bills or automobile insurance. But payments on loans are also included. What is excluded? The full costs of long-lived purchases—automobiles, houses, or boats—are not shown as expenditures, though the loan payments on them are. Exhibit 2.3 summarizes expenditures you might list in an income statement.

How many categories of expenditure you include in the income statement depends upon how complex your finances are and how much detail you need. Generally, 12 to 15 categories is the minimum, 25 to 30 the maximum. Remember, the more categories you list, the more record keeping and preparation involved.

The lower part of Exhibit 2.2 summarizes Frank and Mary Swanson's expenditures. Their 20 categories of listed expenditures make their income statement fairly complex. Frank and Mary might determine the amount for each expenditure category from their financial records. If they have a budget, the topic of Chapter 3, it will provide them with expenditure totals. Lacking that, they might review their checkbook record to compute the amounts. If they do that, they will have to add an estimate of what they have purchased for cash.

Does creating such a detailed statement sound challenging? Figuring expenditures is easy if you maintain a detailed budget, and after you finish Chapter 3, you will know how to do that. But even without the budget, it will be reasonably easy if you write checks for most purchases. If you purchase almost everything for cash, figuring your expenditures will be very difficult. Using checks leaves a trail to assist your financial planning.

Surplus or deficit

The difference between the income shown in the first section of your statement and the expenditures in the second measures your financial health. It shows what part of your income was not spent on short-lived items, recurring living expenses, or loan payments. If income exceeds expenditures, you have a **surplus.** You may have deposited that surplus in some investment for future use. Some options would be a savings account, a money market account, a checking account, or a mutual fund account

Exhibit 2.3

Typical Expenditure Categories for an Income Statement

Food	Rent	Utilities	Insurance premiums
Clothing	Taxes	Auto expenses	Travel expenses
Child care	Personal	Entertainment	Education expenses
Repair costs	Loan payment	Miscellaneous	Mortgage payment

(more on these later). Regardless of where it was deposited, the surplus is there for future use.

But what if your expenditures exceed income? Suppose your income statement shows a **deficit.** This means that you have spent more than you have taken in. You can deal with a deficit, of course. One way is to spend money that you accumulated in an investment in the past. Or you could borrow the money through a formal loan or by charging items on a credit card. Regardless of how you handle a particular deficit, there is a limit to spending more than your income. Investments are eventually exhausted. Sooner or later, lenders will say *no* more credit! We discuss this point further in a later section.

The last line in Exhibit 2.2 shows a surplus for the Swansons: their income exceeded expenditures. They are managing their finances to accumulate money for future use.

Analyzing your income statement

Your income statement can tell you if you are living within your income. It can also tell you whether your financial plan is working the way you want. Though the Swansons seem to have a successful financial plan, they may still want to compare their actual and planned surplus to see if they need to change their strategies to meet their goals. If the Swanson's income statement had shown an unplanned deficit, it would have signaled the need for corrective action. The size of the deficit would have shown them how serious their fiscal situation was.

Second, an income statement can show how you have spent your money. Often people are surprised at how much money they spend and what they spend it on. A review will show what portion of your expendi-

tures is for essential items. Reducing your spending on these items may be possible, but it will be difficult. They are likely to be necessary for daily living: food, rent, utilities, insurance premiums. Other expenditures are discretionary and these are usually easier—though hardly pleasant—to reduce: travel, entertainment, or recreation.

Third, you can review the surplus on your income statement to see if it will reach the goals you have set. Estimating the dollar amounts needed for future goals is a major topic of Chapter 3, but for now suppose that Frank and Mary Swanson have decided they want to accumulate $9,000 as a down payment for a house. They figure that will require annual investments of $1,500. Reviewing their income statement can help them decide if they are progressing toward that goal.

Finally, an income statement provides a continuing reminder of the amount of money you manage for yourself, often without a great deal of planning. When people first prepare an income statement, a comparison of total income and total expenditure statements suggests they *should* have a sizable surplus. Yet the balances in their investments rose little, if any, during the year. Why? Often there is an incomplete accounting of last year's expenditures. They have difficulty determining where the money went, but it is gone. Large differences between what *should be* and what *is* highlight the need to manage your finances: that way you *know* where and why the money went.

Strategy

Preparing and analyzing an income statement can help you understand your past spending patterns and assist you in making future spending plans.

Balance Sheet   A **balance sheet** summarizes your financial position at a specific moment. It is a snapshot of your financial condition. To do this, it lists the major assets you own. Next, it lists all of the amounts that you owe to other people or organizations. Finally, it compares those two amounts; the result is an estimate of your net worth. You should construct such a balance sheet each year, at about the same time of the year; comparing one year to the next will let you see your progress.

The three major sections of a balance sheet are:

- *Assets.* The things that you own.
- *Liabilities.* The amounts that you owe to others.
- *Net worth.* The difference between assets and liabilities.

Assets   Assets are the things that you own. They could be items you use on a regular basis; call these **personal assets.** Typically, these are owned for the service and benefit they provide. Some offer both pleasure and income—coin collections, art, or jewelry. **Financial assets,** the second major sort of asset, are held primarily for the income, or rate of return, they provide. They have value because they represent a claim on some other individual or organization.

Exhibit 2.4 lists typical assets you might find on a balance sheet. When listing assets on a balance sheet, certain rules should be observed:

1 All assets are listed at their current market value.
2 An asset is listed in full even if there is an outstanding loan.

An example will illustrate the sense of these rules. Suppose you had purchased a $14,000 auto several years ago and borrowed $10,000 of the price. Today the car is worth $9,800 and your loan balance is $6,700. On your balance sheet the auto would be listed at $9,800—what you would receive if you sold it. The loan appears as a $6,700 liability, since this is your actual debt.

Liabilities   **Liabilities** are the amounts you owe others. Some liabilities may be repaid in a matter of days, but a long-term debt such as a mortgage takes many years to repay.

The following conventions should be observed when you list liabilities:

1 List the current unpaid balance, even though the original debt may have been larger.
2 List liabilities in decreasing order of maturity; those that are repaid quickest come first, and those that will take years to repay are last.

Exhibit 2.5 shows some typical liabilities you might find on a balance sheet.

Exhibit 2.4

Typical Assets for a Balance Sheet

Personal Assets

Clothing	Major appliance	Condominium
Boat	Coin collection	Furniture
Artwork	House	Antiques
Automobile	Jewelry	

Financial Assets

Cash	Checking account	Savings account
Money market account	Common stock	Mutual fund account
Corporate bond	Ownership in a business	Municipal bond
Treasury note or bond	Limited partnership	Life insurance (cash value)

Exhibit 2.5

Typical Liabilities Shown on a Balance Sheet

Short Term

| Credit card balance | Utility bills | Insurance premium |
| Charge account balance | Medical bills | Telephone bill |

Intermediate Term

| Automobile loan | Personal bank loan | Furniture loan |

Long Term

| Mortgage loan | Education loan | |

Frank and Mary Swanson have listed their liabilities at the lower half of Exhibit 2.6. The example illustrates how a balance sheet is constructed. We will talk about how to analyze a balance sheet later.

Net worth
The final calculation on a balance sheet shows your **net worth.** In fact this figure is what makes the statement ''balance'': you compute your net worth by deducting liabilities from assets. The equation is:

Net worth = assets − liabilities

Suppose you sell all of your assets for the amounts listed on your balance sheet—the current market value. The money you receive would be

Exhibit 2.6

Balance Sheet for the Period Ended December 31, 19XX
Frank and Mary Swanson

	Assets*		
Short-term financial assets			
Checking account		$ 550	
Savings account		750	
Money market mutual fund		2,800	
Total			$ 4,100
Long-term financial assets			
Corporate bond mutual fund		$ 1,400	
Common stocks		2,100	
Common stock mutual fund		2,850	
Total			$ 6,350
Restricted financial assets			
Certificate of deposit: IRA		$ 3,670	
Employer's thrift plan		1,375	
Total			$ 5,045
Personal assets			
Automobiles		$13,500	
Furniture and appliances		4,250	
Clothing, jewelry, other		3,450	
Total			$21,200
Total assets			$36,695
	Liabilities†		
Current balances			
Credit cards		$ 570	
Charge account		120	
Total			$ 690
Intermediate-term loans			
Auto loan		$ 7,600	
Appliance loan		1,010	
Total loans			$ 8,610
Total liabilities			$ 9,300
	Net Worth		
Net worth (assets − liabilities)			$27,395

* Amounts shown represent market value at time of balance sheet.
† Represents unpaid balance as of December 31, 19XX.

used to repay your liabilities in full. The money that remains is your net worth.

Most people's net worth will be positive. That is what you would expect, since the assets people own usually exceed their bills and loans. Over time your net worth is likely to increase. That might happen if you use any surplus from your income to purchase personal and financial assets. Or the market value of assets you own (particularly financial assets) may increase over the years; if your liabilities don't change, your net worth will rise. Or you might use surplus income to repay liabilities; when liabilities decline and assets don't, net worth rises.

Frank and Mary Swanson's net worth appears at the bottom of Exhibit 2.6. Since the Swansons' assets exceed their liabilities, their net worth is positive. Compare their net worth to their total assets: it gives a realistic measure of the Swansons' true wealth.

Determining your current financial position

Many people find preparing their balance sheet a revealing exercise. It forces them to systematically inventory what they own and what they owe. It is amazing how many people have only a vague idea of what they have. At the opposite extreme, experts who assist people who are deeply in debt find that few of their clients have ever added up their sizable debts. Most of us will not suffer the "lost" asset problem of the first group or the staggering debts of the second, but preparing a balance sheet is still useful and revealing for financial planning.

Strategy

A balance sheet provides a profile of your current financial status, and it may reveal areas that need better management.

Analyzing your net worth

The first step is for you to find out whether your **net worth is positive.** If it is, how large is your net worth? If you have established some target net worth, you can compare it to your actual amount and judge your progress.

But what about those who have a **negative net worth?** Since their assets are less than their liabilities, they are not going to be interested in selling their assets to pay their debts: it would not work. A negative net worth often suggests the person has not been an effective financial manager.

A negative net worth can arise from many sources; but overuse of debt is a frequent cause. Borrowing to purchase assets that drop quickly in value can cause a negative net worth. Or maybe expenditures far exceeded income each year. The person may have borrowed heavily to allow excessive buying. One common trait in personal bankruptcies is a negative net worth. Negative net worth does not always mean bankruptcy, but it nearly always shows there is a need to improve financial management.

Comparison with prior years

People who prepare a yearly balance sheet will benefit from comparing one year to the next to observe changes. The starting point is to see if net worth rose and how much. Second, you will want to review the makeup of your assets: what proportion of them are financial rather than personal assets (financial assets provide a return and are more likely to increase your future net worth). Third, you should compare your total financial assets to see if they have appreciated or declined. Finally, you should review liabilities for major changes. A sharp rise in your debts could signal borrowing that may not be prudent.

Ability to repay liabilities or raise cash

Most people plan to repay their debts by spending part of their current income. But suppose your income ceases or drops sharply. Suppose one Friday afternoon your employer suggests you pursue your career elsewhere . . . immediately. Or you quit your present job before finding a new one. Or you decide to go back to school for graduate work. Each might require that you sell some of your assets to repay debts that are due.

Which assets would you sell? First you should look at assets which are highly "liquid": ones that can be converted to cash quickly, with minimal commissions or penalties. The easiest assets to liquidate include the balance in your checking account, savings account, money market account, or money market mutual fund. Financial assets such as common stocks or bonds are generally less liquid, present a selling cost, or require you make price concessions so you can sell quickly. Many personal assets such as furniture or cars could take months to sell, involve selling costs, or require you reduce the price in order to sell.

In looking at your balance sheet, check the relationship between your liquid assets and those liabilities you will have to repay in the next few months. This comparison should let you estimate how long the sale of your assets would let you make payments on your debts.

A review of assets will also show you whether you could raise a block of cash on short notice. That ability could let you meet a large unexpected expenditure or grasp an investment opportunity that won't wait.

Projected future balance sheet

In planning for their financial future, people target the net worth they would like to have at various points. Comparing their yearly balance sheets to those targets lets them measure their progress. For example, a goal for a couple in their middle years might be to accumulate financial assets which will generate retirement income. If they establish periodic targets, their balance sheets will help them measure their success.

Personal Property Inventory

Why **inventory your personal property?** Many of us have more personal assets than we realize. If you don't know the worth of your personal property, you can't shop intelligently for insurance coverage. If any of your assets are lost to fire, flood, or burglary, the insurance company will expect a detailed list of the items before it pays a claim. If your loss is major, reconstructing a complete list of assets after the event will be challenging, maybe impossible. Or suppose you hire Harvey Handy Hands to haul your worldly goods to Friendship City and he "loses" them en route; an inventory will help establish your loss for insurers. Such an inventory will also help you summarize personal assets on your balance sheet.

Information that a personal property inventory might contain includes:

- Description of the item
- The purchase price
- Condition of the asset
- Date you acquired the asset
- Approximate current market value
- Location of the item

Special items that have considerable value, such as artwork, antiques, and collectibles, should probably be appraised by an expert in the field. Settling a loss claim on specialized assets is easier and quicker if you have a professional appraisal.

Two good ways of keeping a personal property inventory are in a loose-leaf notebook or on small index cards. Either way, you should be able to add and delete items quickly. Exhibit 2.7 shows how the notebook might look. Never store the inventory where you live. After all, the burglar may not leave it on the table with a nice note. Nor will it be easy to sift out of the ashes if the place burns.

Strategy

Store your personal property inventory off-premises and update it periodically.

Tax Records

Even with good records, tax preparation hardly highlights the spring social season. Without them, there can be frustration, errors, and unnecessary costs. If you miss a deduction that could have lowered your taxes, do not count on the Internal Revenue Service (IRS) calling to remind you. But fail to include part of your income on the return and it may bring a note or call: "Hi, this is the IRS, and we want to *help* you." A good tax file can save you hours in preparing tax returns. Even more important, it may reduce the amount of taxes you pay.

We split **tax records** into two kinds. First, there is the **historical information from your past taxes:** copies of forms submitted, receipts, can-

Exhibit 2.7

Sample Personal Property Inventory

Room: Living Room	Date of Inventory: Oct. 14, 19XX		
Description	*Condition*	*Purchase price*	*Purchase date*
Sofa	Excellent	$1,475	Feb. 1982
Easy chair	Good	700	Mar. 1981
Table lamps (2)	Excellent	150	Apr. 1979
Oriental rug (appraised by J. Smith, Aug. 1984)	Very good	1,500	Aug. 1975
Stereo	Excellent	1,500	Mar. 1986

celed checks, computations. You should keep these old tax returns for at least 4 years, 7 years if you have the space. Then there is the **information you need to complete this year's tax returns:** information on your income, deductions—taxes paid, contributions, loan interest, medical expenses—and other expenses or payments that reduce the income on which you must pay taxes. Chapter 5 will give you a better understanding regarding this file. A file folder, accordion file, or large manila envelope provides suitable storage for tax records.

Strategy

Keep a separate, accessible file where you can store tax-related materials.

Homeowner-ship Records

Homeowners need to maintain **some special records and documents.** The terms *home* or *house* encompass the entire range of ownership options: single-family houses, condominiums, town houses, mobile homes, any unit of which you own part or all. First, we discuss the formal documents that are part of the transfer process when the unit is purchased. Second, we cover what is needed to record improvements and repairs the owner makes to the house.

Formal owner-ship documents

A **deed** is the legal document that conveys ownership of the housing unit to you. It is valuable because you need it to resell the unit. It may be difficult to replace and should be kept in a secure location.

When you purchase a house, there may be a survey to determine the legal boundaries of the property: retain a copy in your records. You may receive the blueprints that were used to construct a newer house. These can be important if you later decide to alter or remodel the house.

Records during ownership

You may be able to sell your house for more than you paid for it: that is the good news. The bad news is that you may have to pay income taxes on the gain. At worst you would pay taxes on the gain. But if you buy another house within a prescribed time, you may be able to postpone the entire tax payment. Sellers who are age 55 or over fare even better: up to $125,000 of their gain is not taxed.

Home improvements. Tax regulations allow you to count what you spend on improving your house and surrounding lot while you owned them. Your gain for tax purposes is reduced by a dollar for each dollar you spend on improvements.

Your tax gain is computed as:

$$\text{Gain} = \frac{\text{sale price}}{\text{of house}} - \left(\frac{\text{original purchase}}{\text{price of house}} + \frac{\text{cost of all}}{\text{improvements}} \right)$$

Improvements are any expenditures that raise the value of your house or extend its useful life. Exhibit 2.8 lists some items that would qualify. To track those expenditures, your records should note the date of the improvement, calculate the amount spent, and contain all receipts for improvements. It is helpful if you keep a summary sheet giving a running total of all improvements.

Good records are crucial, because many people keep a house for 10 or 20 years. Trying to remember when you added that fence could be difficult, and reconstructing its cost, impossible. Fail to include all improvements when you sell your home, and you could pay unnecessary taxes. If the IRS asks you to support your computation of a gain, your record can provide evidence.

Home maintenance. The distinguishing trait of **home maintenance** expenditures is that they merely keep the house in good repair and keep it operating smoothly. They do not enhance the value of the property. Generally maintenance entails repairing, restoring, or preserving an existing part of the house, rather than adding something new. The lower half of Exhibit 2.8 gives examples.

Insurance Record

The major purpose of an **insurance record** is to briefly summarize your insurance coverage. The record typically shows the type of coverage, policy number, insurance company, dollar coverage, and amount and due date of premium. Exhibit 2.9 provides an example.

Exhibit 2.8

Is It a Home Improvement or Maintenance Expenditure?

Improvements
A garage	Trees and shrubs	New furnace
Storm windows	Air conditioning	Pave driveway
A new wing	Remodel kitchen	New plumbing

Maintenance
| Exterior painted | Repair sidewalk | Repair furnace |
| Paint a room | Hire a lawn cutter | Seal coat driveway |

Exhibit 2.9

Insurance Policy Record

Insurance coverage	Policy number	Company	Amount of insurance protection	Due date	Premium
Life	283728	You Bet Your Life	$30,000	June 10	$125
	396278	Last Gamble Life	45,000	July 8	162
Auto	12876243	Fidelity	100/300/25* 250 Ded	Aug. 20	375
Homeowners	4728316	Friendship Mutual HO-3†	82,000	Jan. 15	257
Health	114732	Blue Cross and Blue Shield		Nov. 1	935

* Refers to liability limits (see Chapter 13 for a complete discussion).
† Refers to the type of homeowners policy (also discussed in Chapter 13).

This record gives you advance notice of when insurance premiums are due and their amounts. It helps you plan your expenditures. As your needs change, you may want to alter the coverage before renewing the policy. Or you might want to check on obtaining coverage from a different insurance company. Later chapters in the book will outline specific steps to help you decide what coverage you need.

Investment Records

Investment records track the performance of your investments and give details on purchases and sales. You will want to know how your "winners" are doing. And you *need* to know how poorly your "dogs" are doing. A review of last year's performance can show if your investment strategy needs a revamp. If you decide to sell an investment, the IRS will want to collect income taxes on the interest, dividends, and any gains. Good records can assist all of these purposes.

You should start a separate file folder for each investment. It is a convenient place to collect statements, notices, confirmations, and purchase details. Included in that record should be a summary sheet, similar to Exhibit 2.10, tracking the investment's performance. While we summarize three investments on this exhibit, in practice a separate sheet for each one is preferred.

MAINTAINING YOUR RECORDS

Financial records are too important to stuff in a shoe box or a Twinkies carton. You will need to update them regularly. And you will need the information easily accessible. Why spend hours searching for a record that was last spotted in the vicinity of the kitty litter bag? An orderly, centralized record system means that your time can be spent planning your finances.

Get a small file cabinet to house all of your records: metal, plastic, or fiberboard will do. Next, buy a good supply of standard file folders to segment the material in logical order.

 *Exhibit 2.10*

Record of Your Investments

	Investments		
Line description	Last ditch mutual fund	High flyer common stock	Stoic bond
1. Purchase date	5/1/1985	3/6/1987	7/10/1986
2. Original purchase price	$1,500	$2,000	$3,000
3. Market value, January 19XX	$2,000	$2,500	$3,000
4. Interest or dividends during 19XX	$ 120	$ 50	$ 360
5. Market price, December 19XX	$2,200	$2,400	$3,000
6. Change in value of investment during past year: line 5 − line 3	$ 200	− $100	0
7. Rate of return during 19XX (line 4 + line 6) divided by line 3	16%	−2%	12%

Using a Personal Computer: Income Statement and Balance Sheet

Should you use a **personal computer** for your **financial record keeping?** If you have access to a personal computer, preparing your income statement and balance sheet on the unit may be worth considering. Both records are prepared on a regular basis, and comparisons between periods are helpful. Also, the statements entail some computations. These tasks can be performed readily by a personal computer.

One option you have is to use some form of specialized **personal finance software:** some of the more popular current titles are Managing Your Money, Dollars and Sense, Your Personal Net Worth, Home Accountant Plus, and The Personal Accountant. There will be additional titles by the time you read this. Most of these programs will generate your balance sheet, and some will also prepare an income statement.

Using a specialized personal finance program offers several advantages. The form for the statement has already been designed for you. Many of the required account titles are provided by the software, but most programs allow you to add others if necessary.

Specialized software also has some disadvantages. First is the $100 to $300 cost of the program. Then there is the time and effort you need to put in to learn how to operate the program. Poor or nonexistent instructions can make learning the program frustrating. Limited documentation may make it difficult to figure out why you are getting a particular result and offer no guidance on correcting problems. Programs that have more features and options than you need are a wasteful investment. Programs that lack adequate flexibility mean you end up with a record that does not meet your needs.

Your second option is to use standard **spreadsheet software.** The rows-and-columns format of this software makes it good for income statements and balance sheets. Some of the more popular current programs are Lotus 1-2-3, Multiplan, SuperCalc, and VisiCalc. There will be others by the time you read this. Standard spreadsheets offer several advantages. Because the records constructed are tailored to your needs, you can modify them as your finances become more complex. You may already be familiar with this type of program, making use of the program easy: you don't have to learn how to use a new piece of software. Once the format is established, periodically updating your statements should be easy. Last, the columns of the statement can be defined so as to make comparisons between periods automatic.

Using a general-purpose spreadsheet program also has some drawbacks. First, the program can be expensive. If you are not familiar with it, you will have to spend time learning the structure and commands; fortunately, instructions for major spreadsheets tend to be clear and comprehensive. Initially, it will take you some time to set up your record format.

Whether you should use a personal computer to keep your financial records depends on your circumstances. It certainly can provide a professional-looking income statement and balance sheet. It may provide more subtotals, totals, percentages, and comparisons to prior periods than would manual records. But you may find it takes more time to produce those results, especially at the beginning.

Strategy

If you have a personal computer, consider using it to prepare your income statement and balance sheet. If you don't have one, preparing basic financial records will hardly justify your buying one.

Using a Personal Computer: Other Financial Records

For purposes beyond creating and updating an income statement and balance sheet, the benefits of using a personal computer are less clear. A spreadsheet program can be developed to quickly compute the performance data for each of your investments. But your benefits are going to be greatest when the investments are numerous and diverse. Benefits from using the computer for the insurance record and the personal property inventory are doubtful: it is easy to update and add information to a handwritten list. None of these benefits, of themselves, would justify purchasing a computer.

SAFEGUARDING YOUR RECORDS

There are three locations that need to be considered as possible storage sites for your important documents. Documents that you need almost daily should be carried on your person. Documents that you need less frequently, and that would not be overly difficult to replace, can be stored in your home: the file cabinet we discussed in the previous section would be the obvious choice. Finally, documents that would be very difficult or expensive to replace should be stored in a safe-deposit box.

Exhibit 2.11 summarizes where your important records and documents should be kept. Following each listing is a suggested period of time for retaining that item.

A Safe-Deposit Box

Commercial banks have historically been the major source of **safe-deposit boxes.** Located in the bank's vault, boxes were reasonably secure and fire-resistant. Recently, savings and loans, mutual savings banks, credit unions, and some specialized businesses have also begun offering safe-deposit boxes.

What do you receive for your $20 to $40 annual rental payment? A small box that requires two keys to open: you keep one and the other is held by the bank or institution. Losing a key could mean having to pay $50 or more to have the box opened, since there usually is no duplicate. Generally you will have to sign a form each time you want access to the box. The contents of your box will usually not be covered by the bank's insurance. But losses have generally been rare. For your $20 to $40, you are purchasing security for your most valuable documents.

Strategy

If you have important documents, renting a safe-deposit box is advised. Purchasing insurance to cover the box's contents is not advised unless you store personal assets of high value in the box.

Exhibit 2.11

Storage and Keeping of Important Records and Documents

On Your Person

Auto registration; until renewed	Drivers license; until renewed
Social Security card; permanently	

Filed at Home

Bank statement; prior 3 years	Birth certificate (copy); permanently
Canceled checks; prior 3 years	Guarantees; while item is owned
Health records; permanently	Insurance policies; until new policy
Letter of last instruction (copy); permanently	Major purchase receipts; 6 years
Tax returns; prior 4 years	Will (copy); permanently

Safe-Deposit Box

Adoption paper; permanently	Auto title; until sold
Birth certificate; permanently	Bonds; until sold
Citizenship papers; permanently	Common stock certificate; until sold
Contracts; 6 years after closure	Divorce decree; permanently
Letter of last instruction; permanently	Marriage record; permanently
Military papers; permanently	Personal inventory; until updated
Real estate deed; until sold	Social Security record; permanently
Will; permanently	

Summary

1 An income statement presents an historical summary of your income, your expenditures, and the surplus (or deficit) that is the difference between the two categories.
2 Analyzing your income statement involves reviewing the details on the present year's statement and comparing it with statements for prior years.
3 A balance sheet summarizes your assets (the things you own), your liabilities (what you owe to others), and your net worth (assets minus liabilities) as of a particular moment.
4 Assets are carried on your balance sheet at their current market value, and liabilities at their present unpaid balance.
5 An analysis of your current balance sheet, along with a review of prior years, can reveal potential problems in the management of your personal finances.
6 A personal property inventory should be updated periodically and stored off-premises. It can support insurance claims in the event of a loss.
7 Your tax records should have two components: (1) an historical file for the years you have completed and filed the required tax forms and (2) a file to collect details to be used in filing this year's tax return.
8 Homeownership records include items such as deeds, surveys, and house plans that are transferred at time of purchase. While you own a house, you ought to keep records on all improvements to it.
9 Insurance records provide a brief summary of your coverage together with data on the premiums.
10 Your investment record tracks the performance of each investment: winners and losers. It will provide necessary support for gains and losses you claim on your tax return.
11 A file cabinet and a supply of manila folders makes record keeping easier and more-organized.
12 A personal computer can help you with personal financial records which require computations, frequent replications, comparisons to prior periods, and when a neat record is important. Personal finance software or general-purpose spreadsheet programs can be used.
13 Store personal records and documents that would be difficult or costly to replace in a safe-deposit box.

Review your understanding of

Income statement
Surplus on income statement
Deficit on income statement
Balance sheet
Personal asset
Financial asset
Liability
Net worth
Positive net worth
Negative net worth
Personal property inventory
Tax record: prior years

Tax record: current year
Homeownership record
Deed
Home improvements
Home maintenance
Insurance record
Investment record
Personal computer: record keeping
Personal finance software
Spreadsheet software
Safe-deposit box

Discussion questions

1 What information does an income statement summarize? How can you use it to assist you in your financial planning?
2 If your income statement indicates you have a surplus, what does that suggest? How might that surplus affect your balance sheet? When an income statement shows a deficit, what does that suggest? Is there a limit to how long the deficit can continue?
3 What information does a balance sheet show? How can you use it in your financial planning?
4 Give some examples of events that might cause the net worth on your balance sheet to rise. What conclusions might you draw from a negative net worth on a balance sheet?
5 What information should your personal property inventory contain? How can it assist in managing your finances?

6   What sorts of items should your tax file of the past several years contain? How would the tax file for the current year differ? What purpose does it serve?

7   How does a home improvement expenditure differ from a home maintenance expense? Which would you want to track most carefully? Why?

8   Why should a person have an insurance record? How can it help you plan your personal finances?

9   What is the purpose of an investment record? Name two ways in which the record can assist you.

10 List advantages of using a personal computer to help you prepare your financial records. Are there disadvantages? What records are the best candidates for computer assistance? Why?

11 What features make a safe-deposit box secure from unauthorized people? Are such boxes widely available? How would you decide if a record should be stored in your deposit box?

Problems

2.1 Charlie Closecount needs some help finishing his income statement for the year. So far Charlie has summarized the year's information as follows:

Wages	$19,000	**Medical expenses**	$ 440
Checking account	400	Personal expenses	280
Taxes	3,300	Miscellaneous expenses	600
Rent and utilities	5,750	Travel	2,100
Unpaid loan balance	1,300	Clothing	780
Auto expenses	2,100	Insurance premiums	600
Credit card balance	300	Loan payments	800
Food	2,120	Money market account	1,200

Prepare an income statement for Charlie.

2.2 Wayne and Wendy Worth went to prepare a balance sheet for the end of the year. Their balances and details for the year are:

Checking account	$300	House	$80,000*
Unpaid bills	800	Mortgage	60,000†
Automobile	6,500*	Mutual fund, common stock	3,400*
Mutual fund, money market account	1,500	Personal property	4,300
		Auto loan	5,200†

* Current market value.
† Present unpaid balance.

Can you help the Worths with their balance sheet?

2.3 To do this problem, you must have completed Problem 2.2. Please show how the following two items would impact on the Worths' balance sheet:

a The Worths use $1,000 from their money market mutual fund to repay $1,000 of their present automobile loan.

b The Worths borrow $13,000 to purchase a new $13,000 automobile.

2.4 Dennis Disorganized is reviewing the possible gain on the recent sale of his house. Details from the 3 years he owned the house include:

Original purchase price	$50,000	Painting exterior and interior at time of purchase	$ 4,000
Cost of adding new bedroom	9,000	Sale price	78,000
Remodeling kitchen	7,000	Replacing two broken sections of sidewalk	300

a Which of the above items will qualify as home improvements?

b Using the improvements you have listed in part (a), figure Dennis's potential gain on the sale.

2.5 Summarized below are Connie Comparison's balance sheets for the past 3 years.

Year	12/31/85	12/31/86	12/31/87
	Assets		
Cash	$ 300	$ 300	$ 300
Money market, mutual fund	4,300	2,000	400
Automobile	500	9,500	12,900
Personal property	2,000	4,000	6,000
Total	$7,100	$15,800	$19,600
	Liabilities		
Current bills	$ 300	$ 800	$ 1,800
Auto loan	0	8,000	12,000
Cash loans		2,500	3,500
Total	$ 300	$11,300	$17,300
	Net Worth		
	$6,800	$ 4,500	$ 2,300

a What has happened to Connie's net worth during the 3 years?
b What has caused the change in her net worth?
c Might you suggest any changes for Connie's personal finances?

2.6 Show the effect of each transaction listed below on the following balance sheet categories: total assets, total liabilities, and net worth. For each category, show the likely dollar amount and the direction of change: use (+) for increases, (−) for decreases, and a (0) for no change or an indeterminate change. Be prepared to support your position.

Transaction	Assets $ change	Liabilities $ change	Net worth $ change
Buy a $12,000 car with $9,000 loan and $3,000 from checking account.	_____	_____	_____
Draw $500 from checking account to repay credit card balance.	_____	_____	_____
Market value of your mutual fund account rises $250.	_____	_____	_____
Uninsured bicycle is stolen: original cost $300; current value $100.	_____	_____	_____
Bank deposits $50 interest in your savings account.	_____	_____	_____
Charge $400 ski trip to your credit card.	_____	_____	_____
Deposit $100 from paycheck in money market mutual fund.	_____	_____	_____
Borrow $1,000 from credit union to repay credit card balance.	_____	_____	_____
Market value of car was $5,000 last year; now car is worth $3,400.	_____	_____	_____

2.7 Sidney Sunset has summarized selected totals from his income statement for the past 3 years. Those totals are shown in the table on the next page.
a What surplus or deficit does Sidney have for each of the 3 years?
b What has happened to Sidney's living costs and taxes during the 3 years? His discretionary expenses?
c Discuss the strengths and weaknesses you observe in the above income statements. Support your position.
d What suggestions for future action might you give Sidney?

Details	Current year	1 year earlier	2 years earlier
Total income	$24,500	$22,700	$21,000
Expenditures			
Living costs and taxes	$18,400	$16,720	15,200
Discretionary expenses	11,100	9,650	8,400
Loan payments	4,025	2,600	740
Total	$33,525	$28,970	$24,340

Case problem

Gloria Schultz is planning to start her junior year in college this September. She has lived at home during the 2 years she spent at a community college. Working part time at the school bookstore, she earned sufficient income to pay her community college expenses. But when she transfers to the main campus of the state university, she will need financial aid. Since she is claimed as a dependent on her father's tax return, she will need to provide information on the family's finances on the aid application. The application requires a balance sheet and income statement for the family.

Gloria's father is busy, so he has asked that she prepare the two statements. He has provided the following details. Last year he earned $36,000, on which he paid Social Security taxes of $2,574, federal taxes of $3,900, and state taxes of $950. The family's present house was purchased 3 years ago for $79,900; its current market value is $92,500. The unpaid balance on the mortgage is $62,070. Estimated living costs for the past year are:

Monthly amounts		Annual Amounts	
Food	$350	Real estate taxes	$1,900
Mortgage payment	605	Health care	600
Utilities	130	Entertainment	1,700
Clothes	120	Life insurance	300
Loan payments: car	240	Homeowners insurance	320
Auto operating expense	180	Home maintenance	900
Miscellaneous	200		

In addition to the house, assets include a money market fund with a balance of $3,100 and a checking account with a balance of $350. There are two cars: an 11-year-old compact worth $800 and a 3-year-old station wagon worth $8,600; its original price was $12,750. The unpaid balance on the car loan is $7,300. Other current bills include $750 due on various credit cards and a dentist's bill for $120 (not covered by insurance). Personal assets are currently worth $15,300.

1   Help Gloria complete an income statement.
2   Help Gloria complete a balance sheet.

Developing and managing your income

PART 2

CHAPTER 3

Developing financial goals and integrating them into your budget

AFTER COMPLETING THIS CHAPTER YOU WILL HAVE LEARNED

- The importance of developing financial goals
- How to develop a plan for long-range and short-range goals
- How to convert a goal's total cost to a monthly amount
- How to judge whether you can complete your planned goals
- The four major steps in the budgeting process
- How to estimate income available for your budget
- How to develop dollar estimates for your major budget categories
- How to integrate your financial goals into your budget
- The major purpose of your budget summary sheet
- How to analyze differences between your actual results and your planned budget amounts
- The purpose of an emergency cash reserve

Managing personal finances without a financial plan is like trying to drive to Casablanca without tracing your route on a map. You may know enough to turn left at the end of your driveway, but you will be very lucky if you reach your destination. Planning your personal finances is essential in order for you to reach *your* goals. The noted financial advisor Venita Van Caspel notes that most people arrive at retirement with little, "not because they planned to fail, but because they failed to plan." People fail to meet many other goals because they don't develop adequate financial plans.

Designing your personal financial plan is a lot like planning a trip. First, you need to specify what **financial goals** you want to reach—your destination. Next, you need to outline the steps which will take you to your goals—a route to your destination. Then you need to ask the question: Do I have the resources to get me where I want to go? The answer to the question will tell you whether you have set reasonable goals or whether you have to change them. Finally, you need a "log book" to monitor your progress; your budget is that log.

This chapter will teach you how to draw up an organized financial plan that will let you achieve what *you* want.

DEVELOPING YOUR FINANCIAL GOALS

In this chapter we will focus our attention on longer-term financial goals involving sizable amounts of money. There are four steps in developing your financial goals:

- Decide what you want to do.
- Decide *when* you would like to attain each goal.
- Estimate the approximate cost to reach each goal.
- Ask yourself: Do I have or will I have the resources to achieve my goals? If not, what revisions are needed to better balance what I want to do with what I *can* do.

You will find it easier to decide what you want to do if you set goals for two periods. Your goals for the next 15 to 25 years will be your long-range plan. The second period should cover the next 5 years; this plan will be more detailed, since these goals will be reached relatively soon.

Plan for Long-Range Goals

Your **long-range plan** should contain all the financial goals you wish to complete over the next 15, 20, or 25 years. Why the range? People who have a stable and predictable financial situation can generally plan for the longer period. Those in less certain financial situations must opt for the shorter period.

You may consider 10 years to be forever, and 20 years nearly beyond comprehension. But a good financial plan should not concentrate on the short term alone. Many long-term goals, such as building a retirement fund to provide 20 years of income, require large amounts of money. You cannot accumulate that amount in a few years. You need to plan for this goal early so you have time to reach it. If long-term goals are ignored, they can never be reached. Remember the phrase about not planning to fail but failing to plan.

A time line will help you place your goals in perspective. A sample is shown in Exhibit 3.1. You can divide the line any way it works for you: most find 5-year segments work well. Most people, particularly those who are young and starting their careers, have a lengthy list of goals on their time line. Don't attach a price tag to your goals now; that is done later. An example will illustrate how a long-range plan is developed. Since you were introduced to Frank and Mary Swanson in Chapter 2, we will use them as our example.

Frank and Mary Swanson: An example

Recall that Frank and Mary Swanson both earn considerable income. And they have prospects of even higher incomes in the future. Both have received sizable raises during the past 3 years. This may partially explain the ambitious goals the Swansons list in Exhibit 3.1. Frank and Mary certainly have elevated financial expectations for the next 20 years.

Your list of goals will probably differ significantly from the Swansons'. It should. A Mercedes-Benz may epitomize one person's automobile goal; others might think it woefully overpriced transportation. The trendy new house in a pretigious suburb that is one person's dream is someone else's cement overshoes. Though everyone needs to develop financial goals, yours will be personal and reflect your values and choices.

After summarizing their long-term goals (Exhibit 3.1), the Swansons will develop a plan for the next 5 years. Here they take a detailed look at their goals for the next 5 years.

 **Exhibit 3.1**

Projected Time Schedule for Frank and Mary Swanson's Long-Term Financial Goals

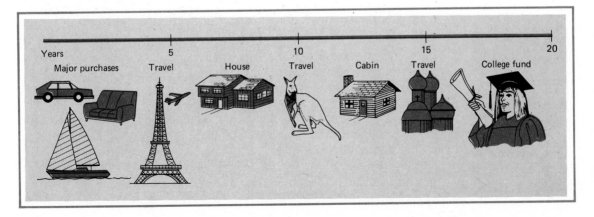

Plan for Short-Term Goals

Your **short-range plan** includes the goals you expect to complete in the next 5 years. Though you might choose a period other than 5 years, you should develop your goals for the near term. Sample goals for such a plan might include:

- Accumulate the down payment on a house that you will purchase in 5 years.
- Accumulate the money to trade in your automobile in 3 years.
- In 5 years, accumulate one-half the money you need to let your child attend college in 10 years.

Some goals may be scheduled for completion quite early; others will not be implemented until the end of 5 years. Some that entail a sizable amount may not be completed until after 5 years. If the cost of your financial goal is high, start accumulating the money now. Include any goal that you expect to launch during the next 5 years. Goals you do not plan to begin until year 6 or later can wait for some future plan.

Our time line is also useful for planning your short-term goals. Exhibit 3.2 illustrates how one might look. Since the period is only 5 years, single-year increments work well. Though a price tag will be attached later, Frank and Mary Swanson illustrate such a plan.

Frank and Mary Swanson: An example

Frank and Mary have summarized their goals for the next 5 years. Like Exhibit 3.1, this plan shows numerous goals. The Swansons may find they need to revise their goals once they attach a dollar cost to each. That will be the topic of the next section.

The Swansons' goals (Exhibit 3.2) reflect their joint values and choices. My list certainly would look different, and so would yours. It is important that everyone affected be involved in planning the goals. Whether single, a young couple, or a couple with children, your plan is far more likely to succeed if everyone affected by it helps develop it.

Exhibit 3.2

Projected Time Schedule for Frank and Mary Swanson's Short-Term Financial Goals

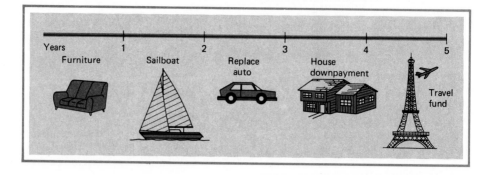

Estimating the Cost of Each Financial Goal

Now estimate what it will cost to implement each goal in your short-term plan. The cost should include all of the expenditures you expect to make.

Don't be like Delbert Dollarshort: though he saved the $9,000 he needed for the down payment on a town house, he overlooked the $2,000 he needed for closing expenses. Delbert will need several more years in his apartment to save that $2,000. Hopefully he planned for the cost of furnishings, moving, and yard and patio equipment for the town house. Avoid the Dollarshort dilemma: include *all* costs of a goal.

You may ask: What about inflation's impact on these future costs? Should they be adjusted upward? For the moment, accept my word that it probably is not necessary; later we will see why. Since the Swansons have shared their short-term plan, it will serve as our example for this step.

Frank and Mary Swanson: A continuing example

Note that Frank and Mary Swanson list each of their short-term goals in column 1 of Exhibit 3.3. These are the same as in Exhibit 3.2, but they are now ordered by time of completion. Column 2 shows the estimated cost for each: this is based on current cost. Finally, the Swansons list the projected number of months until completion in column 3. A couple of quick notes: (1) The "net difference" is what Frank and Mary expect they will have to pay to trade their present second car for a new one; (2) if you look at Exhibit 3.1, you will note that the Swansons plan to actually purchase the house in year 8, but due to the sizable amount, they will accumulate half of the estimated cost during the next 4 years.

Converting a Goal's Total Cost to a Monthly Amount

Usually, personal budgets use monthly segments for planning purposes. There are excellent reasons for that, as we will see later. Since a budget is a basic part of a well-developed financial plan, you should integrate your financial goals into your budget. That means **reducing each goal's cost to a monthly amount.** You can do that by dividing the goal's total cost by the

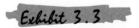

Exhibit 3.3

Developing Cost Estimates for Frank and Mary Swanson's Short-Term Financial Goals

Financial goal	Estimated total cost	Proposed completion date	Monthly amount needed	Rank among goals
New furniture	$ 3,600	12 months	$300	3
Sailboat	9,600	24 months	400	5
Replace auto: net difference	12,960	36 months	360	4
House down payment: ½ of $9,120	4,560	48 months	95	1
European travel	5,100	60 months	85	2

projected number of months until completion:

$$\frac{\text{Monthly}}{\text{amount}} = \frac{\text{total cost of goal}}{\text{months to complete goal}}$$

The following example will illustrate this process.

Frank and Mary Swanson: A continuing example

Mary and Frank want to convert each goal's cost (Exhibit 3.3) to a monthly amount. Dividing the total costs in column 2 by the projected months to completion in column 3 gives the monthly amount. Column 4 of Exhibit 3.3 shows the results.

The large amounts in column 4 suggest the Swansons will need to save a considerable amount each month. You will recall we earlier said the Swansons seemed to have ambitious goals. When each goal's total cost is stated as a required monthly savings figure, you see more clearly.

Interpreting the monthly dollar amounts

The last section illustrated one reason for converting to monthly amounts: it lets you integrate your financial plan into your monthly budget. The process also highlights just how much money you will need to save each month to reach your goals in the desired time.

You might accumulate that money in one of several ways:

- Buy a lottery ticket; some jackpots have been enormous.
- Hope that Aunt Agatha names you in her will, preferably sooner rather than later.
- Or save the money on a regular basis and invest it until the goal is reached.

That's a list of my long-term financial goals including my retirement plan. You can jump in anywhere it seems appropriate.

As a financial planner, I have a decided preference for the last; it certainly is more controllable than the first two. (My Aunt Agatha will probably outlive me by years.) Most important, though, is that the last alternative lets you implement a *plan* to attain your goals.

What about the interest the money earns while it is invested? The observant individual is likely to ask: What about the interest or dividends the money will earn while it is invested? Why not reduce the amount you must save by the "bundle" the money will earn while it is invested? The interest, dividends, and possible rise in market value on your investments could be sizable, especially if you invest for a long time. But your actual earnings may be less than you imagine. Recall that Chapter 1 noted that your partners, the Internal Revenue Service and your state income tax department, want to share your "good times." Some of your earnings—perhaps 30 percent or more—will be needed for federal and possibly state income taxes.

Also consider the impact of inflation on a goal's final cost. As inflation pushes up future costs, carrying out a goal will cost you more. Take the Swansons' planned house purchase from Exhibit 3.3 as an example. The current cost for their house of choice is $81,000. One major cost of purchasing that house will be the 10 percent down payment. If inflation averages 5 percent annually over the 10 years until they buy the house, the home's price will have risen to about $132,000. They will need $13,200 for a 10 percent down payment, not $8,100. Where will the extra $5,100 for the down payment come from? A good part of it could come from the interest and dividends their investments earn. Even after taxes, those earnings can offset much of the inflationary cost increase. A high return on investments before taxes is desirable because it lets you cover taxes and offset inflation.

I hesitate to generalize that after-tax earnings will always cover inflation, because many factors can affect real earnings. Your tax rate, for instance, affects the amount you keep to offset inflation. The time remaining until your goal will be completed also affects the interest you earn. Certainly the rate of return affects your earnings. Coming chapters on investments and retirement planning will develop more sophisticated models that consider other factors that can influence your "required" monthly savings. For now, dividing a goal's total cost by the months until completion will give us an adequate estimate.

If you don't take interest earnings into account, you automatically provide for inflation, or a large portion of it. And the process is much simpler than predicting what inflation might be 5, 10, or more years from now.

Does that mean you can ignore the rate of return on a prospective investment? Not at all. Your earnings on investments must pay taxes and offset much, if not all, future inflation. A substandard return on the money you invest could mean your final savings will be insufficient; inflation might push the goal's cost beyond what they will cover.

Can You Carry Out Your Financial Plan?

The monthly amounts you estimate you need to reach your goals raise a question: Do I have the resources I need to achieve the goals? Most people could give an unqualified *yes* if they postponed eating for 3 years, their landlord "overlooked" their rent for about 5 years, and Hertz leased a car for $5 a month for 4 years. The hard fact is that many find their resources are insufficient to reach their ambitious goals. Either they must adjust their goals (the easiest—if not the most pleasant—option), or they have to increase their monthly income (like winning the lottery, a good idea but often difficult).

You must start by estimating the monthly income you have available to achieve your goals. Since much of your income will be needed for living expenses and loan payments, only a fraction is available for savings. The surplus, or deficit, from your income statement is your starting point. Recall from Chapter 2 that you compute that total by deducting the sum of your living expenses, discretionary expenditures, and loan payments from your total income. A deficit obviously means you have nothing to meet future goals. If you have a surplus, you will be able to reach some or all of your goals, depending on the size of the surplus. Your income statement is only a starting point: it summarizes your "past" spending. You will also need to know available income based on "planned" future spending. This is discussed later.

If you compare your available income to the amount needed for your goals, you can judge how many of those goals you can reach. If you have enough income to complete all the goals in your plan, congratulations. That is an easy "problem" to handle. But what if your income is inadequate for your goals? First, you are not alone. But what are your options? You could eliminate some goals in the plan. Maybe you could pick them up in next year's plan, or later. You might also lengthen the period planned to attain one or more goals. That would lower the required monthly amount since the cost is spread over more months. Or you could review your present income and expenditures to see if some changes would make more money available to you. The budget material from the second part of this chapter reviews that option. Often, a combination of two or more of these options will work.

Let's see how Mary and Frank Swanson could plan to reach the goals in Exhibit 3.3.

Frank and Mary Swanson: Continuing the example

Frank and Mary first need to estimate how much income they have for their goals. If you look back to Exhibit 2.2, you will see that the Swansons' income statement shows a $6,600 surplus. Assume that their spending plans for next year are unchanged; the $6,600 surplus will continue. Dividing that $6,600 by 12 shows the Swansons have $550 each month for their goals.

An examination of Exhibit 3.3 reveals that the Swansons' resources are not adequate to reach their goals. The monthly amounts in column 4 show they need more than $1,200 each month to attain their ambitions.

The $650 difference between needed savings and their actual resources suggests revisions are needed.

Remember, the Swansons ranked their goals in column 5 of Exhibit 3.3, with the most important goal ranked as 1 and the least ranked 5. Now they can see which goals they can reach if they make no adjustments. The required monthly amount for goals 1 through 3 is $480 ($95 + $85 + $300). They would have no difficulty doing these; in fact the $70 ($550 − $480) left over could start them toward their fourth goal; however, it would take them more than 15 years to accumulate the required $12,960 at $70 monthly. Further revisions are in order.

They have three options:

1   Drop one or more goals.
2   Extend the completion date for one or more goals.
3   Review their present income and expenditures for possible changes.

The Swansons decide to revise their plan using a combination of the first two. They extend the completion date on the furniture purchase from 12 to 36 months, which drops the monthly amount to $100 ($3,600 cost/36 months). They decide to wait 12 more months to replace the second car: with a target of 48 months, the monthly amount drops to $270 ($12,900/ 48). Finally, they decide to postpone the sailboat purchase. Adjusting the timing on the furniture and the car, and giving up the sailboat, reduces the required monthly amount for goals 1 through 4 to $550 ($95 + $85 + $100 + $270), their available income.

The strategies you use to adjust your financial plan are likely to be quite unlike the Swansons' because your values, aspirations, and willingness to sacrifice are probably different. But when your available income is insufficient, you must review and make adjustments. If you want to reach your goals, your plan must be realistic. If you match your ambitions to your financial ability, you *can* have what you want, but it will take time, discipline, and foresight.

PURPOSE OF A BUDGET

The second topic of this chapter is developing a budget. Do not file the material you just covered: you will need to integrate the financial goals you just developed into your budget.

No one publishes a master budget to tell you how to "best" spend your money. You are the only one who can decide how to obtain the greatest satisfaction from your income. What a budget can do, however, is help you plan your spending for maximum satisfaction. This applies whether you have $15,000, $30,000, $50,000 a year, or are one of those poor devils fending off the tax collector because your income exceeds 6 digits.

A major distinction between a budget and an income statement is the time period each covers. A budget looks to the future. Income statements record the past.

A budget can help you answer two related questions: What do I want to do with my income? What can I reasonably expect to achieve with my income? A budget encourages you to address these questions in advance. Potential problems can be spotted while there is enough time to make the adjustments.

BUDGETING: THE PRELIMINARIES

Exhibit 3.4 illustrates the four steps in the **budgeting process:**

1   Estimate your available income.
2   Define the major expenditure categories for your budget and set spending levels for each.
3   Use a budget summary sheet to track your actual income and expenditures.
4   Review and analyze your budget summary sheet periodically to see if your actual experience matches your plans; if not, take corrective action.

The Budgeting Process

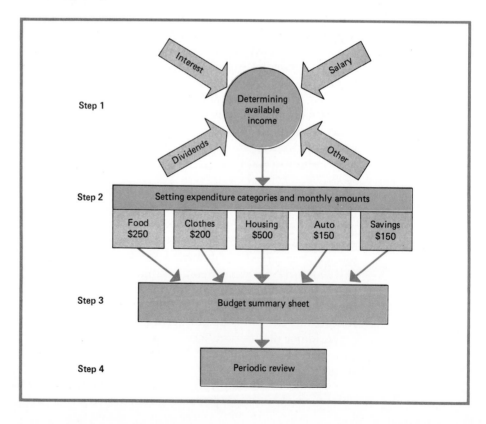

Your clerical work is primarily concentrated in step 3. Still, maintaining a well-developed budgeting system should take no more than 1 to 3 hours a month. Using a personal computer, you might cut that considerably; more on this later. People often think a budget's major purpose is capturing the past; budgeting becomes a clerical exercise as they try to hunt down every penny spent. Yet budgeting's largest roles in financial planning rest on steps 1 and 2: deciding what you have and what you want to do with it. The secondary benefit of budgeting is in step 4: providing a guide for managing your finances. These benefits far outweigh the clerical effort required.

Step 1: Estimating Available Income

Identifying your available income is the first step of the budget process. But you can't use gross income, the annual amount divided by 12. You must adjust gross income to reflect what you actually receive. Suppose Norma Newhire accepts a job at a monthly salary of $2,200. After one month, Norma nervously opens her first pay envelope. Is it a check for $2,200? No. Aha! Too many coffee breaks Norma? No, deductions make the check much smaller. What Norma receives is her net pay, or **take-home pay.** Some deductions are nonvoluntary; even if she wanted to say no, she could not stop them. The rest are voluntary; she can stop these at any time.

Nonvoluntary deductions

Nonvoluntary deductions are withheld from your salary whether you want them to be or not. Heading the list are taxes: Social Security contributions, federal income taxes, state income taxes, and possibly city income taxes. Other examples are required contributions to a pension plan and premiums for health or life insurance. All share a common feature: you cannot stop them except by stopping your income. Social Security will take a dim view if you say: ''I gave last year; skip me this year because I need the money.''

Voluntary deductions

Voluntary deductions are amounts you asked to have deducted from your wages. Examples are contributions to your employer's savings plan, a monthly deposit to your credit union account, or premiums for optional insurance coverage. Their common feature is that you could stop or alter them if you decided to.

Available income

Your **available income** is what you have left after subtracting nonvoluntary deductions. This is the income you have available to spend. Your budget starts here.

To illustrate how you compute available income, we will use the example of Sam and Nancy Swift (Exhibit 3.5). The Swifts have identified all sources of income they expect to receive during the *coming* year; remember, a budget concentrates on future events. Beside salary and wages, other employment-related payments—bonuses, commissions, and profit sharing, for example—can be included *if* they are reasonably certain. The list can also include earnings from a savings account, shares of common stock, mutual funds or other investments. As before, we will use a monthly planning period. Sam and Nancy have divided their annual amounts by 12

Exhibit 3.5

Estimating Available Monthly Income for Sam and Nancy Swift

	Sam	Nancy	Total
Monthly gross salary	$1,800	$1,600	$3,400
Interest	20	20	40
Dividends	15	15	30
Bonus		225	225
Gross monthly income	$1,835	$1,860	$3,695
Less: nonvoluntary deductions			
Federal income tax	$ 148	152	300
State income tax	65	65	130
Social Security	135	137	272
Pension	18	32	50
Medical and life insurance	34	19	53
Total available income	$1,435	$1,455	$2,890
Less: voluntary deductions			
Credit union	$170		$ 170
Stock purchase plan		$ 135	135
Total take-home income	$1,265	$1,320	$2,585

to compute the monthly amount shown in Exhibit 3.5. They expect a monthly gross income of $3,695 for the next year.

In the middle section of Exhibit 3.5, Sam and Nancy have subtracted their projected nonvoluntary deductions and estimated their available income as $2,890. This will be the starting point for their budget. Since you can stop or reduce voluntary deductions and reallocate the money, do not subtract them from your income.

One special caution as you calculate your available income: the above computation assumes the amount you have withheld for taxes will actually pay your tax bill for the year. People sometimes find their federal or state income taxes exceed the amount withheld. They must use some "available" income to pay the balance. Realistically, these payments should be part of a planned budget; a later section will discuss this further. Suppose too much federal or state income tax is withheld and you receive a refund. Is this good planning? No. Unless something unexpected causes overwithholding, large tax refunds signal poor management. Chapter 5 will show why.

The bottom section of Exhibit 3.5 computes Sam and Nancy's take-home pay.

Strategy

Find the available income for your budget as:

$$\text{Available income} = \left(\begin{array}{c}\text{gross}\\\text{salary}\end{array} + \begin{array}{c}\text{interest}\\\text{earnings}\end{array} + \begin{array}{c}\text{dividend}\\\text{payments}\end{array} + \begin{array}{c}\text{bonus and}\\\text{commissions}\end{array}\right) - \begin{array}{c}\text{nonvoluntary}\\\text{deductions}\end{array}$$

Step 2: Establishing the Major Expenditure Categories

How much detail should you have in your budget? Limiting yourself to 10 or fewer major **expenditure categories**—food, housing expenses, automobile costs, insurance, loan payments, and personal expenses, for instance—simplifies the process. A short budget is easy to prepare and maintain. But there is a trade-off: fewer categories provide less detail. That could make it more difficult to identify the cause of some problem. Increasing the number of categories to 20 or 30 would provide a detailed spending plan. Such a budget breaks expenditures into smaller units: housing costs might be split into rent, utilities, and insurance, for example. Analyzing an expenditure overrun is easier with the added detail. But a more complex budget is more work to prepare and maintain.

Strategy

Choose the number of budget categories that gives you detail on how your money is spent, yet does not frustrate your budgeting effort with minute detail.

The budget period

Most people use the year ahead as their total planning period. If a budget is to be effective, the year should be divided into smaller **budget periods.** Monthly periods seem to work best: they match the billing pattern on many expenditures and permit enough detail so that you can monitor your spending, yet updating of the budget is not so frequent that it requires excessive clerical effort.

Include all of your expenses

A good budgeting system should plan *all* of your spending. Living expenses, such as food, housing, or transportation, must be paid on a reg-

ular basis. Dividing the category into monthly amounts is reasonably straightforward. But you should also plan a monthly amount when an expense—such as an insurance premium—is paid only once or twice a year. This way you make certain these items are part of your spending plan. Furthermore, saving regular monthly amounts helps ensure you will have the funds for the payment.

A later section gives a more formal plan for handling timing differences between your income and payments.

Strategy

Your budget should include monthly amounts for regular expenditures and for those bills that are paid only once or twice a year.

How do you want to spend your money?

Once you decide on your expenditure categories, you need to determine the amount for each category. Some find their spending plan exceeds their income. Then hard choices have to be made as to how to spend resources. How can you set guides for your spending?

Expenditure estimates: past spending. Start by assessing how you spent your income last year. Your past expenditures can help you set reasonable levels for this year. If you used a budget last year, total your actual expenditures from it. For instance, Sam and Nancy Swift summarized seven of their expenditure categories in Exhibit 3.6 using last year's budget. To save space, only seven categories, and monthly detail for only 3 months, is shown. However, total expenditures for the year appear in column 6. In the final column these totals have been divided by 12 to find the

Exhibit 3.6

Historical Record of Spending* in 19XX: Sam and Nancy Swift

Expenditures	January	February	March	Quarter	Total	Average
Food	$ 375	$ 400	$ 385	$1,160	$ 4,620	$ 385
Housing						
Mortgage payment	770	770	770	2,310	9,240	770
Real estate taxes	930	—	—	930	1,860	155
Utilities	215	185	170	570	2,100	175
Homeowners insurance	—	—	228	228	228	19
Maintenance	—	310	20	330	780	65
Total housing	$1,915	$1,265	$1,188	$4,368	$14,208	$1,184
Clothing	$ 170	$ 70	$ 130	$ 370	$ 1,620	$ 135
.	.	.	.	.	.	.
.	.	.	.	.	.	.
Grand total	$2,675	$2,195	$2,220	$7,090	$28,200	$2,350

* All amounts rounded to the nearest dollar.

average monthly expenditure. Exhibit 3.6 is a guide to help Sam and Nancy plan their budget.

Expenditure estimates: Your checkbook. Suppose you did not prepare a budget last year. What then? Use your checkbook to estimate your expenditures. The checks you wrote during the past 3 to 6 months should tell you where your money went. Don't worry about the pennies; you only need an estimate. How frequently you use checks significantly affects the accuracy of your estimate. If you often pay cash, only a fraction of your spending will be captured. The next section has a solution.

Expenditure estimates: Use a trial period. Suppose your records are incomplete or many payments were made with cash. Now what? First and foremost, don't conclude a budget is impossible. Instead, estimate how much you would *like* to spend in each category; include that in your budget. Over the coming months you can track your expenditures and use the results to adjust your estimate. Don't be surprised if you must make revisions, often increasing the planned amount rather than decreasing it. The important thing is that you have started planning how you want to spend your money. Starting to budget is crucial to managing your finances.

Payments on your outstanding loans

Payments on consumer loans—used to purchase automobiles, major appliances, recreational items, furniture, etc.—must be considered in your budget. These payments are separated from other expenditures for several reasons. First, loan payments are generally fixed: sending a $145 check instead of the required $245, noting you are a bit short this month, will bring a response—but you may not like what it says. Second, a loan's fixed period allows you to predict when the payments start and stop. If payments stop midyear, your budget simply eliminates them. Last, highlighting loan payments shows you one part of your fixed obligations.

Integrating your short-term financial goals into your budget

Up to now, your short-term financial goals have not been considered in your budget. Let's add them. We noted earlier that an essential step in setting your goals was to ask: Do I have the resources to meet my planned financial goals? Initially you used your income statement to answer the question. But the income statement is an historical record. You really need to consider future income to get a good answer. A budget—which looks ahead, not back—will help you see whether your resources are adequate. It compares your expected available income to your planned expenditures, telling you how much income will remain to meet your financial goals. The contrast between what you want and what you can afford will show you whether your goals are too ambitious. As you develop your budget, include the monthly amount for each financial goal. Even if you will not spend the money for a goal within the period covered by the budget, include it in your spending plan. Some goals may not be reached for several years, but the money can be accumulated in some investment so it will be there when needed.

Let's use Sam and Nancy Swift's plan to show **how financial goals are integrated into a budget.** Exhibit 3.7 summarizes Sam and Nancy's short-term financial goals (their goals for the next 5 years). The exhibit shows

Exhibit 3.7

Cost Estimates for Sam and Nancy Swift's Short-Term
Financial Goals

Financial goal	Estimated total cost	Proposed completion date	Monthly amount needed	Rank among goals
Landscaping	$ 900	12 months	$ 75	1
Sailboat	5,040	48 months	$105	2
College tuition fund	5,100	60 months	85	3
Total	$11,040		$265	

each goal's total cost and the number of months until it will be reached. Dividing the total cost from column 2 by the number of months in column 3 produces the monthly amount needed for each goal.

Including the monthly amount needed for each of the Swifts' financial goals accomplishes several things. First, it formally sets aside a fraction of their monthly income for each goal. Second, the budget can help them track their progress toward their target. Finally, since many financial goals tend to be longer-term, it forces the Swifts to use current resources to attain more distant objectives.

Strategy

Compute the monthly amount needed to achieve each of your short-term financial goals, and include it in your budget.

Step 3: Developing the Budget Summary Sheet

Your **budget summary sheet** should highlight:

1   Your *planned* income, expenditures, loan payments, and monthly amount needed for your financial goals.
2   Your *actual* income, expenditures, loan payments, and monthly contributions toward your goals.
3   The difference between the planned and the actual amount for each item. Label these as surpluses or deficits.

Let's continue the example and look at the budget summary sheet for Sam and Nancy Swift (Exhibit 3.8).

The top section of their budget sheet summarizes expected monthly available income. Since Sam and Nancy have already summarized their various income sources (Exhibit 3.5), they carry their $2,890 of available income to the second column of their budget summary sheet.

The middle section of the budget shows the expense categories established in step 2 of the budgeting process. Each category shows planned monthly spending. Sam and Nancy Swift used their spending summary from Exhibit 3.6 as their guide.

Exhibit 3.8

Budget Summary Sheet for Sam and Nancy Swift

	Budgeted amount	January Actual	January Surplus (deficit)	February Actual	February Surplus (deficit)	March Actual	March Surplus (deficit)	Quarterly Budgeted amount	Quarterly Actual	Quarterly Surplus (Deficit)
Available income	$2,890	$3,290	($400)	$2,640	$250	$2,740	$150	$8,670	$8,670	—
Food	$ 405	$415	($ 10)	$ 390	$ 15	$ 430	($ 25)	$1,215	$1,235	($ 20)
Expenditures										
Housing										
Mortgage payment	770	770	—	770	—	770	—	2,310	2,310	—
Real estate taxes	170	1020	(850)	—	170	—	170	510	1,020	(510)
Utilities	185	225	(40)	195	(10)	180	5	555	600	(45)
Homeowners' insurance	20	—	20	—	20	240	(220)	60	240	(180)
Maintenance	70	—	70	—	70	—	70	210	—	210
Clothing	135	15	120	180	(45)	85	50	405	280	125
Medical expenses	35	—	35	39	(4)	20	15	105	59	46
Auto: gas and maintenance	145	115	30	265	(120)	115	30	435	495	(60)
Auto: repairs and insurance	80	30	50	70	10	110	(30)	240	210	30
Contributions	90	70	20	105	(15)	70	20	270	245	25
Life insurance	50	—	50	—	50	150	(100)	150	150	—
Personal	50	40	10	70	(20)	20	30	150	130	20
Entertainment and travel	170	60	110	110	60	80	90	510	250	260
Miscellaneous	100	50	50	110	(10)	65	35	300	225	75
Total expenditures	$2,475	$2,810	($335)	$2,304	$171	$2,335	$140	$7,425	$7,449	($7,449)?

	Budgeted amount	January Actual	January Surplus (deficit)	February Actual (Loan payment)	February Surplus (deficit)	March Actual	March Surplus (deficit)	Quarterly Budgeted amount	Quarterly Actual	Quarterly Surplus (Deficit)
Auto	$ 150	$ 150	—	$ 150	—	$ 150	—	$ 450	$ 450	—

Monthly amounts for goals

	Budgeted amount	January Actual	January Surplus (deficit)	February Actual	February Surplus (deficit)	March Actual	March Surplus (deficit)	Quarterly Budgeted amount	Quarterly Actual	Quarterly Surplus (Deficit)
Landscaping	$ 75	$ 75	—	$ 75	—	$ 75	—	$ 225	$ 225	—
Sailboat	105	105	—	105	—	105	—	315	315	—
College tuition fund	85	85	—	85	—	85	—	255	255	—
Total monthly amount	$ 265	$ 265	—	$ 265	—	$ 265	—	$ 795	$ 795	—

Expenditures, loan payments, and monthly goal amount

	Budgeted amount	January Actual		February Actual		March Actual		Quarterly Budgeted amount	Quarterly Actual	Quarterly Surplus (Deficit)
	$2,890	$3,225		$2,719		$2,750		$8,670	$8,694	($ 24)

Emergency cash reserve

	Budgeted amount	January Actual		February Actual		March Actual		Quarterly Budgeted amount	Quarterly Actual	Quarterly Surplus (Deficit)
Deposits or (withdrawals)	$ 0	$ 65		($ 79)		($ 10)		$ 0	($ 24)	($ 24)

Next, the budget summary sheet shows consumer loan payments for the coming year. The Swifts have included the one loan payment they will make in the middle section of Exhibit 3.8.

Now the Swifts integrate the monthly amount for each of their short-term financial goals. Generally, you should include a separate line for each goal; it makes it easier to adjust one or more of the amounts if necessary. Sam and Nancy developed the necessary monthly amounts in Exhibit 3.7; those are carried straight to their summary sheet.

At this point in the budget process, all planned income and expenditures should have been listed. If we total the expenditures, loan payments, and monthly goal amounts, we find total outflows. Take as an example the line "expenditures, loan payments, and monthly goal amounts" in Exhibit 3.8. If total outflows are reasonably close to the income available, nothing further needs to be done. Since outflows equal inflows, the Swifts' planned spending matches their income.

But what happens when expected income does *not* equal or exceed planned expenditures? Well, you can do nothing and *hope* it works out. Winning the lottery or Aunt Agatha's untimely demise would help. Far better, you should review your plans and take specific corrective action. For a limited period, you can spend more than you make; borrowing the money or selling some of your assets will allow this. More often, you will need to reduce your expenditures, revise your financial goals, or do both. An alternative is to raise your expected income, but that is often difficult. Regardless of which strategy you choose, choose one. You will need to make adjustments *before* you set your budget. There is no sense in building a budget that is doomed to fail.

Recording actual income and payments

Each month you should record, or "post," your actual income, expenditures, loan payments, and monthly contributions to financial goals. The sample summary sheet in Exhibit 3.8 has a separate column for each month's actual results. To conserve space, only the first three months are actually shown in the exhibit. Posting the actual results shows how well you are doing. Just as you would not set off on a 12-month trip by consulting a map on January 1 and then folding it neatly away for 12-months, you should take regular budget readings during the year to measure your progress toward your objectives. Adjustments may be needed along the way.

The information for your budget summary will come from a number of sources. Data on income could be from the stub attached to your paycheck, from deposits to your checking account, and perhaps from investment records. Three sources can help you summarize your expenditures: (1) payment listings in your checkbook; (2) credit card receipts—when you use a credit card, immediately write on the charge slip what the expenditure was for and use the slip as a source; (3) your record of items purchased for cash. The last are the hardest to track and the easiest to overlook, so use a check where possible. Or you might want to summarize your cash purchases in a notebook. Together, the three sources will provide an excellent record of expenditures. Using their checkbook, charge slips, and cash payment summary, Nancy and Sam Swift summarized the monthly amounts in columns 3, 5, and 7 of Exhibit 3.8. They totaled their expenditures, loan payments, and monthly financial goal amounts to compute their outflow.

Most people find that the best time to post their expenditures is when they are paying their monthly bills. Unless your finances are highly complex, or your records poor, 30 to 60 minutes should be all it takes.

Comparing actual results with budgeted amounts: Surplus or deficit?

One way to measure your financial planning success is to compare your actual results to your budgeted amount. The four columns labeled "Surplus (deficit)" in Exhibit 3.8 do just that. To distinguish, deficits are enclosed in parentheses. Compute a surplus or deficit by deducting the actual expenditure from what you budgeted. When the budgeted amount exceeds the actual, you have a **surplus.** When the actual amount exceeds the budget, there is a **deficit.** Sam and Nancy Swift's budget summary sheet (Exhibit 3.8) illustrates the process.

Look at Exhibit 3.8, which has separate surplus and deficit columns for each month and one for the 3-month quarter. First, concentrate on the individual months. What does a surplus in the "available income" category mean? Budgeted must have exceeded actual income. Actual income was less than planned. That would be considered unfavorable because if it continued, spending would have to be adjusted downward to cover the shortfall. A deficit would, of course, carry the opposite connotation.

Suppose your actual expenditures exceed the amount budgeted? First, it would show as a deficit. Is that favorable or not? If you said unfavorable, we agree. Your spending exceeds what you planned to spend. There may be a good reason why it occurred. Maybe it is not serious. Perhaps half of your annual auto insurance premium was paid that month, or inclement weather boosted your monthly utility bill. As a general rule, continued spending deficits will cause problems at some point. The opposite occurs when spending is less than you budgeted. Generally, that will be a favorable development.

A surplus or a deficit in an *income* category does not have the same meaning as a surplus or deficit in an *expenditure* category; they are exactly opposite. When actual income exceeds your plan—a deficit—that is favorable. That seems reasonable. But when actual spending exceeds your plans—also a deficit—that is unfavorable. Once you understand this distinction, interpreting a surplus or a deficit is easier.

Loan payments and the monthly amount for each financial goal are treated differently in Exhibit 3.8. Neither shows a surplus or deficit. You should expect the planned and actual loan payment to be alike. The payment is predictable; differences are rare. Likewise, the monthly amount actually contributed toward each financial goal is as planned. Does that mean everyone always keeps up with financial goal objectives? No. But rather than show a surplus or deficit, you will use your short-term cash reserve to make up any difference between planned and actual deposits for your goals. A later section will demonstrate how that reserve operates.

Step 4: Review and Analysis of Your Budget Summary Sheet

Once your budget sets your spending plans, you will want to monitor how you are doing. You just computed the surplus or deficit for each category. Now you will measure your progress by **reviewing and analyzing those results.** Your major concern will be instances where the real result differs significantly from your plan. What is "significant"? As a rule of thumb, when the difference between actual and planned exceeds 5 to 10 percent of the budgeted amount, it is significant. A $10 deficit on an item budgeted at $300 is probably not worth analyzing. The same $10 difference on an item budgeted at $25 deserves your attention. Once you find significant differences, you should analyze them to determine the cause.

Period for the review and analysis

Most people find that a budget review every 3 months is adequate. It is long enough so short-term, special factors are less likely to trigger an analysis. It holds clerical effort down. But if corrective action is needed, the period is not so long that you will find it hard to recover.

For instance, Nancy and Tom use the final three columns of Exhibit 3.8 for their review. They multiply the budgeted amount by 3 to compute the quarterly budget figure. Totaling the actual results for January, February, and March provides the actual amount for the quarter; the next-to-final column shows that total. Deducting the actual amount from the budgeted amount gives the surplus or deficit for the quarter; this is shown in the final column.

However, some people do their budget review monthly. This entails more work. More frequent reviews focus your attention on financial planning. If this is your first experience at budgeting, monthly reviews might be wise. Your desire to closely monitor your budget progress is another case for monthly reviews.

Does your analysis suggest corrective action?

The goal of your analysis is to determine why a particular surplus or deficit occurred. Once you do that, ask yourself: Do I need to take any corrective action? For many surpluses and deficits, the answer is no. Take automobile insurance premiums that are billed every 6 months. The month you pay those premiums, you will show a sizable deficit. Yet as long as the premium equals what you planned for 6 months, no action is needed. In the same vein, utility bills fluctuate considerably between summer and winter in most areas. A high bill in a cold month is to be expected: no action is needed.

But what if your analysis suggests corrective action is required? Several approaches are available.

Modify future spending. You may decide to leave your budget unchanged; you planned it this way, and you expect to carry through. But to do that, you must modify future spending to balance to the planned amount. If you overspend on clothes during the first 3 months of the year, you must spend less than the planned monthly amount for the remaining 9 months.

Revise your original budgeted amount. You may have to revise your original budgeted amount if it did not accurately reflect your plans. Your actual spending for the year should approximate the revised amount.

Before you proceed, you must consider what the revision has done to the balance between your available income and total planned spending. If you revise your planned spending, it probably no longer equals available income.

Suppose you raise the $200 you budget for travel each month to $300. But if your spending approximated your income, an upward revision means expenditures will exceed your income. To balance the two, you will have to reduce spending in some other category. Your other alternative is to revise the planned amount for one or more financial goals.

Sam and Nancy Swift: A sample review and analysis

Let's use the final three columns of Sam and Nancy Swift's summary in Exhibit 3.8 to practice our new skills. Their $20 deficit in the food category is not significant. But their sizable deficit on property taxes requires attention. The deficit is caused by the Swifts paying half of their annual taxes in January: at $1,020 every 6 months, the total payment for the year will be $2,040 as budgeted (12 months $\times$ $170 = $2,040), so no corrective action is needed. Now skip down to the $125 surplus in the clothing category. Since the Swifts' actual spending lagged behind their budgeted amount, they should ask: Do we plan to spend the $135 we budget each month? Suppose they revise it to $100 monthly: Planned spending is reduced $35. The Swifts should review their budget to decide how to use the $35.

Emergency Cash Reserve

We have intentionally delayed discussion of the emergency cash reserve (the final section of Exhibit 3.8). Now let's talk about it. An **emergency cash reserve's** major purpose is to bridge the gap between what you receive and what you spend. While a reserve has many roles, we will focus on how it can help you manage your budget:

1   It can provide the funds to cover large, unexpected expenses that cannot easily be paid from current income.
2   It can provide funds to handle those months when your expenses exceed your receipts. This can happen in any month when one or more major payments are due. Later, receipts will probably exceed expenditures, and you will be able to restore your emergency reserve.

Your cash reserve will help even out short-term differences between your actual receipts for a month and that month's payments. In months when what you receive exceeds what you spend, deposit the money in your cash reserve. Money will be withdrawn when you fall short. The cash reserve entry at the bottom of Exhibit 3.8 illustrates that role.

Sam and Nancy Swift's experience (Exhibit 3.8) illustrates the use of a cash reserve. In January the Swifts' income exceeded their expenditures, loan payments, and monthly financial goal contributions. The extra was deposited in their cash reserve. In February they found their expenses exceeded income, so they drew the needed funds from their cash reserve. In March they also drew funds from their reserve. They will probably make deposits and draws from their cash reserve for the remaining 9 months. As long as their actual spending approximates their actual income and both parallel their budgeted amount, the year's deposits and withdrawals will net to zero. Remember, a cash reserve will not make up chronic shortfalls; at some point it will be exhausted. But it can help you manage your budget by covering temporary shortages.

How large should your cash reserve be? An amount equaling 2 or 3 months' available income is a minimum. This assumes your employment is secure, you have a good credit rating, and you have adequate insurance coverage. If you do not meet these criteria, you should raise the amount to 6 months' available income.

Strategy

Your cash reserve should equal 2 to 3 months of available income. Raise that to 6 months if you change jobs frequently, your employment is not secure, your credit rating is poor, or your insurance coverage has gaps.

Tailor Your Budget to Your Needs

Budgets requiring excessive detail quickly kill your interest. Structure your budget to provide information with minimum clerical work. Second, include a "miscellaneous" category so you are not trying to account for every penny: start by setting the category at 5 percent of your income. Third, round off all amounts to the nearest $1, $5, or $10.

Your quarterly review should not be an exercise in self-punishment: unrealistically low budget amounts look good and may let you think you are thrifty. Living with such a budget may be so discouraging that you drop the whole budget after your first few quarterly reviews. Your budget should be a planning tool that helps you reach your objectives.

PREPARING YOUR BUDGET ON A PERSONAL COMPUTER

A personal computer with the proper software can be ideal for preparing your budget. Since budgeting involves repetitive steps—posting monthly results, computing surpluses and deficits, and totaling amounts quarterly—a personal computer can reduce your clerical effort and save you time. Furthermore, a computer makes revising and updating easy. If you have a printer, you can print monthly and quarterly detail. But computers cannot do your initial planning; you still have to. Likewise, you will still have to do the review and analysis. And you will still need to determine any corrective action for your budget.

Initially, it takes time and effort to adapt your budget to a personal computer. This is especially true if you are using general-purpose spreadsheet software rather than specialized personal finance software. But once set up, a computer program can reduce your clerical work. When you develop next year's budget, a considerable part of last year's budgeting effort can be used.

You can prepare your budget on a personal computer in several ways. One is to use software specifically developed for personal finance: Manag-

Exhibit 3.9

Advantages and Disadvantages of Using Specialized Personal Finance Software or General Spreadsheet Software to Prepare Your Budget on a Personal Computer

Specialized Personal Finance Software

Advantages	*Disadvantages*
Setup work will be done	Could be challenging to modify to fit your circumstance
Most budget categories will have been created	You must learn steps to operate
May integrate with income statement and balance sheet	Limit to range of tasks covered
Instructions may include numerical examples	Purchase cost can be sizable
	Documentation on some is weak

General Spreadsheet Software

Advantages	*Disadvantages*
Flexibility may allow it to meet your specific needs	You must create the budget application
Software can be used for other applications	You must learn steps to operate
Purchase cost has declined	You will have to diagnose and correct your problems

ing Your Money, Dollars and Sense, Your Personal Net Worth, Home Accountant Plus, and The Personal Accountant come to mind. Or you can use a standard spreadsheet program: Lotus 1-2-3, Multiplan, Supercalc, and Visicalc are examples. Exhibit 3.9 highlights some of the strengths and weaknesses of each approach. In choosing, you will need to consider what software you currently have access to, your present computer skills, experience with some of the software, and what programs are available for your computer.

Strategy

If you have access to a personal computer and the necessary software, consider using it to prepare your budget.

Summary

1. Developing financial goals requires you to:
   - Decide what you want to do.
   - Estimate the cost of the goal.
   - Decide when to finish the goal.
   - Ask: Can I complete these goals?
2. The typical plan for reaching long-range goals covers 15 to 25 years.
3. Your short-term goals should cover the next 5 years.
4. Financial goals typically require that you save a set amount each month to ensure that the funds will be available when needed.
5. Interest and dividends earned on your investments for a goal can offset most, or all, of the potential future rise in that goal's cost.
6. A budget outlines your future income and expenditure plans.
7. The budget process has four steps:
   - Estimate your available income.
   - Define major budget categories, and set a spending level for each.
   - Use a budget summary sheet to track actual income and expenditures.
   - Analyze differences between your plans and actual results.
8. Available income includes income from all sources, less nonvoluntary deductions.
9. Spending levels for each budget category can be based on the prior year's expenditures, spending during the last 3 to 6 months, or

your estimate, which can be revised after several months.

10 Your short-term financial goals should be integrated into your budget.

11 Your budget summary sheet should highlight:
   - Your planned income and spending
   - Your actual income and spending
   - Surpluses or deficits—that is, differences between your plans and your actual results

12 An analysis of the differences between your actual results and your plans can help you decide if corrective action is needed.

13 Your emergency cash reserve is intended to cover:
   - Major unexpected expenses that cannot be covered by current income
   - Months when expenditures temporarily exceed your cash inflows

Review your understanding of

Financial goals	Expenditure categories
Long-range plan	Budget period
Short-range plan	Integrating financial goals
Monthly goal amount	Budget summary sheet
Budget process	Surplus
Nonvoluntary deductions	Deficit
Voluntary deductions	Budget analysis
Available income	Emergency cash reserve
Take-home pay	

Discussion questions

1 What are the four steps in developing your financial goals? Briefly discuss what each step entails.

2 What are the principal differences between a plan for long-range goals and one for short-term goals? Which is likely to be more detailed? Why?

3 Al and Janice Lee want to accumulate approximately $18,000 for their daughter's college education in 10 years. If they expect to start saving now, should it be in their plan for short-term goals? Why?

4 Sam Higgins plans to buy a townhouse in 4 years; at today's prices he would need $9,840 to complete the purchase. Will the final cost exceed that $9,840 4 years from now? Why? Where will the extra money come from?

5 Ann Ambitious's list of short-term goals would require $570 each month to reach; she only has $260 of income that can be used. Should she be concerned? Why? What options might she use to balance the two?

6 How would you compute your monthly available income? What could you learn from such a calculation? Would it be part of your budget?

7 What are the trade-offs in limiting the categories in your budget? What are the trade-offs in expanding the categories?

8 How can you integrate your financial goals into your budget? Why is it important to do so?

9 What information does a budget summary sheet contain? What is its principal purpose?

10 What sources would you use to post actual expenditures to your budget summary sheet? Which type of expenditure is the most difficult to track?

11 When an expenditure category shows a surplus, what does that suggest? How about a deficit?

12 Give examples of expenditure categories where a deficit for a quarter might not suggest corrective action. Give some examples of categories where a surplus might not require corrective action.

13 Oliver Overspent budgeted $100 each month for entertainment; his actual spending totaled $1,200 during the first 3 months.
   a Outline some options that Oliver might use to correct this situation.
   b How much can Oliver spend in each of the remaining months and still stay within his budget?

14 How can your emergency cash reserve assist you in managing your budget? What kind of month might cause you to withdraw funds from your reserve? Add deposits to it? On balance, what should your total withdrawals and deposits equal for the year?

Problems

3.1 Connie New has outlined the following list of financial goals she expects to work toward during the next 5 years:

Financial goal	Estimated current cost	Months to completion
Redecorate apartment	$2,400	18 months
New furniture	3,000	24 months
Extended vacation cruise	3,960	36 months
Trade for a new auto	6,000	48 months

Connie also plans to purchase a condominium in 8 years; current estimated purchase cost is $10,080. Since that goal extends beyond 5 years, she is unclear if it belongs in her plan.
a What amount will she have to save each month to achieve each goal?
b Should her condominium goal be in the plan? Why?
c Since there is no explicit consideration of interest earned on the invested money, she plans to keep it in her non-interest-paying checking account. Do you agree? Why?

3.2 Sidney Shortfall estimates that next year he will have $395 each month that can be saved toward his financial goals. His top-ranked goal is $9,840 to purchase a house in 4 years. His second choice is a $1,800 fund for his planned trip in 12 months. Third on his list is $3,600 for a motorcycle in 3 years. Last is $4,800 for a European extravaganza in 5 years.
a Can he carry out all of his plans? Why?
b What corrective actions might he take to better balance his resources and his plans? Outline several options for Sidney to consider.

3.3 Agnes Twine wants your help to estimate the monthly available income she should use for her budget. Details on her income include:

Voluntary deductions (monthly)	$ 150
Gross monthly salary	1,400
Annual interest income	288
Nonvoluntary deductions (monthly)	360
Annual bonus from employer	1,080

What is Agnes's monthly available income?

3.4 Ed and Edna Endpoint have detailed the following financial goals:

Goal	Amount	Months to completion	Monthly savings
Auto	$6,000	36 months	?
Condominium down payment	7,000	60 months	?

During the accumulation period, the Endpoints expect to earn 10 percent on any invested money. What monthly savings will they have to set aside to achieve their goals?

3.5 Shown below is a portion of Fred and Francine Freshstart's budget summary sheet:

| | | April | | May | | June | |
Category	Budgeted	Actual	Surplus (deficit)	Actual	Surplus (deficit)	Actual	Surplus (deficit)
Income	$1,245	$1,205	($40)	$1,200		$1,340	
.	.	.	.	.		.	
.	.	.	.	.		.	
Rent	420	420	—	420		420	
Utilities	80	90	(10)	60		30	
Renter's insurance	7	—	7	—		84	
Clothing	30	20	10	70		—	
.	.	.	.	.		.	
.	.	.	.	.		.	
.	.	.	.	.		.	
Loan payments	175	175	—	175		175	
Financial goals	80	80	—	80		80	
Total expenditures	$1,245	$1,200	$45	$1,300		$1,400	
Emergency cash reserve	—	5					

a Complete the surpluses and deficits for this budget summary sheet.

b If the Freshstarts had $2,000 in their emergency cash reserve on April 1, what will be the balance at the end of June? (Assume that the only withdrawals and deposits are those shown in their budget summary sheet.)

3.6 Carl and Jan Tryzinski need your help to complete the review and analysis of their budget summary sheet. The quarterly totals for some expenditure categories are:

| | Quarterly Summary | | |
Category	Budgeted	Actual	Surplus (deficit)
Rent	$1,080	$1,080	_____
Utilities	330	390	_____
Renter's insurance	30	0	_____
Clothing	90	30	_____
Entertainment	300	1,200	_____

a Complete the surplus (deficit) column for this quarterly summary.

b Analyze the surpluses and deficits and write an explanation for the major ones.

c What corrective actions, if any, do you suggest?

3.7 The following table summarizes the totals in the quarterly summary for Steve and Sally Spendit's budget summary sheet.

| | Quarterly Summary | | |
Category	Budgeted	Actual	Surplus (deficit)
Available income	$6,200	$5,800	_____
Total expenditures	4,220	4,645	_____
Loan payments	830	830	_____
Total financial goals	1,150	1,150	_____
Emergency cash reserve	—	—	_____

a Compute the surpluses and deficits needed to complete this summary.
b Briefly describe what happened during the quarter in the Spendits' category for:
    Available income
    Total expenditures
    Loan payments
    Financial goals
    Emergency cash reserve
c What has likely happened to the balance in the Spendits' emergency cash reserve? Why?
d What corrective action, if any, would you recommend for Steve and Sally? Why?

Case problem

Kevin González recently graduated from college and started work as a management trainee for a large retail firm. He is single, but plans to be married in about 18 months when his fiancée, Janice, graduates from college. She expects to go to graduate school.

His salary is $1,575 per month, and after deductions for Social Security, health insurance, and federal and state income taxes, his available income is $1,160. He plans to share an apartment this year with a college friend. His share of the monthly rent and utilities will be $210. By cooking most of his meals, he expects to hold his food cost to $140 per month. His other major expenses include (unless otherwise noted, all are annual amounts):

Operating auto (monthly)	$ 110	Entertainment	$540
Life insurance premium	312	Contributions	360
Auto insurance premium	360	Renter's insurance	96
Personal	240	Miscellaneous (monthly)	50
Clothing	1,020		

At present Kevin is making monthly car payments of $170 and must do so for 22 more months. During the next 18 months, he would like to accumulate $2,500 so that he and Janice can travel next summer. In addition, he would like to accumulate $2,000 during the same period to purchase some new furniture.

Kevin recognizes the need for a budget but is unsure how to proceed.

1 Can you prepare Kevin's budget?
2 Can Kevin achieve his proposed spending plan? Why?
3 Does he have much latitude in his spending plan? Will his actual spending have to closely parallel his planned spending?
4 If your answer to 3 was no, please explain.
5 Should Kevin decide to reduce his spending below the amounts listed, which categories would be the easiest to reduce? The hardest?
6 If Kevin does not save for the travel and furniture, how could he still be able to have them? Would your alternatives have an effect on his future spending? Are there advantages to saving for the two items?

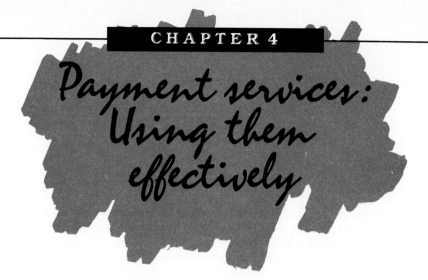

CHAPTER 4

Payment services: Using them effectively

AFTER COMPLETING THIS CHAPTER YOU WILL HAVE LEARNED

- Which financial institutions offer checking accounts, negotiable order of withdrawal (NOW) accounts, and share draft accounts
- The features and costs of the major payment accounts
- How to select the account that best meets your needs at the lowest cost
- How to open a payment account
- When a particular endorsement is appropriate
- How to handle an overdraft on your account
- Why a certified check is necessary in some cases
- How to use a stop-payment order
- The objective of reconciling your payment account
- The steps to reconcile your payment account
- When a central asset management account should be considered
- What services an automated teller machine (ATM) provides
- Why a cashier's check or money order is needed in some cases
- The specialized service a traveler's check provides

*f*inancial institutions bombard us with TV, radio, print media, billboard, even city bus advertisements. Each trumpets its claim to provide the financial services *we* need. Institutions claim to be *the* one-stop center for every financial service. Some go after the mass market with cries of low cost, high interest, convenience, and service throughout a wide area. Others take the boutique approach, targeting specific groups, mostly the affluent. Both types may provide payment accounts, investment alternatives, borrowing options, credit and debit cards, automated teller machines (ATMs), trust services, even financial counseling.

This chapter concentrates on the payment services financial institutions offer. Using these payment services, you can pay individuals or businesses, whether by means of a standard checking account, cash drawn from an ATM, or a check issued by the financial institution.

You should understand payment services for several reasons. First, they can help you manage your finances. Second, the deregulation of financial institutions has produced an explosion in payment services. As financial institutions expand from local markets to regional and even national ones, your choices will expand further. Increased competition means institutions must recover the costs of providing a particular service. This means charging fees for what were once free or low-cost services. Cost differentials among competing institutions can be sizable. Finally, knowing what a service involves lets you single out those you need.

MAJOR FINANCIAL INSTITUTIONS THAT OFFER PAYMENT SERVICES

Let's briefly examine the major types of financial institutions that offer payment services to individuals: commercial banks, savings and loan associations, mutual savings banks, and credit unions. All take your deposits and place them in an account. Each promises to make payments from that account to an individual, business, or governmental unit at your request.

Commercial Bank

Commercial banks have long offered a range of financial services to individuals. Checking accounts are the traditional payment option for individuals, and banks once had exclusive claim to offering them. This and other services made them the premier one-stop financial center, but they are losing that distinction as other institutions offer expanded services. Because banks are so common, they are very accessible, but the number of "small" banks which can adjust to individual needs or community interests is decreasing as independent banks are merged into larger regional banks.

Savings and Loan Association

Originally, **savings and loan associations (S&Ls)** primarily loaned money for home purchases. Now larger ones offer the services needed to qualify as one-stop personal financial centers. S&Ls are common throughout the United States except for the Northeast. Mutual savings banks dominate there.

Mutual Savings Bank

Like S&Ls, **mutual savings banks (MSBs)** began by loaning customers money to purchase homes and other major items. Now their array of financial services has broadened, and many qualify as one-stop centers. Those who have not lived in one of the New England or mid-Atlantic states may not be familiar with this institution. There are relatively few MSBs outside these two areas.

Credit Union

A **credit union** is made up of a group of members who share some common bond. The bond can be working for the same employer, living in a particular neighborhood or district, or affiliation with some group. Only members sharing the "common bond" can use the credit union's services. Credit unions originally specialized in moderate-sized, short-term loans to members. Money for those loans came from the funds other members deposited in their accounts. Later, members were allowed to write share drafts—like checks—against their accounts. Larger credit unions have expanded their services and approach being one-stop financial centers.

To join a credit union, you need to have the necessary "common bond." Some larger, more aggressive credit unions have made that easier by defining the common bond quite liberally—for example, "everyone living within a specified municipality" or "all those living within a stated county."

PAYMENT ACCOUNTS

Let's start by examining the different payment accounts the four major institutions offer individuals. For the typical account, the financial institution accepts your deposits, keeps a record of your balance, and pays it out as you direct. You make a written order (the check) telling the institution to whom the payment is to be made and for how much.

A few years ago you had one choice: the traditional checking account. Then negotiable order of withdrawal accounts and share draft accounts joined the list. Let's review the major features of each.

Checking Account

The check you write on your **checking account** instructs the bank to remove money from your account and pay it to someone: the payee. Until the check is presented to your bank, the money remains in your account. It earns no interest, however, because a 1933 federal regulation prohibits interest on checking accounts.

Virtually all commercial banks offer checking accounts, but not all S&Ls and MSBs do.

Negotiable Order of Withdrawal (NOW) Account

The negotiable order of withdrawal you write looks like a check. It instructs the institution that has your **negotiable order of withdrawal (NOW) account** to pay a prescribed amount to a specific payee. Unlike checking accounts, though, NOW accounts can pay interest.

NOW accounts were created for two reasons. Since they permit you to draw against a savings account, mutual savings banks (and later S&Ls)

could offer them. And since they used a savings account, they avoided the prohibition on interest payments. That gave NOWs an added attraction.

NOW accounts can be offered by commercial banks, MSBs, and S&Ls. Each institution can set the interest rate on its NOW accounts at whatever level it chooses and can adjust the rate up or down as it needs. Institutions have only been able to set interest rates on NOW accounts at any level since 1986; before then there was a ceiling. Current NOW account interest rates are in the 5.25 percent range.

Share Draft Account

Credit unions pioneered the **share draft account** so they could offer a payment account to individuals. The payment order (the share draft) looks and works like a check: it instructs the credit union to pay an amount to some payee. When that draft is presented at the credit union, the money is deducted from your share account balance. Up until the draft is paid, however, you earn interest on the money. Again, the prohibition against interest on checking is avoided.

Only credit unions offer share draft accounts, and smaller ones might not offer the service. Credit unions can pay whatever interest rate they choose and change it whenever they want, but experience suggests rates will likely be stable. Share draft accounts currently pay 5 to 6 percent interest.

BENEFITS OF A "CHECK-ING" ACCOUNT

Throughout the remainder of this chapter, *payment account* will be used when a particular idea applies to all three types of accounts. When a point is unique to one account, *NOW, share draft,* or *checking account* will be used. Likewise the more familiar *check* will be used for checks, negotiable orders of withdrawal, and share drafts.

Checking accounts are widespread, with 80 percent of all households having one or more. Why are they so popular? First, there is convenience. You can pay bills by mail. No need to carry cash and wait in line to pay. A checking account is much safer than keeping large amounts of cash. Someone finding your lost checkbook will be hard pressed to get to your money, short of forgery. Not so for the finder of your "wad" of crisp tens. Most businesses in your area will accept a check if you have suitable identification.

Second, a checking account can help your financial record keeping. Your checkbook, with its list of payees and amounts, is a summary of your expenditures. It makes preparing budgets, income statements, and tax records much easier. In fact, developing adequate financial records without a checking account is difficult. People without checking accounts can start the week with a bundle of cash and end wondering where it went; your checkbook provides a spending "trail" you can follow.

Finally, a canceled check provides a receipt that proves you made a particular payment. The payee's endorsement on the check (more on this later) is evidence the money was received.

PRINCIPAL TYPES OF PAYMENT ACCOUNTS

Commercial banks, MSBs, S&Ls, and credit unions currently offer several kinds of payment accounts. Differences center on the services provided and the fees charged. The next sections will discuss the major payment options. Exhibit 4.1 summarizes the major features and service fees for each.

Minimum Balance Account

The identifying feature of a **minimum balance account** is that if you maintain a specified balance, you eliminate service fees for the account. Checking accounts, NOW accounts, and share draft accounts are available this way. Commercial banks generally require a higher minimum on a NOW account than on a checking account; MSBs and S&Ls often require a smaller minimum; and credit unions often have the lowest minimum.

To determine if you have met their minimum, institutions can either examine your lowest account balance during the month or compute an average of the daily account balance. The latter is preferred. Suppose Vera Volatile's checking account requires a $500 minimum to avoid all fees. On the days when Vera deposits her twice-monthly salary check, her balance is large. But it drops quickly as she writes checks on the account. If her bank bases its minimum on an average of her daily balances, her balance can drop below $500 for several days if she offsets that shortage with days above $500. But a single day below $500 would subject her to service fees if the minimum were based on the lowest *daily* balance; 29 daily balances well above $500 would not save Vera.

What happens if Vera's balance is less than the account's minimum? The service fee might be a flat dollar amount: $5 to $10 is typical. Or she might be assessed a fee for each check that month plus a flat fee.

Exhibit 4.1

Features and Service Fees for the Major Payment Accounts

Payment account	Minimum balance	Service fees and special features
Minimum balance account		Maintain minimum balance to avoid fees. Allows unlimited check writing.
Checking	$300–$3,000	Pays no interest.
NOW	$200–$4,000	Pays interest on account balance.
Share draft	$100–$1,000	Pays interest on account balance.
Minimum investment account	$500–$5,000	Hold the required investment to avoid fees and minimums on checking account. Investment earns a return. Allows unlimited check writing.
Service fee account	None	$0.10–$0.50 processing fee per check. $2–$8 monthly maintenance fee. NOW and share draft accounts pay interest.
Unconditional free account	None	No service fees on the payment account. NOW and share draft accounts pay interest.

Even if you maintain the required minimum in a checking account, it is not really "free." Suppose Vera's daily account balance averaged $700 for the month. Remember, interest is prohibited. Had she invested that $700 in her 6 percent money market account, she would have earned interest: $700 × 6% = $42 in a year. That $42 "lost" interest is the account's cost. The larger the required balance, the larger the loss.

Even a NOW or share draft account may have a cost. Suppose Vera averaged a daily balance of $700, but had a NOW account paying 4 percent interest. She loses interest because she has to accept 4 percent when her savings account offers 6. Her yearly loss is $14: ($700 × 6%) − ($700 × 4%). The higher the account's minimum, or the lower its interest rate, the higher the cost.

Estimates suggest that more than one-half of the households with a payment account pay no service fees. Minimum balance accounts are probably a popular way to do that. If you have sufficient funds, a minimum balance account is often a prudent choice, particularly if you write many checks or the minimum is low.

Strategy

Consider the minimum balance, how the balance is computed, and the interest rate when selecting a minimum balance account. Check what local credit unions, MSBs, or S&Ls offer; their minimums and their fees for missing the minimum may be lower.

Minimum Investment Account

With a **minimum investment account,** you must maintain a specified investment to qualify for a payment account without service fees. Investments may include a savings account or a certificate of deposit (CD). Since it is primarily commercial banks that offer this option, you generally receive a checking account.

This account lessens the disadvantage of the non-interest-paying account. The investment that qualifies you for the account usually pays the going rate of interest. If you manage the checking account so the balance remains low (dropping below zero is not allowed), you minimize "lost" interest. But though you earn interest on the required investment, even good management will not eliminate all the interest lost on the checking account.

Unless the required investment is excessive or its rate of interest disappointingly low, a minimum investment account is superior to minimum balance checking. Several things can make this account more desirable:

- If you already hold the required CD or savings balance as an investment, the no-fee checking account becomes a secondary benefit.
- If competing NOW accounts require a larger minimum balance or offer lower interest, the CD's added return may offset your "lost" interest on the checking account.

Still, a minimum balance NOW account is usually a better choice.

Strategy

Before deciding on a minimum investment account, compare it to local minimum balance NOW accounts.

Service Fee Account

A **service fee** account does not have a set minimum balance, but customers are charged two fees. First, there is the **processing fee** for each check charged against your account: the more active the account, the more you pay. Second, there is a **monthly maintenance fee** whether you write checks or not. Both checking and NOW accounts are available in this form.

An example will demonstrate. The account's processing fee is $0.25 per check with a $4 monthly maintenance fee. You expect to write 28 checks in an average month. A typical month's total fee is $11: (28 checks × $0.25) + $4 fee. The year's fee would be $132.

The interest paid on a NOW account would offset only part of these costs. A $250 NOW account balance paying 5 percent interest earns only $12.50 in interest ($250 × 5%). That does little to balance an annual fee of $100 or more.

Strategy

Substantial annual costs make a fee account a poor choice if you can qualify for a minimum balance account or a minimum investment account. If your institution's minimum seems excessive, check others in the area.

"Economizer" Service Fee Accounts

Some financial institutions offer reduced service to people who write only a few checks each month but want a payment account. The account's processing fee on the first 5 to 10 checks each month might be 20 to 50 percent below the standard fee. Beyond those 5 or 10 checks, the fee may be much higher, so savings disappear as your check volume rises. At some point, the standard fee account is cheaper.

Strategy

People who write few checks should consider this account rather than a standard fee account. But a minimum balance or minimum investment account is often still a better choice.

Unconditional Free Account

An **unconditional free account** allows you unlimited checks with no minimum balance or service fees. Before you set off on a search, be warned this is a vanishing breed. Some credit unions offer "free" share draft accounts and a few MSBs and S&Ls offer "free" NOW accounts.

Strategy

Unconditional free payment accounts are an excellent choice. But they are scarce.

SELECTING YOUR PAYMENT ACCOUNT

Selecting a payment account requires you to do some investigative work. To compare accounts, you need data on minimums, interest rates, fees, overdraft privileges, and other services. There are no published summaries. Even a friend's recommended account may be suspect: your friend's mother-in-law may be president of the bank. Keep your options open; look at accounts from commercial banks, MSBs or S&Ls, and credit unions (if you qualify). The right account can provide you sizable benefits. In any area, service fees and minimum balances can vary widely.

To narrow your field of eligible accounts, ask: Can I meet the account's minimum balance? After that, estimate the cost for each of the remaining accounts. Finally, consider any other financial services the institution provides.

Minimum Required for the Account

Decide the maximum amount you could realistically keep in the payment account. Sidney Smallbuck hardly need consider the "Ultra" account—$5,000 minimum balance—when $500 is his maximum. You can quickly single out accounts whose minimum is near your maximum. If none of the account minimums are in your range, then your only choice is a service fee account. On to step 2.

Annual Cost of the Account

To compare competing payment accounts, figure the annual cost based on your projected use. You will need to estimate how many checks you will write each year.

For minimum balance accounts, calculate the minimum. Second, does the account pay interest on the balance? Payment on daily balances is best. What is the interest rate? It should be competitive with what other institutions offer. If it is not, the "lost" interest is a cost of the account. When the account pays no interest, its cost is the interest "lost" by not investing the money. This process should let you single out which option is best.

If there are service fees, compute the estimated processing fees and monthly maintenance fees for the year. Use your projected account usage for the year to make all estimates comparable. You should be able to select the best fee account by comparing these costs.

You have narrowed the field, but how do you decide between a service fee account and a minimum balance account? Use the cost you have calculated for your "best" fee account, following the process just described. Then estimate what your money would earn if it were not tied up in that "best" minimum balance account. Does the interest exceed the cost of the service fee account?

If it doesn't, take the minimum balance account. If it does, take one more step. Deduct the total service fees from your projected interest earnings. Does the remainder exceed the interest you could earn by having it in the minimum balance account? No? Take the minimum balance account. If the answer is yes, take the service fee account.

Assume Bob's two choices are a $1,000 minimum balance checking account or a service fee account costing $112 annually. He could invest his $1,000 and earn 8 percent: $80 annually. That $80 does not match the

Exhibit 4.2

Key Features on Your Personal Check

Phil Fast
1456 Deadend
Leadpoint, USA 98765

No. 517

(a) _____ 19 _____

Pay to the
Order of _____ (b) _____ $ _____ (c) _____

_____ (d) _____ Dollars

Last National Bank
Leadpoint, USA 98765

Memo _____ (f) _____   _____ (e) _____

⊞0123 ▪ 0098 ⊞11 ▪ 56 ⊞1133311 ▪ 517
(g)

$112 service fee. Bob selects the minimum balance checking account. Want a bigger challenge? Suppose Bob's options are a $1,000 minimum balance NOW account paying 5 percent or a service fee account costing $80 annually. He could invest that $1,000 to earn 10 percent: $100 a year. That exceeds the service fee total, so Bob moves to the next step. Deducting the $80 service fee from the projected $100 in interest leaves $20. Since that does not exceed the $50 in interest ($1,000 × 5%) the NOW account would pay, Bob selects the NOW account.

Range of Financial Services Provided

A secondary consideration when selecting an account is the institution's other financial services. Those may include loan options, credit or debit cards, home mortgage, safe-deposit box, and financial counseling. You may have need for one or more of these. Even if an institution does not offer these services, it may still be a candidate, since you could obtain the services elsewhere.

OPENING YOUR PAYMENT ACCOUNT

Opening a payment account is simple. You first fill out an account registration card showing the account owner(s). You sign the card so the institution has a facsimile of your signature. This is used to verify that the signature on a check is indeed yours. Anyone else sharing your account will also have to sign the registration card.

Most checks are personalized with your name, your address, and possibly your telephone, Social Security, or driver's license number. You generally pay the printing costs. Options range from single-color "banker blue" to the scenic extravaganzas. The more elaborate, the higher your cost. Likewise the book for carrying your checks can be staid and inexpensive or spectacular and costly. You decide.

USING THE ACCOUNT

Writing a check is also easy and straightforward. But there are several things to do to ensure your check will be cashed for the amount you intended. Exhibit 4.2 illustrates a sample check; the key points are explained below.

a   *Current date.* Write the current date here; it makes no difference if it is a Sunday or holiday. **Postdating** a check (writing June 13 when it is June 10) is generally not acceptable to persons or businesses or to most financial institutions.
b   *Payee.* The **payee** is the person or business you want to receive the money.
c   *Dollar amount.* Write in numerals the amount of the check. Place the numbers close to the dollar sign.
d   *Dollar amount.* Write the amount in words here. Begin at the far left of the line and fill the space at the end with two parallel lines.
e   *Signature.* Sign your name the same as on your signature card.
f   *Memo.* You can write the purpose of the payment here. The bank does nothing with this information, but it can help you with your record keeping.

g   Magnetic ink character recognition (MICR) numbers. This series of numbers identifies the financial institution the check is drawn on, your account number, the number of the check, and the check's dollar amount. Optical scanning machines use this information to sort the check, charge your account, and prepare your statement.

Recording Checks and Deposits

Whenever you write a check or make a deposit, promptly record it in your checkbook. A typical checkbook record, such as the one in Exhibit 4.3, contains columns where you can write (a) check number, (b) date, (c) person or business to whom the check is written, (d) check amount or account charge, (e) deposit or account credit, and (f) current account balance. The need for prompt recording seems obvious, but many people fail to do it. When they do go to enter a check, they may not recall the payee or amount. Without an up-to-date record, they may overdraw their account. Banks charge a sizable fee to discourage such behaviors. Further, balancing a checkbook with checks and deposits missing is impossible.

Making a Deposit

The personalized deposit slips you received when you opened the account are marked with an MICR code carrying some of the same information as your checks. They are used whether the deposit is made in person, at an ATM, or through the mail. The slip ensures correct posting of the deposit to your account.

Always promptly deposit checks you receive. First, the person who wrote the check may wonder if you received it if it is not cashed. Second, many institutions will not accept a check dated more than 60 to 90 days ago. Finally, you immediately begin earning interest if yours is a NOW or share draft account.

Before depositing a check you must endorse it (sign your name) on the reverse side. All that signals is that you, the payee, want to collect the money from the institution on which it is drawn. Exhibit 4.4 illustrates the three widely used endorsements discussed in the following sections.

Blank endorsement

A **blank endorsement** (top of Exhibit 4.4) converts the check to a bearer instrument: anyone who has the check becomes the ''bearer,'' and can cash it. The finder of a lost check with a blank endorsement could cash it. This endorsement is best used on deposits you are making in person.

Exhibit 4.3

How to Record a Deposit and a Check in the Checkbook Record

Check number	Date	Check issued to	Amount of check	Deposit	Balance
					$254.00
	5/15	Deposit		$300	$554.00
517	5/15	Sunken Swamp Estates	$400.25		153.75

Restrictive
endorsement

A **restrictive endorsement** limits how the check can be used. For example, the two checks in the middle of Exhibit 4.4 can only be deposited in the account of the check's payee: Fred Bear's account for the left check, the account of Wiloms Schultz for the right check. This is a suitable endorsement for a deposit at an ATM or by mail.

Special
endorsement

A **special endorsement** limits who can cash the check to the person named in the endorsement. Sally Jones, the payee on the check in the lower left corner of Exhibit 4.4, endorsed it to Jack Winter. Only he can cash it, endorsing it below Sally's signature. Bjorn Anderson, the payee for the check in the lower right corner, endorsed it to Last National Savings and Loan Association. Only that S&L can cash it. This endorsement is well suited to ATM and mail deposits.

The Missing
Deposit?

Igor Innocent deposits his salary check on Friday and writes checks on his NOW account over the weekend. Several businesses call on Wednesday, saying the bank returned his check because of insufficient funds; it "bounced." They are not pleased. Embarrassed, irked, and puzzled, Igor calls his bank to ask what happened. The bank replies that **deposits are**

Exhibit 4.4

Types of Endorsement

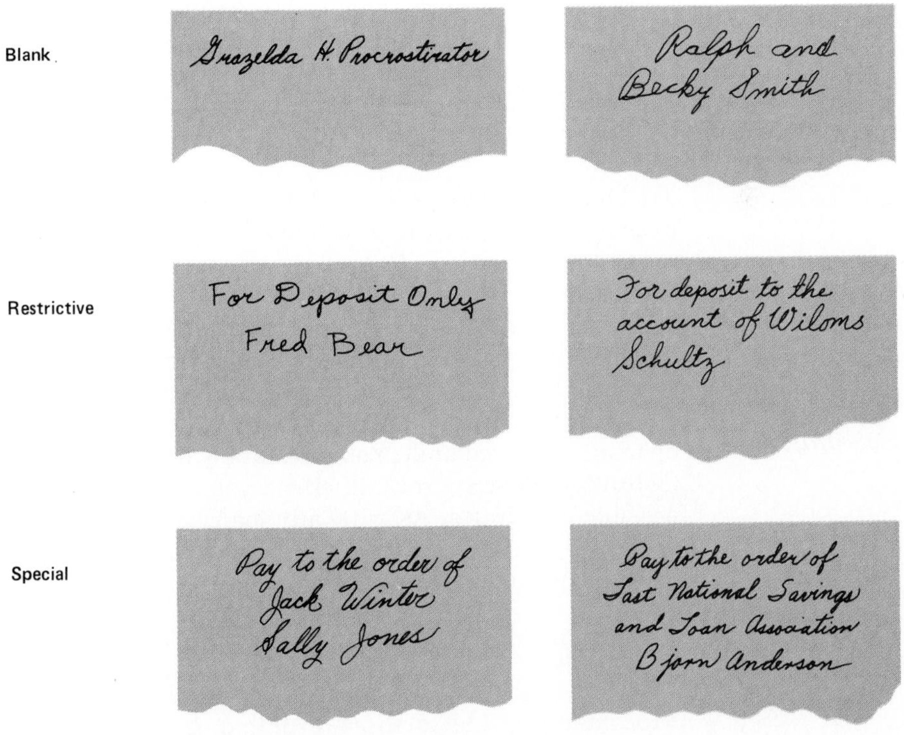

Blank	*Grazelda H. Procrostirator*
	Ralph and Becky Smith
Restrictive	*For Deposit Only Fred Bear*
	For deposit to the account of Wiloms Schultz
Special	*Pay to the order of Jack Winter Sally Jones*
	Pay to the order of Last National Savings and Loan Association Bjorn Anderson

placed on "hold": funds from local checks are not available for 5 days and from out-of-state for 10.

Many institutions "hold" the funds from a deposit so you cannot use them immediately. A typical "hold" on a local check is 3 to 5 days. Out-of-state checks might be held more than a week. Is that "hold" fair? No, but institutions can "hold" deposits for whatever time they decide. That complicates managing your account. An adequate account balance may not be enough. You also must decide if a recent deposit is still covered by a "hold."

Strategy

Ask the institution what "holds" it places on deposits. Long holds are cumbersome and unfair, so you may want to look elsewhere.

PAYMENT ACCOUNTS: SPECIAL FEATURES

Since payment accounts tend to be similar, many accounts now offer some added features in their attempt to attract customers. Depending on your own situation, these added services may help you manage select personal finance areas. Let's briefly review each one to see what it might be able to do for you.

Overdrawing Your Account

When you write a check for more than your account balance, your bank, MSB, S&L, or credit union has two choices. It can return the check to the institution where it was deposited, indicating there are not sufficient funds (NSF) in your account. The person or business that deposited your check will be charged $6 to $30 and will not collect any money. They will quickly contact you, asking you to cover the check. Having paid $6 to $30 for "experience," they are not likely to want a second check. Your bank, MSB, S&L, or credit union also charges you a fee of $5 to $30 to discourage future NSF checks.

The institution's second choice is to advance the money to cover your **overdraft.** The institution will ask that you immediately deposit money to repay the advance. Charging you a $5 to $30 fee confirms their displeasure.

Some overdrafts are intentional: the writer knew the check exceeded the account's balance. Some are caused by an error: a deposit added incorrectly, a check that was never recorded or recorded incorrectly.

Automatic overdraft

An automatic overdraft privilege allows you to overdraw your account up to an approved limit. You must apply for the overdraft privilege and the institution must approve. In effect, you arrange an open-end loan to cover possible overdrafts. As with any loan, you pay a finance charge on the overdraft until it is repaid. Your monthly bank statement summarizes any use of your overdraft privilege.

Strategy

Request an automatic overdraft for your payment account. It covers errors and provides a short-term loan source.

*Credit card
cash advance*

Some institutions use the cash advance feature on a VISA or MasterCard credit card to give overdraft protection. These credit cards allow holders to draw a cash advance up to their account limit. Institutions that offer this option ask you to authorize a cash advance from your credit card if needed for an overdraft. A finance charge is assessed, based on the amount of the advance and the time until it is repaid.

Strategy

*If your account offers a credit card cash advance instead of a
separate advance, it is a feature worth having.*

**Certified
Check**

If your financial institution takes one of your regular checks and guarantees your account has funds to cover it, the bank creates a **certified check.** It stamps *certified* across the check's face, and a bank officer initials the check. For this service you pay $5 to $20. Most institutions segregate the money upon certification; it cannot be withdrawn or paid to someone else.

**Stop-Payment
Order**

Suppose Jan wrote a $1,500 check to Arnold's Antiques for a 1790 Welsh tall case clock. At home Jan finds "Made in Hong Kong" on the clock's case. Rather than call "Ernie the Enforcer," Jan calls her bank and places a **stop-payment order** on the check. If the check has not been cashed, the bank makes its "best" effort to not cash it. Information from that stop order—check number, payee, amount, and date—is circulated to bank personnel to alert them. But stop orders have a clause exempting the bank from liability should the check be cashed through oversight or error.

Most institutions will accept a written or telephone stop order, though you may have to confirm the latter with a written order. The service fee ranges from $5 to $30. The order remains in effect for a prescribed time; extending it costs more.

**RECONCILING
YOUR PAY-
MENT
ACCOUNT**

The objective of **reconciling a payment account** is to confirm that the balance shown in your checkbook (Exhibit 4.3) agrees with the balance your financial institution has recorded for your account. If you adjust your checkbook balance and do the same to the balance your institution shows in your account, the two should be equal. You might ask: Why would the two differ? You may have written checks the bank does not yet have; your account has not been charged. You may not know fees the bank charged to your account or interest credited to it. Or the bank may have not received your recent deposit. Let's look at how to adjust your account.

Your reconciliation should accomplish three things: (1) Test the accuracy of your records and those of the financial institution; (2) update your records for service fees, finance charges, or interest earned on the account during the period; (3) the final product, your *adjusted account balance*, should accurately reflect the account's true balance.

Period Covered by the Reconciliation

The account statement that your financial institution sends you each month is your starting point. It gives you the period covered by the report, a beginning and an ending date. Though the statement covers approximately 30 days, it probably will not coincide with the end of the month. Institutions stagger the closing dates on their customers' accounts to spread them throughout the month.

The Monthly Bank Statement

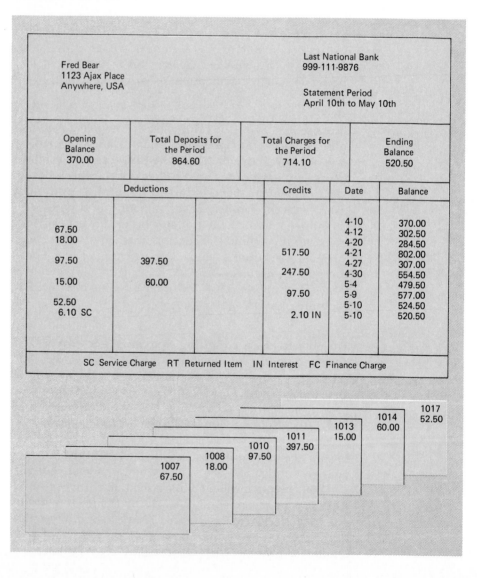

Fred Bear
1123 Ajax Place
Anywhere, USA

Last National Bank
999-111-9876

Statement Period
April 10th to May 10th

Opening Balance 370.00	Total Deposits for the Period 864.60	Total Charges for the Period 714.10	Ending Balance 520.50

Deductions			Credits	Date	Balance
				4-10	370.00
67.50				4-12	302.50
18.00				4-20	284.50
			517.50	4-21	802.00
97.50	397.50			4-27	307.00
			247.50	4-30	554.50
15.00	60.00			5-4	479.50
			97.50	5-9	577.00
52.50				5-10	524.50
6.10 SC			2.10 IN	5-10	520.50

SC Service Charge   RT Returned Item   IN Interest   FC Finance Charge

| 1007 67.50 | 1008 18.00 | 1010 97.50 | 1011 397.50 | 1013 15.00 | 1014 60.00 | 1017 52.50 |

Reconciling your account requires five components:

1   Balance shown on your account statement.
2   Balance shown in your checkbook.
3   Service fees and interest.
4   Outstanding checks (you wrote these but they have not been charged to your account).
5   Deposits in transit (they have not been added to your account).

Let's use the details on Fred Bear's account for our example. Fred's monthly account statement is shown in Exhibit 4.5, his checkbook in Exhibit 4.6, and his final reconciliation in Exhibit 4.7. Activity in Fred's account is moderate, but reconciling an account with double or triple the activity involves the same steps.

Balance shown on the account statement

The typical account statement summarizes the account activity for the past month. It lists checks that were charged against your account, deposits recorded in your account, service fees on the account, and interest credited to the account. Fred's account balance was $520.50 on May 10, the date of the reconciliation.

Balance shown in your checkbook

You will use the balance shown in your checkbook as of the closing date on the bank statement. Fred's checkbook shows a balance of $382.00 on May 10. More work needs to be done, because that differs from the bank statement's $520.50.

Service fees and interest

Depending on the type of account and your activity that month, your bank statement may show a monthly maintenance fee, processing fee for checks, finance charge for an overdraft, or a charge for printing checks.

Exhibit 4.6

Checkbook Details

Check number	Date	Check issued to	Check amount	Deposit amount	Balance
1007	4/9	Ace Plumbing Supply	$ 67.50 ✓		$302.50
1008	4/11	Valley Telephone	18.00 ✓		284.50
	4/19	Deposit		$517.50	802.00
1009	4/19	Ralph Smith	22.50		779.50
1010	4/20	Electric and Gas Co.	97.50 ✓		682.00
1011	4/21	First Savings and Loan	397.50 ✓		284.50
	4/28	Deposit		247.50	532.00
1012	4/29	John Waldo, M.D.	90.00		442.00
1013	4/31	Swift Drugs	15.00 ✓		427.00
1014	5/2	Shopper's Market	60.00 ✓		367.00
1015	5/4	Central TV Repair	52.50		314.50
1016	5/8	Douglas Dog Hospital	30.00		284.50
	5/8	Deposit		97.50	382.00
1017	5/9	Cash	52.50 ✓		329.50
	5/10	Deposit		52.50	382.00
1018	5/11	Sully Oil Company	37.50		344.50
1019	5/15	Jones Nursery	9.00		335.50

NOW and share draft accounts will show the interest earned. The abbreviations at the bottom of the statement in Exhibit 4.5 identify the fee or interest.

List of outstanding checks

An **outstanding check** is one you have written and given to the payee, but that has not been cashed and charged against your account. Comparing the canceled checks returned with your statement to your checkbook does two things. You confirm that the MICR amount encoded at the bottom of the check, (it is the last digits in MICR characters) is the same as your checkbook amount. Place a mark (✓) beside each check as you do this. Checks without that mark are the ones you wrote but which have not been charged to your account; they are outstanding checks. Fred's outstanding checks in Exhibit 4.5 are #1009—$22.50, #1012—$90.00, #1015—$52.50, and #1016—$30.00. They total $195.00.

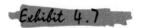
Exhibit 4.7

Checking Account Reconciliation

Line	Description	Amount
	Per Bank Statement	
1.	Balance per bank statement	$520.50
2.	Add: deposits in transit	52.50
3.	Subtotal	$573.00
4.	Less: outstanding checks	195.00
5.	Adjusted cash balance per bank	$378.00
	Per Checkbook	
6.	Balance per checkbook	$382.00
7.	Less: service charges	6.10
	Add: interest earned	2.10
8.	Adjusted cash balance per checkbook	$378.00

Checklist
1. If line 5 equals line 8, you are done. If not, proceed to steps 2 through 6.
2. If line 5 is greater than line 8:
   a. Recheck your list of outstanding checks.
3. If line 8 is greater than line 5:
   a. Recheck your list of outstanding checks.
   b. Check your deposits in transit.
   c. Review bank statements for additional bank charges.
4. If line 8 and line 5 still do not agree:
   a. Test the addition and subtraction in your checkbook.
   b. Recompare the amounts on the returned checks to the amount recorded in the checkbook.
5. If line 5 and 8 still do not agree:
   a. Compare the dollar amount that you wrote on each check with the dollar amount that the bank coded in magnetic ink (MICR) at the bottom of that check.
6. If the two lines still do not agree:
   a. Take a short break; you are probably overlooking an obvious error.

Your bank, MSB, S&L, or credit union may not return the canceled checks. To reduce costs, some institutions no longer return canceled checks to the customer. Your institution retains a copy of each. They will send you a copy if you need it. In place of the checks, your account statement lists all checks cashed this period by check number and amount.

In this case, you still have a facsimile of each check because the check blank your institution issues you has two parts: the check itself and a duplicate on carbonless paper. As you write the check, you create the duplicate. The copy is marked "not negotiable" so no one can cash it.

Outstanding checks are identified by comparing each check's dollar amount on the account statement to your checkbook duplicates. The account lists checks in numerical order to simplify the process. Place a (✓) mark on those duplicate checks that were cashed. Those without the (✓) mark are outstanding.

Deposit in transit

A **deposit in transit** is one you have made but which your bank has not credited to your account. Your bank may not have received the deposit you made just before they sent out the statement. When Fred compared the deposits on his statement, Exhibit 4.5, to his checkbook, Exhibit 4.6, he discovered the $52.50 deposit of May 10 was in transit.

Completing the Reconciliation

Your completed reconciliation should show the "true" balance in your payment account. You first compute an adjusted balance using the balance from your checkbook. Next you compute an adjusted balance using the balance shown on your bank statement. Those two balances should be the same if the account does not have errors. Let us examine the process and summarize the details in Exhibit 4.7.

First, compute the adjusted balance using the bank statement (top section of Exhibit 4.7). Start with the closing balance from the statement. Next add any deposits in transit. That amount will be credited to your account in a few days, so that is justified. Now deduct the total of your outstanding checks: eventually your account will be charged for them. The resulting figure is the adjusted balance for the bank statement.

Now we compute the adjusted balance using your checkbook (lower section of Exhibit 4.7). Start with the checkbook balance on the closing date of the account statement. Subtract any service fees. Then add back any interest earned. Your bank has already charged or credited you for these amounts, so this updates your record. The resulting balance is the adjusted balance for your checkbook.

Are the two adjusted balances—lines 5 and 8 in Exhibit 4.7—equal? Yes? That is the account's "true" balance. No? Then you have an error. The checklist at the bottom of Exhibit 4.7 can help you locate it. If the error is in your checkbook, correct it. If it is the bank's error, request corrective action from their accounting department.

Once you are satisfied that the two adjusted balances are equal, deduct the service fees and add any interest to your checkbook. It now shows the adjusted balance in your account.

OTHER PAYMENT METHODS

There are several payment methods that can supplement or be substituted for checking, NOW, or share draft accounts.

Central Asset Management Accounts

Existing **central asset management accounts** combine financial services and investment services. Because the accounts centralize those services, they are labeled all-in-one accounts. They are offered by brokerage firms, financial institutions, insurance companies, and mutual funds. A typical account provides a payment account, money market investment, credit or debit card, brokerage service, and access to an ATM. Let's look at the payment account.

Typical minimum account balances range from $5,000 to $25,000. Many count both your cash balance and your investment securities for that minimum balance. Beside the minimum, most charge an annual fee of $25 to $100. For this you receive a payment account with no service fees. Any extra dollars in the payment account are invested in some short-term investment. The prevailing market interest rate on this type of investment is what you receive. Your monthly statement summarizes the account balance, securities held, the checks charged against the account, your credit or debit card activity.

Who should consider one

Because of the large minimums, only people with sizable cash or security holdings need apply. Unless you need the wide range of services offered, the annual fee makes central asset management accounts a poor choice if you only need a payment account. People who expect to use the services extensively may find these an option. Concentrating financial and investment activity in one place is a decided advantage.

Strategy

For those who meet the minimum and need the services, central asset management accounts are a reasonable choice.

Money Market Mutual Fund

When you invest in a **money market mutual fund,** you purchase shares, just as you do in a credit union. The fund invests your and other customers' money in short-term investments: large certificates of deposit (CDs), Treasury bills, and commercial paper, for example. It allows you to write checks on your account when you want to withdraw money. The funds do not limit the number of checks or charge a fee, but each check must be for at least $250 or $500. Unless you only write large checks, the account serves only as a supplement, but it can be a good place for the cash reserve discussed in the budgeting section of the last chapter. A later chapter will discuss these funds in detail.

Automated Teller Machines

The **automated teller machine (ATM)** is designed to provide financial services at convenient locations and at all hours. An ATM will accept deposits, dispense cash, transfer money between accounts, pay loan or credit card balances, or give a cash advance on a credit card. ATMs are placed in shopping centers, in office buildings, in small freestanding facilities, and outside financial institutions. Many operate around the clock, 7 days a week.

You use a plastic identification card to access your account at an ATM. Some require a special card; others accept major credit cards. In addition to the card, you type in a personal identification number (PIN). Someone finding your card would also need that PIN to access your account. Don't make that easy by writing the PIN on the card or by carrying it in your wallet. ATMs have the added safeguard of only permitting a few attempts at your PIN. If they are incorrect, the ATM locks up the account and keeps your plastic card. You must go to the institution to recover it.

If you lose your ATM card, immediately notify the institution that supplied it. If you notify the institution within 2 days of discovering the loss, your liability for missing funds is $50. Beyond 2 days and up through 60 days, your liability is $500. Beyond 60 days it is unlimited. Prompt notice is essential.

Strategy

Banking with an institution that offers a network of ATMs can make managing your finances easier. Access to an ATM should be a factor when selecting an account.

Cashier's Check

A **cashier's check** is drawn against the financial institution that issued it. Backed by that institution's promise to pay, it is readily accepted as a payment. It can be used when a payee does not accept personal checks.

Commercial banks, MSBs, S&Ls, and credit unions sell cashier's checks. Some provide them as a "free" customer service; others charge a $2 to $10 fee.

Once cashed, the cashier's check is retained by the issuing institution. You retain the duplicate you received when you purchased it. Most institutions will supply a copy of the check if you need it.

Money Order

Money orders are issued by the U.S. Post Office and a number of financial service firms. The financial strength of the issuer makes them an acceptable means of payment. Money orders can be used when a payee does not accept personal checks.

You pay for the money order at time of purchase, and the issuer pays when it is cashed. A typical fee is $0.75 to $10. You send the draft part of the money order to the payee but retain the duplicate. The issuer retains the cashed draft but will send you a copy if you need it.

Traveler's Checks

Businesses and individuals outside your immediate area will rarely accept your personal check. If you are traveling or temporarily working out of town, that is a hurdle. **Traveler's checks** cover it. They are issued by large national and international banks, credit card companies, and financial service companies. Backed by the issuer's promise to pay, they are accepted throughout the United States and abroad. If your checks are lost or stolen, the issuer will replace them.

In the past you purchased these checks at a financial institution for the check's face (stated) value plus a 1 percent sales charge. Now they can be purchased at many locations, and some sellers waive part or all the sales charge as a customer service.

Strategy

Check financial institutions and other issuers in your area to see if any offer traveler's checks at a reduced fee.

Many people hold unused traveler's checks for future use. The checks have no time limit, but your money earns no interest. If you have access to "free" checks, always cash any leftover checks. Even if you must pay the full 1 percent fee, you should generally cash the checks. Suppose Ned had $500 in checks from his vacation. Holding the checks eliminates a future $5 fee ($500 × 1%). But if it will be 6 months until he used them, he could have earned $15 interest ($500 × 6% × 6 months/12 months) by cashing them and investing the money in his 6 percent money market savings account.

Strategy

Immediately cash unused traveler's checks if new ones are "free." Unless you expect to use them within 70 days, cash even those with a fee.

Summary

1 Commercial banks, S&Ls, MSBs, and (to a lesser extent) credit unions have broadened their service offerings in a push to become one-stop personal finance centers.

2 Checking accounts, NOW accounts, and share draft accounts are the major payment accounts used by individuals. The latter two pay interest on your account balance.

3 Benefits from a checking, NOW, or share draft account include:
- Convenience of making mail payments
- Avoids risk of carrying large amounts of cash
- Provides a detailed record of your spending
- Canceled checks are a valid receipt

4 The four major payment accounts are:
- Minimum balance account
- Minimum investment account
- Service fee account
- Unconditional free account

5 Three criteria should be considered when selecting a payment account:
- Minimum balance required by the account
- Estimated annual cost based on your projected use
- Range of other financial services the institution provides

6 Most checks are personalized with name, address, and perhaps your telephone or driver's license number. Customer pays for printing.

7 Use a blank endorsement only on checks to be deposited or cashed immediately.

8 Checks deposited at an ATM or by mail should have a restrictive or special endorsement.

9 When an institution places a "hold" on your deposit, the money cannot be withdrawn until it has been on deposit for the specified number of days.

10 Many payment accounts offer an automatic overdraft privilege. Customer can overdraw the account, but a finance charge is assessed.

11 Your financial institution "certifies" your account has adequate funds for the certified check.

12 A stop-payment order may prevent payment of a check you wrote.

13 Reconciling your payment account entails computing two "adjusted" balances, one based on your checkbook, the other on the account statement. When those two are equal, the account is reconciled.

14 ATMs will accept a deposit, dispense money, transfer between accounts, make payments, and advance cash from your credit card.

15 Payees who will not accept a personal check often will take a cashier's check or a money order.

16 Traveler's checks are a convenient payment option while away from home.

Review your understanding of

Commercial bank
Savings and loan
Mutual savings bank
Credit union
Checking account
Negotiable order of withdrawal (NOW) account
Share draft account
Minimum balance account
Minimum investment account
Service fee account
Processing fee
Monthly maintenance fee
Unconditional free account
Payee
Postdating
Blank endorsement

Restricted endorsement
Special endorsement
"Hold" on deposits
Overdraft
Certified check
Stop-payment order
Reconciliation of account
Outstanding check
Deposit in transit
Central asset management account
Money market mutual fund
Automated teller machine (ATM)
Cashier's check
Money order
Traveler's check

Discussion questions

1 Despite the wide availability of traditional checking accounts, NOW accounts and share draft accounts were developed. Why? How are the three accounts similar? Do NOW or share draft accounts offer any advantage(s)? Disadvantages(s)?

2 Fran Wallinski has narrowed her payment account choices to two:

  a A NOW account that pays 5 percent interest; she must maintain a $600 balance to eliminate service fees.

  b A checking account with no service fees if she maintains a $600 balance in the bank's 5 percent savings account.

What are the strengths of each option? Which would you choose? Why?

3 Ron McGee's twice-monthly salary check is directly deposited in his minimum balance NOW account. From that NOW account he writes checks for all expenses and investments. Would he prefer that the account's minimum balance be based on the lowest daily balance during the month or on the average of those daily balances? Why?

4 Can you give some reasons why checking, NOW, and share draft accounts are so popular? What type of person would benefit most from using one?

5 An area commercial bank claims: "Totally *free* checking when you maintain a $500 balance in your checking account." Do you agree? Why or why not?

6 Give several situations where a service fee checking account might be the best choice. Would it likely be best for most people? Explain.

7 Describe a circumstance where a blank endorsement is appropriate; one where a restricted endorsement is appropriate. What is the major difference between the two?

8 Don Smith has an ingenious system for managing his checking account. He records no checks and never computes the account balance. Instead he deposits $700 in the account and writes checks until the bank notifies him he is overdrawn. He has an automatic overdraft on the account to avoid the bank's $20 overdraft fee. An 18 percent finance charge is assessed on the overdraft amount until he deposits another $700 to repeat the cycle. What is your opinion of Don's system?

Can you suggest any improvements? What would they accomplish?

9 Last National Bank has the following policy for "holds" on customer deposits:

  a Money from checks drawn on local banks will not be "available" for 3 days.

  b Checks drawn on an out-of-state bank will not be "available" for 8 days.

Explain what this means and how it complicates managing a checking account.

10 Why is an automatic overdraft often a worthwhile option? Briefly explain its operation and its cost, if any.

11 Does a stop-payment order eliminate the possibility of a check being cashed? Give several examples of situations where the order might be useful.

12 How would you handle the following when reconciling your payment account?

  a Your bank credited you with $6.25 in interest.

  b Several checks you wrote during the month have not been cashed.

  c The deposit you made near the end of the month does not appear on the account statement.

13 Brad Botch notices his ATM card (PIN written upside down on the back) is missing on Monday. A check of the account balance on Friday at the bank shows $0.60 not the $600 he expected. He asks the bank to restore the missing $599.40 to his account. Will he succeed? Any hints for Brad?

14 A section of a sales contract stated: "Payment must be by cashier's check, money order, or certified check; personal checks not accepted." Why does the contract make that distinction? What makes the first three options more acceptable than the prohibited one?

15 Why do the banks and companies that issue traveler's checks not place an expiration date on them? If most or all of the 1 percent commission goes to the institution or business selling the checks, how does the issuer make a profit?

Problems

4.1 **Nick and Kathy O'Brien are evaluating three payment options:**

Bargain check. No minimum balance; $0.15 per check processing fee; $2 monthly maintenance fee.

Charge free. Maintain a $700 minimum balance in the checking account and there are no service fees.

Investor special. Maintain a $2,000 balance in a savings account paying 5 percent interest and receive a checking account that charges no fees.

Presently the O'Briens have $2,500 in a credit union account that pays 7 percent interest.

  a What is each account's monthly cost if they write 5 checks per month? Which one do you prefer?

  b Would you recommend the same account if they expect to write 20 checks per month? Why?

4.2 To reconcile her checking account as of August 27, Susan Weber summarized the following information:

  ■ The August 27 balance in her checkbook is $56.10.

- A search of her bank statement shows the following checks were neither charged to her account nor returned by the bank: #513—$75.00, #517—$13.50, #523—$37.75, #524—$6.50, and #527—$17.25.
- Service fees of $1.35 were deducted on her bank statement. Her statement also indicates that she earned $0.25 interest for the month.
- Her bank statement shows a $205.00 balance on August 27.

a What is the total of Susan's outstanding checks?

b What is the account's adjusted balance based on the bank statement? What is the adjusted balance based on her checkbook?

c What adjustments should Susan make to her checkbook to complete the reconciliation?

4.3 Ralph DiCassa is considering two options for $500 of unused traveler's checks:

- Cash the checks and deposit the proceeds in a 5 percent savings account. Pay a $5 fee to repurchase them 180 days from now.
- Retain the checks until needed in 180 days.

a What does each option cost? Which would you recommend?

b Would your advice for part (a) differ if Ralph expects to use the checks within 30 days?

c At what length of holding period will the two options cost the same? (*Hint:* Compute the daily cost of holding.)

4.4 Last Chance Bank offers the following three payment options:

Feature of payment account	Service account	Minimum checking	NOW account
Required minimum balance	None	$700	$1,500
Processing fee per check	$0.20	None	None
Monthly maintenance fee	$4.00	None	None
Interest rate paid on account	None	None	5 percent

Connie Confused expects she will write 25 checks each month. Currently she has $1,500 invested in a money market mutual fund that pays 8 percent interest; the money for any required minimum balance would be drawn from it.

a What is the net cost of each option? (*Hint:* Compute each account's fees. Then compute interest earned on the $1,500: part may be tied up in the account's minimum, part in the mutual fund. Combine those two for the net cost.)

b Which one do you recommend? Support your choice.

4.5 Maynard Moreorless has two competing payment account offers. One provides a checking account with no service fee if he maintains $500 in a 5 percent savings account; checking account pays no interest. The competing NOW account pays 5 percent interest and requires a similar $500 minimum. Past experience suggests Maynard will keep a working balance of $200 over and above the payment account's minimum.

a What is the cost for each account?

b Maynard has noticed it may be a week or more before a check is cashed. Should he consider that in his selection decision? Why?

Case problem

Phil Fast has recently opened a personal checking account. Being new to the checking account world, he is having more than a few problems with his monthly reconciliation. To date, his reconciliation consists of:

Balance from bank statement $142.50

Balance from checkbook $121.00

The fact that the two do not agree disturbs him, but he is unclear about how to proceed. His checkbook, bank statement, and returned checks are shown on the next two pages so you can help Phil solve his problem.

Check number	Date	Check issued to	Check amount	Deposit amount	Balance
					51.00
1511	10/7	Central Food Mart	$ 10.00		41.00
1512	10/14	Leadpoint Public Service	40.00		1.00
	10/14	Deposit		$320.00	321.00
1514	10/15	Ajax Retail Service	155.00		166.00
1515	10/15	Quick Charge, Inc.	25.00		141.00
1516	10/15	Leah Schwartz, M.D.	10.00		131.00
1517	10/15	Red Dot Insurance	40.00		91.00
1518	10/18	Central Food Mart	15.00		76.00
	10/21	Deposit		90.00	166.00
1519	10/25	Fred's Auto Repairs	37.00		129.00
1520	10/30	Tony's Clothes	25.00		104.00
1521	10/30	Cash	12.00		92.00
1522	11/2	Central Food Mart	16.00		76.00
	11/4	Deposit		45.00	121.00
1523	11/6	Western Beverage Spot	13.50		107.50

1 Why is the balance per bank statement, $142.50, different from the balance in Phil's checkbook, $121.00?
2 What information is needed before the account can be reconciled?
3 Using this information, compile a list of outstanding checks. Why is this needed?
4 Are there any deposits in transit?
5 Complete the reconciliation of Phil's account.
6 What corrections, if any, should Phil make in his checkbook?

Phil Fast					Last National Bank
1456 Deadend					Leadpoint, USA 98765
Leadpoint, USA 98765					

Statement Period: October 5 to November 5

Beginning Balance	Total Deposit		Total Charges			Ending Balance
51.00	410.00		318.50			142.50
Charges			Credits	Date	Balance	

Charges			Credits	Date	Balance
				10-6	51.00
10.00				10-11	41.00
			320.00	10-15	361.00
40.00	60.00	155.00		10-17	106.00
25.00				10-20	81.00
			90.00	10-22	171.00
15.00				10-24	156.00
12.00				11-4	144.00
SC 2.45			IN .95	11-5	142.50

SC Service Charge	FC Finance Charge	DM Debit Memo	IN Interest

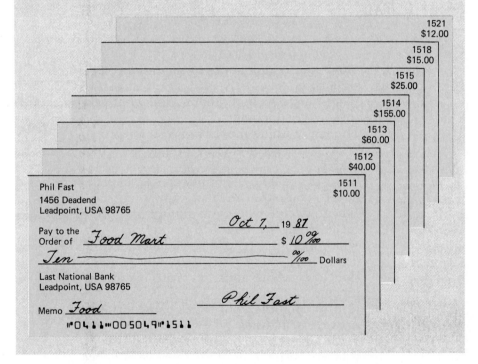

1521
$12.00

1518
$15.00

1515
$25.00

1514
$155.00

1513
$60.00

1512
$40.00

1511
$10.00

Phil Fast
1456 Deadend
Leadpoint, USA 98765

Pay to the
Order of *Food Mart*

Oct 7, 19 *87*

$ *10 00/100*

Ten ———————————— *00/100* Dollars

Last National Bank
Leadpoint, USA 98765

Memo *Food*

Phil Fast

⑈0411⑈005049⑈1511

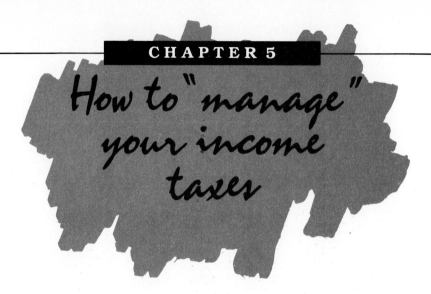

CHAPTER 5

How to "manage" your income taxes

AFTER COMPLETING THIS CHAPTER YOU WILL HAVE LEARNED

- The major components of the federal income tax structure
- What has to be included in, and what can be excluded from, gross income
- The major adjustments to gross income
- What the standard deduction is and when you should take it
- What expenditures qualify as itemized deductions and how to compute the most common ones
- How to decide when you should use itemized deductions rather than the standard deduction
- What eligibility tests must be met to claim someone as a dependent
- How to compute adjusted gross income and taxable income
- How to compute your taxes using either the tax table or tax rate schedules
- What a tax credit is and how it lowers your tax bill
- How you can qualify for the more common tax credits
- When you have to estimate your income and make quarterly tax payments
- How to avoid the penalty for underpaying income taxes
- What a marginal tax rate is and how it is used
- Tax planning techniques that can reduce your tax bill
- How to survive an audit by the Internal Revenue Service

*D*espite sweeping changes contained in the Tax Reform Act of 1986 (the TRA), you still have a partner to "share" your income. The reduction in the top tax rate from 50 to 33 percent may mean some people pay a bit less on their last dollar of income, but many will still work from January into May just to pay their taxes.

Just who are our "tax partners"? First, there is the federal government. Depending on your income level, the feds may take from $0.28 to $0.33 of your last income dollar. Then there are state and local income taxes. Live in "taxland" U.S.A., and they could take another $0.08 to $0.12. Last, plan on paying about $0.07 of each dollar for Social Security taxes. Together, your "partners" may take over half of the last dollar you make! Tax authorities may not "kill" the golden goose—anyone who pays taxes—but they sure grab a lot of its food.

You need a working knowledge of taxes. First, it can make it possible for you to use perfectly legitimate options to minimize your tax bill. Second, taxes affect your financial decisions; understanding how they work will help you make better decisions. Third, violating some tax limit or rule may result in penalties. If you miss a possible tax break, the Internal Revenue Service (IRS) will not insist you take it, but if you take one you don't deserve, the IRS will let you know. Finally, the quality of some tax advice and preparation services is poor, and even the toll-free tax line provided by the IRS can be wrong more than 20 percent of the time. Even if someone else prepares your tax returns, you still need to understand taxes to be a good personal financial manager.

This chapter provides basic information regarding federal income taxes. State and local income tax structures are so diverse that they cannot be covered in our limited space. We will focus on the issues that affect most taxpayers. Though the pages that follow can't make you a tax "pro," few of us need to be one anyway. When a point involves highly detailed rules (and many tax issues do), we will suggest you consult one of the tax reference manuals listed at the end of the chapter. One thing we will *not* do is to lead you line by line through tax forms. They change so frequently that our examples would quickly be dated. When you understand the basics of taxes, filling out a form is nothing more than an exercise in applying that knowledge.

Avoiding, Not Evading, Taxes

Through a combination of oversight, confusion, error, timidity, and plain fear, many people overpay their taxes. Some avoid anything that might be challenged. Others are so poorly informed, or their tax advisors are, that they miss major tax reduction opportunities. Still others hesitate to claim an item, believing that if they do it will subject their entire return to a detailed audit by the IRS. (More on this point later.) A good financial planner does not spend money on extra taxes.

The Supreme Court has confirmed that taxpayers have the right to use all the options in the tax regulations to reduce taxes. **Tax avoidance** is using all available legal means to cut your tax bill. **Tax evasion** is quite different—Understating income, claiming bogus deductions, inflating the number of exemptions, and other illegal manuevers can mean a fine and even a temporary federal address which will *not* improve one's résumé.

Strategy

If you qualify for a particular tax reduction alternative, use it. At worst, you may have to support your claim to the IRS.

BASIC INCOME TAX STRUCTURE

Our discussion of taxes builds on the basic tax structure summarized in Exhibit 5.1. Taxes would be a lot simpler if you could just multiply your total income by some tax rate. Unfortunately some income has to be included in the total, some excluded, and some partially excluded. There are also some qualifying expenditures you may deduct from your income. Sound complex? It is, but we will explain the options available for reducing your tax bill.

Let's examine some terminology and review major points from Exhibit 5.1. We'll work from the top down.

Gross Income

Gross income includes all of the income items you must include on your tax return: wages, interest, dividends, and profits from a business you own, for example.

Exhibit 5.1

Basic Income Tax Structure

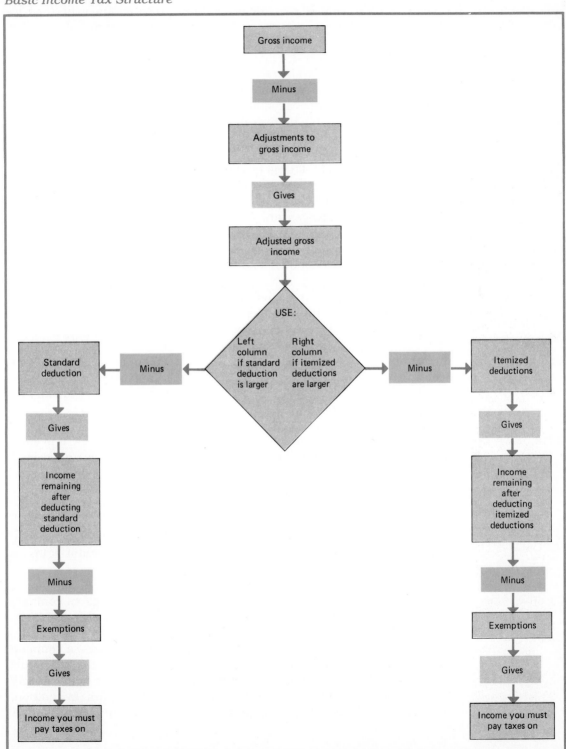

Adjustments to Gross Income

Some expenditures qualify as **adjustments to gross income;** they can be deducted from your gross income. Those minus boxes in Exhibit 5.1 are especially helpful. The more you can reduce your gross income, the lower your taxes: that is successful tax management.

Adjusted Gross Income

Deducting adjustments from your gross income gives you your **adjusted gross income** (sometimes called AGI). This amount is shown midway down Exhibit 5.1. It is used in a number of tax computations, so you need to calculate it.

Itemized Deductions

A select group of expenditures qualify as **itemized deductions;** you can deduct these from your adjusted gross income. They add to the "minus" box on the right side of Exhibit 5.1. Examples include state income taxes, interest on home mortgages, and charitable donations.

Standard Deduction

Suppose Ed has few qualifying itemized deductions: his state's income taxes are low, he does not own a home, and Ebenezer Scrooge's donations look generous in comparison. Not to worry. Every taxpayer can take a **standard deduction** rather than itemize (a nice "minus" on the left side of Exhibit 5.1). Those with many itemized deductions should elect the right side; those without should choose the left side of Exhibit 5.1.

Exemption

An **exemption** allows you to subtract a flat dollar amount from your income. If you provide the majority of someone's support, you may be able to claim an exemption. Later in the chapter we develop the qualifying points for an exemption.

Taxable Income

Taxable income is the amount on which you have to pay taxes. It is what remains after the standard deduction (or itemized deductions) and exemptions are deducted from your adjusted gross income. The lower your taxable income, the lower your tax bill. That is why those "minus" blocks are so valuable.

GROSS INCOME

Exhibit 5.2 gives an alphabetical list of major items that must be included in gross income. Most entries are straightforward, but capital gains or losses and Social Security benefits need explanation.

Capital Gains and Losses

Capital gains and losses arise from the sale of such things as common stocks, corporate bonds, municipal bonds, mutual fund shares, and Treasury securities. (Selling your home may generate a gain which receives special treatment: we cover it in Chapter 9.) Sell a capital asset—a common stock, bond, or mutual fund share—for a price different from your purchase price, and you have either a gain or loss. You need to know the net purchase price and net sale price to compute the gain or loss. In addition, you need to distinguish between short- and long-term gains and losses.

Net purchase price

An asset's **net purchase price** is the sum of its price and any commissions paid to buy it. If you bought 100 shares of Zug Products from a broker for $15 per share plus a $40 commission, your net purchase price was $1,540: (100 shares × $15 per share) + $40 commission.

Net sale price

The **net sale price** is the sale price minus any commission. Suppose your 100 shares in Zug are sold for $20 each, and the broker charges a $50 commission. Your net sale price is $1,950: (100 shares × $20) − $50 commission.

Capital Gains: Short-Term and Long-Term

When an asset's net sale price exceeds its net purchase price, you have a **capital gain.** The IRS wants to share in your good fortune: the entire gain has to be included in gross income and is taxed whether it is short- or long-term.

For tax purposes, gains on any capital asset owned for 6 months or less are considered **short-term.** All others are **long-term.** The IRS treats both identically. Then why distinguish between them? In the past, only 40 percent of long-term gains had to be included in income. Yes, Gert, the other 60 percent was tax-free; long-term gains used to be *very* attractive. The TRA of 1986 made the *entire* gain taxable. Stay tuned, however: there is a better than even chance that some special tax treatment for long-term gains will be revived. Even if the tax treatment is identical, the tax form for gains and losses still requires they be split.

Computing the capital gain

Exhibit 5.3 contains several examples of capital gains situations. Suppose the net purchase price for the Zug Products shares on the top line is $1,540, and the net sale price is $1,950. Since they were held 5 months, the short-term gain is $410: $1,950 − $1,540. The entire $410 must be included in gross income. Likewise, all of the $175 long-term gain on the XQ bonds—second line of Exhibit 5.3—is included in gross income.

Exhibit 5.2

Items That Must Be Included in Gross Income

Alimony received
Business profits
Capital gains and losses
Commissions
Contest winnings
Dividends
Gambling winnings, but only to the
　extent they exceed losses*
Interest on savings, bonds, certificates
　of deposit (CDs), Treasury securities
Lottery winnings

Partnership income
Payments from retirement accounts:
　IRA and Keogh plans
Pension payments
Salaries
Social Security benefits (may be
　partially taxable)
Tips
Unemployment benefits
U.S. savings bond interest
Wages

* If gambling losses were $500 and winnings were $600, only the $100 excess of winnings would be included. If the opposite were true—winnings were $500 and losses were $600—none of the winnings would be included. But *none* of the $600 loss could be deducted.

Capital Losses: Short-Term and Long-Term

When an asset's net sale price is less than its net purchase price, you have a **capital loss.** Since the government is so willing to share in the good times, it seems fair that they join in the bad times too. Deducting the loss lowers your gross income, so you pay less tax. Those tax savings can offset as much as 30 or 40 percent of your loss. The tax treatment of **long-term losses** and **short-term losses** is similar: you can *usually* deduct the entire loss (we will look at the "usually" later).

Computing capital losses

The last two lines in Exhibit 5.3 show several examples of situations that generate capital losses. Assume the net sale price of Slug common stock is $4,675. Since that is less than its $4,975 net purchase price, the taxpayer has a $300 short-term loss (short-term because the asset was only held 6 months). All of this loss can be deducted from gross income. Likewise, all of the $1,050 long-term loss on the QT Bond can be deducted from gross income.

Strategy

Consider selling losing investments to create a capital loss; the tax savings will offset part of the loss.

Limits on deduction of capital losses

You have to have some other source of income to deduct capital losses. Since most people have wages or salary, this is not a serious problem. Even if you have no other income, the loss can be carried forward to future years when you do.

If you have both capital gains and losses, deduct the losses from the gains and use the net amount. What if gains were minimal or zero, yet losses were large? You cannot deduct more than $3,000 of losses from your other income in any year; unused capital losses should be carried forward to future years.

Delbert Downdraft had no gains and $2,500 in capital losses this past year. He can deduct the entire amount. If Penelope Pits amassed $7,000 in losses this year (investments are *not* her forte), she can deduct $3,000 this year, another $3,000 next year, and the remaining $1,000 the following.

 **Exhibit 5.3**

Computation of Short-Term and Long-Term Gains and Losses

Capital asset	Asset held for	Short-term (ST) or long-term (LT)	Net purchase price	Net sales price	Gain that is taxed	Loss that can be deducted
Zug Stock	5 months	ST	$1,540	$1,950	$410	—
XQ Bonds	2 years	LT	1,825	2,000	175	—
Slug Stock	6 months	ST	4,975	4,675	—	$ 300
QT Bonds	27 months	LT	4,050	3,000	—	1,050

Social Security Benefits

Social Security benefits range from partially taxable to nontaxable. At worst, one-half of the benefit is taxable. If Sidney has extensive income from other sources, he might have to include as much as $4,000 of his $8,000 Social Security benefit in his gross income. For single people whose total income—including one-half the Social Security benefit—is $25,000 or less, none of the benefit is taxable. Couples that file jointly can earn $32,000 from all sources—including one-half their Social Security benefit—without including any benefits in gross income. Above those limits part of the Social Security benefit has to be included in gross income. Specific details of that computation are explained in Chapter 10.

Sources of Income You Do Not Have to Include

After looking at Exhibit 5.2, you may wonder: Does anything escape being taxed? In fact, there are a number of ways you can receive money that is not included in gross income. Exhibit 5.4 summarizes major items that can be excluded.

ADJUST-MENTS TO GROSS INCOME

There is a select group of expenditures that can be deducted from gross income, thereby lowering your taxes. These adjustments differ from the itemized deductions we will discuss later in the chapter: you can subtract these items whether you itemize or not.

Contributions to Pension Plans

Contributions to certain pension plans qualify as adjustments to gross income; these include those which self-employed persons make to Keogh plans. Some people may be able to deduct contributions to Individual Retirement Accounts (IRAs). Let's look at the potential advantages of making these voluntary contributions.

First, you lower your income when the contribution qualifies as an adjustment to gross income. Contribute $1,000 to a Keogh or IRA, and you postpone paying taxes on that $1,000. You contribute **before-tax dollars** to these plans. Second, the earnings on contributions are shielded from taxes until you make withdrawals from the plans. Since no tax was paid on the original deposit or on earnings, the entire amount is subject to taxes on withdrawal.

 Exhibit 5.4

Income That Is Not Counted as Part of Gross Income

Annuity payments: the portion that represents your original cost
Child support payments
Disability benefits (if you paid the premiums for the policy)
Dividends paid in common stock and stock splits
Gifts and inheritances
Health and accident insurance payments
Interest on notes and bonds issued by states and cities
Insurance payments for damage to your automobile, house, or personal belongings
Life insurance payments
Scholarship and fellowship awards (but there are some limits)
Welfare benefits
Workers compensation

Self-employed person's pension plan: The Keogh plan

Individuals can contribute up to 20 percent of their self-employment earnings to a **Keogh plan;** maximum contribution is $30,000. Self-employment need not be your sole source of income, but you can only contribute on the self-employment portion. Sandy earned a $20,000 salary and an additional $5,000 as a self-employed consultant. She could contribute up to $1,000 ($5,000 self-employment income × 20% maximum) to her Keogh account. Keogh plans are a major topic of Chapter 18.

Strategy

If you qualify, a Keogh contribution reduces your taxes while building a retirement fund.

Individual retirement account (IRA)

Anyone who earns an income can contribute to an **Individual Retirement Account (IRA).** The maximum contribution is the lesser of your total income or $2,000. But *not* everyone can deduct that contribution as an adjustment to gross income. Those not covered by a pension plan from their employer can deduct the entire amount regardless of income. Even if covered by a pension plan, they can still deduct the full amount if adjusted gross income is $25,000 or less if single—$40,000 or less for those filing jointly. Part of the contribution is deductible when adjusted gross income is between $25,000 and $35,000 if single—between $40,000 and $50,000 for joint returns. Above $35,000 single, and $50,000 joint, none of the contribution can be deducted. IRAs are covered in Chapter 18.

All earnings on your IRA are shielded from taxes while the money remains in the account. This tax deferral holds whether all, part, or none of the contribution can be deducted.

Strategy

Seriously consider an IRA, since contributions reduce your taxes while you build a retirement fund. Even when the IRA contribution is not deductible, taxes are deferred on the interest and dividends the money earns.

Alimony Payments

Alimony or maintenance payments to a spouse or former spouse may qualify as an adjustment to gross income. The rules are complex; professional tax help is recommended.

Child support

Payments made to support a child from a prior marriage do *not* qualify as an adjustment to gross income. But the payment of child support may allow the person making those payments to claim the child as a dependent.

DEDUCTIONS FROM ADJUSTED GROSS INCOME

Now you know your adjusted gross income. As our sketch of the tax structure in Exhibit 5.1 shows, the next step is to subtract all allowable deductions from your AGI. The diagram shows that you have two options: to take a standard deduction or to itemize deductions. You can do whichever gives you the largest total deduction, but you can only do *one*. In the sections that follow we'll explain each option and show how you choose which is best for you.

Standard Deductions

The **standard deduction** is a flat dollar amount that can be deducted from adjusted gross income. For 1988 those amounts are:

- $5,000 for married couples filing jointly (more on this later)
- $4,400 for heads of households (defined later)
- $3,000 for single individuals
- $2,500 per person if a husband and wife file separate tax returns

Those amounts do not vary with income, nor do you have to show some list of "qualifying" expenditures. You automatically qualify for a standard deduction.

Beginning in 1989 those amounts are scheduled to rise with inflation. Check a reference book for the current amount.

Standard deduction: additional amount

Taxpayers who are 65 or older and those who are blind qualify for an additional standard deduction. Single individuals who are 65 or older or blind can add $750 to the standard deduction. Those 65 or older *and* blind add $1,500. Individuals filing a joint return who are age 65 or older, or who are blind, can add $600 to the regular amount. A couple can add $1,200 if both qualify.

Itemized Deductions

For some, **itemizing, or listing, their deductions** may be the better choice. If the total of those qualifying items is larger than the standard deduction, deducting that total will reduce taxes more. Let's look at the major qualifying items.

Interest charges

Home mortgages and home equity loans. **Interest on a home mortgage qualifies** as an itemized deduction. Depending on the interest rate, total interest on a $60,000 mortgage could top $6,000 for the year.

Interest on second mortgages and home equity loans is usually deductible, but the home has to be security for the loan. Additionally, the total of all "home-based" loans cannot exceed the home's original purchase price plus improvements. That means that the total of the unpaid balances on the first mortgage, second mortgage, and all home equity loans has to be less than the purchase price plus improvements. Ed paid $75,000 for his house and has made $5,000 worth of improvements. As long as the total unpaid balance on his mortgages and home equity loans is less than $80,000, all interest is deductible.

Consumer loans and credit cards. **Interest and finance charges on consumer loans and credit cards are losing their deductible status.** The deductible portion of the interest and finance charges is 40 percent in 1988, 20 percent in 1989, 10 percent in 1990, and then nothing. During 1988, Phil Plastic ran up $200 in finance charges on his credit cards. Only $80 qualifies as an itemized deduction. By 1991, none of it will qualify.

Taxes

The following tax payments generally qualify as itemized deductions:

- *Property taxes.* Amounts paid on your home, car, and other personal property.
- *Income taxes.* Amounts paid to the state or city where you live based on your income; foreign taxes paid on income also usually qualify.

For homeowners, property taxes are often a major deduction. Likewise, taxes on personal property may be sizable in some states. Last, state and local income taxes can range from zero in those few states that have no such tax to several thousand dollars in others. For many, this is one of the largest categories of itemized deductions.

Contributions

Most contributions to religious, charitable, educational, and philanthropic organizations **qualify** as itemized deductions. Examples of eligible groups include (1) churches, synagogues, and other religious groups; (2) United Way, Community Chest, and similar groups; (3) colleges, universities, and other educational institutions; (4) public broadcasting, environmental groups, and medical research groups. Contributions to family members, fraternal groups, professional groups, social clubs, and lobbying organizations do not qualify. If you are not sure whether a group qualifies, ask the organization whether the U.S. Treasury has approved its deductible status.

Contributions are deductible whether paid in cash or by check. Canceled checks serve as receipts and are preferred. Even if you do not have a receipt, the IRS will usually accept a reasonable claim of cash contributions.

Donations of property. Property donated to a qualifying organization can be deducted. You can deduct the property's fair market value, but there are special rules for some items. Fair market value is the amount the property would sell for in the open market. Property that has appreciated in value can be especially attractive as a donation. You avoid recognizing the gain (and paying the associated taxes), yet still claim a deduction for

the full market value. Check the rules to make sure your donation qualifies.

Donations of services. Donations of personal services *cannot* be deducted, but the expenses associated with donating your time—mileage at $0.12 per mile, postage, phone, supplies, and others—are deductible.

Medical and dental expenses

Deductible **medical expenses** include professional services (doctor, dentist, nurse, etc.), medical equipment, prescription drugs, medical treatment, hospital services, and health insurance premiums. Transportation expenses incurred for the medical treatment also qualify; you can claim $0.09 per mile for using your car. Only those expenses paid for yourself, spouse, or dependents can be included. You cannot deduct any expenses your health insurance paid.

Your deduction is limited to expenses in excess of 7.5 percent of your adjusted gross income. That restriction sharply reduces what can be deducted, as Exhibit 5.5 shows. During the past year, Helen incurred the sizable expenses shown at the top of Exhibit 5.5. With an adjusted gross income of $15,000, however, she can only deduct $975 out of the $2,100 total.

Strategy

The 7.5 percent limit, along with health insurance coverage, generally constrains your medical and dental deductions.

Casualty and theft losses

A **casualty or theft loss** to your property may be deductible. To qualify, a casualty loss must be sudden, unexpected, or unusual in nature. If Grezelda Bushbacker skips washing her car and it turns to a rusty hulk, that is a gradual loss; it fails to qualify. But if a falling tree drops the car's top 48 inches, Grezelda is out a car but has a casualty loss. Storms, earthquakes, fires, riots, vandalism, and accidents often give rise to qualifying casualty losses.

Even if you meet the "casualty" standard, two hurdles remain. The first $100 of the loss cannot be deducted; that is a nuisance more than a serious restriction. Now the biggie: only the loss exceeding 10 percent of adjusted gross income is deductible. Suppose Grezelda's $6,000 car is a

Exhibit 5.5

Computation of Medical Costs That Can Be Taken as Itemized Deductions

Medical and dental expenses	$1,150
Prescription drugs	200
Health insurance premium	750
Subtotal	$2,100
Less: 7.5% of adjusted gross income: $15,000 × 7.5%	1,125
Allowable deduction	$ 975

total loss. First, she subtracts $100 from the total. Next, she subtracts 10 percent of her $20,000 adjusted gross income. That leaves $3,900 she can deduct on her taxes *if* she has no insurance. Exhibit 5.6 summarizes the details.

Few people qualify for casualty or theft losses. The amount of the loss has to be *very* large. Second, reimbursements from your insurance lower the loss. What remains? Uninsured, catastrophic losses. And a good insurance plan—we will develop one in Chapters 10 to 13—should minimize these.

Strategy

Few taxpayers qualify for a deduction for casualty or theft loss.

Moving expenses

Part of all of the **costs of moving** to a new job or being transferred to a new location for your present job may qualify as an itemized deduction. There are two restrictions. The move must be more than 35 miles, measured as the distance from your present home to the new job minus the distance from your present home to your old job. If Jean's old job was 13 miles from her present home and her new job is 65 miles away, her "52-mile move" (65 miles from present house to new job − 13 miles from present house to old job) exceeds the minimum.

In addition, you must work for at least 39 weeks (any combination of weeks) during the year following the move. Meet both qualifications, and you can deduct moving expenses. Major qualifying expenses include the following.

Travel expenses. Costs of traveling—transportation, meals, and lodging—to the new location can be included.

Moving costs. Costs of packing, storing, and transporting your possessions can be deducted. In-transit storage up to 30 days and insurance on the items also qualify.

House-hunting trips. The cost of finding housing in the new location can be deducted, including transportation, lodging, and meals. There is no limit on the number of trips, and they do not have to be successful.

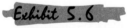

Computing the Portion of a Casualty Loss That Can Be Taken as an Itemized Deduction

Amount of casualty loss		$6,000
Less: $100 exclusion on all losses	$ 100	
10% of adjusted gross income: 10% × $20,000	$2,000	$2,100
Amount deductible as casualty loss		$3,900

Temporary living quarters. If you have to stay in temporary quarters before you can move into your permanent residence, costs for lodging and meals qualify. Deductions for temporary living quarters are limited to 30 consecutive days after you obtain employment.

Expenses of leaving present residence. Costs of selling your present home can be deducted as a moving expense. Renters can deduct the costs of settling the lease, or rental agreement.

Maximums on the amount of deductible expenses. Many of the above qualifying expenses have complex dollar limits that constrain your total deductions. Consult a reference book for specifics.

Reimbursement from employer. If an employer pays part of your moving costs, the reimbursement is counted in your gross income. You should deduct all qualifying moving expenses, so that you do not pay taxes on the reimbursement.

Miscellaneous deductions

As Exhibit 5.7 shows, the number of qualifying miscellaneous itemized deductions is considerable, but the TRA of 1986 placed a hurdle in the way: only the amount of these expenses exceeding 2 percent of adjusted gross income can be deducted. If Stanley's miscellaneous deductions total $750 and his adjusted gross income is $15,000, he can only deduct $450: $750 total miscellaneous − ($15,000 adjusted gross × 2%). That requirement sharply reduces or eliminates what can be deducted.

The list in Exhibit 5.7 includes the more common miscellaneous items. One of the tax reference books can provide a complete list. Since most items are self-explanatory, we will only discuss employee business expenses, education expenses, and job search costs.

Employee business expenses

Employees can generally deduct **business expenses** that are not reimbursed by their employer. Such expenses include auto mileage (currently $0.21 per mile), transportation costs, meals, and select entertainment expenses. Only a portion of meal and entertainment expenses is deductible. Consult a tax reference book for details.

Education expenses

Some **educational expenses** can be deducted. However:

- You must currently be employed.
- You *cannot* deduct the expenses if the program's purpose is to help you meet the minimum education level for your occupation.

Exhibit 5.7

Miscellaneous Expenses That Qualify as Itemized Deductions

Appraisal fees	Investment counseling fees
Specialized clothing	Job search expenses
Dues—union, professional societies, trade associations	Periodicals and books used in business or profession
Education expenses	Safe deposit box rental
Employee business expenses	Tax preparation fees
	Tools used in profession

- The program must (1) maintain or improve your skills for your current occupation, or (2) be required by your employer, or (3) be required by a current regulation for your occupation.

The list is restrictive, so many people do not qualify.

The education program does not have to lead to a degree. Nor is it limited to university study: vocational schools, correspondence courses, professional seminars, and other educational programs qualify. The fact that you may be promoted once you complete the program does not void the deduction.

You can deduct course fees, books, supplies, and transportation costs. The costs of living away from home to take courses also qualify.

Job search expenses

The **costs of searching for a new job** in your present occupation may qualify as a miscellaneous deduction. They include such things as transportation costs for interviews, preparing a résumé, employment agency fees, and career counseling. There are two criteria. First, you have to be currently or recently employed; those seeking first-time jobs do not qualify. Second, the new work has to be in the same field as your present occupation.

Should You Itemize Deductions?

You should calculate a rough total of your itemized deductions before starting to fill out your tax form. If the total is woefully low, stick to the standard deduction. If the total is close, make a more precise and detailed estimate. If the total of your itemized deductions exceeds the standard deduction, itemize.

Do not be surprised if the standard deduction comes out best. The TRA of 1986 has made "itemizing taxpayers" an endangered, if not vanishing, breed. That legislation boosted the standard deduction by 20 to 30 percent, making it the choice for more people. In addition, hurdles like the 7.5 percent for medical or 2 percent for miscellaneous reduce the amounts that can be deducted for some qualifying deductions—in some cases, to zero. Finally, some itemized deductions were simply phased out.

Strategy

Compute your total itemized deductions before deciding whether to take the standard deduction. If the itemized deductions are larger, then you should itemize.

EXEMPTIONS

An **exemption** allows you to deduct a fixed dollar amount from income. Since that lowers the taxes, you want to claim all the exemptions you are entitled to. For 1988, an exemption is worth $1,950. In 1989 it will be $2,000, and will continue to rise thereafter with inflation.

The first step is to determine how many exemptions you are allowed. You always have one: yourself. Couples who file a joint return (more on this later) always have two. Dependents must meet the five tests summarized in Exhibit 5.8. You must be able to give at least one yes answer from each of the five in order to claim another person as a dependent. Question 1 of Test 1 requires that the person be one of the relatives listed in Exhibit 5.9. Question 2 of Test 2 applies when several taxpayers support the same person. First, the entire group has to provide more than 50 percent of the total support. Second, only those taxpayers who pay more than 10 percent of the person's total support are eligible. Last, everyone in the "10 percent"

Exhibit 5.8

Five Tests That Must Be Met to Claim Someone as a Dependent

	Yes	No
Test 1: Relationship or Member of Household		
1. Is the person one of the relatives listed in Exhibit 5.9?	( )	( )
or		
2. Did the person reside in your home, and was the person a household member during the entire year?	( )	( )
Test 2: Support		
1. Did you pay more than half of the person's support?	( )	( )
or		
2. If the person received support from several people:		
a. Did combined support from these people exceed 50 percent of the person's total support?	( )	( )
b. Did you provide more than 10 percent of the person's total support?	( )	( )
c. Has everyone who provided more than 10 percent of the person's support agreed to your claiming the dependent?	( )	( )
Test 3: Gross Income		
1. Was the dependent's gross income less than $1,950 (1988)?	( )	( )
or		
2. Is the dependent your child and under 19 or a full-time student? (If yes, the $1,950 (1988) gross income test does not apply.)	( )	( )
Test 4: Citizenship or Resident		
1. Is the dependent a U.S. citizen or a resident of the United States, Canada, or Mexico?	( )	( )
Test 5: Joint Return		
1. If married, does the dependent file a separate, rather than a joint, return?	( )	( )

Exhibit 5.9

Relatives Who Qualify as Dependents

Child, stepchild, or adopted child
Grandchild
Parent, grandparent, or stepparent
Aunt or uncle if related by blood
Son-in-law or daughter-in-law
Father-in-law or mother-in-law
Brother or sister

Brother-in-law or sister-in-law
Stepbrother or stepsister
Niece or nephew if related by blood
Foster child who resided in taxpayer's home the entire year as a member of taxpayer's family

group has to agree on who claims the exemption. Support includes lodging, meals, medical costs, transportation, entertainment, and other costs of living. Gross income in Test 3 includes all those items we noted back in Exhibit 5.2.

You do not have to itemize in order to take exemptions.

Strategy

Claim all the exemptions you are entitled to.

FILING STATUS

Federal income tax regulations recognize four **filing statuses:** single, married—joint return, married—separate returns, and head of household.

Single

Taxpayers who are unmarried on December 31 are considered **single** for the entire year.

Married— Joint Return

Taxpayers who are married on December 31 are considered **married** for the entire year. They have the choice of filing jointly or separately. A **joint return** combines the gross income, adjustments to gross income, deductions, and exemptions of both partners on one tax return. Generally this status provides the lowest tax bill.

Married—Separate Returns

A **married** couple also has the option of filing two tax returns. In that case, each spouse's income, deductions, and exemptions are kept separate. Only in special circumstances is it advantageous for a couple to file **separate returns.**

Head of Household

Head of household is a special category for people who maintain a rented or owned residence for a parent or for one of the qualifying relatives in Exhibit 5.9. There are three qualifications. The taxpayer has to be unmarried on December 31; the taxpayer must pay more than half the cost of maintaining the home; and both the taxpayer and qualifying relative must occupy that home more than half the year. Parents are an exception. They can live in a different home as long as the taxpayer still pays more than half of the costs of maintenance. Finally, except for children, the qualifying relative must be a dependent of the taxpayer. That requires meeting the tests in Exhibit 5.8.

BASIC INCOME TAX STRUCTURE REVISITED

Let's take a moment and review the points and features of the tax system discussed thus far. Exhibit 5.10 is similar to Exhibit 5.1 but provides some added detail.

Assume that Chet Hunt has (1) $20,650 gross income, (2) $2,000 in adjustments to gross income, (3) itemized deductions of $3,500, (4) a $4,400 standard deduction, and (5) one $1,950 exemption for himself. His adjusted gross income is $18,650: $20,650 gross − $2,000 adjustment to gross. The standard deduction is larger than his itemized deductions.

Exhibit 5.10

What to Consider When Starting Your Tax Report

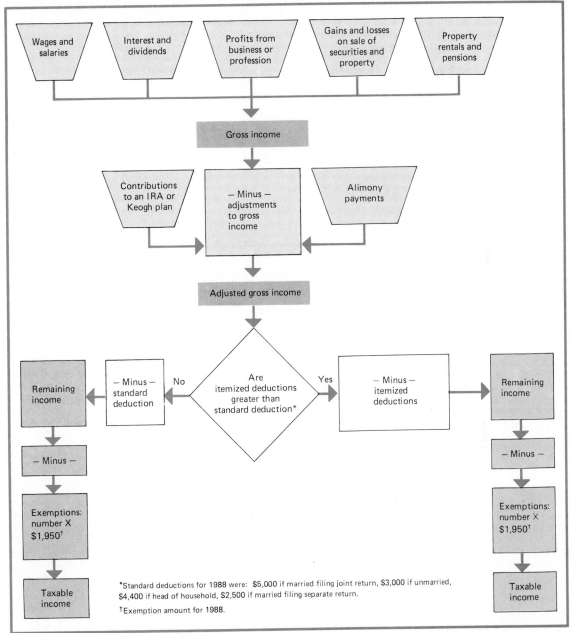

*Standard deductions for 1988 were: $5,000 if married filing joint return, $3,000 if unmarried, $4,400 if head of household, $2,500 if married filing separate return.

†Exemption amount for 1988.

Chet's taxable income is $12,300: $18,650 adjusted gross − $4,400 standard deduction − $1,950 exemption. Since he is unmarried, Chet will pay the tax rate for singles.

Or take the case of John and Ann Swift. During 1988 they had (1) combined gross income of $42,100, (2) $4,000 in adjustments to gross income, (3) itemized deductions totaling $8,500, (4) $5,000 total standard deduction, and (5) exemptions for themselves of $3,900. They file a joint return, so their adjusted gross income is $38,100: $42,100 gross income − $4,000 adjustments. They take the larger itemized deductions. Their taxable income is $25,700: $38,100 adjusted gross − $8,500 itemized deductions − $3,900 exemptions.

METHODS USED TO COMPUTE INCOME TAXES

Once you know your taxable income, you are ready to compute the amount of tax you will pay on it. There are three principal methods of computing income taxes. Those with lower incomes can use the tax table. Taxpayers with higher incomes generally use the tax rate schedule. A few high-income taxpayers will pay the alternative minimum tax.

Tax Table

Using the **tax table** requires a minimum of computation, so it is the easiest of the three methods to use. All you have to do is find your income, then go to the column that describes your filing status. Exhibit 5.11 will give you an idea how this table might look. Actual tables cover a wider income range than the one in the exhibit.

An example will illustrate use of the tax table. Suppose Carol's taxable income is $14,830 and she is single. Reading across the line "$14,800 to $14,850" to the "single" column, you see that her taxes are $2,224.

Tax Rate Schedules

Taxpayers whose income exceeds the tax table's upper limit compute their taxes using the **tax rate schedule.** Exhibit 5.12 summarizes part of the rate schedule for three filing statuses: single, married—joint, and head of

Section from the Tax Table

Range of Taxable Income		Tax Filing Status			
Over	But not over	Single	Married—joint	Married—separate	Head of household
$14,700	$14,750	$2,209	$2,209	$2,209	$2,209
14,750	14,800	2,216	2,216	2,216	2,216
14,800	14,850	2,224	2,224	2,224	2,224
14,850	14,900	2,231	2,231	2,231	2,231
14,900	14,950	2,239	2,239	2,245	2,239

Note: Amounts are based on proposed 1988 rates.

household. Since the income cutoffs differ, each has a separate rate schedule.

As with the rate table, you begin with your taxable income figure. But when you use the rate schedule, you do the computations. Suppose Chantile's taxable income is $25,900, and she qualifies as a head of household. Her total tax, $4,145, is made up of two parts: $3,585 base + [($25,900 − $23,900) × 28% tax rate]. What is the total tax on a joint return with a combined taxable income of $34,250? Total tax is $5,723.

A review of the tax rate schedule

A couple of things stand out if you examine Exhibit 5.12. First, there are only three tax rates. The lowest is 15 percent, the middle is 28 percent, and the top is 33 percent. That is far simpler than the 14 or more tax rates that existed prior to the TRA of 1986.

Second, at moderate levels of taxable income—less than $14,000—all three groups pay the same tax. But at higher income levels—above $30,000—the taxes differ significantly. Given the same income, a couple filing a joint return pays the least, a head of household pays more, and a single person pays the most.

Exhibit 5.12

Tax Rate Schedules

If Your Taxable Income Is:		You Will Pay:		
Over	*But not over*	*This base amount*	*Plus your tax rate will be:*	*On income over this amount*
Single				
$ 0	$ 17,850	$ 0	15 PERCENT	$ 0
17,850	43,150	2,678	28 PERCENT	17,850
43,150	100,480	9,762	33 PERCENT	43,150
100,480	Unlimited	28,681	28 PERCENT	100,480
Married—Joint Return				
$ 0	29,750	$ 0	15 PERCENT	$ 0
29,750	71,900	4,463	28 PERCENT	29,750
71,900	171,090*	16,265	33 PERCENT	71,900
171,090	Unlimited	48,998	28 PERCENT	171,090
Head of Household				
$ 0	$ 23,900	$ 0	15 PERCENT	$ 0
23,900	61,650	3,585	28 PERCENT	23,900
61,650	145,630*	14,155	33 PERCENT	61,650
145,630	Unlimited	41,868	28 PERCENT	145,630

* For these income brackets it is assumed that there are two exemptions. The 33 percent rate will still apply to additional income if there are more exemptions.
Note: Tax rates are based on proposed rates for 1988.

Tax table versus tax rate schedule

Will your taxes be the same whether you use the tax table or the tax rate schedule? They may differ by a small amount—$1 to $7—but that is a result of the construction of the tax tables (taxes for each income bracket are based on the midpoint of that bracket).

Tax tables are too lengthy to reproduce here. Instead we will use the rate schedules in Exhibit 5.12 for our computations. Yes, Gert, it is a bit more work, but think of it as honing your tax skills.

Alternative Minimum Tax

We are not going to review the **alternative minimum tax** computation in detail. It is quite complex and it is only relevant for a small number of taxpayers. Its purpose is to ensure that every taxpayer contributes at least a minimum amount of tax. One criticism of the tax system before the TRA of 1986 was that some taxpayers with high incomes were able to pay little or no tax; these were people who had many tax options and used them aggressively. The TRA strengthened the rules for the alternative minimum tax, enacted in 1978. It is still possible to earn a sizable income without paying taxes, but it is increasingly difficult.

TAX CREDITS

A **tax credit** reduces the taxes you owe on a dollar for dollar basis. You can use a credit regardless of whether you have adjustments to gross income, and regardless of whether you itemize or take the standard deduction. Deductions reduce the income on which you pay tax, but credits directly cut your tax bill. The only one we will examine is the child and dependent care credit. The others are more specialized, so consult a reference book.

Child and Dependent Care Credit

Taxpayers can claim a credit for part of the **costs of caring for a child or disabled dependent.** The credit ranges from 20 to 30 percent of qualifying expenses. The exact rate depends on your adjusted gross income. The 30 percent maximum applies to incomes of $10,000 or less, and the credit drops 1 percent for each added $2,000 of income until it hits 20 percent. For example, the rate is 28 percent on a $13,000 income, 24 percent on $21,000, and 20 percent for incomes above $28,000.

General requirements to qualify for the credit include:

- You must work full or part time.
- You must maintain a residence for the child or disabled dependent.
- If you are married, your spouse must work or be a full-time student.

Two-career households with children usually qualify.

Eligible expenses can be for household services or for direct care of the child or dependent. Payments for child care, whether it is provided at home or at a sitter's house, a day-care center, or a nursery school qualify. Payment for domestic help also qualifies. You may even be able to count payments to relatives.

Total care-related expenses are limited to $2,400 for one child and $4,800 for more than one. Maximum credit for a modest income and high expenses is $1,440: $4,800 maximum $\times$ 30% rate. For higher incomes, the maximum is $960: $4,800 $\times$ 20%. In effect, the tax system pays from 20 to 30 percent of child care expenses up to the maximum allowed.

Strategy

If you qualify, carefully compute your total child care expenses; each dollar you identify can reduce your tax bill by $0.20 to $0.30.

PAYMENT OF TAXES

Most people pay their taxes in one of three ways. The most widely used is payroll withholding. Making quarterly estimated tax payments is another common method. Paying when you file your tax return is less common because so many people receive refunds rather than owe taxes.

Payroll Withholding

Nearly everyone who works for an employer has income taxes **withheld from his or her salary.** The employer sends the money to the U.S. Treasury. The precise amount withheld depends on the Form W-4 you file with your employer. The form shows your filing status, number of exemptions claimed, and additional instructions for withholding. You can file a revised W-4 form at any time.

Overwithholding: a good savings plan?

Almost 75 percent of taxpayers qualify for a tax refund when they file on April 15. That suggests **overwithholding** is common. Many view this practice as a forced savings vehicle. Forced it may be, popular it may be, but it is miserably *unastute* as a financial move. You receive no interest; even a totally insensitive bank would not think of quoting *zero* interest. And you wait weeks or months to obtain the refund.

Strategy

If you need a forced savings plan, sign up for a payroll deduction plan that automatically invests your money in something that pays a return.

Estimated Tax Payments

Self-employed individuals who have no taxes withheld from their salaries have to make quarterly **estimated tax payments** in April, June, September, and January. Likewise, individuals who earn sizable incomes above their salaries may also have to make quarterly tax payments. To avoid penalties, you typically must make a quarterly tax payment that is approximately 25 percent of your estimated total tax bill for the year.

While there are guidelines on who should make quarterly tax payments, there are no specific penalties for not doing so. As we shall see though, there are specific penalties for not having paid in enough taxes during the year.

Payment with Your Tax Return

Some taxpayers find they owe additional taxes when they file their returns. There is no penalty or interest charge for owing taxes unless the amount is sizable. In fact, a small unpaid tax liability is often the mark of a well-managed tax plan. The unpaid tax shown on your return can be as much as 10 percent of your tax bill before you incur a penalty. Above that, you may be subject to an underpayment penalty.

UNDERPAYMENT OF TAXES

If you do not pay enough taxes during the year through withholding and any estimated tax payments, you may be assessed a penalty for **underpayment of taxes.** The intent is to ensure that taxpayers pay their taxes throughout the year rather than waiting until they file their returns. Even if you owe taxes, you may be able to use one of two exceptions to avoid a penalty.

Pay at Least 90 Percent of Total Taxes

As long as you pay at least 90 percent of your total taxes through a combination of withholding and estimated payments, you avoid the penalty. Sam Swift's situation (top line of Exhibit 5.13) illustrates this exception. Sam paid in 90 percent, so there is no penalty.

Strategy

If you are a bit below the 90 percent cutoff near the end of the year, consider changing your W-4 form to have an additional amount withheld in the remaining months.

Current Year's Payments Equal Last Year's Tax Bill

You can avoid the penalty if your total payments this year—withholding plus estimated payments—equal or exceed last year's tax bill. Tammy Wonder's payments (middle line of Exhibit 5.13) illustrate such an exception. Since Tammy's $2,100 payments total exceeds last year's $2,000 tax bill, she avoids any penalty. Unfortunately, the Aces, last line in Exhibit 5.13, miss both exceptions; they will pay a penalty.

FILING YOUR TAX RETURN

April 15 is the day of reckoning for most taxpayers. You're on time if your return is postmarked by that date. Some post offices even stay open late on April 15.

Always file the return on time, even if you lack the money to pay your taxes. At worst you will be assessed some interest for failing to pay on time. Failure to file a tax return on time has some nasty penalties attached; avoid these at all costs.

Strategy

Wait until the last minute to file if you owe taxes. But file as soon as possible if you expect a refund. If you will be assessed an underpayment penalty, early filing is advised to minimize the penalty.

Filing Extension

You can obtain a 60-day extension of the filing deadline by submitting a suitable form to the IRS. You still have to pay all of the taxes by April 15, but you have more time to complete the forms.

MAKING IT EASIER

In many households, the second week of April marks the running of the "tax marathon." Preparation of returns involves several miserable late-night sessions; even the dog dreads it. Tax time will never be the spring season's social blowout, but a little advance planning and preliminary work can make it easier.

Keep Records

Good, detailed records are essential. First, they provide specific dollar amounts. Second, they keep you from missing some attractive deductions. Finally, if you have to support a tax deduction for the IRS, you have the details to do it.

At the start of each year, establish a tax file where tax-related receipts, invoices, and special reminder notes can be accumulated. That file coupled with an early start can ease preparation of your return.

Exhibit 5.13

Underpayment of Income Taxes: Possible Penalty Situations

Individual	Total taxes for current year	Prior year's taxes	Taxes Paid Through:		Possible penalty
			Withholding	Estimates	
Sam Swift	$2,000	$2,000	$1,850	0	No
Tammy Wonder	$2,500	$2,000	$1,500	$ 600	No
Jan and Tom Ace	$3,200	$2,600	$1,000	$1,000	Yes

Think Taxes

Obviously taxes need not be a constant concern. But thinking of the tax consequences of some action may encourage you to collect the needed records. For example, when you make a contribution, note it in your file. The best time to summarize your expenses is when you return from that continuing education conference, not 10 months later.

Use a Tax Reference Book

A good tax reference book is essential; you need it to answer your questions and guide your tax preparation. Some are suggested at the end of the chapter. Most guide you through the complex issues and provide extensive examples to illustrate questionable points.

Prepare Your Return Early

Preparing your return before the mid-April due date gives you several advantages. It is much easier to obtain answers to your questions. If you are missing something from your file, you can request a duplicate. Besides, tax preparation, like reviewing for an exam, is more efficient and less frustrating if undertaken in several short sessions.

Seeking Professional Tax Assistance

Given the complexity of today's tax rules, many people seek help in preparing their returns. The "assistant" can range from someone who merely prepares the return to a CPA or tax attorney who offers extensive tax planning services. Which is best? It depends on what you need and the complexity of your financial situation.

IRS toll-free number

The IRS toll-free help line can be especially effective in answering a question about a specific point. Unfortunately, several studies have found the answers can be wrong more than 20 percent of the time. If you doubt the answer, ask to be connected to the IRS technical services area. For complex issues, this is the suggested strategy.

Strategy

Use the IRS toll-free number; it can often provide the help you need.

Tax preparers

As the name suggests, tax preparers merely fill out your tax return using the data you provide. They generally do not offer tax planning services. Their educational preparation ranges from nil to moderate. Nearly anyone can claim to be a tax preparer. The major advantage is low cost. A simple return will cost less than $100.

Certified Public Accounts (CPAs)

A CPA is likely to have had training in basic taxation; many have specialized in the field, so their credentials are excellent. They handle both preparation and planning. Those who specialize in taxes can handle very complex tax issues. The more specialized the person, the higher the cost: expect to pay $100 per hour and more for high-caliber talent. Even a moderately complex return can cost $500 or more.

Tax attorneys

Tax attorneys deal with the really complex tax issues. They handle both preparation and planning, with the latter as their specialty. Such talent is expensive. Hourly rates of $125 and up are common.

Which is best?   Which should you choose? It depends on your circumstance and needs. There is little point in paying $100 per hour to have a simple return prepared. But it makes little sense to use a storefront preparer for a complex return. In the long run, that may prove expensive.

MARGINAL TAX RATE   When someone mentions the words *tax rate*, they usually mean the **marginal tax rate:** the amount of tax paid on the last dollar of income. (And it's likely to be what will be paid on the next dollar, too.) We will use this concept throughout the book, so let's look at an example that will show us how the marginal tax rate is determined.

Ralph is single and was recently hired by Last Chance Investment Bankers. Exhibit 5.14 will be used to track his marginal tax rate. His taxable income is $14,500, so his marginal tax rate is 15 percent (top portion of Exhibit 5.14). Ralph paid $0.15 in taxes on his last dollar of income; he likely paid taxes on the first dollars of income also, but our concern is with the last dollars. If he receives a $100 bonus, he will pay $15 in taxes. That is the rate he uses in most of his financial planning.

Suppose Ralph is promoted to vice president and his taxable income rises to $25,500. His marginal tax rate is now 28 percent (middle section of Exhibit 5.14). Taxes will take $0.28 of Ralph's last dollar of income. He would now pay $28 on a $100 bonus. Now 28 percent is the rate he uses in financial planning.

Ralph is on a *very* fast track and moves to executive V.P. with a taxable income of $45,500. Now his marginal tax rate is 33 percent (lower part of Exhibit 5.14). He now pays $0.33 of tax on his last dollar of income. Should he receive the same $100 bonus, he would pay $33 in taxes. He will use the 33 percent figure in his financial planning.

TAX PLANNING FOR PERSONAL FINANCE DECISIONS   Income taxes affect many personal financial decisions. They can make options attractive or unattractive. Taxes deserve consideration but should rarely be the exclusive basis for a choice. Some of the bigger investment scams of the past few years have been perpetrated on taxpayers who were mesmerized by possible tax savings, while ignoring the most basic rule: an investment should and must make money at some point. Let's examine several popular tax planning strategies.

Consider Tax-Exempt Investments   **Tax-exempt investments** have been a popular tax avoidance option for many decades, especially for those with higher incomes. Interest on most municipal securities is exempt from taxes. These securities are issued by cities, states, and municipalities; we examine them further in Chapter 15. Because the interest is exempt, they offer rates only 70 to 90 percent of what fully taxable securities pay. The key is the after-tax return. On the municipal security the before- and after-tax returns are identical since there is no tax. On a taxable security the after-tax return equals the security's total return minus your taxes. The "best" choice is the security that provides the highest return after paying taxes.

Ernie has two choices: (1) a taxable security paying 8 percent interest and (2) a tax-exempt security paying 6.5 percent. Ernie's marginal tax rate is 28 percent. After-tax return on the tax-exempt security is 6.5 percent. On the taxable option his return is 5.76 percent: 8% return − (8% return × 28% tax rate). If all else is equal, Ernie's best option is the tax-exempt security.

Marginal Tax Rates: What They Are and How They Are Used

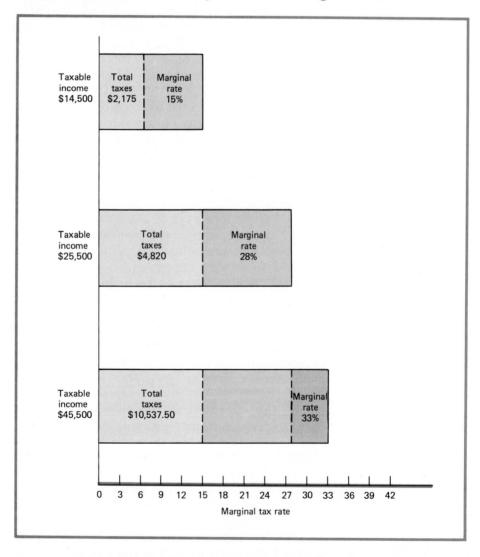

Strategy

Tax-exempt securities often provide a higher after-tax return than their taxable counterparts, especially when your marginal tax rate is high.

Deferring Income Taxes

Investments that allow you to **defer income taxes** on earnings can offer an advantage. Because you pay no tax, all of those earnings can be reinvested. Examples include Series EE Savings Bonds, the cash value of life insurance, annuities, and IRA and Keogh plans. Suppose we have a $1,000 investment that pays 10 percent interest. If we defer the income taxes, the entire $100 can be reinvested. If the $100 interest is taxed at a 30 percent marginal rate, only $70 remains to be reinvested: $100 interest − ($100 interest × 30% tax rate).

However, you must realize that you are only *deferring* taxes. At some future date you will have to pay taxes on those earnings; this is not true for the fully tax-exempt interest of the last section. Still, there are advantages. First, future earnings are based on the $100, not the tax-reduced $70. In the long run, those future earnings are going to be significantly more. Second, when the earnings are ultimately taxed, your marginal tax rate may be lower.

Shifting Income to Children

Parents can shift some income by donating money to their minor children using a Uniform Gift to Minors Act custodial account; the money remains there until the child is 18 or 21. The donation provides no tax savings, but the money can be invested in the child's name. All earnings on those investments are reported in the child's name. We will concentrate on the tax angle here; pluses and minuses of establishing the account are discussed in Chapter 17.

The first $500 of interest, dividends, and capital gains the child earns is not taxed. The next $500 is taxed at 15 percent—the lowest rate. Beyond that, if the child is 14 years or older, earnings continue to be taxed at 15 percent. If the child is under 14, added earnings are taxed at the parent's rate; this negates the advantage of shifting the income to a young child.

Strategy

Shifting income to a child can help reduce your tax bill. You can pursue a much more aggressive shifting strategy once the child is 14. But, as Chapter 17 points out, there are disadvantages.

Take Your Investment Losses

If all investments turned out to be sterling choices that yielded staggering returns, this section would be unnecessary. The real world of investments is not quite so delightful. Investments can and do drop in value. If the drop is significant and prospects for recovery are questionable, taking the loss may be a good tax strategy. Assume John's 100 shares of Unlimited Horizons have plunged from the $2,000 he paid to $1,000 in less than 6 months. Prospects for recovery appear limited. His marginal tax rate is 28 percent. Selling for the $1,000 loss would reduce his taxable income by $1,000 and lower his tax bill by $280. The net effect is to reduce his loss to only $720: $1000 capital loss − ($1,000 loss × 28% tax rate). Certainly that does not match a gain. But it may be better than holding until those shares become candidates for framing.

Strategy

Review any investments that have generated a loss. You may want to use the loss to take advantage of tax savings.

Tax Savings Can Drop the Cost of a Deductible Outlay

Earlier in the chapter we discussed how deductible expenses can reduce your tax bill. You can think of those tax savings as lowering the net cost of the deductible item. Suppose Sue is considering donating $100 to her favorite charity. Her marginal tax rate is 28 percent, and she expects to itemize her deductions. Sue's income drops $100 if she makes the donation. At 28 percent, her tax bill drops by $28. Granted, she writes a $100 check to the charity; but her check to the IRS is $28 less. Net cost of the donation is only $72: $100 donation − ($100 donation × 28% tax rate). What is the net cost of a $500 donation if the marginal tax rate is 15 percent? It is $425.

You can only realize this lowering of net cost if you itemize. The higher your marginal tax rate, the greater the reduction from tax savings, but it only applies to those expenditures that qualify as itemized deductions.

Concentrate Your Deductions in One Year

The higher standard deductions provided by the TRA of 1986 reduced the ranks of those who itemize. If your total itemized deductions are far short of the standard deductions, there is little you can do. If the total is close, **concentrating your deductions** in one year may help. Try to shift some deductions from next year into the current year. Make charitable contributions several months early. Pay as many miscellaneous items as possible this year, especially given the 2 percent hurdle. Or pay two years' property taxes in one year. You can use the allowed installments on one set of taxes while you pay the other one in a lump sum near year-end. We are not suggesting adding new deductible expenditures, just paying some of next year's a bit early.

What is gained? You may be able to itemize those deductions this year. And the tax savings can lower the net cost of the deductions. But won't that "destroy" next year's deductions? Yes. Next year you must settle for the standard deduction. The year after that it's back to concentrating.

An example will show the possible benefit. Exhibit 5.15 outlines the details for Sue and Max. Because their itemized deductions total only $4,800, just short of their $5,000 standard deduction, they decide to concentrate. Rather than pay their $2,000 property tax in four installments next year, they pay all of it now. Likewise, they make $500 of their charitable donations in advance. Now their total itemized deductions are $7,300. With an adjusted gross income of $36,000, total taxes are $3,720 (top line of Exhibit 5.15). Next year's itemized deductions fall by the same $2,500, but then Sue and Max shift to the standard deduction. Taxes for next year are the $4,050 on line 2 of Exhibit 5.15. Total tax for both years is $7,770, considerably less than the $8,115 they would pay without concentrating. The lower section of Exhibit 5.15 summarizes the details. A $345 tax saving makes it worthwhile to pay these expenses a few months early.

Concentrating can also yield tax savings if your total itemized deductions are slightly more than the standard amount. Again the key is to shift some future expenses to the current year. If you concentrate, your tax return will swing from itemizing to standard to itemizing, and so forth.

Strategy

Concentrating itemized deductions can provide tax savings when total itemized deductions are near the standard deduction.

AN AUDIT BY THE IRS

The prospect of an **IRS audit** can trigger sweaty palms in many otherwise calm folks; even a visit for extensive dental work is more desirable. Some people go so far as to ignore legitimate deductions just to ensure they will not be audited. But that should not be necessary. Let's talk about tax audits.

Specific Item

Most IRS audits are directed at one or two specific items that triggered the audit. Often a computer singles out a return for a review. For example, Guendalyn Goodtime's itemized deductions for mortgage interest and prop-

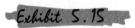

Exhibit 5.15

Potential Income Tax Savings from Concentrating Deductions

Year	Adjusted gross income	Exemption	Total itemized deduction	Standard deduction	Taxable income	Taxes owed (exh. 5.12)
		Total Taxes with Concentrating				
1988	$36,000	$3,900	$7,300	$5,000	$24,800	$3,720
1989	36,000	4,000	2,300	5,000	27,000	4,050
						$7,770
		Total Taxes without Concentrating				
1988	$36,000	$3,900	$4,800	$5,000	$27,100	$4,065
1989	36,000	4,000	4,800	5,000	27,000	4,050
						$8,115

erty taxes totaled $13,000, which didn't match the typical deduction for a single earning $22,000. Or there may be some item on the return that the IRS has classed as a "flag" for a review. Unfortunately, the IRS zealously guards the criteria its computer programs use to select returns.

The IRS is more likely to audit returns that show a high income, but even then only a small percentage is selected. Chances of an audit rise with the complexity of a return. A return that shows large adjustments to gross income or extensive itemized deductions or business ventures that lost money can trigger a review.

How to Survive an Audit

Accepting a low-paid job, avoiding all itemized deductions, and keeping it simple hardly seems the answer. If you're entitled to a deduction, take it— but make sure you can support it. In fact, on unusual items including a supporting explanation can head off an audit.

If you are selected, review your return to see if you made a simple math error. Correcting it may end the audit. If that is not the case, look over your tax file to confirm you have the receipts, canceled checks, and other materials you need to construct solid support for your position. If evidence is missing, get it.

You may not even have to visit the IRS for a chat. They may simply ask that you send copies of supporting materials to back up the questioned item. But suppose you are invited in for that chat. Remember, the auditor is not questioning your integrity and intelligence, or conducting an inquisition. He or she merely wants to establish if added tax is due. Rule number one is to stick to the item being questioned. Do not volunteer information about the rest of your return. A solid foundation for your position coupled with supporting data should carry the day.

Strategy

A tax audit should not present a major crisis if you appear with a well-documented tax return in hand. Think of it as a way to spice up an otherwise dull Thursday afternoon.

Taypayer compliance measurement program audit

Taxpayer compliance measurement program audit is a long title for a grueling review of your entire tax return. Yes, Johnny, they start at line 1 of the first form and do not finish until the final line on the last form. Some wags have suggested that a "lucky" taxpayer dies just before the process starts. This is the time for those palms to start gushing. Only about 50,000 people are selected for this audit in a given year, and they are, indeed, in for a lengthy process of documenting *everything* in the return. That can and does take months. Some have suggested the strain of working a second full-time job would pale compared with the effort demanded here.

Can this audit be avoided? Unfortunately, the lucky devils that receive this draft are chosen at random. Can it be survived? Yes, but it takes well-documented tax records. If your records are well-organized, and they should be, this audit too will pass.

Summary

1　Good tax management involves using all means available in income tax regulations to reduce your taxes.

2　In the basic federal income tax structure:

You start with:	Gross income
You can deduct:	Adjustments to gross income
That gives:	Adjusted gross income
You can then deduct:	Standard deduction *or* itemized deductions
You can also deduct:	Exemptions
That gives:	Taxable income

This last amount is the income on which you will pay taxes.

3　Long-term and short-term capital gains are treated the same: both are fully taxable. The TRA of 1986 eliminated the earlier, highly favorable, treatment of long-term gains.

4　Contributions to an IRA (for those who qualify) or to a Keogh (for the self-employed) allow you to invest "before-tax" income.

5　All taxpayers can reduce their income by the amount of the standard deduction. The size of the standard deduction depends on your filing status. Taxpayers who are 65 or over or blind can claim an additional amount.

6　If the total of your itemized deductions is larger, you can substitute it for the standard deduction.

7　Common itemized deductions include
■ Interest on mortgages
■ Property and income taxes
■ Donations to eligible groups
■ Medical expenses (if large enough)
■ Casualty losses (if major)
■ Moving expenses
■ Miscellaneous deductions (if large enough)

8　You may claim an exemption for someone who qualifies as your dependent. That requires they meet five tests: relationship, support, gross income, citizenship or residency, and the dependent cannot file a joint return.

9　The four filing statuses for income taxes are:
single, married—joint return, married—separate returns, and head of household.

10　Taxes are most frequently computed using the tax tables or tax rate schedules. You merely "look up" your tax payment in the first. Those with larger incomes have to use the second one and make several computations.

11　The alternative minimum tax attempts to ensure that taxpayers pay at least some tax; but few taxpayers have to use this method.

12　Tax credits can be deducted directly from the taxes you owe; when you are able to take one, you get a dollar for dollar reduction in taxes. Qualifying child care expenses are a common credit.

13　The three usual ways of paying taxes include payroll withholding, estimated quarterly payments, and payment with your tax return.

14　To avoid a penalty for underpayment of income taxes you must either:
■ Pay 90 percent of your current year's tax bill through withholding and estimated payments
■ Pay an amount through withholding and estimated taxes equal to last year's tax bill

15　Overwithholding is a poor financial strategy since you receive no interest and the refund is returned months after you pay your taxes.

16　Advanced planning, complete and well-organized tax records, an early start, and a good tax reference book can reduce the burden of tax preparation.

17　You can obtain assistance in preparing your taxes from the IRS toll-free number, a tax preparer, a CPA, or a tax attorney. As the level of expertise rises, so does the price.

18　Your marginal tax rate is the amount you pay on your final dollar of income.

19　When your total itemized deductions about equal your standard deduction, it may be worthwhile to concentrate the itemized deductions in one year, followed by a year when you take the standard deduction.

20　When the IRS audits a tax return, it usually concentrates on one or two items; good records will ensure your survival.

Review your understanding of

Avoiding taxes	Adjustments to gross income
Evading taxes	Adjusted gross income
Gross income	Itemized deductions

Standard deduction
Exemptions
Taxable income
Net purchase price
Net sale price
Capital gain
    Short-term
    Long-term
Capital loss
    Short-term
    Long-term
Before-tax dollars
Keogh plan
Individual Retirement Account
Standard deduction
Itemized deductions
    Interest charges
    Taxes
    Contributions
    Medical expenses
    Casualty losses
    Moving expenses
    Employee business expenses

Education expenses
Job-search expenses
Exemption
Filing status
    Single
    Married—joint return
    Married—separate returns
    Head of household
Tax tables
Tax rate schedules
Alternative minimum tax
Tax credit
Child and dependent care
Payroll withholding
Estimated tax payments
Overwithholding
Underpayment of taxes
Marginal tax rate
Tax-exempt investment
Deferring income taxes
Concentrating deductions
IRS audit
Taxpayer compliance audit

Discussion questions

1   Which of the following items would be included in gross income?
    a Winnings from state lottery
    b Salary
    c Gift from Aunt Maude
    d Interest on municipal bond
    e Payment from life insurance policy
    f Interest on Treasury notes
    g Short-term capital gain
    h Bonus from employer

2   Jean Whitecloud is self-employed and qualifies for a Keogh but is unclear about what its advantages are. Does it offer anything over a straight investment program? Would you recommend she open a Keogh? Why?

3   Can most people establish an IRA? Will most be able to deduct the contribution to that account? If the contribution cannot be deducted, are there any benefits to opening an IRA?

4   What features distinguish an adjustment to gross income from an itemized deduction? Why would someone who takes the standard deduction want an item classified as an adjustment?

5   Why do most taxpayers take the standard deduction rather than itemize deductions? List several events that might boost a taxpayer's itemized total above the standard amount.

6   What tests must be met to qualify moving expenses as an itemized deduction? List some of the major expenditures that can be included. Would most recent college graduates qualify?

7   What tests must an education expense meet to make it an itemized deduction?

8   Which of the following individuals qualifies as a dependent?
    a The person is the taxpayer's uncle; his gross income is $1,500; he is a U.S. citizen; the taxpayer paid $4,000 toward his $7,000 total support; the uncle is single.
    b The person is the taxpayer's aunt; her gross income is $600; she lives in Canada; taxpayer paid $3,000 toward her $5,700 total support; she is single.
    c The person is a brother; his gross income is $700; he is single; he is a U.S. citizen; taxpayer paid $600 in support; taxpayer and four other brothers and sisters paid $6,000 of brother's $8,000 total support; the other brothers and sisters agree taxpayer should claim the exemption.

9   Are there any advantages to filing as a head of household? What does it take to qualify? Give several examples of people who might use this filing status.

10 Which taxpayers would likely use the tax table? What forces someone to switch to the tax rate schedules? For an income that is covered by both, would the taxes from the tax table and the tax rate schedules be similar?

11 Are you allowed to revise your Form W-4 during the year? What would you change on the form if you wanted more taxes withheld? Less?

12 In addition to her regular salary, Pamela expects

to earn some added income teaching piano. How can she pay income taxes on that income? Is there a specific penalty for not filing quarterly estimated tax payments? How does the IRS "encourage" timely tax payments?

13   Will any of the taxpayers listed below be subject to a penalty for underpayment of taxes?

14   How would you react to the statement: "I do not want to earn that last $500 of income because it would boost me into the next tax bracket; my taxes would soar!"?

Tax-payer	Taxes for current year	Amount of Taxes Paid by:		Taxes for previous year	Penalty for underpayment?
		Withholding	Estimates		
A	$1,800	$1,650	—	$1,850	_____
B	2,650	1,700	$400	1,975	_____
C	1,650	700	600	1,400	_____

Problems

5.1   Becky and Fred Bear sold the following common stocks during the year:

Corporation	QT, Inc.	Pigeon, Inc.	Imports Ltd.	Zug Co.
Net purchase price	$1,200	$1,300	$1,900	$1,500
Net sale price	$1,500	$ 700	$1,100	$2,000
Holding period	13 months	5 months	3 years	11 months

a   What is their net gain or loss on each?
b   What is the impact on their gross income (ignore any implication from having gains and losses within the same year) of each of the following sales: QT, Inc.; Imports Ltd.; Pigeon, Inc.; Zug Co.?

5.2   Sharon Jones had the following medical expenses during the year: health insurance premiums of $550, unreimbursed doctors' and dentists' bills of $700, and prescription drug charges of $125. Her adjusted gross income was $16,000, and she plans to itemize. What is her medical expense deduction?

5.3   Jan Swartz's tax details are summarized for 1988 as follows:
   ■ Her total itemized deductions are $4,000.
   ■ Her adjusted gross income is $19,400.
   ■ She is single.
   a   What is her taxable income?
   b   When computing the tax, does she take an exemption allowance?
   c   Should she use her itemized deductions or the standard deduction?

5.4   Listed below is the tax information for three taxpayers for 1988:

Taxpayer— Filing status	Gross income	Adjustments to gross income	Itemized deductions	Number of exemptions	Taxable income	Amount of taxes
A—Single	$16,600	$ 500	$3,400	1	?	?
B—Married	38,500	2,600	3,000	2	?	?
C—Head of household	18,500	—	2,000	2	?	?

a   What is the taxable income for each taxpayer?
b   How much tax does each taxpayer owe? (Hint: Exhibit 5.12 can help.)

5.5   Al and Susan Bach are reviewing their child care expenses:
   ■ They paid a baby-sitter $2,800 to care for Al, Jr., in their home.
   ■ Al, who works full-time, had an adjusted gross income of $18,000.

■ Susan, who works full-time, had an adjusted gross income of $13,000.

■ Their itemized deductions total $3,000.

a Do they qualify for a child care credit?

b If so, what is the dollar amount of their credit?

c How should they handle the credit on their tax return?

5.6 Ralph Zuggo expects that his taxable income will be $19,000 this year. He is a single person. What are his taxes? What is his marginal tax rate? Due to a great year-end push, he qualifies for a $2,000 bonus. Should he accept it or tell the firm he cannot "afford" it?

5.7 Wilma Smith's taxable income was $16,000. She is single and her itemized deductions were substantially larger than the standard deduction. What is the net cost of the $2,000 in property taxes she paid during the year? What would be the effective cost of her donating $100 to her favorite charity?

5.8 Sang Fu estimates that his taxes for the current year will be $5,000. That is substantially more than the $3,000 withheld from his salary. The shortfall arose because no taxes were withheld from the earnings of his part-time business. Last year, when he did not have the business, his taxes totaled only $2,900; $2,800 of that was withheld during the year.

a Should Sang have filed an estimated tax form? Why?

b Will be pay a penalty for underpayment of taxes?

c Can Sang avoid the penalty? How?

5.9 Mike Stuart is considering three possible $1,000 investments. Option 1 pays 10 percent interest and is fully taxable at Mike's 28 percent marginal rate. Option 2 pays 8.5 percent interest, but is fully tax-exempt. Option 3 pays 10 percent interest that is tax-deferred until retirement. Which option will provide the best return? Discuss the principal tax considerations for each investment option.

5.10 Ned and Noreen Notcertain's total itemized deductions for 1988 are $5,500; they expect them to be about the same next year. While that will allow them to itemize each year, they wonder if they might save on taxes by concentrating deductions. By paying property taxes now and prepaying some of next year's contributions, they could shift another $3,000 of their deductions to this year. Their combined adjusted gross income for 1988 is $40,000 and they expect next year's will be similar. They plan to file a joint return and will claim themselves as exemptions ($1,950 for each exemption in 1988, and $2,000 in 1989). Assume the standard deduction will be the same in 1988 and 1989.

a What will their tax bill be for each of the next 2 years if they do *not* concentrate deductions?

b If they concentrate deductions as outlined, what is their tax bill for each of the next 2 years? (*Hint:* Compare the amount of the itemized deductions that remain for 1989 to their standard deduction.)

c What potential savings does concentrating offer? Are there disadvantages to paying those deductible expenses "early"?

Case problem

Herb and Grazelda Procrastinator are beginning their April 13 income tax marathon; it usually lasts well into April 14, if not April 15. Both work full-time, and they have a young daughter. A glance through their checkbook and scant records reveals the following for 1988.

Outflows

Purchase of new car	$11,000	Health insurance premium	$ 250
Medical expenses (unreimbursed)	100	Contributions	500
Gasoline taxes	75	Property taxes	2,650
Dental expenses	100	Automobile insurance premium	250
Professional teaching dues for Grazelda	550	Life insurance premium	450
State income taxes	1,520	Interest on home mortgage	5,400
Utility bills for the house	1,250	Veterinary expenses for McKenzie, their dog	100
Daughter's nursery school fee	200	Gifts for their parents	300
(monthly)	400	Safe-deposit box rental	30
Finance charges on their home equity		Prescription drugs	50
loan		Tax reference book	15
		Grocery bills	3,800
		Education expenses	380

In past years, the Procrastinators have taken the standard deduction on their joint return. Their combined adjusted gross income for 1988 is $38,000.

1   Based on what you know, should they itemize their deductions this year? Why or why not?
2   What are their total itemized deductions? Will they use the standard deduction or itemize their deductions?
3   What is their taxable income? Based on this figure, what are their taxes?
4   Do they qualify for any tax credits? Based on your answer for their total tax in part (3), how much tax will they actually pay?
5   What recommendations do you have for Herb and Grazelda for next year's tax return? What advantages can they expect if they follow your suggestions?

INCOME TAX REFERENCE BOOKS

With the exception of Publication 17, most bookstores carry the tax reference books listed below. All are updated annually, so they should contain current information. The front cover of each prominently displays the year covered.

Your Federal Income Tax, Publication 17, Department of the Treasury, Internal Revenue Service, Washington D.C., published annually. Very thorough coverage of most tax topics. Has a reasonable number of examples to illustrate major points, but it could use more. It assumes you already have some background in taxes and therefore know what questions you want answered. As might be expected, it contains *no* tax-saving hints and tips. One major redeeming feature: it's free from the IRS.

The Arthur Young Tax Guide, Ballantine Books, New York, published annually. The guide reproduces the official IRS guide, *Your Federal Income Tax*, but then adds its own comments, examples, explanations, and tax-saving tips. To distinguish the two, the latter points are displayed in colored boxes. The final product is a complete, technically accurate manual with numerous examples, explanations, and money-saving tips. As might be expected, it is very long; but then you will not be using all the sections. The prose in the IRS manual is a bit dry, but the volume is well indexed, so it is easy to use.

J.K. Lasser's Your Income Tax, Simon & Schuster, New York, published annually. Provides very thorough coverage of income tax regulations, IRS rulings, and court decisions. Excellent index that is very detailed. Contains numerous examples and exhaustive checklists on various tax points. Has a complete section outlining strategies you can use to save taxes next year. The print may be a bit small, but this book delivers good, solid tax preparation advice.

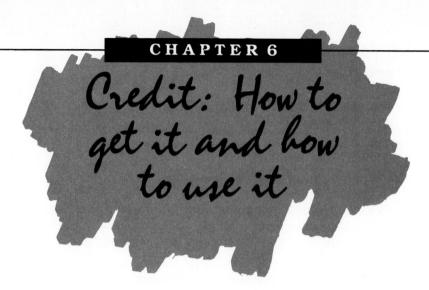

CHAPTER 6

Credit: How to get it and how to use it

AFTER COMPLETING THIS CHAPTER YOU WILL HAVE LEARNED

- Why varying the finance charge or the maturity alters a loan's total finance charge
- How to decide whether you should use credit
- How to use your budget to establish your upper debt limit
- What a loan's annual percentage rate (APR) is and how to use it
- How finance charges are rebated under the "rule of 78"
- How to analyze the cost of using credit against the cost of saving
- How the billing cycle for a credit card operates
- How to use the grace period on a credit card effectively
- How the finance charge on a credit card account is computed
- What disclosures lenders must make under the Truth in Lending Act
- How credit scoring systems operate and why they are used
- What provisions have been enacted to ensure women equal access to credit
- Your rights regarding your record at a credit bureau
- What steps you should take to correct an overuse of credit

*C*onsumer credit is certainly widely available. If you have a reasonable credit record, finding a willing lender is easy. In fact, credit can be too easy to obtain. Lenders may search you out. Once, seeking credit suggested you were a poor manager of your finances. Now it is considered part of many personal financial plans.

Nearly everyone uses credit to purchase a house. The sale price of many homes exceeds $100,000, so most of us find it necessary to borrow in order to buy. We don't want to wait years to save the money.

Individual opinions differ on what is an "appropriate" use of credit. Other than housing, some restrict its use to emergencies. They say: If you cannot afford to pay cash, do without. Others use credit for purchasing costly durable goods: autos, furniture, and appliances. Some suggest credit can be used to purchase almost any product or service. Regardless of which group you belong to, credit can be helpful in implementing some parts of your financial plan.

Before you can decide credit's role in your financial plan, you must know what credit is and how it operates. Unless you understand the advantages and disadvantages of credit, you cannot decide whether to use it in a particular situation. Credit has its own language. *Annual percentage rate (APR), balloon payment, collateral,* and *grace period* are not household words.

But you must understand such terms if you are to use credit wisely. Even if using credit seems reasonable, your finances may not permit it. Finally, you need standards for comparing competing credit offers.

This chapter concentrates on the general features and operations of three types of consumer credit:

- *Consumer cash loan.* The lender gives you a check for the amount of the loan. Usually you make equal monthly payments over the life of the loan.
- *Consumer sales loan.* You borrow money to purchase a big-ticket product: an auto, an appliance, or furniture. You make equal monthly payments over the life of the loan.
- *Open-end consumer credit.* Credit cards and charge accounts are examples of this type. They are open-ended because you decide how much credit to use and how frequently. The lender specifies the maximum you can borrow. Repayment options are quite flexible: you can pay the entire amount, you can pay some minimum and stretch payments over 2 to 3 years, or you can pay something in between.

A fourth type of consumer credit, the mortgage loan, is discussed in the housing chapter. Since a mortgage is a basic part of buying a house, this subject is better covered there.

HOW CREDIT OPERATES

Your immediate purchasing power rises when you use credit. The increase is a temporary one, however, because lenders expect to be repaid. You will have to use future income to make those payments, so you lose future purchasing power. The lender wants you to repay the amount you borrowed, but in addition levies a rental fee, the **finance charge.** It compensates the lender for giving you use of the money.

When you repay the loan and the finance charge, you pay more than you originally borrowed. What does that do to your overall purchasing power? It falls while you are repaying the loan and finance charge. Therefore, using credit causes your total purchasing power to drop.

An example will clarify. Stan expects to earn $21,000 during the next year. We ignore taxes, so $21,000 is his total purchasing power for the next year. This is shown in the top half of Exhibit 6.1. Assume Stan borrows $19,500. His purchasing power immediately rises by that $19,500. But he must agree to repay that $19,500 plus $1,500 in finance charges over the next 12 months; this will take his entire salary. The lower half of Exhibit 6.1 illustrates.

Stan's purchasing power over the next 12 months is $21,000 with the first option. The second boosts Stan's immediate purchasing power $19,500. But he must commit his entire $21,000 salary for the next year to gain this advantage, and he sacrifices $1,500 to obtain immediate use of the money.

Exhibit 6.1

Reduction in Purchasing Power Caused by Finance Charges on a Loan

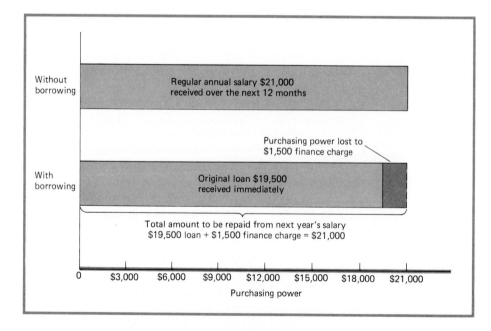

Finance Charge

The mention of *finance charges* may lead you to ask what ever happened to interest charges. They are still around, but they, plus all other costs of credit, fall under the broad heading of *finance charges.* These include such charges as a loan application fee, processing fee, credit check fee, interest, and insurance premiums. Finance charges can be stated in dollars or as an annual percentage rate.

Repayment Terms

Two things define a credit offer's **repayment terms:** the number of months until the loan is paid and the payments required during that time. The time between when a loan is made and when it is repaid is called **maturity.** Consumer credit maturities range from days to many years.

Required payments on a credit offer can be equal monthly amounts, uneven amounts, or a lump sum. Equal monthly payments are typical, but a few loans have pleasantly small monthly payments up to the final one: a whopping "balloon" payment equaling the remaining unpaid loan balance.

You usually have much latitude on payment size and timing with open-end consumer credit. You may choose to pay the entire amount or to make several monthly payments on the balance. Nearly all lenders require that you pay some "minimum."

Varying the Finance Charge Alters the Payment

The finance charge affects what you pay for a particular loan. Let's vary the annual finance rate from 9 to 30 percent to show what happens to your payments on a $1,000, 24-month loan. At the same time we will look at the total finance charge. The left-hand portion of Exhibit 6.2 shows the required monthly payment at different rates, and the right summarizes the loan's total finance charge. For example, an 18 percent loan has monthly payments of $49.92 and total finance charges of $198.18.

Raising the finance charge boosts your monthly payment by a deceptively small amount. Only $2.85 ($49.92 − $47.07) per month separates the payments on a 12 percent and an 18 percent loan. But you pay that $2.85 24 times. All of it goes for the added finance charge. Total finance charges for the 18 percent loan are 52.7 percent higher than for the 12 percent loan.

Remember, our sample loan was only $1,000. The monthly difference on a more typical $9,000 to $12,000 loan is 9 to 12 times that $2.85—it would range from $25.65 to $34.20. Over 24 months, the total is significant.

This section's message: even a moderate change in the annual finance rate affects your finance charge considerably. You must compare the rate on competing credit options.

Strategy

You can save money by selecting the credit option with the lowest finance rate.

Impact of Maturity on a Loan's Payment

Altering a loan's maturity also affects your monthly payment. The total finance charge also changes. To illustrate, let's use a $1,000 loan with an 18 percent finance charge and maturities of 12 to 60 months. The left side of Exhibit 6.3 shows the monthly payment for each maturity (middle of the exhibit). The total finance charge appears on the right side.

You can see that lengthening a loan's maturity reduces the monthly payment. But the percentage reduction is not uniform throughout the maturity range. Stretching an 18-month loan to 24 months reduces the payment nearly 22 percent. The same 6-month extension on a 54-month loan drops the payment only about 6.5 percent. The longer the initial maturity, the smaller the reduction for a given increase in maturity. If you seek to reduce payments by lengthening the maturity, you reach a point of diminishing returns.

What happens to the total finance charge with the longer maturity? Hertz will not let you keep their car for extra months without charging more, nor will a lender let you keep their money without paying for it. Look at the right side of Exhibit 6.3. You pay for the privilege of taking longer to

Exhibit 6.2

Monthly Payments and Total Finance Charges on a 24-Month, $1,000 Loan with 9 to 30 Percent Finance Charge

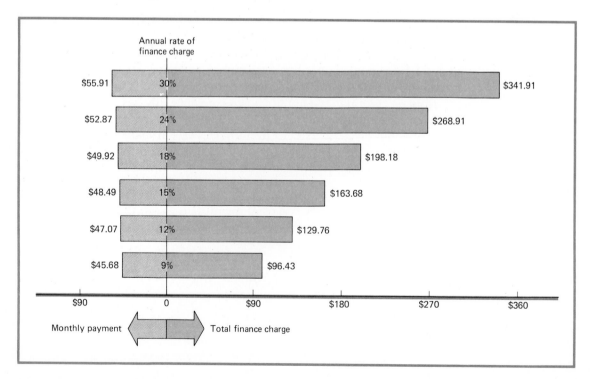

repay a loan. The monthly payment drops, but the total you must repay rises.

Strategy

Before seeking a long repayment period, consider the added finance charge. Is the lower payment worth sacrificing future income for?

USING CREDIT   The difference in credit use among individuals suggests what may be "appropriate" for some is not right for others. No single rule or magic equation will tell you what is an "appropriate" use of credit. But there are some

 **Exhibit 6.3**

Monthly Payments and Total Finance Charges for $1,000 Loan with 18 Percent Finance Charge and 12- to 60-Month Maturity

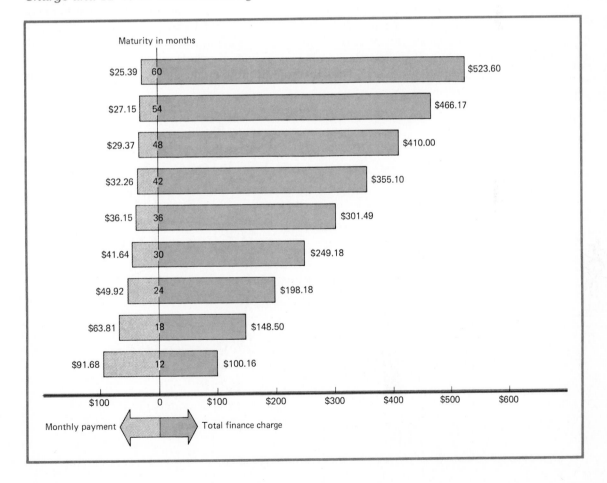

guidelines to help you decide if credit is justified in *your* particular circumstance.

Cost-Benefit Trade-Off

The primary cost of using credit is the lender's finance charge. As Exhibit 6.1 showed, today's credit use means sacrificing future income.

But there is a secondary cost: reduced flexibility and increased risk. You lose flexibility because you are committed to make a series of payments. This reduces your discretionary income. Risk is increased because most credit options require fixed payments. That sweet pitch, "Dudley, our loan can help you enjoy life's 'good' things," can become the gruff, relentless demand: "Pay the damn bill now, Dudley, or *else*." Late payments will almost certainly stain your credit record and destroy your peace of mind; they may affect your health and even your employment.

Credit also offers some benefits. First, using credit to buy an auto, appliance, or recreational vehicle means you receive the service it provides immediately. Second, credit often permits you to purchase a product or service at a favorable price: waiting until you have the money could mean missing a bargain. Third, buying now may let you avoid inflationary price increases. But be careful: moderate inflation rates make this benefit small and elusive. Fourth, credit can provide a bridge when your expenditures temporarily exceed your income. Finally, credit may provide convenience:

It's just amazing what you can charge on these plastic cards...

it substitutes for cash or your checking account, while giving you a detailed record of purchases.

To decide whether you should use credit, examine the **cost-benefit trade-off** for each credit situation. If costs appear to exceed benefits, avoid credit.

Is Credit Justified in This Situation?

The questions in Exhibit 6.4 should help you decide whether to use credit for a particular product or service. If most of your answers are yes, then using credit is probably justified. It is surprising how many people never stop and ask these basic questions before proceeding. Too often, they are lured by a claimed bargain—price reduced 30 percent, just say "charge it"—or the "easy" credit terms—only $49 per month and this antenna dish is yours. First ask: Do I really need it? Then consider the option: defer the purchase until you save (yes, save) the necessary money.

I am not suggesting long-lived, big-ticket items such as autos, appliances, and furniture are the only "appropriate" use of credit. But as you consider short-lived goods and services, make certain credit is warranted. The most memorable restaurant, that breathtaking vacation, those designer clothes, may be forgotten long before your payments stop. When you use credit for its convenience, repay it quickly, when billed if possible. Extended repayment periods for short-lived goods and services sometimes mean you never repay one set of bills before running up new ones.

Strategy

Credit is probably justified if you answered yes to most questions in Exhibit 6.4. Several no answers, especially to Questions 2 and 3, suggest you should consider alternatives other than credit.

Exhibit 6.4

Is Credit Justified? A Decision-Making Guide

	(Yes)	(No)
1. Do you really need the item?	( )	( )
2. Is it impossible to postpone the purchase?	( )	( )
3. Is purchasing on credit your only alternative?	( )	( )
a. Is it impossible to draw from savings instead of using credit?	( )	( )
b. Is it impossible to defer the purchase and to save the money to buy later?	( )	( )
4. When the credit has extended payment terms:		
a. Is the item's useful life 3 to 5 years?	( )	( )
b. Does its life equal or exceed the loan's maturity?	( )	( )
c. Is it impossible to fit the purchase price into your monthly budget?	( )	( )
5. When the credit has flexible repayment terms:		
a. Credit for short-lived items such as food, travel, clothing—can you repay the entire amount when billed?	( )	( )
b. Credit for a temporary cash shortage—can you repay the borrowed amount when billed?	( )	( )

SETTING YOUR DEBT LIMITS

You are best qualified to decide your **upper debt limit**—the amount of credit on which you could comfortably make the required payments from current income. Some people expect the lender to set their debt limit: as long as a lender will lend them money, they think they are below their limit. Lenders can be excellent judges of how much credit you can handle, but they face hurdles. Credit is so readily available, lenders may not know how much you already owe. If one lender says no, some people search for another. By the time the most lax lender refuses, the borrower can be grossly overextended with credit.

Rather than rely on a lender's standard, ask the person who knows your finances best: you.

Estimating Your Limits

The questions in Exhibit 6.5 can help you decide whether you are nearing your upper debt limit. If you answer yes to many questions, you are close. Question 1 deserves special attention: few purchases justify continual worry and sleepless nights. Credit should help you manage your finances, not create an unending dilemma.

Generally, if you can readily figure out where the money for the new payment is to come from, you are probably within your limit. Debts that require a major revision of your present expenditure and savings plans signal you are at or beyond your limit.

Your Budget Can Best Set Your Debt Limit

A personal budget is the ideal tool to use for deciding whether you can handle a credit opportunity. First, it summarizes your various resources for the period. Next, its information on your expenses, existing payments, and required savings for future financial goals tells you your planned spending for the same period. Comparing available income with planned spending shows what income you have for credit payments.

Those whose planned spending is already near their projected income have little income for credit payments. If projected income considerably exceeds planned spending, there is discretionary income to allow additional debt.

Exhibit 6.5

Checklist for Upper Debt Limit

	(Yes)	(No)
1. Will you feel uncomfortable with more debt?	( )	( )
2. Will fitting the new payment into your budget be difficult?	( )	( )
3. Will the new payment:		
a Take money from essentials (food, clothing, housing, savings)?	( )	( )
b Make it difficult to meet current debt payments?	( )	( )
c Require major changes in the planned spending in your budget?	( )	( )
d Reduce or eliminate your budgeted savings?	( )	( )
4. Will the added debt reduce your net worth on your balance sheet?	( )	( )

Let us take the example of Gus and Dimitra Alevaro to illustrate the decision process. The Alevaros want to decide whether an $8,100 loan for a boat is within their debt limit. That loan requires $220 payments for the next 48 months. Their budget shows projected income of $2,700 and planned spending of $2,475 per month. They have $225 ($2700 − $2475) of discretionary income; enough for the $220 payment. They are within their debt limit.

Strategy

Before accepting a new credit offer, review your budget to see if you can afford the payment.

Let's alter the details for Gus and Dimitra. We'll raise their present planned spending to $2,625 per month, thus lowering their discretionary income to $75, short of the needed $220. Now the loan would push them beyond their debt limit.

But suppose the Alevaros still want to consider the boat purchase. What do they need to do? They must identify where in their budget the missing $145 ($220 − $75) for the payment is to come from. It is not enough for them to say: "We will simply be more thrifty." Not paying the utilities or rent will hardly do unless a damp park bench is their idea of getting back to nature. Nor will the idle "we'll find the money" work. They should reassess their budget to find out where the $145 could come from. Raising their income would be ideal, but probably one or more spending categories will have to be reduced. If Gus and Dimitra decide the sacrifices are not worth it, they should pass on the loan. If they decide the cuts are warranted, they will fit the loan into their credit limit.

Strategy

If planned spending must be cut to fit a proposed loan payment into your existing budget, identify which categories you will cut and how much.

Longer Repayment Periods

An earlier section examined how extending a loan's maturity lowers the payment. Do those smaller payments expand your debt capacity? In most cases, I would say no. Suppose you extend the maturity on an auto loan. It is possible the loan will not be repaid before you need to buy another auto. Or imagine that Mel finances this year's vacation over the next 36 months. What happens to the next and the following year's vacation as he repays this one? Basically, you mortgage more of your future income by taking on the higher finance charge required by a longer maturity.

Extension is probably warranted when the loan's original maturity was abnormally short: a 12-month, $9,000 auto loan for example. Either 36 or 48 months would be more reasonable.

Strategy

If your only reason for extending a loan's maturity is to make it fit your budget, rethink whether you should use credit.

COST OF CREDIT

Lenders quote the cost of most credit as a dollar charge for lending you the money and as an **annual percentage rate (APR).** The APR arose because lenders used to quote finance rates "creatively." Comparing credit costs ranged from challenging to impossible. APR became a standard measure, and lenders now must quote it on most credit offers.

Annual Percentage Rate (APR)

Lenders must use the finance charge (this includes all costs associated with a credit offer) to compute the APR for a loan. The APR is a comparative measure: it is the cost (as a percentage) per year of borrowing each $1. The loan with the lowest APR has the lowest net cost per dollar borrowed. Comparing APRs lets you single out the lowest-cost credit offer.

To illustrate, suppose Sharon has two 24-month loan offers: a $2,000, 15 percent APR loan and a $2,500, 18 percent loan. Which is best? Loan number one. Each $1 of that loan costs Sharon 15 percent per year; for the other, it is 18 percent per $1. Sharon's cheapest option is loan number one. It may be that because Sharon needs the full $2,500 she takes loan number two, but she will have to pay a premium.

Tom is considering two $4,000 loans: a 48-month, 14 percent APR loan and a 60-month, 16 percent APR loan. At 14 percent per $1 per year, loan number one costs less than the 16 percent of loan number two. If Tom takes loan number two, he pays a premium for its longer maturity.

Strategy

The credit option with the lowest APR offers the lowest cost per dollar per year.

Comparison Shopping

All types of consumer credit have become competitive. Lenders vie to give you a loan or sell you credit. Remember, credit is a service for which you pay a fee—the finance charge—so you should shop for the best offer. If your income is adequate and your credit record reasonable, lenders will likely want to grant you credit. Let them make you an offer. Cost differentials can be significant even within a geographic area. Look for a credit offer that best meets your needs.

In seeking credit, you may be able to bargain with the lender if you have several offers. Few people consider bargaining with a lender for a lower APR. It can help. Sure, some lenders may be surprised when you ask: Is that your best APR? Go ahead, surprise them. Quote a competitor's rate, but be honest about it.

Strategy

Check the APRs of competing lenders for the lowest cost.

Income Taxes Can Lower Your Cost of Credit

Prior to the Tax Reform Act of 1986, the finance charge on virtually all types of consumer credit qualified as an itemized deduction for federal taxes. But TRA changed all that. Now only those loans that use your house as security still qualify. Examples of qualifying loans include first mortgages, home equity loans, and second mortgages. While the actual loans will be examined in Chapters 7 and 9, let's review why that deductible feature can be attractive to some taxpayers.

On those select loans that still qualify, deducting the finance charge lowers your income and that reduces the taxes you have to pay. And the larger the finance charge, the bigger the tax savings. The net cost of credit is reduced because you pay less taxes.

Rose is considering borrowing $2,000 using a home equity loan, on which she expects to pay $300 in finance charges during this year. Her marginal tax rate is 40 percent, and she itemizes deductions. If she deducted the $300 finance charge, her income would drop $300, saving her $120 in taxes ($300 × 40% tax rate = $120 savings). Paying $300 to save $120 may not be a bargain, but it reduces her net credit cost to $180 ($300 − $120).

Deducting the finance charge on your tax return lowers a loan's effective after-tax APR. The higher your marginal tax rate, the larger the drop. But it only works for those select loans which qualify, and only if you itemize. People who do not itemize lose the finance charge deduction.

Strategy

If you can deduct finance charges from your taxes, it lowers the cost of credit.

Computing the Finance Charge on Cash and Sales Loans

Lenders may use two methods to compute finance charges on loans: they may assess either a precomputed finance charge or a simple interest finance charge. Most use precomputed finance charges. Credit unions are an exception, with most using simple interest. Let's illustrate the two methods using a $1,200, 10.9 percent APR loan that requires 12 monthly payments.

Precomputed Finance Charge

A **precomputed finance charge** is set when the loan is made. The finance charge is $72 on our $1,200, 10.9 percent loan. Added to the $1,200 borrowed, it gives us a $106 monthly payment. If the loan were made on the fifteenth of the month, we would be expected to pay by that date each month. If we did not, we would be charged a late payment fee: a set amount or a percentage of the loan. We would receive no credit if we paid several days early.

Simple Interest Finance Charge

The borrower taking out a loan with a **simple interest finance charge** is charged only for the actual time the money is used. Borrow $500 and repay it in 62 days, and the finance charge is computed on $500 for 62 days. Using the $1,200 loan example, first convert the 10.9 percent annual rate to a daily rate: 10.9%/365 days = 0.0299%. Round that to 0.03 percent per day for simplicity.

Exhibit 6.6 shows the results of the computation for the first three payments on this loan. To illustrate the flexibility of this method, our first payment is made after 30 days, the second after 35 days, the third after 25 days (see column 2 of Exhibit 6.6). The loan started at $1,200 (line 1 of column 3) and was to be repaid by $106 monthly payments (column 5). The finance charge on the first payment is $10.80 ($1,200 × 0.03% × 30 days), as shown in line 1 of column 4. If we deduct $10.80 from the $106 loan payment, we have $95.20 to repay part of the loan. Our new balance is $1,104.80 [$1,200 − ($106 − $10.80)], as we see if we look at line 1 of column 6.

When the second $106 payment arrives 35 days later, the finance charge is $11.60 ($1,104.80 × 0.03% × 35 days). We pay an actual finance charge for those extra 5 days (35 versus 30 days). After deducting that from the $106, the remaining $94.40 reduces the loan balance to $1,010.40 [$1,104.80 − ($106 − $11.60)]. Line 2 of column 6 illustrates.

What about the third payment? The finance charge drops: the loan's unpaid balance is smaller, and only 25 days have elapsed since our last payment. We receive credit for paying early. Line 3 reflects these factors.

When the lender uses the simple interest method, the borrower gets credit for paying early. When you pay late, you pay the actual finance charge. Typically, that charge is less than a late payment penalty.

Strategy

If you expect to repay a loan on an irregular schedule, search out a loan at simple interest; it has major advantages over loans with precomputed finance charges.

Exhibit 6.6

Finance Charge on a $1,200 Loan with an APR of 10.9 Percent, Using Simple Interest

Payment number (1)	Days since last payment (2)	Beginning loan balance (3)	Finance charge: col. 3 × col. 2 × 0.03% daily finance rate (4)	Loan payment (5)	Remaining loan balance: (col. 3 + col. 4) − col. 5 (6)
1	30	$1,200.00	$10.80	$106	$1,104.80
2	35	1,104.80	11.60	106	1,010.40
3	25	1,010.40	7.58	106	911.98

A caution   On simple interest loans, always ask how early and late payments are handled. Some lenders restrict the benefits of paying early. Others assess a late payment penalty in addition to the finance charge. Either lessens the benefits of the simple interest method.

Rebate of Finance Charges   If you repay a loan with precomputed finance charges early, the lender rebates a portion of the charges. Many lenders use the **rule of 78** to compute your prepayment refund.

Assume a 24-month loan is to be repaid after 4 months. Here's how it works:

1   Number each month of the loan consecutively; assign the largest number to the first month and the smallest number to the last. On a 24-month loan, the first month is 24, the second is 23, and the last month is 1.
2   Add the numbers for all those months: 24 + 23 + 22 + . . . + 1 = 300.
3   Add the numbers for the months you have had the loan: 24 + 23 + 22 + 21 = 90.
4   Total months you had loan divided by total months of the loan, equals the percentage of the finance charge you pay. In this example, it is 90/300 = 30 percent.
5   Multiply the percentage from step 4 by the total finance charge to find what you pay.

Suppose this 24-month loan had been for $4,125 with a 15 percent APR; monthly payments are $200. Total finance charges are $675: ($200 × 24) − $4,125 = $675. Suppose you pay 4 months at $200 each and now want to repay the entire loan. Your share of the finance charge is 30 percent; you pay $202.50 ($675 × 30%). Deduct that $202.50 from the $800 you have paid; the $597.50 that remains reduces the original $4,125 loan. You will pay $3,527.50 to repay the entire loan: $4,125 loan − ($800 payment − $202.50 finance charge) = $3,527.50.

The finance charge computation using the simple interest method is quite similar. Some lenders skew the result in their favor by levying a prepayment penalty which makes early payment of the loan unfavorable.

Though early payment saves finance charges, there are other ways you can reduce your encounters with the rule of 78. Concentrate on loans at simple interest; no refund need be computed, since finance charges are assessed on each payment. Second, tailor the maturity of your loan to your ability to repay. Finally, avoid loans that assess a penalty for prepaying.

ESTIMATING MONTHLY PAYMENTS   To estimate the monthly payment on a loan, you need to know the dollar amount of the loan, its APR, and its maturity. To assist you, a portion of a loan table is reproduced in Exhibit 6.7. (Appendix A.1 gives a complete one.) Various APRs run across the top and maturities down the side of the table. Payments shown in the table are for a $1,000 loan; all amounts are rounded to the nearest penny. While not precise, the figures are adequate for our needs.

Let's see how the table operates. Exhibit 6.7 shows the payment on a $1,000 loan, but the table works for any amount. Larger or smaller loans are merely multiples of the base amount. A $2,600, 24-month loan with a 12 percent APR demonstrates. The loan's approximate payment is $122.38: $47.07 × ($2,600/$1,000). What is the payment on an $800, 12-month, 12 percent APR loan? It should be $71.08.

Total Finance Charge

Exhibit 6.7 and Appendix A.1 can also be used to compute a loan's total finance charge. First, multiply your estimated payment (from the section above) times the loan's maturity to compute the total payment. Next, deduct the original loan amount from the total payment to find the total finance charge. Take the $2,600, 24-month loan with a 12 percent APR from the last section. Paying $122.38 for 24 months means you pay $2,937.12 ($122.38 × 24 months) in total; $2,600 repays the original loan, so the finance charges total $337.12 ($2,937.12 − $2,600). What is the total finance charge on the $800 loan? If you said $52.96, we agree.

SAVING: AN ALTERNATIVE TO CREDIT

Unless you need a product or service immediately, you might save the money and purchase the item for cash rather than using credit. The major advantage is that you avoid finance charges. To decide which is better, let us review the cost differential between using the credit option and saving for the item. Initially, we will estimate the cost of each option. Later we will refine the analysis by considering income tax implications.

Cost of the Credit Option

Suppose Fred and Becky Vanderhoop want to buy $2,500 worth of furniture. One option is to use a $2,500, 12-month home equity loan with an 18 percent APR. To pay the required $229.20 (the $91.68 from Exhibit 6.7 ×

Exhibit 6.7

Monthly Payments on a $1,000 Sales or Cash Loan with Different Maturities and APRs*

Months to Maturity	Annual Percentage Rate (APR)							
	9%	12%	15%	18%	21%	24%	27%	30%
12	$87.45	$88.85	$90.26	$91.68	$93.11	$94.56	$96.02	$97.49
18	59.60	60.98	62.38	63.81	65.24	66.70	68.18	69.67
24	45.68	47.07	48.49	49.92	51.39	52.87	54.38	55.91
30	37.35	38.75	40.18	41.64	43.13	44.65	46.20	47.78
36	31.80	33.21	34.67	36.15	37.68	39.23	40.83	42.45
48	24.89	26.33	27.83	29.37	30.97	32.60	34.28	36.00
60	20.76	22.24	23.79	25.39	27.05	28.77	30.54	32.35

* Payments rounded to the nearest penny.

$2,500/$1,000) for the next 12 months requires a total of $2,750.40. Of that, $250.40 ($2,750.40 − $2,500) is the finance charge (see column 2 of Exhibit 6.8).

Cost of the Savings Option

If Fred and Becky decide to save the $2,500, they can set aside less than the full $2,500 over the next 12 months. The money they deposit in their 6 percent savings account will earn interest and generate part of the needed $2,500.

How can we estimate the interest? While we could look ahead to the investment chapter and use its compound interest table to compute it exactly, we don't need that precision. As Fred and Becky save money over the 12 months, their balance will grow from zero to the $2,500 target. Let's say the average account balance will be about $1,250. On an average $1,250 balance, the Vanderhoops will earn $75 in interest ($1,250 × 6% = $75). The $75 is a rough estimate (actual interest would be a bit less) but it will do.

Exhibit 6.8

Cost Differential: Saving the Money to Buy a $2,500 Item vs. Borrowing $2,500 to Buy It

Description	Credit	Saving
Cost Differential—Ignoring Income Taxes		
Loan	$2,500.00	
Finance charge	250.40	
Savings balance needed for purchase		$2,500.00
Savings deposits: 12 payments $202.08		2,425.00
Interest earned on savings deposits		75.00
Total cost of credit alternative:		
Repayment of loan and finance charge	$2,750.40	
Total cost of saving alternative:		
Required savings deposits		$2,425.00
Cost differential:$2,750.40−$2,425.00	$ 325.40	
Cost Differential—Considering Income Taxes		
Total cost of credit alternative:		
Loan repayment and finance charge	$2,750.40	
Less: Reduction of income taxes due to finance		
charge: $250.40 × 30%*	75.12	
Net after-tax cost of credit alternative	$2,675.28	
Total cost of saving alternative:		
Required savings deposits		$2,425.00
Add: Additional deposit needed to offset income tax		
on interest earnings: $75.00 × 30%		22.50
Net after-tax cost of savings alternative		$2,447.50
Cost differential: $2,675.28 − 2,447.50	$ 227.78	

*Finance charge would only be deductible on those loans that still qualify under the TRA of 1986, and only then if the individual itemizes deductions.

The $75 in interest drops the Vanderhoop's contribution to $2,425. That $2,425 is the net cost of the savings option. (Column 3 of Exhibit 6.8 summarizes).

Cost Differential: Credit versus Saving

When you borrow, you pay the lender "rent" on the money. When you save, the financial institution pays you "rent" on your money. Saving should cost less, and it does. The difference is computed as:

Added cost of credit = total cost of credit − total cost of saving

For the Vanderhoops, credit's added cost is $325.40 ($2,750.40 − $2,425). You might consider this $325.40 the savings from not using credit. (See the top section of Exhibit 6.8.)

Strategy

Calculate the added cost of credit to decide if immediate use of an item justifies using credit rather than saving for it.

Impact of Income Taxes

Up to this point the effect of income taxes has been ignored. Because finance charges on select loans qualify as itemized deductions, taxes reduce the cost of credit if you itemize deductions. Taxes reduce the net cost of credit, but only on loans that use your house as security.

Conversely, interest earned on investments is taxed. That raises the net cost of saving, because you must contribute more to meet the target balance. The net effect is to raise the cost of the savings option.

The last example can demonstrate the impact of income taxes. Assume Fred and Becky's marginal tax rate is 30 percent and they itemize deductions. If they deduct the $250.40 finance charge on their home equity loan, their taxes drop $75.12 ($250.40 × 30% tax rate). Net cost of the credit option declines to $2,675.28 ($2,750.40 original cost − $75.12 tax savings). See column 2 at the bottom of Exhibit 6.8.

Taxes raise the cost of the Vanderhoops' savings option $22.50 ($75 × 30% tax rate), since 30 percent of the interest goes for taxes. The savings option's net cost rises to $2,447.50 ($2,425 original cost + $22.50 lost interest). Column 3 of the lower section of Exhibit 6.8 shows this.

To use our earlier "rent" analogy, you get back part of the "rent" paid on the credit, and lose part of the "rent" earned on savings. That lowers the added cost of credit. Saving still has the lower cost, however. For Fred and Becky, the benefit of using the savings option drops to $227.78: $2,675.28 cost of credit option − $2,447.50 cost of the savings option. The final line of Exhibit 6.8 summarizes the savings.

Make note: The higher your marginal tax rate, the greater the reduction in the cost of credit, the greater the rise in the cost of savings, and the smaller the cost differential between them. Income taxes actually encourage the use of select types of credit by lowering the cost of borrowing.

FINANCE CHARGE: CREDIT CARD ACCOUNTS

The discussion which follows relates to three types of credit cards: cards issued by major retailers (such as Sears, Roebuck or J. C. Penney), cards issued by oil companies (such as Exxon, Mobil Oil, Standard Oil), and the two bank-affiliated cards (MasterCard and VISA). Finance charges on credit cards are calculated much like simple interest. Usually there is not one but a series of transaction dates. People charge things on an ongoing basis. In effect, they borrow money each time. The payment is not always the same each month. To estimate how much a payment reduces the account's balance, the finance charge has to be computed first.

Before examining the actual computation, let's review how a credit card generally operates.

Billing Cycle

The **billing cycle** covers the period from the closing date to the date your payment is due. These key dates are discussed below. Exhibit 6.9 shows the sample statement we use to demonstrate a billing cycle.

Closing date or billing date

Your **closing date** or **billing date** is the final day any transaction was posted to your account statement for this cycle. The transaction could be a purchase, payment, or credit. The billing date on the statement in Exhibit 6.9 is 9-2-8X. Most credit card accounts use a calendar month, so last month's closing date was probably 8-2-8X. The statement in Exhibit 6.9 summarizes all account activity—purchases, payments, charges, and credit—for the period from 8-3 through 9-2. If your payment arrives on September 3, it will not appear until the October statement.

Due date

The **due date** is generally 25 to 30 days after your statement's closing date. Your payment must arrive by then to be on time. For the statement in Exhibit 6.9, the payment must arrive by 9-27-8X. Missing the due date could subject you to a penalty, a finance charge, or both.

Grace period

Some credit card issuers grant a **grace period** for the 25 to 30 days between the closing and due dates if you meet certain conditions. Qualify, and there is no finance fee for those days. You may qualify if:

- The entire balance on the last month's statement has been paid by its due date.
- The unpaid balance on this month's statement is due to goods and services purchased during the billing period.
- The entire balance on the current statement is paid by its due date. In effect you use the card issuer's money to purchase the items and pay no finance charge. This is an exception to the statement that borrowing always entails a finance charge.

Some credit card issuers are working hard to add on finance charges. A few eliminate the grace period entirely: finance charges begin when the purchase is posted to your statement. Others have shortened the grace period to less than the usual 25 to 30 days.

The sample in Exhibit 6.9 illustrates how the grace period operates. Since Ralph's "previous balance" is zero, he must have paid the balance on his last bill. Ralph will have to pay the entire $100 balance shown on this statement by 9-27-8X to qualify for the grace period. Assuming his payment is on time, he will not pay a finance fee this month. But what if Ralph still owed $200 from last month? Even if he paid that $200 plus this month's $100 by September 27, he would be assessed a finance charge on both balances.

Maximizing the grace period. You can extend your grace period beyond 25 days by charging an item on or just after your statement's clos-

Exhibit 6.9

Sample Monthly Statement for a Typical Credit Card Account

MONTHLY STATEMENT

Ralph Smith
456 Dead End St.
Nowhere

Account Number
123-4567-890

Date	Reference Number	Description	Amount	
8-23-8X	305F-402319	Ajax Lumber Co.	100	00

Previous Balance	New Purchases	Finance Charge	Payments	New Balance	Past Due Balance	Minimum Payment
0	100.00	0	0	100.00	0	10.00

Annual Percentage Rate	Billing Date [A]		Payment Due Date [B]	Card Limit	Balance of Limit Remaining
18 percent	9-2-8X		9-27-8X	500	400

ing date. Look at Ralph's statement in Exhibit 6.9. An item purchased on September 3 will not appear until the October statement: billing closed September 2. He has use of the money for 29 days, between September 3 and October 2. If Ralph pays the September bill on time and in full, he qualifies for the added 25 days until he must pay on October 27. Ralph's total grace period: 54 days.

Strategy

Concentrate your purchases on or shortly after your statement closing date to maximize your grace period.

Computing the Finance Charge

Credit card finance charges are computed in one of three ways: on the basis of previous balance, average daily balance, or adjusted balance. Take Ralph's statement in Exhibit 6.9. Assume Ralph makes a $50 payment on September 17, leaving $50 unpaid. Exhibit 6.10 summarizes the finance charge based on each of the three methods.

Previous balance

The **previous balance** method gives no credit for partial payments. Unless the balance is paid by the due date, a finance charge is assessed on the entire balance. In Ralph's case the finance charge is assessed on the $100 as of September 2. Even though he paid $50 on September 17, he receives no credit for it. The previous balance method often results in the highest finance charge of the three methods. It is still used by some credit card issuers.

Average Daily Balance

As the name suggests, here the finance charge is based on the **average daily unpaid balance** during the period. That average is computed by adding the unpaid balance each day of the billing cycle, then dividing that total

Exhibit 6.10

Computation of Finance Charge Using the Previous Balance, Average Daily Balance, and Adjusted Balance

	Previous balance	Average daily balance	Adjusted balance
Closing balance, September 2	$100.00	$100.00	$100.00
Payment, September 17	50.00	50.00	50.00
Ending balance	50.00	50.00	50.00
Balance on which finance charge is based	100.00*	75.00†	50.00‡
Finance charge for September (1½% per month)	1.50	1.13	0.75
Credit for partial payment	None	Partial	Complete

* Represents unpaid balance on September 2, 198X.
† Represents average daily balance during the period:
    15 days (9/3 to 9/17) @ $100 = $1,500
    15 days (9/18 to 10/2) @ $50 =   750
      Total $2,250
    Average daily balance = $2,250/30 days = $75
‡ Represents unpaid balance on October 2, 198X.

by the number of days in the cycle. In Ralph's case that works out to the $75 shown at the bottom of Exhibit 6.10. Partial payments during the period reduce the daily balance from that point forward, so you receive some credit for them. This is the most widely used computational method.

Adjusted balance

Using the **adjusted balance** method, the finance charge is based on the account balance at the end of the billing cycle. Full credit is given for any partial payments made before the due date. In Exhibit 6.10, Ralph's finance charge is based on the $50 balance as of October 2. While the method usually gives the lowest finance charge of the three, it is the least used.

Minimizing Your Finance Charges

You can do several things to minimize your finance charges. First, pay within the grace period if at all possible: even if you have to borrow the money for a few days (the automatic overdraft on your checking account would do), the loan's finance charge will be less than the credit card's. Mail your payment so it arrives on time: paying a penalty of 1 to 2 percent of the balance is a stiff price for being tardy. Finally, if your payment will be only a day or two late, call the card's issuer and explain; the charge might be canceled.

TRUTH IN LENDING

Before the passage of the **Truth in Lending Act,** consumers often lacked the information needed to make informed credit decisions. Information provided often could not be compared, and some of it was downright misleading. The central intent of the Act is to require disclosure of uniform and meaningful information by lenders.

Coverage

All consumer credit transactions under $25,000 are covered. Mortgages used to buy personal residences are covered, regardless of the loan amount. The Act applies to any institution or business that regularly offers credit: banks, credit unions, S&Ls, MSBs, retailers, service businesses, and professionals are examples.

Required Disclosures

Lenders must disclose specific information for each credit offer. Exhibit 6.11 summarizes specifics for three types of credit. Often the disclosure is contained in your credit contract. Read and understand it. Never accept the assurance: "We never enforce that section." If the lender doesn't, ask that it be removed from the contract.

Strategy

Review your credit contract before signing anything. Ask the lender to explain unclear points.

QUALIFYING FOR CREDIT

In the past, lenders relied heavily on subjective judgment to decide whether you were a good credit risk. Information on your income, length of residence, and existing debts, and other financial data on you influenced their decisions, but there was no fixed measure to separate good and poor credit risks.

Now, lenders rely on credit scoring techniques; under their **credit scoring systems,** they assign points for certain characteristics. If your total score is high enough, you qualify; if not, into the reject pile. Each lender singles out characteristics which separate applicants into two groups:

- Good credit risks. They have a record of repaying promptly and borrowing wisely. Accept these.
- Poor credit risks. They have been late in paying, required considerable collection effort, or—worse—part of the debt was never collected. Reject these now. Let some ''lucky'' competing lender get them.

The scoring method is more objective than its predecessor: it relies on 5 to 10 **borrower characteristics** and weights them by importance.

Which Characteristics Are Used?

All lenders do not use the same characteristics. Lenders develop individual lists that work best with their applicants. Lenders rarely discuss the details of their systems. These are expensive to develop, and a good one can reduce the lender's credit losses. Lenders also claim that applicants could manipulate the outcome if the system were published. Nevertheless, some shared characteristics seem to appear in most scoring systems. Column 1 of Exhibit 6.12 lists frequently used factors.

Assigning Points to Each Factor

When you apply for credit, you will fill out an application that requests personal and financial information. The lender uses the data to assign you points. The higher your score, the more likely you will be accepted. Columns 2 and 3 of Exhibit 6.12 provide some guidelines as to what deter-

Exhibit 6.11

Required Disclosures on Consumer Credit Transactions

Required disclosure	Type of credit	Required disclosure	Type of credit
Finance Charge		Payments	
Annual percentage rate (APR)	1, 2, 3	Number of payments	1, 2, 3
Total dollar finance charge	1, 2	Amount of each payment	1, 2
Method to compute charge	3	Due date of payments	1, 2, 3
Description of grace period	3	Total amount of payments	1, 2
Method to refund charge	1, 2	Minimum payment	3
Penalties		Security Pledged	
Fee for late payment	1, 2	Borrower's asset pledged as	1, 2, 3
Fee if paid before maturity	1, 2	security	

Key to type of consumer credit disclosure is required on:
1 First mortgage on a home; discussed further in Chapter 9.
2 Consumer cash and sales loans.
3 Charge accounts and credit cards.

mines your score. Column 2 summarizes the situation that might net you a low score for a particular factor; Column 3 does the same for high scores.

Deciding Who Qualifies

Lenders total your points on the scoring system to see if you meet their minimum. You generally have to score 60 to 70 percent of the maximum number of points to be accepted. Individuals on the borderline may be reviewed by the lender. Some lenders adjust your score using your **credit record at the local credit bureau.** Negative information in your credit report—slow payment on present debts, legal action on past debts—could lower your previous score. Enough negatives, and you receive form letter number 23: "We regret to inform you that you have been rejected, but have a nice day."

Lender Notifies You

Under the **Equal Credit Opportunity Act,** lenders must notify you of their decision within 30 days after you submit a complete credit application. Retain a copy of your application as proof that you completed it.

If you are rejected, you have the right to request a written statement of the reason or reasons for rejection, if not included in the rejection letter. Those reasons may suggest your next course of action. If you scored low, some extenuating circumstance might have caused it. Frequent job transfers can cause low scores on residence or on your time in the area. Calling the lender to explain the circumstance might lead to your application being accepted. Possibly a negative report from a credit bureau figured in the rejection. If so, the lender must tell you the credit bureau's name and address.

Since scoring systems differ, it is possible another lender will accept you. If, however, your low score is not due to some special circumstance,

Exhibit 6.12

Borrower Characteristics Used in Many Credit Scoring Systems

Factors That Control the Points Assigned		
Borrower characteristics	*Low points*	*High points*
Residence	Renting	Owns residence
Time lived in the area	Less than 6 months	More than 10 years
Level of gross income	Less than $15,000	More than $100,000
Occupation	Low-skill job	Profession
Time employed	Less than 3 months	More than 10 years
Number of credit cards	None	Eight or more
Loan from finance company	Several	None
Debt payments as a percentage of gross income*	More than 30 percent	Less than 5 percent
Checking and/or savings account maintained	None	Both
Age	Less than 30	Over 50

* Excludes payment on home mortgage.

or several lenders rejected you, ask yourself: Was the rejection warranted? Are there specific weaknesses I need to correct? Am I pushing my upper credit limit already? Yes answers suggest you may need to take corrective action.

Credit Rights for Women

The Equal Credit Opportunity Act also requires that potential creditors treat men and women equally when judging applicants. The criteria used to judge an applicant's creditworthiness must be uniform for both sexes. A creditor cannot reject a woman's application solely because she is a woman. Nor can the lender impose higher qualifying standards on women than men. The act does not guarantee your application will be approved, but it has helped ensure far fairer treatment than in the past.

Applying for credit

Single women who apply for credit do not have to disclose whether they are or ever were married. Married women do not have to disclose their husband's income when applying for credit. Jane Smith does not even have to reveal old Fred exists, unless she is pledging some of the couple's assets to secure the loan. An exception is creditors in community property states, who can ask marital status and spouse's name.

Married women should apply for credit in their own name. That way, they establish a personal credit record. Too often, couples apply for all credit in the husband's name, and divorce or death leaves the woman with little or no credit history, even when her salary was a major part of the household's income. A later section shows how joint reporting lessens this problem.

A woman's income

The loan officer Sam and Betty Dewit are meeting with asks for gross income. They reply: "Forty thousand dollars." He fills in the blank, but then asks: "Your income, Sam?" Sam answers: "Twenty thousand dollars." The lender crosses out $40,000 and writes in $20,000. Legal? Not today, but done in the past. A woman's income was considered transitory. Now prospective creditors must consider both the husband's and wife's income on joint applications. Questions about childbearing plans are off limits, too.

Lenders must consider all sources of income for unmarried women or those who are separated. That includes alimony, Social Security benefits, welfare benefits, wages (part- or full-time), pensions, and investment earnings. You cannot be rejected solely because you list income other than wages and salaries.

Personal credit history

Anyone who has applied for and used credit is likely to be studied by a credit bureau. Married women once had a special problem because only the husband had a record. Now you can ask that all credit records be reported in both the husband's and the wife's name. The wife can also ensure she has a record by applying for credit in her name alone. Either way, use your legal name: Becky Bear is acceptable; Mrs. Fred Bear is not.

Strategy

Married women should always establish their own credit record. Best is to have your own credit. Lacking that, have jointly used credit reported in both names.

What happens to a single woman's established credit record if she marries? Nothing. She can keep her present credit accounts. If she changes her name, she should tell her creditors.

YOUR CREDIT BUREAU FILE

When you use and apply for credit, a local credit bureau will keep a file on that activity. Usually, it contains your payment record for the past 12 to 24 months, credit limits on your accounts, inquires to the credit bureau, disputed credit amounts, debts written off as uncollectible (if any), and personal bankruptcy (if applicable).

Fair Credit Reporting Act

The **Fair Credit Reporting Act** was enacted to ensure that your credit report contains accurate and up-to-date information. First, it is intended to protect you against the circulation of inaccurate, incomplete, or obsolete information. Second, it outlines steps you can take to correct or remove inaccurate, dated, or biased data from your file.

Your rights

If a lender denies you a loan because of your credit record, the lender must disclose the reporting bureau's name and address. You can call and arrange to review your file. The bureau must disclose the file's contents and tell you the sources of its information. Though not required, it may give you a copy of the file. The bureau must also tell you what organizations or individuals requested information from your file in the past 6 months. There is no fee for this service.

Strategy

Always review your file when you have been denied credit. You can single out negative points that caused the rejection.

Even if you have not been denied credit, you can ask to review your file. You will have to pay a fee of $5 to $15 for the service. Always call ahead for an appointment. If you do not know which bureau has your file, ask your bank or a retailer where you have a credit card.

Strategy

Review your credit file before you apply for a major loan such as a home mortgage. To ensure its accuracy, you may want to review it every couple years.

Incorrect information

You can request that the bureau investigate information that appears to be incorrect or incomplete. If the information cannot be substantiated, it must be removed. If you ask, the bureau must send—for free—corrected information to anyone who received your credit report during the past 6 months.

Disputed information

If you disagree with an item in your file, ask the credit bureau to place your comment in the file; the comment is limited to 100 words. Future credit reports must contain your comment. For a nominal fee, the bureau will send your version to those who recently requested your credit report.

Obsolete information

Adverse information must be deleted after 7 years, with one exception: bankruptcy information can be retained for 10 years.

OVEREX-TENDED WITH CREDIT

People who find themselves buried under a mound of credit card payments, loan payments, charge accounts, and balances due to professionals and stores have become overextended with credit. A loss of job, a cut in salary, "easy" credit, poor management of finances, or the fanciful "hope" the money will come from somewhere may have led to the overextension. Regardless of the cause, corrective action is needed.

Overextended?

The questions in Exhibit 6.13 may provide some early warning signs of impending credit problems. Yes responses to five or six of the questions suggest you need to review your use of credit.

Self-Study and Evaluation

If you presently do not have a budget, prepare one. Make a detailed list of payments; include the total balance, minimum payment, and the payment you would like to make. Compare your projected monthly available income with the combined total of your planned spending and your required debt payment. Then you can judge how serious the overextension is. Depending on its severity, decide whether you have a:

- **Short-term cash flow problem.** This is a temporary problem you may be able to correct over the next few months.
- **Major financial crisis.** You will have to curtail your spending. Even then, it could take more than a year to correct.
- **Situation in which bankruptcy is the sole option.** Your credit obligations surpass your current and future ability to pay. Correcting the overextension may be impossible.

You are the one who knows your finances, resources, and obligations best. Once you decide the severity of the situation, *you* can take appropriate corrective action.

Temporary Overextension

Correcting a temporary overextension requires surviving the next few months. First, remain calm. Develop an emergency budget that reduces all your expenditures to a minimum. Second, pay some amount on all your debts. On credit cards, pay the minimum: if you cannot, at least pay something. Third, call or write your creditors to explain that your problem will be corrected within several months. Finally, use credit sparingly, if at all.

A Major Credit Crisis

Corrective action on a major credit crisis requires the steps listed in the last section. Use your emergency budget to estimate how much you can pay each month. Then you can estimate how many months repayment will take. Anticipate your creditors: call or write to explain your repayment

Exhibit 6.13

Early Warning Signals of Credit Problems

	(Yes)	(No)
Savings		
1. Has your cash reserve decreased sharply?	( )	( )
2. Are you forced to draw on savings each month?	( )	( )
3. Do you rarely make deposits in savings?	( )	( )
Monthly Payments		
1. Do you pay just the minimum on credit cards?	( )	( )
2. Has your bill paying slowed?	( )	( )
3. Are any of your debts delinquent?	( )	( )
4. Do you need overtime or an extra job to make ends meet?	( )	( )
5. Are you unclear where your money goes?	( )	( )
6. Are you always short of money before payday?	( )	( )
7. Do you use the overdraft on your checking account frequently?	( )	( )
Use of Credit		
1. Do you have many charge account and other debts?	( )	( )
2. Are you uncertain how much you owe?	( )	( )
3. Have you started receiving past due notices or calls?	( )	( )
4. Do you have debt consolidation loans?	( )	( )

plan. Happy they will not be: willing to compromise they may be if you demonstrate you can correct the problem. Be realistic, don't claim you will repay in 2 or 3 months if that is impossible. Review your assets to see if there are some things you can sell or redeem. If there is a significant fee or penalty for selling—the penalty for early withdrawal from an Individual Retirement Account (IRA), for example—consider this a last resort. Can you increase your income? A second or part-time job might help. As a final step, you may want to consider a debt consolidation loan.

Debt consoli-
dation loan

A **debt consolidation loan** provides money to repay existing debts and concentrates payments with one lender. If the payment is less than for your existing debts, it provides some breathing room. That may give you time to work out a long-term solution. Second, the loan may carry a lower APR than your present debts; less of each payment goes for finance charges, so you pay off the debt quicker. A lower APR is typical on many credit union and some bank, MSB, and S&L loans.

But use extreme care. Lenders may shout: "End your debt problems by consolidating them into one easy-to-pay loan." End the problem? Often people merely postpone it. Use no credit while repaying that loan. Avoid loans whose APR is even higher than the price you are already paying.

Strategy

At best, a debt consolidation loan assists a well-developed repayment plan. Keep the maturity as short as your budget will permit.

Deciding who
should be paid

Suppose you have decided against a debt consolidation loan, and you lack the funds to make minimum payments on all your debts. How do you decide who gets paid? One option is to try and minimize the damage to your credit record. Creditors that report to the credit bureau immediately are prime (number 1) payment candidates. Creditors who report less readily are second (number 2) priority. Last are those who only report when legal action is taken (number 3). Debts in each category might include:

1   Bank-affiliated credit cards, major national retailer credit cards
2   Credit cards from regional department stores, finance company loans
3   Utility charges, bills from professionals, landlord, credit cards from oil companies

Until you have the needed funds, you might want to first pay creditors in groups 1 and 2. Pay something, however small, to the rest.

If you can pay more than the minimum, pay debts that have the highest APR.

Outside Assis-
tance: Credit
Counseling

Those who need outside assistance should consider *nonprofit credit counseling organizations.* If you cannot find one in your area, call the National Foundation for Consumer Credit for information. The number is (301) 459-8766. You will be asked to complete a questionnaire detailing your income, expenses, and total debts. Then you will meet with a counselor who will review your finances. If the overextension is very serious, the counselor may suggest you see an attorney. If a payment plan seems feasible, the counselor may help develop a payment plan you can carry out on your own. Or the counselor may suggest you turn over part of each month's income to the agency for it to repay your debts. Counselors generally call your creditors to explain the proposed plan. The fee for the initial review is usually $20 to $30. If the agency manages your payments, expect to pay a $10 to $20 monthly fee.

There are also some for-profit credit counseling and debt consolidating businesses. Their fees are higher; several hundred dollars is not unusual. And by reputation, some are suspect; they may achieve much less than nonprofit agencies.

Strategy

If you want outside assistance, search out a nonprofit credit counseling organization.

Bankruptcy: A Last Resort

At some point you may find a debt repayment plan just is not possible. You may be so deep in debt that you lack the current and future income to repay your debts. You may want to consider what relief **bankruptcy** can provide. It is a last resort. It will most certainly reduce, if not eliminate, your creditworthiness. It will likely be costly. And there are limits to how often you can file for bankruptcy. You have two options: wage earner's plan (officially, Chapter 13) and straight bankruptcy (officially, Chapter 7). Both are highly technical and require a knowledgeable attorney. This is not do-it-yourself territory.

Wage earner's plan

A **wage earner's plan** is designed to allow you to repay your present debts from future income. Under a court-approved plan, the maturity of your debts may be extended, finance charges can be reduced or eliminated, and the debt itself may be reduced. You do not surrender your assets with this plan.

Less of a stigma is attached to a wage earner's plan, since you are repaying your debts, even if not on the original terms. The plan sets the amount you must pay to a trustee each month. The trustee, in turn, distributes that money to your creditors. To qualify for such a plan, you have to show your income exceeds your expenses. Further, you will have to show that the amount available can repay your debts within a "reasonable" time: 3 years is usual.

There are sizable costs to a wage earner's plan (your attorney, court costs, and trustee's fees), reason to consider it a desperate measure. There is no time limit between filings. Once should be more than enough.

Strategy

A wage earner's plan may be appropriate where the overextension is so serious that the individual cannot manage a full repayment plan, but is not so bad that some form of repayment is hopeless.

*Straight bank-
ruptcy*

Straight bankruptcy corrects a credit overextension by taking your assets in return for canceling your debt obligations. It is advised if your income is less than your monthly living expenses or if the amount you could repay is so limited it would take years to cover your debts.

A court-appointed trustee takes title to the debtor's assets and sells them to raise money for repayment. Assets that are necessary for "continued life" plus a specified dollar amount are exempted by federal and state regulations. Money raised from the sale will be much less than total debts; lenders must settle for a few cents for each dollar owed. The unpaid portion of most debts is canceled. Exceptions include student loans, child support, alimony, most unpaid taxes, and debts from intentional injury or property damage.

The costs of straight bankruptcy are high: your attorney, court costs, and trustee's fees. Many creditors are very reluctant to extend credit to someone who has declared bankruptcy in the past. Bankruptcy remains on your credit record for 10 years. Furthermore, if Boris Bumbler filed for bankruptcy in 1987, he cannot file for it again until 1994: 7 years is the minimum between filings. Are there positive features? It gives a fresh start to someone whose credit problems virtually defy a workable solution. But it is a very serious move.

**Debt Collec-
tion Agencies**

Collection agencies assist creditors in collecting on consumer and credit card debts. When creditors have exhausted their normal collection efforts, they may turn an account over to one of these agencies. The agency's fee is a percentage of the amount collected; one-half of each dollar is not uncommon.

To "encourage" payment, agencies once used tactics that were questionable, if not outright illegal. Now, the Fair Debt Collection Practices Act limits what agencies can do to collect a debt. They cannot harass you, call at unusual times, or contact you at work if your employer objects. They cannot falsely represent themselves or the status of your debt. Even with those limits, a collection agency's effort can be unrelenting and discomforting. Be aware that the employees of some agencies will stretch the rules to the limit, and sometimes beyond, to collect. Employees of creditors are not covered by this act. So they can use some of the tactics this legislation ruled off-limits.

Strategy

Avoid being subject to the tactics of debt collection agencies by managing your debts so you do not become overextended.

Summary

1   Borrowing increases your immediate purchasing power, but simultaneously reduces future purchasing power by a larger amount.

2   The finance charge on credit includes all costs: interest, application fee, credit check, insurance premiums, processing fee.

3   Extending the maturity of a loan lowers its

monthly payment but raises the total finance charge.

4 Deciding if credit is appropriate involves assessing the cost-benefit trade-off it entails.

5 A personal budget is the best way to establish an upper debt limit because it helps you answer the question: Where will the money for the payment come from?

6 The APR is the cost per $1 per year for a credit offer. It can be used in comparing credit offers, even if their terms are not identical.

7 The wide availability of consumer credit and the intense competition in the field mean you can shop for credit.

8 Two methods are used to compute the finance charge on consumer loans: precomputed and simple interest methods.

9 Many lenders use the "rule of 78" to compute rebates of the finance charge when a loan is repaid before maturity.

10 Deferring the purchase of an item until you save the money is an alternative to using credit.

11 Many credit cards provide a 25- to 30-day grace period with no finance charge when certain conditions are met.

12 The finance charge on a credit card can be based on the previous balance, the average daily balance, or the adjusted balance.

13 Lenders must disclose enough information about a credit offer so that consumers can make an informed decision.

14 Many lenders use a credit scoring system to decide who qualifies for credit.

15 The provisions set forth in the Equal Credit Opportunity Act are intended to ensure that women have the same access to credit as men.

16 A credit bureau must review the contents of your credit file with you. There is no charge if the file was the basis for a lender refusing you credit; otherwise there is a nominal fee.

17 Many people can correct an overuse of credit through financial planning. Nonprofit counseling agencies can assist with this.

18 Bankruptcy is an expensive, final step to correct or eliminate a serious overuse of credit.

Review your understanding of

Finance charge
Repayment terms
Maturity
Cost-benefit trade-off of credit
Upper debt limit
Annual percentage rate (APR)
Precomputed finance charge
Simple interest finance charge
Rule of 78
Billing cycle
Closing date
Billing date
Due date
Grace period

Finance charge on credit card:
    Previous balance
    Average daily balance
    Adjusted balance
Truth in Lending Act
Credit scoring system
Borrower characteristics
Equal Credit Opportunity Act
Credit bureau file
Fair Credit Reporting Act
Debt consolidation loan
Nonprofit credit counseling
Bankruptcy
    Wage earner's plan
    Straight bankruptcy

Discussion questions

1 If someone polled households on (a) whether they use credit, (b) what is an appropriate item to purchase with credit, and (c) the type of credit used, would you expect reasonably uniform answers? Why or why not? What could account for some differences?

2 What does it mean to use credit as a "convenience"? Are there any rules that should be observed when using credit this way? What are the potential problems?

3 Describe the function of a budget in defining upper debt limits. What are the strengths of using a budget for this task?

4 Comment on this statement: "Extending the repayment period expands your debt capacity."

5 Is there a difference between a loan's interest charges and its finance charges? Explain. What does it mean if a loan's APR is 15 percent? What will the APR tell you about different loans?

6 What is the difference between the calculation of a loan's finance charge using the simple interest method and using the precomputed method? What might make simple interest advantageous to the borrower? Why?

7 Heidi is considering two options for her new sailboard:
a Wait one year to save the $2,000, then buy it.
b Buy it now by borrowing the $2,000.
Which option will likely cost more? Why? How

might Heidi decide which one to use? If the price of the item is expected to rise 5 percent during the next 12 months, how would that affect her decision?

8   Some people argue that the federal tax system encourages the use of certain types of credit while at the same time discouraging saving. What points support this position?

9   Wilbur Worldly noticed his credit card statement shows a due date and a closing date; he is unclear what these terms mean. Can you present an example to help Wilbur understand the significance and workings of each?

10 How does a grace period work? What is its significance? How can you get maximum benefit from it?

11 What benefits do you see in Truth in Lending legislation? How can a consumer best use the information?

12 Why do you think it was necessary to pass legislation to ensure credit rights for women? Can you cite improvements it provided?

13 How can you find out what your credit file contains? What can you do if it contains inaccurate or obsolete information?

14 What are the early warning signs that you may be overextended with credit? What steps might you take if you think you are nearing your upper credit limits?

15 Cite the major differences between straight bankruptcy and a wage earner's plan. In what situation would each be appropriate? What advantages might a wage earner's plan provide over a plan developed by the borrower? Disadvantages?

Problems

6.1 Ralph is considering two credit options to finance $2,000 worth of new furniture. The furniture dealer offered a 24-month loan with a 24 percent APR. Ralph's credit union offered a 24-month loan with a 12 percent APR. When asked about the difference, the dealer suggested it probably was not a good comparison. Besides, the monthly payments differed by only slightly more than $10.
   a Is the APR comparison valid?
   b What is the monthly payment for each loan?
   c How much more will Ralph pay each month for the dealer's loan than for the credit union's loan? How much more will Ralph pay over the loan's total life?
   d Which loan would you recommend?

6.2 Ann has loan offers from three different lenders:

	Lender X	Lender Y	Lender Z
Amount of cash from loan	$2,000.00	$2,000.00	$3,000.00
Monthly loan payment	$ 94.14	$ 99.84	$ 137.04
Number of months	24	24	24

   a What is the APR for each loan (*Hint:* Exhibit 6.7 may be helpful.)
   b Can Ann compare the APRs of the three loans?
   c Which loan would you recommend?

6.3 Burton Swift plans to repay her 12-month, $2,000 cash loan at the end of 4 months. Refunds are made using the rule of 78.
   a What portion of the loan's original $156 finance charge will be returned?
   b Since Burton has had the loan for one-third of its original maturity, why is her refund less than two-thirds of the original fee?

6.4 Susan Banks is considering two $4,000 loans for her new car: (1) a 36-month loan with an APR of 18 percent, and (2) a 60-month loan with an APR of 18 percent. The lender has stressed how much "easier" the payments will be on the loan with the longer repayment period.
   a What are the monthly payments on the loans?
   b Is the 60-month loan cheaper?
   c If Susan can make the payments on either loan, which should she take? Why?

6.5 Clyde Padro is comparing two purchase alternatives on a $2,000 rug.
1   Purchase immediately with a $2,000, 12-month home equity loan at 12 percent APR.
2   Save the money over the next 12 months in his 6 percent credit union account. A $162.13 deposit at the end of each month and his accumulated interest will equal $2,000 at the end of the twelfth month. Clyde's current marginal tax rate is 40 percent, and he itemizes deductions.
   a If income taxes are ignored, what is the cost differential between options one and two? What is the cost differential between options one and two when taxes are considered? (Assume the finance charge is a deductible expense.)

  b Which would you recommend? Why?

  c Without working through a detailed solution, how would that differential change if Clyde's tax rate were 30 percent?

6.6 Lee Chang has offers from three car dealers for a new Piggo sport coupé.

	Dealer A	Dealer B	Dealer C
Cash price	$9,000.00	$10,000.00	$11,000.00
Credit option monthly payment	$ 293.40	$ 278.30	$ 289.64
Number of payments	48	48	48

All three dealer prices are for the same model, similarly equipped. Lee expects each dealer will provide comparable service.

  a If Lee were buying the car with cash, which dealer should he choose?

  b If Lee selects the credit option, which dealer should he choose? Why?

  c What is the APR quoted by each dealer? (*Hint:* Exhibit 6.7 may help.)

  d Can the APRs be compared for the three credit alternatives? Which option has the most attractive APR? Why?

Case problem

Ralph and Grazela Smith are thinking of buying a $7,200 camping trailer. Although they want the trailer, they are unsure whether the loan will push them beyond their upper debt limit.

Both work full time and have no dependents. The combined available income on their budget is $33,480 ($2,790 monthly). Average monthly expenses include rent, $525; utilities, $125; food, $350; clothing, $190; transportation (excludes the auto loan payment), $340; entertainment, $200; donations, $70; insurance premiums, $55. Their monthly savings for long-term financial goals are $180.

Present monthly debt payments include (months until each loan matures shown in parentheses) auto loan (30), $360; furniture (20), $180; and home entertainment center (35), $126. Since their savings balance is limited, they would finance $6,575 of the trailer's cost. The dealer has offered a 36-month, $6,575 loan with a 24 percent APR; monthly payment is $258.

1 Should the Smiths take on the new debt? What alternatives, if any, would you suggest?

2 Prepare a budget for the Smiths to see whether they are nearing their upper debt limit. What is your conclusion?

3 If the Smiths are still interested in the trailer, what is their next step? Why is your suggested step important?

4 What are the advantages and disadvantages of extending the loan's 36-month maturity? Should Ralph and Grazela shop for other credit offers? Why?

5 Ralph's friend has suggested a debt consolidation loan from Friendly Bob's Finance Shop to "clean up" all their present debts. Its maturity is longer than their present debts, so the monthly payment is less. Its APR is higher, however. What is your opinion of this loan?

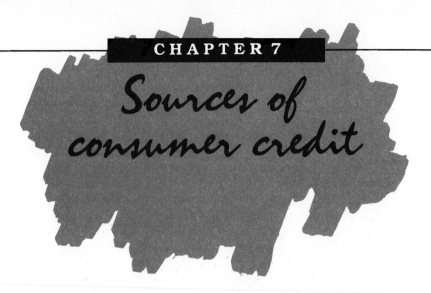

CHAPTER 7

Sources of consumer credit

AFTER COMPLETING THIS CHAPTER YOU WILL HAVE LEARNED

- What a consumer loan is and how it operates
- How an unsecured cash loan differs from a secured cash loan
- How a second mortgage loan operates and when it should be used
- Why a home equity loan differs from a second mortgage loan
- How to decide if a loan with a fixed finance charge is better than one with a variable rate
- The major sources for consumer cash loans and the advantages and disadvantages of dealing with each
- What a consumer loan is and how it operates
- How to evaluate credit life and disability insurance coverage on consumer loans
- What open-end consumer credit is and how it operates
- How to obtain the benefits from credit cards and charge accounts, while avoiding their potential pitfalls
- What to do when you lose a credit card
- What a debit card is and how it operates

Consumer credit vendors include all the sources people use to purchase products, obtain cash, and acquire needed services. Consumer debt continues to grow because purchasers are willing to use credit freely. Recent trends in the credit area contribute to this growth.

First, consumers are now using credit for an expanded range of purchases. No longer do they limit credit to big-ticket products and financial emergencies. Many people see credit as a convenience, not just a way to expand their purchasing power. For many, credit cards are a substitute for cash or a personal check. When they use credit for smaller purchases, they plan to repay the balance when billed. That way, they use credit to help manage their finances. Much of the growth in credit purchasing can be attributed to such use.

Lenders have encouraged the use of credit by introducing new options. For example, they allow homeowners to use the equity in their homes as security for loans. Borrowing against one's home used to be considered a last resort. People's present willingness to take advantage of such offers signals a shift in how credit is viewed. Liberalized lending rules have also inspired lenders to introduce variable interest rates. Rather than charging a fixed rate over the loan's life, lenders adjust interest as a specified financial market interest index changes.

The expansion in consumer credit has attracted new lenders to the market. For instance, brokerage firms now lend money to individuals. Savings and loans have supplemented their traditional mortgage lending with consumer credit. Finance companies have broadened their loan options to reach a larger clientele.

The net effect of these changes is that you have many credit options. Sorting through the bewildering array takes time, is challenging, and requires detailed analysis. But a good choice can be rewarding. Credit use is not without risks. Careful management is essential; you need to avoid overuse, to refuse expensive "easy" options, and to recognize high origination costs that sharply boost borrowing costs.

CONSUMER CASH LOAN

When you borrow cash, you receive a check. While you may plan to buy some product or service with the money, purchasing the item is not a prerequisite for the loan. Loans can range from less than $100 to more than $20,000. Maturities run from a few days to more than 10 years. The finance charge APR can range from 10 to more than 30 percent. Small loans with short maturities have the highest APRs. Most require equal monthly payments, but some have a series of uneven amounts.

Unsecured Personal Loan

The borrower's promise is the lender's only assurance that an **unsecured personal loan** will be repaid. The lender will therefore carefully review your credit record and payment ability before granting an unsecured loan. You must have an adequate income and a good record of paying past loans on time to qualify. Often the loan will be limited to a moderate dollar amount. Lenders will suggest a secured loan for larger amounts.

Since the only security is the borrower's repayment promise, the lender is exposed to some risk. Thus, finance charges on unsecured loans are moderately high. Lenders often quote a lower rate on a secured loan to encourage its use.

Strategy

If you need a smaller loan and have an established, top-grade credit record, an unsecured cash loan can be a good credit option.

Automatic overdraft

The **automatic overdraft** privilege on your checking, NOW, or share draft account (see Chapter 4) is just a special unsecured cash loan. More accurately, it is a "line of credit" rather than a loan. You apply to the financial institution to establish the overdraft privilege. Your dollar limit is set using the same qualifying criteria as for a loan. You draw on your credit line by writing a check for more than is in your account. Some advance the precise amount. Others advance money in even $100 multiples.

Most institutions charge no annual fee or maintenance charge to maintain your overdraft privilege. But you pay a finance charge on each dollar you borrow until the overdraft is repaid. Fees are computed using the simple interest method. Assume Wanda qualifies for an overdraft up to a $1,000 maximum at an 18.25 percent APR. She drew $400 on it 15 days ago. What is her finance charge? First, convert that 18.25 percent to a daily rate: 18.25%/365 days = 0.05%. Some lenders use 360 days as the base

"year"; their daily rate would be a bit higher. Having used $400 for 15 days, Wanda's finance charge is $3: $400 × 0.05% × 15 days. What if she repays the $400 in several installments? The logic is the same; the mechanics are similar to those for the loan repayment in Exhibit 6.6.

Payments on overdrafts take two forms: you may send your payment to the institution, or the institution may deduct the payment from your deposit. The second is more convenient. Overdrafts are an easy way to bridge a temporary cash shortage. Once you have the money, you can repay the entire amount. Overdrafts that extend for several months require monthly payments. Most lenders specify a minimum monthly amount.

The overdraft privilege is highly flexible. Once established, you can use it when you want. Because your institution uses the simple interest method, you pay a finance charge only for the time the money is used. Right now, 15 to 20 percent is a typical finance fee. Within limits, you tailor the repayment to your needs.

Some argue this flexibility invites misuse. Earnie Easygo's attorney solemnly reads from his will: "To my bank, I finally repay the overdraft; a feat I never quite managed before drawing the next one. Now, please send an application to my new address. I plan . . . "

Strategy

Properly used, an automatic overdraft provides a convenient, flexible, short-term source of credit.

Secured Personal Cash Loan

When you take out a **secured personal cash loan,** you must either pledge some asset or have someone else, **the consigner,** promise to repay the loan. The lender has added assurance the loan will be repaid. Fail, and the lender repossesses the pledged asset or asks your cosigner to pay.

Lenders look for two attributes in a pledged asset: (1) Can the item be controlled and tracked? (2) Is it reasonably easy to sell if necessary? The first choice is financial assets: common stocks, certificates of deposit, or bonds. Next come autos, recreational vehicles, boats, or camping units. Less desirable would be furniture, appliances, and general household goods. The pledged property's value usually must exceed the amount of the loan.

Lacking suitable assets, the borrower may have someone cosign the loan as security. If the borrower cannot repay, the lender expects the cosigner to pay the loan. A cosigner must have a reasonable credit record. But never casually agree to cosign someone's loan: if the borrower misses one payment, some lenders quickly proceed against the cosigner. You may end up paying the loan to maintain your credit reputation. The quickest way to lose a friend is to cosign a loan.

Even with security, lenders consider your ability and willingness to repay the primary criterion. Most require you meet a minimum on their credit scoring system. Some adjust the score using your credit history. Even excellent collateral will not lead some lenders to approve borrowers with substandard credit records, since the costs of repossessing assets or pursuing cosigners are high.

Finance charges on a secured loan are often lower than on an unsecured loan. The assurance of the security reduces the lender's risk. Lenders will often make a secured loan for a large amount and for a longer time.

Secured loans expose borrowers to losing pledged assets or having the lender pursue the cosigner for repayment. Make certain you are within your debt limits before proceeding with a secured loan.

Strategy

Secured loans are attractive because they may offer a lower APR, higher upper dollar limits, and a longer maturity. However, if an unsecured loan offers comparable terms, take it.

Second Mortgage Cash Loan

Before discussing second mortgages, let's first look at what a mortgage is. Mortgages give a lender an interest in your property (typically a house and the surrounding land) as security on a loan. If you fail to repay the loan, the lender has the right to take the property. Then it is sold to repay the loan. Nearly all home purchases involve use of a first mortgage to obtain the loan needed (Chapter 9 examines this in detail). The "first" designation indicates the lender has primary claim on the property if you do not repay.

A **second mortgage** gives a lender the "second" interest in the property. Fail to repay the loan, and the lender may repossess the property. However, the holder of the first mortgage has to be repaid before the lender with the second mortgage receives anything. Suppose a house has a $65,000 first mortgage and a $20,000 second mortgage. The borrower fails to pay one of the loans: the house is seized and sold for $80,000. The lender with the first mortgage collects $65,000. The holder of the second mortgage collects only $15,000.

Amount you can borrow

To minimize their losses, lenders limit the combined first and second mortgages to less than the value of the house. A typical limit might be computed as follows:

■ Estimate the current market value of the property.	$ _____
■ Deduct current unpaid balance on first mortgage.	$ _____
■ The remainder is the owner's equity, or ownership value, in the property.	$ _____
■ Maximum loan is 60 percent (a conservative limit) to 80 percent (a liberal limit) of that equity.	$ _____

An example will illustrate. Helen purchased her house, current market value $90,000, using a $70,000 first mortgage. Her unpaid balance is now $66,000. How large a second mortgage can Helen obtain? Her equity is $24,000: $90,000 value − $66,000 first mortgage. Depending on the lender's limit, she can borrow from $14,400 (60% × $24,000) to $19,200 (80% × $24,000).

Why the increased popularity?

The increased popularity of second mortgage loans has several causes. One is that homeowners can tap their increasing home equity as security for a cash loan. Suppose Helen, from our last example, decides against the loan, but she reconsiders it in 5 years. Her potential loan will rise. Two forces raise the amount. Inflation and the housing market will push up the home's $90,000 value. A rise of 5 percent a year for 5 years would raise it to $114,865. That boosts her equity and with it the potential loan. Furthermore, continued payments lower the first mortgage loan's balance to $56,960. What can she borrow with a second mortgage (round the numbers to $115,000 and $57,000)? She can get from $34,800 to $46,400.

Another attraction of second mortgages is the large amount you can borrow. Our examples show that a reasonable equity in a home permits a large loan. This is especially true when your home's market value has risen sharply.

Competitive interest rates on second mortgages can be another attraction. The lender's secured position (the second mortgage) should limit the losses from nonpayment. That can be reflected in a moderate finance charge.

Possible tax savings is the final reason for their increased popularity. Under recent tax regulations, finance charges on most consumer cash and sales loans no longer qualify as an itemized deduction. But finance charges on housing-related loans—first and second mortgages, home equity loans—still qualify. While there are limits on loan size, the potential tax savings from deducting the charge may lower the net cost of the qualifying loans.

Costs of obtaining the loan

Obtaining a second mortgage often involves costs that most cash loans do not. First, the lender may impose an origination fee; 1 to 3 percent of the loan (the industry would say 1 to 3 "points") is typical. Second, the lender will probably want a current appraisal on the property. Third, you must pay for title insurance on the property. Finally, there are the costs of closing and recording the second mortgage. Because these costs must be paid to obtain the loan, they must be included in the loan's APR.

In practical terms, these fixed costs make small second mortgage loans too expensive. These loans are best if you need a large amount.

Are there risks?

Remember, you are pledging your house. Fail to repay the second mortgage, even if you make the payments on the first mortgage, and you could lose it. Unless the vista provided by living under a freeway overpass appeals to you, this is a disconcerting prospect. Second, some lenders have a series of payments like the following:

- Monthly payments for all but the last month merely cover the finance charge. On a $10,000 loan with a 15 percent APR that is a pleasantly low $125: $10,000 × 15%/12 months.
- But the last payment! It is $10,125! That is the entire $10,000 loan and the last's month's finance charge. That is called a "balloon" payment (there are other names for it, but we cannot print them). Rare is the borrower with the discipline to save for a "balloon." Insist

on equal monthly payments. If you cannot manage to fit them into your budget, you are at your upper debt limit.

Carefully compare a second mortgage's APR with those of comparable credit offers. Some second mortgage lenders specialize in granting credit to high-risk borrowers, but their high collection costs and losses force them to quote a very high APR.

Home Equity Cash Loan

A **home equity cash loan** takes your house as security. In fact, like a second mortgage, it gives the lender an interest in your property. The comments about second mortgages in the last section apply here. But a **home equity loan** also has some unique features that warrant separate consideration.

Home equity loans generally provide an open-ended **line of credit.** Once this is established, you can draw as much or little money as you need, up to the lender's established maximum. You pay a finance charge on the amount borrowed only for the time it is borrowed. Home equity loans resemble overdraft accounts in this regard, but the dollar amount can be higher because the lender has your property as security. Typical loan maximums are 60 to 80 percent of your equity in the property. A large equity will support a large loan.

To draw on your home equity, you notify the lender who issues the check. Since the loan is open-ended, you could make a number of small withdrawals. Your required monthly payments are computed when you draw the money. Usually, they are equal monthly amounts that extend the maturity over 10 years or more, though some offer the undesirable balloon payment with its whopping final payment.

Popularity of home equity loan

Like that of second mortgages, the popularity of home equity loans rests on several points. Owners can tap the equity in their homes to secure loans, often in large amounts. Lenders generally quote competitive APRs on these loans, since they are secured. Flexibility is an added advantage; you only borrow what you need, when you need it. But an assessment of the costs and risks suggests that the actual benefits may be more modest than they appear. Last, the finance charge on the loan may qualify as a deductible expense on your tax return.

Cost of obtaining a home equity loan

A home equity loan carries all the costs of a second mortgage: origination fee, appraisal cost, title insurance, and closing costs. You pay all of those costs just to establish your line of credit; $500 is not unusual. The loan's APR will *not* reflect that cost. Why not include them? To include these costs we would need to know the loan amount. But this is a line of credit; you decide how much to borrow once the loan is established. Add those costs to a short-term $500 loan, and the APR is breathtaking. Spread them across a long-term $10,000 loan, and the effect is minimal. That is why home equity loans are best for medium to large amounts: $5,000 and up.

Comparing a home equity loan to another credit offer. Let's compare a home equity loan's total cost to that for a secured cash loan. Lyle has two 48-month offers: (1) $5,000 home equity loan, carrying a 12 per-cent APR once Lyle pays $500 to establish the loan, or (2) $5,000 consumer cash loan with a 15 percent APR and no added costs. The first loan's annual percentage rate looks attractive, but what about the $500 fee? To end up with the $5,000 the second loan provides, Lyle will have to borrow $5,500; the additional $500 covers the fee. That is how we will compare costs: loan number 1 (adjusted for the $500 fee) and loan number 2 as is.

Payments on the adjusted $5,500 home equity loan are $144.81 ($26.33 payment per $1,000 from Exhibit 6.7 × $5,500/$1,000). Pay-ments on the second $5,000 loan are only $139.15 ($27.83 payment per $1,000 from Exhibit 6.7 × $5,000/$1,000). Despite its higher APR, the 15 percent cash loan has lower payments and is the best choice.

Suppose Lyle planned to borrow $10,000 rather than $5,000, but all other costs were the same. The home equity loan's $276.47 payment (we've adjusted for the $500 fee) is less than the cash loan's $278.30. The relative desirability of a home equity loan depends on the amount you borrow.

Strategy

Do not be misled by a home equity loan's APR. You must also include the cost to establish the loan.

Suitable uses for an equity loan

Equity loans are special in a number of ways. First, the setup costs restrict equity loans to larger amounts. Second, once it's established, you may tap the line of credit you establish on an ongoing basis. Third, pledging your house is a serious step; be certain you plan to use the credit wisely. Though the maturity on these loans can be 10 years or more, you should not use long-term loans for short-lived services and products. Finally, you must use this credit wisely. Having access to a line of credit may lead some borrowers to overuse it.

FINANCE CHARGES: FIXED OR VARIABLE RATE?

Once, consumer cash loans had **fixed finance charges.** The rate you were quoted when the loan began was what you paid throughout its life. Some lenders have added a new option: **a finance rate that varies.** The loan con-tract spells out how the "new" rate is determined and how often the rate can be changed. The rate is usually tied to some financial interest index over which the lender has little control; the prime interest rate and the rate on Treasury securities are both widely used. The "prime interest rate" is what banks quote on a business loan to large corporations with superior credit ratings.

A variable rate loan contract might specifiy:

- Interest rate is reset 6 months after the loan begins and every 6 months thereafter.
- The new interest rate will equal the prime interest rate on that date plus 2 percent.

Points to Consider: Fixed-Rate Loan

You know the finance charges and payments for a fixed-rate loan before you accept it. If interest rates change, you are unaffected; the lender accepts the risk of rate increases. But if rates drop, you can benefit only by repaying the loan early and refinancing; that may not be worth doing.

Points to Consider: Variable or Floating-Rate Loan

Generally, floating-rate loans have lower finance charges than fixed-rate ones. In return, you accept the risk of rate increases. If market interest rates decline, you benefit: the loan's cost drops. Conversely, as rates rise, so do your borrowing costs. And you will not know your total finance charge in advance. Likewise, your payments will not be fixed. A rise in rates may boost your monthly payments or force you to make an extra payment at the end. Of course, a rate decline lowers your payments.

Variable rate consumer cash loans are not universally available, and it is unclear how common they will become. Lenders prefer them; borrowers seem to favor fixed rates. If variable rate mortgages are any indication, it will be some time before borrowers accept variable rate consumer loans.

Fixed-Rate versus Variable Rate Loans

Your personal preference will be the basis when you decide between a fixed-rate and a variable rate loan: some people are uncomfortable with the uncertainty of the variable rate. Another factor is future interest rates; predicting the direction and magnitude of interest rates changes is difficult. If you believe future rates will be lower, a variable rate loan is the choice. If rates are expected to rise, a fixed-rate loan will be best. Finally, remember that a variable rate loan should have a lower APR than a fixed-rate loan. If it does not, you accept the risk of rate changes without being compensated.

MAJOR SOURCES OF CONSUMER CASH LOANS

Before you start shopping for a consumer cash loan, you need to know what options are available to you. Column 1 of Exhibit 7.1 summarizes the major sources for consumer cash loans. We'll discuss each of these in the sections that follow. Column 2 outlines the principal loan types each lender offers. Columns 3 and 4 of Exhibit 7.1 summarize the principal advantages and disadvantages of the various lenders. These are generalizations; lenders in your area may operate differently. Also, your personal credit record affects how lenders treat you. A brief strategy statement accompanies each listing.

Financial Institutions

- *Commercial banks.* Commercial banks have come far from the days when your income had to be high and credit record pristine for you to qualify for a loan. While hardly high-risk lenders, their definition of a "qualified" borrower is now more liberal. They offer a number of loan options. Collectively, they are one of the largest consumer lenders.
- *Mutual savings banks.* Mutual savings banks (MSBs) have expanded their options and become more aggressive lenders. But MSBs are almost exclusively found in the New England and the mid-Atlantic states.
- *Savings and loan associations.* Savings and loan associations

(S&Ls) are relative newcomers to consumer lending. Only in the last few years have they been allowed to offer consumer loans. Some S&Ls have become aggressive lenders. Others have been more cautious: the APR and maturity on their loans are little better than the competition's. The rest concentrate on issuing mortgages rather than on consumer lending.

- **Credit unions.** Credit unions have long granted consumer loans; that is, and is likely to remain, their principal business. To borrow money from a credit union, you must be a member. Some credit unions have made borrowing easier by liberalizing membership; everyone living within some area may qualify. If you qualify, definitely include a credit union among your potential lenders: their APRs are among the lowest.

Consumer Finance Companies

Consumer finance companies' initial specialty was lending to borrowers with weaker credit records. That involved extensive collection efforts and losses on uncollectible loans. For that reason, finance companies often charge higher fees than other lenders. To broaden their customer base,

Exhibit 7.1

Principal Advantages and Disadvantages of Major Consumer Lenders

Source of loan	Types of loans offered	Principal Factors to Consider		
		Advantages	Disadvantages	Strategy
Commercial bank	1, 2, 3, 4	APR is competitive. Borrower develops credit record and can use other financial services.	Requires established credit record. Marginal borrower may not qualify.	Commercial banks are a good place to begin your search.
S&L or MSB	1, 2, 3, 4	APR is usually competitive. Borrower develops credit record and can use other financial services.	Requires established credit record. Marginal borrower may be refused.	Check S&Ls or MSBs; some are aggressive lenders with low APRs.
Credit Union	1, 2, 3, 4	APR is among the lowest. Credit life is included as part of APR. Small loans and short maturities available.	You must be a member to qualify. Range of financial services is often limited.	Include a credit union; they often have the best APRs.
Consumer finance company	1, 2, 3, 4	Accepts borrowers with poor or limited credit record. Small loans available. Accepts variety of assets as security.	APR is often the highest among these lenders. Restrictive regulation can limit loan's usefulness. Offers no services beyond loans.	May be only choice for those with weak or limited credit history.
Brokerage firm	2, 4	APR is very competitive. Good source when you want to pledge financial assets as security.	Sizable cost to set up home equity loan. Offers no services beyond loan options.	May be a reasonable source if you have the required assets.

Key to types of loans offered:
1 Unsecured cash loan   3 Second mortgage home loan
2 Secured cash loan   4 Home equity loan

some have recently targeted loans to customers with average or better credit records. If you are in this group, they may quote more competitive finance charges.

Some states narrowly regulate consumer finance companies. They restrict loans to some limit, specify the maximum finance charge, or set the loan's maximum maturity. Others leave most of those decisions to the finance company.

Brokerage Firms

Brokerage firms have traditionally concentrated on selling investments such as common stocks, bonds, and mutual funds. They advanced money so customers could purchase investments with a partial payment: this is called "buying on margin." Recently, they have started making cash loans unrelated to any investment purchase. They will make cash loans using your common stocks, bonds, or mutual funds as security. Some also lend through home equity lines of credit.

Specialized Consumer Lenders

There are three specialized lenders you might consider when seeking a cash loan: the life insurance company, the loan broker, and the loan shark. Since they are rather specialized, not everyone can qualify.

Life insurance companies

Life insurance companies will only lend you money if you have accumulated a cash value in your insurance policy. You must have an insurance policy that accumulates a cash value: whole life, straight life, universal life, or limited-pay life, for example. That limits availability: many people have term insurance, which has no cash value. The accumulated cash value sets the loan maximum. Small policies or ones that have only been owned a few years have built little cash value.

Strategy

A life insurance loan can be a good short-term cash source if your policy has the cash value you need.

Loan brokers

Loan brokers do not lend money. Instead, they act as intermediates; they bring borrowers and lenders together. Brokers claim they have access to many lenders who are anxious to lend to people like you. For this service, brokers charge a fee.

Proceed with extreme caution when dealing with a loan broker. Tales of misrepresentation, exorbitant finance charges, breathtaking fees, phantom lenders, and other sordid practices are numerous. People who are so burdened with credit that they must resort to brokers need to take corrective action. One more debt is not going to rescue them.

Strategy

If your credit record is reasonable, you should not need the services of a loan broker. If it is not, turn your efforts to correcting the situation, not searching out brokers.

Loan sharks

A **loan shark** is an unlicensed, unregulated lender who makes loans that offer several special touches. Astronomical finance charges with three-digit APRs are typical. Maturities are as short as a few weeks or even days. The loan and all finance charges are due at once. Qualifying standards are often low. But the lender's idea of "security" for the loan can range from your possessions to your kneecaps. In their collection efforts, loan sharks tend to ignore the Fair Credit Collection Act.

Strategy

Don't use loan sharks. *There are plenty of reputable lenders. If they turn you down, you need major assistance with your finances.*

Shopping for Your Cash Loan

Exhibit 7.2's top checklist shows what you need to do before beginning a loan search. Loan applications always ask questions about your current income and debts, so update your records. An income statement and balance sheet (see Chapter 2) will provide that information. Before visiting lenders, list what you want: loan amount, maturity, type of payments, approximate finance charge, what you are willing to offer as security.

The lower section of Exhibit 7.2 summarizes the information you should get from each lender. It can be the basis for a comparative analysis. Write the facts down. Lenders should willingly provide this data; if they hesitate, look elsewhere.

Check at least three lenders, even if the first offer sounds attractive. You can then confirm that Friendly Fred's offer really is as good as claimed. Few credit offers are so good, or their life so short, that they cannot wait.

Exhibit 7.2

Checklist to Use When Shopping for a Cash Loan

Preliminaries List
1. Know how the money will be used.
2. Know how much money is needed.
3. Know how long a maturity you need.
4. Know what security you can pledge on the loan if required.
5. Collect current data on yourself (income, rent, present debts, monthly payments, savings).

6. List prospective lenders and rank by preference.
7. Prepare a current balance sheet and income statement. Does the balance sheet show all your assets?

Questions to Ask Prospective Lenders
1. What is the loan's finance charge (APR)?
2. What are the repayment terms?
3. Does the loan require security? What?
4. Are there late payment penalties?

5. Is there a prepayment penalty?
6. If loan is repaid early, how is the finance charge refund computed?
7. Is credit life insurance required?

CONSUMER SALES LOAN

Consumer sales loans appear in your life when you use credit to purchase some big-ticket item such as a car, furniture, or a major appliance. No cash changes hands; instead, you receive the merchandise in return for your promise to repay. The loan is secured by the purchased item.

You pay a part of the purchase price as a down payment. The balance is financed by the sales loan. Loans can be less than $100 for a small appliance or more than $20,000 for an auto, boat, or similar item. You repay in equal monthly installments, with maturities ranging from 6 to more than 60 months. The APR for the finance charge can range from 12 to more than 30 percent.

Most sales loans originate with the selling dealer, but few stop there. Nearly all dealers sell loans to a finance company, bank, or other lender. That way, the dealer receives cash without waiting 12 to 60 months for the borrower to repay the loan.

Role of the Lender Who Purchases the Loan

Most sales loans involve three parties: the buyer, the selling dealer, and the ultimate lender. The buyer and the dealer originate the loan agreement. Then the dealer sells the loan to another party. The buyer is expected to send the payments to that lender. But the buyer has had limited, if any, contact with the lender. This raises several issues.

Rebate

The purchasing lender rebates a portion of each loan's finance charge to the dealer for originating the loan. Offering an attractive rebate is one way a lender can encourage dealers to sell their loans. If the rebate is attractive, the dealer may push a sales loan hard, but the loan will not necessarily be to the customer's benefit. The dealer may select the lender offering the best rebate rather than the lowest APR.

Strategy

Avoid subsidizing the dealer's rebate. Compare the sales loan's APR with that of a similar cash loan to ensure the rate is competitive.

Corrective action from the dealer

Suppose Thelma Thrifty has used a sales loan to purchase a freezer from Fast Fred's Appliance. As part of the deal, it was to be "chuck full" of select beef. One meal convinced Thelma that the freezer was chuck full, but the beef was not tasty; her dog even preferred Wuffo Chow. Blessedly, the freezer soon quit working, reducing the meat to pulp. Unfortunately, when she called Fred, he argued *she* had a problem and suggested she solve it.

Thelma is furious. Can she withhold payment on the sales loan? Yes! Until Fred takes the necessary corrective action, Thelma can stop her payments. This makes the lender a party to the original sale. The lender must assist the buyer if payments are to resume. Since buyers can withhold payments, lenders have become more selective in choosing dealers; they want a dealer who will perform satisfactorily.

A few years ago, Thelma's tale would have had a different ending. Lenders would have claimed they were not party to the original sale. It would have been a battle between Thelma and Fred. The lender could force Thelma to repay the loan, even though the freezer was defective and the beef misrepresented.

Strategy

Buy from dealers who will perform satisfactorily. But if there is a dispute, withhold payment to force corrective action.

Repossession by the lender

The precise steps a lender must take to **repossess** an asset depend on state rules and regulations. But the results are universal: the lender takes physical possession of the property, though this must be done by legal means.

Once repossessed, the item is usually sold, with the money being used to repay the underlying loan. State regulations determine whether the sale must be public or private. In the unlikely case that the sale proceeds exceed the loan, the borrower receives the balance. If the proceeds are less than the balance owed, the borrower must pay the difference.

Repossession is a poor way to close a loan. First, you may have to repay part of the loan if the proceeds of the sale are inadequate. Second, some lenders make little effort to obtain the highest sale price. Third, if you really need the item, you may have to buy a replacement. Some repossession tactics may be legal but are questionable. Finally, repossession can seriously flaw your credit record.

If repossession looks possible, discuss your credit problems with the lender. Maybe a small, but steady, payment will forestall action. Failing that, see if the lender will let *you* sell the asset: you are far more likely to obtain a fair price. Or try to get a short-term cash loan to repay the lender. Then sell the asset and repay the temporary loan with the proceeds.

Strategy

Arrange your own rescue plan rather than let an asset be repossessed.

Balloon note on a loan

An earlier section introduced the **balloon note,** enticingly small monthly payments through the loan's life and a final giant one. For example, a 24-month, $4,000 loan with an APR of 24 percent could have the following terms:

- 23 monthly payments of $80 (essentially the finance charge on the loan)
- 1 final payment of $4,080 ($80 for the final month's finance charge plus the entire $4,000 loan)

It takes one *very* organized financial planner to handle that final payment. That $80 payment is so much less than for a loan with 24 equal payments—that $211.48 payment is according to Exhibit 6.7—that people convince themselves they will systematically save the needed money. Few do. If a balloon note is necessary to let you handle the loan, you simply cannot afford to borrow.

Acceleration clause

An **acceleration clause** in a contract makes the entire loan due immediately if you fail to make a payment on time. People who cannot make a payment are in no position to repay an entire loan. Fail to repay, and the lender moves to repossess the security. Acceleration clauses are widespread, so avoiding them is difficult.

CREDIT LIFE INSURANCE ON CONSUMER LOANS

Credit life insurance repays the balance on your loan at the time of your death. The policy pays the lender directly, so your survivors are not involved. The policy's payment is equal to the loan's unpaid balance.

Credit life insurance is frequently offered as an extra-cost option on loans. When the insurance is optional, premiums are *not* included in the loan's APR. If the lender requires you take the insurance, its cost becomes part of the quoted APR. Note that many credit unions include credit life insurance as a free benefit.

Coverage

Delbert Doomed borrows $9,000 in the form of a 48-month cash loan; he buys optional credit life coverage. As he leaves the bank, Delbert fails to notice the crosstown bus speeding up the street: credit life pays $9,000. But suppose Delbert makes 25 payments, leaving the unpaid balance at $5,111.95; that is what the policy pays if Delbert expires. Or, Delbert heads for the mailbox clutching his final payment, only to be flattened by a runaway steamroller. Credit life pays the final $264.33. Coverage is never more than the loan's outstanding balance.

How Premiums Are Computed

Most states specify the maximum premium on credit life insurance, typically $0.30 to $1 per $100 of loan. Lenders cry, "All that peace of mind and financial security for only pennies per week," but credit life is very expensive insurance.

Use Delbert's $9,000, 48-month, 18 percent APR loan as an example. The lender assured Delbert the premium was a low, low $0.80 per $100 of loan. Surprise one: the premium is based on the loan *plus* its finance charge. On the $9,000 loan, that totals about $12,687.84: ($29.37 payment per $100 from Exhibit 6.7 × $9,000 loan/$1,000) × 48 months. Delbert's annual premium is $101.50: ($12,687.84 total amount/$100 base) × 0.$80 premium per $100. Raise the APR or lengthen the maturity, and the premium rises because of the finance charge.

Surprise two: Delbert pays the same premium each year of the loan, even though his coverage declines with the balance. Over 4 years, Delbert's premiums total $406 ($101.50 per premium × 4 years).

Now for surprise three. Delbert must pay the entire premium immediately. Many borrowers do not have the necessary cash. "Don't worry," counsels the lender. "We will just toss that amount into your loan." The borrower pays a finance charge on top of what has become very expensive insurance. Delbert's $406 premium boosts the monthly payment $11.92. Over the loan's 48-month life, he will pay $572.16 in premiums.

What is no surprise is that this is exorbitant life insurance. Let's look at an inexpensive substitute.

Term Life Insurance: An Alternative to Credit Life

Let's glance ahead to a major topic of Chapter 11: **term life insurance.** First, term life is simple insurance: it only pays off when you die. It offers no savings plan, accumulates no cash value, and promises no annuity payment. This is precisely what you need: something to pay your debts if you die.

Let's compare the premiums on term life and credit life to see what you can save. For now, we will ignore the declining coverage of credit life insurance, $9,000 initially but only several hundred dollars at the end. For our calculation, we will use the initial $9,000 throughout.

A typical annual cost per $100 of coverage with term life insurance is:

- $0.20 for borrowers whose age is in the twenties
- $0.30 for borrowers who are in their thirties
- $0.45 for borrowers who are in their forties

If Delbert is 35 years old, premiums for 4 years' coverage on a $9,000 loan are $108: ($0.30 premium per $100 × $9,000 loan/$100 base) × 4 years. This is far less than the $406 credit life insurance premium. Would you substitute term life for a 75 percent cut in premiums? Certainly. Even better, this term life insurance's coverage is $9,000 throughout the life of the loan. And Delbert would pay $27 at the start of each year, not a $108 lump sum. He needs no financing.

Let us refine the calculation. Make the first year's coverage equal to the initial loan, the second year's equal to the unpaid balance at that time, and also use the unpaid balance for years 3 and 4. Required coverage for the 4 years is $9,000, $7,313, $5,296, and $2,884, respectively. Premiums for the 4 years total $73.48. Now term life is even more attractive.

Strategy

Before you accept credit life insurance, consider substituting term life insurance coverage.

Is Separate Credit Life Coverage Necessary?

A well-developed life insurance plan, such as the one we will discuss in Chapter 11, includes coverage for your unpaid loans. Any separate policy may be costly and unnecessary.

There are two times when credit life may be a worthwhile option. Borrowers whose health is too poor for term life insurance may find credit life a "cheap" policy. Or borrowers who are 55 to 64 years old may find the premiums to be competitive with those for term life. Even here, borrowers need to ask: Do I really need the coverage?

DISABILITY INSURANCE

Disability insurance is an extra-cost option on some sales and cash loans. If you become disabled and unable to work, the policy makes your loan payments. Some policies begin payments immediately. One with a 90-day waiting period will make no payment until you have been disabled for at least 90 days. Waiting periods reduce your premiums.

Is Disability Insurance Needed?

Do you need general disability insurance? Definitely. Do you need a policy that covers only one financial need? No. It's more sensible and much cheaper to meet all your needs in one policy. You may already have disability coverage through your employment, so no additional policy may be needed. If you don't, a single disability policy is a far better choice; more on this in Chapter 12.

OPEN-END CONSUMER CREDIT

With **open-end consumer credit,** you decide when you'll use credit and how much of it you'll use. Credit cards and charge accounts are examples of widely used types of open-end credit. The lender grants you a line of credit for future use: the lender sets your maximum.

Repayment terms for open-end credit are generally flexible. You can pay the entire balance, a major portion of it, or a minimum amount set by the lender. If you pay the full balance, you are often entitled to a 20- to 30-day period of free credit. If you pay only a part, you are assessed a finance charge based on the balance.

Charge Accounts

Department stores, drugstores, utility companies, doctors, and other firms and professionals offer **charge accounts.** You can only use the credit for the products and services they provide. However, many businesses eliminated charge accounts when they started accepting credit cards.

Regular charge account

Your purchases on a **regular charge account** accumulate and are billed once each month. You are expected to pay the balance within 30 days. Failure to pay within that period may subject the user to a finance charge of 1 to 1.5 percent per month.

Revolving charge account

A **revolving account** allows you to extend payments over more than 30 days. You pay for the privilege: there is a finance charge of 1 to 1.5 percent per month. Required minimum payments can be a fixed dollar amount ($30 payment on a $300 balance) or a percentage (pay at least 10 percent of the balance). Remitting the minimum lets you repay the account in 12 to 24 months.

Credit Card Accounts

Credit cards range from those that can only be used at one business to general-purpose cards that can be used at a whole range of national, even international, firms. Credit cards have become one of the most widely used types of consumer credit. Let's look at three types of cards:

1 Bank-affiliated cards

2   National retail store cards
3   Travel and entertainment cards

Bank credit cards

Bank credit cards (MasterCard, VISA) are offered by affiliated financial institutions throughout the United States. While they are called "bank" cards, they are also offered by S&Ls, MSBs, and credit unions. Your bank credit card account will be administered by a financial institution or service company in your area; it will send out billings, collect payments, and handle your special account needs.

The entity that administers your account decides your upper limit. Your income and other credit characteristics determine that maximum. The usual minimum is around $300; maximums in excess of $5,000 are common for those with excellent credit records. If you exceed your limit, many institutions assess a fee, and they require you to pay enough to drop the balance below your limit.

You typically pay an annual fee of $15 to $25 for a credit card. Those that do not carry an annual fee may charge every time you use the card, but the practice is not widespread. Most cards provide a grace period during which there is no finance charge. Some assess a finance charge from the moment an item is charged.

Strategy

A bank credit card is convenient consumer credit. It is especially useful when a personal check is unacceptable.

Is it for convenience or credit? The financial institution or service company that administers a bank credit card sets its own terms: grace period, annual fee, APR, credit limit, and other fees. Compare competing cards to see which best meets your needs. If you plan to use the card for convenience, seek a long grace period and low annual fee. Since you will pay in full each month, a low finance charge means little. The opposite holds if payments will extend for months: a low finance charge is paramount. The grace period is of little concern.

Strategy

You may want two bank credit cards: one for "convenience" (long grace period and low annual fee) and one for "credit" (moderate finance charge and high credit limit).

Extended-payment supplement. Bank credit cards such as MasterCard and VISA provide the option of charging big-ticket items to a separate **extended-payment supplement.** If you use the supplement, the seller must obtain approval from the company that administers your card. If approved, you specify the desired repayment period: 6 to 36 months is usual. Finance charges begin immediately; there is no grace period.

Strategy

Compare the APR on an extended-payment supplement with a similar cash or sales loan to make certain it is competitive.

Cash advance. You can obtain a **cash advance** using your credit card. The maximum you can borrow is the unused portion of your credit limit. Finance charges will begin immediately. A similar short-term cash source is the automatic cash advance on your payment account. Either can give you quick access to cash, but an advance on your credit card is easier to get when you are out of town.

Strategy

An advance from your credit card can provide a quick source of cash. If your checking account has an automatic overdraft, compare the two APRs to select the best.

"Silver," "gold," and other "precious" cards. Bank credit card vendors offer "premium" cards that entitle you to added services. To qualify, you meet higher credit standards and pay a larger annual fee: $30 to $50 is typical. Extra services include a higher credit limit, free traveler's checks, travel insurance (Harvey Sweatypalm's relatives collect if he "departs" while riding on public transportation), free credit life, and plain old *snob* appeal.

Will they really say "Ah!" when Harvey flashes his gold card? Perhaps. Is it worth it? Unless you need and use the extra services, no.

National retail credit cards

Credit cards from national retailers and oil companies (Sears, J. C. Penney, Shell) provide credit over a broad geographic area. But you are limited to the products and services these retailers offer. Usually there is no annual fee, and most offer a grace period of 20 to 30 days. If you do not pay the entire balance, the finance charge is around 1.5 percent per month. Some oil credit cards offer extended terms only on large purchases.

Strategy

People who drive extensively should consider one or more oil company cards. People who make many purchases at one of the national retailers should consider using their charge card.

Travel and entertainment cards

Travel and entertainment (T&E) cards such as American Express are widely accepted by hotels, restaurants, airlines, rental car companies, and other travel-related businesses here and abroad.

For you to qualify for these cards, your income must exceed some minimum: $20,000 or more should do it. The annual fee for the basic card is $40 to $50. Except for certain major purchases, you are expected to repay the entire balance within 30 days of billing. Pay the account late, and you will be assessed a fee. Chronic late payments are grounds for your leaving home *without* your card.

If you choose to make extended payments, expect to pay a finance charge of 1 to 1.5 percent per month. Several cards offer cash advances, but their terms are more restrictive than with a bank credit card.

Strategy

People who travel extensively may want a T&E card. For others, a major bank credit card will do nearly as well.

Credit Cards and Charge Accounts: Potential Benefits

Properly used, credit cards can help you manage your finances. We have mentioned before the usefulness of credit card receipts in helping you track your spending. The cards also provide other benefits. For many people, the chief of these is the opportunity to make use of the issuer's money without paying a finance charge by taking advantage of the grace period. Many value the convenience and flexibility the card provides when they make purchases.

Finance charge—free grace period

With most credit cards, if you pay the entire balance by the due date, you avoid finance charges. There are usually 20 to 30 days between your card's billing date and its due date, but you may have more time. Remember, your purchase is not posted until the merchant submits your charge slip for collection. Large retail stores do that immediately; smaller ones may accumulate charges for days before submitting them. Then the charge is posted to your statement, but it may be days or weeks before the statement is closed and you are billed. As a result, you can have anywhere from 20 to more than 50 days from the time you make the purchase until you pay for it. During that time, you use credit without paying a finance charge.

Reduce the cost of a temporary cash shortfall. Suppose your checkbook balance is a bit short when your credit card payment is due. Late payment means a finance charge, perhaps a large one. You expect to have the funds in a few days, but where can you get the money immediately? Why not tap the automatic overdraft on your payment account? Midge's average daily balance on her credit card is $500; failure to pay on the due date subjects her to a $7.50 finance charge ($500 balance × 1.5% monthly finance charge). She expects to repay her overdraft within 10 days. Drawing the needed $500 from her payment account only costs $2.06: $500 advance × 15% finance fee × 10 days/365 day year.

Strategy

To avoid credit card finance charges, consider drawing the money from your automatic overdraft for a few days.

Convenience   A credit card or charge account can be a convenient payment option. You don't have to carry large amounts of cash. Second, credit cards are often more readily accepted than personal checks, especially if you are outside your home area. Third, a credit card can bridge a temporary difference between your income and your debts. Finally, the cash advance feature of some cards can provide funds while you are traveling.

Improved record keeping   Credit card and charge account billings and charge slips give you a detailed record of your spending. This is especially useful when you build your monthly budget. You can pay for many purchases in a month and only use one or two checks. That simplifies your payment account reconciliation and can lower your fee for that account.

Credit Cards and Charge Accounts: Potential Problems and Pitfalls   Credit cards and charge accounts are not all benefits. They present some problems and pitfalls. Some of these you can't guard against—for instance, the possibility that you'll buy a defective product with your credit card or end up with an erroneous charge on your statement. But you do need to know what your rights are in these situations and what procedures to follow. There are other pitfalls that it's your responsibility to avoid "falling" into: specifically, giving in to the seductions of "easy" credit and overusing your accounts, and getting mired in the "minimum payment rut."

Billing disputes   The Fair Credit Billing Act has done much to improve your bargaining position if you dispute an item in your account. You might dispute an item charged to your account that you didn't purchase, a charge for the wrong amount, a credit not posted to your account, even a simple arithmetic error. Creditors must establish procedures customers can follow to resolve **billing disputes.**

Exhibit 7.3 summarizes the steps and timetable specified in the Fair Credit Billing Act. The left side of the exhibit outlines the creditor's actions. Your role as the customer is shown on the right side of that exhibit. Many creditors maintain toll-free telephone numbers that you can use to inquire about your account.

Strategy

You must write the card issuer to explain your billing dispute. But if the lender has a toll-free number, use it to check on the problem or to clarify the steps you need to take.

Defective articles or services

If you purchase a deficient product or service using your credit card, you may be able to withhold payment. First, you must give the seller a chance to correct the problem. The purchase must be for more than $50; small items are not covered. And the purchase must have been in your home state or within 100 miles of your home. If all of these conditions are met, you can withhold payment until the seller corrects the problem.

Excessive use of credit

The availability and acceptability of credit cards and charge accounts can cause problems. Some people find it easy to charge items or services rather than paying immediately. They ignore the fact that they will have to pay at some future date. When the bill arrives, they are astonished by what they owe. You can avoid this problem.

First, know what you have charged to your account. If you use it extensively, jot down the amount for each use in your checkbook, personal calendar, or a small notebook.

Second, don't charge items on impulse. Rationalizations like "I deserve a treat" or "it will be weeks until the bill comes" can produce whopping credit card bills.

Third, don't buy a sale item just because its price is reduced. Large savings do not create bargains if you do not need the product. Resist the urge to "stock up" on an item unless you have definite need for it in the future.

Fourth, fully pay your credit card bills on the due date or as soon as you can. Don't let your credit balance creep up on you.

Finally, if you cannot control your urge to charge, close your credit card accounts. Drastic? Yes. But some people need to do it to get off the credit card cycle.

"Minimum payment rut"

The minimum payment on credit cards and charge accounts is small. That helps when you are short of funds, but it also stretches the payments out over 24 to 36 months. Because your payment is minimal, much of it goes to pay the finance charge. Small payments can trap you in a **minimum payment rut;** you send in money, but the balance hardly declines.

You might use a cash loan to repay a credit card balance, if it will take months to repay. Often the loan's APR is lower. Meanwhile, use your credit card only when you can pay the entire balance on the due date.

Exhibit 7.3

Steps to Take to Resolve a Billing Dispute on a Credit Card or Charge Account

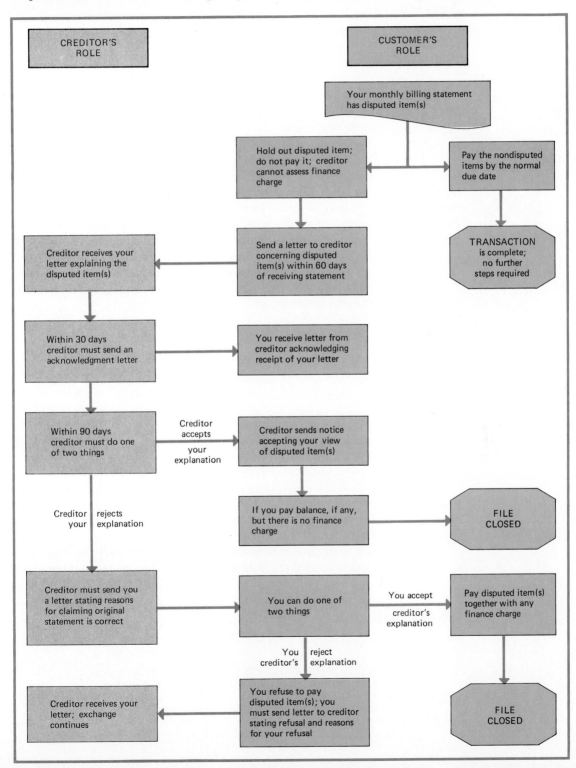

Strategy

Use the minimum payment option only during temporary financial emergencies. If you need more than 6 months to repay a credit card balance, get a cash loan.

Offers of credit life and disability coverage

Credit cards and charge accounts often provide insurance coverage. Most of the time, you are covered for the account balance by one or more insurance policies. The insurance is optional, so you will be billed for the premium.

If you believe the advertising copy, you wonder how you survived this long without insurance. Even motherhood and apple pie sound suspect compared to the claimed benefits. Should old Sidney expire while sipping margaritas by moonlight, his relatives need not worry: his $38.13 credit balance will be paid. Let a wayward 747 obliterate the pool and Sidney, and his heirs will receive double indemnity—$76.26! Ask yourself: Do I need this coverage? Will it duplicate insurance I already have? Even if you need this protection, it is usually cheaper and more logical to address all your needs with a single policy. A well-developed insurance program (see Chapters 11–13) makes far more sense.

Strategy

Avoid the fragmented coverage of credit card and charge account insurance. If you need coverage, consolidate insurance in a single policy.

Lost or stolen credit cards

Lose a credit card and you may be liable for up to $50 of any unauthorized charges to your account. But if you notify the card issuer before the card is used, you owe nothing: immediate notification of the card issuer is essential.

Exhibit 7.4 shows the steps you take to report a lost card. You can prepare yourself. For each credit card, keep an index card showing the name, address, and telephone number of the issuer. Keep only those credit cards you use frequently; cancel the others.

A credit card notification service: Needed? There are firms that specialize in notifying issuers if you lose a credit card. For an annual fee, they

Exhibit 7.4

Steps to Take to Report Missing Credit Cards

1. Call card issuer and report loss.
2. Take down the name of the person with whom you discuss the loss.
3. Send card issuer a certified letter. Save receipt to prove notification.
4. Examine subsequent billings for charges made by someone else.
5. *Note:* Homeowners or renter's policy may cover losses up to $500.

promise to inform each issuer of your loss. Necessary? We doubt it. If you have a good record-keeping system (see the preceding section), you should be able to do that quickly. While these firms suggest you could lose big with a stolen card, remember $50 is the maximum.

Debit Cards

Debit cards are offered by MasterCard and VISA, and by some large ATM networks. They look like credit cards; you would be hard pressed to tell the two apart. But they operate quite differently. A credit card generally gives you 20 or more days to pay for an item. Not so with a debit card; your account is charged immediately.

Some issuers proudly point out that debit cards lack the credit card's annual fee. But remember, no credit is extended. Unlike a credit card, a debit card does not expand your purchasing power. Those who pay the entire balance on their credit cards appreciate the grace period. Debit cards have none.

Debit cards have the same effect writing a check on your account does. A check gives you a "float" while it clears. Unfortunately, debit card charges often clear your account more quickly. Though issuers argue that debit cards are more acceptable than personal checks outside your home area, so are credit cards, and they give you more time to pay. Another supposed benefit is that debit cards offer reduced fees. Still, a good minimum balance payment account has no fees to "save." And you can't use a debit card to make mail payments: you still need a payment account.

Lose your debit card and discover another difference. Notify the issuer within 2 days of discovering your loss, and you are liable for no more than $50. Wait more than 2 days, and that rockets to $500. Wait more than 60 days after a bogus transaction appears on your account statement, and your losses are unlimited. Yes, Mildred, they can and will take the whole farm.

Strategy

Two words say it all for debit cards: totally underwhelming.

Summary

1   Consumer cash loans can be secured or unsecured. Usually, security is either a pledged asset or the pledge of a cosigner to pay the note if the borrower defaults.

2   A second mortgage loan is secured by your house. If your home equity is sizable, the loan can be large.

3   A home equity loan typically has a line of credit which you can draw on as needed.

4   There are significant costs for establishing second mortgage or home equity loans. They are included in the second mortgage loan's APR but not in the APR for a home equity loan.

5   Usually, cash loans have a fixed APR, but some now offer variable, or floating, APRs.

6   Major sources for consumer cash loans are commercial banks, S&Ls, MSBs, credit unions, consumer finance companies, and brokerage firms. All offer at least two types of loans.

7   Major features of a sales loan are:
   ▪ The loan is used to purchase a costly item.
   ▪ It provides no cash.
   ▪ The borrower, the dealer, and the lender are parties to the loan.

8   Borrower can withhold payment on a sales loan to force corrective action from dealer.

9   Allowing lender to repossess the pledged asset is not a good way to repay a loan.
10 Loans with balloon payments offer low monthly payments until the final one, which may be the entire amount borrowed.
11 Credit life is often much more expensive than term life coverage.
12 Most borrowers should purchase one large life or disability insurance policy rather than the coverages offered on cash loans, credit cards, and charge accounts.
13 The lender establishes the credit limit on open-end credit, but you decide how and when to use the credit.
14 A credit card can be used as a "convenience" or as a source of credit.
15 Benefits from credit cards and charge accounts include:

- Grace period with no finance fee
- Convenience
- Improved records

16 Major problems and pitfalls that you may run into with credit cards and charge accounts are:
- Billing disputes with issuer
- Excessive use of credit
- Becoming trapped in the "minimum payment rut"

17 The most you pay for unauthorized use of a lost credit card is $50; once the card issuer is notified, you are no longer responsible for losses.
18 Debit cards extend no grace period to the user; checking or savings account is charged immediately.

Review your understanding of

Unsecured personal loan	Acceleration clause
Automatic overdraft	Credit life insurance
Secured personal loan	Term life insurance
Cosigner	Disability insurance
Second mortgage cash loan	Open-end consumer credit
Home equity cash loan	Charge account:
Line of credit	Regular
Fixed finance charge	Revolving
Variable finance charge	Bank credit card:
Consumer finance company	Extended-payment supplement
Brokerage firm	Cash advance
Loan broker	Grace period
Loan shark	Billing dispute
Consumer sales loan	Minimum payment rut
Repossession	Debit card
Balloon note	

Discussion questions

1   What are the advantages and disadvantages of taking out a secured rather than an unsecured cash loan? Would the lender prefer one over the other?
2   Yvonne Yuppie has asked her friend to cosign her loan. Her friend asks: Why do you need that? What is involved? Explain this "routine" request to Yvonne's friend.
3   How is a second mortgage loan like a home equity loan. How do they differ?

4   Why is it relatively expensive to establish a second mortgage loan or a home equity loan? How do these costs affect their APRs? Explain.
5   What are the advantages and disadvantages of fixed-rate loans? Variable rate loans? Which would you prefer? Why?
6   The APR on many consumer finance company loans is high. Why?
7   Helmut Maki has the three offers for a 12-month, $1,000 cash loan that are shown below:

	Loan 1	Loan 2	Loan 3
Lender	Commercial bank.	Credit union.	Consumer finance company.
Special points	Will use automatic overdraft on NOW account.	Unsecured personal cash loan.	Unsecured personal cash loan.

What are the principal differences between the loans? What advantages or disadvantages should Helmut be aware of?

8   What steps should a prospective borrower take before visiting potential lenders?

9   How does a consumer sales loan differ from a cash loan? Can the two be interchanged? What factor(s) would you take into account if you had to decide between the two?

10 The auto Ron purchased from Ageless Auto Sales has never run right, despite Ageless's repair efforts. Ron still has more than 45 months to go on his 48-month automobile sales loan. What would you suggest he do? Could Ron have taken your suggested action in the past? How might Ron minimize such problems in the future?

11 Why is it a poor idea to allow repossession of an asset pledged as security for a loan? What options might the borrower use to avoid repossession?

12 How should you decide if you need credit life insurance? What are its advantages? Disadvantages? How can you reduce the cost of the coverage you need?

13 What are the advantages to the holder of a bank credit card? What do banks gain by offering the cards? What might explain their rapid growth? What do you see for the future?

14 Betty Perfection noted that her May credit card statement showed a payment of $135.35; yet she had written the check for $135.37, which equaled her unpaid balance. She was assessed a $2.03 finance charge because she did not pay the entire balance. What should Betty do?

15 While vacationing in Deadwood, Juan purchases a "rare" emerald ring. At home, a jeweler appraises it as a nicely cut piece from a Heineken bottle. Does Juan have to pay the credit card charge for the ring? Explain.

16 Fred Forgetful just discovered he "mislaid" a credit card. What should he do? Fred's next statement has a $2,475 charge for 2 one-way tickets to Casablanca. Fred cannot remember being there. Discuss the consequences.

17 A recent advertisement from Last Ditch Savings states: "Our new debit card: it has all the convenience of a credit card, but no annual fee and you never pay a finance charge." Is this card a "cheap" substitute for a credit card? Discuss.

Problems

7.1 Orphial Parchenski has three offers for the $1,000 loan she wants:

	Loan 1	Loan 2	Loan 3
Lender	Bank credit card	Mutual savings bank	Credit union
Type of loan	Cash advance	Cash loan	Cash loan
Security	None	None	Auto
APR	18%	12%	11%
Period to repay	1–24 months	12 months	12 months
Computation of finance charge	Simple interest	Precomputed	Simple interest

Orphial expects to repay the loan in 12 months, but if her finances permit, she may repay sooner.

a What is the monthly payment for each loan, assuming a 12-month maturity? (*Hint:* Exhibit 6.7 or Appendix A.1 may help.)

b What is the total finance charge for each loan?

c Which loan would you recommend? Why?

d Do any of the loans have special features that Orphial should consider?

7.2 Eliot Sanderman recently received a brochure extolling the merits of using his "trapped" equity to back a home equity loan. The brochure noted:

■ The lender establishes a credit line the borrower can use as needed.

■ The credit line cannot exceed 70 percent of the owner's equity.

■ The borrower pays a 2 percent origination fee and second mortgage closing costs.

■ Amounts drawn on credit line carry a 12 percent APR

Eliot estimates his house's current market value is $93,000; he paid $78,000 5 years ago. Payments have reduced his mortgage balance from $64,740 to $53,930.

a Explain to Eliot the difference between a line of credit and a loan.

b What is Eliot's maximum line of credit? (*Hint:* The example in the chapter may help.)

c Why is the lender willing to make the sizable loan? *Optional question:* What is the minimum the house could be sold for and still repay both the mortgage and Eliot's maximum loan in (b)?

d What are the advantages of this loan? Disadvantages?

e How does the cost of setting up the credit line affect Eliot's cost of credit?

7.3 Morris Bumbler cannot decide whether to take credit life insurance on his $6,000, 3-year, 18 percent APR loan. The lender volunteered that the premium is $0.80 per $100 per year, small price for "peace of mind." That premium is assessed on the initial loan plus its associated finance charges. The lender notes: "Most of our borrowers finance the premium and pay it off over the life of the loan. Your monthly payment is a low, low $6.77."

  a What dollar amount would the premium be assessed on? (*Hint:* Exhibit 6.7 or Appendix A.1 may help.)
  b What is the total insurance premium if Morris makes the monthly payment?
  c Monthly payments drop the loan's approximate unpaid balance to $4,345 at the end of 1 year, and to $2,366 at the end of 2 years. How much insurance coverage will Morris receive?
  d An insurance agent offered Morris term life with premiums of $4 per $1,000 of coverage per year. What is the annual cost of purchasing term coverage equal to the original $6,000 loan? For the entire period?
  e What would you suggest Morris do? Why?

7.4 Liz Krantz has price quotations from two dealers on the new camera and accessories she wants for her vacation:

	Local camera dealer	*Mail-order dealer*
Total cash price	$700	$650
Credit offered	Credit card or sales loan	None

Liz does not have the money; she will finance the purchase for about 12 months. Her credit alternatives include:

	Credit Alternative			
	1	*2*	*3*	*4*
Source	Dealer	Credit card	Commercial bank	Credit union
Description of credit offer	Sales loan	Extended payments	Automatic overdraft	Unsecured cash loan
Maturity	12 months	12 months	12 months	12 months
APR	15%	18%	15%	12%
Special notes			Will accept more rapid payment	Includes credit life insurance

  a What is the monthly payment for each alternative? What is the total cost of each one?
  b What are the strengths of each credit alternative? The weaknesses?
  c Which option would you recommend? Why?

7.5 Ken Montgomery's bank credit card account currently has a $415 balance that is due July 20. Because his vacation cost more than he intended, Ken cannot make the entire payment.

       He can make the $15 minimum payment. That subjects him to a finance charge of 1.5 percent per month on the average daily balance. (Ken's daily balance is $415.)

       Ken could draw the required $415 from his automatic overdraft checking account. Its 15 percent APR finance charge is based on the daily balance of the outstanding overdraft. Ken expects to repay the overdraft in about 20 days.

  a What finance charge will Ken pay for missing the grace period? (*Hint:* Exhibit 6.10 may be of interest.)
  b Is the checking overdraft an option? Is it cheaper?
  c Assume Ken continues to make the $15 minimum payment. How many months will it take to repay the balance? What total finance charge would Ken pay? (*Hint:* The 18 percent APR column in Exhibit 6.7 should help.)

Case problem

Eric and Ingrid Svensen have decided to replace their kitchen stove and refrigerator. The replacement units they want are handled by the local appliance dealer. The dealer's price is $1,800 and he will handle all the financing problems. Eric and Ingrid think the dealer's sales loan is a bit costly: a 24-month loan, an APR of 30 percent, with credit life and disability insurance included as extra-cost items. The monthly payment, with extras, would be $103.88. But they feel they are fortunate that the dealer will make the small loan. Both doubt their bank or credit union would make an $1,800 loan.

1   Is a sales loan their only option? What would be an alternative?
2   What is your opinion of the above loan? Do you see any problems with it?
3   What would be the saving if the Svensens could find the same 24-month loan with an APR of 12 percent? Of 15 percent? (*Hint:* Exhibit 6.7 may be helpful.)
4   The Svensens could charge the two units on their bank credit card (their limit is $2,000) and make the minimum monthly payment. What are the strengths and weaknesses of this option?
5   How should the Svensens decide about the credit life and disability insurance? If they decide that the coverage is needed, what would you recommend?

Consumer expenditures

PART

3

CHAPTER 8

Major consumer purchases: Automobiles and appliances

AFTER COMPLETING THIS CHAPTER YOU WILL HAVE LEARNED

- The five major categories of automobiles
- What it costs to own and operate an automobile
- Why buying a smaller-size auto often reduces the total ownership cost
- How to estimate the ownership costs for your auto
- How to compute a "fair" price on a car before visiting dealers
- How to compare the costs of ownership and leasing
- The four criteria for evaluating major home appliances
- What a service contract offers and who should have one
- How to interpret appliance energy-cost labels
- When the added cost for a high-efficiency appliance is justified
- How to select a payment option for major appliance purchases

*P*urchasing, maintaining, and operating automobiles and home appliances is expensive. The purchase price is your most obvious cost. Still, what you pay for operating and maintaining these goods often exceeds the original cost.

We need a way to rationally assess purchasing, maintaining, and operating expensive products. Auto ownership requires a major financial commitment and appliance purchases are not far behind. Proper selection is important. Once, cosmetic engineering created little more than an appearance of difference. Now there are substantive differences between different brands and models; they affect the service you receive and your costs.

Automobile ads would make us believe our auto confers social status, reflects our success, and makes us attractive. But remember, an auto's primary purpose is to carry you from place to place.

Purchasing an auto means looking beyond its price. Two autos might have the same price tag, yet involve radically different costs. Maintenance and operating costs are large and they continue. If you choose wisely, those costs can be reduced.

We will develop a model to help you calculate the costs of car ownership. Even if, in a fit of vehicular lust, you decide the high priced Piggo coupé is the real "you," at least you will know its costs.

CLASSIFYING AUTOMOBILE MODELS

The federal government **classifies automobiles** according to passenger and luggage space. Mark that a major improvement over the previous classification based on exterior size with no concern for how efficiently that "space" was utilized. **Five classifications are used: minicompact, subcompact, compact, midsize, and large.** Each category has a minimum combined passenger and luggage space (see Exhibit 8.1). To help you classify cars, the government publishes an annual "Gas Mileage Guide" that lists each model's available space; most car dealers can provide a copy.

COST OF AUTOMOBILE OWNERSHIP

Most car owners underestimate their cost for driving. Why? They include fuel, maintenance, and repairs, but few remember depreciation, insurance, taxes, and license fees.

Fixed Costs of Ownership

The **fixed costs of ownership** vary little with miles driven. The largest fixed cost is depreciation: the decline in your car's market value over time. The decline is mostly due to age; older cars, except for antique autos, are worth less than new ones. If you drive more than the "average"—about 9,000 miles annually—depreciation accelerates.

Financing the purchase is your next largest fixed cost. The finance charge on your auto loan could be with you for 5 years. Even paying cash costs you. You lose the interest on the money you tied up in the car. With a loan, you also have "lost" interest—in this case, on your down payment.

Other fixed costs include insurance, personal property taxes, and license fees.

People who drive little—Maude just drives to church on clear days—will have almost the same fixed costs as an average driver of an equal car. Even those who drive 20 to 30 percent more than average may not have much higher fixed costs, though those who drive 2 or 3 times the average will.

Variable Costs of Ownership

The **variable costs of ownership** rise with mileage. Fuel is usually the largest variable cost, but maintenance and repairs can be high if you drive a great deal.

Those who drive a large number of miles will have high variable costs. But Maude, who drives little, will pay little for gas, maintenance, and repairs.

Combined Cost of Owning and Operating an Auto

Several different groups publish studies on the costs of automobile ownership. One of the more useful is compiled by Hertz Corporation; it will be used here. Exhibit 8.2 gives the approximate cost per mile to operate subcompact, compact, midsize, and large cars which are kept 5 years and driven 10,000 miles annually.

Exhibit 8.1

Comparison of Vehicle Weight, Vehicle Length, and Usable Passenger and Luggage Space for the Five Major Automobile Size Classifications

Car model		Typical overall length	Typical total weight	Usable passenger and luggage space
Minicompact		152 inches	1,880 pounds	Less than 85 cubic feet
Subcompact	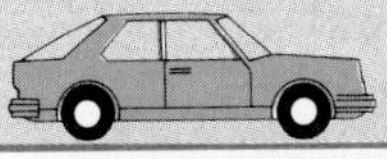	165 inches	2,158 pounds	85 to 100 cubic feet
Compact		175 inches	2,500 pounds	100 to 110 cubic feet
Midsize		185 inches	2,800 pounds	110 to 120 cubic feet
Large	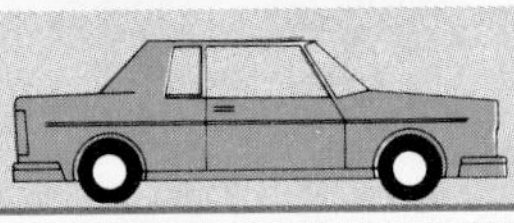	200 inches	3,500 pounds	More than 120 cubic feet

Source: Gas Mileage Guide and author's estimates.

Exhibit 8.2 suggests costs rise with the size of car. Subcompacts are cheapest and large cars most expensive. Second, owning and operating a car costs far more than many people imagine. The 40 to 50 cents it costs per mile far exceeds the 5 to 10 cents in fuel costs. If you are average, driving 9,000 miles annually, you have major automotive expenses.

Comments on the study

No study can account for all the variables that make up auto ownership costs; certain assumptions and compromises are made to find an average. Exhibit 8.2's costs are for 1985; they may have been increased by inflation since then. Hertz assumed the car was kept 5 years; extending or shortening the time will lower or raise costs. Raising or lowering purchase prices affects costs. Even the area where you live has a bearing on your costs.

The Hertz study is still valuable. It shows the high cost of auto ownership. Even with inflation, the differential it lists between models will continue. You can always update costs with the CPI. Finally, the costs are accurate enough for our decision models.

FACTORS THAT CAN AFFECT YOUR TOTAL COSTS

A number of factors affect your costs, but you can control some of them. Purchase price affects your depreciation losses as well as what you pay in finance charges. The size of your car affects your costs in ways you may not be aware of. So does the choice you make about when to trade in your car. This can push your total costs up or down by as much as one-fourth. You can control these costs only if you make informed, rational decisions.

Exhibit 8.2

Per Mile Cost of Owning Different-Size Cars for 5 Years While Driving a Total of 50,000 Miles

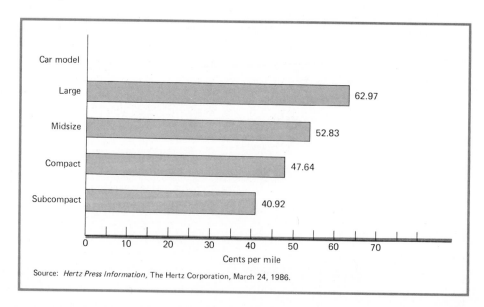

Source: *Hertz Press Information,* The Hertz Corporation, March 24, 1986.

Length of Ownership

For a number of reasons, the **ownership period** affects your costs for owning the car. Autos depreciate most rapidly when they are new. A car can lose 20 to 30 percent of its value in the first year. The often-made claim that "your first drive around the block costs $2,000 to $3,000" is not without merit. Generally, the longer you own a car, the lower its annual depreciation. Finance costs also decline over time and end when the loan is repaid. Insurance premiums lessen as the car's value sinks. However, repair and maintenance costs rise as the car's age and mileage increase. On balance, your per mile cost declines through the tenth year of ownership.

Exhibit 8.3 illustrates ownership costs for 1 year, 3 years, 5 years, and 10 years. Trading annually rather than every 5 years boosts your per mile cost 15 to 20 percent. Hold your car for 10 rather than 5 years, and the per mile cost drops 20 to 25 percent. That "new car" smell comes dear.

Which ownership period?

People often trade cars frequently to avoid "expensive" repairs. They seem to think spending $6,000 to trade cars beats paying $60 for a new battery. Trading to avoid regular maintenance expenses makes little sense, but trading to avoid recurring major repair expenses is probably justified. Use your experience as a guide. A string of $300 to $500 repairs may signal that it's time to trade. Ask the service manager where you have your car serviced whether you should put more money into your present car.

Strategy

Your repair experience can signal when to replace your car. Costly, recurring repairs can signal it is time.

Purchase Price of the Automobile

The most prestigious auto's market value will fall over time, but some resale values drop more slowly than others. The higher the purchase price, the larger the depreciation. The percentage decline on a $15,000 car is about the same as on a $10,000 model. But the price is 50 percent higher, so more money is lost. Options can raise a car's price and mean more depreciation. Should every one drive the "plain vanilla" model? No. But only a fraction of the money the "grand luxe" model costs will come back when you trade or sell.

Size Category of Automobile

Exhibit 8.2 shows that ownership costs and auto size are directly related. Smaller cars generally have lower costs for fuel, insurance, maintenance, and repairs. Less expensive models also have lower depreciation.

Exhibit 8.4 summarizes the potential savings for smaller models. Savings are possible. Does a shift from a midsize to, say, a compact *always* save money? Not quite. A Jaguar is a compact—ah, the leather, the walnut—but its stratospheric price and high operating costs make it as expensive to operate as a full-size car.

Exhibit 8.3

Cost of Owning and Operating Different-Size Automobiles Over Four Different Ownership Periods

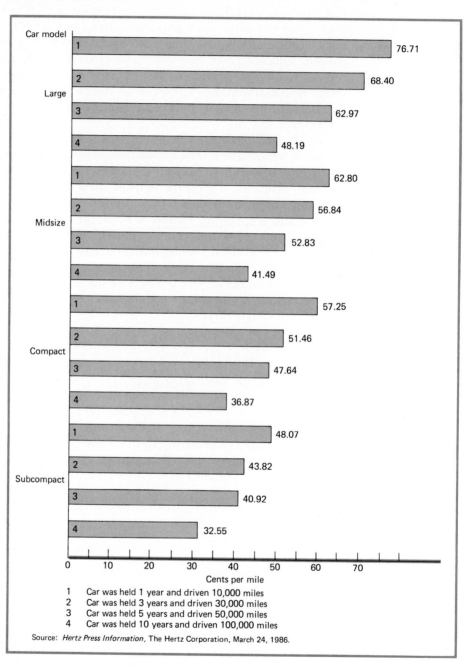

Car model		Cents per mile
Large	1	76.71
	2	68.40
	3	62.97
	4	48.19
Midsize	1	62.80
	2	56.84
	3	52.83
	4	41.49
Compact	1	57.25
	2	51.46
	3	47.64
	4	36.87
Subcompact	1	48.07
	2	43.82
	3	40.92
	4	32.55

Cents per mile

1 Car was held 1 year and driven 10,000 miles
2 Car was held 3 years and driven 30,000 miles
3 Car was held 5 years and driven 50,000 miles
4 Car was held 10 years and driven 100,000 miles

Source: *Hertz Press Information,* The Hertz Corporation, March 24, 1986.

**Area Where
You Live**

Where you live affects ownership costs. When she moves, Grezelda may find her annual insurance premium in Fish Creek now covers barely a month in Boston. Repair cost differentials can be equally traumatic. Someone accustomed to the mechanic's hourly rate at Friendly Fred's in Poland

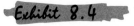

*Annual Cost Savings from Swtiching between Four Different-Size
Automobiles for Three Different Holding Periods*

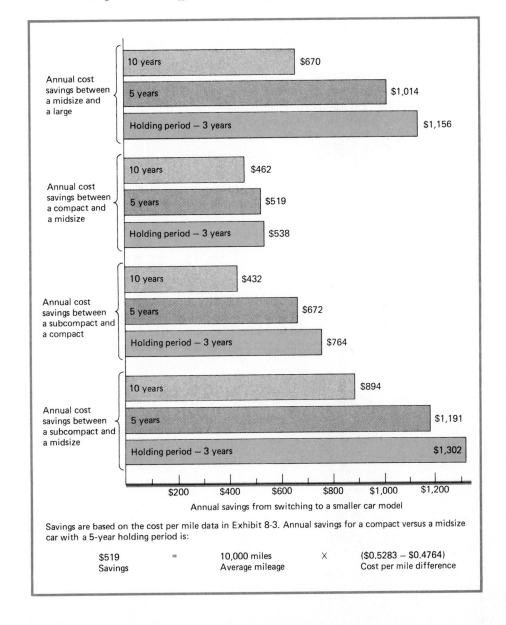

Springs may wonder if a renowned heart specialist worked on her car in San Francisco. Even purchase price can vary. Should all of us commute from the Fish Creeks and Poland Springs of the world? No. But consider these costs when deciding where to live.

ESTIMATING YOUR TOTAL COSTS

Exhibit 8.2 gave ownership costs for a "typical" car in each size group. It can be modified to estimate the costs for a specific auto if the purchase price is adjusted to better reflect depreciation and if that purchase price is used to compute new finance charges and lost interest expense.

All Ownership Costs but Depreciation and Financing

You can take ownership costs for everything but depreciation and financing directly from the Hertz study. Your actual costs may differ slightly from those given in Exhibit 8.5. If the car's mileage is poor, your fuel costs will be higher. If its repair record is a nightmare—the service manager not only knows how you like your coffee, she stocks your favorite chocolate doughnuts in the customer waiting room—your costs will be much higher. Nevertheless, Exhibit 8.5 is a starting point.

Depreciation Costs

An auto's annual **depreciation** is determined by purchase price and the annual percentage decline in value. The higher the initial price, the larger the depreciation. Percentage declines in market value are not uniform, ranging from 20 to 30 percent the first year to 5 percent or less later. Exhibit 8.6 depicts this drop: its lower section tracks what remains of the original price, and the upper summarizes depreciation. After 5 years the car's value is only 20 percent of its original price. Doris's $13,000 compact will be worth about $2,600 ($13,000 × 20%) after 5 years; depreciation has claimed the remaining $10,400 ($13,000 × 80%).

To estimate depreciation on a specific car, you need to know its purchase price and how long you expect to keep it. Use the percentages in the top section of Exhibit 8.6 to compute depreciation. Divide that total by your projected mileage to figure the depreciation cost per mile. Suppose Doris

Exhibit 8.5

Ownership Cost in Cents per Mile, Excluding Depreciation and Financing Costs, for Various Automobile Size Categories

	Ownership Period and Miles Driven				
Car size	1 year 10,000	3 years 30,000	5 years 50,000	7 years 70,000	10 years 100,000
Large	26.51	28.49	29.04	28.81	28.66
Midsize	24.65	26.52	27.04	26.80	26.65
Compact	21.55	23.08	23.51	23.21	22.98
Subcompact	20.18	21.65	22.07	21.80	21.70

Source: Hertz Press Information: The Hertz Corporation, March 24, 1986, and author's estimates.

expects to drive 50,000 miles during the 5 years she has the $13,000 compact. Per mile depreciation cost is $0.208: $13,000 cost × 80% depreciation/50,000 miles.

Costs of Financing the Auto

For our analysis we need two more components: the finance charge on the loan and the lost interest on the down payment. First establish your down payment (the lender may set a minimum).

Doris pays 25 percent down for her $13,000 compact car ($3,250) and borrows the rest. She computes the interest she loses on the down payment. To find the going interest rate, she checks the rate on a 1- to 3-year certificate of deposit (CD) at several banks or S&Ls; assume it is currently 8 percent. Her lost interest will total $1,300 over 5 years: $3,250 down payment × 8% × 5 years.

To estimate the finance charge, Doris checks the APR on auto loans from local lenders. She finds the APR is 15 percent. Doris computes her finance charge using the method introduced in Chapter 6. First, she decides the loan's maturity. Set it to equal your planned period of ownership, but no longer than 5 years, since that is usually the maximum for automobile loans. Then Doris computes her monthly payment using Exhibit 6.7. She plans to keep the car 60 months, so the payment on her $9,750, 15 percent APR loan is $231.95: $23.79 payment from Exhibit 6.7 × $9,750 loan/$1,000. Her total payments are $13,917: $231.95 payment × 60 months. Of that total, $9,750 was the original loan, so her finance charges total $4,167 ($13,917 − $9,750).

If lost interest and finance charges are added, you end up with the total **financing costs.** In Doris's case, the lost interest ($1,300) and finance

Exhibit 8.6

Impact of Depreciation on the Market Value of Your Automobile

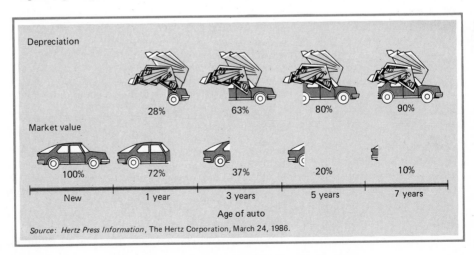

Source: Hertz Press Information, The Hertz Corporation, March 24, 1986.

charges ($4,167) add up to $5,467. Over 50,000 miles, her per mile finance cost is $0.1093: ($1,300 + $4,167)/50,000 miles.

Estimating Total Costs

Exhibit 8.7 brings together all three cost components. Let's see how it works. Chuck needs to estimate the ownership cost of a $14,000 midsize auto driven 30,000 miles over 3 years. His down payment will be $3,500; the other $10,500 will come from a 15 percent APR loan. This data is entered on lines 1 through 5.

Exhibit 8.6 shows depreciation will be 63 percent during the first 3 years; for a $14,000 car, it is the $8,820 ($14,000 × 63%) on line 7. Over Chuck's 30,000 miles, that would be $0.294 per mile (line 13).

Chuck estimates an 8 percent rate on savings. Chuck's lost interest totals $840: $3,500 down payment × 8% interest × 3 years. His proposed 15 percent APR, $10,500 loan carries a monthly payment of $364.04: $34.67 from Exhibit 6.7 × $10,500 loan/$1,000. Finance charges for the 3 years equal the $2,605.44 on line 10. Total financing costs are $3,445.44 ($840 lost interest + $2,605.44 finance charge), as shown on line 11. For 30,000 miles, that is $0.1148 per mile (line 14).

Chuck's total ownership cost of $0.6740 per mile, line 15, has three components:

Line 12. *Ownership costs except depreciation and financing from Exhibit 8.5.*

Line 13. *Depreciation based on purchase price and ownership period.*

Line 14. *Financing cost (lost interest and finance charges).*

Exhibit 8.7

Worksheet for Estimating Ownership Costs for a Specific Automobile

Line	Description of Cost	Data
1	Purchase price: midsize car plus options	$14,000.00
2	Ownership period	3 years
3	Projected total mileage	30,000 miles
4	Down payment for car: 25% of price	$ 3,500.00
5	Loan for balance of auto's cost	$10,500.00
6	Percent of original cost lost to depreciation: Exhibit 8.6	63%
7	Total depreciation expense: line 1 × line 6	$ 8,820.00
8	Lost interest on down payment: $3,500 × 8% × 3 years	$ 840.00
9	Monthly payment if loan's APR is 15%: $34.67 from Exhibit 6.7 × $10,500 line 5/$1,000	$ 364.04
10	Finance charge on loan: $364.04 (line 9) × 36 months − $10,500 (line 5)	$ 2,605.44
11	Total financing costs: line 8 + line 10	$ 3,445.44
12	Operating cost per mile without depreciation and financing costs: Exhibit 8.5	26.52 cents
13	Depreciation cost per mile: line 7/line 3	29.40 cents
14	Financing costs per mile: line 11/line 3	11.48 cents
15	Total ownership cost per mile: line 12 + line 13 + line 14	67.40 cents

Chuck will spend almost $6,740 a year to drive 10,000 miles: $0.6740 ×
10,000 miles. Each year's cost will not be identical, of course, but Chuck
now has a far better idea of his likely costs.

Strategy

*Use a worksheet like Exhibit 8.7 to compute the projected ownership
cost for any car you are considering.*

Does the Projected Ownership Cost Fit Your Budget?

Car costs are often the third largest item in a household budget; only housing and food expenditures are greater. Avoid being car-poor by drafting a
budget *before* you buy the car. Generally auto costs should not be more
than 12 to 15 percent of your available income.

An example can illustrate the merits of a preliminary budget. Sandra
is considering buying a car that would cost $0.40 per mile to own and oper-
ate. At 10,000 miles per year, her costs would average $4,000—that will
take 20.5 percent of her $19,500 of available income, a sizable fraction.
By including that $4,000 of auto expenses in a preliminary budget, she can
decide if it is workable. If it is going to be a problem, Sandra can look at
other options.

Sandra has several choices. She might switch to a less expensive car.
Possibly shifting from a compact to a subcompact will reduce costs. Or she
may decide to buy the original car and accept the cuts she will have to make
in her budget.

Strategy

*Develop a preliminary budget to decide if you can afford a car before
you buy it.*

SHOPPING FOR YOUR AUTOMOBILE

The discussion thus far should help you decide which autos might be right
for you. Now let's talk about how to select a car to meet your needs, single
out a particular brand, estimate a fair price, and pick a dealer to purchase
from.

Selecting an Auto to Meet Your Needs

Two criteria can help you decide which size car will meet your needs. First,
how much space do you want for yourself, passengers, and luggage? Even
as autos shrink on the outside, usable space often equals or exceeds that
of their larger predecessors. The "Gas Mileage Guide" mentioned previously gives the combined passenger and luggage space on most models.
The guide is updated annually. The April issue of *Consumer Reports* summarizes the comfort and convenience features of most new models and
gives interior and exterior dimensions.

Second, match the auto to your regular needs. Why should Otto Out-
doors purchase a "large" auto just to stow gear for his annual 1-week
camping foray if the rest of the year he carries only one passenger? Good
economy suggests the model that's adequate for your regular needs; limit
size and keep ownership costs down.

Strategy

Select the model that meets your regular passenger and luggage needs.

Selecting an Automobile Brand

Selecting a car with moderate repair and maintenance needs can do much to reduce your costs. You want a brand with a dealer network that gives you access to service and replacement parts. No one wants a car sidelined while the elves of Sherwood Forest make and ship a special part.

Owner surveys are a good source of reliability and maintenance information. Several periodicals regularly report their readers' experience with different cars. *Consumer Reports* gives the most comprehensive coverage. Their April issue rates frequency of repair on each car's major components and provides a relative cost index for each model's repair and maintenance expenses. Surveys in *Popular Mechanics* and *Road and Track* concentrate on single models, domestic and foreign. These surveys can help you choose dependable cars that do not require a second mortgage on the house to keep running.

Picking a Dealer

Friends and coworkers can help you select an automobile dealer. They, or someone they know, may have had experience with various dealers. Questions of interest include: Did the dealer handle warranty items quickly and fairly? Is the service department competent? Fair and honest? Would you buy from the dealer again?

Unless the savings are large, buy from a local dealer; traveling 100 miles for warranty or adjustment work is time-consuming. Read the deal-

er's ads skeptically. Claims of "lowest price in the area," "tremendous discounts," and "near invoice cost" may be true, half true, or untrue.

Strategy

Select a dealer who provides customer support after the sale. You want a dealer who is interested in keeping you as a customer.

Estimating a Fair Price for Your Car

You can visit many dealers to determine a **"fair" price,** but there is an easier, more accurate method. You need to have three pieces of information:

- Wholesale price on the car you plan to trade
- Dealer's invoice price on the car and options you plan to buy
- An estimate of the dealer's profit margin

With these you compute a fair price before visiting any dealers.

Wholesale price of a used car

Current market values of most domestic and foreign cars are compiled in national publications such as the *NADA Official Used Car Guide* and *Kelley Blue Book.* Some state automobile associations publish regional used car prices. The typical guide lists three prices:

Loan value. *What a lender will loan to purchase the car.*
Wholesale value. *The price a dealer will pay for the car.*
Retail value. *The price a dealer will ask when selling the car.*

Check your credit union, public library, bank, or savings and loan for one of the used car publications or ask a local used car dealer if you can look at a copy.

Dealer's invoice cost for the new car and associated equipment

The **invoice price** is what the dealer pays the car manufacturer. Guides like *Edmunds New Car Prices* and *Consumer Guide 1986 Autos* compile and print dealer costs on domestic and foreign cars and optional equipment. The April issue of *Consumer Reports* and the December issue of *Changing Times* also publish this information. Larger public libraries generally have one or more guides.

You can also approximate the dealer's cost using the **sticker price,** which is the manufacturer's suggested retail price. A typical car costs the dealer 85 to 90 percent of that sticker price. Domestic compacts and subcompacts are nearer 90 percent. Midsize and large domestic models and most foreign models are about 86 percent. Optional equipment costs the dealer about 85 percent of its sticker price.

Car dealer's profit margin

The difference between the dealer's cost and your price is profit. **Profit margins** range from $200 to $800, with most in the $400 to $600 range, but there are exceptions.

Competition in your local auto market affects the margin. If there are few dealers or little competition, the profit margin is higher. Very popular cars also carry a higher profit margin. Foreign car dealers often have high profit margins; if demand is heavy and supply short, some dealers will tack

$1,000 or more on the suggested retail price—all of it straight profit. Finally, some dealers are content to sell a few cars with a large profit on each.

What you pay: the net cash difference

The worksheet in Exhibit 8.8 uses the costs discussed thus far to estimate a car's "fair" price. The left column assumes a "low" profit margin, and the right is based on a "high" margin.

Suppose Fred wants to trade his present car for a new compact. One of the price guides lists a sticker price of $10,195 and a dealer cost of $8,770. The options Fred wants total $2,500, with a dealer cost of $2,125. Destination charges are $425. These costs are listed on lines 1(a), 1(b), and 1(c) of Exhibit 8.8.

A guide lists a $2,500 wholesale price for Fred's present car; he enters this on line 3. Profit margins of $400 and $600 go on line 5(a). Other purchase costs go on lines 5(b) and 5(c).

The costs from line 4 and line 5 give the **net cash difference** (line 6). The worksheet suggests Fred can expect to pay somewhere between $9,836 and $10,046, assuming a dealer profit of $400 to $600. Fred now has a price range when he goes to a dealer.

Completing Exhibit 8.8 took work, but it is faster and more accurate than running to three or four dealers trying to compile the same information.

When you have no car to trade, modify Exhibit 8.8: leave line 3 blank.

Exhibit 8.8

Computing the Net Cash Difference for Purchase of a New Car

		Dealer's Profit Margin	
Line	Description of cost item	Low markup	High markup
1	Dealer's cost:*		
	a Basic car	$ 8,770	$ 8,770
	b Options and extras	2,125	2,125
	c Destination charge	425	425
2	Total dealer cost	$11,320	$11,320
3	Less: Current wholesale value of car to be used as a trade-in*	2,500	2,500
4	Cost difference that remains	$ 8,820	$ 8,820
5	Add:		
	a Dealer's profit margin*	400	600
	b Sales tax (if applicable)†	586	596
	c Title and license transfer§	30	30
6	Net cash difference for new car	$9,836	$10,046

* See discussion in text for source of estimate.
† Sales tax of 5% on dealer's cost plus profit margin ($11,320 + $400) × 5% = $586 and ($11,320 + $600) × 5% = $596.
§ Set at $30, but it will vary for different states.

Bargaining with the Dealer

Before you visit dealers, decide on the model and optional equipment you want. If you want immediate delivery, you will have to accept a model from the dealer's inventory. You may get a few options you do not want, drop some you did want, and settle for an available color and trim combination. But first ask the dealer to check other dealers for the car you want. Better yet, order what you want: it will take 4 to 6 weeks—more for high-demand and foreign cars—but you will get your preferred model, options, color, and trim.

Strategy

Do not let a dealer push you into a car loaded with options you do not want: electronic tinsel can be a repair nightmare. Likewise, do not let the dealer sell you a car that does not fit your needs.

A promise to sell cars with "hundreds cut from the list price" may reflect nothing more than an inflated sticker price. The important number is the net cash difference for the new car. Some dealers claim they give "top dollar" for your trade-in. Sandra Salesperson at Fast Phil's Dealership might offer Fred Bear $300 or $400 more than his car's wholesale value, but if she tacks $500 onto the new car's price, Fred breaks even or loses.

Ask the salesperson to write down each detail of the new car's price. That way you can compare different offers. Some salespeople claim they never quote a price unless you first agree to purchase the car. If you encounter this, go elsewhere. And remember, financing is a totally separate decision from buying; Chapters 6 and 7 can help you with it.

Strategy

*Know approximately what the car and options cost **before** you meet the dealer. Concentrate on the net cash difference you must pay for the new car.*

Will a Used Car Do the Job?

The question of a new versus a used car has no simple answer. A carefully purchased used car can save money, but a poor choice may make hiring a chauffeur and limo seem cheap.

The major saving with a used car is lower depreciation. Since cars depreciate most rapidly when new, if you buy one when it has reached a gracious middle age, someone else has paid the largest share of depreciation. But maintenance and repair costs rise with age and mileage. On some cars these can wipe out the advantage.

Selecting a used car

Your first criterion should be minimizing repair and maintenance costs. The owner surveys in *Consumer Reports* can guide you to a model with a good repair record and moderate repair costs. Picking a car for your major needs is important, but you also want one that meets them at a reasonable cost. Exhibit 8.9 can assist you in your search.

Strategy

Carefully evaluate any used car to avoid buying someone else's repair problems.

Pricing a used car

One of the used car price guides can help you decide what is a "fair" price. Most guides price the car and its major options. If you buy from a dealer, you will probably have to pay retail price. Purchase from a private owner and your price is generally between wholesale and retail. Cars that are in mint condition usually sell for a premium.

Where to buy a used car

The four major sources for used cars are new car dealers, used car dealers, rental car companies, and private owners. Exhibit 8.10 lists the major advantages and disadvantages of buying from each.

CAR WARRANTIES

Warranties provided by the manufacturer promise to replace or repair defective components and cover a car for a specified number of months or miles. The usual warranty is 12 months or 12,000 miles, though some war-

Exhibit 8.9

General Guidelines for the Used Car Purchaser

Guideline	Comment
1. Concentrate on brands with good repair records.	The owner surveys in *Consumer Reports, Road and Track,* and *Popular Mechanics* are good resources.
2. Stay with basic model rather than one loaded with options.	Initial cost is less and options can become a repair nightmare.
3. Look for a car with low mileage on the odometer.	Recent legislation has curbed some dishonest practices, but it does not yet guarantee an honest odometer reading.
4. Buy from a reputable dealer.	An unscrupulous dealer can make a junker look superb and run perfectly until the sale is complete.
5. If required, the car should have a valid inspection certificate or safety sticker.	Cost of correcting safety problems can be sizable.
6. Read books from the library on how to judge a used car.	These books discuss the points to check and items you should look for in a used car.
7. Once you have read one or more books, do an exhaustive check on the car's overall condition.	Inspect everything to see whether it works properly; drive the car in the city, on the expressway, and in the country to see how it performs.
8. Have a mechanic you know and trust examine the car.	A professional can help you avoid major mechanical pitfalls; the fee is nominal.
9. Carefully review the used car dealer's disclosure sticker if your state requires one.	Some states require each dealer-sold used car to carry a sticker indicating the condition of the car's major mechanical components.

ranties last 24 months or more and offer unlimited mileage. A few cover the power train for as long as 5 years or 50,000 miles.

Covered Components

Most warranties cover a car's major components: engine, transmission, drive axle, suspension, brakes, and cooling, electrical, and steering systems. Items with a limited life are excluded: tires, brake pads, paint, upholstery, hoses, and belts.

When You Have a Warranty Problem

Promptly report problems to the dealer. Keep going back until you are satisfied. Be skeptical of the claim that it will take a few thousand miles for things to "settle in" or the contention that the problem is "normal." If it takes longer than the warranty lasts to solve the problems, you pay the cost from *your* pocket. If you do agree to wait, ask for a written commitment to fix the problem.

When the dealer cannot fix the problem

If you have exhausted all avenues of redress, contact the manufacturer either through the manufacturer's representative or the central office.

The manufacturer's representative is the link between the dealer and the manufacturer's zone office for your area. Ask the dealer's service manager to arrange a three-way meeting, involving the dealer, you, and the manufacturer's representative, to discuss the problem. Come prepared with details on the complaint, copies of repair orders, and a clear idea of what you want done.

Another avenue is writing or calling the customer relations department at the manufacturer's central office. Provide complete details on the problem, repair efforts, and a statement of what you want done. Your request

Exhibit 8 . 10

Major Sources for Used Cars

Source	Advantage	Disadvantage	Comments
New car dealer	a, b, c, f	1, 2, 6	Good source for a 1- to 4-year-old car of the brand the dealer sells.
Used car lot	d, e, f	1, 3	Source for older, high-mileage cars.
Rental car company	a, c, g, h	2, 3, 4, 6, 7,	Excellent source of cars that are 1 year old or less.
Private owner	e, g	2, 3, 4, 5	Good source for older cars without refurbishing. *What you see is what you buy.*

Key to advantages:
a Concentrates on late model cars.
b Has facilities to service car.
c Typically offers a reasonable used-car warranty.
d Usually has a good cross section of car brands.
e May have some older, high-mileage cars.
f Probably will take existing car as a trade-in.
g Frequently sells car at wholesale price.
h May provide car's detailed maintenance record.

Key to disadvantages:
1 Price is full retail plus, possibly, a premium.
2 Selection of car brands is limited.
3 Limited or nonexistent repair facilities.
4 Existing car cannot be traded in.
5 Car is not professionally refurbished.
6 Few older, lower-priced cars are offered.
7 May not have sales office in your area.

for corrective action will probably be routed to the zone office in your area. That office will set up an appointment to discuss the problem with you.

Strategy

If the dealer cannot or will not correct a warranty problem, take your case to the manufacturer. Be persistent and unrelenting when pressing your claim.

LEASING: AN ALTERNATIVE TO PURCHASING

When you lease a car, you actually rent it for a specific period of time and pay a set amount. Is leasing worth considering? It depends on your circumstances.

What a Lease Includes

Leases can cover any period, but most run from 2 to 5 years. The lease specifies the maximum number of miles you can drive: exceed it and you pay more. Otherwise, you have unrestricted use of the car. You pay for fuel, maintenance, repairs, and insurance.

Leasing is like owning in some ways. When Cindy calls the lease company from the pay phone to report her stalled car, the representative says, "Sounds like *you* have a problem with *your* car. As soon as *you* get it fixed, *you* can be on your way." For an extra $30 to $50 per month she could have purchased a maintenance contract covering repairs, and another monthly fee would provide insurance coverage.

You need to negotiate a "fair" lease price as carefully as a new car's purchase price. Since you bear responsibility for repair and maintenance, leasing is hardly "hassle free," no matter what the ads say.

Types of Leases: Closed-End or Open-End

A **closed-end lease** relieves you of all responsibility for the car's market value. Pay the agreed amount each month, and the only conditions you have to meet are that you not exceed the maximum mileage and that you return the car in "reasonable" condition for a vehicle of its age and mileage. These leases are sometimes called "walkaway," "straight," "net," or "flat rate."

An **open-end lease** subjects you to considerably more responsibility. You can be responsible for part of the car's decline in value at the end of the lease. When you first lease the car, the company computes your monthly payment using its estimate of the car's market value at the end of the lease. Suppose the value was set at $3,000: if the car's market value is only $2,500 at the end of the lease, you pay the $500 difference. If it is worth $3,400, you receive a $400 refund. Your maximum liability cannot exceed 3 months' lease payments. Other names for this lease include "participating" and "cost plus."

Since you accept more risk with an open-end lease, its monthly payments should be less.

Strategy

An open-end lease may be desirable if its monthly payment is considerably lower and you expect stable auto prices during the lease.

Cost of Leasing versus Cost of Owning an Automobile

In many cases leasing is more expensive than owning, but not always. Fuel, insurance, maintenance, and repairs can be ignored in the analysis because you pay them in both instances. We assume you also pay sales taxes and licensing fees whether you lease or buy.

Exhibit 8.11 shows a sample worksheet for computing the costs of owning and leasing. The cost of owning is shown in the top half; leasing costs are summarized in the lower section.

Wanda wants to compare the cost of purchasing a $10,900 midsize car with the cost of leasing it. If she buys the car, she will pay $2,000 down and finance the rest with a 48-month, 12 percent APR auto loan. The down payment is entered on the top line of Exhibit 8.11. Monthly payments on the auto loan are $234.34: $26.33 payment from Exhibit 6.7 × $8,900 loan/$1,000. Over 48 months, her payments total $11,248.32. This is entered on line 2 of the ownership section.

Wanda also loses the interest on her $2,000 down payment. At 8 percent she could have earned $640 over the next 4 years: $2,000 down payment × 8% × 4 years. Enter that on line 3 as a cost of ownership. Combine these and they total the $13,888.32 on line 4.

After 4 years Wanda expects to sell the car for $3,720. Deduct that amount on line 5 to reduce the cost of ownership. Wanda's net ownership cost over the 4 years will be $10,168.32, as is shown on line 6.

Exhibit 8.11

Comparing the Costs of Ownership and Leasing

Cost of Owning Car for 4 Years

Down payment	$ 2,000.00
Total payments on $8,900, 48-month, 12% APR loan: ($26.33 from Exhibit 6.7 × $8,900/$1,000) × 48 months	11,248.32
Lost interest on the $2,000 down payment: $2,000 × 8% × 4 years	640.00
Total cost of owning car	$13,888.32
Less: Proceeds from sale of used car after 4 years	3,720.00
Net cost of owning car	$10,168.32

Cost of Leasing Car for 4 Years

Security deposit: 2 months' lease payments	$ 440.00
Lease payments: 48 months at $220 per month	$10,560.00
Lost interest on security deposit: $440 × 8% × 4 years	140.80
Less: Return of security deposit at end of lease	440.00
Net cost of leasing car	$10,700.80

A large leasing company has offered Wanda a 48-month closed-end lease on the same car for $220 per month. She must give them an amount equal to two payments, $440, as a security deposit: see line 1 of the leasing section. Over 48 months Wanda will pay a total of $10,560 ($220 payment × 48 months). This total is shown on line 2. Wanda's lost interest on her security deposit totals $140.80 at 8 percent: $440 × 8 percent × 4 years. It appears on line 3. Wanda's deposit is returned to her at the end of the lease, so it is deducted on line 4 of the analysis. Wanda's net cost to lease is the $10,700.80 shown on line 5.

In this case it is cheaper for Wanda to buy the car than to lease it. But other factors might enter into the decision. If she does not have the $2,000 down payment, leasing might prove her only option. If she expects the car she is considering to depreciate rapidly, that could make leasing attractive. (Of course, if she expected slow depreciation, ownership would be more attractive.) Finally, if Wanda is uncertain how many miles she will drive, she might want to avoid a lease's mileage cap.

Until now, we have ignored income taxes. Part of the interest lost on the down payment and the lease deposit would have gone for taxes. Taxes actually reduce your "lost" interest. Since ownership has more of this component, its total cost drops more. Your marginal tax rate can be used to estimate the exact decreases.

If you borrow the money using a real estate loan, the finance charge may be deductible on your tax return. That lowers the cost of ownership since you pay less tax; the cost of leasing is unaffected. You can incorporate one or both of these tax adjustments into your cost analysis.

Strategy

Leasing is often more expensive than ownership. But prepare a cost analysis like the one shown in Exhibit 8.11 to determine which is best for you.

Caution: Lease Payment versus Loan Payment

Selma Shifty tells her prospective lease customers that comparing the lease payment with the auto loan payment is the best way to decide whether to lease or buy. She claims the smallest payment is the "clear winner." If it were, Exhibit 8.11 would have only two lines. Ignore the owned auto's resale value, and leasing will almost always look best. You need to factor in all the cost components shown in Exhibit 8.11 to decide intelligently.

Caution: Down Payments and Deposits Are Not the Same

Some leases require a down payment. Unlike a deposit, your down payment will *not* be returned. But it permits the leasing company to quote attractive monthly rates. Don't be misled. If it *is* a down payment, it becomes one more leasing cost. And you will still lose interest on the money. Exhibit 8.11 can be adjusted to handle this kind of lease.

Caution: Excess Miles Cost You Money

You pay $0.06 to $0.15 for each mile beyond the maximum set in your lease. Generally the fewer the miles you expect to drive, the lower your lease payment. But understating your expected mileage is costly.

Joan set the mileage at 50,000, even though her experience suggested it would be 60,000 over the 4 years. Her lease charged $0.10 for each mile over the maximum. Any savings the 50,000 estimate might have offered will be eliminated by the extra mileage charge of $1,000: 10,000 extra miles × $0.10 per mile.

Strategy

Be realistic when estimating your total mileage under a lease: the charge for exceeding the maximum will be larger than any savings from lower payments.

SELECTING MAJOR HOME APPLIANCES

Major home appliance purchases deserve careful consideration. Appliances last a long time, as Exhibit 8.12 shows. Operating and service costs can total far more than the appliance's original purchase price. Most people would rather not win the "customer of the year" award because of their frequent service calls to fix their clunker. Owning a lemon is inconvenient and aggravating, as well as costly.

Life-Cycle Ownership Costs

An appliance's **life-cycle ownership cost** includes all your cash outlays from the date of its purchase to the day it burrows into the local landfill. That cost includes service expenses, operating costs, and the purchase price. The left side of Exhibit 8.13 summarizes those categories.

As the right side of Exhibit 8.13 suggests, you will balance cost considerations with desire for particular operating features and capabilities as you make your purchase decision. Some people seek low life-cycle costs. Others look for design and operating features. Though life-cycle costs need not be the sole concern, they deserve consideration. Price, operating costs, and service costs, combined with the unit's operating features and capa-

Exhibit 8.12

Life Expectancy of Major Home Appliances

Appliance	Years	Appliance	Years
Automatic clothes washer	11	Refrigerator	15
Clothes dryer—electric	14	Kitchen range—gas	13
Clothes dryer—gas	13	Room air conditioner	7
Dishwasher	11	Television—black and white	11
Freezer	20	Television—color	12
Kitchen range—electric	12	Water heater—electric or gas	10

Source: Marilyn Doss Ruffin, "Consumer Appliance Decisions: Using Energy Labels," *Family Economics Review,* Summer 1978, p. 12.

bilities, can guide your selection of a reasonably priced unit that meets your needs.

Strategy

When selecting an appliance, consider its life-cycle cost as well as design and operating features.

SERVICE ON HOME APPLIANCES

Service costs can comprise more than 10 percent of life-cycle costs. Fortunately, modern appliances are more reliable than ever. But the cost of a basic service call starts at $40, and replacement parts seem to be made of precious metals, so the amount spent on service is still large.

Service Frequency

If the appliance needs frequent service, your costs are going to be high. A good service record may justify paying an extra $50 to $100 for an appliance. The savings from buying a cheaper model vanish after a few service calls.

Each year, *Consumer Reports* polls its subscribers on their repair experience with major appliances. They publish each brand's repair index

Exhibit 8.13

Four Areas to Consider When Selecting Major Home Appliances

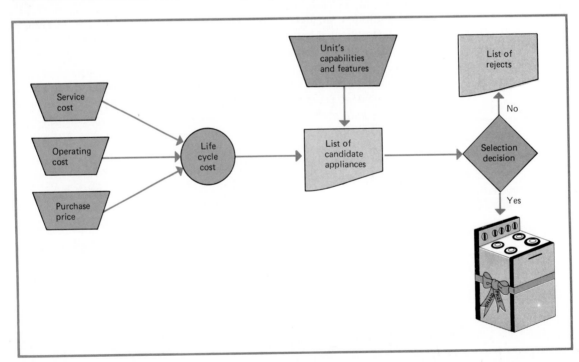

in their comparative appliance tests. This compilation can help you single out brands or models which will minimize your service costs.

Service Availability

Even the most trouble-free appliance will likely need service at some point. Time and mileage charges are *very* expensive, so you want to have competent service in your area. You also want to avoid a second mortgage to resuscitate "Albert," the dishwasher. Friends and coworkers can be valuable information sources on the quality and price of local service.

Strategy

When shopping for an appliance, check the dealer's service policy:
- *Is work done locally?*
- *What is the minimum fee?*
- *How long does it take?*
- *Does the dealer stock parts?*

Appliance Warranties: What Service Work Is Included?

Most major appliances include a **warranty** that covers labor and replacement parts for a specified time. The warranty can cover as little as 90 days or more than 5 years, but the period is usually much shorter than the unit's expected life. You should plan on paying for some service calls.

Nearly all appliance warranties are "limited": the coverage varies for different parts and may not include labor and parts. The seals on your new refrigerator may be covered for 3 months, even though its compressor is warranted for 6 years. Some manufacturers offer longer or more generous warranties than others, and you should consider that in your search among competing models.

But do not place undue emphasis on an appliance's warranty. Any well-designed new unit should need minimal repairs initially. Most warranties have expired by the time a unit reaches midlife and service needs increase. Once the warranty expires, you will be paying the bills. A unit with a low frequency-of-repair rate is worth more to you then than an "impressive" expired warranty.

Service Contracts: Are They Worthwhile?

A **service contract** covers specific repairs and maintenance after the warranty expires. Some contracts are limited to replacement parts, others include some labor, still others cover all labor and parts. You pay an annual fee for the contract; the fee depends on your coverage and the appliance's age.

Service contracts are offered by appliance manufacturers and independent service firms, and are purchased when you buy the product. You cannot buy some contracts unless the unit has been covered continuously since its sale: you cannot obtain coverage when the appliance is 8 years old unless you had it covered for the first 7 years. Why? There are considerable opportunities for abuse when a customer can wait until the unit is aged and needs repairs before buying the contract. Grazelda calls Fast Phil's Appliance Emporium—she purchased her refrigerator there 6 years ago—

and announces: "Phil, I am taking that service contract you offered me."
She glances at the food oozing from her silent refrigerator. Two hours later,
Grazelda calls back: "Phil, please send a repair person. Seems the fridge is
broken."

What the contract provides

A typical contract covers all of the service needs of your appliance for
1 year for a flat annual fee, whether it takes 1, 5, or 10 service calls. You
have an insurance policy, trading unknown future repair costs for the fee.
Contracts are at their best when the appliance is at its worst, but usually
we would quickly trade collecting on the contract for a dependable
appliance.

Carefully check the terms on service contacts. The best cover all parts
and labor. Excluding labor can be expensive; it is a large part of many
repairs. If you must pay a large deductible, your coverage is effectively lowered. Will the unit be repaired at your home? If not, you go without the unit,
and this can be inconvenient.

Cost of service contracts

The annual fee rises as the appliance ages. Rising service needs boost
the cost. The first 2 years of coverage are often combined, making the fee
seem small, but remember that the original warranty covers part of this
period. Beyond the third or fourth year, the annual increase can be sizable.
By the tenth year, the fee might equal 25 percent of a new appliance's cost.

Exhibit 8.14 shows annual fees for sample contracts covering a color
television and a clothes washer; service costs on these two can be a significant part of their life-cycle cost. As Exhibit 8.14 attests, service contracts
are *not* cheap. In 7 years, total fees may exceed the original purchase price.
The contract's daily rate—"only $0.21 per day to end your television service worries"—suggests low cost. Some salespeople downplay the high fees
of later years by noting you can always cancel, but by doing so, you may
drop coverage when you most need it.

Who should buy a contract?

Service contracts are expensive for several reasons. Unlimited visits
encourage people to call: they seek "free" service rather than looking for
simple problems—putting the plug back in the outlet may be enough. Second, the salesperson may receive a commission, and the dealer has a profit
margin for selling contracts. Finally, people who abuse appliances or
ignore regular maintenance find contracts attractive. When Harvey Heavy-

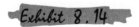

Annual Cost of Two Appliance Service Contracts

| Appliance | Annual Cost by Ownership Year | | | | | | Total cost |
	1 & 2*	3	4	5	6	7	
Color television	$78	$78	$80	$90	$104	$117	$547
Clothes washer	56	63	63	72	80	88	422

* The first 2 years are often combined; part of that period is covered by appliance's warranty.

hands's lawnmower does not start, he uses his hammer to "fix" it. Now, $82.50 in service contract repairs and Harv is back mowing.

Strategy

Service contracts are best reserved for the appliance abusers. Unless you fit the mold, skip the contract.

COST OF OPERATING APPLIANCES

As appliances have become more complex and larger, and cheap energy has turned into nothing more than a warm remembrance, manufacturers have made a concerted effort to reduce **operating costs,** some more successfully than others. The most dependable and efficient appliance might run 2 or more years on what the least efficient costs in 1 year.

Energy-Cost Labels: Your Guide to Operating Costs

Manufacturers are required to attach an **energy-cost label** to seven major appliances: room air conditioners, clothes washers, dishwashers, freezers, furnaces, refrigerators, and water heaters. The labels' format is set by the Federal Trade Commission (see Exhibit 8.15). The standardization makes comparison between competing units simple; it allows you to shop for a **high-efficiency appliance.**

Manufacturers provide three cost components:

1   Estimated annual operating cost based on the current national average cost of energy
2   Comparative annual operating costs for similar models
3   Range of operating costs based on different energy costs

Estimated annual operating cost

Point (1) in Exhibit 8.15 shows the estimated cost to operate the appliance for 1 year, assuming it's used an "average" amount. This cost is based on the national average cost of energy. Tags on electrical appliances show the cost per kilowatt hour (kwh). For natural gas units, the cost per therm is used, and for those operating on fuel oil, the cost per gallon. If your energy costs are "average" and your usage likewise, point (1) shows what you will pay to operate the appliance each year.

Comparative operating costs

Point (2) in Exhibit 8.15 gives the range of operating costs for similar models; the most efficient, lowest-cost unit is compared to the least efficient. All units ranked have similar size and capacity, and use the same type of energy.

Note that the label uses a triangle to show where a particular appliance falls on the cost line. You can assess the relative efficiency of competing products; using the line, you know where a unit ranks in efficiency, and you can calculate the savings from switching to a more efficient unit.

Range of operating costs

Energy costs in the United States are not uniform, of course. The lower half of the label—point (3) in Exhibit 8.15—displays a series of annual costs based on a range of possible energy costs. You can estimate your cost using the local energy cost supplied by the electric or gas utility in your area.

Potential Savings from High-Efficiency Units

The more energy-efficient the appliance, the lower your annual operating costs. Exhibit 8.16 summarizes the savings for two types of appliances: refrigerators and freezers. Each unit's energy efficiency is shown in column 2 of Exhibit 8.16. Annual operating cost for each is shown in column 3.

Exhibit 8.15

Energy-Cost Label for Refrigerator-Freezer

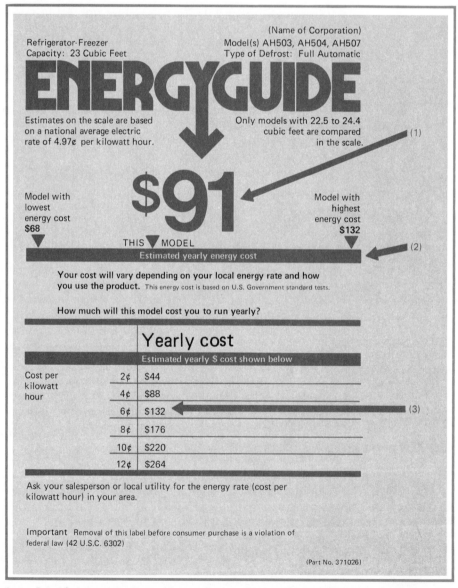

Source: Federal Trade Commission, Bureau of Consumer Protection, Division of Energy and Product Information.

Note the sizable difference. Operating cost for the least efficient is nearly twice what it is for the most efficient. The right-hand section of Exhibit 8.16 summarizes the potential saving over the unit's life.

Strategy

Compare the efficiency of an appliance to that of competing units; lifetime savings from a more efficient unit can be large.

High Efficiency: How Much Is It Worth?

Energy-efficient appliances often cost more than their less efficient counterparts. How much additional expense can you justify for extra efficiency? You could total the savings in operating costs over the unit's life; if it exceeds the added cost, purchasing the more expensive unit may be justified. But this is too simplistic; let us see why.

You pay the added price right now, but the operating savings are spread over future years. We could take a complex route: adjust all of those future savings to a "present value" using some assumed interest rate and compare the adjusted savings to the added cost of the more efficient appliance. Instead, let's develop a simple decision table based on the time-value principle; all of the computations will be done assuming an interest rate of 7 percent. This table will meet our needs.

Time needed to recover the added purchase price

Exhibit 8.17 shows the number of years it takes to recover an appliance's higher purchase price through lower operating costs. Column 1 gives the unit's projected life: 15, 12, or 10 years. Column 2 lists the years it takes to recover the added costs. Column 3 shows whether purchasing the more costly unit is justified.

An example will illustrate. Suppose Thelma has narrowed her choice to Model X—$800 price and $70 per year to operate—or Model Y—$710 price and $85 per year to run. It will take her 6 years to recover X's $90

Exhibit 8.16

Potential Annual Operating-Cost Savings with Use of Energy-Efficient Appliances

Appliance	Relative efficiency rank	Cost per year*	Potential Savings in Operating Cost					
			Most Efficient vs Midrange		Most Efficient vs Least		Midrange vs Least	
			Annual saving	Life-time	Annual saving	Life-time	Annual saving	Life-time
Refrigerator: Top-freezer (capacity 16.5–18.4 cubic feet)	Most	$ 61	$29	$435	$59	$885		
	Midrange	90					$30	$450
	Least							
Freezer: Upright (capacity 13.5–15.4 cubic feet)	Most	48	25	375	50	750		
	Midrange	73					25	375
	Least	98						

* Computed using $0.082 per kwh. Savings are larger where cost is higher. Annual cost rounded to nearest dollar.

higher price: $90 added cost/$15 annual operating savings. Since refrigerators are expected to last 15 years—Exhibit 8.12—the top section of Exhibit 8.17 applies. Model X is Thelma's clear choice. It could have taken as long as 9 years to recover the difference and X would still have been acceptable. Need practice? Brand Z price is $100 higher, but its annual operating cost is $15 less than for Brand Q; they will both last 10 years. Which one is best? It is Z.

Strategy

The time needed to recover any added purchase price tells you whether a more efficient unit is justified.

PURCHASE PRICE OF APPLIANCES

Establishing a fair price for a particular appliance model is more difficult than for a car. Unlike autos, appliances carry no suggested sticker price. In addition, the large number of models available, even from the same manufacturer, greatly increases the choices. Even determining the year an appliance was manufactured can be hard; it is often coded into the serial number (and nearly indecipherable); a model just might be a year or more old. Some dealers do not even post prices, and when they do, that "asking" price may be negotiable. Taken together, these factors make pricing an appliance difficult.

Estimating a Reasonable Price

The best starting point we could have would be a list of typical selling prices for appliances. No such list appears to exist. *Consumer Reports,* however, generally gives prices in its comparative appliance tests. An **"average" price,** "low" price, and "high" price are compiled from dealer price quotations. A price spread of $100 to $200 is not uncommon on large appliances. That is significant when the unit's price is often less than $1,000. Comparison shopping among dealers is financially wise.

Good as *Consumer Reports* is, it has some limitations. Prices may be outdated and are given for only a few models; that provides little guidance for the other models. Manufacturers change models often, so the ones the

Exhibit 8.17

When is an Appliance's Higher Efficiency Worth Its Added Cost?

Expected life of appliance	Years required to recover unit's added purchase price	Is added cost justified?
15 years	9 years or less	Yes
15 years	More than 9 years	No
12 years	8 years or less	Yes
12 years	More than 8 years	No
10 years	7 years or less	Yes
10 years	More than 7 years	No

magazine publishes facts on may be outdated. What should you do? The only choice is to check prices at several dealers in your area.

Haggling on price

Should you haggle over the quoted price? Dealers tend to two extremes. Salespeople at large department stores and nationwide retailers usually cannot bargain on price, but salespeople at local and regional dealers often have some latitude.

If you want to try bargaining, do your homework. Check prices on the models you are interested in through *Consumer Reports* or at another local dealer. Otherwise you may suffer Boris Bumbler's fate. The dealer sized up Boris and quoted $850 for a stereo. Sensing a quick $100 saving, Boris countered with $750. After feigning great distress—she noted her children might go shoeless—the dealer accepted. The next week Boris found the same unit priced at $700.

"Trading you up"

Dealers and salespeople can gain profits and commissions if they **"trade you up"** to a higher-priced, more option-laden model. Compare your needs to what the unit offers you. Most people are well-served by a model midway between the most basic and the most deluxe.

Strategy

Before accepting a model the dealer is pushing, ask: Do I really need, and will I use, the added features?

Bait and switch

The **bait-and-switch** sales tactic is illegal in its most blatant form, but there are still some dealers who use subtler versions. First comes the "bait"—a heavily advertised unit carrying an enticing price. Next comes

the "switch"—the customer is encouraged to switch from the advertised version to a more expensive model.

Switch techniques are ingenious. The salesperson may claim to have just sold the last "bait" model in stock. He or she may expound on the bait's weaknesses and shortcomings. Or the bait may be displayed in the worst possible environment: poor arrangement, ghastly color, a 26-pound plastic turkey gobbling up the limited space.

Regardless of the ploy, resist being switched. If you want the bait, demand it; unless the ad noted "limited quantities," you can probably force the issue. If you want something other than the bait, look elsewhere. If the switch is blatant, report it to the consumer protection agency in your state or to the better business bureau.

Judging claims about price

Most people think "price" when they go appliance shopping. That is understandable since most advertisements focus on it. Claims of "close-out," "inventory reduction," "cash distress" are commonly used to announce sales. But are they really sales? Have prices really been "sliced to the bone"? Is it truly a once in a lifetime opportunity? Or will next week's sale offer the same price? True sales probably occur much less frequently than claimed. Judge the merits of a "sale" by comparing competitors' prices.

DESIGN AND OPERATING FEATURES

Features and design in appliances are a matter of personal preference. Sensing this, manufacturers offer models ranging from basic units to ones offering many options. Take refrigerators. Bernard Basic may want a unit to cool leftovers, keep his ice cream from oozing, and freeze an occasional ice cube. Yvonne Yuppie expects all of this plus a water-and-ice dispenser in the door, a separate "entertaining" cooler, a special chiller, and push-button controls. Yvonne may pay 2 to 3 times what Bernard does. Even without the added cost. Bernard might think Yvonne's fancy machine a repair "nightmare." Let's examine how you can evaluate a unit's features in light of your preferences.

Information Sources

The comparative appliance test reports in *Consumer Reports* provide extensive data on the design and operating features of models tested. They also list major advantages and disadvantages and discuss how well each model performed its basic task. The reviews note how well the unit's supplemental and convenience features performed. Carrying test results which are updated every 2 to 3 years, *Consumer Reports* can be found in most libraries.

Evaluation of Competing Units

The comparative test results in *Consumer Reports* generally rank the tested models in declining order of quality. You should check the advantages and disadvantages of each unit and ask yourself: How important is this shortcoming or defect to me and what I want? These comparative tests can provide the background you need to begin visits to dealers in your area. Once you have the background information, you can start looking at available units, at prices, and at service issues.

Strategy

Evaluate each appliance's design and operating features to decide if it meets your needs. Ask yourself if the extra features are worth the added cost.

PAYING FOR THAT NEW APPLIANCE

Most dealers offer at least two or three payment options: cash and consumer sales loans are nearly universal. Some dealers add another option: **deferred payment same as cash.** Let's look at how each works, and its advantages and disadvantages.

Cash

Paying cash means you avoid finance charges, but don't expect a lower price for cash. The dealer may be able to make more money on a loan (see rebates in Chapter 6), and may actually discourage cash purchases. Also, once the appliance is paid for, you have less leverage with a dealer when you try to persuade him or her to make adjustments or repairs.

Consumer Sales Loan

Since many dealers receive a finance charge rebate on sales loans, they push this option. Before accepting the dealer's loan, you will want to check its APR and terms against competing loan sources. If you have problems with a financed appliance, you can withhold payment until they are corrected; that provides considerable leverage.

Deferred Payment Same as Cash

Deferred payment plans usually require a down payment, with the balance due in 30, 60, or 90 days. You gain immediate use of the appliance, and there is no finance charge if you pay by the due date (hence the "same as cash"). Until the entire balance is paid, you have some leverage to force corrective action. This is an excellent option, if you can fit the payments into your budget.

SHOPPING FOR AN APPLIANCE

The four selection criteria—service, operating costs, purchase price, and design plus operating features—are not equally important for all appliances. Service is very important for a complex appliance like a television set, but it is of limited concern for a basic kitchen stove. Exhibit 8.18 provides some guidelines on the relative importance of the four criteria for different appliances. These were developed to minimize life-cycle costs; you may or may not agree with that criterion. When you select an appliance, you may want to modify the relative weights in Exhibit 8.18.

Exhibit 8.18

Relative Importance of Service, Operating Cost, Purchase Price, and Design Features

			Criteria	
Appliance	Service	Operating costs	Minimizing purchase price	Design features— advantages and disadvantages
Air conditioner	V	E	M	M
Clothes washer	V	V	M	M
Clothes dryer	L	L	V	L
Dishwasher	V	V	M	M
Freezer	M	E	M	L
Kitchen range	L	L	V	M
Refrigerator	M	E	M	M
Television	E	M	M	V
Water heater	L	E	V	L

Key to letter codes:
E Extremely important   M Moderately important
V Very important   L Little importance

Summary

1   Automobiles are classified according to passenger and luggage space. The size categories are minicompact, subcompact, compact, midsize, and large.

2   The yearly decline in a car's market value, its depreciation, is a major ownership cost.

3   The market value of an auto drops fastest in the early years and more slowly later on; that slow decline reduces ownership costs for longer holding periods.

4   Generally, the larger the automobile, the higher its ownership costs.

5   The optimum holding period for most cars ends when repair expenses become large and frequent.

6   To estimate a "fair" price for a new car, you need to know:
   ■ Dealer's cost of the car and options
   ■ Wholesale value of the car you will trade in, if any
   ■ Dealer's likely profit margin on the new car

7   If a used car's ownership cost is to be less than a new car's, repair costs must be minimized.

8   All costs must be considered when comparing owning and leasing; comparing monthly payments is not enough.

9   Four criteria need to be applied when selecting a major home appliance:
   ■ Service cost
   ■ Operating cost
   ■ Purchase price
   ■ Design and operating features

10   An appliance's life-cycle cost includes its purchase price, operating costs, and service.

11   A service contract lets you trade uncertain repair costs for a set annual fee, but the cost can be high.

12   Certain major appliances must carry an energy-cost label. It shows the cost to operate the unit, operating cost for competing units, and cost to operate the unit at different energy costs.

13   Decide whether buying a more efficient appliance is worth the extra cost by calculating how long it will take to recover that amount through the savings in annual operating expenses.

14   Price differentials of $100 or more on the same appliance are not uncommon among competing dealers.

15   The comparative appliance tests in *Consumer Reports* can provide useful price data.

16   Comparative appliance test reports in *Consumer Reports* discuss the design and operating features of tested units.

17   The purchase options on appliances include paying cash, using a dealer loan, and "deferred payment same as cash"; the last is attractive if you can fit the payment into your budget.

Review your understanding of

Automobiles:
  Size classification
  Variable costs of ownership
  Depreciation
  Financing costs
  Ownership period
  Estimated "fair" price
  Wholesale car value
  Sticker price
  Dealer's invoice price
  Dealer's profit margin
  Net cash difference
  Warranty coverage
  Closed-end lease
  Open-end lease

Ownership cost
Fixed costs of ownership
Appliances:
  Life-cycle ownership cost
  Service cost
  Warranty coverage
  Service contract
  Operating cost
  Energy-cost label
  High-efficiency appliance
  Average purchase price
  Haggling on price
  Trading you up
  Bait and switch
  Deferred payment same as cash

Discussion questions

1   How do present criteria for classifying cars differ from past practice? Why do you think the change was made? Do you think the new system has benefited the prospective car buyer? How?

2   What is the major difference between the fixed and the variable ownership costs of an auto? Give examples of each. Are variable costs of greatest concern to high- or low-mileage drivers?

3   Do automobiles decline in value at a steady rate throughout their lifetime? Explain. What implications does that have for ownership costs?

4   What steps do you take to estimate the ownership costs for an automobile? Why is depreciation calculated separately? How is it calculated? Why would it differ from auto to auto? Why are financing costs computed separately?

5   What is meant by "fitting the auto to your budget"? Would it be best to do this after buying the car so that you have accurate cost data? Stanley Shortfall estimates that the operating costs on his proposed auto will not fit his budget. What are his options?

6   What do you need to know to estimate the net cash difference when you want to trade for a new car? Where can you obtain the needed information?

7   Which cost—fuel, insurance, price, etc.— should be the major concern when selecting a used car? Why? Where would you obtain that information?

8   Nel Naive wonders if "open" or "closed" in a lease refers to the car's sunroof. Please explain. Is the monthly payment likely to be the same on both leases? Why?

9   Which cost do you think consumers emphasize most when shopping for major appliances? Why? What is meant by "life-cycle costs"? Should they be a criterion when selecting appliances? Why?

10 Will a service contract end your service worries for "only a few pennies a day"? What are a contract's major strengths? Weaknesses?

11 Which appliances carry energy-cost labels? Why do you think all appliances do not have them? How can the information on these labels be used when shopping for an appliance?

12 Pricing appliances is more challenging than pricing autos. Why? How would you go about establishing a price?

13 What does "trading up" an appliance customer mean? Why is it a problem? How do customers lose when they are traded up to a deluxe model that has more features and extras than needed?

14 Fast Phil's Appliance Outlet recently announced a sale to "clear out our inventory." How do you judge whether it is a legitimate sale?

15 The dealer quoted Ralph and Grezelda two payment options for a $700 appliance: (1) 90-day deferred payment same as cash or (2) a 24-month sales loan with a 24 percent APR. Which would you recommend? Why? Which one is the dealer likely to stress? Why?

Problems

8.1 Susan Lee wonders if switching from a large car to a compact would cut her ownership costs. She generally keeps a car for about 5 years and drives about 10,000 miles each year. What are her annual savings if she makes the switch? Total savings for the 5 years? If Susan decided to trade the car every year rather than every 5 years, would her savings be larger or smaller? (No computations are required for this part.) Why are the savings different?

8.2 Boris Bumbler is having difficulty deciding what a fair price is for the new car he plans to buy. After checking a source that gives used car prices, he finds the following details on his present car: wholesale price $3,000, retail price $3,500, loan value $2,750. He also knows that the dealer's cost on his new car with all the options he wants would be $11,350; transportation cost is $400. The sales tax will be 5 percent of the total price of the new car. What net cash difference should he expect to pay? What additional factors may influence the actual "cash difference" quotes he receives from dealers?

8.3 Tom Whitefoot has narrowed his choice of new cars to two models, one a compact and one a midsize model:

	Compact	Midsize
Price	$12,040	$12,740
Ownership period	7 years	7 years
Expected mileage	70,000 miles	70,000 miles

Tom has decided that either model would be acceptable for his needs. He plans to make a $2,000 down payment; currently that money is earning 6 percent interest. The balance will be financed with a 60 month loan; its APR is 12 percent. What will the ownership cost per mile be for each of the cars? Assuming he drives an equal number of miles each year, what will Tom's annual automobile expense for each car be? What additional noncost points should Tom look at when considering the two cars?

8.4 Tim and Margaret Sudowski have been offered a service contract on a new clothes washer: it costs $55 for the first and second year, $58 for the third, $63 for the fourth. The cost rises $5 each year beyond the fourth.
a What is the total cost if the Sudowskis keep the contract in force for the washer's expected life?
b The dealer says they can reduce the total by dropping the contract once the annual fee becomes sizable. Discuss the merits of that suggestion.
c Assume a typical service call in the area averages $50. How many calls will it take to make the contract a "bargain"? Do you think contracts are bargains for most people? Why?

8.5 Susan McKenzie plans to replace her refrigerator with one of three models:

Model	Purchase price	Estimated monthly operating cost
Standard (freezer on top)	$840	$7.15
Standard (freezer on side)	960	8.45
Superefficient (freezer on top)	960	5.20

a What is the annual operating cost for each?
b How long will it take to recover the added cost for the superefficient model? For the standard with freezer on side?
c Which would you recommend? Why?
d What is the highest purchase price you could justify for the superefficient refrigerator? (*Hint:* Consider the maximum recovery period for an appliance with a 15-year life.)

 a

Fred and Becky Bear plan to purchase a new, large station wagon costing $13,750. They expect to keep it for 5 years and average 10,000 miles per year.

Most of their travel is within the medium-size metropolitan area where they live, but they make an annual 1-week camping trip. In fact, one of the attractions of the large wagon is its ability to carry their camping gear. They have two children, so their passenger needs are moderate. Fred and Becky have always assumed that operating costs for most models are about the same; consequently, they have never seriously considered a smaller car.

Their combined disposable income is $30,000, but their house takes a considerable part of that. The money for their 20 percent down payment would come from their credit union account, which currently earns 6 percent interest. The credit union will finance the balance for 5 years with a 12 percent APR loan.

1   What will it cost them to own and operate the car they have chosen? (*Hint:* Exhibit 8.7 may be of interest.)
2   Does their choice fit within the suggested budget guidelines?
3   If Fred and Becky switched to a compact station wagon costing $11,250, what would the projected ownership cost per mile be for the same 5 years and 50,000 miles?
4   At 10,000 miles per year, will the compact provide significant savings? Over the 5 years, what will the savings total?
5   Which model would you suggest the Bears consider? Why?

Case problem b

Bob and Jan Smith need major appliances. A dealer has quoted them a price of $3,900 for a package which includes refrigerator, kitchen range, washer, and dryer. The dealer has assured them that the appliances are super deluxe models with many options and extras. The dealer maintains that all appliances are basically similar, so the only thing to consider is price. (Of course, she quickly emphasizes, her price is the lowest available.)

Since the Smiths are short of cash, the dealer has offered an "easy" 3-year sales loan (APR 30 percent). The $165.56 monthly payment comes to a "low, low $5.44 per day." "Not much to pay for all that service," the dealer notes. Because they are "good" customers, the dealer has offered them a service contract covering any repair and service needs on all four units for only 50 cents per day. The Smiths' combined annual income is $33,000.

1   Do you agree with the dealer's point that price is the only consideration?
2   How would you recommend that the Smiths shop for each of the appliances?
3   What guidelines would you recommend they use to decide which models best meet their needs?
4   How much will those "easy" terms cost the Smiths? How much is the finance charge?
5   What credit alternatives would you recommend? Why?
6   What is the annual cost of the service contract the dealer offers? Is it likely to remain at that level throughout the lifetime of all the appliances? If the service contract fee remains constant, approximately how much will those fees total over the next 15 years (a reasonable estimate of the appliances' lifetime)?

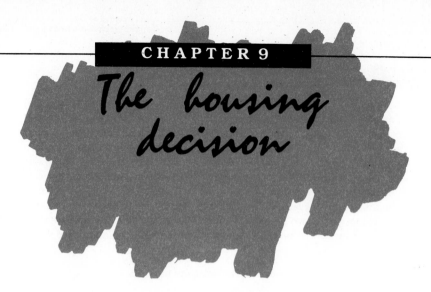

CHAPTER 9

The housing decision

AFTER COMPLETING THIS CHAPTER YOU WILL HAVE LEARNED

- What the principal rent alternatives offer
- The major advantages and disadvantages of single-family houses, condominiums, and mobile homes
- Advantages and disadvantages of renting
- Advantages and disadvantages of ownership
- How to compute the net cost and the long-term cost of renting and owning
- Why current tax rules lower ownership costs but not rental costs
- How a budget helps you decide if you can afford the out-of-pocket costs of ownership
- What to consider when choosing a rental unit
- What you should consider when selecting a single-family house, a condominium, or a mobile home
- The features most mortgages have in common
- Major advantages and disadvantages of the principal types of mortgages
- How to select the *best* mortgage for your situation
- How the closing procedure on a house works

Selecting a house is one of the most important decisions in your life. Although it may be the largest item in your budget, housing involves more than just money. It determines how much time you will spend commuting to work, shopping, and in social or cultural activities. Friends you make in your neighborhood are an important part of your social network. Choose a bad location, and you may live next to Brenda Borrower: after borrowing half your tools, spare food, lawnmower, and first born, she moves to the big items. If you have children, where they live usually determines where they will go to school, which in turn decides many of their friendships. Pride in your home also influences your life. Finally, you spend considerable time in your home; you should be comfortable with your choice.

THE HOUSING ALTERNA- TIVES: RENTAL OR OWNERSHIP

Your two basic housing alternatives are renting or owning. For some, owning is not a serious option. Others view rental as a temporary detour on the way to owning their own house. Like many people, however, you probably do not fit either category exclusively.

This chapter develops guidelines, cost comparisons, and rules to help you answer the question: Should I rent or own at this time?

Rental

Rental options fall into three categories: apartments, duplexes or townhouses, and individual houses. The amount of living space, available recreational facilities, presence or absence of appliances, yard space (if any), degree of privacy, and the renter's responsibility for repairs and maintenance differ considerably.

Apartment

Apartments usually offer the least living space; three bedrooms at most. Newer apartment developments offer swimming pools, tennis courts, community buildings, and putting greens. Older ones have far fewer recreational facilities. Many apartments provide appliances, so you avoid having to purchase them. Larger developments usually have pay laundry facilities. But apartment developments do not provide tenants their own private yard. An apartment's high-density design gives you the least privacy of the rental options.

A major advantage of apartments is that you have few responsibilities for repairs and maintenance. What little yard there is will be cared for; the building will be maintained; and repairs will be taken care of for you.

Duplex and townhouse

Duplex apartments and **townhouses** offer a more spacious layout than apartments, so they offer you more space and privacy. Many provide renters with several levels (including basement storage) and even small yards or an inner court. They rarely provide recreational facilities, and major appliances may not be included. Though you may be responsible for some maintenance and repairs, separation from your neighbors can be a real blessing; you may even have to ask a neighbor if his party was good.

Individual house

An individual house usually provides the most living space and privacy, but special recreational facilities and major appliances are rarely included. Most offer a private yard and a place to park your car, maybe even a garage. The individual lot separates you from your neighbors. The tenant is often expected to do some, or all, of the repairs, maintenance, and yard work.

Ownership

Let's look at three ownership alternatives: single-family house, condominium, and mobile home. For simplicity, we will make "home" the generic term that encompasses all three.

Single-family house

The **single-family house** is the most popular housing unit in the United States, despite the inroads made by condominiums and mobile homes.

When you buy a single-family house, you generally purchase the living unit and the land it sits on. Single-family homes range from one-bedroom units of less than 1,000 square feet up to manors exceeding 6,000 square feet. Only a few feet may separate one house from the next, or the home may have acres of land to itself. Prices cover the whole spectrum: $20,000 to $30,000 "handyperson's specials" crop up in ads next to mansions that start at $1 million. Size, quality of construction, location, and amenities vary greatly.

Advantages and disadvantages of a single-family house. Exhibit 9.1 summarizes the major advantages and disadvantages of a single-family house.

Condominiums

When you purchase a condominium, you acquire two property areas: your individual living unit and an undivided interest in the "common property."

Exhibit 9.1

Advantages and Disadvantages of Owning a Single-Family House

Advantages
1. Large selection of houses in different designs, sizes, and locations.
2. Lengthy history of home prices lets purchasers value a particular single-family house and predict its price will appreciate with inflation.
3. Freedom to redecorate and remodel the house and to change landscaping as you wish.
4. Widest range of financing alternatives; lending institutions have extensive experience with financing houses.

Disadvantages
1. Large monthly mortgage payment and sizable property taxes can make a single-family house prohibitively expensive.
2. Owner is responsible for all repairs and maintenance on house and surrounding property.
3. Down payment and other costs at time of purchase that can easily exceed $8,000 to $12,000.
4. Unavailability or undesirability of units near the business district of major cities.

Individual living unit. A **condominium** purchase gives you title (ownership) to an **individual living unit,** usually part of a multiunit building; your deed gives a precise description of its boundaries. You finance your condominium with a standard home mortgage, and real estate taxes are assessed on your unit the same as on a house. Each owner is responsible for the unit's mortgage payment and real estate taxes; you cannot be assessed for or forced to pay anyone else's obligations.

Common property area. The **common property** is the land where the condominium development is located plus all property items shared by the owners: exterior walls, stairways, roof, hallways, sidewalks, parking lots, and recreation facilities. Because they are used by all owners, they are paid for by all.

All owners have access to and responsibility for the common area; no one can claim any particular part of it is his or hers. Greta Greenthumb cannot spade up the lawn for her radishes. Every owner pays a monthly **maintenance fee** to cover upkeep and repairs on common property as well as ongoing services such as security, lobby personnel, and parking attendants.

Mobile homes

Advantages and disadvantages of a condominium. Exhibit 9.2 summarizes the major advantages and disadvantages of condominium ownership. The points in Exhibit 9.2 relate primarily to year-round residential units; vacation developments are not covered here.

Mobile homes qualify as homes, but are they truly mobile? Most are moved once, from the dealer's lot to a permanent lot. Low purchase prices make mobile homes popular. Fully equipped, a new mobile home can cost as little as $12,000 or as much as $50,000. High-priced units provide more than 1,000 square feet of comfortable, sometimes opulent, living space—comparable to many single-family houses, but at a considerably lower price.

Zoning regulations often limit mobile homes to specially designated mobile home parks, where owners rent a site. Some parks limit occupancy to homes that are purchased from the dealership that operates the park. Others accept all owners but restrict the type of unit accepted. All repairs and maintenance in the park are covered by the monthly rent. Repairs and maintenance for individual units are the owner's responsibility.

You can also purchase a lot in some mobile home parks. The buyer receives title to the ground on which the unit stands. The purchase also generally includes an undivided interest in common property: roadways,

Exhibit 9.2

Advantages and Disadvantages of Owning a Condominium

Advantages
1. All maintenance and repairs of common property area are someone else's responsibility.
2. Condominium developments frequently offer extensive recreational facilities.
3. Limited use of land, coupled with cost savings from the building's high-density design, generally means a square foot of living space in a condominium costs less than it would in a comparable single-family house.
4. Since only a limited amount of land is needed, condominiums can be placed near downtown businesses.
5. Some condominiums target a select clientele—e.g., singles, married without children, retired.

Disadvantages
1. High-density living means less privacy; you will probably have to make compromises in your living style.
2. Monthly cost of ownership—mortgage payment, maintenance fee, and property taxes—can be high.
3. Personal choice in decorating and landscaping is limited; condominium owners jointly decide how to decorate the common property and landscape the grounds.
4. Some developments limit how and to whom you can sell your unit.
5. Down payment and costs associated with purchasing a condominium, though less than those for a single-family house, can be sizable.
6. Owner is responsible for repairs, maintenance, and cleaning of individual living unit.
7. Condominiums are a relatively new housing option; no long-term price information is available that would make it possible to predict how market value will react to moderate or high inflation.

parking lots, recreation facilities, some utility lines, and meeting rooms. Owners are assessed a monthly fee for repair and maintenance of the common property.

Advantages and disadvantages of a mobile home. Exhibit 9.3 summarizes the major advantages and disadvantages of mobile home ownership.

THE BASIC DECISION: RENT OR BUY

Let's start by dividing the factors in the rent or buy decision into nonmonetary and monetary categories. While not all factors have equal weight, each needs to be considered. Our goal is to develop guidelines that will let you combine both sets of factors as you make your decision.

Renting: Nonmonetary Factors

Putting economics aside, what are the advantages and disadvantages of being a renter as opposed to a homeowner? Let's look first at some nonmonetary advantages of renting. Then we'll enumerate some of the disadvantages.

Advantage: Extensive recreation facilities

Newer apartment developments usually offer you swimming pools, tennis courts, clubhouses, exercise facilities, even putting greens. Few homeowners can afford such amenities; certainly not the tempting array developments offer.

Advantage: Restrictions on types of tenants

Some complexes only rent to a select clientele; couples without children, singles, mature couples with grown children. Though housing regulations limit this practice in some states, where it is allowed, the renter can match his or her life-style with the other tenants'.

Exhibit 9.3

Advantages and Disadvantages of Owning a Mobile Home

Advantages
1. Cost per square foot of living space is the lowest for any of the ownership alternatives.
2. Most mobile home units include major appliances and some furniture. This minimizes the initial purchase cost.
3. Monthly net cost of owning is the lowest for any of the ownership options.

Disadvantages
1. Unlike market values of single-family houses and condominiums, a mobile home's market value may decline.
2. Potential decline in market value may offset some, or all, of the savings from the unit's lower purchase price.
3. There are fewer financing options for mobile homes; available options often have a shorter maturity and a higher finance charge.
4. Materials and quality of construction in some units have been substandard. Questions have also been raised about the safety of some units.
5. Availability of sites is limited because some parks accept only units purchased from the park's dealership.
6. Poor maintenance and poor management have made some parks resemble slums.
7. Mobile homes are hardly "mobile." Few are ever moved to a new location.

Advantage: Repairs and maintenance

Renting does not eliminate the cost of repairs and maintenance; they are buried in the rental cost. But you avoid the work and responsibility associated with them. Responsibility for handling repairs is a "joy" many people don't want.

Advantage: Greater flexibility

Vacating a rental unit is generally fast and easy. Once the lease expires (12 months is a fairly common period), you are free to go. Negotiating an early end to the lease is possible, but it may mean you have to pay a cancellation fee.

Disadvantage: Restrictions on personal freedom and lifestyle

Rentals put lots of people in a limited space. You may learn of your neighbor's loud, boisterous, 3:00 A.M. party through your bedroom wall. You may not share the landlord's love of *shocking pink*, but there it is on the lobby walls; the battleship gray in the hallways may remind him sentimentally of the Navy, while you might think it suitable for a mortuary. When a fellow tenant's friend parks in your spot, you can end up on the street. You sacrifice considerable freedom and choice when you rent, and may end up sharing the development with people you dislike.

Ownership: Nonmonetary Factors

Let's look at another part of the picture now. What are the principal factors that make some people long to become proprietors of "the house with the white picket fence," while others are happy to decline the honor?

Advantage: Psychological factors

The psychological rewards of homeownership can't be measured, but they are real. There is pride and personal satisfaction in owning your home. Ownership offers a feeling of permanence. No landlord can refuse to renew your lease, and no exorbitant rent increase or tenant restriction can force you to move. Your home is yours until *you* decide to sell; the old claim that "your home is your castle" is not wholly an exaggeration.

Unlike renting, ownership allows you to change the home to suit your taste, and you have more freedom to pursue the life-style you prefer.

Disadvantage: Repairs and maintenance

Whether you rent or own, you pay the costs of repairs and maintenance. Owners do it in the open; you write the checks. When your furnace dies, you can either skip the heat (pray for a January heat wave) or write the check for a new one.

The owner of a single-family home is responsible for maintaining it. That means you do, or hire someone to do, all the exterior and interior work. As Fred gently sways on his 28-foot ladder, he pauses with the 40-pound storm window gripped in his cool knuckles—20 mph, 38° breeze—to see his neighbor's wave from a rented townhouse. The neighbor is taking a break from watching Saturday's football game. In a condominium, you only have to handle repairs and maintenance on your individual living unit: clogged toilets, totally silent appliances, and other gems . . . Exterior work is contracted to someone else.

For people who lack the time or inclination, repairs and maintenance are a decided disadvantage of owning.

Disadvantage: Reduced flexibility

When you own a home, changing locations is much more involved. Selling the house can take considerable time. You can end up living in Buffalo and selling your house in Sausalito. Second, plan to pay 6 percent or so of the selling price as a commission. Finally, anticipate weeks or months of upset and anxiety while your house is on the market.

If you do not plan to own a home for at least 2 or 3 years, renting may be the best choice. It takes several years for a home to appreciate enough to cover the sales commission and to justify the disruptions caused by selling.

If you are being transferred, your employer may have a relocation program that minimizes the effort and covers the cost of selling your home.

Renting: Monetary Factors

Now let's start looking at the economic side of the rent or buy question. What are the factors—both in terms of immediate costs and in terms of the way the economic and tax system as a whole treats "nonownership"— that affect the overall cost of renting?

Advantage: Low initial cost to rent

Most leases require that renters advance 1 to 3 months' rent as a security deposit. Should the unit be damaged or left unusually dirty, repair and cleanup costs will be charged against this deposit. Many rental units come provided with major appliances and carpeting, but furniture is the tenant's responsibility. Without furniture costs, $1,000 to $2,000 will cover the initial cost of most rentals.

Advantage or disadvantage? Cost of rental unit

No, the heading is not a misprint. First, we will estimate the cost of renting. Then we will estimate the cost of owning. We will bring the two together to decide whether rental costs are an advantage or a disadvantage.

The worksheet in Exhibit 9.4 will accumulate the costs of renting. It includes amounts spent during a "typical" year. Estimates are used, since the worksheet is usually done prior to renting.

If the costs in Exhibit 9.4 are to be compared to those for owning, it is essential that the units be comparable in size, facilities, location, and amenities. Our example will be a three-bedroom house that rents for $900 per month. The tenant pays all utilities—heat, light, and water—and the landlord handles all repairs and maintenance.

Exhibit 9.4

Worksheet for Estimating the Annual Cost of a Rental

Line	Description	Rental: House
	Costs	
1	Rent	$10,800
2	Mortgage payment	—
3	Maintenance and repairs	—
4	Utilities	2,400
5	Insurance	200
6	Property taxes	—
7	Interest lost on security deposit:	
	$1,800 × 7% × (100% − 32% marginal tax rate)	86
8	Gross cost: Total of lines 1 through 7	$13,486

Several points about the worksheet. First, all amounts are rounded to the nearest dollar. Second, lines 2, 3, and 6 will not be used: the worksheet will be used later to calculate ownership costs, and they will be used then. The line 2 figure is zero because the tenant has no mortgage. Maintenance and repairs are the landlord's responsibility, so line 3 is zero also. Had the tenant paid part of these costs, the amount would be entered here. Line 6 is zero because the building owner pays the property taxes.

The estimated rent (line 1) is easily obtained. You can obtain utility cost estimates from the landlord, building manager, or (sometimes) the local utility company. Your insurance covers your furniture, appliances, and personal goods and gives you liability coverage if someone is injured in your unit. This insurance is essential; it covers things not handled by the landlord's policy. An insurance agent can provide an estimate for line 5.

On Line 7 you calculate interest lost on your security deposit. A few states require that interest be paid on security deposits. Here we assume the $1,800 security deposit—2 months' rent—could have earned 7 percent in a savings account. Federal and state income taxes would take some of that interest—let's assume 32 percent. Therefore, the potential lost

Exhibit 9.5

Worksheet for Estimating the Annual Cost of Owning a Home

Line	Description	Ownership: House
	Cost	
1	Rent	—
2	Mortgage payment	$9,408
3	Maintenance and repairs	$1,000
4	Utilities	$2,400
5	Insurance	400
6	Property taxes	2,200
7	Interest lost on down payment:	952
	$20,000 × 7% × (100% − 32% marginal tax rate)	
8	Gross cost: Total of lines 1 through 7	$16,360
	Tax Savings	
9	Property taxes	$2,200
10	Interest paid on mortgage	8,800
11	Total deductible amount: Line 9 + line 10	$11,000
12	Marginal tax rate	32%
13	Tax savings from deductions: Line 11 × line 12	$ 3,520
	Net Cost	
14	Net cost: Line 8 (gross cost) − line 13 (tax savings)	$12,840
	Long-Term Cost	
15	Appreciation in market value:	$ 3,000
	$100,000 × 3% annual appreciation	
16	Repayment of mortgage balance: Line 2 − line 10	608
17	Long-term cost: Line 14 (net cost) − line 15 − line 16	$ 9,232

interest after taxes is $86: $1,800 deposit × 7% interest × (100% − 32% tax rate).

The combined amounts on lines 1 through 7 give a gross rental cost of $13,486 (line 8 of Exhibit 9.4).

Disadvantage: Rental costs not deductible

Deducting an amount on your federal or state tax return saves you money. As we noted in Chapter 5, a deductible item reduces your taxable income and therefore your taxes. Unfortunately, the rental costs in Exhibit 9.4 are not deductible; the before- and after-tax costs of renting are identical. That is a major disadvantage.

Disadvantage: No appreciation in market value

Over time, the market value of most living units rises, especially when inflation is high or housing costs are rising. Renters receive none of this benefit; the landlord receives it. Historically, real estate investments have earned reasonable returns. Since renters have no investment in the living unit, there is no return. To add to the insult, your rent is likely to increase as the building's value rises.

Disadvantage: Housing cost is less predictable

During the lease period, monthly rent is fixed. But at renewal time the rent can be changed because of cost of living increases or at the owner's discretion. Whether inflation, higher demand in the rental market, or both, push up rents, your cost increases. Predicting the magnitude of these changes is difficult.

Ownership: Monetary Factors

Let us look at the economic aspects of homeownership. As you will see, it takes some effort to fully evaluate the costs of owning. In the following sections, we'll work through those calculations. When we're done, you should understand how to compare ownership costs for a particular home with those for a specific rental unit.

Cost of owning: Advantage or disadvantage?

To decide whether the cost of owning is an advantage or a disadvantage, we have to compare the costs of renting and owning.

A worksheet like the one in Exhibit 9.5 will be used to summarize ownership data. The top section is similar to Exhibit 9.4.

To keep the comparison valid, we will use a three-bedroom, $100,000 house as our example. The down payment is $20,000; the remaining $80,000 is financed with a 25-year, 11 percent fixed-rate mortgage. The monthly payment is $784; that was computed using Exhibit 9.11. A later section will show how.

Line 1, rent, is blank for most homes. Mobile homes on a rented lot will have an entry here. Mortgage payments for the year go on line 2. Here they are $9,408 (12 months × $784).

Maintenance and repair costs depend on the home's construction, age, previous care, location, and design. Expect to spend 1 percent of the home's purchase price annually. On a turn of the century Victorian home, 2 to 3 percent is more realistic. If you want a solid estimate, talk to a builder or to the owner of a similar home. Line 3 includes a 1 percent allowance for our sample house.

For a condominium, two costs must be added to arrive at the line 3 figure: the monthly maintenance fee for the common property, and repairs and maintenance on the owner's unit. If you report your garbage disposal has ceased disposing, the owner's association may answer: When *you* get *your* unit fixed, it will probably dispose again. Allow 0.5 percent of the condo's purchase price per year for its maintenance.

Mobile homes can have one or two components for line 3. In all cases you will pay the cost of maintaining the living unit; figure on 0.5 percent of the mobile home's price. If you rent the lot, that is your sole entry. But if you own the lot, you have to add the monthly fee for maintaining the common areas.

Estimated utility costs go on line 4. The present owner might be able to give you historical information. If not, the owner can sign a release, and many utility companies will provide details on recent billings. On a new home, you will have to rely on the builder's estimate. Costs are set at $2,400 for the sample.

When you own a home, homeowner's insurance covers it, its contents, and your liability for injuries on the premises. Premiums are higher than a rental policy's, but adequate coverage is essential. A local insurance agent can provide an estimate based on the value of the home and its contents. Here we set the cost at $400.

Property taxes depend on a home's value, where it is located, and the local tax rate. Mobile home taxes may have two components: one in the monthly rental (the property taxes), the second in a separate billing (tax on the unit's value). On existing homes, the realtor's sales sheet will usually list current taxes. For new homes, the builder or the local assessor's office should be able to supply an estimate. Line 6 of Exhibit 9.5 shows annual taxes of $2,200.

It is a rare home that does not require a down payment. While that money is tied up in the home, it earns no interest and therefore has to be considered a cost of owning—even though it is part of your home equity. The 20 percent down payment on the $100,000 house could have earned 7 percent interest. 32 percent of the earnings on that $20,000 would have gone for income taxes. Line 7 shows the lost interest at $952: $20,000 down payment × 7% interest × (100% − 32% tax rate).

Line 8 of Exhibit 9.5 pulls all ownerships costs together into one gross cost. For rentals the analysis stopped here. Because there are no tax deductions for rental costs, the gross cost of renting and the **net cost of renting** are the same. But here we need to take into account the effect of tax regulations on ownership costs.

Tax savings reduce ownership costs.   Federal income tax regulations have long favored ownership, and the current law does too. Owners can deduct all payments for mortgage interest and property taxes on their returns. The deductions reduce your income taxes. The savings depend on how much you pay in taxes and interest, and your marginal tax rate.

To start, estimate the property taxes and mortgage interest. Taxes are easy; take the amount from line 6 of Exhibit 9.5. Interest calculations require that you split total mortgage payments on line 2 into interest—

deductible and by far the largest fraction—and principal. An estimate will serve. To compute the interest, multiply the mortgage balance at the start of the year by the interest rate. An $80,000 mortgage balance at 11 percent involves approximately $8,800 interest: $80,000 balance $\times$ 11% interest (actual interest would be $8,768.33, so our $8,800 estimate is fine). Interest payments will decline over time, but the decline is glacially slow. Even after paying on that $80,000 mortgage for 5 years, your annual interest exceeds $8,300.

Line 11 of Exhibit 9.5 summarizes qualifying deductible expenses—$11,000 for our sample. Line 12 shows the combined federal and state marginal tax rate: 32 percent. Multiplying that tax rate times the deductible expenses from line 11 gives the tax savings on line 13: $3,520 for the example ($11,000 $\times$ 32%). Those savings reduce the cost of owning. In our example the **net cost of owning** drops to $12,840 (line 14): $16,360 gross cost $-$ $3,520 tax savings. Look back to the rental option in Exhibit 9.4, and you will find the net costs are quite similar.

Advantage: Some ownership costs are tax deductible

The deductibility of property taxes and mortgage interest lowers the cost of owning. In effect our tax system subsidizes homeownership. That benefit is likely to continue. The higher your marginal tax rate, the greater your subsidy. The higher the cost of the house you buy, the more you can deduct. Those savings are never enough, however, to drop the net cost of an expensive house below that of its less expensive counterpart.

Advantage: Price appreciation lowers ownership cost

As an owner you benefit from any increase in your home's market value—from its **appreciation.** Selling a home for more than you paid for it lowers your cost of owning. How much will a house appreciate? Most homes increase in value, but the amount depends on the home's location, its construction and design, supply and demand in the local housing market, inflation, and how much time you have to sell it. Single-family homes have appreciated as much as 10 percent annually during the last 10 years. Statistics on mobile homes and condominiums show widely divergent trends. Condominium prices have risen sharply in some areas, while others are flat. Appreciation in mobile home prices is far less common. In their early years, the value of these units actually declines. That raises the cost of owning. What looked like a bargain may not be one in the long run.

To include appreciation in your analysis, you need to forecast *future* appreciation. You can begin by building on historical records. Ask owners, realtors, mortgage lenders, builders, and the municipal or county tax assessor's office about the appreciation of similar units. Developing an appreciation estimate for a single-family house is easiest; for a condominium it is more challenging, and for a mobile home most difficult.

An analysis of appreciation trends suggests the following broad guidelines. Future appreciation for:

Single-family house. *2 to 5 percent per year.*
Condominium. *1 to 5 percent per year.*
Mobile home. *−5 to 2 percent per year.*

These rates are considerably lower than actual appreciation during the late 1970s, but inflation has slowed since then, so a more conservative estimate seems in order. Yes, that is a minus for mobile homes; depending on the unit's age and location, its value might rise, stay the same, or decline.

Let us return to Exhibit 9.5 and incorporate price appreciation. Suppose we expect prices in the market where the sample home is located to go up 3 percent annually. On a $100,00 house, that is about $3,000 yearly; this is entered on line 15.

Advantage: Limited taxes on gain from sale of home

When you sell assets at a profit, the gain is usually taxed. Houses receive special treatment. If you purchase another house of equal or greater value within 2 years before or after the sale, you can defer the tax on your gain. "Deferred" means taxes are postponed, not canceled. Even if you buy a less expensive house, you may be able to defer part of the tax. However, if you sell at a loss there is no deduction.

What if Schmedly Successful amassed a heap of deferred gains by his astute home purchases and sales? Will the tax agent finally get his due? Maybe not. Homeowners can exempt up to a $125,000 gain on a home sale if they are 55 or older. That means up to $125,000 of Schmedly's past gains will not be taxed. This forgiveness can only be used once, even if you do not use the entire $125,000 exclusion.

Strategy

If you are 55 or older when you sell your home and do not expect to purchase another, or if you are buying a much cheaper house, consider using your $125,000 one-time gain exclusion.

Cost Comparison: Renting versus Owning

Let's use the costs developed in Exhibits 9.4 and 9.5 to decide the question of whether renting or owning is cheaper. The costs of renting (Exhibit 9.4) are complete. Since renting bears no tax benefits and there is no price appreciation to consider, the gross cost on line 8 is your long-term rental cost.

Our ownership costs in Exhibit 9.5 are not complete. Look at line 16 of the exhibit. Total payments on the mortgage were $9,408 (line 2), yet interest paid was only $8,800 (line 10). The $608 difference repaid part of the $80,000 mortgage. That is a small amount, but remember, payments continue for 25 years. When the house is sold, you should recover that money. Repayments of borrowed funds are not a true cost of owning but an investment; they should be excluded. Line 16 deducts the mortgage repayment.

Now we are ready to compute the long-term cost of owning for line 17: it is $9,232. This figure is called the long-term cost because the owner will not receive the profit represented by appreciation in the market value and the equity represented by the mortgage repayments until the home is sold.

How does the figure on line 17 differ from the net cost (line 14)? Line 14 shows the out-of-pocket cost of owning. Line 17 shows the final cost of owning, compiled after the house is sold. Price appreciation and mortgage repayments make this less than the net cost.

Exhibits 9.4 and 9.5 show owning is cheaper than renting. The net cost of owning is $12,840 (line 14 of Exhibit 9.5), but that of renting is $13,486 (line 8 of Exhibit 9.4). In this particular case, ownership is preferable from a monetary standpoint, though nonmonetary considerations could shift the decision. Ownership is not always the better choice. You need to complete a cost comparison like Exhibits 9.4 and 9.5 to decide which option is best for you.

In cases where it is cheaper to buy, long-term costs will be even lower. Compare line 8 in Exhibit 9.4 and line 17 in Exhibit 9.5. Price appreciation and mortgage repayments combine to drop ownership costs, but only an analysis will give you the information you need. Again you should develop detailed cost estimates to decide which option is cheaper.

RENT OR BUY: IT'S YOUR DECISION

Both renting and owning have impressive advantages and some significant disadvantages. There is no clear winner. Weigh the factors you consider important to decide what is best for you. Renting and buying are very individual choices. Renters are not necessarily frustrated homeowners merely waiting for the chance to be owners. Nor is ownership the exclusive domain of families with children.

Line 8 of Exhibit 9.4 summarizes the cost of renting, and line 14 of Exhibit 9.5 the cost of owning. If you decide to own, you will have to fit this amount into your budget. That means answering the question: Can I afford to own?

Can You Afford to Own?

Once you have analyzed the costs of owning, you can work out a detailed budget to see if you have the income you need. When you make out your budget, consider the effect the purchase will have on your expenditures—auto, commuting, and education expenses, for instance. Tax savings should be taken into consideration.

Strategy

Use a budget to decide whether you can afford to own a particular house.

The long-term cost (line 17) can help you decide whether buying a home is wise, but the net cost (line 14 in Exhibit 9.5) shows if it is feasible. A homeowner forced into bankruptcy by housing expenses will never make it to the "long run." Remember, predicting price appreciation is difficult; err on the side of the conservative when you do your analysis.

Historical guides to affordability

Some financial advisors and lenders still use two historical guides to determine affordability:

1 You can afford the house if its price is less than 2½ times your annual income.

2 You can afford the house if your related expenditures are less than 28 percent of income.

Both calculations are quickly done, but these two neat rules are of questionable worth.

If you decide whether you can afford a home based solely on its purchase price, you are ignoring the costs of owning it. The annual cost of owning a home depends on the size of your down payment, local property taxes, your marginal tax rate, maintenance and repairs, and current mortgage interest rates. If one or more of these change, payments can go from manageable to very difficult to make.

The rule that limits housing payments to a percentage of income—25 to 30 percent—concentrates on the right thing: the payments required. However, note that usually only the mortgage payment and property tax are compared to gross income. And the approach ignores one major item: *you.* Depending on your spending habits and debts, 25 to 30 percent may be too high.

A budget is a far more accurate way to gauge affordability than historical rules of thumb.

Which is best for you?

Cost comparisons are not the final "answer" in the rent or purchase decision. You must consider all the advantages and disadvantages. Even if

owning costs less, its disadvantages may be such that you choose to rent. If renting is cheaper, you may still decide owning's advantages justify its cost.

SELECTING A RENTAL UNIT

If your analysis shows renting is best, the challenge is finding a good rental unit. A careful search increases the likelihood that you will be content after you move in. Problems with leases and landlords can often be minimized by a detailed check.

Investigating the Rental

The questions in Exhibit 9.6 highlight points to check in a prospective rental unit. While specifically designed for apartments, 80 to 90 percent of the points apply as well to houses, duplexes, or townhouses.

Rental Agreement

Most rental units require a formal agreement between the renter and land-lord: the **lease.** It specifies the starting date, length of the lease—a 1-year lease is standard, but 2- and 3-year leases are sometimes offered—monthly rental, security deposit, and rules and regulations. Read the lease's contents carefully. Key points include:

Exhibit 9.6

Checklist for Selecting an Apartment

Building and Grounds
Attractive, well-constructed building with professional landscaping
Good maintenance and upkeep
Locked, secure entrances
Clean, well-lighted, and uncluttered lobby, halls, and stairs
Reliable building management and supervision

Services and Facilities
Laundry equipment
Adequate parking space (indoor or outdoor)
Locked mail boxes and receiving room for packages
Reliable and convenient trash collection and disposal
Accessible fire escapes
Storage lockers
Elevators
Engineer on call for emergency repairs
Extras—window washing, decorating, shops, lobby attendant

Living Areas
Adequate room sizes and storage space
Convenient floor plan with good traffic pattern
Suitable wall space for furniture
Soundproof (Can you hear talking, footsteps, running water, and the operation of equipment in other apartments and in hallways?)
Attractive decorating and fixtures
Pleasant views, good natural light
Agreeable size, type, and number of windows, affording good ventilation
Windows equipped with blinds or shades, screens and storm windows
Easy upkeep, including attractive low-maintenance floors
Furnished appliances in good operating condition
Clean, effective heating, thermostatically controlled
Up-to-date and sufficient wiring
An adequate number of electrical outlets, conveniently placed
Well-fitted doors, casings, cabinets, and built-ins
Extras—air conditioning, carpeting, dishwasher, disposal, fireplace, patio

Source: Money Management Institute Booklet, *Your Housing Dollar.* The Money Management Institute, Household Financial Services, Prospect Heights, IL.

What utilities, if any, are included in the rent payment?
Who do you contact for repairs and maintenance?
What happens if you have to terminate the lease early?
How is the rent determined if you want to renew the lease?

If a section is not clear, ask for an explanation. Promises of redecoration and repairs should be in writing, as should any waivers of the rules.

Strategy

Read the lease carefully; know what you receive and what the landlord expects of you.

Security deposit

The **security deposit** can be troublesome. A deposit of 1 month's rent is a minimum; 2 to 3 months is increasingly common. Problems center on several issues: What can and should be charged to the deposit? When is the deposit returned? What recourse does the tenant have if the treatment seems unfair? Deposit practices are regulated by some states. Call the consumer affairs office of your state to get information on the rules.

Strategy

Carefully examine the treatment of security deposits in the lease. Ask what can be charged against your deposit; have this put in writing if the lease is not clear.

BUYING THE RIGHT HOME

Suppose you decide to own; how do you go about choosing a suitable home? Some factors are common to all ownership units.

Location

There is an old axiom in real estate that the three most important concerns in buying a home are *location, location,* and *location.* This overstates matters, but location is crucial. A well-designed, well-built, well-maintained home in a deteriorating neighborhood, next to major highways, or near heavy industry, will appreciate slowly if at all, will be hard to sell, and will always be worth less than a comparable home in a good location.

Strategy

Make certain the home you buy is in a desirable location.

Zoning

Zoning regulations spell out what types of buildings can be constructed in an area; they can be important in maintaining the value of a home. A good bratwurst, the morning paper, and steel-belted radials are fine things, but few want the smell of a meat packer, a paper mill, or a smelter wafting over their backyard fence. Good zoning separates industrial and residential areas. Within that residential area, single-family units may be separated from multifamily homes.

Strategy

The area where you are considering a home should be zoned for residential units comparable to your choice.

Value of surrounding property

The value of surrounding property influences the value of a home. A $150,000 home in a neighborhood of $80,000 houses is not going to be as valuable as it would be in a neighborhood of $150,000 and $200,000 units. It is to the owner's greatest advantage if a home's value is about the same, or slightly less, than values of those around it.

Strategy

Concentrate on houses whose value is comparable to that of others in the neighborhood.

Convenience

Consider distance to shopping, schools, church or synagogue, and work. Living in an inconvenient location in a large metropolitan area can entail considerable travel costs.

Selecting a Single-Family House

Single-family homes have long been the main housing unit in the United States. There is usually a wide selection available. Start your search using the previous four criteria. Then narrow your choice to specific houses.

The criteria in Exhibit 9.7 can help in the systematic evaluation of the house, the yard, and the neighborhood. A few hours of inspection should reveal things like damp basements, inadequate insulation, decrepit windows and doors, and "vintage" plumbing. You may not spot all the problems, but you will have far fewer "surprises."

Considering an older house?

An older house can offer unique design, location, and amenities, quality construction, and generous living space. But the potential shortcomings and problems are such that you may want to go beyond the checklist in Exhibit 9.7. Some excellent books on evaluating an older home can help you. Second, get a qualified builder or contractor to evaluate the house. The modest fee is money well spent. Finally, consider having an independent appraisal of the house's value.

Selecting a Condominium

There are fewer condominiums for sale than single-family homes. They are fairly recent developments, and have only been built in some locations. They are often targeted to a specific clientele. The four general criteria—location, zoning, value of surrounding property, and convenience—apply equally to condominiums, but recognize that you may have less latitude in your choice.

Before evaluating specific units, let's review the added features of condominiums. The checklist in Exhibit 9.8 can help you decide the relative importance of each one. A series of yes responses suggests a condominium

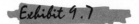

Exhibit 9.7

Checklist for a House

House Exterior and Yard
Attractive, well-designed house
In harmony with natural surroundings and
  neighboring houses
Lot of the right size and shape for house and
  garage
Desirable orientation on lot
Suitable use of building materials
Attractive landscaping and yard
Good drainage with dry, firm soil around the
  house
Mature, healthy trees, providing shade when
  needed
Well-kept driveway and walks
Patio, porch, deck, or yard
Convenient parking—garage, carport, or
  street
Enough distance between houses to afford
  privacy
Sheltered entry—well-lighted and large
Convenient service entrance with access to
  kitchen

Outside Construction
Durable siding materials in good condition
Solid brick and masonry free of cracks
Solid foundation walls, 6 inches above
  ground level, 8 inches thick
Caulked and weather-stripped windows and
  doors
Noncorrosive gutters and downspouts,
  connected to storm sewer or splash block to
  carry water away from house
Copper or aluminum flashing used over
  doors, windows, and joints on the roof

Inside Construction
Sound, smooth walls with invisible nails and
  taping on dry walls; without hollows or
  large cracks in plaster walls
Well-done carpentry work with properly
  fitted joints and moldings
Well-fitted, easy-to-operate windows

Level wood floors with smooth finish
Good possibilities for improvements,
  remodeling, expanding
Built-in cabinets with properly fitted and
  easy-to-work doors and drawers
Dry basement floor with hard smooth
  surface and adequate drain
Stairways with sturdy railings, adequate
  head room, not too steep
Leakproof roof, in good condition
Adequate insulation for soundproofing and
  year-round comfort

Living Space
Satisfactory floor plan
Attractive entry with foyer and closet
Work areas (kitchen, laundry, workshop)
  with adequate storage and counter space,
  lighting and electrical power
Bedrooms and bathrooms located far
  enough from other parts of the house to
  afford privacy and quiet
Inviting social areas (living, dining, and
  family rooms, play space, yard, porch,
  deck, or patio) spacious enough for
  family and guests
Certain rooms conveniently located—
  foyer and living room, dining room and
  kitchen, bedrooms and baths
Adequate storage—closets, cabinets,
  shelves, attic, basement, garage
Rooms of sufficient size to accommodate
  furnishings
Agreeable size and type of windows,
  placed to provide sufficient light and
  ventilation
Attractive decorating and fixtures
Usable attic and/or basement space
Extras—fireplace, air conditioning,
  porches, new kitchen and baths, built-
  ins, skylights, deck

Source: Money Management Institute Booklet, *Your Housing Dollar*, The Money Management Institute, Household Financial Services, Prospect Heights, IL.

may be right for you. Many negative responses indicate you need to reconsider.

The prospective buyer selecting a condominium has to focus on the same concerns as a buyer looking at a single-family house does. The checklist in Exhibit 9.7 outlines the major points. Even through the yard is common property, it should be evaluated.

Caution: Problem areas ahead

There are enough abuses and questionable practices in condominium sales to suggest caution. Some developers don't deliver promised recreation facilities; the four-color brochure of planned swimming pools and putting greens is no substitute for the real thing. Others quote attractively low monthly maintenance fees, but when the condominium owners take con-

Exhibit 9.8

Evaluating a Condominium's Added Features

	Yes	No
1. Is the reduced maintenance feature		
a. An appealing one?	( )	( )
b. Critical to you?	( )	( )
c. A means of eliminating work you dislike?	( )	( )
2. Are the recreational facilities		
a. What you enjoy?	( )	( )
b. Sufficient for everyone to use without long waits?	( )	( )
c. Such that you will use them extensively?	( )	( )
d. Such that you can drop your recreation club membership?	( )	( )
3. Will the unit's location		
a. Reduce your commuting effort and expense?	( )	( )
b. Put you closer to social and cultural interests?	( )	( )
c. Benefit your family's interests and activities?	( )	( )
4. Do your present housing needs not require the		
a. Larger living area of a single-family house?	( )	( )
b. Private yard of a single-family house?	( )	( )
5. Can you live where you		
a. Have limited control over the common property?	( )	( )
b. May have to alter your life-style (regarding noise, entertaining, hours, and pets, for example)?	( )	( )

trol they find no provision for major repairs and replacement, so fees have to double or triple. Some developers retain title to the recreation facilities and lease them to the development for exorbitant rents. The moral? Always check out the development and the developer thoroughly. Exhibit 9.9 can help you do that. If you answer many questions no, look elsewhere.

Selecting a Mobile Home

A sizable number of manufacturers produce a wide array of mobile homes, from stripped-down models to some very well appointed ones. Unfortunately, there are few places to park mobile homes. Zoning regulations often limit them to designated parks, and some of those accept only units purchased from their own sales outlet. Location, value of surrounding homes, and convenience have a place in the initial selection process, but you will have to make some compromises.

The person selecting a mobile home uses some of the same criteria as the buyer of a single-family house; the questions in Exhibit 9.7 can help. Of course, questions about the yard and neighborhood do not apply. Select a mobile home carefully. In the past, the quality of materials and construction has been suspect. Certainly, many high-quality units have been pro-

---

Exhibit 9.9

Judging a Condominium Development

	Yes	No
General Development Plans		
1. Are the neighbors compatible (singles, parents with children, mature couples)?	( )	( )
2. Does the overall development		
a. Appear attractive and well thought out?	( )	( )
b. Provide adequate facilities and common area?	( )	( )
3. Is the design suitable for your climate?	( )	( )
4. When you want to sell		
a. Are there restrictions?	( )	( )
b. Must you work through a particular realtor?	( )	( )
5. Are the number of units and the final completion date set?	( )	( )
6. Are there many vacant units? If so, why?	( )	( )
Common Facilities		
1. Do the facilities meet your needs?	( )	( )
2. Are recreation facilities part of common property?	( )	( )
3. If leased, are the fees reasonable?	( )	( )
4. If unfinished, is the completion date guaranteed?	( )	( )
Maintenance		
1. Are the units well built?	( )	( )
2. Does the maintenance fee cover replacement of major items (roof, painting, sidewalks)?	( )	( )
3. Is the estimated fee per unit based on a realistic number of units?	( )	( )
4. Have the developer's previous condominiums been of high quality and successful?	( )	( )
5. Can owners be forced to pay their maintenance fee?	( )	( )
6. If a new development, is the projected budget reasonable?	( )	( )
7. If an established complex, has the maintenance fee per unit remained relatively stable?	( )	( )

duced, but there have been enough shoddy ones to warrant taking extra care.

Strategy

Concentrate on reputable mobile home manufacturers. Talk to people who have purchased mobile homes made by a particular manufacturer.

FINANCING YOUR HOME

With the price of a "typical" home approaching $100,000, nearly everyone borrows to buy a house. Penelope Persistent may be willing to save for 20 or 30 years, but most people want to enjoy their home much sooner. The federal government has long encouraged an active mortgage market to help people buy homes.

Common Features of Mortgages

Since all mortgages have some common features, let's review these. Then we'll move to the specifics of the various types of mortgages. These points can help you decide whether a particular mortgage is appropriate.

Self-amortizing

A **self-amortizing loan** is one for which the unpaid balance is repaid over the life of the loan. The balance is gradually reduced through a series of periodic payments. Nearly all mortgage loans will self-amortize.

Exhibit 9.10 illustrates how the payments on a $1,000 loan reduce the

Exhibit 9.10

Unpaid Balance on a $1,000 Mortgage Loan at 12 Percent, with Maturities of 15, 20, 25, and 30 Years

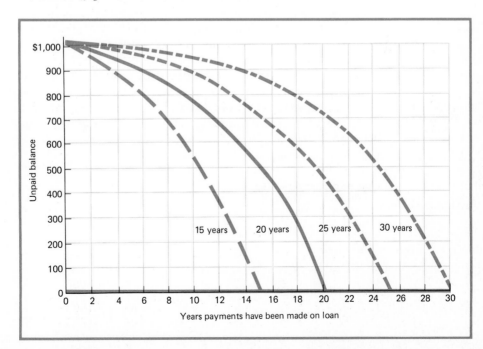

balance over time. Four loan maturities are shown: 15, 20, 25, and 30 years. All these loans self-amortize, since the payments drop the balance to zero by the loan's maturity, but the rate of repayment differs. The early, flat section of Exhibit 9.10 shows that interest consumes 83 to 97 percent of those early payments; little remains to repay the mortgage. But in the final years of each mortgage much of the money goes to pay off the principal; the sharp drop of the curves in Exhibit 9.10 confirms this. The longer the maturity, the longer it takes to enter this faster payment segment.

Mortgage payment table

You can calculate the monthly payment for a particular mortgage in several ways. The easiest is to use tables like those in Exhibit 9.11 or Appendix A.1. Both show the required payment for a $1,000 loan at different interest rates. To use either one, divide the amount of the desired loan by $1,000 and multiply the result times the payment in the table. For a $65,000 mortgage loan at 11 percent for 25 years, the payment is $637: ($65,000 mortgage/$1,000 loan) × $9.80 (Exhibit 9.11). This is only an estimate, but it is close enough to the actual $637.07 payment for our use.

What if the quoted rate is 11.25 percent? Do you wait until rates rise to 12 or drop to 11? No. Prorate the difference between 11 and 12 percent. Payment on a $1,000, 25-year, 11.25 percent loan would be $9.9825: $9.80 from the 11% loan + [0.25 × ($10.53 for a 12% loan − $9.80 for an 11% loan)]. From there you can compute the monthly payment for a mortgage of any size.

Acceleration clause

Many mortgages have **acceleration clauses** which make the balance of the loan due if the monthly payment is 60 to 90 days late. The lender can foreclose and begin repossessing the property. Lenders are not willing to negotiate on this provision; purchase a house that fits your budget, and it should not be a concern.

Nonassumption clause

A **nonassumption clause** says a new buyer cannot take over the existing mortgage. Why would a buyer want to? If interest rates have risen sharply since the current owner financed the home, the mortgage may carry a bargain rate. Recognizing this, many lenders routinely include this clause, although some federally supported mortgages prohibit it.

Prepayment penalty

A **prepayment penalty** is a fee charged if the buyer decides to repay a mortgage before its maturity. There are exceptions. Some loans allow you to repay 10 percent of the balance each year without penalty, and there

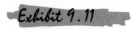

Exhibit 9.11

Monthly Payments to Amortize a $1,000 Loan at Different Interest Rates and Maturities

Years to maturity	Finance Rate on Loan (APR)							
	8%	9%	10%	11%	12%	13%	14%	15%
15	9.56	10.14	10.75	11.37	12.00	12.65	13.32	14.00
20	8.36	9.00	9.65	10.32	11.01	11.72	12.44	13.17
25	7.72	8.39	9.09	9.80	10.53	11.28	12.04	12.81
30	7.34	8.05	8.78	9.52	10.29	11.06	11.85	12.64

generally is no penalty if you sell the house. Some states restrict prepayment penalties.

Suppose Bob Banker, local mortgage loan officer, signs a customer to a 30-year, 15 percent loan and the market rates drop to 10 percent in 4 years. The 15 percent borrower will want to refinance at the lower rate. But if Bob placed a stiff prepayment penalty in the original loan, refinancing could be too costly to be attractive.

Strategy

Search for a mortgage with no prepayment penalty. Negotiate with the lender to have it removed if the contract has one.

Tax and insurance escrow accounts

Some lenders require that borrowers include one-twelfth of the home's property taxes and homeowners insurance premium in each monthly payment. The money accumulates in a **tax escrow account** or a tax and insurance escrow account, which often earns little or no interest. Some states require interest be paid. Tax and insurance bills are paid by the lender from the escrow account.

Lenders assure you the escrow account makes your life "easy." Rest assured this is not a charity. Even if it is not "required," many lenders encourage you to use one, arguing escrow accounts are needed to ensure that taxes and insurance are paid. Most home buyers can manage their finances to ensure the necessary money will be there. Little or no interest on your savings is hardly attractive. Last, an escrow account prevents you from timing your property tax payment to take advantage of federal income tax regulations.

Strategy

Try to avoid tax and insurance escrow accounts on a mortgage. They can be cumbersome, pay limited or no interest, and limit your flexibility.

Features That Distinguish Different Mortgages

The six major types of mortgages we will review differ in three respects:

1 Size of the required down payment
2 Variability of the interest rate
3 Stability of the payments

Required down payment

Home buyers are normally required to pay a percentage of the purchase price as a down payment. Some government-guaranteed or -insured mortgages require 3 percent or less. A conventional mortgage may require 20 percent or more down.

Home buyers and mortgage lenders view down payments differently. Lenders prefer large down payments so the buyer has a "stake" in making the home purchase a success; if the buyer defaults (fails to repay), the down payment may be lost. If the lender repossesses the unit, the down payment will help cover any losses. In contrast, buyers see the down payment as a barrier to ownership; they want it low.

Government insurance and guarantees, along with insurance from private companies, allow lower down payments. Lenders will accept less down when insurance or a guarantee program protects the lender against large losses if borrowers default.

Interest rate over life of mortgage

Ten years ago this section was not necessary: mortgages had fixed interest rates. A mortgage that started at 10 percent stayed there until it was repaid. Lenders were locked into a fixed rate, but borrowers could refinance the loan if interest rates dropped.

Now the interest rate on many mortgages is adjustable. If interest rates in general rise or fall, so do the rates on these mortgages. The sharp rise in interest rates during the late 1970s and early 1980s showed lenders the danger of long-term fixed-rate mortgages. To encourage borrowers to accept a variable rate contract, many lenders quote lower interest on adjustable rate mortgages.

Most frequently, adjustment of the mortgage's interest rate is automatic. The rate is tied, or **indexed,** to some interest rate in the financial marketplace. An increased demand for funds, or reduced supply of them, causes interest rates in the financial markets to rise. Reduced demand or increased supply causes a decline. A mortgage that has an indexed interest rate follows interest rates in the marketplace. The rate on an adjustable rate mortgage may be adjusted at an interval that ranges anywhere from every 6 months to every 5 years.

Sometimes mortgage rates are adjusted through negotiations between the lender and the borrower. Instead of an automatic adjustment, the mortgage is built on a series of 1- to 5-year notes (the buyer usually chooses their length) covering the full 20 to 30 years of the mortgage's maturity. Each time a note comes due, the new interest rate is negotiated. The level of interest is still affected by what is happening in the marketplace. If rates are high, the mortgage's rate will increase, and if they are low, it will fall.

Monthly payment over life of mortgage

The traditional fixed-rate mortgage had a set payment throughout its life to self-amortize the loan. Many newer mortgages allow payments to change as the interest rate is reset.

Some mortgages are set up with a series of graduated payments. Payments begin small to lessen the burden for first-time buyers. At prescribed times during the life of the mortgage, payments rise. The initial payment is not high enough to repay the mortgage, so later ones are considerably larger to catch up. The underlying assumption of these mortgages is that the buyer's income will rise, thereby increasing the ability to pay. Increases in the payment may continue for 5 to 10 years or for the life of mortgage.

MAJOR TYPES OF CURRENTLY AVAILABLE MORTGAGES

The entire mortgage field has changed considerably during the past decade. New types of mortgages continue to be introduced: a few succeed and become generally available; others disappear. Some traditional kinds of mortgages will also disappear. One or more of the mortgage types discussed below may have vanished by the time you read this, only to be replaced by new ones.

Not all these mortgages will be available everywhere. While more spread out than ever, mortgage markets are still somewhat regional. The mortgages offered to you may have some unique features, but you should be able to find one that matches your needs.

Exhibit 9.12 uses down payment, variability of interest rate, and stability of payments to highlight major differences and similarities of six widely available mortgages.

Conventional Mortgage

Lending institutions have offered **conventional mortgages** for years; these mortgages are the traditional home loans. The lender is assured of repayment by the borrower's promise to repay, the pledge of the house as security, and the down payment. While maturities of 20, 25, and 30 years have always been popular, lenders currently quote attractive rates on 15-year mortgages. As Exhibit 9.11 shows, repaying over the shorter period requires considerably higher payments.

FHA-Insured and VA-Guaranteed Mortgages

Federal Housing Authority (FHA) mortgages are available to the general public. Veterans are eligible for **Veterans Administration (VA) mortgages.** Neither organization actually lends money: that is done by a financial institution, a third party to the transaction. The role of the FHA is to insure, and the VA to guarantee, the repayment of the loan if the borrower defaults. Because the lender's loss is partially or completely covered, smaller down payments are acceptable: near zero on some VA loans and around 5 percent on FHA loans. Both are far short of the 20 percent needed for most conventional mortgages.

There is a cost, however. Borrowers pay a mortgage insurance premium (MIP) of 2.4 to 3.8 percent of the mortgage at the start of the loan. The amount can be added to the mortgage balance; most people take this option. On a $70,000, 25-year FHA mortgage, the present MIP is $2,520: $70,000 mortgage $\times$ 3.6% premium.

Exhibit 9.12

Features of Currently Available Mortgage Loans

Type of mortgage	Typical down payment	Interest rate on mortgage	Monthly payments over life of mortgage
1. Conventional	20% or more	Fixed when loan is obtained	Fixed when loan is obtained
2. FHA and VA	0% to 5%	Fixed when loan is obtained	Fixed when loan is obtained
3. Conventional, insured	5% to 10%	Fixed when loan is obtained	Fixed when loan is obtained
4. Graduated payment (GPM)	5% to 15%	Fixed when loan is obtained	Increases each year during first 5 to 10 years
5. Growing equity (GEM) (rapid payoff)	5% to 10%	Fixed when loan is obtained	Increases 2.5% to 7.5% each year of mortgage loan
6. Adjustable rate (ARM)	10%	Varies with interest rates in the marketplace	Varies as the interest rate on the mortgage changes

The size of an FHA or VA mortgage is limited. The FHA has a loan maximum, presently around $80,000. If you choose an expensive house, that may be a problem. VA loans do not have a direct limit, but the very low down payment makes it difficult to obtain loans above $100,000.

Interpreting the quoted interest rate on a VA loan is not simple. The maximum VA loan rate is set by government regulation and is often slightly below the market rate on mortgages—a 9.5 percent rate when the market is charging 10 percent, for example. Arnold Astute, local mortgage lender, is not about to make VA loans at 9.5 percent when other mortgages offer a 10 percent return. To make VA loans attractive, the regulators created "points"; we will discuss those shortly.

The interest rate on FHA loans is not capped but floats with prevailing market interest rates. But what if the rate is set somewhat below the market? Arnold Astute would view this gem like the VA one: "My favorite competitor deserves both." Points encourage Arnold to reconsider.

Points

Points are widely used in mortgage lending. Fees, discounts, premiums, and other costs may be quoted as so many points. One point equals 1 percent of the mortgage balance. So three points on a $70,000 loan would be 3 percent of the balance, or $2,100. Let's see how points are used on FHA and VA loans.

Points can bring an FHA or VA loan's interest rate up to the prevailing market rate. Each point charged raises the mortgage's effective interest rate roughly one-eighth of a percent. Why not do it directly? The maximum rate on a VA loan is regulated, and lenders are often reluctant to quote a higher rate on FHA loans for fear of losing customers. Though the quoted rate is unchanged, points raise the effective rate and boost the lender's return.

An example will illustrate. Bob plans to buy Sue's house using a $70,000 VA mortgage. The maximum VA rate is 9.5 percent (the market rate is near 10). The lender will not settle for 9.5 percent. If one point raises the lender's return about one-eighth of a percent, charging four points will bring the return to 10 percent. But someone will have to pay that four-point, $2,800 fee: $70,000 mortgage × 4%.

On a VA loan, the seller pays the points. On an FHA loan, the buyer and seller negotiate who pays. Since the loan in our example is a VA loan, Sue pays. She receives $67,200 from the mortgage lender: $70,000 loan minus the $2,800 point fee. In effect, the lender collects payments on a $70,000 loan but pays out $67,200, raising the return from 9.5 to 10 percent. Sue will be so "impressed" (maybe depressed) by all this that next time she will boost the sale price by about 4 percent, neatly shifting the payment to the buyer. Had it been an FHA loan, Bob and Sue could have negotiated who pays the points.

Strategy

VA or FHA mortgage interest rates are less attractive if you have to pay points. As the buyer, you can pay openly on an FHA loan or indirectly through an inflated sale price on a VA loan.

Conventional Mortgage: Insured

Both buyer and lender benefit from a **conventional mortgage backed by private insurance.** Buyers get a mortgage with 5 or 10 percent down. Lenders have insurance to cover part or all of the loss if the borrower defaults. Another advantage is speedy approval or denial of loan requests; this mortgage does not involve a 1- or 2-month wait as FHA and VA loans often do. Since there is no interest ceiling, no points have to be juggled.

The insurance company uses the premiums from many borrowers to cover losses from a few. Borrowers pay an initial premium of 0.5 to 1.25 percent of the mortgage when the loan is granted. Someone who put 10 percent down and borrowed $70,000 might pay about $385 ($70,000 × 0.55%). Once the home has been purchased, the buyer's annual premium equals 0.4 to 0.6 percent of the unpaid mortgage balance.

Graduated-Payment Mortgage

Graduated-payment mortgages (GPMs) are targeted to people who have difficulty fitting a conventional loan payment into their current budget. Initial payment on a GPM is less than what is needed to amortize the loan. To catch up, payments rise over the next 5 or 10 years; annual increases of 2.5 to 7.5 percent are typical. On some loans, early payments may not even cover the interest, so the loan balance actually rises; this is called negative amortization. It may be several years before the payment reaches the point where it begins repaying the principal. Once all the planned increases are in place, remaining payments will cover the entire balance by the final maturity date.

Two of the mortgages in Exhibit 9.13, the conventional and the GPM, will illustrate. Both are for $70,000, at 11 percent interest, for 30 years. The payment on the conventional mortgage is $666.40 per month, but beginning payments on the GPM start at only $509.79, nearly $160 less. Those savings gradually disappear as the payment rises 7.5 percent each year, and by the end of year 4 the GPM payment exceeds the conventional loan's. At the end of year 5, the GPM reaches $731.86, where it remains for the balance of the mortgage. The later payments, nearly $66 higher than the conventional mortgage's, make up for the low early installments.

Growing-Equity Mortgage

Payments on a **growing-equity mortgage (GEM)** increase by a specified percentage each year over the mortgage's life. First-year payments are identical to those on a conventional mortgage for a similar amount; then the payments increase by 2.5 to 7.5 percent each year. The larger monthly payments mean more is applied to the principal and the mortgage is repaid in much less than 25 or 30 years. A payment increase of 2.5 percent annually repays a mortgage in about 14 years. At 7.5 percent it takes only 10 years. Of course, raising the payment 7.5 percent more than doubles it by the end.

Buyers who expect their incomes to rise quickly and consistently find GEMs attractive. By agreeing to the higher payments, buyers are committing part of their future income to early repayment. A slower than planned growth in income could leave them scrambling to make the payments.

Let's finish Exhibit 9.13 with a GEM example. The loan is still $70,000

Exhibit 9.13

Monthly Payments during First 9 Years on a Conventional, Graduated-Payment, and Growing-Equity Mortgage

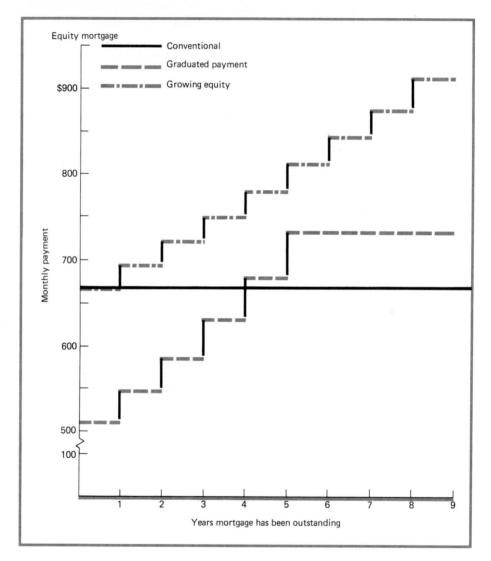

at 11 percent; payments are scheduled to rise 4 percent annually. With a 30-year maturity, the $666.40 initial GEM payment is the same as the conventional mortgage's. It rises to $779.86 by the fifth year, and $912.32 by the ninth, nearly 37 percent higher than initially. Those extra dollars go to repay the mortgage; the balance will be repaid near the end of the thirteenth year.

Adjustable Rate Mortgage

As the name suggests, the interest rate on an **adjustable rate mortgage** (ARM) is not constant. When market interest rates are rising, the mortgage rate does too. Good news for the lender—the return on the mortgage is rising—but not so good for the homeowner. A decline in rates lowers the borrower's cost but drops the lender's return. An ARM follows interest rates in the financial markets.

To protect borrowers from sharp interest rate swings, ARMs may include limits. Many contracts promise not to raise or lower the rate by more than 1.5 to 2 percent each year. An ARM that starts at 10.5 percent and limits the annual change to 1.5 percent cannot exceed 12 percent nor drop below 9 at the end of the first year. It can, however, continue to change by the allowed maximum every year.

As further protection, some contracts place a cap on how high or low an ARM's rate can go over the loan's lifetime; typically the cap is 5 percent. So the rate on a 10.5 percent ARM with a 5 percent cap could not rise above 15.5 nor drop below 5.5 percent. But note that regulations do not *require* any cap; that is the lender's decision. A cap is desirable since it makes borrowing costs more predictable.

Strategy

Always try to find an ARM with a cap: 5 percent is acceptable. Limits on the annual rate change, while desirable, are less critical.

Your payments change with the interest rate. Usually the payment is adjusted each time the rate changes; rising when rates rise, dropping when they fall. A second option is to keep the same payment but change the repayment period; lengthening it if rates rise, shortening it if they drop. However, if a mortgage is relatively new and rates rise sharply, it may not be practical to lengthen the maturity.

An ARM's rate can be indexed to some prevailing market interest rate, or it may be set by negotiations between the lender and the borrower.

Indexed rate

Some ARMs are indexed to an interest rate in the financial markets that is independent of the lender. One widely used index is the interest rate on selected Treasury securities. Since this rate reacts quickly to changes in the financial markets, using it means an ARM's rate will track the market quite closely. Another option is to base the rate on a weighted average of the interest rates the savings institutions in a region are paying on certificates of deposit and savings accounts. The Federal Home Loan office compiles statistics and computes such rates for different regions of the country. This index lags the financial markets a bit, not rising until after the market has been going up for a while and not declining as quickly. So ARMs based on this rate also lag market developments a bit.

Negotiated rates

Some ARMs rely on negotiations between the borrower and the lender to set the interest rate. Generally, the initial rate remains in effect for 1 to 5 years. Then the lender quotes a rate for the next period. If the quoted rate is not acceptable, the borrower can try to negotiate a lower rate or refinance with another lender. The latter can be expensive, since the entire closing process has to be repeated.

LAND CONTRACT: AN ALTERNATIVE TO A MORTGAGE

Under a **land contract** the seller finances the sale of a house by agreeing to accept a series of monthly payments as part of the purchase price. Interest rates on land contracts are generally fixed, although some do permit adjustments. Some have equal payments over the life of the loan. Others have attractively small payments during the loan's lifetime and one very, very large balloon payment at the end. Recall from Chapter 6 that this final payment usually constitutes a major part of the loan. With land contracts at tens of thousands of dollars, the buyer can end up with a gigantic last payment.

A major difference between the land contract and a mortgage is the point at which title passes to the buyer. With a mortgage, the buyer receives title when the loan is made, though the title has a lien against it. With the usual land contract, title remains with the seller until the final payment is made. If the entire contract is not repaid, the buyer has little recourse if she or he tries to recover money already paid. Because the buyer does not have title, the house cannot be sold by the buyer.

Strategy

Consider a land contract only if (1) you are certain you can make all payments and (2) you have exhausted all other sources for a mortgage.

SELECTING THE RIGHT MORTGAGE

Begin by examining your own financial circumstances using an up-to-date income statement, balance sheet, and budget. You will need this financial data when you apply for the loan, but it can also guide your search. An estimate such as the one in Exhibit 9.5 can give you a general idea of the costs of ownership. Some issues you must deal with when selecting a loan are financial, some involve value judgments, others depend on your personal preference.

1 How large is your proposed down payment?
2 How much can you spend on housing?
3 How long are you likely to own the house?
4 Will your future income rise?
5 How fast will that income increase?
6 Will the uncertainty a flexible loan entails be a problem?
7 Is repaying quickly important?
8 Will you consider several lenders?

As you answer these questions, you will likely find that one or two of the loan options are best for you.

When selecting a mortgage, you need to consider the current state and future direction of the overall economy. Pertinent questions include:

1   Are current rates historically high or low?

2   Have interest rates been rising or declining recently?

3   Is the number of lenders increasing or dropping?

4   Are interest rates likely to rise or fall in the future?

Answers to these questions can help you narrow the choice among mortgage loans.

To help sort out the six mortgages discussed earlier, Exhibit 9.14 summarizes the major strengths and weaknesses of each. Guidelines given in

Exhibit 9.14

Guidelines to Help You Evaluate Currently Available Mortgage Loans and Decide Which Mortgage Is Best for You

Strengths	Weaknesses	When to Select
Conventional Mortgage Widely available. Payment remains fixed. Predictable future cost. Higher down payment may lower interest rate.	Very large down payment. Interest rate may be higher than on ARMs.	Future interest rates will likely be higher. Buyer wants fixed terms.
FHA and VA Mortgages Extremely low down payment. Payment remains fixed. Predictable future cost.	Long wait for approval. Seller may refuse if points are high. Insurance premium for FHA or VA coverage.	Future interest rates will likely be higher. Buyer needs low down payment.
Conventional Mortgage, Insured Very low down payment. Widely available. Payments remain fixed. Predictable future cost.	Interest rate higher with small down payment. Initial and annual insurance premium.	Future interest rates will likely be higher. Buyer needs lower down payment.
Graduated-Payment Mortgage Lowers initial payment. Payments are fixed. Payment rises with buyer's ability to pay. Predictable future cost.	Interest rate may be higher than on conventional. Not offered by all lenders.	Buyer needs lower initial payments. Buyer expects income to rise.
Growing-Equity Mortgage Rapid payoff reduces interest paid. Lender may offer "bargain interest rate" to promote GEM.	Very large payment in later years. Repayment is difficult if income rises slowly.	Buyer's income to rise sharply. Buyer wants to repay quickly. Buyer expects to sell in 7 years or less.
Adjustable Rate Mortgage Interest rate falls with market rates. Interest rate may be lower than on conventional. Widely available.	Interest rate rises with market rates. Sizable payment increase if rates rise sharply. Future cost hard to estimate.	Future interest rates will likely be stable or fall. Buyer expects to sell in 7 years or less.

the far right column suggest who would be best served by each mortgage. The combination of these guidelines, your own circumstances, and overall economic conditions can help you select a mortgage.

LEGAL ASPECTS OF THE ACTUAL PURCHASE

Purchasing a home is a complex process involving several legal and procedural issues. For the first-time buyer, these can be formidable. Let's review the major steps to familiarize you with the process.

Asking Price and Counter offer

When a home is offered for sale, the seller sets its asking price. That price is usually the collective effort of the seller, the realtor handling the sale, and sometimes an independent appraiser. It is the starting point from which the prospective buyer and seller begin to hammer out an agreeable price. To provide room for negotiation, the asking price is often set 5 to 10 percent high.

The actual process may go like this. The asking price on the house Fred wants is $91,500. He decides to **counteroffer** $80,500; his realtor submits this in a purchase contract with other terms of the offer. The seller rejects this, counteroffers $87,900, and alters some terms. Fred can counteroffer again. Buyer and seller exchange offers until they reach a final price or negotiations fail. Where will the "final" price be? It depends on such things as:

1   Is it a seller's (few houses) or buyer's (many houses) market?
2   Is the house or its location highly desirable? Both?
3   Does the seller need a quick sale?
4   How badly does the buyer want the house?
5   Are both the seller and the buyer willing to compromise on price?

The agreed-upon price may be less than the original asking price, equal to it, or even higher in some cases.

Earnest Money

Once the buyer and seller agree on price, they sign a purchase contract. To show good faith, the buyer makes a deposit, called **earnest money.** This can be as little as $500 or as much as 5 or 10 percent of the price. The seller is assured the house is sold. But what if the buyer does not complete the sale because no lender will approve the necessary mortgage? Then the seller is entitled to keep the earnest money. Buyers should protect themselves by including a contingency clause in the purchase contract; making the offer contingent upon obtaining satisfactory financing is sensible.

Deed, Title, and Abstract

A **deed** is the written document that conveys **title** (the right of ownership) to a piece of property from the seller to the buyer. The deed is registered with a local unit of government to notify interested parties of the property's status.

An **abstract** is a historical record of the transactions on a piece of property. When a title search is made, the abstract and other documents are reviewed to make certain the title to the property is clear. Your attorney does this. Lenders will require the attorney's unqualified opinion on the title before granting a mortgage.

Title Insurance

When Carol Colonial purchases her house, she is concerned about whether its title is free of all claims. Maybe the title search missed the lien that a home improvement firm placed on the house for unpaid remodeling costs. Even though Carol was not a party to the original work, the lien still remains against the property. **Title insurance** will protect the buyer and lender against claims on the property.

Title insurance is purchased at the time of sale. There is usually one policy for the buyer and another for the lender. The first protects the buyer's down payment, but as that equity increases over time not all of the potential loss is covered. The second policy covers the lender's investment in the property. Premiums are based on the home's sale price and the buyer's down payment.

Closing Costs for the Purchase

Before you can move into your new home, you must pay **closing costs:** these are the various costs involved in transfer of ownership and completion of the sale. Exhibit 9.15 lists the major closing costs along with probable amounts for a $70,000 house. Depending on where you live, total cost could be as little as $500 or over $3,000. There may be additional closing costs in your area.

When you apply for a mortgage, the lender must supply an estimate of closing costs. When the actual closing of the sale takes place, the lender provides exact figures. Obtaining estimates from several lenders may save you considerable money.

Legal Assistance

Even a seasoned buyer will want a lawyer to be present at the closing when title is transferred. A lawyer can ensure you receive clear title, review the prorating of taxes, and handle other details of closing. Ask your lawyer for an estimate of his or her fees.

Strategy

Before signing any purchase agreement, consult an attorney. For the first-time buyer, an attorney can outline the steps in the purchase process.

Exhibit 9.15

Estimated Price Ranges for Closing Costs on a $70,000 Home

Cost	Price range	Cost	Price range
1. Title search fee	$ 50–150	6. Recording fee	$15–30
2. Title insurance	$200–600	7. Credit report (on buyer)	$25–75
3. Attorney's fees	$ 50–700	8. Termite inspection	$50–150
4. Survey of property (if required)	$200–400	9. Lender's origination fee	1% to 3% of mortgage
5. Appraisal fee	$100–300		

OWNERSHIP: AN INVEST- MENT OR A SHELTER?

When inflation rose to double digits in the late 1970s and early 1980s, owning a house was touted as a near certain investment. In some markets, it became a "bigger fool" investment: buy a house today and in a short time sell it for a tidy profit; the next buyer does the same. It goes on and on because there will surely be a "bigger fool" to pay the next inflated price. Unfortunately, sometimes you run out of fools, and the end of the line is no place to be standing. As Exhibit 9.16 demonstrates, the late 1970s were indeed a "good" time for housing. Home prices rose faster than inflation, providing a profit greater than many conventional investments.

Annual Percentage Increase in Consumer Prices and the Median Price of an Existing Home

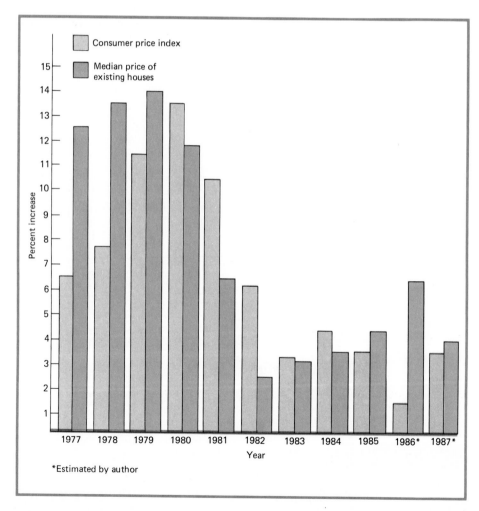

The second half of Exhibit 9.16 shows the market's correction in action. Since 1981, housing prices have often risen with or a little more slowly than the general rate of inflation. The real rate of return dropped to close to zero. No longer was homeowning a "sure" investment. Price appreciation was not completely uniform; houses in some areas continued to surpass inflation, and some will no doubt continue that trend. However, ownership should be considered as *shelter* first, an investment second. If your home turns out to be a "good" investment, be happy. But investment return should not be your sole motive for buying.

Summary

1   The three major rental options are apartments, duplexes or townhouses, and single-family houses.
2   Major ownership options include the single-family house, condominium, and mobile home.
3   Major advantages of renting include:
   - Extensive recreation facilities
   - No responsibility for maintenance and repairs
   - Possible lower cost of renting
   - Restrictions on type of tenant
   - Greater flexibility to move
   - Low initial cost to rent
4   Major advantages of ownership include:
   - Psychological satisfaction.
   - Some costs can be deducted on income tax return.
   - Limited income taxes when unit is sold.
   - Possible lower cost of owning.
   - Owner captures any appreciation in unit's market value.
5   Major disadvantages of renting include:
   - Restrictions on personal freedom and lifestyle.
   - Rental costs cannot be deducted on income tax return.
   - Tenant does not share in the unit's market value increase.
   - Long-term cost is less predictable.
6   Major disadvantages of ownership include:
   - Owner is responsible for repairs and maintenance.
   - Reduced flexibility when owner wants to move.
7   Both mortgage interest and the property taxes on a home can be deducted on your tax return. The tax savings can substantially lower the net cost of owning.
8   Appreciation in a home's value reduces the long-term cost of owning.
9   Revising your budget to include the projected costs of owning is the best way to decide if you can afford to own a home.
10 Four factors should be evaluated when buying a home:
   - Location of the unit
   - Zoning rules for the area where the unit is located
   - Value of surrounding property
   - Convenience of location
11 Three criteria differentiate the major types of mortgages:
   - Size of the minimum down payment
   - Whether the interest rate is fixed or variable
   - Whether the monthly payment is constant
12 Major types of currently available mortgages include:
   - Conventional mortgage
   - Conventional with insurance
   - Growing-equity mortgage (GEM)
   - FHA or VA mortgage
   - Graduated-payment mortgage (GPM)
   - Adjustable rate mortgage (ARM)
13 When selecting a mortgage, the borrower should consider his or her present and likely future financial position, as well as the present and likely future condition of the economy as a whole.
14 A home's selling price is usually set through a series of offers and counteroffers exchanged by the seller and the prospective buyer.
15 Closing costs to complete the transfer of ownership can equal 3 to 5 percent of the home's price.
16 Purchasing a house is primarily a shelter decision; investment considerations should be secondary.

Review your understanding of

Apartment	Townhouse	Condominium	Common property
Duplex apartment	Single-family house	Individual living unit	Maintenance fee

Mobile home	Acceleration clause	Conventional insured	Counteroffer
Net cost of renting	Nonassumption clause	Graduated payment (GPM)	Earnest money
Net cost of owning	Prepayment penalty	Growing equity (GEM)	Deed
Price appreciation	Tax escrow account	Adjustable rate (ARM)	Title
Long-term cost of owning	Mortgages:	Points	Abstract
Lease	Conventional	Indexed	Title insurance
Security deposit	FHA	Land contract	Closing costs
Self-amortizing loan	VA		

Discussion questions

1 How might the features and facilities of an apartment differ from those of a townhouse?

2 What advantages might a condominium have over a single-family house? Disadvantages?

3 In your opinion, are some advantages of ownership more important than others? Why? Which disadvantages would you rank near the top?

4 Some argue that tax regulations favor ownership over renting.
   a Can you give examples?
   b How do income tax regulations reduce the cost of ownership?
   c What breaks does the tax system offer renters?

5 What costs does ownership involve that renting does not? What, if any, tax savings does it provide over renting?

6 Why does the long-term cost of ownership differ from its net cost? Which cost is likely to be more predictable?

7 Gus Gullible cannot decide if he should accept the lender's voluntary tax escrow account.
   a What are the account's advantages?
   b Are there disadvantages?

   c Can you suggest an alternative Gus could use?

8 What do FHA, VA, and conventional insured mortgages have in common? What are the major differences? Describe a borrower who might consider each.

9 What common feature is shared by graduated-payment and growing-equity mortgages? How do they differ? Describe a borrower who might consider each.

10 Lenders have encouraged borrowers to shift from conventional to adjustable rate mortgages.
   a How do the two mortgages differ?
   b Why have lenders pushed ARMs?
   c Describe a situation in which the borrower might gain with an ARM. The lender.

11 How does a land contract differ from a mortgage?

12 At times homes have been touted as "good" investments.
   a Why was this theme popular in the late 1970s?
   b Based on recent trends, is a home becoming a better investment?

Problems

9.1 Orelia Option is deciding between two $60,000 conventional mortgages: a 20-year, 14 percent loan and a 30-year, 14 percent loan.
   a What is the monthly payment for each loan?
   b Over the life of the mortgage, what are the total payments on the 20-year loan? On the 30-year loan?
   c Why is the total for the 30-year loan so much higher? What happens to those additional payments?
   d How should Orelia decide between the two loans?

9.2 Assume Harve Hightax (whose marginal tax rate is 40 percent) and Ron Recentgrad (whose marginal tax rate is 25 percent) are both considering a particular condominium. Annual costs for the condominium include:

Mortgage payments	$7,235	Interest on mortgage	$7,005
Property tax	1,035	Homeowners insurance	240
Utilities	960	Maintenance cost	600
Interest lost on down payment (after tax)	400		

   a What is Harve's net cost of owning? Ron's net cost of owning?
   b Why are the two net costs different?

9.3 Betty Bungalow plans to use a 30-year, $45,500 VA mortgage to purchase a house. Currently, the maximum interest rate on VA mortgages is 11 percent; the prevailing interest rate on conventional mortgages is 11.75 percent.
   a Will the lender charge points on the VA mortgage? If so, how many?
   b If there are points, how many dollars are involved and who pays?
   c Why would a lender accept an 11 percent VA mortgage when conventional mortgages offer an 11.75 percent return?

9.4 Hal Halfdone has developed the following cost worksheet on his two housing options:

	Rental	Ownership
Housing unit	Duplex	$60,000 house
Net annual cost*	$5,880	7,155

* Amount from line 14 on a worksheet similar to Exhibit 9.5.

Based on information on a comparable house in the area, Hal expects the house will appreciate approximately 3 percent per year. During the early years, Hal repays approximately $120 of the mortgage each year.
   a What is Hal's long-term annual cost of ownership?
   b Which option offers the lowest long-term cost?
   c When will Hal receive the benefits of long-term ownership?

9.5 Wilma Dixon is considering the following apartment:

Monthly rental	$350	All maintenance and repairs
Annual premium on renter's insurance	110	provided by landlord
Monthly utilities	95	Security deposit of 2 months' rent in advance

Money for the security deposit will come from Wilma's money market fund, which currently pays 7 percent interest. Her marginal tax rate is 30 percent.
   a What is the net annual cost of the apartment?
   b Does the apartment give Wilma any tax benefits?
   c Will the apartment's long-term cost differ from the net cost in part (a)? Why?

9.6 Fran Fasttrack, who recently graduated with an M.B.A., has two mortgage options for her condominium:

Mortgage	Interest rate	Maturity of mortgage	Annual rise in payment	Payments will increase:	Initial payment
Graduated payment	12%	30 years	7.5% per year	During first 5 years	$338
Growing equity	12%	30 years	7.5% per year	Each year of mortgage	$458

   a Compute the annual payment on each mortgage for the following years (round to nearest dollar):

Mortgage	Year					
	1	2	3	4	5	6
Graduated payment	$338	____	____	____	____	$485
Growing equity	$458	____	____	____	____	$658

   b Which loan will be repaid most quickly?
   c How should Fran decide between the two loans?

Case problem

Alice Crosely earns $28,500 annually as a buyer for a major department store. She is certain her income will keep pace with inflation, but expects promotions to boost it well above the minimum.

Alice presently rents a one-bedroom apartment she finds convenient to work, cultural activities, and shopping. Her rent is $500 per month, and heat and electric bills average $80 monthly. Insurance on her possessions costs $100 per year. Because her lease will expire in several months, she wants to reevaluate the rent versus buy decision. Alice plans to remain in the area for the next 5 to 10 years.

Single-family houses do not appeal to her because of their extensive yardwork and exterior maintenance responsibilities. She does not want to give up the convenience of being near the city center. She would, however, like the freedom to decorate and furnish a home to her taste. Several of her coworkers have mentioned that a house is good tax shelter. Alice is not clear whether ownership at her present 30 percent marginal tax rate would provide any "tax breaks."

Near her apartment building a new development is offering one-bedroom condominiums for $58,500. Those units have about the same features and amenities as her apartment. If she decides to buy a unit, her $5,900 down payment would come from a money market fund; this currently pays 7 percent interest. Alice can obtain a 25-year insured conventional mortgage at 11 percent interest to finance the $52,600 balance. Estimated property taxes on the unit are $820 annually. Her monthly maintenance fee for the common property would be $75. Annual premiums on an insurance policy covering the unit and contents would run $140. Projected utility costs are $85 per month. The developer has suggested that owners can expect annual maintenance and repair costs on their living units to average 0.5 percent of the unit's price. Similar condominiums in the area have been appreciating at about 4 percent annually.

1   What is the annual net cost of the condominium? The apartment?
2   What percentage of her income will Alice spend on housing if she buys the condominium? How should she decide if she can afford the unit?
3   What is the projected long-term cost of the condominium? (*Hint:* You will need to consider appreciation.)
4   What happens to Alice's long-term cost if the condominium only appreciates 3 percent annually? If it appreciates 5 percent? Does the assumed appreciation rate have a major effect on the unit's long-term cost? Why?
5   When, if ever, will Alice receive the benefits of appreciation? Of repaying the mortgage?
6   If you faced the same decision as Alice, what would you do? Why?

Safeguarding your resources

4

PART

CHAPTER 10

Risk management, insurance, and Social Security

AFTER COMPLETING THIS CHAPTER YOU WILL HAVE LEARNED

- How personal risk management operates
- Why insurance is just one option for managing personal risks
- What insurance is and how it operates
- How to avoid underinsurance and overinsurance
- Why a deductible is often a good way to reduce premiums
- How to select an insurance agent and company
- Ways to reduce insurance costs
- When to review your insurance program
- Why Social Security should be integrated into your insurance plan
- How Social Security can reduce the amount of insurance you need

*I*nsurance allows people to pool their risks through a premium that covers the losses of a few. All who participate know that if they have a loss, they will collect. Some might claim that the lucky devils with the losses are the only ones who benefit from their premiums. Not so. Those with a loss are compensated, but the rest had the assurance they would have been compensated if they had a loss.

Let's use a fictional town with 200 homes to illustrate how insurance operates. The estimated value of each house and its contents is $100,000. Though only one house is lost to fire every other year, it is a devastating loss for the owner. The citizens decide everyone will share the losses of the few by contributing to a "pot" to cover projected losses. They anticipate a $100,000 loss every second year, so each of the 200 owners pay $250 in annual premiums: $50,000 loss/200 homes. Now any unlucky victim can draw funds from the "pot" to rebuild. Our imaginary owners have developed and used a form of insurance.

To develop a sound insurance program, you must understand risk management; then you can purchase insurance to meet your needs. Unfortunately, many people do not use insurance wisely. They spend premiums on insurance for losses they could afford and fail to protect themselves against large losses. Should the worst happen, they or their survivors face severe financial hardship. An insurance plan tailored to your needs offers you both economy and protection.

To make an informed insurance decision, you must know:

1   What should be insured
2   How much coverage you need
3   How to pick an insurance company and an agent
4   What special insurance needs you have

First we need to examine risk management, because purchasing insurance is only a part of managing your protection.

PERSONAL RISK MANAGEMENT

When you do a risk management analysis, you take an organized and systematic approach to the potential losses you face. You begin by identifying and analyzing your risks. Then you assess the best method for dealing with each one. Finally, you must conduct a periodic review to update the program. Managing your insurance program is but one component of risk management.

A risk management program anticipates losses. When you know your options in advance, you have peace of mind, conscious that if a loss occurs you will be covered.

Personal Risk Management: An Overview

Developing a sound personal **risk management program** involves the four steps in Exhibit 10.1:

1   Identifying your potential risks
2   Evaluating the possible effect of each risk

3   Determining how to manage each risk
4   Selecting the correct insurance coverage

**Step 1: Identi-
fying Your
Potential Risks**

Begin your risk management plan with **risk identification;** that is, by listing situations in which a loss could occur. These include:

1   Expenses arising from sickness or accident
2   Losses resulting from personal liability
3   Loss of property through fire, theft, accident, or other causes
4   Loss of income because of premature death
5   Loss of income through sickness or accident

Most of us face losses in several of these categories.

Steps in Personal Risk Management

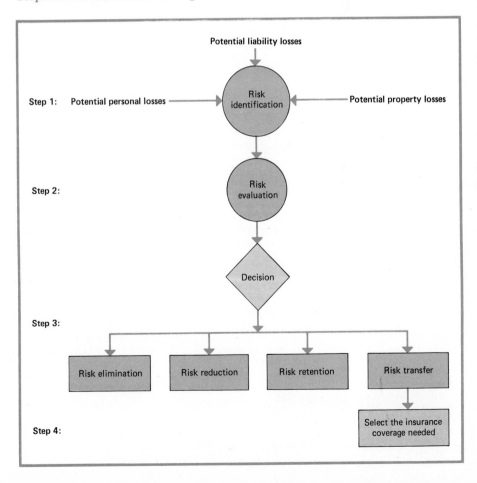

Step 2: Evaluating the Potential Effect of Each Risk

After pinpointing the potential risks you face, you need to **evaluate their financial impact** by first estimating the potential loss for each situation, and then estimating how frequently such a loss might occur.

Examples will illustrate this two-step process. The potential dollar loss of damage to your home and its contents is large; it would rank as severe. At the opposite extreme, having to pay the first $50 for unauthorized use of your credit card is unpleasant but hardly severe. In general, the more money involved, the more severe the loss will be.

The second aspect of the evaluation centers on calculating how frequently a loss might occur. Paul Poorhealth, who routinely ignores warning labels, exercise, and life-style guidelines, is a prime candidate for frequent health care expenses. On the other hand, even Greta Goodluck has a remote chance of being hit by a satellite plunging out of the sky. In general, the greater the likelihood a loss will occur, the more importance it has.

To determine the effect if a risk becomes reality, we need to consider the potential dollar loss as well as the likelihood it will happen. The greatest losses come when the possibility and dollar amount are both high, but even very low probabilities can lead to important losses if the amount at stake is very large.

Exhibit 10.2 analyzes the potential losses for different situations. Potential dollar losses are given, and the next column reviews the likeli-

Exhibit 10.2

Risk Evaluation: Losses Faced by Individuals

Potential loss situation	Maximum possible loss for risk	Likelihood of loss occurring	Who should consider it important
Loss of income due to premature death.	Depends on income; may exceed $200,000.	Low, but increases as you grow older.	Wage earners with dependents.
Medical expense due to illness or injury.	Can range from a few hundred dollars to more than $100,000.	Small losses almost certain; large losses are less frequent.	Everyone; especially if family has prior history of problems.
Loss of income due to illness or accident.	Depends on income, but annual losses of $20,000 are common.	Chances are 1 in 10 you may be disabled before age 65.	Everyone who earns an income.
Liability for damages due to negligent auto operation.	Losses exceeding $100,000 are common.	Fairly limited if you drive prudently.	Everyone who owns an auto.
Damage to auto from collision, theft, and other causes.	Maximum is value of your auto.	Reasonably high; rises with miles driven and location of auto.	All owners whose auto is worth more than a nominal value.
Liability arising from injury in the home or rental unit.	If serious, damages can exceed $100,00.	Limited chance of loss.	All who own a home or rent a living unit.
Damages to home or contents in home or rental unit.	Value of the home and the contents.	Limited chance of loss.	All who own a home or rent a living unit.
Loss of personal assets.	Values of those assets.	Generally limited, but depends on asset.	Owners of valuable assets.

hood of the loss occurring. A combination of the two factors is used to judge the relative importance of each loss. The final column lists individuals who might rank a loss as ''important.''

Step 3: Deciding How to Manage Each Risk

Once you have decided a loss's relative importance, you have a series of options for managing the risk. Some of these options involve insuring yourself against the risk, but there are other possibilities. Let's look at some of those first.

Eliminate the risk

Your first option is to eliminate the risk entirely. When you are no longer vulnerable to a loss, nothing more need be done. Selling your boat or all-terrain vehicle eliminates it as a risk.

Strategy

If you can eliminate a risk without undue hardship, that may be the best way to manage it.

Reduce the risk

If you can't eliminate the risk, you may be able to reduce its importance by reducing the potential dollar loss or the likelihood of its occurring. Drive an older, less valuable auto, and a total loss may cost less than damages on a new car. Using public transportation to commute to work means you will drive fewer miles and avoid traffic congestion, reducing your chances of an accident. Such actions do not eliminate risk, but they diminish its impact and importance.

Strategy

Some risks can be managed by lessening their severity, usually through reducing the likelihood of the loss occurring.

Retain the risk

When you **retain a risk,** you accept the financial consequences of a potential loss, entirely or in part. Retaining the potential $50 loss for unauthorized use of your credit card is an illustration of accepting the whole risk. The deductible on an insurance policy is a classic example of retaining part of a risk. Retaining a loss should not be undertaken lightly: make certain you understand *what* you are accepting.

Strategy

Accepting part, or all, of a risk can be an effective management tool, especially when the amount is small.

Transfer the risk

Some risks involve such a large loss that neither reduction nor retention is enough. **Transferring the risk** to someone else may be the best option. When you purchase insurance, you pay a premium to transfer the risk to the company. If a loss occurs, the insurance company pays. As you would expect, the amount of the premium depends on the size of the potential loss (as the amount rises, so does the premium) and on the likelihood of the loss occurring (the more likely, the higher the premium).

Strategy

Transferring part, or all, of a risk to an insurance company is often the best way to manage your risks.

Step 4: Selecting the Right Insurance

If you decide to transfer the risk, you will need to select the appropriate insurance. You want a policy that covers the potential loss yet does not waste premium dollars. Identical coverage may cost significantly more from some insurance companies. Comparison shopping among competing companies can reduce your cost considerably.

Major types of insurance for individuals

Exhibit 10.3 summarizes insurance coverage under three headings: property, liability, and personal. We will briefly look at the more common ones here. Specifics on each will be covered in Chapters 11 through 13.

Health insurance. Illness can be costly; a brief stay in the air-conditioned splendor of a hospital can easily cost several thousand dollars. Some or all of the medical costs associated with an illness or accident can be covered by good health insurance.

Exhibit 10.3

Major Types of Personal Insurance

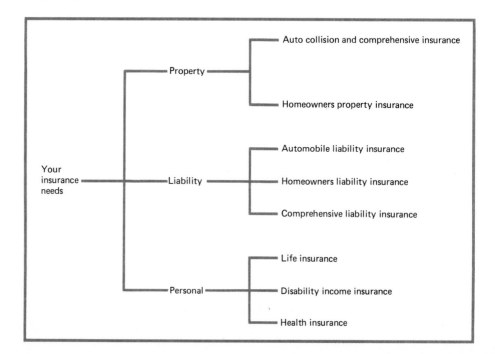

Liability insurance. Damages arising out of your improper or negligent actions is covered by liability insurance. The two most frequent sources of such claims are autos and houses. Either can generate large losses if another person is injured or their property damaged. Demolish a new Mercedes, and the loss could top $50,000. Seriously injure someone, and medical costs, lost income, and other losses can easily pass six digits.

Property insurance. Property insurance protects you from losses if your auto, boat, home, or personal assets are damaged or lost. It covers losses arising from natural causes, theft, fire, and vandalism, and other hazards. What you own and what it's worth determine your potential loss. For most people that loss is sizable.

Life insurance. Life insurance pays a beneficiary if the insured dies. As such, it can replace your income for your dependents. The amount of coverage you need depends on your income, the age of your dependents, and what percentage of your income you need replaced.

Disability income insurance. Should you be unable to work because of illness or accident, disability insurance provides a monthly income. You are more likely to be disabled than to die prematurely, so disability coverage is important. How large a disability loss might be depends on your present income and the length of time you are unable to work.

Pure risks are your principal concern

Risk management is concerned with the pure risks you face. A **pure risk** has only one outcome: you suffer a loss. Examples include premature death, major medical expenses for an illness or injury, disability that causes loss of income, and damage to property from fire, wind, or other perils. Insurance companies generally only insure against pure risks.

A **speculative risk,** on the other hand, can result in either a loss or a gain. Putting $40 on Fleet Foot to win the fifth race is an example. In the worst case, you lose $40. If Fleet Foot wins, you could profit handsomely. Insurance companies avoid situations where you might profit from the risk.

INSURANCE: REIMBURSE-MENT FOR YOUR LOSSES

You do not carry insurance to make money. Instead, you are **indemnified**—compensated—for a loss covered by the policy: a homeowners policy indemnifies you for losses to your home or its contents. If you negligently injure someone while driving, your auto policy indemnifies the victim for the injury you cause.

A central operating principle of insurance is that it restores you to approximately the *same* financial position as before the loss. You are paid the amount of the actual loss or the policy's dollar limit, whichever is less. If Cindy Closecall insures her $70,000 condominium for $60,000, the most she can collect is $60,000; she set the **policy limit** at $60,000 and that is the most she collects. Suppose Ronald Resourceful takes the opposite tack: he insures his $80,000 house for $160,000. Will it take $160,000 to "restore" Ronald if the house is destroyed? No! His maximum loss is $80,000, and $80,000 is all he can collect. Insurance companies have to limit payments; if people could profit from their losses, the Ronald Resourcefuls of the world would find losses all too "convenient."

Nor will purchasing policies from several insurance companies make Ron rich. He is free to buy several $80,000 policies and pay the premiums, but each of those policies will contain a clause stating that the loss will be split if there are multiple insurers (and they will *work* to find each other). Ronald is not likely to collect more than $80,000.

You can set your own "cash value" with life insurance. Want to be worth $1 million when you die and impress Uncle Bob with your solid rosewood casket? All you need to do is pay the premium and—maybe—pass a medical examination. And you can spread your business around if you wish: all insurers will pay when you depart the gene pool permanently.

Life insurance companies protect themselves in several ways. First, people cannot call the agent from their deathbeds, whispering, "Sandra, I have decided to take that $100,000 policy you wanted to sell me." Most policies disallow claims resulting from suicide during the first 1 or 2 years. Likewise a policy will not pay if the beneficiary caused the insured's demise . . . so even if Aunt Agatha is the beneficiary, it is safe to devour those cookies she gave you before the plane departed.

What Can You Insure?

A risk has to meet certain conditions to be insurable. First, it has to be a pure risk. Second, the loss has to be measurable in dollars; further, the moment of the loss has to be definite. Third, the loss must be accidental; insurance companies could not survive if they had to cover losses caused by the insured. Finally, the loss cannot affect all of those covered by insurance simultaneously; the "pool" of premiums just would not be big enough. If only those who faced the greatest possibility of flood losses in a single high-risk location purchased flood insurance, the insurance company would quickly go broke.

Protect against Large Losses

The primary purpose of insurance is to protect against large, financially devastating losses which have a limited likelihood of happening. The chance of your being involved in a serious auto accident in which you are negligent is limited, but that is no consolation when you are being sued for $250,000. The costs of defending yourself can be enormous; lose, and you can spend years paying the judgment.

Protection against large losses is basic to a good personal insurance program. Set your policy's dollar limits well above what you might expect to pay. That assures you that even the worst possibility will be covered. Fortunately, the added premium to raise a policy's coverage limit is usually moderate.

Do Not Under-insure

Some people make the mistake of leaving themselves without enough insurance. A prime example of **underinsurance** is having a mere $10,000 liability limit on an auto policy. Even a minor accident that injures two or three people could push damages above $10,000. If major medical expenses, lost wages, and pain and suffering are involved, $10,000 will hardly cover miscellaneous items. Limits of $100,000 or $300,000 are not out of line for automobile liability.

Strategy

When the potential dollar loss is large, high insurance coverage limits should be standard.

Avoid Overinsuring

Buying insurance to cover small losses is wasteful. The $50 lost contact lens, the $72 dent that mysteriously appears on your auto, the $15 hose that disappears from the front lawn are not pleasant to pay for, but they hardly cause financial hardship. Yet some people spend scarce dollars to cover such losses rather than retaining them. They are **overinsured.**

Lenna Loselens may think contact lens insurance is a good buy (she loses a lens almost every week). But why should you subsidize her losses by joining that pool? Even if her coverage is canceled, other Lenna look-alikes will make the coverage expensive for what you receive.

To decide if coverage is overinsurance, ask yourself: Can I pay this loss out of current income (unpleasant though it be)? How likely is this small loss to occur? Is the loss quite small? Any yes answer suggests overinsurance.

Strategy

Rather than overinsuring, spend your premium dollars to fill significant insurance gaps.

MANAGING YOUR INSUR-ANCE PRO-GRAM

Once you decide insurance is appropriate and desirable, you need to manage your insurance program. First, you must choose an insurance company. We will discuss several criteria that can help focus your choice. Second, you will want to hold down premiums; we will discuss several ways that can be done. Finally, you need to know—and we will cover—the details of the procedure for submitting a claim for a loss.

Selecting an Insurance Agent

A good agent can help you build an insurance program that complements and protects your financial plans. You still need to complete a risk management analysis to determine the risks and decide how they are to be managed. You provide this background information, along with an estimate of your basic insurance needs; the agent designs a program to address them.

Agents often specialize. Some concentrate on personal "lines": life, health, and disability insurance. Others concentrate on property and liability lines: auto and homeowners insurance. You may find several agents better serve your needs. These guidelines can help you select an agent:

1   Avoid agents who have little—or no—experience in developing programs. You want a professional, not last week's used car salesman.

2   Require the agent to work for you. He or she should be willing to quote rates, find alternatives, answer questions, and work with you to develop *your* program.

3   Consider both the agent and the company. Even the best agent cannot help you if the coverage is issued by an expensive or disreputable company.

4   Deal with an agent who has passed one of the professional examinations. For life insurance agents the designation is **Chartered Life Underwriter (CLU),** and for property and casualty agents, **Chartered Property and Casualty Underwriter (CPCU).**

5   Ask your friends and coworkers for recommendations. They may know an agent who provides good, professional advice.

Selecting the Right Insurance Company

Many companies sell insurance: most have the resources to cover the losses of their customers, and most provide reasonable service. But some stand out. Their finances are not just adequate, they are top-grade, and

What luck, honey.. It's our insurance agent!

they go that extra step to satisfy customers. Those A+ companies are the ones you want to deal with. You want to avoid any company whose finances are marginal or that has the attitude it is doing you a favor by selling you insurance. Some guidelines to help you pick the winners are detailed in the following sections.

Financial strength

You want an insurance company with enough money to cover losses. You purchased insurance to transfer risk; you do not want it passed back by a bankrupt insurance company. A. M. Best and Company publishes two excellent rating guides on insurance companies: *Best's Insurance Reports* and *Best's Life Reports.* Most public libraries have them. Each guide rates insurance companies using a "General Policyholder Rating" based on a number of criteria. Rather than list them all here, we suggest you consult the guide itself. The rating uses a truncated grading scale: A+ and A are excellent, B+ is very good, B is good, C+ is fairly good, and C is fair. Most financial advisors recommend limiting yourself to firms rated A+ and A.

Strategy

Concentrate on insurance companies with a strong General Policyholder Rating; premiums are no higher, so buy the best.

Customer satisfaction with claims service

Given a choice, few of us want to be one of those "lucky devils" who collects on an insurance policy. But if you do have a claim, you want it settled quickly and fairly. A loss is traumatic enough without having to battle your insurance company. It is interesting to note that some companies just seem to be more customer-oriented; differences in satisfaction are large. When assessing particular types of insurance, be aware that *Consumer Reports* compiles a satisfaction index for companies based on the responses of its readers.

A second source of customer satisfaction information is your state insurance commissioner's office, the place customers report disputes with companies. Call to find out which companies have accumulated large numbers of complaints.

Last, a good agent should be willing to offer a candid assessment of a particular company's settlement policy.

Reducing Insurance Costs

There are steps you can take to hold down the costs of insurance; many of these are the same for most types of insurance. They require some effort on your part but the payoff, better insurance coverage for lower premiums, make it worthwhile.

Compare premiums on competing policies

Comparative studies and surveys have resoundingly confirmed that differences in premiums between similar policies are often significant. Comparing premiums on competing policies can save you money. You don't need to worry that only low-rated firms quote attractive rates. In reality, firms with both strong finances and satisfied customers often quote the lowest premiums.

Strategy

Obtain rate quotations from several insurance companies before purchasing. Often the lowest premium will offer you real savings.

**Use deducti-
bles for most
coverage**

A **deductible** is the part of the loss you agree to pay; the insurance company is to pay the balance. Deductibles are available in differing amounts; the higher the deductible, the lower your premium. The higher your deductible, the more risk you retain.

Deductibles lower your premiums for several reasons. First, the insurance company pays less because you retain part of the loss. Second, the insurer avoids the administrative and settlement costs of small claims. Processing costs about the same on a claim for a $75 parking lot ding as on a claim for a $1,750 crumple. Last, deductibles place the insured at risk: nothing fosters driving discipline like knowing *you* pay the first $250 or $500 for your carelessness.

Selecting a deductible. Typical deductibles range from zero to $500, but some go to $2,000 and beyond. Trying to avoid any and all deductibles is wasteful and a form of overinsurance. In choosing a deductible, consider three factors: the financial resources you have to cover the deductible amount; the amount your premium is reduced by the higher deductible; and the potential cost of your added risk with the higher deductible. Note that in two of the three cases we mentioned a "higher" deductible. That means most policies should have some deductible.

Begin by asking: Can I afford the deductible? Your cash reserve (discussed in Chapter 3) can help you answer that question. Also look at your financial assets to see if they could be tapped for the necessary amount. Paying a deductible is not pleasant, but having none means you are paying extra for limited coverage.

If you decide you can handle a particular deductible, calculate how much it will save in premiums. Those savings should be compared to your **added risk exposure** with the higher deductible.

The following example illustrates how to compare the premium savings to the added risk exposure. Suppose you are offered a choice of two deductibles on your auto collision coverage: collision insurance covers damage to your car when the accident is your fault. Premiums on a $100 deductible are $149 annually. A $200 deductible costs $120 yearly. How long will it take to recoup the $100 of added risk exposure from the $29 premium savings? Exhibit 10.4 compares the total cost of the two policies under four different conditions. Column 2 assumes an accident every year, a disastrous record. Column 3 assumes a 2-year period with one accident. The succeeding columns assume premiums were paid for 3 years with one accident or 4 years with one accident.

Exhibit 10.4 shows it takes more than 3 years for the savings to balance the added risk exposure. If you expected to have an accident every 3 years or less, the smaller deductible would be best. However, at 4 years and beyond, the savings more than offset the higher deductible. If you go 4 years or more without an accident, the higher deductible pays off. For any-one who has only one accident in 10 years—about every 8 years is aver-age—$290 saved (10 years $\times$ $29) far exceeds the $100 added risk exposure.

One last comment about Exhibit 10.4. If Fran Fenderbender averages an accident a year—her agent knows her voice all too well—is a low deductible best? Not necessarily. With her record, Fran may have difficulty finding *any* insurance, let alone quibbling over the deductible. Her premi-ums will be high because she is a high risk.

A worksheet similar to Exhibit 10.4 can be used to analyze any deduct-ible. You need the cost of competing policies and an estimate of how fre-quently you may have to pay the deductible; your recent experience can help with that estimate.

Strategy

Decide which deductible is best for you by computing how long it takes for the lower premium to break even with the added loss from the higher deductible.

Some insurance agents discourage higher deductibles. They consider $100 a "large" deductible. Given the inflation of recent years, $250 or $500 is probably realistic. Some agents also worry that a policyholder will be unhappy at having to pay a sizable deductible.

Strategy

If your analysis shows a larger deductible is workable, stick to your decision even if your agent seems lukewarm.

Exhibit 10.4

Premium Savings from Raising Deductible

	One Auto Accident within			
	1 year	*2 years*	*3 years*	*4 years*
Cost: $200 Deductible				
Total premiums paid	$120	$240	$360	$480
Deductible payment	200	200	200	200
Total cost (A)	$320	$440	$560	$680
Cost: $100 Deductible				
Total premiums paid	$149	$298	$447	$596
Deductible payment	100	100	100	100
Total cost (B)	$249	$398	$547	$696
Added cost (savings) with $200 deductible:				
Cost (A) − Cost (B)	$ 71	$ 42	$ 13	($ 16)

Retain the risk on small losses

Small losses are best handled by retaining the risk yourself. You can generally cover those losses from your current income and your emergency cash. Insurance is best reserved for severe financial losses. General rules on insurance include:

1   The poorest insurance buys are those that cover probable risks involving small losses. The high cost of administering frequent, small claims guarantees a ''poor'' insurance buy.
2   The better insurance buys are usually those that cover risks with potentially severe dollar losses and a moderate to limited likelihood of occurring. This allows the insurance pool to spread potentially large, infrequent claims of the unfortunate few over large numbers of policyholders who have no claim.

A fictional dental policy illustrates the point. The policy covers only annual examinations and cleaning. The potential loss—the fee for the exam—is not large, but nearly every participant will have a claim. The cost of administering and processing those small, frequent claims inflates the premium. The sheer volume of claims could push the cost beyond that of the exam. This extreme example underscores the importance of retaining small risks.

Strategy

Retain risks where the dollar loss is limited. Generally, any loss of less than 25 percent of your cash reserve should be retained.

Pay premiums annually or semiannually

Insurance companies usually offer different premiums for annual and semiannual payments. When they are available, you pay extra for the convenience of monthly payments. A service fee of a few dollars per payment may seem minor, but as a percentage of the total, the fees make finance charges seem like bargains.

Strategy

Pay your premiums annually or semiannually to eliminate service fees.

Use group insurance

When a company can sell similar insurance to a group of people, it can often offer a lower premium. Many group policies also offer better coverage than that available to individuals. Two examples of **group insurance** are the policies employers offer in their fringe benefit packages and the coverage available to certain professionals—attorneys, doctors, accountants—through their professional organizations.

It is rare for an employee not to participate in an insurance program if the employer pays the premium. Even if the employee must pay part of the premium, such coverage is generally attractive. However, if the employee is already covered by a similar policy through a spouse's employer, or if the employee is a single person who has no need for a life insurance policy, a group policy should be rejected.

Several words of caution are in order about group insurance coverage. If your employment is terminated or you drop your membership, your coverage eventually ceases. If you change jobs, you may face a waiting period (6 months is common) before new coverage begins, leaving a gap in your protection. Before you change jobs, check whether your group insurance can be converted to an individual policy; that will close the coverage gap, but the premiums may be high. Second, investigate your options for replacing your policy *before* it expires. You may have to accept much higher deductibles on the replacement coverage to keep premiums reasonable; review your finances to determine the worst case you could handle. Finally, do something. Don't just procrastinate until you have no coverage.

Concentrate coverage in a big policy

There are economies of scale in purchasing insurance. One large, all-encompassing life insurance policy will almost always cost much less than a fistful of small policies. That is one reason credit life and disability insurance make little sense; if you need the coverage, you are usually better off covering your needs in one large policy.

Consider purchasing directly from the firm

Some insurance companies sell direct to the public: no agents. You have to seek out the company and request information, since there seems to be no central source that compiles the names and addresses of companies that sell this way. Nor will you have an agent to help you develop an insurance program; however, some of the companies maintain toll-free telephone numbers you can call for assistance.

There are a number of companies that offer auto and home insurance directly. Life insurance is not widely available in this form, and health insurance is hardly ever offered direct.

Strategy

Check to see whether some companies sell the insurance you need direct. While this entails more work, it can lower premiums.

When to Review Your Insurance Coverage

A good insurance program should not be static; you should review and reassess your insurance needs every 2 or 3 years. Specific events that call for a review include:

- A change in marital status
- Moving to a different home
- Buying a car or boat
- Revision of your employer's insurance plan
- Resignation of your current insurance agent
- A change in the number of dependents
- Acquisition of new personal asset(s)
- A job change for you or your spouse

An insurance review is definitely in order when your net worth rises. First, deductibles should be raised to reflect your increased ability to pay.

Second, you may want to raise your coverage limits, since you have more to lose. Third, reconsider whether some additional risks should be retained. But unless your net worth has moved to seven digits, you still should not retain large losses, even infrequent ones.

Submitting an Insurance Claim

You submit a claim to the insurance company to be reimbursed for loss or damage to insured property. If the claim is large, by all means submit it. But if the loss is small, there are times when you may want to ignore your right to file a claim. Fred Frequent carries these deductibles: $100 on auto collision, zero on auto comprehensive, and $50 on homeowners. He could collect $35 when a $135 dent mysteriously appears in his auto. Likewise, he could collect the full $10 when a passing truck cracks his car's head-light, or get $20 when $70 worth of lawn furniture disappears. Should Fred really submit these small claims? Frequent small claims might net him letter number 233 from the insurance company: "Your coverage will *not* be renewed, so you may want to consider other coverage. Have a nice day." A small claim hardly justifies risking the loss of a policy.

However, *always* notify your insurance company of any loss, even a minor one, that arises from an accident involving injury to others. If you fail to notify the company, you may not be covered. That can cause you severe problems if someone involved later claims serious injury and the accident is considered your fault.

Documenting claims

Supporting documentation is required on most claims, especially large ones. On claims arising from accidents, documentation helps determine which party was at fault. Names and addresses of witnesses can be helpful, and you should always request a copy of the police report on an accident. Canceled checks, paid invoices, and receipts can support your losses. A picture of the damages, taken immediately after the accident, is very effective. Always submit a copy of the documentation; that way you retain the original. A good agent can guide you on what is needed.

SOCIAL SECU-RITY: AN INTEGRAL PART OF INSURANCE PLANNING

Social Security is a "pay as you go" program. The Social Security taxes that Fred Bear paid on this week's payroll check are *not* accumulated in his account. Instead, they pay the benefits of today's Social Security recipients. Benefits paid to Fred or his survivors will come from the Social Security taxes of people who are working when Fred becomes eligible. Today's workers pay the benefits of yesterday's workers; tomorrow's worker's will pay the benefits of today's.

Social Security means retirement to most people, but the program is broader. It pays benefits if you are disabled. And your survivors may collect a benefit if you die prematurely. By transferring part of the risk of disability and premature death to the Social Security system, you lower your need for insurance.

You cannot avoid paying into Social Security, so make the best of it by using it in your risk management plan. We will show you how that can be done in the life and disability insurance chapters.

Who Is Covered?

Participation in Social Security is mandatory, and you cannot withdraw from the system. Currently, you pay about 7.5 percent of each dollar you earn into the system. Your employer contributes a matching share. Self-employed individuals pay both parts: their rate exceeds 13 percent.

Only earnings up to the amount of the **maximum wage base**—set by the Social Security system—are subject to the tax. In 1987 that maximum was $43,800, but it will continue to rise. Since your annual Social Security tax bill can easily top $1,500, you should understand what your money buys.

How Benefit Levels Are Determined

The benefit level is the amount of the payment you or your survivors receive from the Social Security Fund. Three factors determine the amount, beginning with your past earnings; in general, the higher they are, the larger the benefit. Only those wages up to the maximum wage base are counted: If Fran earned $30,000 when the maximum was $24,000, her benefit is based on $24,000 because Social Security taxes were paid only on that amount.

Second, your benefit is based on how long you have worked. The longer the time, the higher the benefit. Very young workers who have not had time to accumulate a lengthy work history are covered by special rules to lessen the impact of that short history.

Third, the age of your dependents affects benefits. Minor children usually receive benefits until age 18. Spouses are treated less generously. Surviving spouses receive benefits only if they are caring for a minor child under age 16 or are retired. Even that benefit may be reduced if the spouse works.

Benefit Payments Are Indexed

Benefit payments are indexed to the consumer price index (CPI); as it rises, benefits rise. A 5 percent rise in the CPI during the year could boost a recipient's $400 benefit to $420. This increment keeps the recipient's purchasing power constant. If the CPI changes by less than 3 percent, an adjustment is not required (Congress has so far chosen to give increases anyway).

Taxability of Benefits

Social Security benefits are not necessarily tax-free. According to the rules, single people who earn $25,000 or less and married couples who earn $32,000 or less pay no income taxes on their benefits. On amounts over those limits, one-half is subject to income taxes. In no case will more than one-half of the benefit be subject to tax. The taxable portion is the lesser of:

1 One-half of the dollar amount over the allowed limit:

$$\frac{\text{Taxable}}{\text{portion}} = \frac{\text{total income}}{\text{from all sources}} - \frac{\text{dollar}}{\text{allowance}} \times \tfrac{1}{2}$$

2 One-half of the entire Social Security benefit:

$$\frac{\text{Taxable}}{\text{portion}} = \frac{\text{Social Security}}{\text{benefit}} \times \tfrac{1}{2}$$

Exhibit 10.5

Taxability of Social Security Retirement Benefits for 1987

Single or married	Social Security benefit × ½	Total income from all sources	Dollar allowance	Amount over limit	Benefit Subject to Tax	
					½ × benefit	½ × excess
Single	$3,000	$21,000	$25,000	—	—	—
Single	3,600	26,000	25,000	$ 1,000		$ 500
Single	4,200	35,000	25,000	10,000	$4,200	
Married	5,400	30,000	32,000	—	—	—
Married	7,200	35,000	32,000	3,000		1,500
Married	8,400	50,000	32,000	18,000	8,400	

Total income from all sources includes wages, pensions, interest, dividends, interest on municipal securities, and one-half of the Social Security benefit. Yes, municipal interest and one-half of the Social Security benefit are included in that total.

Exhibit 10.5 was developed to demonstrate how Social Security benefits are taxed. The final two columns of the exhibit summarize the portion of Social Security that is taxed, if any. Exhibit 10.5 suggests you can earn a considerable amount and not be taxed. Because the $32,000 allowance for marrieds is far from double the $25,000 for singles, a two-career household is more likely to pay taxes on benefits.

Potential Benefit Payment

Are benefits really large enough to include in an insurance plan? Yes. Monthly disability benefits can easily top $600; since there will be little or no taxes, that is more than it appears. Add dependents and the benefit can exceed $1,000. Ignoring this benefit source means wasting money to buy excess insurance.

Monthly payments to the survivors of someone who dies prematurely may exceed $1,000, replacing a considerable amount of life insurance. Social Security should be included in your insurance plan if you want to avoid unnecessary premiums.

Some might ask: Will Social Security be there when it is needed? I take a more positive view than those who predict that the whole system is headed for financial collapse. Granted, the system has had to be rescued several times in the past two decades, and several of the rescue plans that were touted as "lasting into the next century" barely made it through a decade. But the system was rescued *before* it collapsed, and its finances, at least for now, appear to be reasonably secure. For these reasons I think Social Security should be part of a well-developed insurance plan.

Summary

1   Personal risk management involves four steps:
   - Identify the risks.
   - Evaluate their seriousness.
   - Examine options for managing risk.
   - If needed, select the correct insurance coverage.

2   The four ways you can manage a risk are:
   - Eliminate it.
   - Reduce it.
   - Retain it.
   - Transfer it.

3   Insurance indemnifies, or pays, the insured for a loss. The maximum payment is the dollar loss or the upper policy limit, whichever is less.

4   Insurance will only pay for actual losses. Even if property is insured for more than its current value, its value is the maximum payment. If property is covered by multiple policies, the loss is split among them.

5   Insurance is primarily intended to cover major financial losses; small losses should be retained.

6   To gain the CLU or CPCU designation, an agent must pass a professional examination.

7   A. M. Best and Company rates insurance companies using a General Policyholder Rating ranging from A+ to C; most professionals suggest concentrating on A+ and A companies.

8   Cost studies have confirmed that there are large differences between premiums of competing insurance companies. Comparison shopping can reduce costs.

9   Selecting a high deductible means the insured retains more of the risk; but a high deductible lowers premiums.

10　To decide whether a higher deductible is warranted, you need to compare the premium savings and the added risk exposure.

11　Small losses are best handled by paying them from current income and cash reserves rather than using insurance.

12　Some ways of reducing insurance costs include:

- Paying premiums annually or semiannually
- Directly purchasing insurance
- Combining coverages in a single policy
- Using group insurance if available

13　Rather than requesting reimbursement on small claims arising from nonaccident losses, you may want to pay them yourself.

14　Social Security pays benefits for disability and for premature death. Both need to be considered when planning insurance coverage.

15　Once Social Security benefits begin, they rise with the CPI to maintain a constant purchasing power.

16　Unless total income from all sources exceeds an allowed limit ($25,000 for a single person and $32,000 for both partners in a married couple), Social Security benefits are not subject to income taxes.

Review your understanding of

Risk management
Risk identification
Risk evaluation
Risk retention
Risk transfer
Pure risk
Speculative risk
Indemnification
Policy limits
Underinsurance

Overinsurance
Chartered Life Underwriter (CLU)
Chartered Property and Casualty Underwriter (CPCU)
Deductible
Added risk exposure
Group insurance
Maximum wage base
Total income from all sources

Discussion questions

1　Would you develop an insurance plan or a risk management plan first? Why? How can a risk management plan help you identify your insurance needs?

2　Is insurance the only option for managing a risk? What are the other options? Can you name a risk that might best be handled by insurance? Name several risks that would likely be better handled by one of the other techniques.

3　What factor is most important in deciding whether a risk should be retained or transferred? Give an example of a risk that should be retained. One that should be transferred.

4　Who provides the money an insurance company pays out in claims? Why aren't premiums refunded to people who have no claims?

5　What benefit(s) do you expect to receive from purchasing insurance? Do individuals who never make a claim receive any benefit?

6　What does it mean to underinsure? How does overinsurance differ? Give several examples of each.

7　Sue Smalltime's insurance strategy is to (1) insure against small losses that happen frequently, so that part of her premiums are returned through her claims, and (2) never insure against large losses that happen infrequently, because she is not likely to collect on these. What do you think of the strategy? Would you suggest any changes?

8　What are some of the criteria that should guide you in your search for an insurance agent?

9　How would you go about selecting an insurance company? What sources would you use to obtain the needed information?

10　Why does a deductible lower the cost of insurance? Should most policies have a deductible? Why?

11　Some people maintain that a small deductible is best; they use this rationale: "It minimizes the cost, since the insurance company pays the entire amount." How would you respond?

12　What steps should you, the insured, take to decide whether raising a deductible is justified?

13　Name events that would trigger a review of your insurance plan. Which types of coverage would be affected in each case? Why should changes in your financial status require an insurance review?

14　What factors should be considered when deciding whether to submit a claim? Give several examples of situations in which you might decide not to submit a claim.

15　Your need for which type of insurance coverage is likely to be most affected by potential Social

Security benefits? Is Social Security likely to increase or decrease the amount of required coverage? Why?

16 Does Social Security need to be considered in the risk management process? Which step, or steps, does it have a major impact on?

17 Comment on this statement: "Most people pay little or no income tax on their Social Security benefits." Give the worst case scenario for taxation of annual Social Security benefits of $6,000.

Problems

10.1 Brenda Ross is concerned that losing a contact lens could be financially devastating. Her friend's contact lens insurance—annual premium, $25—replaces a lens once the friend pays a $25 deductible. A replacement lens currently costs $50.
   a What would Brenda lose if she had to replace a lens without insurance? What is the loss if she purchases the $25 insurance?
   b Should she purchase the insurance? Why?

10.2 Ron Avery plans a complete review of his insurance needs. The list that follows summarizes his potential loss situations, the projected dollar loss for each, and the likelihood of each loss happening.

Potential loss situation	Projected dollar loss	Likelihood of loss
Theft of personal property from apartment	$12,000	Moderate
Prolonged illness	$20,000 or more if lengthy	Limited
Annual dental examination	$ 45	High
Disability that prevents him from working	$20,000 or more	Moderate
Loss from raising $100 deductible on auto collision coverage to $200	$ 100	Limited
Loss of a contact lens	?	?
Liability for unauthorized use of credit card	?	?
Rusty 1972 Ford Pinto auto if destroyed in a collision that is Ron's fault	?	?

   a Should Ron transfer or retain each of the first five risks?
   b Estimate the projected dollar cost of each of the last three risks and its likelihood of occurring. Which ones should be retained and which ones transferred?

10.3 Debra Diligent has two deductible options on her auto collision policy. The premium for 6 months on a $100 deductible policy is $135. If the deductible is raised to $250, the 6-month premium is $110. During the past 5 years she has had one accident that was her fault.
   a Which deductible should she select? Why?
   b What other factors should Debra consider (if any) before selecting the deductible?

10.4 During a party, Arnold Sweatypalms conducted a quick poll (suave he is not) and found that most of the guests had one to two dental examinations and cleanings each year at $60 each. Arnold figures a new insurance product, Sweatypalms Dental Limited, to cover just those charges would be a great idea. Arnold believes over 1,000 of his friends (he is very gregarious) would likely be interested. He predicts each person would have 1.5 exams each year. As an astute planner, he wants your opinion on the following points.
   a Is an annual dental exam a pure risk? Why?
   b Is this a risk that should be transferred to an insurance company? Why?
   c With 1,000 policyholders, what total benefits will Sweatypalms Dental Limited pay annually?
   d What premium will each policyholder have to pay?
   e What "lucky" participants will benefit from the plan? Which ones will lose?
   f Projected costs of administering Sweatypalms Dental Limited will be about the same as its total annual benefit payment. What will that do to the quoted premium?
   g Based on the premium calculated in part (f), will Arnold's friends join?

10.5 At a recent cookout in the Golden Years Recreation Center, Ron Allan, Bob Sweet, and Tom Young were talking about what portion of their Social Security benefits would be subject to federal income taxes. Ron is single. Bob and Tom are married and file joint tax returns with their spouses. Details on their respective incomes include:

Individual	Total income other than Social Security	Social Security benefit	Age	Filing status for taxes
Ron	$20,000	$8,400	66	Single
Bob and	11,000	7,200	67	Joint return
Alice	14,000	8,400	68	
Tom and	23,000	8,000	66	Joint return
Joan	20,000	7,400	65	

a   What portion of Ron's Social Security benefit is taxable? How about Bob and Alice's benefit? Tom and Joan's benefit?

b   Had Bob and Alice been single, what amount of their Social Security benefit would have been subject to income taxes? Are two people filing as single people or the same two people filing as a married couple on a joint return most likely be subject to income taxes? Why?

Susan Shortfall wants to conduct a detailed review of her current insurance program. She has avoided several types of insurance because she thought she was already paying more premiums than necessary. She hopes the review might produce savings which would permit her to add missing coverage or to increase her present coverage.

Insurance coverage	Details on current policies
Homeowners insurance on $70,000 condominium.	Two policies with $70,000 coverage on each; neither policy has a deductible. Premiums are paid monthly.
Auto collision coverage.	Policy has a $50 deductible. Premiums are paid monthly.
Life insurance.	Five policies; the dollar coverage on each is very limited. Premiums are paid monthly.
Insurance to cover unauthorized use of credit card.	Premium included on monthly credit card bill. Homeowners policy provides similar coverage.
Dental insurance: maximum annual payment is $100.	Premiums are paid monthly. Policy has no deductible.

Susan has listed the following areas where she thinks she may need additional insurance. Her personal observations follow each item on the list.

Insurance coverage	Comments on that coverage
Health insurance.	Premium seems so costly. Susan feels she is very healthy.
Disability insurance.	Given she is not sick much, is it needed?
Auto liability.	To minimize premiums, her upper policy limit is only $20,000.
Auto comprehensive (covers theft, fire, wind, vandalism, other).	Should this be substituted for the present collision coverage?

1   Does Susan have any gaps in her present insurance coverage? What are they?
2   What changes would you recommend in her present policies?
3   Will the changes you suggested in (2) reduce Susan's present premiums?
4   Have Susan and her insurance agents developed a comprehensive program, judging from your review? What guidelines might she use when selecting an insurance agent in the future?

CHAPTER 11

Life insurance

AFTER COMPLETING THIS CHAPTER YOU WILL HAVE LEARNED

- Three major reasons for purchasing life insurance
- Why all policies provide death protection but only some provide an investment component
- How the features of six popular life insurance policies differ
- The difference between participating and nonparticipating insurance policies
- What the major policy options, or riders, provide
- The payment options beneficiaries can elect for the proceeds from a life insurance policy
- How life insurance proceeds and the policy's cash value are taxed
- How to estimate what life insurance you should have, using the needs approach
- The seven major categories of life insurance needs
- How inflation affects your life insurance needs and your plan
- Guidelines for developing an insurance plan that meets your needs
- How to single out reasonable policies and helpful agents

*P*urchasing life insurance is part of managing your personal finances. Often, people do not know what they need, let alone how to meet that need, and the insurance industry has not helped. High commissions encourage agents to push policies that are profitable, even if they do not meet customers' needs. Many brochures and annual statements might as well be in Sanskrit; they defy intelligent analysis. Insurance policies often prove the axiom: What the large print giveth, the small print taketh away.

Yet there is hope. You can find insurance that meets your needs and at a reasonable cost. Increased competition has encouraged the development of customer-oriented companies that offer you the information you need for a good decision. They help you estimate your required coverage and select the best insurance, rather than putting you in the position of relying on questionable advice.

This chapter will provide you with background and skills to design and manage your life insurance plan. It:

- Gives you background information on major types of life insurance.
- Tells you about the principal provisions in most policies.
- Provides a worksheet for estimating the coverage you need.
- Lists guidelines for the insurance purchaser.

HOW LIFE INSURANCE OPERATES

Let's use a simplified example to show how insurance works. Suppose 1,000 members of the Loyal Order of Lost Moose Lodge establish a life insurance company for themselves. Each member is 27 years old and wants $1,000 of coverage. Each has named the beneficiary to collect the $1,000 if he dies.

In the last chapter we learned that insurance companies collect premiums from a large number of people to cover the losses of a few. What premium should this $1,000 policy carry? First, we need to estimate how many Moose will permanently miss future meetings. Mortality tables predict the number of deaths per 1,000 people for each age group: for 27-year-olds, 2 out of each 1,000 people will die. Projected total losses for our fictitious insurance company are $2,000 (2 people × $1,000) each year. Spread over 1,000 members, the premium should be $2.

A real-world insurance company would charge more than $2: it needs to pay administrative costs and agents' commissions. There would also be far more than 1,000 members in the insured pool (mortality tables are only accurate if the pool is large). Not everyone would want $1,000 of coverage, so premiums would differ. Finally, participants would be of different ages.

Before we leave Lost Moose Insurance, we need to know what happens to premiums as the members grow older. Clearly, the "permanent" departures from the membership roll will rise. At age 48, the mortality table says 7 people out of 1,000 will die. At $1,000 coverage per member, losses would be $7,000, and annual premiums would rise to $7 per member.

Standard Provisions and Terms

The life insurance business has its own language. Before going further, we need to define some of the terms used in the business and explain the provisions often written into life insurance policies.

Face amount

A policy's **face amount** is what the insurance pays if the insured dies.

Insured

The **insured** is the person covered by the policy; the death of the insured triggers the payment. Generally, the insured is the person who pays the premium.

Beneficiary

The **beneficiary** receives the payment when the insured dies. Several beneficiaries can be named and the payment divided among them. The policy owner—usually the insured—names the beneficiary. A minor child who is a beneficiary must have a guardian or trustee, since minors cannot transact business.

Strategy

Review your beneficiary designation every 2 to 3 years, or if your circumstances change.

Owner

Generally the insured is the **policy owner,** though in special cases (estate planning and divorce settlements, for example) ownership may be held by someone else. Ownership is important because the owner names the beneficiary.

Premium

To obtain insurance coverage, you must pay an annual **premium.** Doubling a policy's face amount boosts the premium, but it may not double it. Life insurance offers some economies of scale, so that the cost per $1,000 of coverage often drops as the face amount increases. As our Lost Moose example showed, premiums rise with the age of the insured.

Premiums can be paid annually, quarterly, even monthly, but you pay extra for quarterly or monthly billings.

Insurability

Insurability describes whether the company considers you a good risk. If you are in good health, you will be classified as a **standard risk.** Most people qualify for this group.

Individuals who are unusually good risks may qualify for **preferred risk** rates; not all companies offer this classification. Possible qualifying points include not smoking, regular exercise, having long-lived parents, and avoiding risky hobbies and pursuits.

At the opposite extreme, **substandard risks** are persons with major health problems or dangerous occupations. Their premiums are higher because losses are more likely. Some companies have several substandard categories.

Cash surrender value

Some insurance policies add an investment or savings feature to the standard death protection. The accumulated investment in a policy is called its **cash value.** If you surrender the policy, you receive its cash value. Premiums are higher on this type of policy, since part of the money is invested to accumulate the cash value.

Double indem-
nity

Some insurance policies have a provision that doubles the death ben-efit if the insured dies in an accident. This **double indemnity** provision is also sometimes called an accidental death rider.

Major Reasons
for Purchasing
Life Insurance

There are three major reasons for purchasing life insurance:

1   To replace the income the insured would have earned
2   To provide money to settle the insured's estate
3   To accumulate cash value as an investment

Let's look at each.

Replace the
insured's
income

Providing income for your survivors is the principal reason for buying life insurance. Proceeds from the policy replace the income you would have earned. For someone with minor children, this is important.

A later section has a worksheet for estimating how much life insurance you need. Someone earning a substantial salary and who has one or two children might find $200,000 or more is needed. Not everyone needs such coverage, but do not be surprised if you need $50,000 or $100,000.

Settle an
estate

When people die, there are costs to settle their financial affairs. Burial, medical costs, and other bills have to be paid. A mortgage, auto loan, or credit card balance may have to be repaid. There may be legal and probate fees or other court costs. If the deceased's assets are large, there may be federal estate taxes and state inheritance or estate taxes to pay. Life insur-ance can provide money for these expenses. For most people, this purpose is not as important as replacing income.

Insurance as
an investment

Life insurance policies that have a cash value feature can serve as investment vehicles. When you no longer want the insurance, you can withdraw the accumulated cash value. Most people consider the invest-ment feature a secondary reason for buying insurance.

TYPES OF
INSURANCE
CONTRACTS

All life insurance provides death protection that pays beneficiaries if you die. Some add an investment feature, cash value. Let's look at the major types of insurance.

Pure Death
Protection

Death protection pays the face amount of the policy if the insured dies. Usually, the amount is fixed. To raise or lower it, you must buy a new pol-icy. But there are exceptions. Decreasing term insurance lowers the death protection in a series of steps over time; the policy specifies the timing and size of the drop. Universal life policies allow the insured to raise or lower the face amount, but the amount of the change is usually limited.

Investment
Feature

Some life insurance policies provide cash value. The insurer puts part of each premium payment into an investment account. The money accumu-lates, and interest adds to the policy's cash value.

On traditional policies, such as whole life, the amount going to the investment account is fixed, as is the annual premium. The policy provides a table showing the cash value at various points.

On newer policies, such as universal life, the annual premium is often flexible; the deposit to the investment account varies with the premium. Pay a large premium, and the deposit is sizable. Make a small payment, and nothing may be deposited in the cash value. Most insurance companies send regular statements showing the current cash value.

Let's review how six popular life insurance policies combine death protection and investment. The list is not exhaustive, since insurance plans continue to be started, modified, and dropped.

Level Term Insurance

Level term insurance provides only death protection. To collect, you have to die. Term insurance is so named because during the "term" of the policy—1, 5, and 10 years are common—your annual premium for the policy's face amount remains constant. A person who purchases a $50,000, 5-year term policy with a $150 annual premium pays $150 in each of the next 5 years for $50,000 of protection. When it's time to renew, coverage remains at $50,000, but the premium rises because the person is older. If the policy is a 1-year term policy, premiums will change annually.

Many term insurance policies cannot be renewed after age 65. The insured can either convert the policy to some type of cash-value insurance that can be continued past 65 or find a term policy that can be renewed past 65 (some go to age 75, a few to 100). This problem is not as serious as some would have you believe. Insurance needs often drop at age 50 or 60, sometimes to zero. A later section will show why life insurance may become less important as you age.

Decreasing Term Insurance

Decreasing term life insurance also provides only death protection; there is no investment component. Its major distinguishing feature is that premiums remain constant over the life of the policy, but insurance protection declines. When you reach the end of the policy, coverage will be much less than initially.

The term of a policy can be as little as 5 years and as much as 30. Suppose Wanda purchases a $10,000 policy with a 20-year term. Her premium is $450 per year for the whole term. If she dies in the first year, her beneficiaries collect $10,000. In the tenth year, they would collect only $7,200 if she died. By the twentieth year, the death protection is only $1,000. After that she has no insurance coverage.

Many companies will not sell a policy that extends past age 65, so age 55 may be the latest time at which you could purchase a 10-year policy.

Whole Life Insurance

Whole life insurance provides both a death benefit and an investment component: the cash value. If you die, your beneficiaries receive the policy's face amount as the death benefit (later you will see that the cash value pays part of the benefit). Whole life is also called cash-value, ordinary life, or straight life insurance. Until recently, it was the most common type of life insurance.

The premiums on a whole life policy remain constant from the time of purchase. The premium purchases the needed death protection, and the remainder accumulates with interest as the policy's cash value. The insurance company decides how to split the premium. It's a forced savings plan, because you have to pay the premium or the policy lapses. But buried in that premium is your investment in the cash value.

Cash value accumulates in a whole life policy because the premium is intentionally set above the amount needed for death protection. The example in Exhibit 11.1 illustrates. Two $50,000 policies for a 25-year-old male are shown: a 5-year level term and a whole life. The annual premium for the term policy starts at $110 and rises in steps as the insured grows older. Premiums on the whole life policy are a steady $460. What happens to the extra $350? Some is deducted for expenses, but most is deposited in the whole life's investment component. Over time these deposits continue, although not at the same $350; they combine with the interest earned to provide the cash value.

One question arising from Exhibit 11.1 is: How can the premium remain constant when the cost of $50,000 of death protection—the term insurance premium—eventually exceeds the whole life premium? The reason is this: should the insured die, the cash value pays part of the death benefit; the premium no longer has to buy $50,000 of death protection. Suppose that Duane Destiny purchased the $50,000 whole life policy in Exhibit 11.1. The lower section of Exhibit 11.2 shows that policy's accumulating cash value. When Duane has been paying premiums for 35 years, the cash value reaches $21,500. While dreaming about that balance, Duane steps in front of a crosstown bus to become a traffic statistic. His beneficiaries collect the $50,000. Of that amount, cash value provides $21,500 and the remaining $28,500 comes from insurance. At age 60, Duane's $460 premium had to buy only $28,500 of death protection.

Exhibit 11.2 demonstrates how the rising cash value (lower section) allows the death protection in the top section to decrease. The two components combine to equal the policy's face value. If Duane continues paying premiums to age 100, the policy's accumulated cash value will equal its $50,000 face value.

Exhibit 11.1

Comparison of Premiums on a $50,000 Level Term Policy and on a $50,000 Whole Life Policy, Both Purchased at Age 25

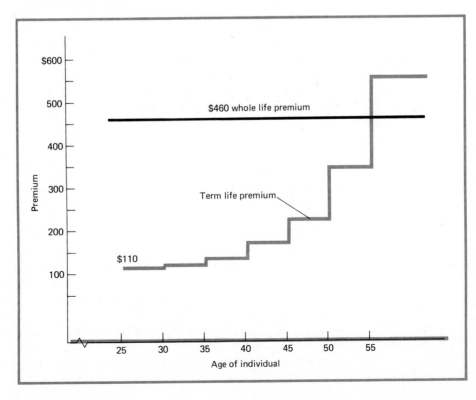

Exhibit 11.2

Accumulated Cash Value on a $50,000 Whole Life Policy Purchased at Age 25

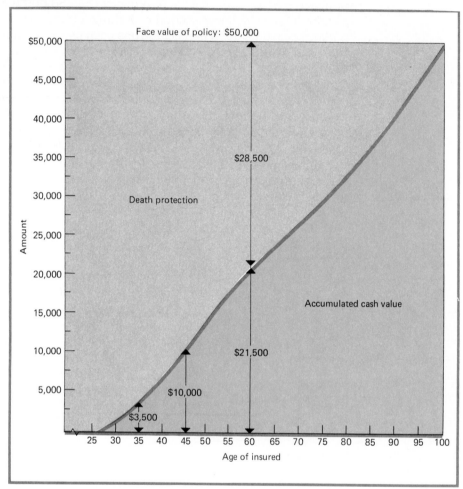

What happens to the cash value if the insured survives? Suppose the bus swerves, leaving Duane shaken but unscathed. He can surrender the policy for its cash value at any time. Of course he loses his life insurance coverage. He can calculate the rewards, because each policy includes a schedule showing the buildup of cash value.

Limited-Pay Life Insurance

Like whole life, **limited-pay life insurance** provides both death protection and a cash value or investment component. Its distinguishing feature is that the fixed premium is paid for a set period. A limited-pay policy might require payments for 20 or 30 years or until age 65. Regardless of the period, coverage equals the policy's face amount right to age 95 to 100.

The premiums on these policies are high. The fewer premium payments have to be large in order to provide the death protection while cash value accumulates. The shorter the payment period, the higher the premium.

Endowment Policy

Endowment policies provide both an investment component and death protection, but they are primarily investment vehicles. Cash value accumulates quickly, with a large annual premium providing the deposit for the investment program. The policy specifies the number of years of premium payments: 10 years, 20 years, and to age 65 are common. At the end of that period the policy's cash value usually equals its face value. That is a much faster buildup than with a whole life policy, which has to run to age 95 or 100 to equal its face value.

Death protection ensures that your beneficiaries receive the policy's face value. Suppose Carol Careless purchased a $10,000, 20-year endowment policy with annual premiums of $430. If Carol survives to make all 20 payments, she can surrender the policy for $10,000 after 20 years. But suppose after paying 10 years, Carol drives through a red light, earning a nice obituary. Her beneficiaries receive the full $10,000; $4,000 comes from the cash value and $6,000 from the death protection.

Since the cash value has to accumulate quickly, annual premiums are high. An endowment policy is expensive life insurance.

Universal Life Insurance

Universal life insurance provides both death protection and an investment component. But it differs significantly from the three previous types of life policy. First, it allows the insured to increase or decrease the face amount of the policy, though many policies limit how much you can raise coverage. The insurance coverage can be tailored to your current needs, but a medical exam may be required if you want to raise the amount sharply.

Second, the insured has some flexibility on annual premiums—this is not true for traditional life insurance. You might pay a large premium one year and much less the next year if your financial situation changes. The insurance company will deduct an amount for the death protection you request. Whatever remains is invested in the policy's cash value. With a large premium payment, that cash value deposit is sizable. If you pay no premium, the insurance company deducts enough from the accumulated cash value to cover the cost of that year's death protection. If that deduction continues, it eventually exhausts the accumulated cash value.

You do not have total discretion on the premium. Most policies set a minimum initial premium. Some extend that minimum for several years to ensure a buildup in cash value. Beyond that, many provide a "target" premium for the policy. Nearly all policies limit how much you can pay for a given amount of insurance. This prevents you from turning a small insurance policy into a major investment vehicle.

Most universal life policies guarantee a fixed rate of interest: 3 to 5 percent is usual, but the actual rate paid is often higher. Each company sets the rate of interest for its policies. Rates can change monthly, quarterly, or (most common) annually.

Universal life policies generally provide you with a detailed statement showing current coverage, premiums paid, expenses charged, the cost of the death protection, deposit to cash value, balance in cash value, and earnings on the policy.

Since neither the premium payment nor the interest rate is fixed, estimating a policy's future cash value is nearly impossible. When interest rates are high, your policy will show high earnings. If you make large premium payments, the cash value will rise rapidly. At the opposite extreme, minimal premium payments along with moderate to low returns will limit cash value buildup.

Universal life coverage continues in force as long as you pay the premium or your policy has sufficient cash value to cover the death benefit. You can continue the policy as long as you want.

PARTICIPATING AND NON-PARTICIPATING POLICIES

Insurance policies come in two forms: nonparticipating and participating. Insurance companies that are owned by shareholders offer nonparticipating policies. These "stock" companies are organized to make a profit for their shareholders. Mutual insurance companies are owned and controlled by their policyholders; they issue predominately participating policies.

Participating Policies

With a **participating policy** you share in the fortunes of the company. Your initial premium is an estimate, and it is usually generous; in other words, the policyholder pays an overcharge. Once the insurance company has computed its final costs, it pays its policyholders a nontaxable **dividend** which can reduce the net cost for the policy considerably. Dividends change from year to year. Factors that affect the dividend you receive include investment earnings, actual mortality experience, and operating expenses.

A caution

Dividends can lower a participating policy's net cost. Often the participating policy is less costly than a comparable nonparticipating policy. Some agents claim the "dividend" is the rate of return you receive, but the dividend does nothing but return part of *your* own money. Only Gert Gullible would consider a $20 refund on her $100 premium a 20 percent rate of return ($20/$100). If this was true, someone who paid a $200 premium and then received a $120 dividend would be getting a 60 percent return.

Dividend options

Most insurance companies will let you do one or more of the following with your dividend: (1) be paid; (2) reduce next period's premium; (3) leave it on deposit to earn interest; (4) purchase additional insurance. Option 2 can reduce your insurance cost. You might choose option 4 if you need more insurance and the amount is appropriate.

Nonparticipating Policies

Nonparticipating policies do not rebate part of the premium as a dividend. Predicting the future cost of a nonparticipating policy is easy since you do not have to predict dividends.

In comparing premiums on participating and nonparticipating policies, you first need to subtract any dividends from the quoted premium. Studies suggest participating policies are usually less expensive.

Strategy

While the initial premium for a nonparticipating policy may be less, compute the net cost of the participating policy—premium less dividend—before you decide.

MAJOR POLICY RIDERS

Like automobiles, life insurance policies come with options. You pay extra for these **options**—or **riders**—and it is not a one-time cost: you continue to pay with each premium. Select with care. Let's examine the more common options.

Waiver of Premium

When you buy the **waiver of premium** option, the company forgives the policy premium if you are disabled and unable to work. Cost of the option depends on the premium, your age, sex, and the policy's definition of *disabled*. If you have a good general disability policy (the next chapter will argue you should), this option duplicates existing coverage.

Strategy

One large, general disability policy that covers all your needs is generally better than small, fragmented policies.

Guaranteed Insurability

A **guaranteed insurability** rider gives you the right to purchase additional life insurance coverage in the future. At specified times you can add coverage at the same rate as a standard health risk, even if you develop health problems. The amount you can buy is some percentage of the policy's face amount. If your future insurance needs are likely to rise and your health fail, this option is worthwhile.

But make certain the option's terms meet your likely needs. Will you need the insurance when you have the option to buy it? An option to buy every 2 years over the next 6 years means little if your need arises in 10 years. Second, will the added coverage meet your needs? If you can only add $2,000, yet your needs rise by $40,000, the option is worthless.

Accidental Death Benefit

The **accidental death benefit** is another frequently offered option. Your beneficiaries collect 2 or 3 times the policy's face amount if you die in an accident and have this special coverage. Die in an accident, and a $50,000 policy pays $100,000 or $150,000; this is called double or triple indemnity. Note two things. If your survivors need $100,000, then buying a $50,000 policy and hoping for an accident is hardly good planning; you are far more likely to die from natural causes. Second, a sound insurance plan meets your needs regardless of how you depart this world.

Strategy

Avoid the accidental death option; it duplicates coverage in a well-developed insurance program.

Selected Special Options

Insurance policies with a cash value—whole life, limited-pay life, endowment, and universal life—offer other options, some free. Term life insurance never offers these options.

Policy loan option

You can borrow part or all of a policy's accumulated value through a **policy loan.** There is no credit check, but the loan is limited to the cash value. Interest on the loan ranges from 5 to 10 percent, with newer policies usually nearer 10. Repayment terms are very flexible; on many of these loans you have to pay only the interest.

Since a policy loan reduces the accumulated cash value, outstanding loans reduce the death payment. Borrow $5,000 on your $50,000 policy, and your beneficiaries would receive only $45,000.

Nonforfeiture options

Most policies offer nonforfeiture options to ensure that cash value is not lost if the insured stops paying premiums.

Cash surrender value. One widely used option is to **surrender the policy and receive a check for its cash value.** Insurance coverage ceases when the policy is "surrendered" or turned over to the insurance company. Column 2 of Exhibit 11.3 illustrates the possible cash value built up in a $100,000 policy purchased at age 25.

Strategy

Use the cash surrender option if you no longer want the coverage.

Paid-up insurance. The accumulated cash value can be used to purchase another insurance policy. No premium payments are required on this

Exhibit 11.3

Approximate Nonforfeiture Values per $100,000 of Insurance for a Whole Life Policy Issued at Age 25

Premiums paid to age	Cash value	Paid-up insurance	Extended term insurance
30	$ 2,340	$ 9,050	7 years—183 days
35	7,850	26,200	20 years—300 days
40	15,200	39,400	25 years—110 days
45	23,400	54,600	24 years—211 days
55	40,500	64,300	20 years—175 days
65	61,000	86,700	16 years— 83 days

paid-up policy; your accumulated cash value pays the premium. Insurance coverage continues at a lower level. Column 3 of Exhibit 11.3 shows the paid-up insurance that the accumulated cash value on a $100,000 policy might buy.

Strategy

Use this option if you want to continue the insurance and the coverage amount is adequate.

Extended term insurance. The policy's cash value can also purchase term life insurance. With **extended term insurance**, your coverage remains unchanged; the new policy's face value equals the old. The length of coverage depends on your policy's cash value and your age. The higher the cash value, the longer the new policy will run. The older you are, the shorter the time you will be covered.

The fourth column of Exhibit 11.3 shows the approximate duration of a $100,000 term policy at varying ages, using the cash value in a $100,000 whole life policy.

Strategy

Use the extended term option if you want to retain the same insurance coverage using a term policy.

SETTLEMENT OPTIONS

When the insured dies, most policies provide several options for payment to beneficiaries.

Lump-Sum Payment

The lump-sum option pays beneficiaries the entire death benefit as soon as a claim is filed and a copy of the death certificate is sent to the insurance company. Beneficiaries then decide how the money will be used; many invest it for the future.

Strategy

The lump-sum payment option is chosen on the assumption that the funds will be prudently invested and managed to meet future needs.

Interest Option

Under the interest option, the proceeds of the policy are left with the insurance company. Interest earned on the proceeds is sent to the beneficiary each month.

Strategy

The interest option is usually temporary; the company pays the interest while the beneficiary is choosing a settlement option.

Series of Installment Payments

Most insurance companies offer beneficiaries the option of converting the death benefit into a series of installment payments, usually monthly. Part of each payment comes from the initial death benefit and part from interest that is earned while the unpaid benefit remains on deposit.

The size of the payment depends on the value of the policy and the period over which payments are received. There are several choices for how long the benefits continue.

Installments for a fixed period

The beneficiary can receive payments over a set number of years or months. During that time, the entire balance and interest will be used. The longer payments are spread out, the more interest the balance will earn.

Strategy

This option is best when a beneficiary needs income for a period and that period can be specified with some certainty.

Installments of a fixed amount

The beneficiary can also specify how large a payment he or she wants. Payments continue until the policy's proceeds and interest are exhausted. Large payments will deplete the balance faster than small ones.

Strategy

Installments over a fixed period are often more desirable than a fixed-dollar option.

Installments for the beneficiary's lifetime

None of the previous options guarantees the beneficiary an income he or she cannot "outlive": this one does. Under the straight life option the insurance company makes installment payments as long as the beneficiary lives. Companies can provide a guaranteed lifetime income because people who die "early" fund payments for those who die "late."

The age of the beneficiary at the time payments begin is a major determinant of the payment's size. The younger the beneficiary, the lower the payments, since they will continue longer.

Strategy

Beneficiaries who need and want a monthly income they cannot "outlive" may want this option.

The death of a beneficiary shortly after payments begin can be a disadvantage of this option. Some insurance companies offer an option here: you can specify a guaranteed period for payments to continue—5 or 10 years perhaps. Payments are made for at least the guarantee period, longer if the beneficiary survives.

Assume Bennie Bummer elects the settlement option of $200 monthly for his lifetime but with a 5-year guarantee. If Bennie dies after 2 months, the person he named as beneficiary will receive payments for the 58 months that remain in the guarantee period. If Bennie survives beyond 5 years, payments continue until his death. The potential payment is less when you include a guarantee period.

Strategy

Beneficiaries who want to ensure at least a minimum number of payments should elect one of the guarantee periods.

TAXES ON LIFE INSURANCE PROCEEDS AND CASH VALUE

In general, life insurance escapes taxation, but in certain cases it can be subject to federal income or estate taxes. Since most state and local governments track the federal rules on income taxes, we do not cover them in detail. Unfortunately, state inheritance and estate taxes vary so widely that they cannot be covered here.

Three issues related to life insurance taxation will be covered:

1   Taxation of proceeds paid to a beneficiary
2   Taxation of proceeds when the owner surrenders a policy for its cash value
3   Taxation of interest earned as the policy's cash value accumulates

Benefit Paid When Insured Dies

All death benefits paid by a life insurance policy are exempt from federal income taxes. When Marvin Mishap dies, no income taxes have to be paid on his $50,000 life insurance benefit; his beneficiary receives it all.

Whether a policy's death benefit is subject to federal estate taxes depends on two things. First, if someone other than the insured owns the policy, there are no estate taxes: if Marvin's sister owns the $50,000 policy, it isn't part of his estate, so there is no tax. Second, even if the insured owns the policy, there may be no estate taxes. Marvin's $50,000 policy and all of his other assets become part of his estate. Currently, everyone receives an estate tax credit that allows you to pass on a $600,000 estate without paying taxes. Given that sizable limit, few people pay estate taxes.

The top half of Exhibit 11.4 summarizes the income and estate tax treatment of death benefit payments.

Exhibit 11.4

Taxability of Proceeds from a Life Insurance Policy

Situation	Policy owner	Income tax	Estate tax
Death of insured.	Insured.	None.	Included in insured's estate.
Death of insured.	Other than insured.	None.	None.
Surrender for cash value.	Anyone.	Only the excess of cash value over the total premiums paid is taxed.	
Interest on policy's cash value.	Anyone.	None.	None.

Proceeds from a Policy's Cash Value

When you surrender a life insurance policy for its accumulated cash value, you pay income taxes only on the portion of the cash value that exceeds the total premiums you have paid. Liz recently surrendered a whole life policy for its $3,520 cash value. She paid premiums of $532 for each of the 10 years she had the policy (total premiums of $5,320), so none of the cash value is taxed. If the cash value had been $5,500, the $180 that exceeded total of the premiums would be subject to income taxes.

There is never an estate tax when you surrender a policy. Exhibit 11.4 summarizes the income and estate consequences of surrendering a policy.

Interest Earned on Accumulated Cash Value

As noted earlier, part of a policy's cash value comes from interest earned on accumulated money. These earnings are sheltered from income taxes while they remain in the policy. With no taxes to pay, all the interest accumulates in the cash value as long as the money remains in the policy.

None of the interest earned on the policy's cash value is subject to federal estate tax. Exhibit 11.4 summarizes the income and estate tax treatment of interest earned on a policy's cash value.

DETERMINING YOUR LIFE INSURANCE NEEDS

Rather than just picking some insurance amount and hoping it's adequate, a wise financial planner estimates how much is required. Some insurance brochures advise multiplying your salary by some figure—4 to 6 times is common—to reach an estimate. For a $25,000 salary they suggest $100,000 to $150,000 coverage. That formula is simplistic, since it does not take into account the number of dependents, their ages, other financial resources, income the survivor may earn, and estate settlement costs. This rule could mean excessive coverage for someone with no dependents and woefully inadequate protection for someone with several young dependents, limited financial resources, and a spouse with no current income. By analyzing your current situation, you can develop a **needs approach** to insurance planning. Let's see exactly how you do that.

Coordinating Life Insurance and Social Security

A good insurance plan should count any Social Security benefits the survivors might receive. Since such benefits could easily top $1,000 monthly if the deceased had several minor children, they need to be part of the plan. They can replace a considerable part of the deceased's income.

Who qualifies for benefits?

Children of the deceased worker qualify for benefits until they reach age 18 (19 if still in high school), and benefits are not reduced by any investment income the child might receive. Even a child's wages have minimal impact unless they are large.

The deceased's spouse may qualify under two conditions. Benefits begin immediately if he or she is 60 or older. A spouse under age 60 may receive a benefit if he or she is caring for a child under age 16. For the spouse to receive the full benefit, his or her income cannot exceed the specified limit: $6,000 in 1987. Once income goes over the limit, the benefit drops $1 for each $2 over. Earn $3,000 over the limit, and your benefits drop $1,500. Once a spouse's earnings approach $20,000, the reduction

usually eliminates the benefit. Only wages and salary count; you can have any amount of investment income, pension payments, and insurance proceeds. Benefits cease when the youngest child is 16 and can restart when the spouse is 60.

Estimating social security benefits for the survivors

The calculation of the precise benefit for survivors relies on the deceased's historical earnings and the length of time he or she had worked. The logical source for an estimate would be the local Social Security office, but they claim they cannot do that. Once old Jeanine is gone, the office readily computes the benefits for her survivors. But if the benefits prove too small, Jeanine cannot return to buy the needed life insurance. Life insurance is not planned A.D. (after death). So let's see how to overcome the problem.

Table of estimated survivor benefits. Appendix A.2 provides an estimate of benefits your survivors might receive upon your death. At the top of that table is a Survivor Category, and under it different survivor situations. Down the side of the table are a series of age groups and within each is a range of incomes. Look at the top of the table for a minute. Column 3 shows the benefit a single child under 18 receives. Benefits for two children are in column 4; a surviving spouse caring for one child under 16 receives the same benefit. Column 5 shows the maximum a family can receive when there are three or more children under 18 or when a spouse cares for two or more children.

The table allows you to estimate the Social Security benefit. An example will show how it works. Assume John is 35 years old and currently earns $17,000 annually; he does not have a spouse. If John dies, his 3-year-old child will receive $443 each month. If he has two children under age 16, the combined benefit is $886.

A spouse can complicate things. Assume Joan, who is 25 years old, earns $24,000. Her husband Sid would care for their 4-year-old child if Joan died. Sid and the child would receive $1,156 if Sid's earnings were less than the maximum. He would lose $1 of benefits for every $2 he earned over that limit. In no case would the child's benefit drop below the $578 shown in column 3. If there were two children, Sid and they would receive the $1,348 family maximum if his earnings were below the limit. But significant earnings could drop his benefit to zero. The children would always receive the $1,156 in column 4.

The estimates in A.2 are based on the assumption that you have worked steadily and have received roughly "average" wage increases during that time. If so, the estimates are reasonably accurate. Violate one or both premises, and the accuracy drops. If you want to use A.2 for years after 1987, raise the benefits by the approximate change in the CPI since 1987 for a rough estimate that is adequate for planning.

Request an estimate from social security. You might try writing the Social Security Administration, Office of Public Inquiries, Baltimore, MD 21235, and request an estimate of your survivor's benefits.

Make a detailed computation of your likely survivor benefits. The detailed booklet *Guide to Social Security* outlines the steps you need to take to compute your benefit, using a series of worksheets. These worksheets can make an involved, complex estimate manageable. You can purchase the booklet from William M. Mercer-Meidinger Inc., Compensation and Benefit Services, 2600 Meidinger Tower, Louisville KT 40202-3415.

The Needs Approach to Life Insurance Planning

When you use the needs approach, you concentrate on the two most important reasons for having life insurance: to settle your estate, and to provide replacement income for your survivors. These two requirements can be split into seven broad needs categories:

1   Settling the estate
2   Repaying debts
3   Emergency fund
4   Education fund
5   Income: family years
6   Income: middle years
7   Income: retirement

The first two relate to settlement of the estate, the remainder to replacement of the deceased's income.

To demonstrate how the needs approach operates, let's use a mythical couple, Carl and Connie Green, as an example. Carl is 30 while Connie is 32 years old, and they have one child, 2 years old. First, we will estimate how much insurance Carl should have to cover the possibility of his dying. Then we will project Connie's insurance needs.

The Greens' case is going to be complex, but we make no apologies. Once you master a complex problem, others are easy. Our planning centers on how much insurance Carl needs right now; this will change over time.

The worksheet in Exhibit 11.5 summarizes the life insurance needs for each of the seven broad categories in the list above. For now we are concerned with the dollar amount of insurance needed in each area. Later we will show how existing insurance and financial assets together can cover the amount.

Settling the estate
Expenses for settling an estate include funeral expenses, medical costs not covered by insurance, federal estate taxes, state inheritance or estate taxes, probate costs, and the executor's fees for administering the estate. For a complex estate with many assets, the survivors will have to pay most of these costs, while simple estates entail but one or two. Regardless, the insurance plan needs to provide money to cover these items.

Carl Green's estate is simple, so settlement costs are moderate. He has good health insurance to cover his medical costs. Because of the small size of his estate, there will be no federal or state estate taxes. Based on local costs, the Greens estimate that $7,000 would be needed to settle the estate; this amount is entered on line 1 of Exhibit 11.5.

Exhibit 11.5

Needs Analysis Worksheet for Estimating the Life Insurance Required to Settle Estate and Replace Carl Green's Income

Reason why life insurance is needed	Total amount needed	Amount Provided by		Amount still needed	Time period covered	Potential insurance required
		Spouse's earnings	Social Security benefit			
1. Settle estate	$ 7,000	—	—	$ 7,000	One time	$ 7,000
2. Repay debts	74,000	—	—	74,000	One time	74,000
3. Emergency fund	4,000	—	—	4,000	One time	4,000
4. Education fund	22,000	—	—	22,000	One time	22,000
5. Family years (until child is 18)	2,100	1,300	558	242	192 months	46,464
6. Middle years	1,500	1,300	—	200	144 months	28,800
7. Retirement years	1,100	493	532	75	300 months	22,500
Total required life insurance						$204,764

Repayment of debts

A good insurance plan should provide money to repay all debts. Many people have consumer credit charges ranging from cash loans to credit card balances. Your unpaid loan balances plus your credit card balances equal your required coverage from insurance.

If you have a home mortgage, you have two choices. You can include the entire unpaid balance in the insurance plan. Survivors can then use the money to repay the mortgage and remain in the home. Or the monthly living expenses for the survivors can include an amount to continue regular mortgage payments. The first option offers more flexibility, so we will use it.

Currently, $66,000 remains to be repaid on the Greens' $70,000 mortgage; its remaining life is about 19 years. In addition, the Greens' consumer loans and credit card debts total $8,000. See line 2 of Exhibit 11.5 for the total.

Emergency fund

An emergency fund provides money for major, unexpected expenses such as auto repairs, home maintenance, and uninsured medical expenses. It removes some of the uncertainty for your survivors. You can use the guidelines for creating a cash reserve from Chapter 3 here as well. A reserve equal to 2 months' income would be minimal, and 6 month's income the most needed.

Carl and Connie decide a $4,000 emergency fund is needed. They already hold that $4,000 in their general cash reserve, but we include the entire amount on line 3 of Exhibit 11.5. Later that money and other assets will be incorporated into the insurance plan.

Education fund

The education fund covers the children's costs for a private primary or secondary school, a private or public university, or other educational programs. You need to estimate the costs of the desired education to decide how large a fund to provide. Also consider whether the child might qualify for financial aid.

The effect of inflation. The costs at the time a child's education begins may be substantially higher than at present. We can cover those increases by having the money in the education fund invested until it is needed. Even after taxes, the rate of return should exceed inflation. Thus, if one invests enough money to pay for 1 year at a public university today, it should increase enough to meet rising university costs, assuming they rise at the rate of overall inflation.

The Greens want to provide their child 4 years at a public university: estimated current cost is $22,000 ($5,500 × 4 years). If Carl died, that $22,000 would be invested so that it would be sufficient to cover education costs when the child enters school in 17 years. Line 4 of Exhibit 11.5 shows the education fund.

Income: family years

The family income years last until the youngest child reaches age 18. You might subdivide this period into two portions. The first part extends until the youngest child reaches age 16, when the spouse's benefit ends. The second runs until that child is 18, when his or her benefits end.

When there are young children, life insurance during the family years is essential, especially if the spouse's earning capacity is limited. Social Security benefits combined with life insurance become the major income sources. Life insurance needs will be lower when the surviving spouse has substantial earnings.

Projected income needs and possible sources. We start by estimating the monthly income survivors need for living expenses. Your current budget (with some adjustments) is a good starting point. First, one less person in the household should lower expenses. Second, the mortgage payment can be eliminated if a lump sum is provided to repay it; all other housing costs remain. Third, include any additional child care and domestic help that may be required. As a rough estimate, 75 percent of the current budget is generally adequate.

There are 3 sources of income for the family period: the surviving spouse's earnings, Social Security survivor's benefits, and life insurance. For a two-career family, the first source will be major. Regardless of the spouse's earnings, the children will receive Social Security benefits until age 18, but when those earnings are large, the spouse's Social Security benefit will be sharply curtailed or even eliminated. (Remember that it drops $1 for each $2 of income over the limit.) Life insurance must provide any income not covered by the first two sources.

Let's project Connie Green's income needs if Carl dies. Exhibit 11.6 highlights that income as well as its potential sources. After-tax income is plotted on the vertical axis, while the horizontal shows Connie's age. The Greens estimate Connie and their child would need $2,100 of after-tax income each month during the family years. Since their child is now age 2, the family period extends for 16 years until the child is 18. At that point Connie will be 48; a line is drawn at $2,100 to that age.

Connie expects to continue her full-time career. With Carl gone, she would qualify as a head of household. She expects a monthly income of $1,300 after deducting federal and state income taxes. That amount is entered in both Exhibit 11.5 and Exhibit 11.6.

Rather than make a detailed estimate of her Social Security benefits, Connie uses Appendix A.2 at the back of this book. To estimate the Greens' benefits, they use Carl's $23,000 salary and his age—30. Based on Appendix A.2 the estimated benefit is $558 for Connie and the child. Their child will receive the benefit, but Connie's $20,500 income means her benefit will be zero. Only $558 is entered in Exhibits 11.5 and 11.6.

Connie's $1,300 after-tax earnings and the child's $558 Social Security benefit cover all but $242 of the $2,100 a month they need. That $242 is entered as required income in Exhibit 11.6 and in column 5 of Exhibit 11.5.

The family income period in Exhibit 11.5 covers the 192 months until the Greens' 2-year-old child is 18. As we noted, the family period extends until the youngest child is 18; then Social Security benefits cease. We

Exhibit 11.6

*Projected Future Income Needs and Possible Sources for the Family,
Middle, and Retirement Years*

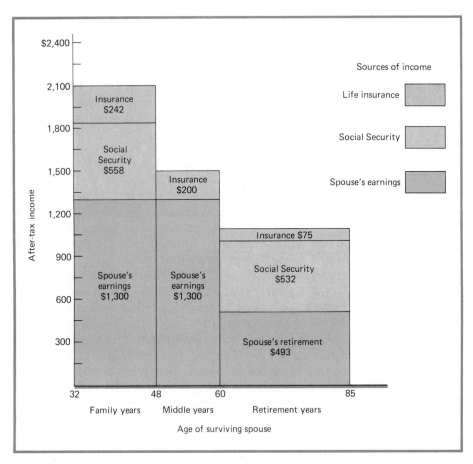

assume the child is self-supporting or using the education fund at that
point. We enter 192 months in column 6 of Exhibit 11.5.

*Income: middle
years*

The middle years span from the youngest child's reaching 18 to the
spouse's retirement. The earliest a surviving spouse can qualify for retirement benefits is age 60, but retirement can be delayed to age 62, age 65,
or later; the longer the delay, the higher the benefit. A spouse has only two
sources of income during the middle years: earnings and life insurance proceeds. For a spouse with sizable earnings, life insurance will be less important, but even with high earnings, some insurance may be advised as a
safety margin.

Projected income needs together with possible sources. First estimate the after-tax income the surviving spouse requires. Any children are

assumed to be self-supporting at this point, so they are not part of the analysis. The Greens decide that Connie would need $1,500 monthly. Column 2 of Exhibit 11.5 shows that amount.

The middle section of Exhibit 11.6 identifies where that $1,500 income will come from. Connie's $1,300 of after-tax earnings is the major source; only $200 has to come from life insurance. That amount is entered in column 5 of Exhibit 11.5.

As noted earlier, the middle years extend until the surviving spouse retires. The Greens expect Connie to retire at age 60. That makes a total of 144 months until Connie reaches age 60. That total is entered in column 6 of Exhibit 11.5.

Income: retirement years

This period begins with retirement and ends at death. Major income sources during this time include pension payments, Social Security retirement benefits, and life insurance. The surviving spouse's earnings give rise to the pension, and the size of the payments depends on the quality of that plan and the level of salary earned. At age 62 or 65, Social Security benefits can either be based on the deceased person's earnings or on the survivor's. A survivor can elect to take whichever benefit is larger. The benefit at age 60 is based on the deceased's record, however.

Projected income needs together with possible sources. Projecting income needed for retirement comes first. When making the estimate, we need to consider the special circumstances of retirement: work-related expenses stop, but travel expenses might increase, for example. The Greens estimate Connie would need $1,100 of after-tax retirement income each month (see column 2 of Exhibit 11.5 and the analysis in Exhibit 11.6).

Start by reviewing the surviving spouse's pension plan, if there is one, and estimating its benefit. A rough estimate will serve. Depending on the individual's work history, a pension may replace 20 to 40 percent of working income. If the pension payment is highly uncertain, you might project no income. The Greens estimate that Connie's present pension will provide $493 each month after taxes. This amount is entered in the last section of Exhibit 11.6; it is also entered in column 3 of Exhibit 11.5.

If the estimated Social Security benefit is based on the deceased spouse's record, his or her income would be used in Appendix A.2. If a benefit will be based on the survivor's work record, we use the survivor's income for the estimate. If Connie is to retire at 60, her benefit must be based on Carl's record. Using his $23,000 and age of 30, Appendix A.2 gives a monthly benefit of $532. This amount is entered in Exhibits 11.5 and 11.6.

Life insurance is the element which completes the income profile in Exhibit 11.6. A reasonable pension joined with good Social Security benefits lowers the need for life insurance. But for those with small (or no) pensions and limited Social Security, life insurance will be a major resource. The Greens fit the first category: only $75 of the required $1,100 monthly income ($1,100 − $493 pension − $532 Social Security) has to come from life insurance. This amount is shown in Exhibit 11.6 and Exhibit 11.5.

The last step is to project how long retirement will last. That entails estimating how long the survivor will live. A mortality table (it was discussed earlier) shows how long a man or woman is expected to live at a given age. Add some years to that projection to ensure the person does not "outlive" the income. The Greens decide to provide income to age 85; this is the cutoff for Exhibit 11.6. A total of 300 months is entered in Exhibit 11.5 to cover Connie from age 60 to 85.

What life insurance is required?

The final column of Exhibit 11.5 shows the amount of life insurance required to cover all seven of the needs categories. The required amounts in column 5 were multiplied by the periods in column 6 to yield the required insurance coverage amounts in the final column. Since the first four categories are one-time expenses, computing the final column is easy. The total amounts in the final column show the Greens' insurance needs: the total is $204,764.

What about inflation? Shouldn't those income needs for the middle and retirement years be raised to cover inflation? No. Granted, inflation will boost the cost of living, but the sources of income we identified should also rise. The surviving spouse's salary should increase, and Social Security benefits are indexed to rise with inflation. What about the life insurance segment? We expect that any insurance money intended for future use will be invested and that its after-tax return will exceed inflation. As those balances grow, they should provide future benefits large enough to offset inflation. Thus, no special adjustment is needed for inflation.

How Much Life Insurance?

Start with the potential total life insurance shown at the bottom of Exhibit 11.5. You may not need $100,000 just because it shows that amount. First, any existing life insurance reduces that total. Second, your present financial assets—savings accounts, money market funds, mutual funds, and common stocks—further reduce those needs. Net required insurance becomes:

Total required   current   existing   new
life insurance from   −   life insurance   −   financial   =   life insurance
"needs" analysis   coverage   assets   needed

For example, the Greens' needs analysis in Exhibit 11.5 shows Carl should have about $205,000 of insurance. Carl has $36,000 of life insurance; that should be subtracted from the $205,000. The Greens' current financial assets total $14,000; that too will be deducted. Carl needs the following:

Required life insurance (Exhibit 11.5)	$205,000
Existing life insurance	−36,000
Present balance in financial assets	−14,000
New life insurance for Carl	$155,000

While the net insurance amount will vary widely, the steps you take to arrive at that amount are the same. Your survivors' needs and the cost of settling your estate form the basis for a logical estimate of your insurance needs.

Life Insurance Planning for Women: Are Their Needs Different?

Do women have different life insurance needs than men? In a word, *no*. A woman should also consider whether life insurance is needed to settle her estate. If she has dependents, she will want to analyze the income needs of her survivors to see what part of her income must be replaced by life insurance. Analyzing Connie's insurance needs involves the same steps as analyzing Carl's: only the dollar amounts differ.

Strategy

Women should estimate what life insurance they require, using a needs analysis like the one in Exhibit 11.5. This holds for women with full-time or part-time careers, as well as those who remain at home to care for minor children.

Inflation and Life Insurance Needs

Inflation has a continuing effect on your life insurance needs. As prices rise, the costs for loan repayments, emergency funds, and monthly income for the survivors also increase. Therefore, you should review and update your life insurance coverage every 2 to 3 years. Exhibits 11.5 and 11.6 can be reworked using current dollar amounts for each of the seven major categories. Not all categories rise: as you repay your mortgage and other loans, your debt repayment needs should drop. As prices rise, the monthly income needed by survivors will increase, but total needs may drop because the period covered is getting shorter. Do not just assume increases and decreases will offset one another, however: reestimate your insurance needs.

Strategy

Review your life insurance every 2 to 3 years to ensure your coverage is adequate. Too much coverage wastes premium dollars; too little leaves your dependents without protection.

SELECTING THE LIFE INSURANCE YOU NEED

Simple rules to guide life insurance purchases, such as "Always buy term insurance" or "Never buy endowment policies" would be convenient. But there are no such general rules that work. Given the right circumstances, any one of the six policies discussed here could be "best." But there are some guidelines.

Buy Your Life Insurance— Don't Be Sold It

The rule seems straightforward. Yet it is amazing how few insurance policy purchases are initiated by the insured.

Fran Fastbuck, local agent for Last Bet Life Insurance, calls Ed Easytouch: "How ya doing, Ed?"

After some small talk she asks: "Ed, have you thought about how much your survivors need you?"

There is a pause. "We have this great new insurance policy."

Ed notes: "I'm short of dough right now."

"Not to worry," Fran intones: "We have this tiny, tiny policy. You can always buy more in 2 to 5 years."

Chances are the policy is woefully inadequate for Ed's needs. But the Eds of the world too often say yes without determining their needs or doing any comparison shopping. You can and should be different. The general features summarized in Exhibit 11.7 provide a start. The guidelines of the next sections provide further help.

Strategy

Buy the life insurance that you want and need; do not let an agent sell you a policy.

Pure Death or Death Protection with an Investment Plan?   Volumes have been written extolling the virtues of purchasing just death protection. Unfortunately, a sizable stack of learned verbiage would also refute the notion. Some would claim that policies which combine death protection with an investment component are best: whole life, endowment,

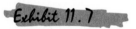

Exhibit 11.7

Features of the Basic Life Insurance Policies

Type	Coverage period	Annual premium	Amount paid at death	Cash-value component
Level term.	Terms of 1 to 20 years; typically not offered past age 65.	Fixed for the term, but rising at each renewal.	Fixed for life of policy.	None provided.
Decreasing term.	Periods of 5 to 30 years; typically not offered past age 65.	Fixed for period of policy.	Declines to zero over period of policy.	None provided.
Whole life.	Until age 95, 100, or death.	Fixed and continuing to age 95 or 100.	Fixed at policy's face value.	Increases at fixed rate set by policy.
Limited-pay life.	Until age 95, 100, or death.	Fixed; continuing for set period—e.g., 20 years.	Fixed at policy's face value.	Increase at fixed rate set by policy.
Endowment.	Set period, such as 10 years, 20 years, or to age 65.	Fixed for period of policy.	Fixed at policy's face value.	Increases at fixed rate set by policy.
Universal life.	Until age 95, 100, or death.	Flexible: within limits, insured can specify.	Variable: insured can decide.	Flexible; buildup depends on premium and rate of return.

limited-pay, and universal life insurance. Neither generalization is wholly true. For many, a policy providing only death protection is not only best, but may be the only sound option. Those who have greater resources may be interested in adding an investment or cash value component. You need to decide what is best given your circumstances.

Can You Afford Life Insurance with an Investment Feature?

Combining life insurance and an investment program is attractive, but there are additional costs. Add the investment feature, and your premiums could be 3, 5, or even 10 times greater than those for a straight death benefit policy. Exhibit 11.8 shows typical premiums you pay for competitively priced insurance policies. It has one dramatic message: premiums on term insurance—it provides just a death benefit—are vastly less than those for whole life and universal life, both of which add an investment component. The exhibit is not meant to suggest that the "low" cost of term insurance makes it the "best" buy. Remember, term insurance premiums rise with your age. But one thing is clear: your premiums are going to be very large when a policy has an investment component.

Faced with high premiums, people are tempted to buy small policies. That is wrong. If your survivors need $150,000 of protection to meet their needs, a $20,000 policy, even if it is affordable, is useless. Stick with a straight death policy: with its much lower premium, you can buy the dollar coverage you need.

Strategy

Buy enough insurance to meet your needs. Don't settle for an inadequate cash-value policy just to keep the premiums manageable; your survivors deserve better.

Selecting Term Life Insurance

Let's first examine the common features of level term and decreasing term. Major strengths and weaknesses of the two policies are summarized in

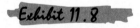 **Exhibit 11.8**

Approximate Annual Premium for a $50,000 and a $200,000 Insurance Policy Purchased at Three Different Ages*

Type of life insurance	Age at Purchase of $50,000 Policy			Age at Purchase of $200,000 Policy		
	25	35	45	25	35	45
Level term (5 year)	$110	$126	$ 218	$ 324	$ 332	$ 586
Decreasing term (20 year)	96	135	268	283	356	719
Whole life	456	700	1,023	1,938	2,680	3,912

* Premiums shown are for a typical policy; your actual premium may differ.

Exhibit 11.9. The strengths are self-explanatory, but several weaknesses require comment.

The fact that coverage on many policies cannot be extended past age 65 is touted as a "near fatal" shortcoming. But is it? Recall the seven major needs listed in Exhibit 11.5: how many of those remain for the typical person at age 65? Children are grown, so there is not need for child-rearing and education funds. Most people will have accumulated financial assets to settle their estate, repay debts (the house is probably paid for), and provide an emergency fund. At age 65 there are no middle years. There is only one need left: retirement income. If you have planned your retirement (Chapter 18 will show why and how that's done), that should also be covered. In short, many people do not need insurance after 65. Except in special situations—e.g. young children, heavy debts coupled with a limited net worth, large costs to settle estates—the lack of coverage after 65 may not be a major weakness.

What about the lack of an investment feature? As later chapters will show, you have many different investments other than life insurance. Even if the investment feature looks appealing, it may be unaffordable. Finally, if you are managing your finances, you should not need forced savings.

Strategy

Level and decreasing term insurance policies excel at providing maximum death benefits at the lowest cost. For those who need high dollar coverage and a minimal premium, they are often the best choice.

Level term insurance

Level term insurance is best when you need high coverage for an extended period. As Exhibit 11.8 shows, its premium is generally low; the

Exhibit 11.9

Strengths and Weaknesses: Level Term and Decreasing Term Insurance Policies

Strengths
1. Policies provide the largest insurance protection for each premium dollar; for that reason, term insurance is often the best option when the required insurance coverage is large.
2. Comparison shopping is reasonably easy.
3. Cost per $1,000 of coverage often declines as size of policy rises.
4. Many professional groups and associations offer these policies.

Weaknesses
1. Many companies will not renew policy past age 65 or 70.
2. Policy does not accumulate any cash value.
3. Premium rises as you grow older; once you are past age 45, those increases can be sizeable.
4. Death protection under decreasing term policy declines to zero during the policy's set period.

premium does, however, rise considerably once you reach age 50. Many policies offer true economies of scale: the annual premium for a $100,000 policy is often far less than 4 times that for a $25,000 one. These features make it ideal for covering needs that are currently sizable, but which will drop at age 50.

For people who will need some insurance past age 65, term may still have a major role; it could easily be the choice to cover those needs that end before 65.

Strategy

For many people, term insurance will be the major component of their insurance plan. It provides high dollar coverage at a reasonable premium.

Renewable and convertible—essential points. A good term insurance policy is **renewable;** *you* have the right to renew the policy at the end of its present term. Granted, the premium will be higher, but you shouldn't have to pass a medical exam. Give the insurance company the option to renew you, and you risk Bunky Bummer's fate. His policy was renewable at the company's option. Just when deteriorating health made continuation imperative, his company refused to renew. This option is not acceptable.

Find a policy that is **convertible**—i.e., one that you can convert from term insurance to one of the cash value policies if you choose. Conversion allows you to extend coverage past age 65 if the need arises. The new premiums may be high, but you avoid a medical exam. A good conversion option provides several policy choices and permits you to switch until age 60 or so.

Decreasing term insurance

The death benefit under decreasing term insurance declines over time. It is suitable to meet an insurance need that likewise declines over time: repaying your mortgage, for example. Or it might cover an education fund; as you accumulate money in that fund, your insurance needs drop. To make this system workable, you need to find a policy with coverage that declines at the same rate as your need does.

Strategy

Use decreasing term insurance for needs that decline predictably over time.

Selecting Whole Life, Limited-Pay Life, and Endowment Policies

Exhibit 11.10 summarizes the major strengths and weaknesses of these three policies. Several need further explanation.

A frequent selling point for these policies is their near "magical" buildup of cash value. A few agents go so far as to claim premiums paid for term insurance are "wasted" because you never build a cash value. On the contrary, term insurance provides death protection, the *main* reason for

Exhibit 11.10

Strengths and Weaknesses: Whole Life, Limited-Pay Life, and Endowment Policies

Strengths
1. You can continue coverage to age 95 or 100 by paying premium.
2. Once you purchase the policy, the premium remains constant.
3. Policy accumulates a cash value as the investment component.
4. You are "forced" to save, since you must pay the premium to keep the policy in force.
5. Income taxes are deferred on the interest earnings that accumulate in the policy's cash value.
6. Owner of policy can borrow against its cash value.
7. On a limited-pay policy, you only pay the premium for the specified time period.
8. Endowment policy accumulates a cash value equal to the policy's face value reasonably quickly (but premiums can be very high).

Weaknesses
1. Premium can be prohibitively expensive for a policy with a large face value.
2. Limited buildup of cash value during the first 5 years; rate of return is often negative.
3. When the policy is held 10 to 20 years, its rate of return ranges from reasonable to dismal.
4. Estimating a policy's rate of return is difficult.
5. Endowment policies provide limited death protection for each premium dollar: a very expensive life insurance vehicle.
6. Shortened payment period on limited-pay life policies boosts premium significantly.

purchasing life insurance. And, far from appearing magically, Exhibit 11.8 confirms that the cash value comes from *you*. Some agents stress that these policies force you to "save": you must pay the premium or coverage stops. But a serious financial manager does not need a forced savings plan.

To decide whether cash value makes sense for you, ask: Do I want and need an investment vehicle? If the answer is no, stick to policies that provide just death protection. Why wouldn't you want an investment? Maybe you (1) already have an adequate investment plan, (2) do not currently have the money to begin an ambitious plan, or (3) do not need an ongoing plan.

Even if you want an investment plan, whole life, limited-pay life, or an endowment policy may not be your choice. You have to decide how good the typical cash-value life insurance policy is as an investment. The risk is low, but how good is the rate of return? Computing that return requires some assumptions, since the typical life insurance contract never mentions a rate: in fact, even if asked, most companies will not provide one. But a well-documented study by *Consumer Reports* gives some insights.[1] Hold it 20 years, and a "good" whole life policy may yield an 8 to 10 percent return, a "medium" policy 5 to 6 percent, a "poor" policy less than 4 percent. Shorten that to 5 years, and you will be hard pressed to find a policy that

---

[1] *Consumer Reports*, "Life Insurance, Ratings of Whole-Life Policies," July 1986, pp. 458–469.

provides a positive return: most are decidedly *negative*. If you paid $1,000 into one of these gems over 5 years and then retrieved your "prize," you wouldn't receive any interest, your original $1,000, or even the holiday candle the local S&L had offered.

Strategy

Avoid these three policies if you plan to hold the policy less than 10 years; the return is dismal.

A comment on "tax advantages"

Recent changes in federal income tax regulations left life insurance relatively untouched:

- Your cash value accumulates tax-free in the policy.
- Only that portion of cash value that exceeds the total premiums paid is subject to tax when withdrawn.

Capitalizing on this, cash-value life insurance is being touted as the "last great tax shelter." Is it? First, since the top tax rate is now 28 percent, you are not avoiding mountains of taxes. Even after paying taxes, the 9 percent before-tax return on a general investment—that's 6.48 percent after taxes [9% × (100% − 28%)]—may better the mediocre return of many policies. Second, not all tax-advantaged investments are gone. Salary reduction plans, Keogh plans, and Individual Retirement Accounts are still open to many (see Chapter 18). Likewise, tax-free municipal bond mutual funds, savings bonds, and common stock mutual funds provide opportunities to defer or even avoid taxes altogether (more on these in Chapters 14 through 17). Life insurance is hardly the *only* tax-advantaged investment. Finally, if you are paying insurance premiums to gain a tax advantage and you do not need the coverage, you are wasting money.

Strategy

Don't be oversold on the tax-shelter feature of whole life, limited-pay life, and endowment policies. A dismal tax-sheltered return is still dismal.

Selecting a cash-value policy

How can you incorporate the above concerns into your decision? Proceed with caution. Make certain you want, and can afford, the policy's investment component. Too many policies are purchased and then let lapse after several years. Don't take on a policy you cannot reasonably expect to sustain. Second, plan to hold the policy at least 10 (preferably 20) years. Carefully consider other investment options to see if one of these might better meet your needs. Last, and most important, review a comparative study like the one previously cited from *Consumer Reports* to single out policies that have provided reasonable returns. Past performance may not be repeated, but why pick a confirmed loser and hope it becomes a winner?

Whole life insurance

Whole life is ideal for someone who wants the traditional combination of death protection and an investment component. Its forced saving feature may appeal to some. Its tax-sheltered accumulation of cash value can be attractive to someone who has exhausted other tax-advantaged investment options and still faces a high marginal tax rate. And coverage can be continued to age 95 or 100 if you wish.

If your analysis suggests you need a large amount of insurance, the premiums on a whole life policy may be prohibitive; they can run several thousand dollars a year. If you start a policy only to drop it in several years, you may lose money. Some policies are consistent: they keep that dismal return going.

Strategy

Select a whole life policy only if you need and want the investment component and you plan to keep the policy 10 years or more.

Limited-pay life insurance

Limited-pay life is designed for the person who wants to avoid paying premiums after a certain point, age 65 for example. The purchaser should want an investment component and expect to hold the policy for 10 years or more. Shortening the payment time boosts premiums; for many it is simply unworkable.

Strategy

The high premiums and limited-pay feature of this policy limit its appeal to those who can afford the costs.

Endowment policy

An endowment policy is first and foremost an investment vehicle. It adds some death protection; this provides funds to reach a goal if you die before doing so. The central question is: how good are endowment policies as investments? The answer is not encouraging: low returns often sink to disastrous levels if the policy is cashed in early. Many policies do not provide competitive returns. An alternative is to set up your own investment program and cover yourself with term insurance until your goal is reached. A carefully selected investment program can outperform many endowment policies.

Unless your life insurance needs are very limited, an endowment policy is prohibitively expensive. Consider it an investment with enough term life insurance to cover untimely death.

Strategy

Unless you want or need the forced savings feature of an endowment policy, you can probably do better by selecting your own investment vehicle.

*Selecting a
universal life
policy*

     Exhibit 11.11 summarizes the major strengths and weaknesses of universal life insurance; it should help you decide whether this policy is suitable. Several of those points need elaboration.

     The flexibility of this policy is a decided advantage. By altering the death protection, you can tailor the coverage to your needs, although most policies limit how much you can change the coverage. The policy can help you through a temporary shortage with a reduced premium. Conversely, if you are flush, you might raise the premium.

     Second, agents will willingly and openly quote a current return on most universal life policies—light years better than the "trust us" approach for traditional whole life policies. Furthermore, on the better policies quoted rates are competitive with other returns.

     The final major advantage is in the area of disclosure. Policyholders receive complete disclosure in such key areas as (1) expenses being charged, (2) cost of the death protection, (3) earnings credited on cash value, (4) deposit to cash value, and (5) accumulated cash value, as well as (6) an annual statement summarizing all this. With the typical whole life policy none of this is disclosed. The philosophy seems to be: Trust us, we will take care of you. Maybe, but which are you more comfortable with?

     Watch the expenses as well as the interest rate. Lest we give too rosy an impression of universal life policies, there are drawbacks. There

Exhibit 11.11

Strengths and Weaknesses: Universal Life Insurance

Strengths
1. Insured can, within limits, change the amount of insurance coverage.
2. Insured can vary the size of premium payment; the larger the payment, the larger the amount added to the policy's cash value.
3. Policy's accumulated cash value can be used to pay premium.
4. Income taxes are deferred on the interest earnings that accumulate in the policy's cash value.
5. Policy owner can borrow against the policy's cash value.
6. By paying premium, insured can continue coverage to age 95 or 100.
7. Insurance company discloses rate of return being paid; most reset it every 6 months to 2 years.
8. Policyholder's detailed statement shows complete information on the policy.

Weaknesses
1. There may be an initial setup fee.
2. There may be a deduction of 5 to 10 percent from each premium payment—a "front load"—to cover fees and expenses.
3. Insurer may charge a fee—a "back load"—if policy is surrendered within the first 5 to 10 years.
4. All policies charge a fee—the mortality charge—to provide the required death protection.
5. Some policies are not offered in amounts less than $50,000.
6. Variable interest rate makes it nearly impossible to predict policy's future cash value.

are some large expenses: many insurers deduct a fee—5 to 10 percent is common—from each premium, leaving less to be added to the cash value. To reduce or avoid these fees, some charge a back load fee that you pay if you surrender the policy during the first few years. Most back loads decline over time so they reach zero after about 10 years. Some policies have an application fee, or a monthly administrative fee, or there may be a charge for a cash-value withdrawal. You need to review all fees and expenses carefully.

The amount you are charged for death protection can vary. If that fee—called the mortality charge—is high, less of the premium goes to your cash value, resulting in lower returns.

Even the interest rate quote can be problematic. Some policies quote a very attractive rate—called a teaser—but only guarantee it for a few months. Beyond the guarantee period, the rate is adjusted downward. You need to review all aspects of the policy, not just its "promised" return. Remember: What the large print giveth, the small print can so, so easily take away.

Should you buy universal life? As with all cash-value policies, ask yourself: Do I want and need an investment component? If the answer is yes, ask whether you can afford premiums sufficiently large to allow you to utilize the investment feature. If not, then level term is likely a better choice. If you intend to use the investment feature, plan to hold the policy for at least 10 years. If you don't, back load fees could drop your return. Remember, universal life is just one of many investment options; review the others before you decide.

The process of singling out a "good" universal life policy is involved, time-consuming, and technical. The excellent, detailed study in *Consumer Reports* could be a good starting point for your review.[2] Not only does it assess major points you should consider in selecting a policy, it ranks some existing policies.

I have a decided preference for a universal life over a traditional whole life policy. As a financial planner, I find that the disclosure feature of a universal life policy is not just "convenient," it is essential; the "black box" approach of whole life is unacceptable. Furthermore, universal life's flexibility makes it far more useful and workable. A "poor" universal policy may not top a "good" whole life policy, but a "good" one will in my opinion. Better disclosure on universal life should make it easier to single out the good ones.

Strategy

Universal life is appropriate only if you need life insurance for an extended time, want and need the investment component, and can afford the sizable premium such a policy entails.

---

[2] *Consumer Reports,* "Life Insurance, Universal Life Insurance." August 1986, pp. 515–527.

SHOPPING FOR LIFE INSURANCE

There are some things you can do to be an effective life insurance shopper. First, use a needs analysis like the one in Exhibit 11.5 to decide how much insurance you need.

Second, review the strengths and weaknesses summarized in Exhibits 11.9 through 11.11 to narrow the field. Ask whether a particular strength or weakness is important to you. Usually, there are some economies of scale when purchasing life insurance; the cost per $1,000 of coverage for a large policy is often much less. Single out the one best for you.

Third, observe the axiom that says that the three most important things you can do when purchasing a policy are to compare, compare, and compare. That may look like a misprint, but it dramatizes the need to shop for life insurance. Cost differentials between essentially similar policies are tremendous. Pick the wrong policy, and you could end up paying premiums that are 2 to 3 times those for a low-cost policy. The possibility of cutting premiums by 50 percent or more should encourage you to shop for coverage. Exhibit 11.12 demonstrates what the premium differential between a low-cost and a high-cost policy can amount to if invested over a number of years.

Exhibit 11 . 12

Premium Differentials for a $100,000 Policy Issued at Ages 25, 35, and 45

		Annual Premium		Differential:	Differential Invested Annually to Age 65	
Age of insured	Type of insurance	Highest	Lowest	Highest − lowest	6%	9%
25	Term	$ 264	$ 109	$155	$23,988	$ 52,372
25	Whole life	1,347	849	498	77,071	168,265
35	Term	325	152	173	13,677	23,581
35	Whole life	1,919	1,302	617	48,779	84,102
45	Term	647	245	402	14,788	20,566
45	Whole life	2,758	2,465	293	10,778	14,990

Fourth, use published comparative cost information to start your search. *Consumer Reports* completes a detailed cost review every several years that is highly useful.[3] Also a recent copy of *Best's Flitcraft Compend* (published by A. M. Best Company and revised annually) can help you single out reasonable policies; your local library likely has or can obtain a copy.

Last, make certain you can fit any proposed premium into your budget. Don't be forced to let that expensive cash-value policy lapse because you can't pay the premium.

SELECTING AN INSUR- ANCE AGENT

A good agent can help you with your insurance plan. He or she can confirm that your needs approach seems on target, and should be willing to dig into your finances to develop an insurance plan. Agents want to sell, of course, but a good one will not try to sell you excessive or unsuitable coverage. Your friends or coworkers may be able to recommend someone.

CLU Designa- tion

To use the **Chartered Life Underwriter (CLU)** designation, an agent must pass a series of tests. While not a guarantee, the certification does show the agent's commitment to the field, as well as being a measure of technical skills.

Agent's Sales Presentation

An agent should be willing to spend some time with you discussing your needs. Agents who will not do this are likely looking for a quick sale. Just because you have listened to the pitch, you do not have to buy.

Strategy

Take several days to consider a life insurance proposal. If the agent insists you have to sign immediately, look elsewhere.

---

[3] At the time this was written, the most recent review of life insurance by *Consumer Reports* was a three-part series in 1986. The article in the June issue reviewed term life insurance, the July issue reviewed whole life policies, while the August issue examined universal life policies.

Agent's Willingness to Sell Term Insurance

Commissions on term insurance are generally much less than on a cash-value policy. That encourages agents to avoid the sale of term insurance, even though it is just what many people need. An agent who really wants to "serve" your needs should discuss term insurance.

COMMON MISUNDERSTANDINGS

Let's examine several common misunderstandings about life insurance. Some agents may take advantage of these misconceptions to manipulate consumers into buying unnecessary life insurance.

Buy Life Insurance When You Are Young

Some agents will claim you "save" money by buying a whole life policy when you are young. True, the annual premium is lower, but you are going to pay that lower premium for much longer. Worse, you are probably buying coverage that you do not need.

Strategy

Buy insurance when you need it, not because the premium is lower.

Do Not Switch Policies

Some insurance representatives would have you believe that dropping an existing policy is akin to damning motherhood and apple pie. If you have a policy you don't need, drop it. Likewise, if an existing policy is a "loser," move to a better one. This is especially true on term insurance. But make certain the new policy is in place before dropping the old one.

Insure Your Children

Shortly after his son was born, Sidney received this telephone call.
"Congratulations on your son," says the voice.
Sidney mumbles "Thanks," as he tries to identify the caller's voice.
"Bet you're really happy," says the caller.
"Oh yes," mumbles Sidney, now frantically searching his memory.
"Have you thought about your son's financial future?" asks the voice.
Smiling, Sidney now has it: just one more agent peddling life insurance. He says, "Thanks, but no thanks."
The message: most children do not need life insurance. Agents may claim it's needed for burial expenses, but is it? The death rate for children is low, and funeral expenses are far less than the costs of raising a child.
One exception is the child who is likely to develop a serious illness that will make him or her uninsurable. But we suspect such cases are far fewer than agents claim.

Insurance for College Seniors

Some insurance companies aggressively sell life insurance to graduating seniors. They quote a "bargain" first-year premium to entice them to buy, and encourage them to sign a promissory note for the balance. Later the buyers have to pay off that balance plus its sizable finance charge. Such insurance is not only costly, it is unnecessary. Most college seniors simply do *not* need insurance.

Summary

1   Life insurance serves two major purposes in your financial plan:
   - It replaces your income for those who are dependent on it.
   - It provides money to settle your estate and financial affairs.
2   All life insurance policies provide a death benefit, typically equal to the face value. Some include an investment component that accumulates a cash value.
3   Six popular life insurance policies are:
   - Level term
   - Decreasing term
   - Whole life
   - Limited-pay life
   - Endowment
   - Universal life
4   Participating policies refund part of the annual premium as a nontaxable dividend.
5   On nonparticipating policies you pay the net premium; there is no dividend.
6   Many policies offer one or more of these extra cost options:
   - Waiver of premium if disabled
   - Guaranteed future insurability
   - Double or triple benefits in case of accidental death
7   Accumulated cash value in a policy can be:
   - Collected as cash
   - Used to purchase a smaller paid-up policy
   - Used to buy extended term insurance coverage
8   Upon death, the proceeds from an insurance policy can typically be:
   - Taken as a lump-sum payment
   - Left to earn interest
   - Paid as installments for a set period
   - Paid as installments of a set amount

   - Paid as installments over the beneficiary's lifetime
9   Income taxes are deferred on the interest earnings that accumulate as part of a policy's cash value; when withdrawn, only the excess—cash value minus total premiums paid—is subject to taxes. That is often a small amount or zero.
10 When the insured dies, the policy's proceeds are not subject to income taxes.
11 On large estates, there may be some federal estate taxes on insurance proceeds.
12 Planning life insurance requires estimates of your needs for seven major categories:
   - Settling your estate
   - Repaying debts
   - Providing an emergency fund
   - Funding an education
   - Income for family years
   - Income for middle years
   - Income for retirement years
13 New life insurance required is computed as:

   Total required life insurance from "needs" analysis
   Less: Current insurance coverage
   Less: Existing financial assets

   Equals: New life insurance needed
14 Steps for planning life insurance are identical for women and men.
15 Reestimate life insurance needs every 2 to 3 years to account for inflation.
16 Review each policy's strengths and weaknesses to decide which is best for you.
17 Comparison shopping is essential given the large cost differentials between policies.
18 A good insurance agent should help you develop a life insurance plan.

Review your understanding of

Face amount	Death protection	Waiver of premiums
Insured	Level term	Guaranteed insurability
Beneficiary	Decreasing term	Accidental death benefit
Policy owner	Whole life	Policy loan
Premium	Limited-pay life	Cash surrender value
Insurability	Endowment	Paid-up insurance
Standard risk	Universal life	Extended term insurance
Preferred risk	Participating policy	Needs approach
Substandard risk	Dividend	Renewable
Cash value	Nonparticipating policy	Convertible
Double indemnity	Option, or rider	Chartered life underwriter (CLU)

Discussion questions

1   Can someone other than the insured own a life insurance policy? When might that be appropriate? What are the risks of naming someone else owner?

2   Name the two principal reasons for buying life insurance. For some policies there is a third reason as well; what is it?

3   What component do all insurance policies provide? Is the dollar amount of that component constant on all policies? Explain. What other component do some policies add? Does it differ from policy to policy?

4   What do level term and decreasing term insurance have in common? How do they differ? Describe a situation ideally suited for decreasing term.

5   Whole life and limited-pay life have several common elements. What are they? How do the two differ?

6   What features of universal life are similar to features of traditional whole life policies? Name some differences.

7   Gail Gullible is impressed that the premium on a $100,000 "Sure Thing" Insurance Co. nonparticipating policy is only $275, while a competing $100,000 "Refund National Life" participating policy is $375. Are you equally impressed? Why? What do you suggest Gail do?

8   Why do some policies provide nonforfeiture options? Give a situation where each type of nonforfeiture option is appropriate. Why doesn't term insurance have them?

9   One touted advantage of whole life, limited-pay life, endowment, and universal life is the option of borrowing against a policy's cash value. What are the advantages? Any disadvantages?

10 Sidney Startup's present life insurance needs are limited, but they will likely rise in the future. How might he make sure he can purchase additional insurance even if his health deteriorates? Please provide some guidelines for implementing your recommendation.

11 Ted Troubled included $24,000 of life insurance in his plan to provide $100 monthly for his survivors' middle years. Ted is concerned with what inflation will do to the purchasing power of that $100 during the 10 years until the middle years begin. Should he be concerned? Why or why not?

12 What are the seven major categories that comprise the needs approach to determining your required life insurance? Will everyone require insurance for each category? Why?

13 Sue and Stan Equal, a two-career household, recently completed an insurance plan for Stan. Should they use the needs approach to plan Sue's required insurance? Why?

14 Why do some people claim that far too much life insurance is sold and not enough is purchased? Are there advantages to "buying" rather than being "sold" a policy?

15 During his sterling sales pitch to Linda Lamb, Hal High Commission notes that his $125,000 whole life policy "always provides a cash value, while a term policy only gives a pile of paid premium receipts." Will Linda always receive the cash value? Are there other points she should consider before buying whole life?

16 Can you name several advantages universal life offers over a traditional whole life policy? Does it have disadvantages? Can you profile a buyer that might be well served by this policy?

Problems

11.1 Rodney Rogers has estimated the following life insurance needs:

Type of insurance	Insurance protection	Annual premium	Cash value at age 65
Whole life	$25,000	$300	$14,725
Term to 65	25,000	145*	0

* Premium remains constant to age 65.

- *Settle estate.* $3,000.
- *Emergency fund.* $2,000.
- *Middle years.* $300 per month during 20 years.
- *Retirement years.* $200 per month during estimated 30 years.

a How much life insurance is required for these needs?

b Does your plan assume interest will be earned on the proceeds from that life insurance? Why?

11.2 Marvin Matched (age 25) is considering two nonparticipating insurance policies:
   a If Marvin keeps each policy until age 65, what is his total premium for each?
   b If he dies at age 45, what would each policy pay his beneficiaries?
   c What are the strengths and weaknesses of each policy?
   d Approximately what rate of return would Marvin have to earn on the premium savings (whole life minus term to 65) from the term policy to match the whole life policy? (Hint: Appendix A.4 will help you solve this problem.)

11.3 Wade and Wanda Welch want to estimate how much life insurance Wanda should have on herself to meet her survivors' income needs during the family period. The couple have a 6-year-old child. Other details include:
   ■ *Monthly after-tax income required during period.* $1,400.
   ■ *Child's Social Security benefit.* $375.
   ■ *Wade's monthly before-tax earnings.* $1,235.
   ■ *Social Security benefit to surviving spouse.* $375. This is reduced $1 for every $2 that annual earnings exceed $5,760.
   ■ *Wade's monthly after-tax earnings.* $950.
   ■ *Wanda's monthly before-tax earnings.* $1,300.
   Wade would continue to work if something happened to Wanda.
   a How much of the monthly income must life insurance provide?
   b How many years will the family period last?
   c How much insurance should Wanda consider buying?

11.4 Clem and Ann Tomkin estimate that to provide $1,200 for each year of Ann's 25-year retirement period, he currently needs $30,000 of life insurance. The Tomkins are concerned about what benefit Ann can actually draw when that period begins in 30 years.
   a If Clem dies tomorrow, what amount will that $30,000 have grown to if it is invested at 8 percent? (Hint: Appendix A.3 may help.)
   b Based on your answer in (a), how much can Ann draw during the retirement period? (Ignore any interest she might earn during the retirement period.)
   c Does your answer in (b) mean that Clem can lower his insurance coverage? Why?

11.5 Ed Exact's completed, detailed needs analysis indicates he requires $75,000 of life insurance. Details on his finances include:

Ed's present life insurance coverage	$20,000
Savings account balance	400
Wholesale value of car	750
Balance in common stock mutual fund	6,000
NOW account balance	600

   a What amount of life insurance should Ed purchase?
   b How can it be less than $75,000 and still meet his needs?

11.6 Delbert Doubtful (age 25) wants you to compute what income taxes might be due on his $25,000 whole life policy (annual premium, $300) if:
   a He surrenders it after 10 years for its $1,780 cash value.
   b Delbert should die at age 45 and the $25,000 be paid to his beneficiary.
   c He surrenders it at age 65 for its $12,900 cash value.

Case problem

Jason and Jan Logan both have full-time careers; Jason's annual salary is $20,000, while Jan's is $23,000. Both are 35 years old and they have a child, age 5. Because Jan contributes a sizable fraction of the family's income, they wonder whether she has adequate life insurance. Her present insurance consists of the policy provided by her employer; its coverage is twice her salary.

Jason's graduation from college during the past year has encouraged a flurry of proposals from local insurance agents. One suggested they begin with an endowment policy to provide a fund for their daughter's education. Another stressed the wonderful accumulation of cash value in the whole life policy she was selling; it was far better than just "throwing away your premiums on term insurance," she claimed. Another agent took quite the opposite position; she claimed term insurance was the ideal foundation on which to build their insurance plan. Needless to say, the Logans are far from clear on how to proceed.

In fact, they are not even clear whether any insurance is required at this point. A friend has suggested they estimate how much life insurance Jan should carry by estimating what income the survivors need plus the cost of wrapping up her financial affairs. They decided to work on Jan's life insurance needs first because her income is larger.

They have summarized the following information:
- Money needed to settle estate is $3,000.
- Their debts total $2,745; they rent, so there is no mortgage.
- Desired emergency fund is $2,000.
- Jason and his daughter would need $2,250 monthly during the family years.
- Social Security benefit for the child is $550.
- Jason qualifies for a matching $550 Social Security benefit, but it drops $1 for each $2 his annual earnings exceed $5,760.
- Jason expects to work to age 65; his projected Social Security benefit is $600; his projected after-tax pension benefit is $650.
- Jason expects he would need after-tax income of $1,500 during the middle years; required income drops to $1,300 during the retirement years.
- Jason's projected after-tax income is $1,300 during both the family and middle years.
- Jan and Jason want an education fund that covers $16,000 of the child's $24,000 in college costs; the balance will come from other sources.
- In planning retirement, Jason wants to provide benefits for at least 15 years.
- Presently the combined after-tax household income of Jason and Jan is $2,800 a month.

Jan and Jason have developed the following list of their financial assets:

NOW account	$ 500
Money market account	1,500
Common stock mutual fund	1,800

They are unclear as to how these amounts should be integrated into the analysis, if at all.

1   How much life insurance should Jan carry to meet her survivors' needs in each of the seven broad needs categories: settle estate; repay debts; emergency fund; education fund; family years; middle years; retirement years?
2   What is the total amount of insurance required to meet all of the survivors projected needs?
3   How much additional life insurance will Jan have to consider buying?
4   What guidelines should Jan and Jason use to decide whether they should concentrate on policies that provide just a death benefit or policies that provide both a death benefit and an investment component?
5   Assume it's 5 years later, and both Jan and Jason are in good health. They decide it's time to rework her insurance plan. Normally all dollar amounts would be reestimated. But let's use the original dollar amounts for simplicity; note, however, that the time periods are altered. Rework a needs analysis to see how the passage of 5 years affects their required insurance total. Why did the total change?

CHAPTER 12

Health insurance and disability income insurance

AFTER COMPLETING THIS CHAPTER YOU WILL HAVE LEARNED

- How health insurance and health maintenance organizations protect you against catastrophic medical costs
- How deductibles and coinsurance operate
- The major features of popular forms of health insurance
- How breadth of coverage, performance on small to moderate claims, and performance on high-dollar claims can be used to judge health insurance policies
- Guidelines to use when selecting health insurance or picking a health maintenance organization
- What supplemental health policies offer
- Why disability insurance is essential
- How to estimate the amount of disability insurance you need
- How to calculate your Social Security disability benefit
- How to coordinate the provisions of a disability policy to obtain adequate coverage
- Why disability insurance limits the percentage of lost income that can be replaced

A visit to the doctor and a few medical tests can turn into a major expenditure; several days in the hospital constitute a financial crisis; hospitalization under intensive care can be a full-blown financial catastrophe. Ours is not to decide who is to blame for these high health care costs; what you need is a sound financial plan to protect you against catastrophic losses. A health insurance program or membership in a health maintenance organization (HMO) can do that.

The possibility of using disability insurance to replace income if sickness or an accident prevents you from working is our second concern. The likelihood of disability is surprisingly high: one out of every three workers will likely suffer a lengthy disability before age 65. Beyond a few weeks, the financial consequences are serious. Most workers need disability coverage, but too few have it, and when they do, the benefits do not last long enough. The second part of the chapter discusses the steps needed to avoid these problems.

HEALTH INSURANCE OR AN HMO

Health insurance and health maintenance organizations (HMOs) share an objective: protecting you from catastrophic health expenses. Let's see how each operates.

Health Insurance

Health insurance is the traditional way of protecting against major health care costs. It involves three parties: the insured, the provider of the health care (a doctor, hospital, nurse), and the insurance company. As the insured, you select the doctor or hospital that will provide services. Those health care professionals decide what is needed and deliver it. The bill for services is sent directly to the insurance company or to you (if it is sent to you, you submit the expense to the insurance company for reimbursement). The insurance company is the "third party" that pays the costs.

You pay a premium for insurance coverage. The more generous the coverage, the higher your premium. As with any insurance policy, your premium is pooled with others to reimburse those who have expenses.

Health Maintenance Organizations

A **health maintenance organization (HMO)** protects you from catastrophic medical expenses by providing you with health care services. You pay a set fee, whether you use only a few or many of those services. Because of its fixed fee, an HMO wants to keep you healthy. Many stress preventive care, health checkups, and special programs to keep you well. HMOs have a financial incentive to keep health care costs low.

HMOs take two forms: there may be a group practice, or individual practitioners may deliver health care services. Let's look at each.

Group practice

The traditional HMO structure for delivering health care services is a Group Practice. The HMO employs doctors and other health care professionals who receive salaries and fringe benefits. Often the HMO centralizes its services in a single building.

Some HMOs further integrate the health care process by owning a hospital. The HMO's doctors and other professionals work from this facility. Any hospitalization you need will be in the HMO's facility. In either case, your choice is restricted to doctors and other professionals employed by the HMO, and some see this as a major disadvantage.

Individual practice associates

Under the Individual Practice Associates (IPA) structure, the HMO contracts with a number of individual practitioners in an area to deliver medical services to its clients. These doctors and other professionals are not employees of the HMO; they usually maintain independent offices and treat some patients who are not part of the HMO. While your choice is limited, you usually have more options than in a Group Practice plan. Large HMOs have many "associates" in an area.

COMMON PROVISIONS: HEALTH INSURANCE POLICIES AND HMO CONTRACTS

The lack of a standard contract makes it difficult to compare health insurance plans, and there is no standard HMO agreement to simplify analysis. But many contracts have provisions covering deductibles, coinsurance, policy exclusions, waiting periods, renewability, upper dollar limits, and benefit payments. Let's review some terms and provisions that are common to most health insurance contracts and HMO agreements.

Deductibles

Many health insurance contracts require the insured to pay part of a medical claim, the **deductible,** before the insurance company begins paying. Deductibles can range from $25 to more than $5,000. In effect, you self-insure for the deductible amount. Because you are required to pay part of the cost, deductibles discourage unnecessary medical services. With fewer small claims, the insurer can reduce administrative costs.

How is the deductible met?

Most health plans allow you to accumulate medical expenses for 3 to 12 months to meet the deductible; the longer the period, the better for you. Hazel Hypochondriac's policy only counts payments from the past 3 months to see if she meets the $100 deductible. Though she paid $98 during the first 3 months and $90 during the next 2 months, she collected nothing.

Second, a good plan counts charges for all illnesses and accidents during the deductible accumulation period. More restrictive plans set separate deductibles for each illness or accident. Thus, if Hazel's policy has a $100 deductible for each illness and she pays $80 for each of her three illnesses in October, she will not meet the deductible.

HMOs usually do not have a deductible, but they charge a small fee for each office visit: $5 to $10, for example. The charge is intended to discourage frivolous visits.

Coinsurance Clause

Some health insurance contracts require that the insured pay a percentage of the medical costs beyond the deductible. The company may pay 70 to 90 percent of costs, leaving you the rest. A sample policy with a $100 deductible and an "80/20" **coinsurance clause** will show how it works; the 80/20 means the company pays 80 percent and you pay 20 percent. If you had a $500 medical claim: (1) You would pay $100 for the deductible and an additional $80 (20 percent of the remaining $400). and (2) the insurance company would pay $320 (80 percent of the $400 balance). Exhibit 12.1 illustrates how the policy's deductible and coinsurance clause determine what the company pays and what you pay.

Paying a deductible is unpleasant, but it rarely causes major hardship. Not so with coinsurance. If Sue's medical bills total $10,100, her $100 deductible, 80/20 coinsurance health policy will only cover $8,000; she must pay $2,100. A coinsurance clause can be trouble when the medical claim is large.

Coinsurance with a maximum

Many policies cap what you have to pay. The policy might state that the coinsurance only applies to the first $2,500 of expenses beyond the deductible; the insurance company pays 100 percent above that. Had Sue's policy limited the 80/20 coinsurance to the first $2,500 beyond the deductible, she would have had to pay only $600 (the $100 deductible and 20 percent of the next $2,500). Even with a claim of $100,000 or more, her payment would not exceed $600.

Some policies set a maximum dollar amount the insured pays. For example, a policy might set $1,000 as the maximum the insured has to pay through coinsurance and deductible.

Exhibit 12.1

Summary of Health Insurance Deductibles and Coinsurance.

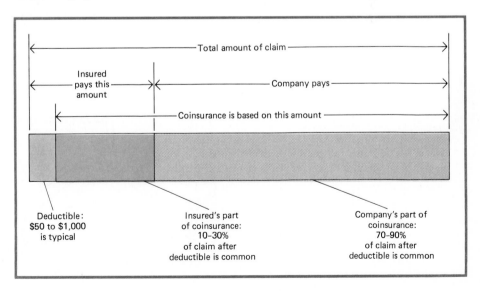

| Deductible: $50 to $1,000 is typical | Insured's part of coinsurance: 10-30% of claim after deductible is common | Company's part of coinsurance: 70-90% of claim after deductible is common |

Strategy

Avoid policies with open-end coinsurance clauses. Pay the small added premium for a policy with a maximum or coinsurance cap.

Few HMOs have coinsurance clauses. They provide medical services but do not require you to pay part of the cost. That is an advantage of HMOs.

Policy Exclusions

Health insurance policies and HMOs sometimes list exclusions—specific medical procedures that are not covered. Frequently excluded services are cosmetic surgery, some dental procedures, self-inflicted injuries, and some transplant procedures. Pregnancy may be excluded or only covered if the policy has been in force for a specified time. Most exclusions are justified and sensible; you would not want to pay high premiums to a plan that pays for frivolous or questionable medical procedures.

Strategy

Carefully review the exclusions in any insurance policy or HMO agreement you are considering. You should be satisfied that a basic medical need is not being excluded.

Waiting Periods

Some insurance policies require that you have the coverage for some minimum time before certain expenses will be paid. During this **waiting period,** you pay the entire cost of the procedure. An example is the common exclusion of pregnancy costs until the policy has been in force for 9 months or more.

A moderate waiting period is reasonable, since it prevents someone from purchasing insurance to cover an existing medical need. Imagine Stanley calling to say he and his wife have decided to buy health insurance from an agent just as Edna is leaving for the hospital with childbirth contractions 5 minutes apart.

Renewability

A good insurance or HMO policy is **renewable;** you have the right to renew as long as you wish, regardless of how many claims you have filed. Giving the insurance company the option of renewing is unacceptable. The insurance company or HMO can use the option to purge those with major claims. Your insurance could be canceled just when you need it most.

Strategy

Choose an insurance company or HMO that gives you the option to renew.

Upper Dollar Limits

Most insurance policies place a ceiling on the expenses they will pay. Some set a maximum for the life of the policy, but others apply it to each illness. Still others use the lifetime maximum approach but "restore" part of the available coverage each year the policy is in force. The first and last options for the **upper policy limit** are most prevalent; the second is the best for the insured.

Regardless of how it is set, a high dollar maximum is essential. To protect you against catastrophic losses, you need high limits. A decent starting point is $100,000, but $250,000 to $500,000 is not unreasonable. The likelihood that you'll live long enough to accumulate several hundred thousand dollars in medical bills is slim, but this is possible, and the cost of raising the limit is small.

HMOs and some health insurance policies offer essentially unlimited coverage when you pay the required annual fee. When you buy a policy with unlimited benefits, that policy will pay for all reasonable medical services required.

Strategy

HMO agreements and health insurance policies that offer unlimited medical benefits protect you from catastrophic losses.

Benefit Payments

A health insurance policy can pay for benefits in one of three ways: flat amount, cash benefit, or service benefit. Since HMOs provide needed medical services directly, they make no payments.

Flat dollar amount

Some health policies pay a **flat dollar amount** per day. To collect, you have to be hospitalized. For example, the policy might pay $40 for each day you are in the hospital; you can do whatever you want with the money.

Cash benefit

Some health insurance policies set a maximum amount, a maximum **cash benefit,** for a particular service—$400 for a surgical procedure or $180 per day for a hospital room. If your actual costs are less, you are reimbursed for the lesser amount; you cannot "profit" from your loss. If your actual cost is more than the maximum, you pay the excess.

Strategy

You must have a means for judging the adequacy of the listed payment maximums in order to be able to analyze the merits of the policy.

Service benefit

A **service benefit** pays the "usual, customary, and reasonable costs" for a procedure. You do not have to judge some list of payment maximums. If your health care provider charges "unusual, uncustomary, and unreasonable" fees, the insurance company will often assist in negotiating those fees downward.

Strategy

Judging the adequacy of a policy that provides a service benefit is easier than judging one with a cash benefit.

POPULAR HEALTH INSURANCE POLICIES

Health insurance policies can be divided into three broad categories: basic health coverage, major medical policies, and comprehensive policies. We will review what each offers, discuss some strengths and weaknesses, and provide some guidelines for purchasing.

Basic Health Care Coverage

Basic health coverage is the title we will use for traditional health policies. You purchase a policy for hospitalization, one for surgical expenses, and one for regular medical expenses. Most have modest limits: $2,000 to $5,000. Unless you have all three plans, some of your health care costs will not be covered.

Hospital expense insurance

The typical **hospital expense insurance** policy covers such things as hospital room and some operating room expenses, lab fees, drugs, and diagnostic fees. Limits include a maximum amount per day for a set number of days. The insured pays all charges above the limit.

Surgical expense insurance

Surgical expense insurance covers the surgeon's fee and associated charges. Some policies provide a service benefit, while others set a maximum cash benefit for each procedure. This coverage may be optional on a hospitalization policy.

Regular medical insurance

Regular medical insurance pays the physician's fee for nonsurgical services; it covers services in the hospital, office, or home. Since there are many health care situations that do not involve surgery, this plan complements the surgical policy.

Shopping for basic health insurance

Some basic health policies combine all three components into a single policy; in other cases, separate policies are required. Either way, you need all three types of coverage. The dollar maximums on most policies are limited, and the policies have moderate deductibles, often with coinsurance, to help reduce premiums.

Exhibit 12.2 provides a checklist for evaluating basic health policies. Your major concern should be adequacy of coverage. Three criteria can be used to judge a policy: (1) breadth of coverage, (2) adequacy for moderate claims, and (3) adequacy for a large claim.

Basic health policies rate reasonably high on breadth of coverage. Combining all three components into a single policy closes "coverage gaps" that can leave you with a sizable bill. When there are separate policies, you will want to review each for possible major gaps in coverage.

For a moderate medical claim—several days in the hospital and total charges of less than $5,000—basic policies perform reasonably well. The deductible and coinsurance provisions mean you have to pay several hundred to several thousand dollars.

On major medical bills—$20,000 or more—basic health coverage does very poorly. Just when you need it most, coverage is exhausted. Because you pay 100 percent of the bill beyond the policy's maximum, you can face financial ruin.

 *Exhibit 12.2*

Checklist for Analyzing Basic Health Insurance Policies

Areas of concern	Recommendations
Hospital Expense Coverage	
1. What is the maximum number of days covered?	Desirable policies cover 365 days.
2. What is the daily benefit?	Benefits should equal daily hospital cost in your area.
3. Are additional services, such as x-ray, lab work, and medication covered?	Desirable policies include these extras.
4. What is the deductible?	It should match your ability to pay.
5. Is the policy automatically renewable?	It should be renewable at your request.
6. Is there a waiting period for certain illnesses?	Desirable policies set a short waiting period for illnesses
7. Are there policy exclusions?	Desirable policies have few exclusions.
Surgical Expense Coverage	
1. Does the policy pay a cash or service benefit?	Desirable policies have a service benefit.
2. Does the policy cover surgery only when you are hospitalized?	Desirable policies include outpatient procedures.
3. What are the exclusions?	Desirable policies have few exclusions.
Regular Medical Coverage	
1. What is covered?	Policy should pay all nonsurgical medical expenses except routine office visits.
2. Are prescription drugs covered?	Desirable policies pay for drugs after a minimum has been exceeded.

Strategy

Basic health coverage does not protect you from major medical expenses. Supplement it with major medical insurance.

Major Medical Insurance

Major medical insurance combines broad medical coverage into a single policy. Coverage includes hospitalization, diagnostic tests, drugs, physician's fees, surgical costs, nursing care, and other expenses.

The upper limits on major medical policies are high: $50,000, $100,000, and beyond. Deductibles are sizable: $300 to $1,000 or more. You self-insure by paying for routine health care services, and the payoff is a lower premium. Coinsurance—from 10 to 30 percent of the charge—is nearly universal. While this cuts the premium, it exposes you to a sizable payment on a major claim. A good policy will set a maximum on what you pay for the deductible plus your share of coinsurance.

Shopping for major medical insurance

Exhibit 12.3 provides a checklist you can use to analyze a major medical insurance policy. Carefully consider the policy's deductible and the coinsurance clause; a cap is desirable.

Major medical plans can stand alone as health insurance, but some compromises are required. The plans provide broad coverage, but fall short on moderate to small claims. Until your out-of-pocket payments exceed the deductible, you receive nothing. Even then, the coinsurance provision means you still pay part of the costs. On a small or moderate claim, you may pay a significant fraction. On large claims, major medical performs well, especially when there is a cap. The deductible and coinsurance you pay will be only a fraction of the total.

Strategy

For those willing to pay a significant fraction of a small to moderate claim, major medical can be a reasonable "stand-alone" policy.

 **Exhibit 12.3**

Checklist for Analyzing Major Medical Policies

Areas of concern	Recommendations
1. Upper policy limit?	Maximum should be at least $100,000; $250,000 is suggested.
2. Size of deductible?	Should match your ability to pay.
3. Provisions of coinsurance clause?	80/20 or 90/10 is recommended; there should be a cap or maximum.
4. Renewability of policy?	Should be renewable at your option.
5. Method of computing maximum limit?	Maximum per illness is best; per calendar year, second; over your lifetime, is less desirable.
6. Policy exclusions?	There should be few exclusions.

Major medical insurance can also supplement basic health plans. Its high maximum picks up when the basic policy runs out and covers gaps in the basic policy. A high deductible is quite appropriate, since the basic policy covers the initial charges. A good insurance agent can coordinate the two policies.

Strategy

A major medical policy can cover the deficiencies of a basic health policy.

Comprehensive Medical Insurance

A **comprehensive medical insurance** policy provides the broad, high-dollar coverage of a major medical policy without the high deductible—$50 to $100 is typical. Some policies provide "first dollar coverage" (i.e., they eliminate the deductible), and most have no coinsurance clause. While the "payment pain" of a claim is removed, premiums for these policies are high. Comprehensive insurance is the most expensive: premiums can easily be 50 to 75 percent higher than for major medical.

Comprehensive medical policies are frequently offered as an option by employers. Some employers offer a major medical policy as standard; you have to pay the added premium for a comprehensive plan.

Shopping for comprehensive health insurance

Exhibit 12.4 gives guidelines for analyzing a comprehensive policy. Comprehensive policies provide excellent breadth of coverage. With a limited (or no) deductible and no coinsurance to pay, the policy is adequate for small or moderate claims. And with upper dollar limits of $100,000, $250,000, and more, the policies are good for large to very large claims. Of the policies reviewed thus far, comprehensive policies have the best composite score on our three criteria.

Strategy

Comprehensive medical insurance policies provide excellent coverage for everything from small to catastrophic claims.

With such a sterling record, why not give comprehensive a blanket recommendation? There are a couple of reasons. You usually have to be affil-

 **Exhibit 12.4**

Checklist for Analyzing Comprehensive Health Policies

Areas of concern	Recommendations
1. Upper policy limit?	Maximum should be at least $100,000; $250,000 is desirable.
2. Size of deductible?	Should match your ability to pay.
3. Provision for coinsurance?	There should be no coinsurance provision.
4. Renewability of policy?	Should be renewable at your option.
5. Policy exclusions?	Coverage should be broad, with few exclusions.

iated with a "group" to purchase comprehensive health insurance. Costs are high, with premiums on a family policy sometimes over $2,600 annually! Of course, if your employer pays most or all of the cost, that's no problem.

Strategy

If premiums are a major consideration, a major medical policy may be a better choice than comprehensive.

SPECIALIZED HEALTH INSURANCE POLICIES

In addition to general health policies, some insurance companies offer specialized plans that cover a specific illness or a narrow range of conditions. These policies are usually not good buys, and they don't substitute for broad coverage. Let's look at what they are, though, since some of them are heavily advertised and you need to know what the "good deal" doesn't give you.

Accident Insurance

Accident insurance pays for medical losses resulting from an accident. Often the policy lists specific amounts that will be paid for each result: loss of leg, loss of sight, or a maximum amount if the insured is killed.

Accident insurance is a poor buy. First, coverage is far too narrow. Suppose Fran Fastidious faints while painting her ceiling and topples from the ladder. Her claim to the accident insurance company describes the loss; the company's reply states: "Sorry for your misfortune, but your claim is rejected. Had you plunged from the ladder first, then fainted, you would be covered. You did it in the wrong order. Have a nice day." A good health policy covers medical costs regardless of why or how the loss occurred. You need life insurance to protect against untimely death and disability insurance to replace income caused by a loss of earning capacity.

Strategy

Avoid accident policies. A combination of health, life, and disability insurance provides far better coverage.

Dread Disease Insurance

Dread disease insurance covers the medical costs associated with specific diseases—cancer, heart condition, and kidney disease, for example. Upper dollar limits on the policies look generous, and premiums are often less than $400 a year. Advertisements for the policies note the devastating costs of such illnesses.

Do you really need such a policy? No. Any good health insurance policy covers "dread" diseases plus a broad range of illnesses.

Strategy

Rather than buy a dread disease policy, use the premium to upgrade your general health insurance policy.

Supplemental Hospitalization Insurance

You have seen the insert from a Sunday paper that sings the praises of **supplemental hospitalization insurance.** It prominently displays the claim that you can collect $600, $1,200, or more each month to use "however you wish." It may even announce an upper limit of $50,000 or $100,000. All in bold print!

But the fine print reveals more. You only collect the $30, $40, or more per day while *in* the hospital. Daily charges for a hospital stay far exceed these amounts; the coverage will do little more than provide nice flowers for your stay.

Then there is the waiting period. Many of these policies will not begin payment until you have been hospitalized 5 days, and the average hospital stay is only a bit more than 5 days. As to that $50,000 maximum, think of how many $40 days it takes to collect it. Can anyone survive standard hospital fare that long?

Strategy

Coverage under the standard supplemental hospitalization policy is too limited to be meaningful. Use the premium dollars to enhance your general health insurance policy.

DENTAL INSURANCE

Dental insurance covers most customary charges: annual exams, restorations, dentures, even orthodontia. Many policies include a deductible, however, coupled with coinsurance. The insurer may set a maximum amount the policy will pay in a given year as well.

So far, most of the growth in dental policy sales has been through employer-provided coverage. Few individual dental policies are sold.

Should You Buy Dental Insurance?

Without dental insurance, do you face catastrophic expenses? Several thousand dollars for orthodontia is not the sort of bill we would like to pay, but it won't result in financial ruin. Some major dental work, especially if related to an accident, is covered by your health policy. Dentures and orthodontia can be anticipated and included in your budgetary goals. You may be better off just paying regular dental expenses as they arise.

On balance, dental insurance is not essential, though it is nice to have if someone else pays all or most of the premium. But when dollars come from your pocket, there are better uses for them than dental insurance premiums.

Strategy

Consider a dental policy only if you have been unsuccessful in budgeting for these expenses.

Group Dental Practices

Using the HMO model, some companies structure dental practices along similar lines. These groups provide services for a set fee; they compete with dental insurance providers. Some cover only routine annual services in their fee; if you require more work, you pay extra. Others charge a higher fee but include a broader range of services. There has not been sufficient experience to determine whether a group practice dental plan costs less than dental insurance.

WHERE AND HOW TO BUY HEALTH INSURANCE

The two major sources of health insurance are nonprofit Blue Cross and Blue Shield organizations and private insurance companies. Either can provide good coverage. Let's fill in some basic background information on each, and try to get a handle on the expected costs for good, broad health coverage; then we'll review some guidelines to follow when choosing a policy.

Blue Cross and Blue Shield Organizations

Nonprofit Blue Cross and Blue Shield organizations are the largest providers of health insurance. Most of the Blues, as these organizations are called, offer group as well as individual policies. Coverage is usually very broad, and upper limits are usually generous, so the policy is adequate for large claims. Premiums are set to cover claims submitted and the costs of administration.

Blue Cross is the hospitalization plan, covering direct and indirect costs of your stay in the hospital. Generally the policy pays for a limited number of days at a maximum amount per day. Premiums vary depending on where you live; subscribers living in high-cost metropolitan areas are charged more than those in less costly rural areas.

Blue Shield covers the physician's fees, covering all "necessary and reasonable charges," a service benefit that lets you avoid judging a cash benefit policy. If the physician bills are higher than Blue Shield considers appropriate, the company will negotiate with the physician.

Strategy

Broad coverage, reasonable upper dollar limits, and competitive premiums make the Blue Cross and Blue Shield policies attractive.

Private Insurance Companies

Private insurance companies offer some excellent health insurance contracts that cover a broad range of services and have reasonable upper dollar limits to cover catastrophic losses. They do so for a reasonable premium.

But some private health insurance contracts have a generous profit margin as their primary goal. Understanding the language of some policies is a major hurdle. A combination of exclusions, waiting periods, and limits on current health conditions can restrict coverage. Make certain you understand what is and (more important) is not covered.

Strategy

Select health care policies from private insurance companies with care. If the premium is far less than for a comparable Blue Cross and Blue Shield policy, the "good deal" may be too good to be true.

What Should You Expect to Pay?

It is difficult to generalize about health insurance costs. A single person might pay annual premiums of $500 to $700 for a major medical policy with a sizable deductible and coinsurance. Premiums for a comparable family policy might range from $1,200 to $1,700. Lowering the deductible boosts premiums $100 to $200 for the single and $300 to $500 for the family policy. Upgrade to a comprehensive policy, and premiums on the single policy could range from $900 to $1,200—$2,000 to $2,500 for the family. If you live where health care costs are high, costs will be greater.

Guidelines for Purchasing Health Insurance Policies

If your employer provides a good comprehensive health policy and pays most of the premium, breathe a sigh of relief. But if you must purchase your own health coverage, remember these guidelines:

- Use a Blue Cross and Blue Shield policy as a reference point.
- If there is coinsurance, it should have a cap, or maximum.
- Avoid narrow, specialized health policies.
- Select the highest deductible you can afford.
- Choose an upper limit of $100,000 or more.

**SELECTING
AN HMO**

Exhibit 12.5 outlines some points you should consider in judging an HMO. Customer satisfaction with the HMO's service should be an important issue. Coworkers or friends who are members of the HMO may be able to help. You might also check the personnel office of a local employer who offers membership in the HMO as a health care option.

**Costs of HMO
Membership**

The annual cost of an HMO membership depends on the HMO's location and the number of people covered. But you are buying comprehensive, first-dollar health care, so expect to pay a sizable annual fee: $900 to $1,200 for a single person and $2,000 to $2,500 for a family.

**UPDATING
YOUR
HEALTH
CARE COVER-
AGE**

Review your health care coverage every 2 years. If it is provided by your employer, new options which better suit your needs may have been added. Several events suggest an immediate review is called for.

- *Change of jobs.* When you change positions, avoid a lapse in health coverage. You may have to temporarily convert your group policy to an individual one until your new employment begins. Not possible? Then buy a policy. Make sure the health plan provided by the new position is adequate before allowing your present policy to lapse.
- *Change in family status.* If you add or drop a dependent, notify your insurance company promptly. Failure to do so could compromise that dependent's coverage.
- *Children reach age 19.* Most family policies cover children until they reach age 19. Some policies continue coverage past age 19 if the child is a full-time student. When a child approaches age 19, review the policy to see if separate coverage is needed.
- *Retirement.* When you qualify for Social Security retirement benefits, you also become eligible for Medicare insurance. While

Exhibit 12.5

Checklist for Evaluating a Health Maintenance Organization

Area of concern	Recommendations
1. Range of services offered?	Should provide broad range of health care services at a convenient location.
2. Present HMO members satisfied with services?	Ask current members if they are pleased with services. Check your state consumer affairs office for complaints.
3. Qualifications of staff?	Majority of doctors and staff should be certified in their specialty. High staff turnover may signal a problem.
4. Delivery of services?	Waiting time for an appointment should not be excessive. Ideally a physician should see you on each office visit.
5. HMO a member of professional groups?	HMO should meet federal guidelines; if state guidelines are more rigorous, it should meet them. Membership in the Group Health Association of America is desirable.

Medicare provides some basic coverage, you will want an insurance policy tailored to cover the gaps in coverage. Identifying that policy is part of a well-developed retirement plan; we will have more to say on this in Chapter 18.

DISABILITY INCOME INSURANCE

Disability income insurance replaces your income if you are unable to work because of illness or accident. Under age 65, the chance of being disabled for an extended period is far greater than the likelihood of death, yet most people have far better life insurance than disability insurance. One of the basic insurance principles is to cover the major potential losses and self-insure on the small ones, but much disability coverage operates in just the opposite way: coverage starts fairly soon, but only lasts a short time. Your small losses are covered, but a major disability could exhaust your protection.

Social Security disability benefits rarely cover your complete needs, as we will see. Social Security is a supplement: it is not designed to cover your entire need.

Should You Have Disability Insurance?

Do you need disability insurance? Yes. Unlike life insurance, disability insurance is not intended to take care of someone else: it takes care of *you*. Whether you are married or single, you need disability insurance to provide income and to maintain your household if you are unable to work. Let's review a worksheet to help you estimate what you need.

Calculating Your Disability Insurance Needs

There are three steps in estimating your disability insurance needs. Begin by estimating how much income you would need if you were disabled. Then determine how much, if any, of that income would be provided by Social Security or by a working spouse. What remains has to be provided by disability insurance. The worksheet in Exhibit 12.6 summarizes these steps.

Required monthly income

Enter the amount of income you need for living expenses on line 1 of Exhibit 12.6. This should be the total expenses of the household, including recurring expenses for food, shelter, insurance, and so forth, and less frequent expenditures for autos, appliances, and other big purchases. Work-related expenses should drop, as should income and Social Security taxes,

Exhibit 12.6

Worksheet for Computing Disability Income Needs

1	Required monthly after-tax income		$2,550
2	Less:		
	a Social Security benefits for:		
	Disabled person	$600	
	Dependent's benefit	$300	
	b Spouse's after-tax income	$1,300	$2,200
3	Income to be met with disability income insurance (line 1 − line 2)		$ 350

since some of the replacement income—your Social Security benefit, for example—is not likely to be taxed. Your total living expenses will probably be less than your present budget.

Bob and Sue Vinton will be our example for this section; they have one child, age 8. Based on their present budget, they project monthly living expenses of $2,550 if Sue were disabled. That is entered on line 1 of Exhibit 12.6.

Social Security disability benefits

You must meet three criteria to qualify for **Social Security disability benefits.** First, you must have earned the minimum number of quarters of work credit; since you only have to earn about $500 in a 3-month period for one quarter of credit, you probably have earned one credit each quarter you have worked. The older you are, the more quarters of credit it takes to qualify. If you have worked one-half time or more since age 25, you probably have the requisite number. Second, you have to be unable to perform *any* job to qualify for Social Security benefits, and the disability must be expected to last 12 months or cause death. If a disability forces you to switch from a $40 per hour to a $4 per hour position, Social Security considers the latter substantial work, so you do not qualify. Even if you qualify, the limited payments may mean you must make major changes in your lifestyle. Finally, the minimum waiting period for benefits to begin is 5 months: during that time you have *no* income. Qualifying can require a time-consuming, frustrating crawl through a bureaucratic maze. And it can be costly: you may have to retain an attorney.

Children under age 18 receive a separate benefit equal to 50 percent of the disabled person's benefit. But the maximum family disability payment is 150 percent of the disabled person's. Effectively the family's benefit is the same with one, two, or more children. If Tom qualifies for a $600 monthly Social Security benefit, a son or daughter under 18 will receive $300, but a son *and* daughter together receive the same $300!

Your spouse also qualifies for a benefit, but the earliest he or she can draw it is at age 62, and it is only 37.5 percent of the disabled person's benefit. Because of the delay, this benefit plays a minor role in disability insurance planning.

Impact of income taxes and inflation. Social Security disability benefits, once obtained, are reasonably secure from income taxes and inflation. Under current standards, your benefit is not taxed unless your income is over $25,000 (if single) or $32,000 (if married). At most, one-half of the benefit is subject to tax.

Currently, Social Security benefits rise with the Consumer Price Index in years when the CPI rises more than 3 percent, so their purchasing power is protected. Even when the CPI rose less in the past, Congress passed special legislation to raise benefits.

Estimating your potential benefit. The administrators of the Social Security system would have us wait until we are disabled before disclosing our benefit. This is bureaucratically convenient, but a dead end for planning—kind of like Bernie Broadsided finding out what his auto insurance covers after his 1988 auto has been rendered a large mass of scrap metal; too little, too late Bernie! It is impossible to plan after the fact.

Visit your local Social Security office, or write the Social Security Administration, Office of Public Inquiries, Baltimore, MD 21235, and ask them to estimate your likely disability benefit. Their policy may change to one of providing an estimate by the time you read this.

A second choice is to use a benefit table like Appendix A.2. It gives estimates of your potential benefit based on age and current earnings. The table depends on some assumptions—they are noted in the Appendix—but relying on it is better than waiting until you are disabled to discover your benefit. The disability part of the table has two columns. The first shows the disabled person's benefit, the second shows the benefit for any children.

Based on Sue's age and present income, she would receive $600 if she qualified for Social Security disability benefits. Her child would receive $300. This is entered on line 2(a) of Exhibit 12.6.

Spouse's after-tax earnings

When the disability involves a couple, the nondisabled partner may provide part of the needed income. He or she will probably continue working outside the home, or, if not presently employed, might decide to enter the work force. Any income the nondisabled partner earns can be deducted from required income. Reduce the amount of the partner's earnings by the appropriate federal and state income taxes as well as Social Security taxes and enter the result on line 2(b) of Exhibit 12.6

Bob would continue to work if Sue were disabled, so his income becomes part of the analysis. His after-tax $1,300 monthly income is entered on line 2(b) of Exhibit 12.6.

Required disability insurance

Replacement income from disability insurance is the amount that completes the worksheet in Exhibit 12.6. After deducting the Social Security benefits on line 2(a) and any spouse's earnings on line 2(b), we see that the disability policy would have to provide the income on line 3. Since policy limits are stated as an amount per month, purchasing the needed coverage is easy.

Exhibit 12.6 suggests Sue Vinton needs a disability policy that provides $350 per month. She may already be covered under a policy provided by her employer. If not, she will have to buy the required coverage.

Provisions of Disability Policies

Whether you are choosing a disability insurance policy or assessing one provided through an employer, you need to know the basic provisions that are part of most plans.

Definition of disability

Each policy defines *disability* differently. The more liberal the definition, the more likely you will be able to collect. Highly restrictive policies tend to cost less, but they can leave you poorly protected.

The best definition is: "If sickness or an accident reduces your income, you are disabled." If sickness forces Dawn Doloop to reduce her work load so that she no longer earns her present $30,000, she is considered disabled and eligible for benefits.

Second best is "You are disabled if sickness or an accident prevents you from doing the main duties of your present occupation." If Dawn can no longer continue her computer programming duties, she is considered disabled.

Least desirable is: "You are disabled if you are unable to perform any gainful work." If Dawn can work 40 hours a week at anything paying minimum wage, she is *not* disabled under this definition.

Some policies define *disability* as "inability to carry out your present occupation" for the first 2 years, then switch to "inability to perform any gainful work" from that point on. This is a common provision; it ranks between the second-best and the least desirable alternative.

Strategy

Concentrate on policies that have a reasonably liberal definition of **disability**; *the premium may be a bit higher, but it's worth it.*

Duration of benefits

A policy states how long payments will continue while you remain disabled; the **duration of benefits** can range from 6 months to "until age 65." The longer the period, the better the protection. A policy offering benefits for only a few months can leave you woefully underinsured. Again you're like the nonswimmer wading the river that averages 6 inches deep: it's easy going when it's 3 inches deep, but that 13-foot drop in the center is *big* trouble.

Strategy

Disability benefit payments should extend at least 20 years; continuing to age 65 is even better. Your added premium is usually small.

Elimination, or waiting, period

Benefits do not begin immediately. You must remain disabled during a **waiting period** (or elimination period), which can be as short as 2 weeks or as long as 6 months. The period is a deductible, since you accept the lost income for short-term disabilities. Extending the period usually lowers the premium.

A review of your cash reserves and other financial assets should tell you how long you could get by with no monthly income if you cut your expenditures to the minimum.

Strategy

A long elimination, or waiting, period is best. It may impose minor hardships, but it lowers premium costs, and so lets you buy extended benefits for any long-term disability.

Limits on replacement of your working income

Imagine the potential abuse if people could buy unlimited disability insurance. An unscrupulous person might collect more disability income than he or she earned working. To prevent such abuses, insurers place **limits on income replacement.** For example, a disability policy might state that your combined Social Security benefit and payments from *all* disability policies cannot exceed 60 percent of your predisability working income. If Jan earned $1,600 a month, her Social Security benefit plus disability insurance payment or payments could not exceed $960; $1,600 × 60%. Note that interest and dividends are not included in the limit, nor are her children's Social Security benefits. But if Jan had several disability policies, all benefits would count toward the limit.

Once you are done with a worksheet like Exhibit 12.6, you should check the income limits in the policy. Your combined Social Security benefits plus planned disability income should not exceed the policy's percentage limits.

Strategy

Do not attempt to replace more of your working income than the disability policy allows; you will never collect the excess.

Offset with Social Security benefit

Some disability policies coordinate their total benefit with your Social Security benefit. Rather than promise $400 per month, they might promise a total benefit of $1,000, including any Social Security benefit. If Social Security paid $600, the policy would make up the $400 shortfall. Once the benefit is set, however, a good policy will not reduce it just because the Social Security benefit rises with inflation.

When purchasing coverage under these policies, total coverage should include both the Social Security benefit and the planned disability income from the worksheet in Exhibit 12.6.

Will Your Employer-Provided Disability Policy Meet Your Needs?

Is the disability coverage your employer provides adequate to your needs? Determine what benefit your employer-provided policy offers. Many promise to replace 60 to 70 percent of your working income rather than a set dollar amount. That total includes Social Security and disability income payments. Let's use Sue Vinton's disability needs from Exhibit 12.6 to illustrate. Assume she is covered by a policy that replaces 60 percent of her regular working income. With an $1,800 monthly income, Sue can expect $1,080 if disabled. Since her worksheet in Exhibit 12.6 shows a total need of $950 ($600 Social Security benefit + $350 disability insurance benefit), that $1,080 is adequate.

Next, check how long the benefits last. Unless it's for 20 years (preferably to age 65), consider buying a supplementary long-term policy.

You have fewer options when it comes to the waiting period or the policy's definition of *disability.* Suppose your cash reserves will last 3 months, but the policy has a 6-month waiting period. You may be able to pay a premium to shorten that to 3 months. If not, then work at increasing your cash reserve or cutting expenses. You have two choices when it comes to the definition of *disability*. If it is restrictive but workable, accept it. If *disability* is so narrowly defined that coverage is not adequate, purchase a separate policy.

Buying Disability Insurance

Premiums on a disability policy vary with elimination period, duration of benefits, and definition of *disability*, but they may also be affected by your occupation, age, and sex. Many insurance companies divide occupations into four or five groups. Those groups with a higher incidence of disability, such as construction-related jobs, carry a higher premium. Since older individuals are more prone to disability, they pay higher premiums. Last, some companies quote a 25 to 75 percent higher premium for women than men.

Importance of comparison shopping

Even when policies offer comparable coverage, premium differences can be substantial. A comparative analysis by *Consumer Reports* suggests that a high-cost policy could easily cost 50 percent more than the lowest-cost option.[1]

Strategy

When shopping for disability insurance, request price quotations from several agents; the savings can be sizable.

Impact of inflation on future disability payments

Many disability insurance policies include no provision for increasing future payments if a disability is long-term. Once started, the benefit payment is fixed. Some policies offer an extra-cost rider that raises payments with changes in the CPI.

Strategy

If offered, a cost of living rider is worth having, especially if disability insurance benefits will provide a major part of your income if you are disabled.

Renewability

The last thing you need to be is searching for disability coverage after your policy is canceled because of your ill health. The best policy guarantees renewal without a premium increase; it is called a **noncancellable** policy. Second best is a **renewable** policy—one that guarantees renewal but allows premium increases. Least desirable is the provision that the insurance company cannot cancel your individual coverage but can cancel coverage of the entire policyholder group you are part of.

---

[1] "Disability Income Insurance," *Consumer Reports*, March 1983, pp. 122–126.

Summary

1   Health insurance or membership in an HMO is essential; the likelihood of your needing health care services is high, and a major, extended illness could produce catastrophic costs.

2   For a fixed annual fee, an HMO delivers the health care services you need.

3   Health insurance has three parties: yourself, the health care provider, and the insurance company that pays part or all of the associated costs.

4   A deductible forces you to self-insure for small claims. It should match what you can afford.

5   Coinsurance forces you to pay part of the costs beyond the deductible. A coinsurance clause should have a maximum, or cap.

6   Given the size of potential claims, an upper limit on health policies of $100,000 is essential; $250,000 or more is desirable.

7   Five popular types of health insurance policy are:
- Hospital expense insurance
- Surgical expense insurance
- Regular medical insurance
- Major medical insurance
- Comprehensive medical insurance

8   Narrow health policies that cover only a few situations or specific diseases do not provide the coverage that you need.

9   Dental insurance is not essential; catastrophic losses are unlikely, and you can budget for most expenditures.

10   A policy from one of the Blue Cross and Blue Shield affiliates is a good reference point for judging competing health policies.

11   Two important criteria for judging HMOs are adequacy of services and customer satisfaction with the care provided.

12   Disability insurance replaces your income if an illness or accident prevents you from working.

13   Most working individuals should have disability insurance.

14   Social Security will provide disability benefits, but the qualifying standards are rigid and the process can be protracted.

15   To determine your disability insurance needs, follow these four steps:
- Estimate the income you will need if disabled.
- Deduct: Social Security benefit you might receive.
- Deduct: Other potential sources of income.
- Purchase disability income insurance equal to the remaining need.

16   The more liberal a policy's definition of *disability,* the more likely you will collect.

17   A policy's waiting period functions like a deductible. Select the longest one you can afford.

18   Disability benefits should extend for at least 20 years; having them continue to age 65 is even more desirable.

Review your understanding of

Health maintenance organization (HMO)
Deductible
Coinsurance
Exclusions
Waiting period
Renewability
Upper policy limit
Flat dollar benefit
Cash benefit
Service benefit
Hospital expense insurance
Surgical expense insurance
Regular medical insurance
Major medical insurance
Comprehensive medical insurance

Accident insurance
Dread disease insurance
Supplemental hospitalization insurance
Dental insurance
Blue Cross
Blue Shield
Disability income insurance
Social Security disability benefit
Definition of disability
Duration of benefits
Waiting period
Limits on income replacement
Noncancellable disability policy
Renewable disability policy

Discussion questions

1   Discuss the similarities and differences between the delivery of health care services under traditional health insurance and under an HMO. List several strengths and weaknesses of each.

2   Why do many health insurance policies specify

a deductible? How would a $100 deductible hold down the premiums on a policy? Would it make the policy unacceptable?

3   How does coinsurance operate? Why would a policy include it? Why is coinsurance a problem on large claims? How can that problem be rectified?

4   Why do many health insurance policies require a waiting period? Would policyholders who have already finished the waiting period benefit from such a requirement?

5   How do the three benefit payment methods differ? Which would you prefer? Why?

6   What are the major strengths and weaknesses of basic health insurance policies? What kind of health care situations do they handle reasonably well? What type do they handle poorly?

7   What are the similarities between a major medical and a comprehensive medical policy? How do they differ? How should a person decide between them?

8   What makes a "dread disease" policy unacceptable as a person's principal insurance? Should a standard health policy be supplemented with one of these? Why?

9   Why is dental insurance less critical than health insurance? Should you consider such a policy?

10 A recent ad for Peace of Mind Health, a supplemental hospitalization policy, noted: "For a modest premium, you are assured a generous $40 daily cash benefit that will continue up to a $50,000 maximum." Is this a good policy? Would you suggest an alternative?

11 Why should you review your health insurance options if you are leaving your present employment? How can you avoid lapses in coverage?

12 Some claim that adequate disability income insurance may be more important than life insurance. Why?

13 Why might a disability insurance policy limit the total benefits you can collect while disabled? Give an example to illustrate how such a limit might operate.

14 What three major features determine the adequacy of a disability income policy? Which one is most important? Least?

15 Why is the definition of *disability* in an insurance policy important? What are some key points to look for?

Problems

12.1 Ronald Rollo spent 14 days in the hospital with an illness that doctors had difficulty diagnosing. The hospital room cost $150 per day. In addition, he incurred physician's charges of $1,200 and laboratory fees and x-ray charges of $750. Ronald has a major medical insurance policy with a $250 deductible and an 80/20 percent coinsurance clause. How much will he pay on the bill? How much will the insurance company pay?

12.2 For each of the two policies described below, calculate the reimbursement for medical expenses incurred as follows: January, $150, February, $400, March, $0, and April, $900.

Policy 1	Policy 2
1. $100 deductible	$100 deductible
2. 80/20 coinsurance	80/20 coinsurance
3. 90-day deductible period	Calendar year deductible period

12.3 Alberta Woo has narrowed her choice of major medical policies to the following three:

	Policy 1	Policy 2	Policy 3
Deductible	$100	$300	$500
Coinsurance	75/25	80/20	80/20
Maximum insured must pay	Unlimited	Unlimited	$2,500
Policy limit	$10,000	$25,000	$100,000

All the policies have similar annual premiums. They will allow Alberta to accumulate her medical expenses over the calendar year to meet the deductible provision.

a What would Alberta pay under each policy if her medical expenses totaled $800 for the year?

b What would she have to pay under each policy if her expenses totaled $20,000 for the year?

c Which policy do you recommend? Why?

12.4 Philbert Piecemeal has the following three basic health insurance policies:

	Policy 1	Policy 2	Policy 3
Expense covered	Hospital	Surgical	Medical
Policy limit	$100 per day for 20 days	$700 per surgery	$25 for each day in hospital
Deductible	$100	$50	$50

Philbert recently incurred the following expenses for surgery: (1) hospital room, $150 per day for 10 days; (2) surgeon's bill, $1,500; (3) doctor's fee, $45 per daily visit in the hospital.

a   What amount will Philbert have to pay on these bills?

b   After this experience, Philbert is considering switching policies. What guidelines would you give him for his search?

12.5 Sonya Single is calculating the disability income she would need to replace her present earnings of $1,500 before taxes and $1,160 after taxes. She estimates that, were she disabled, her monthly after-tax income would have to be $960. On the basis of her prior earnings, she estimates her Social Security disability benefits would be $570.

a   What disability income insurance should Sonya purchase?

b   The policy Sonya is considering limits her combined Social Security benefits plus disability income payment to 60 percent of her predisability income. Will that be a problem?

c   Assume that she expects to receive $75 (after taxes) each month from the rental property she owns. What are her revised disability income insurance needs? Will the policy's 60 percent maximum replacement be a problem now? Why?

12.6 Fran and Earl Grey are outlining the disability income insurance Fran should carry. Selena, their daughter, is now 6 years old. They have compiled the following estimates:

Total family after-tax income required if Fran is disabled	$1,950
Fran's Social Security disability benefit	$ 540
Earl's after-tax earnings (if Fran is disabled)	$1,040
Fran's present after-tax income	$1,020

a   How much disability income insurance should Fran have?

b   A local insurance agent suggests that since most disabilities do not last long, the Greys should concentrate on a policy that has a very short elimination, or waiting, period and a short benefit period. Do you agree?

c   The Greys are concerned that inflation may erode the purchasing power of those projected sources of disability income. Will it erode all the sources? Can the Greys compensate for this possibility in their insurance plan?

12.7 Clyde Closecall is considering two disability income policies:

	Policy 1	Policy 2
Maximum benefit period	1 year	20 years
Elimination, or waiting, period	30 days	90 days
Monthly benefit	$200	$200
Maximum income replacement allowed	60%	70%

Both policies define *disability* similarly, and their annual premiums are comparable. Clyde presently earns $1,350 monthly before taxes; he estimates that his monthly Social Security disability benefit would be $600.

a   Will Clyde have a problem with either policy's income replacement percentage?

b   What is the maximum benefit with each policy?

c   Clyde is confused as to why the two policies have similar premiums. Can you explain, given your answer in (b), why they do?

Case problem

Neal and Nancy Shaw are considering several health insurance alternatives. One option is not to buy any insurance. While they are both healthy at the present time, they are not certain that being uninsured is such a good idea. Therefore, they have gathered details on four possible insurance policies:

			Policy	
Feature	Basic health	Major medical	Comprehensive	Supplemental hospital
Deductible	$50	$500	None	None
Coinsurance	None	80/20 with $2,000 maximum	None	None
Benefit payment	Cash benefit	Service benefit	Service benefit	$40 per day after sixth day in hospital
Policy limit	$5,000	$200,000	$200,000	$50,000
Premium	$400	$1,600	$2,600	$300
Waiting period	10 days	20 days	10 days	2 years

1   Should the Shaws buy insurance? Why?
2   What are the strengths and weaknesses of each of these health insurance policies?
3   If Neal incurred $800 of medical expenses without requiring hospitalization, what amount would the Shaws have to pay under each policy?
4   If Nancy had a serious illness that included a 30-day hospital stay with expenses totaling $19,500, what amount would the Shaws have to pay under each policy?
5   List the guidelines you believe the Shaws should use to decide which policy they should choose.
6   If you were faced with the above choices, what policy would you choose? Why?

CHAPTER 13

Property and liability insurance

AFTER COMPLETING THIS CHAPTER YOU WILL HAVE LEARNED

- What coverage a homeowners insurance policy provides
- How coverage provided by the six principal homeowners policies differs
- Steps to take to tailor homeowners coverage to your needs
- What protection you receive for the loss of personal property
- Why special personal property items require separate coverage
- What coverage the standard auto insurance policy provides
- How to get adequate auto policy coverage for a manageable premium
- How a deductible can lower your insurance premiums
- Which factors determine your auto insurance premiums
- How no-fault auto insurance operates
- What coverage an umbrella liability insurance policy offers

*P*roperty **insurance** protects you against the loss of your car, home, and other personal assets. If a covered asset is damaged or stolen, the insurance reimburses you for part or all of the loss. How much you collect varies with the policy you buy.

Liability insurance protects you from financial loss arising from injuries or damages you cause. If someone is injured on your property or because of your actions, liability insurance may cover the costs. The same holds true if you damage someone else's property. Liability insurance usually pays the cost of defending you if the other party sues.

Though property and liability insurance cover different types of loss, they are often combined in a single policy. The policies are specialized: if you have one for your auto, you need another for your home. We will focus on three representative policies: homeowners, automobile, and umbrella liability coverage.

HOME OWNERS INSURANCE

Homeowners insurance provides protection against both property and liability losses. Property losses arise if a fire damages your house or someone steals your stereo system. Homeowners insurance will also cover your liability for a friend's medical costs and lost wages after she trips over a rug in your apartment or pay the bill when Fang, your guard Siamese, "shreds" the leg of your mail carrier's new blue uniform.

Homeowners Property Coverage: The Six Standard Policies

Most insurance policies use standard numerical designations to indicate the type of coverage provided. Owner-occupied, single-family houses are covered by HO-1, HO-2, HO-3, or HO-5 policies. HO-4 policies are for renters, and HO-6s for condominium owners. Each covers a different range of personal property; they differ in what **perils,** or loss situations, they protect against. Exhibit 13.1 summarizes what each policy covers.

Owner-occupied single-family house

When you own your house, you want to protect both the building and your personal property in it: HO-1, HO-2, HO-3, and HO-5 policies do that. The four policies differ in the perils they protect against. An **HO-1 policy** (the most basic) covers the building and your personal property against the 10 perils listed in Exhibit 13.1. The **HO-2 policy** adds 7 more perils. The two highest-level homeowners policies are known as **all risk.** An **HO-3 policy** protects the building against all perils except those specifically excluded—usually floods, earthquakes, war, and nuclear accidents; personal property is covered for the 17 perils listed in Exhibit 13.1. **HO-5 policies** protect both the building and personal property against all risks except events like war, flood, earthquake, and nuclear meltdown. The premium rises with the number of perils covered, but broadening the range has little effect on the actual dollar protection you get.

Rental unit

An **HO-4 policy** is specifically tailored to those who rent an apartment, house, townhouse, or duplex. As a renter, you need to protect your personal property; the owner insures the building. As Exhibit 13.1 shows, HO-4 policies cover perils 1 to 17.

Condominium
Condominium owners have unique needs. Most of the building is "common" property, so it is protected by a single policy paid from the monthly maintenance fee. The **HO-6 policy** covers the condominium owner's personal property and the parts of the living unit he or she owns. The policy covers perils 1 to 17.

Summary of Property Coverage Provisions
The upper part of Exhibit 13.2 summarizes property coverage for each homeowners policy. Even an HO-1 policy provides broad protection, but higher up the scale the coverage is more generous. Most personal property protection limits are tied to the dollar coverage on the building. Since HO-4 and HO-6 policies provide no coverage for the building, their protection is a set dollar amount.

Building: provision a
Your house and all attached structures are covered by this section of HO-1, HO-2, HO-3, and HO-5 policies. You decide how much the house must be insured for: the policy's face amount. If you buy too little, you may not collect the full amount of a loss; but if you buy too much you waste money, since the insurance company will not pay more than the actual replacement value of the house.

Other structures: provision b
The standard homeowners policy covers detached garages, garden sheds, and other buildings for up to 10 percent of the policy's face value. If your house is insured for $70,000, then your **appurtenant structures** (as they are called) are covered for a maximum of $7,000. You could collect as much as $77,000 if the house and detached structures were destroyed. Only HO-1, HO-2, HO-3, and HO-5 policies provide this coverage.

Personal property: provision c
All six homeowners policies cover **personal property** in your living unit: furniture, appliances, clothing, and other items. Standard coverage is 50 percent of the policy's face amount; if your house is insured for $80,000, then you have $40,000 of personal property coverage, though you can purchase more. On HO-4 and HO-6 policies you specify what dollar coverage you want; the insurance company does not ask for a detailed list of your possessions before issuing the policy, but simply writes protection for a blanket amount.

Your personal property is also covered when it is off-premises. If your luggage disappears from your hotel room in scenic Red Granite, your homeowners policy covers it. However, coverage is limited to your policy's personal property limit. Most policies also cover items stolen from your car if there is evidence of forced entry.

Additional living expenses: provision d
All homeowners policies provide an allowance to cover your additional living expenses if a fire or other covered peril forces you to find temporary quarters. Most cover expenses such as lodging, meals, and laundry. HO-4 and HO-6 policies set the amount based on your personal property coverage: the others use the policy's face amount to set limits.

Exhibit 13.1

Perils Covered by Each Homeowners Insurance Policy

Perils Covered When the Policy Is:

Coverage on	HO-1: basic form	HO-2: broad form	HO-3: special form	HO-4: renter's form	HO-5: comprehensive form	HO-6: condominium form
Buildings	1–10	1–17	All risks*	None	All risks*	None
Personal property	1–10	1–17	1–17	1–17	All risks*	1–17

Key:
1 Fire or lightning
2 Windstorm or hail
3 Explosion
4 Riot or civil commotion
5 Aircraft
6 Vehicles
7 Smoke
8 Vandalism or malicious mischief
9 Theft
10 Breakage of glass in building
11 Falling objects
12 Weight of ice, snow, or sleet
13 Collapse
14 Accidental discharge or overflow of water or steam
15 Explosion of steam or hot water system
16 Freezing
17 Damage from artificially generated current
* Policy lists specific risks that are not covered; see text.

Exhibit 13.2

Typical Property and Liability Coverage for Standard Homeowners Policies

Coverage Provided When the Policy Is:

Coverage on	HO-1: basic form	HO-2: broad form	HO-3: special form	HO-4: renter's form	HO-5: comprehensive form	HO-6: condominium form
Dwelling.	You set amount.	You set amount.	You set amount.	None.	You set amount.	None.
Appurtenant structures.	10% of dwelling.	10% of dwelling.	10% of dwelling.	None.	10% of dwelling.	None.
Trees and shrubs.*	5% of dwelling.	5% of dwelling.	5% of dwelling.	None.	5% of dwelling.	None.
Personal property.*	50% of dwelling.	50% of dwelling.	50% of dwelling.	You set amount.	50% of dwelling.	You set amount.
Personal property off-premises.	Same as property on premises.	Same as property on premises.	Same as property on premises.	Same as property on premises.	Same as property on premises.	Same as property on premises.
Living expenses.	10% of dwelling.	20% of dwelling.	20% of dwelling.	20% of personal property.	20% of dwelling.	40% of personal property.
Personal liability.*	$100,000 or more.	$100,000 or more.	$100,000 or more.	$100,000 or more.	$100,000 or more.	$100,000 or more.
Medical payments.*	$1,000 per person.	$1,000 per person.	$1,000 per person.	$1,000 per person.	$1,000 per person.	$1,000 per person.

* Higher coverage is available.

How Much Should You Insure the House For?

Houses need to be insured for at least 80 percent of what it would cost to replace them. The example of Fred's house can illustrate why this level of coverage is critical. Suppose Fred paid $35,000 for the house a few years ago. Initially, he insured it for $30,000, which was enough for the time. But he never raised the limit. Now his insurance is inadequate to cover the home's $75,000 replacement cost. If Fred's house suffers $20,000 of fire and smoke damage when the furnace overheats, won't the $30,000 policy be sufficient? No. He lacks the required $60,000 of coverage (80% × $75,000), so he is subject to coinsurance. To determine the amount of Fred's **coinsurance liability,** the company applies the **80 percent rule.** They multiply his loss amount by the ratio of his policy amount to the required 80 percent replacement value. He can only collect $10,000: $20,000 loss × [$30,000 policy limit/$60,000 (required 80% replacement cost)]. Had he insured for $60,000, all Fred's losses would have been covered up to that amount. If you fail the 80 percent test, coinsurance can leave you paying a significant part of the loss.

Strategy

Reevaluate your homeowners coverage periodically to make certain it is at least 80 percent of the home's replacement value.

Since 80 percent is the minimum, should you insure for more? Even if there is a major loss, part of the existing house should be usable. The basement, lot improvements, and landscaping may still be salvageable. For peace of mind, you can raise coverage beyond the 80 percent minimum.

Coverage on Your Personal Property

Use your detailed personal property inventory (Chapter 2) as a starting point for determining how much coverage you need. Loss of your personal property is traumatic; why add to it having to reconstruct what you have lost? When she returns from her vacation, Debbie Disaster finds her apartment ransacked and her possessions in a 5-foot mound in the living room. Without a good inventory, it will be nearly impossible for Debbie to figure out what is missing. If she can, she still has to estimate each item's purchase date and cost!

A personal property inventory serves two purposes. First, it lets you estimate how much coverage you need. Total the replacement cost of the items, and add an estimate for the small items not listed. This is the personal property coverage your homeowners policy should provide. Second, if you have a loss, the list can help you determine its size. As advised in Chapter 2, store your inventory off-premises.

Strategy

Update your personal property inventory every 2 years, and check to make sure that your personal property coverage remains adequate.

*Reimburse-
ment for per-
sonal property
losses: stan-
dard policy*

The standard homeowners policy pays far less for lost or damaged personal property than you might expect. Unfortunately, many people do not discover this until after they have a loss.

Suppose that Janice's 6-year-old television is stolen. All she has to do is pick up a new $600 Sony and wait for the reimbursement check, right? Her *actual* check may be about $240, because the company will pay only the current cash value of the set, not its replacement cost. Depreciation is deducted for each year Jan has owned the item. If the insurance company sets the life of Janice's TV at 10 years, it is depreciated 10 percent for each year she owns it. After 6 years of ownership, Jan gets reimbursed for the 40 percent that remains, $240. If the set had been 9 years old, the check would have been for $60.

Different types of personal property have different depreciation rates, and each company can set its own rate. But the net effect is consistent: you pay a part of the replacement cost. It is not hard to imagine a situation in which a person might have to pay thousands of dollars to replace older, fully usable property. The answer? Add full replacement coverage.

*Reimburse-
ment of per-
sonal property
losses: full
replacement
coverage*

Many insurance companies provide **full replacement coverage** on personal property at extra cost: no depreciation is deducted. You are reimbursed the full cost of the new replacement. If Janice had purchased this protection, her check for the TV would have been $600. The option will boost your premium 10 to 20 percent, but it is money well spent.

The policy may place limits on full replacement coverage. First, the company will not pay for a better unit than the one you lost. Second, many companies retain the right to replace or repair your existing unit. Finally, some companies limit your reimbursement to 4 times the current value of

Does our property insurance cover replacement costs on a TV if, in a fit of football fever, my husband dropkicked the set?

the item: if a chair is only worth $50, they would pay $200 (choose a more expensive one, and you pay the difference).

Strategy

If available, add the full replacement option on personal property. Without it, coverage on personal property, especially on items 5, 10, or more years old, may be inadequate.

Coverage for Special Personal Property Items

The standard homeowners policy is intended to cover the personal property an "average" person might own. You may need additional coverage if you own something out of the ordinary. We divide such items into two groups. For the first, the standard policy provides some coverage, but it may be inadequate. For the second, little (or no) coverage is provided.

For high-value items such as jewelry, furs, silverware, guns, coins, and securities, coverage under the standard policy ranges from $200 to $2,500. For someone who has many of these items, added coverage is essential. A personal property inventory can help you decide if you need more coverage. For major holdings and collections of art, antiques, stamps, coins, and guns, coverage under the standard policy is inadequate; additional coverage is required.

Personal articles floater

A **personal articles floater (PAF)** provides added coverage for specialized personal property. A PAF will cover anything from your early American antiques to your prized zircon jewelry. It's all-risk coverage, so only specified perils are excluded. You can either purchase a separate policy or add a PAF as an endorsement to your homeowners policy.

Scheduling your personal property. When you buy a PAF policy, you prepare a detailed list of all the items you want covered; this is called **scheduling** the items. The list includes a description of the items, condition, age, location, manufacturer, and current market value. The insurance company may ask you to have some items appraised by an expert. For recently purchased items, bills of sale may suffice. An accurate estimate is essential, since it sets the maximum you can collect for the loss. Equally important, the dollar coverage determines your premium.

Strategy

If you have many special personal property items, a PAF endorsement or separate policy is probably needed. Update the coverage every 2 years to reflect any changes in market value.

Personal property that is excluded

Some kinds of personal property are not covered by the standard homeowners policy: autos, recreational vehicles, airplanes, and large boats, for example. You need to buy separate policies for these.

Homeowners Liability Insurance

The liability protection provided by a homeowners policy covers injuries or damages that you or your family may cause—and your potential losses are large. Houses and apartments present many hazards: seemingly innocent rugs, stairs, icy sidewalks, patio furniture, fruit trees, and swimming pools. Add a *power* mower, and potential damage to someone else's property is there in spades. No, Gert, that's not the bill for a new Mercedes. It is a bill for repairing those dents in the neighbor's candy-apple-red Ferrari sports cruiser caused by Junior using your 4-horsepower Lawngrazer without its grass catcher. Exhibit 13.2 summarizes coverage on each homeowners policy.

Personal liability

Most homeowners policies provide $100,000 of coverage for injuries or property damage caused by you or your family. They will also pay the cost of defense if you are sued. Pets are not covered as personal property, but your policy's liability section covers their willful actions. So if Agnes's piranha samples her guest's fingertip—picky, picky; it was just the pinky— she is covered.

To repeat: the potential loss for injury and property damage can be sizable. If Aunt Mae slips on a rug in your home and is seriously injured, her loss of wages or loss of future earning capacity, coupled with pain and suffering, could mean an award of $50,000 or more. Even a comparatively small $5,000 to $10,000 loss would be financially devastating. High liability limits are essential.

Strategy

Do not skimp on liability coverage. Raising the limit to $300,000 may add less than $20 per year to your premium.

Medical payments

A standard homeowners policy will pay the medical expenses of anyone (except family members) injured in your home, whether or not you or your family are considered negligent. If someone trips on a hose while cutting across your property, his medical expenses will be covered up to the specified limit; $1,000 is usual, though you can buy more.

Shopping for Homeowners Insurance

There are several major things that hold down the cost of homeowners insurance: (1) the deductible, (2) the type of policy, (3) competition from other insurance plans, and (4) the construction and location of the home.

Selecting a deductible

The property sections of a homeowners policy have a deductible, but the liability part does not. If your policy has a $250 deductible, you pay $250 of a $600 loss and the insurer pays the rest. Boost that loss to $6,000 or even $60,000 (assuming you have that much coverage), and you still pay $250. The deductible does not limit the coverage for catastrophic losses.

Which deductible should you select? A $250 or $500 deductible is probably best for most people. Switching to a deductible of this size can cut premiums 10 to 20 percent, as the final column in Exhibit 13.3 shows.

Furthermore, you are not likely to submit a claim for a $150 loss, since numerous small claims might jeopardize the renewal of your policy. If you can afford a $250 loss, consider a $250 deductible.

Deciding on the type of policy

Exhibit 13.3 shows premiums on three different homeowners policies. It costs little to upgrade from an HO-2 to an HO-3 policy, and that is money well spent. The value of an HO-5 policy is less clear, unless you have extensive personal property. For most people, an HO-3 will be adequate.

Strategy

An HO-3 policy is best for many people. An HO-5 policy provides superior coverage if you have extensive personal property, but be ready to pay.

Comparison shopping for a policy

Once you have decided on the type of policy, you have to select a company. Since coverage is fairly standard, comparisons between policies are simple. Price and policyholder satisfaction become the criteria for deciding. The premium comparison in Exhibit 13.3 shows price differences can be large. The best policy from a low-cost company can cost less than a basic policy from a high-cost one. Use a large company like State Farm or Allstate as a reference point; their rates are often quite competitive.

Policyholder satisfaction is important; coping with a loss is trying enough when you don't have collection problems. The office of the insurance commissioner in your state can tell you whether there have been many policyholder complaints against a company. *Consumer Reports* periodically surveys its readers and ranks insurance companies based on policyholder satisfaction; the most recent compilation was in August 1985.

Construction of the house and its location

You usually can do little to alter the construction or location of an existing house. Both should be considered in your purchase decision. Premiums are usually lower when the house is constructed of a fire-resistant material or located near a water supply. Remote country locations may be lovely, but the lack of fire protection may hike your premium significantly.

Exhibit 13.3

Typical Premiums for Homeowners Insurance Coverage

Type of policy	Annual Premium*			Premium savings for switch from $100 to $250 deductible
	Low cost	Average cost†	High cost	
Broad form HO-2	$218	$262	$340	10%
Special form HO-3	228	275	358	10%
Comprehensive HO-5	N/A	323	N/A	10%

N/A = Not available
* Based on home located in a suburban area with class 3 fire protection.
† Average cost based on sample.

AUTOMOBILE INSURANCE

Automobile insurance is one of the major fixed costs of owning and operating an auto. The amount you pay depends on several factors. Your age, sex, marital status, and location have an effect, but you can't control them. Your driving record, type of car, and what you use your car for also influence insurance costs, and over these you have some control. You can further control insurance costs by carefully choosing your coverage, deductibles, and policy.

This section concentrates on tailoring coverage to your needs, while holding down premiums. Good auto insurance is never cheap, but the financial risks make the premiums money well spent.

Coverage Provided by a Typical Auto Policy

Both liability and property coverage are combined in the standard auto policy. The industry defines four major areas of protection:

1   Liability protection for injury and property damage to others
2   Medical expenses of occupants in the policyholder's car
3   Coverage if another driver in an accident lacks insurance
4   Insurance against collision and other damage

Policy coverage provides for two groups: the policyholder and all other people. Exhibit 13.4 uses this breakdown to summarize coverage for bodily injury (top) and property damage (bottom).

Liability coverage

The **liability** section of your policy covers injuries and property damage you or your family cause while driving: included are such things as the injured person's lost wages, medical costs, pain and suffering, and reduced future income capacity. Property damages cover other cars, buildings, street signs, and utility poles. But injuries to you or your property are not covered by this section of the policy.

You specify the dollar coverage limits, either as a single limit or as separate limits for injury and property damage.

Exhibit 13.4

Insurance Protection Provided by Standard Auto Policy

	Protection Given to:	
Bodily injury coverage	*Policyholder*	*Other persons*
Personal injury liability	No	Yes
Medical payments	Yes	Yes
Injury caused by uninsured motorists	Yes	Yes
Property damage coverage	*Policyholder's car*	*Property of others*
Property damage liability	No	Yes
Comprehensive physical damage	Yes	No
Collision damage	Yes	No

Single limit. Policies with a **single limit** combine coverage for injury and property damage into one amount. A $300,000 policy limit will pay up to that amount without regard for how the loss arose. Any combination of injury or property losses up to $300,000 is covered. If the other party sues, your defense costs are covered; they do not fall under the limit, so total payments by your insurance carrier could exceed $300,000.

Separate limits. Many policies set **separate limits:** two limits for personal injury and one for property damage. A $100,000/$300,000/$50,000 policy (industry shorthand is 100/300/50) will serve as an example. The maximum for any one person's injury claim is $100,000. For all injury claims it is $300,000. And $50,000 is the maximum for property damage. See Exhibit 13.5.

Strategy

Single-limit policies are more flexible; they allocate coverage where it is needed.

Medical payments

The **medical payments** portion of your policy covers medical costs for people in your car—some states require this coverage. If you have health insurance, you can often collect from both policies. If your passengers have no health insurance, their costs are covered up to your auto policy limit. The usual minimum is $1,000 to $2,000.

Uninsured motorist protection

Not all states require drivers to have auto insurance. Where insurance *is* required, often no more than 90 to 95 percent of drivers actually carry it. If an uninsured motorist is legally liable for an accident you have, your policy's **uninsured motorist** section covers injuries to you and your passengers. A few states include damage to your property under uninsured motorist insurance, but usually it is covered by your collision section.

In some states uninsured motorist protection is mandatory. The smallest amount usually equals the minimum liability coverage required in your state.

Underinsured motorist. Even if the other driver has liability insurance, the limits may be so low (10/20/5, for example) that you are not adequately protected. **Underinsured motorist** insurance picks up when the

Exhibit 13.5

Automobile Liability Insurance with Separate Limits

Limits of Liability for Personal Injury				Limits of Liability for Property Damage
$100,000 Maximum for any one person's injuries	/	$300,000 Maximum for all injuries in the accident	/	$50,000 Maximum for damage to property of others

other driver's insurance is exhausted. It applies in accidents where the other driver is responsible. Only bodily injury is covered.

Collision coverage

Collision coverage pays for the damage to your car caused by an accident. If the other driver causes the accident, your insurance company may ask that you file a damage claim directly with his or her insurance company. When you are at fault, your insurance pays. If an uninsured motorist is at fault, damages to your auto are still covered. Premiums depend on your car's value and the area where you live. Collision insurance is optional.

The amount your insurance will pay depends on the market value of your car. If damage to your auto totals $2,000, but its retail value is $1,500, the insurance company will consider it **totaled** and pay $1,500. If you have a "mint" 1972 Slugmobile or a car that's been restored, you need special coverage.

Deductibles. Collision is the first auto coverage discussed so far that has a deductible. If you have a $100 deductible on your $3,000 car and it sustains $950 in damages (your fault), you collect $850. Total it, and you collect $2,900.

Comprehensive coverage

Comprehensive covers damage to your car from causes other than collision: fire, theft, vandalism, hail, wind, flood, glass breakage, and contact with birds or animals. Maude rounds the blind curve to see Henrietta the Holstein in her lane. She leans on the brakes, and—*nothing!* Should she choose the Peterbilt in the left lane, Henrietta up the middle, or that giant pine to the right? Udder amazement! She's covered for each: liability if it's the truck, comprehensive if it's the cow, and collision if it's the tree.

Comprehensive coverage is not required. Usually only the car and its original equipment are covered; personal property and owner-added extras are excluded. Premiums depend on the car's value and how likely a loss is in your area. If vandalism or theft is prevalent in your town, expect high rates. Rising claims have made deductibles of $50 to $500 nearly standard.

Who Is Covered?

You and your family members are covered while driving a car you own. You and the car are covered if you loan it to someone who has an accident. You are covered if you borrow a friend's car and have an accident. In short, you are covered in most driving situations, but there are exceptions. You are probably not covered if you charge someone a fee for the ride or a person uses your car without your permission. Likewise, the deductible on a rental car—often $2,000 or more—may not be covered. Have a unique circumstance? Check the policy or ask your agent *before* you need the coverage.

Cancellation and Nonrenewal of Your Policy

You can cancel your auto policy at any time; your insurance company has less latitude. If you fail to pay the premium, the company can cancel after giving you notice. The company can generally cancel if your license is revoked or suspended.

The insurance company can refuse to renew your policy for a number of reasons. A lengthy list of traffic citations can do the trick. So can frequent claims. Form letter number 13 carries the bad news: "Sorry but you have fallen out of the good hands of Wallstate." Sometimes a company decides to thin its policyholders' ranks. Once you've been dropped, finding substitute coverage may be a challenge, especially if your driving record prompted form letter number 13.

When selecting coverage, you should concentrate on companies that drop only a small percentage of policyholders. *Consumer Reports* usually publishes this statistic for major companies in its periodic review of auto policies.

Strategy

Carefully review the cancellation provisions in any prospective policy; also review the company's drop rate for policyholders.

Designing Auto Insurance Coverage for Your Needs

When designing an auto policy for yourself, you have two objectives. First (and foremost), the policy must protect you against catastrophic losses, even if the possibility of enormous loss is slight. Recall, insurance is at its best when protecting against large losses that have a low likelihood of happening. Only after you cover the major losses should you move on to the small ones, thereby obtaining the best coverage for each premium dollar.

Second, you want to hold premiums to a manageable level. That means avoiding duplicate coverage and not insuring against losses you can't col-

lect for. It also means rejecting coverage where self-insuring makes better sense.

Exhibit 13.6 outlines some sample premiums. We make no claim that these are what you can expect to pay: premiums vary widely depending on geographic area, driver covered, and type of car, so it is impossible to quote a representative premium. A young driver in a large city may pay more each month for basic coverage than Smidley Smalltown pays annually for his "grand luxe" policy. Exhibit 13.6 highlights what it costs to upgrade coverage.

Liability: personal injury

Simple advice here: buy as much coverage as you can. Limits of $100,000/$300,000 ($300,000 if a single limit) are suggested. Even for a moderate injury, the combination of lost wages, medical costs, and rehabilitation quickly exceeds the $10,000 to $20,000 many states require. On serious injuries, losses exceeding six digits are not uncommon. This is no place to cut corners.

As the top section of Exhibit 13.6 illustrates, the cost of upgrading liability coverage is often moderate: doubling the upper limits raises premiums 15 to 25 percent. That is a "good" insurance buy; you can add the catastrophic coverage you need for a small extra premium.

Liability: property damage

With many new cars costing $20,000, with BMWs and others of their ilk double that, damage to someone else's car is costly. There are also signs, traffic controls, houses, and other property waiting to jump in front of the

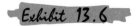

Exhibit 13.6

Representative Premium Increases for Upgrading Auto Policy Coverages

Coverage	Limits (in 1,000s)	Percentage improvement in coverage	Annual premium	Percentage increase (decrease) in premium
Liability:				
Personal injury	25/50/10		$135	
and property	50/100/25	100%	155	15%
damage	100/300/50	200%	186	20%
Medical	$ 2,000		16	
	5,000	150%	22	38%
	10,000	100%	33	50%
Collision	$100 deductible		165	
	250 deductible	*	132	20%
	500 deductible	†	99	25%
Comprehensive	$ 50 deductible		40	
	100 deductible	§	36	10%

* Reduces coverage by $150.
† Reduces coverage by $250.
§ Reduces coverage by $50.

unsuspecting car. You need high dollar limits if that accident is your fault. A minimum would be $25,000, but $50,000 is not unreasonable.

If you increase the personal injury part of a policy, property damage limits often increase automatically. On single-limit policies, injury and property damage is one amount—preferably high.

Medical coverage

If you have a good health policy and rarely carry passengers, then medical coverage on auto insurance is unnecessary. If your health policy is poor, upgrade it rather than covering losses by this section. If you carry passengers frequently, you will want $5,000 or $10,000 in medical coverage; you are not likely to check someone's health coverage before offering them a ride. The usual $2,000 minimum will hardly get someone through the emergency room at today's medical costs. Besides, as Exhibit 13.6 shows, better coverage does not cost much.

Collision coverage

Collision coverage too often takes center billing. Many view the added $150 they would pay if they shift from a $100 to a $250 deductible as akin to financial ruin. Yet their inadequate liability coverage could be exposing them to thousands of dollars of losses. Do you need collision? Yes. We are not advocating self-insuring a car that could be worth $10,000 or more. But choose a deductible that keeps your premiums down.

Which deductible? How often will you end up paying the first $250 or even $500 of a loss if you choose a high deductible? Remember, you only pay when the accident is your fault. Unless you are like Connie Consistent—she averages an accident every Friday the thirteenth and has *major* insurance problems—or drive in a demolition derby environment, you are not likely to have many accidents. Even if you have a $200 encounter with a stop sign on an icy morning, would you submit a claim on your $100 deductible policy if it might result in nonrenewal or a premium surcharge?

Consider a $250 deductible. Use your savings to upgrade liability protection. Going to a $500 deductible is advised if you can deal with it financially and psychologically.

Strategy

Try a $250 deductible as a starting point. Move to a $500 deductible if you are comfortable with it.

Consider dropping coverage on your car when its market value drops to $1,000. With a $250 or $500 deductible policy, you are only buying $750 or $500 of coverage. Is it worth paying $140 or more annually for that protection? We doubt it.

Comprehensive coverage

Comprehensive coverage is important when a car's market value is high, especially in areas where losses due to vandalism, theft, and other perils are common. Comprehensive coverage costs much less than collision. Consequently, shifting to a higher deductible provides small savings; see Exhibit 13.6. Nevertheless, consider a $100 deductible. A boost to $250 or $500 is in order if you can afford the loss.

**Auto Insur-
ance Rates**

Your auto insurance premium depends on a number of factors; some of these you can control by making wise choices. Let's review some of the things you should consider.

Type of car

High-performance cars carry much higher premiums (an extra 20 to 40 percent is not unusual) than some of their lesser brethren. Likewise, cars that are costly to repair or subject to high losses—some Porsche models just seem to evaporate—cost more to insure. Each company sets its own premium. That could add $200, $300, or more to your tab. Ask yourself: Do I really want to pay the extra premium for a performance car?

Strategy

Before you buy a car, ask your insurance agent if it carries a premium surcharge and how much.

Driving record

Insurance companies are not pleased when one of their clients accumulates several traffic violations. Some show their displeasure by adding a 10 to 20 percent surcharge to the premium, a reminder in addition to the $75 speeding fine. To encourage careful driving, many insurers offer "good driver" discounts to the vehicularly pure.

Strategy

A clean driving record can hold down your insurance premiums.

**Record of
claims**

From the insurance company's perspective, a good pool of drivers is one with few claims. To discourage frequent claims, many insurance companies boost the premium for each one. Most define a "chargeable claim" as one with a $200 to $400 loss that was primarily your fault. Submit one such claim and premiums might rise 10 to 30 percent. Add another, and it might cost 30 to 70 percent. Three or more could more than double your premium. The added charge might extend for 3 to 5 years.

Should you refrain from filing a claim? If only your property is involved, and the loss is only a few hundred dollars, you may want to skip the claim. When the accident involves other property, though, proceed with care. You might pay a small loss yourself. But report larger losses to your insurance company, especially if further damages may appear later. Failure to do so may mean your insurance company will not represent you in a damage case. If there are injuries, report immediately: potential liability is just too great to ever consider "going it alone." Unless you report an accident, your insurance company may not represent you if you are sued.

**Use of the
automobile**

The more you drive, the more opportunities for a loss. Insurance rates reflect this risk by basing premiums on the number of miles driven. Commuting long distances raises premiums. Potential auto insurance costs may be a factor to consider when deciding where to live.

Where you live

Auto insurance premiums tend to be higher in metropolitan areas than in rural communities since there are more accidents in metropolitan areas. Areas where theft and other property crimes are a problem also have higher premiums. The differences are significant. A low-cost metropolis might have double the premiums of a small city. Premiums in a high-cost area may be 4 to 6 times more. Consider this factor when weighing the merits of a new job offer.

Credit for driver education

Some insurance companies offer a discount (usually 10 percent) to young drivers who have completed a driver education course. Given the large premiums that many insurance companies charge for young drivers, requiring your child to take driver's education can be good financial planning.

Age, sex, and marital status

In most states, young drivers pay much higher premiums than older ones. Likewise, young men often pay higher rates than women of the same age. Unfortunately, the data on severity and frequency of accidents provides some solid support for these premium differentials. A few states have passed legislation limiting the use of age or sex to set premiums.

Some insurance companies will charge less when a young driver is married. Often the reduction is larger for a young male than for a woman.

Premiums usually drop sharply when the driver reaches his or her mid-twenties. What can be done? Checking the premium for a number of different companies can be a good starting point. Some do not charge nearly as large a differential as others. That search will be much easier for those with a clean driving record. Your options diminish if you have several traffic violations or a chargeable accident.

Buying Auto Insurance

The two criteria to use when selecting auto insurance are cost and policyholder satisfaction. Price differences of 50 to 100 percent are not unusual, so large savings are possible, especially for drivers without a recent chargeable accident or traffic violation.

There are several ways to check policyholder satisfaction. Check the insurance commissioner's office in your state to find out if a company has been the source of consumer complaints. The ratings published by *Consumer Reports* can be helpful too; the magazine's most recent survey of readers' claim experience was published in the September 1984 issue.

Exhibit 13.7 provides guidelines you can use in your search for an auto policy. Time spent in searching can pay off when you find a policy that meets your needs at a fair price.

 Exhibit 13.7

Guidelines for Buying Auto Insurance

Ask friends or coworkers to recommend agents they are satisfied with.

Investigate to see if a company's present policyholders are satisfied.

Ask that each agent develop an auto insurance plan based on your general guidelines.

Obtain premium quotations from each agent, with a breakdown of the cost of each coverage.

Request premium quotations from insurance companies that sell policies by mail or have a toll-free telephone line.

Make certain coverage limits are similar when comparing premiums.

No-Fault Auto Insurance

Traditional auto insurance has long been criticized. The cost of settling claims absorbs a chunk of each premium dollar. A claim can take months or years to settle. And many accident victims collect very little.

No-fault auto insurance was proposed as the solution. Its intent is to deliver better value for each insurance dollar. It eliminates, or severely restricts, attempts to prove which party was at fault in an accident. Each party in the accident collects injury and property damage from his or her own insurance company. To ensure there is something there to collect, generous coverage limits are mandatory. Drivers cannot be underinsured. Medical coverage must be adequate to cover the costs of a serious accident. Property damage coverage is required for major losses. There must be liability coverage for rehabilitation, pain and suffering, and wage loss.

The no-fault picture is mixed. A few states, such as Michigan, have enacted encompassing no-fault insurance laws that deliver the promised benefits. Several others have passed half-hearted programs, and a few have retained traditional auto insurance while tacking on some no-fault coverage. The remaining states, currently more than half, have done nothing. Good no-fault insurance appears to deliver quick and significant benefits to the accident victim, but it is rare. What is needed? A set of national standards for uniform coverage would help, but the likelihood of these being legislated at this time is slim.

If your state has no-fault, do your homework and find out how it operates. A good insurance agent can help here. Just don't forget basic insurance guidelines:

1   Protect yourself against large dollar losses if you injure someone or damage property.
2   Protect yourself with adequate medical and long-term disability coverage.
3   Protect your auto against major loss, but self-insure for the first $250, $500, or even $1,000.

UMBRELLA LIABILITY POLICY

An **umbrella liability policy** picks up where your auto and homeowners insurance policies end. An umbrella policy provides added coverage of $1 million or more. It covers the usual personal injury and property damage losses, but many add libel, slander, false arrest, and defamation of character.

As a first condition, most insurers offering umbrella policies require that you carry high dollar coverage on both your homeowners liability and auto liability: $100,000 on the homeowners and $100,000/$300,000 on the auto, for example. Some companies require that you have both your homeowners and auto coverage with them before they will sell an umbrella policy. You can expect to pay about $100 to $150 annually for $1 million of coverage.

Should you have such a policy? The number of damage settlements exceeding $100,000 is not large—in fact, that is why you can buy this coverage for so little—but they do occur. In my opinion, you are well advised to consider an umbrella policy, and raising the deductible on your home-owners and auto policy from its current $50 or $100 to a more realistic $250 or $500 may provide much of the premium.

Strategy

Consider buying an umbrella liability policy for the high dollar limit to cover rare but devastating losses.

Summary

1 Homeowners insurance and auto insurance combine liability coverage and property damage coverage in single policies.

2 Homeowners insurance covers injury to other people, damage to their property, and damage to your property.

3 Because buyers have widely differing coverage needs, insurance companies offer a number of different homeowners policies. The six popular homeowners policies are divided into three categories:
   - HO-1, HO-2, HO-3, and HO-5 for owner-occupied homes
   - HO-4 for renters
   - HO-6 for condominium owners

4 Upgrading to a better homeowners policy broadens the range of perils that are covered; liability and property damage coverage change relatively little.

5 To avoid coinsurance, you must insure your house for at least 80 percent of its current replacement cost. When coverage does not meet that minimum, reimbursement on a loss equals:

$$\frac{\text{Insurance}}{\text{payment}} = \frac{\text{amount}}{\text{of loss}} \times \frac{\text{actual insurance carried}}{\text{80 percent of replacement cost}}$$

6 Personal property is depreciated when computing reimbursements under the standard policy. Reimbursement is calculated as:

$$\frac{\text{Insurance}}{\text{payment}} = \frac{\text{current}}{\text{replacement cost of property}} - \frac{\text{accumulated depreciation based on age of item}}$$

7 For an extra premium, you can add full replacement coverage on personal property; depreciation will not be deducted.

8 Coverage for special or unique personal property items under a standard homeowners policy is poor at best. A personal articles floater should be added to provide the necessary coverage.

9 The liability portion of a homeowners policy covers claims for personal injuries and damage to other people's property that you might cause.

10 The only deductible in a homeowners policy is on the coverage for your personal property and the home.

11 The standard auto insurance policy covers the cost of personal injury and damage to other people's property, medical expenses for the occupants of your car, and damage to your car.

12 Protection against catastrophic personal injury and property damage losses is by far the most important reason for purchasing auto insurance.

13 Coverage for damage to your auto is provided by the collision and comprehensive sections of your auto policy; both sections usually carry a deductible.

14 Dollar limits on coverage for any personal injury or property damage you might cause should be very high; the cost of upgrading this coverage is usually modest.

15 Deductibles of $250 or even $500 should be used to control auto insurance premiums; your savings can be used to strengthen coverage in other areas.

16 Major factors that determine the cost of auto insurance include type of car, driving record, number of claims, how the auto is used, where you live, age, sex, and marital status.

17 Premium differentials between insurance companies can often exceed 50 to 100 percent; savings from comparison shopping can be significant.

18 Under good no-fault insurance, drivers would look to their own insurance company to cover personal injury and property damage losses. To date, few states have comprehensive no-fault legislation.

19 An umbrella liability policy takes over when personal injury or property damage losses exceed the limit on your homeowners or auto insurance policy.

Review your understanding of

Property insurance
Liability insurance
Homeowners insurance
    HO-1, HO-2, HO-3, and HO-5
    HO-4
    HO-6
Covered perils
All-risk policy
Appurtenant structure

Personal property
Additional living expense
Coinsurance: 80 percent rule
Full replacement coverage
Personal articles floater (PAF)
Scheduled personal property
Auto liability coverage
Single limit
Separate limits

Medical payments
Uninsured motorist
Underinsured motorist
Collision coverage
"Totaled"
Comprehensive coverage
No-fault auto insurance
Umbrella liability insurance

Discussion questions

1   Sue Smalltime and Bill Bigbuck are discussing their homeowners insurance needs. Sue's house is small and moderately priced; Bill's is large and expensive. Bill argues: "Large, expensive houses require an HO-5 policy, while an HO-1 is fine for a less expensive house." Do you agree? Why? What guidlines would you give Sue and Bill for selecting a suitable homeowners policy?

2   Stephanie Studio has always rented an apartment and therefore feels she has no need for homeowners insurance. Do you concur? Why?

3   A recent fire hopelessly damaged $10,000 (current replacement value) of Boris Baddraw's personal property. Boris is confident that the $20,000 of coverage on his standard HO-6 policy will be sufficient. Is he correct? Why?

4   How can a personal property inventory help your homeowners insurance plan? What information should be on the inventory?

5   Ronda Frank recently paid $4,000 for an 1820 table that was made in an upstate New York Shaker community. Will Ronda's present HO-3 policy cover it? What should she do?

6   While delivering the Swifts' mail, Agnes Badback twisted her back when she stepped on a roller skate left by one of the children. As the emergency crew carried her away, her parting words were, "My lawyer will be in touch." Will the Swifts' HO-3 policy cover? If Agnes does sue, who will pay the Swifts' attorney's fees?

7   Fred Firsttime is about to buy his first house. He has heard that the dollar limits on a homeowners policy should be high. He wonders if you would suggest ways to hold down the premium.

8   On her way to a deer hunt in northern Michigan, Brenda Biggame bagged one on the front of her Volkswagen. For $800, the local repair shop will remove it plus the dents and crinkles (she gets the deer, of course). What part, if any, of her auto policy will cover this?

9   While testing the "tenacious winter handling" of her new front-wheel-drive car, Betty Bungle missed a curve, thereby wiping out
  a Her car
  b A fire hydrant
  c Fast Phil's Popcorn Wagon
  d Phil's new 560 SL Mercedes
Both she and Phil were slightly injured. Which sections, if any, of Betty's auto policy will cover each loss?

10   Why are high dollar limits important for the liability section of an auto policy? Since $900 fender benders are far more prevalent than accidents with $90,000 of personal injury and property damage, a small deductible on collision would seem more important than high dollar limits on liability. Do you agree?

11   While Grazelda's car was in the shop, she borrowed her friend's auto for the evening. Due to inattentive driving, she took out a store front and two parked cars. Will her auto policy cover the loss?

12   Tom Morgan currently has $100 deductible collision on his tired 1975 Plymouth; the car's current market value is about $800. If he totaled it, what would he collect? Would you alter the coverage?

13   Marvin Bumpkin wonders if his auto premiums are not unjustly high; they look like a goodly portion of the national debt. Details include
- He drives a "performance" car to support his suave, debonair image.
- Marvin's traffic violations have earned him 11 points; when he hits 12 he will "take the bus and leave the driving to us."
- He is 22 years old and single.
- Marvin keeps all deductibles at $50 to minimize his loss.
- He lives near a major city and commutes a long way to work.

  a Would anything in the above list account for the high premium?
  b What changes would you suggest to lower his premium?

Problems

13.1 Betty Woo's house recently suffered $8,000 of damage from a fire. She had the house insured under an HO-3 policy for $40,000; it would cost $62,500 to replace it.
  a   What will she collect from the insurance company?
  b   To collect the full $8,000, how much insurance should she have?

13.2 The Timms family was forced to live in a motel and eat in a restaurant after their house was extensively damaged by a tornado. Total cost of the 1-month stay was $2,400. The house was covered by a $40,000 (face amount) HO-3 policy.
  a   Will the policy cover this type of expense?
  b   What is the maximum their policy will pay?

13.3 Linda's leather wingback chair was destroyed when her apartment building burned. She paid $600 for the chair 8 years ago and estimates it would cost $1,200 today to duplicate it. Her insurance company told her it uses a 10-year life when depreciating furniture.
  a   What will Linda's HO-4 policy pay?
  b   She was offered full replacement on the personal property for an extra 15 percent of the $150 premium. Had she taken this option, what would she collect?
  c   Which coverage would you recommend? Why?

13.4 While Marie was waiting for a green light, Boris Bankrupt drove into her car. True to his name, Boris has no insurance and there is little likelihood of collecting from him. Marie's policy includes (1) liability of 50/100/25, (2) comprehensive with $50 deductible, (3) uninsured motorist of 15/30, and (4) collision with a $100 deductible. Marie's medical costs total $3,800 and she lost 10 weeks' wages at $380 per week. Damage to her car totaled $2,000.
  a   Will Marie's policy pay any part of the medical cost and lost wages?
  b   Which section, if any, will cover the damage to her car?

13.5 Brian Dale has three coverage options for his automobile policy:

	Policy 1		Policy 2		Policy 3	
Type of coverage	*Dollar amount*	*Annual premium*	*Dollar amount*	*Annual premium*	*Dollar amount*	*Annual premium*
Liability						
Personal injury	$25/$50*	$ 96	$50/$100*	$115	$100/$300*	$138
Property	10*	65	15*	67	25*	69
Collision	50†	194	100†	164	250†	132
Comprehensive	0†	70	50†	52	100†	46

* Amounts in thousands of dollars.
† Deductible amount on policy.

  a   In your opinion, which policy provides the "best" coverage? What would your suggested policy cost?
  b   How can Brian reduce the annual premium? What will a policy that provides good coverage with a minimum premium cost?

Case problem

Randy Jacoby's house recently suffered $22,000 in fire damage; he had it insured for $45,000 under an HO-3 policy. Current replacement cost for the house is $55,000. Randy estimates he lost $8,000 of personal property in the fire. His insurance company has offered to settle those damages for $3,100. A landscaping firm estimates it will cost $2,500 to repair the damage to trees and shrubs around the house.

  The $3,000 detached garage was also a total loss; Randy's auto (current market value about $2,200) and his boat (current market value $5,000) were also destroyed. His auto policy included a $250 deductible on the collision and a $50 deductible on the comprehensive. He did not carry a separate policy on the boat.

Randy lived in a motel during the two months it took to clean and repair the house. That stay cost $2,450.

1   For each loss indicate:
   a Whether it is covered and by what part of the insurance.
   b What amount Randy is likely to collect.
   c If not covered, tell why.
2   Why is the proposed settlement for the personal property loss so small?
3   Which of the losses are likely to leave Randy paying a major part of the cost?
4   What suggestions would you have for improving Randy's insurance plan?

Building for your future

S

PART

CHAPTER 14

Investments: Fundamentals and developing a strategy

AFTER COMPLETING THIS CHAPTER YOU WILL HAVE LEARNED

- The major differences between a lending and an ownership investment
- How a variable-return lending investment differs from its fixed-return counterpart
- The strengths and weaknesses of an ownership investment
- That an investment's return combines interest, dividends, rent, and capital gains or capital losses
- Why long-term and short-term capital gains receive the same tax treatment
- How an investment's risk is measured
- What causes interest rate risk on an investment
- Why investors demand a higher return for higher risk
- How compound return operates and why it is important
- How frequency of compounding affects the rate of return
- How to use a compound rate of return table when there is a single deposit or equal annual deposits to an investment
- How inflation reduces the real rate of return
- Why ownership investments should perform better during periods of high inflation
- How a consideration of risk exposure, rate of return, minimum maturity, minimum dollar amount, tax features, and flexibility can help you decide the suitability of an investment

nvestments are a basic part of a well-developed financial plan. Earlier chapters showed investments as playing a part in financial goals, budgeting, and choice of payment accounts. Chapter 1 discussed how investments could help you accumulate money for financial goals. Whether the goal is months or years away, investments provide a return until then. Chapter 3 advised that your emergency cash reserve should be invested until needed. Even in discussing checking accounts, we noted the advantage of the return on a NOW account.

The range of investment options is large and expanding. You need to understand the basics of investing, because selection is important. Choose the wrong investment option, and you may end up with more risk than you want or a substandard rate of return. The key to success is an informed investment manager: you.

People with significant amounts of money see investments as offering substantial gains. But they can also be important to the someone with limited capital—someone whose assets total less than $50,000 and who invests $500 to $1,000 at a time. These investors need to choose particularly well, since they rarely have a cushion to fall back on if an investment yields an "experience" (a nice term for a near total loss). Since they have less money to invest, they need a good return on their investment. They end up serving as their own investment managers because the professionals frequently expect clients to maintain a minimum balance of $100,000 or more. And they have fewer investment options, since they cannot purchase instruments with large dollar minimums. All these factors make careful, informed investment decisions critical.

Managing investments is challenging, but it promises solid rewards. Obtaining the necessary background and skills takes work. However, a little time and effort will launch you on a pursuit that can be productive and satisfying.

SOME FIRST STEPS

Let's start off with some basic guidelines on developing an investment program.

Expect a Realistic Rate of Return

There is no formula or system that you can use to single out "sure-fire" investments. People like to talk about investments whose price soared, but how many of those stories actually involve investments that were made in advance? And how many misses were there? Annual returns that exceed inflation by 2 to 8 percent are common (differences in risk cause the wide range). Looking forward to this level of return is far more realistic than expecting your money to double or triple. While a quick gain is nice, a sustained, reasonably steady return is more attainable.

Where There's High Return, There's High Risk

Some people insist: "I want to earn the highest return." But do they really? An investment's rate of return and its risk are *directly* related. Yes, Arthur, that 14 percent return sure beats a 5 percent savings account. But boosting the return 9 percent multiplies the risk. And high returns are not guaranteed. Faced with the realities, many people may not want that added risk.

What is needed is a reasonable trade-off between return and risk. Investments should involve no more risk than you are comfortable with.

Use a Systematic Approach

When investors are confused and frustrated, their state of mind often stems from a lack of specific objectives. People try to choose investments before answering such basic questions as:

- How much money is available?
- How much risk do I want?
- Why am I making this investment?
- How long will I hold the investment?

Answering these will quickly narrow your investment options. A wise investor answers the basic questions first.

Start Early and Continue

Letting the return on an investment compound can do wonders. Even a modest balance will grow to a sizable amount if left invested for a time. Recall the "rule of 72": dividing 72 by the rate of return shows how many years it takes for an investment to double. For instance, at 8 percent, the investment doubles about every 9 years.

Early deposits to a plan are important, but so are continued regular deposits. Suppose Becky wants $100,000 when she retires in 40 years. If

I don't usually give advice on long-term versus short-term investments, but.. ..in your case..

she can earn 8 percent, she will need to invest $386 annually. Her first $386 deposit is important; with the reinvestment of interest, it grows to about $8,386 by the end. But the deposits in the second, third, fourth, and following years are essential also. An early start and sustained follow-through can make a large goal achievable.

Are the same early start and sustained follow-through important when the goal is short-term? Assume Winthrop wants to accumulate $14,000 in his daughter's education fund. With an 8 percent return, the required monthly deposit is $190.54 if Winnie begins saving 5 years ahead. If he starts 5 years earlier, the monthly deposit drops to $76.53. If he begins a full 15 years before the money is needed, Winthrop will only have to save $40.46 a month. An "early and sustained" investment program means smaller, more manageable savings deposits.

Strategy

An early start on an investment program and continued regular deposits can ease the way to a goal, especially when the amount is large.

An Investment for Each Purpose

The rapid expansion of investment options for the small investor is a distinct advantage. No longer need you choose between a passbook account offering cookware or another offering an electric blanket. Now you have investment options for long-range goals, for goals 2 to 5 years away, and options for more immediate goals. Unless your goals are homogeneous, no single investment will suit them all. Match your investment to your goal.

Successful Investing Requires Work and Persistence

Most successful investors work diligently at investment planning, taking time to become familiar enough with an area to make informed choices. Few would claim they have had only successes; losses and even an occasional "experience" are part of investing, especially if higher-risk investments are included. Finally, investing when most people are positive (bullish) on the economy's outlook is probably easier, yet some of the best returns come when doom and gloom are rampant.

Strategy

An approach that includes investing during good and not so good times can provide rewarding returns.

TWO BASIC INVESTMENT ALTERNATIVES: LENDING OR OWNERSHIP

Basically, there are two ways to invest your extra funds. You can lend someone the money and be paid for its use; think of the interest you're paid as rent for your money. Or you can use the money to buy part or full ownership in some venture; the venture has to generate your return. Let's look closely at these two major investment options.

Lending Investments

Most **lending investments** (savings accounts, certificates of deposit, savings bonds, corporate bonds, and municipal bonds are examples) have a fixed rate of return and a fixed date of maturity. **Fixed return** means that the interest rate is set at the time you invest. In effect, the borrower agrees to pay a set amount to rent your money, stated as X percent per year. **Fixed maturity** means the borrower sets a specific date when the loan will be repaid. That maturity date is also set when the investment is made.

You are reasonably certain of the results of a lending investment. Since the return and maturity are fixed, you can estimate how much you will get and when. Of course, if the borrower encounters financial difficulty, the promised payment could be delayed, altered, or even missed entirely.

In general, the risk on lending investments is less than on ownership ones. Their lower rate of return reflects their relative safety. There is also a trade-off for the certainty you gain. Your return will be no more than originally promised. Borrowers rarely pay more than the promised rate.

Lending investments with a variable return

The high inflation of the late 1970s and early 1980s caused some to question the wisdom of fixed returns. When a fixed-return investment has a long maturity, high inflation wreaks havoc. Predicting inflation over the full period until the investment's maturity (to ensure that the return adequately offsets inflation) is almost impossible. The solution: vary the investment's promised return during its lifetime by tying (indexing) it to an interest rate in the financial markets that reflects economic and inflation conditions.

Look at an example showing how **variable return** investments operate. Setting Sun Savings offers two 3-year certificates of deposit (CDs):

1   Interest rate is 8 percent and is fixed for 36 months.
2   Interest rate starts at 8 percent; it is reset each month at 1 percent more than last month's interest rate on 3-year Treasury securities.

CD number 1 assures an 8 percent return. But if annual inflation rises to 10 percent after a few months, your real return after inflation is actually −2 percent. If you had bought CD number 2, you would fare better. As inflation rates rise, market interest rates should do the same. Inflation will not have the same dire consequences, because your variable CD's return increases. In an environment where inflation rates are rising or people expect them to, variable rate investments perform better than fixed-rate ones. Of course, if inflation cools and interest rates drop, returns on the variable rate investment will fall.

The restrained inflation of the past several years has reduced the demand for and supply of variable return instruments. If inflation picks up, there will likely be renewed interest.

Strategy

When the inflation rate is rising or highly volatile, a variable rate investment is usually a good choice, especially if you are looking for an investment with a maturity exceeding 3 years.

Ownership Investments

Ownership investments purchase partial or complete interest in a venture that is supposed to make money. Examples include common stocks, mutual funds that invest in stocks, small businesses, partnerships, and rental real estate. Since most business ventures require large blocks of capital, partial ownership is common. Likewise, most investors do not want an active management role, so often someone is employed to run the business.

Under the ownership option, your return depends on the success of the business. If you purchase common stock in Last Flight Airlines, your return comes from any revenues that carrier generates over and above its expenses. Suppose you want more involvement: you buy a rental duplex apartment. Your success will come from keeping the units occupied, finding and keeping tenants who pay fair rents, and holding down maintenance and other costs. At some point you may gain financially by selling the unit for more than you paid for it. In the end, your return on ownership investments depends on the income-producing potential of the underlying venture. If it does well (and not all do), so will the owners.

Ownership investments are unlike lending investments in that there is no upper limit on the return they can provide. But if ownership returns are potentially unlimited, so are ownership losses. Returns can be small, zero, or decidedly negative. At the extreme you can lose your entire investment: ah, another "experience."

Another weakness of ownership investments is that their return is less predictable than that of lending investments. Last, ownership investments by nature tend to require long-term commitments. Though you may be able to liquidate along the way, in many cases it takes a long time for results to materialize.

TOTAL RETURN ON AN INVESTMENT

When you invest money, you give up its immediate purchasing power. To make up for the sacrifice, you not only want the money back, but also expect a return on it. Usually, the rate of return is stated as a certain percentage per year. When you place $1,000 in an investment that promises a 10 percent rate of return, the investment should provide a $100 return each year.

Total Return

Returns on an investment can come from several sources: from interest or dividends, or from a change in the investment's market price (a rise increases the return; a decline lowers it). Part of the income earned can be reinvested so that it generates further earnings (we will look at compounding later). Input from all sources—both positive and negative—is included in the investment's "annual return." Annual return is the measure that should be used when comparing returns on investment options.

Interest Income

When you make lending investments, your return for the use of your money comes in the form of **interest income.** Some investments pay once a year, some twice, some monthly, and some even more frequently. The actual borrower can be a financial institution—bank, S&L, credit union, or savings bank—a corporation, a local or state government unit, or the federal government. Interest is stated as a percentage per year.

Dividend Income

When you purchase common stock in a company, you become part owner. The more shares you own, the greater your interest. As a shareholder, you own a proportionate share in the income the company earns, but not all the income is distributed to the owners. Part is paid to the owners as a cash dividend; that **dividend income** is stated as X cents per share. The income that is not paid as dividends is retained in the company for future use. A small, rapidly growing company may retain virtually all its income for years. Does that shortchange the firm's owners? It should not. Presumably, retained earnings will be used for new or expanded income-producing ventures which enhance the earning potential of the firm. At some future point, the shareholders should receive a significantly higher dividend.

Purchasing shares in a mutual fund that invests in common stocks has the same ownership effect, but indirectly. Your investment dollars purchase shares in the mutual fund; you become a part owner of the fund. The fund buys common stocks with the money and becomes an owner of the firms. A cash dividend paid to the mutual fund is redistributed to those who hold the fund's shares.

Income from a Business

When you own a business directly or as a partner, your share of that venture's **business income** comes directly to you. If you are the sole owner— if the business is a sole proprietorship—you receive the entire income. If the business is a partnership, you receive the share set forth in the partnership agreement. Your rate of return is figured by dividing the income you receive annually by your total investment.

Rent from an Investment

Many real estate investments generate **rent.** Part of those rents will be needed to cover operating and maintenance expenses for the property, but there should be some left to provide a return on the investment.

Capital Gains and Capital Losses

A **capital gain** or **capital loss** arises when you sell an investment for more or less than you paid for it. Suppose you buy 100 shares of Last Flight Airways at $8 a share. Several years later you decide to sell for $9, but you must pay a $25 sales commission. Your capital gain is $75: (100 shares × $9) − (100 shares × $8) − $25 commission. If the price had dropped to $7 per share, you would have had a $125 loss: $700 from sale − $800 purchase cost − $25 commission. In general terms:

$$\text{Capital gain or loss} = \frac{\text{proceeds}}{\text{from sales}} - \frac{\text{purchase}}{\text{price}} - \frac{\text{sales}}{\text{commission}}$$

Capital gains or losses on an investment can range from substantial to zero. Take a savings account or CD. The financial institution promises to redeem it at the full price plus interest. Barring the bank's collapse (financial, not physical), you never receive more or less than the promised rate; even if the bank failed, federal insurance would probably pay. Quite the opposite is true of common stocks. When a company is highly successful, the market price of its shares may rise, and a capital gain result. On the other hand, fierce competition or loss of exclusive products can seriously erode the profits of a company, leaving you with a loss as the market price of its shares drops.

Long-term versus short-term

Before the sweeping Tax Reform Act of 1986, distinguishing between **long-term gains and losses** and **short-term gains and losses** was important. Gains or losses on investments held for more than 6 months were taxed at a special rate. But no more. Now all gains are treated uniformly: the total is included in your income. Yes, Maynard, you have to include the *whole* thing so the IRS gets its share. Capital losses, short- and long-term, can be deducted in their entirety. There is, however, a $3,000 annual cap that may force you to carry part of a large loss to future years.

Strategy

The length of time for which you hold an investment no longer counts for tax purposes: investment decisions should be based exclusively on financial considerations.

Riskiness of an Investment

The standard dictionary definition of **risk**—the possibility of loss, harm, or uncertain danger—can be applied to investments. The 5 percent return on a savings account at an insured bank is a near certainty. Barring a cataclysm, your actual and expected return are identical. There is practically no risk.

But suppose you buy a 5-year Treasury security promising a 7 percent return. If you hold it 5 years, your actual return will be 7 percent. But if you have to sell after 3 years, and the market price has dropped (later we will show why that might happen), your return will fall below the expected 7 percent. There is some small risk.

Now imagine that, throwing caution aside, you purchase the common stock of a company that plans to franchise Tofu Burger restaurants. Perhaps the burgers will equal fried bird in popularity, but the outcome is uncertain. You may hope for a good return, but the reality—and earnings—may be far different. There is some likelihood that the actual return will differ from what you expected. The Tofu Burger investment carries considerable risk.

Risk is reflected in our inability to predict an investment's actual return. The more uncertainty about the actual return, the higher the risk. As risk increases, the range of possible returns on the investment widens, and the actual future returns become less certain.

Measuring investment risk

One measure of risk is the **variability of future returns.** That measure is based on joint consideration of two factors: range of possible returns and likelihood that each possibility will occur. One way to visualize the first component is to plot all of the expected outcomes on a line that runs from positive to negative. Investments with virtually no risk plot as a single point. With one outcome, you know with certainty what the actual result will be. When a small amount of risk is added, the investment develops a range of possible outcomes but they cluster. As risk increases, the range widens until—at higher risk levels—possible returns range from pleasantly positive to dishearteningly negative.

The second graph component shows the likelihood of a particular future return occurring. If a particular return has only a faint possibility of happening, it needs to be considered but its importance is lessened. Returns that are very likely to occur are weighted more heavily when judging an investment's risk.

Variability of future returns will be our measure of risk in this chapter. Exhibit 14.1 uses the two components—range of returns and likelihood of a return occurring—to develop a risk profile for three different investments. Panel *a* shows a very low risk investment: there is just one future return, which is known with near certainty. Panel *b* shows a low-risk investment; there are several possible returns, all closely clustered, so the actual return is still reasonably predictable. Panel *c* shows an investment with still more risk. Possible returns cover a range (one is even negative), and the actual outcome is uncertain.

Risk Profiles of Three Different Investments

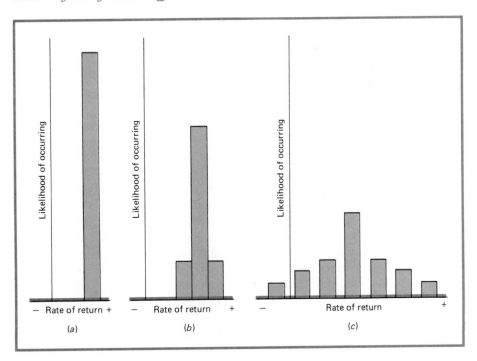

What Causes an Investment's Future Return to Vary?

General economic conditions

There are many **reasons why returns vary,** but they all fall into one of three categories. General economic factors affect many investments. There are also factors that are unique to that particular investment. Finally, changes in interest rates affect many lending investments.

General economic conditions are those which affect many investments. Factors which are negative for the overall economy tend to be negative for investments, but the degree differs. Ownership investments, for example, are usually highly sensitive to general economic factors.

When the overall economy is expanding, borrowers have the resources to repay their obligations. Individuals have money to repay their debts, government collects the taxes and revenues needed to repay its debts, and companies sell enough products and services to provide the funds for repaying *their* debts. Ownership investments are likely to prosper. Sales of goods and services are sufficient to earn a return for the owners.

Quite the opposite occurs during economic contractions. Borrowers may have difficulty repaying; that can lower the investment's actual return. Companies do not earn as much, or even lose money, depending on the severity of the recession. The net effect is to reduce the actual return on many investments.

Factors unique to a particular investment

There are always **factors unique to a particular investment** that can alter its return. For example, a change in health practices, demographics, or increased competition might mean a much lower occupancy than expected in the new hospital wing. If management has borrowed heavily to build the wing, it may have trouble making payments. Or a company's new product line may be poorly received. Plummeting sales may seriously affect the company's ability to repay loans. Owners may find their returns have vanished.

Of course, these unique factors can be positive as well as negative. Heavy demand for a new product or service, a sharp increase in tax revenues, improved income for a group of individuals, all can positively affect returns.

The more sensitive an investment is to such effects—whether positive or negative—or the more numerous the unique risk factors are, the wider the investment's range of possible returns. That means greater risk.

Changes in market interest rates

Interest rates in the financial markets vary greatly over time. In part, these shifts in **market interest rates** reflect changes in the relative demand for loans compared to the supply of funds. Interest rate changes are also partly a result of changes in expectations regarding inflation; more on this later. But we are less concerned with why it happens than with how a change affects lending investments. Unless the borrower encounters financial difficulty, a bond that promises 10 percent should return that amount. But if the bond is sold before maturity, the return will not necessarily be 10 percent. Let's see what **interest rate risk** is and why it occurs.

Suppose Fran pays $1,000 for a bond that has a $1,000 face value, promises 10 percent interest, and matures in 20 years. During each of those 20 years the borrower promises to pay $100 interest. Regardless of whether interest rates in the financial markets rise or drop, the bond pays the fixed rate of $100 annually. At maturity, the borrower will pay Fran the $1,000 face amount. But during those 20 years the bond's price may not stay at $1,000.

Suppose interest rates rise to 15 percent on this type of bond. At 15 percent, a new $1,000 face-value bond will pay $150 annually. Stan, who does not own a bond right now but is considering one, has two choices: he can pay $1,000 for a new one and receive $150 annually, or buy Fran's bond (assuming she wants to sell) and receive $100 per year. He will not offer Fran $1,000 because her bond pays $50 less in annual interest, though both will pay $1,000 at the end. Stan will be willing to pay about $687 for Fran's bond. At that price, his return from the annual $100 interest payment along with the $1,000 at the end is about 15 percent. Since the returns are identical, the bonds are comparable. Point number one: the market price of most lending investments moves in a direction opposite to the movement of prevailing interest rates—as rates rise, prices decline. Since new investments are offering more, the price of old ones has to come down to make them competitive. Conversely, as interest rates drop, the price of existing lending investments generally rises.

These price changes can alter your return. If an investment's market price drops, your return will fall if you sell at a loss. Had its price risen because interest rates dropped, your actual return would rise if you sold at a gain. Even Treasury securities carry some interest rate risk. Granted the Treasury will almost certainly make all interest payments on time, but a change in interest rates can alter the security's market price.

Are there fixed-return investments without any interest rate risk? Yes. The issuer will redeem some at full face value; there are no gains or losses, since price is constant. Savings accounts and CDs are examples. When an investment's maturity is very short—e.g., less than 60 days—interest rate risk is minimal.

Strategy

Most fixed-return investments carry some interest rate risk.

Longer maturities entail more interest rate risk. We are going to add a second bond to the 20-year, $1,000 bond that paid 10 percent interest. It has the same $1,000 face value and 10 percent interest but matures in only 2 years. Suppose prevailing market interest rates on 20-year and 2-year bonds like these rise to 15 percent. Both sample bonds pay $50 a year less than new ones. But there is a great difference in how much the holder loses. You suffer a $50 shortfall for only 2 years on one, but $50 for each of the next 20 years on the other. It takes a far larger price concession to compensate for the extra 18 years. The 2-year bond's price will drop to $919 versus $687 on the 20-year one. If there were a third bond with a 10-year maturity, its price would be $749. Point number two: the longer the maturity of a fixed-return investment, the greater the change in price for a given change in market interest rates.

Fixed-return investments with long maturities carry more interest rate risk. Your potential loss or gain is greater with a long maturity.

Strategy

Shifting to a fixed-return investment with a longer maturity generally exposes you to more interest rate risk.

RISK-RETURN TRADE-OFF

Up to this point we have not made risk seem very appealing. Does it have any redeeming features? Yes. Investors are rational, risk-averse creatures. Given a choice, they will opt for less risk. If they must accept more risk, they want a higher rate of return. High-risk borrowers have to pay more to

Exhibit 14.2

Trade-Off between an Investment's Risk and Its Return

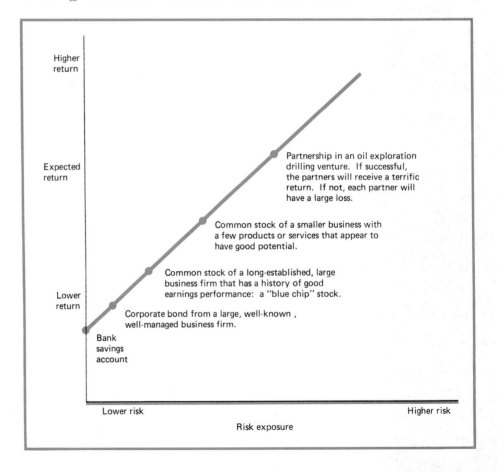

obtain a loan. Likewise, ownership ventures involving considerable risk will have to promise more return to attract investors. That points up the **risk-return trade-off:** in return for risk, an investment should promise a higher return.

Exhibit 14.2 illustrates the risk-return trade-off. Risk is on the horizontal axis; moving to the right increases risk. The vertical axis plots an investment's expected return. Five representative investments are plotted to show how the trade-off might operate. A savings or money market account from an insured bank or S&L carries virtually no risk, so it plots on the vertical axis; with that low risk comes a low return. Next comes a high-grade corporate bond. Its likely outcomes are clustered, but there is some risk; to compensate, it provides a higher return. Further out on the line comes a quality common stock. It holds more risk, so its return rises accordingly. The trade-off continues as we move to still higher-risk ventures.

By connecting the points in Exhibit 14.2 we create a line representing the risk-return trade-off between investments.

Strategy

An investment that promises a higher rate of return generally involves more risk.

COMPOUND RATE OF RETURN

An understanding of **compound rates of return** is basic to intelligent investing, so let's look into the subject. The basic principle of compounding is that all money that stays in an investment will earn a return in the next period. Any future balance in such a compounded investment consists of three parts: (1) your initial investment, (2) the return that initial investment earned, which was then reinvested, and (3) the return on the money

that was reinvested. Over a period of years the contributions of the second and third can be major.

Exhibit 14.3 illustrates the mechanics of compounding. Suppose Jill invests $1,000 in Last Federal Bank at 10 percent interest. During the first year the investment earns $100 (line 1). The interest is reinvested, so the account starts year 2 at $1,100. Earnings for that year are $110—$100 on the initial amount and $10 on the reinvested interest. As the exhibit shows, Jill's year-end balance is $1,210. Interest during the third year is $121; by the next year it's up to $133.10.

Let's move to Exhibit 14.4, where the top line tracks the balance over 20 years. Accumulated interest is important; of the $6,728 final balance, $5,728 is accumulated interest. Note that the line connecting the balances becomes more steeply sloped over time; the balance rises right from the start, but it grows more quickly in later years because the reinvested interest keeps boosting the balance each succeeding year. For example, between years 4 and 5 the account earned $147 interest, but between years 19 and 20 the much larger balance earned $612. Though reinvesting the interest helps throughout, the biggest effect is in later years, when the balance is larger.

Will Earnings Be Different with Simple Interest?

Simple interest works in one of two ways. The investor can decide to withdraw the interest each year, leaving behind only the initial deposit. Or the investment may pay a return only on the initial deposit; subsequent reinvestments earn nothing. The lower line in Exhibit 14.4 shows how the investment performs with simple interest. After 20 years the balance is far less.

Changing the Rate of Return

Does a higher interest rate really matter? Exhibit 14.5 shows the total interest a $1,000 deposit would earn at rates of 7.5, 10, and 12.5 percent. All interest remains in the account and continues to compound for 5, 10, 15, or 20 years. While an extra 2.5 percent return only adds $25 the first year, over 5 years it raises interest earnings considerably. Over 20 years the results are more dramatic; increasing the return from 7.5 to 10 percent—a 33 percent increase—raises total interest more than 75 percent!

Exhibit 14.3

Compound Interest on a Single $1,000 Deposit at 10 Percent Interest

Year	Balance at start of year	Interest for the year at 10 percent	Balance at end of year
1	$1,000.00	$100.00	$1,100.00
2	1,100.00	110.00	1,210.00
3	1,210.00	121.00	1,331.00
4	1,331.00	133.10	1,464.10

Total interest on the 12.5 percent account is nearly triple that on the 7.5 percent investment!

Exhibit 14.5 shows that improving the return increases earnings: the longer the investment remains, the larger the gain.

Strategy

Because compounding significantly raises your return and total earnings, it should be a major consideration in your investment strategy.

Exhibit 14.4

Comparison of Long-Term Return on $1,000 Invested at 10 Percent Compound Interest and 10 Percent Simple Interest

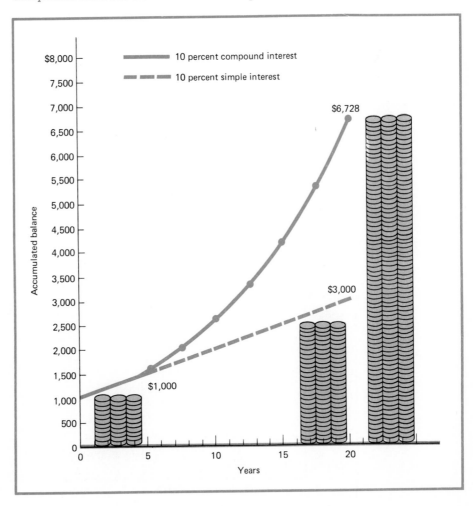

Compounding More Than Once Each Year

Investments that pay returns more than once a year have a greater potential for compounding. Suppose the return on a $1,000, 10 percent investment is split; 5 percent is paid after 6 months, and the remaining 5 percent after another 6 months. You have $50 to reinvest after 6 months. During the second 6 months you earn another $50 on your initial $1,000 and $2.50 on the $50 you reinvested: $50 reinvested interest × 5%. Earnings total $102.50 for the year, so your effective return on the $1,000 is 10.25

Exhibit 14.5

Interest Earned on a $1,000 Investment at 7.5 Percent, 10 Percent, and 12.5 Percent Interest Rates

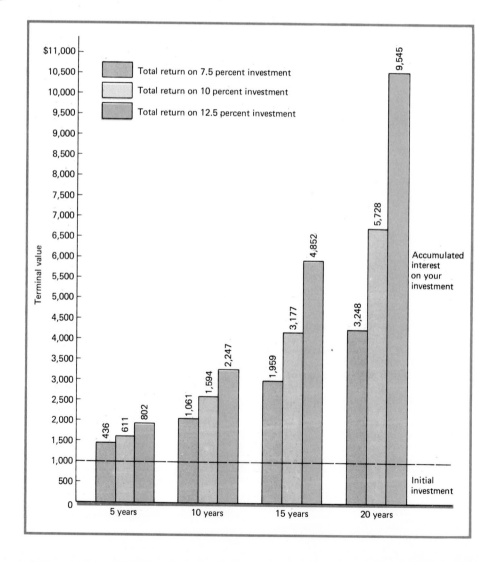

percent: $102.50 interest/$1,000 initial amount. If the 10 percent is paid out in 2.5 percent blocks so it can compound quarterly, the return is 10.38 percent.

The **more frequently a return is compounded,** the higher the **effective rate of return.** Exhibit 14.6 confirms that.

Strategy

The effective annual return is a good measure for comparison of investments since it reflects the frequency of compounding.

COMPOUND RATE OF RETURN TABLES

At times you may want to estimate what the future balance of an investment will be after it has compounded for a period of years. Or you may want to know what amount you must deposit today to reach a future goal. The **compound rate of return tables** in Appendix A.3 and A.4 can help you.

Compound Rate of Return Table: Single Investment

The table in Appendix A.3 shows the future value of a **single lump-sum deposit** of $1 invested today. (The $1 figure is used because you can easily use it to calculate other amounts.) Several assumptions are made in constructing A.3. First, the $1 is deposited immediately; it earns interest the first year. Second, no additional deposits are made. Third, all interest is reinvested, and additional interest is earned on it. Finally, the amounts shown are approximate since all interest factors are rounded to two decimal places.

The table in Appendix A.3 covers interest rates from 1 to 18 percent. They are displayed at the top of the table. Investment periods running from 1 to 40 years are shown at the side.

Future value of an investment

We have reproduced part of Appendix A.3 in Exhibit 14.7; the exhibit shows values for interest rates from 5 to 12 percent and time periods from

Exhibit 14.6

Effective Annual Rate of Return for Different Compounding Periods

Stated rate of return	Effective Annual Percentage Rate of Return When Interest Is Compounded:				
	Annually	Semiannually	Quarterly	Monthly	Daily
5%	5%	5.06%	5.09%	5.12%	5.13%
6	6	6.09	6.14	6.17	6.18
7	7	7.12	7.19	7.23	7.25
8	8	8.16	8.24	8.30	8.33
10	10	10.25	10.38	10.47	10.52
12	12	12.36	12.55	12.68	12.75
14	14	14.49	14.75	14.93	15.02
16	16	16.64	16.99	17.23	17.35

1 to 5 years. Suppose you plan to invest $501 today and leave it for 5 years; you expect to earn 8 percent, and all interest will be reinvested. From Exhibit 14.7 or A.3, we know that $1 will grow to $1.47. The figure for our $501 investment is simply 501 times greater, or $736.47: $501 investment × 1.47 factor @ 8% for 5 years.

Strategy

Appendix A.3 can be modified to compute the future value of any dollar amount that is deposited immediately and left to compound.

What about fractional rates? You can readily modify Exhibit 14.7 or A.3 for fractional interest rates. Suppose your $501 investment promised 8.25 percent. You can interpolate by taking one-fourth of the difference between 8 and 9 percent. Our $501 investment would grow to $745.24: $501 investment × [1.47 factor @ 8% for 5 years + (0.25 × (1.54 factor @ 9% − 1.47 factor @ 8%))].

Required investment to meet future goal

Appendix A.3 can also be used to estimate what you need to invest today to reach some future goal. Suppose your intent is to accumulate $4,200 in 5 years. The investment will earn 7 percent. Since Exhibit 14.7 is at hand, we will use it. At 7 percent over 5 years, $1 grows to $1.40. If we divide our goal ($4,200) by the interest factor, we can compute the required initial deposit. For the example, the required deposit is $3,000: $4,200 target/1.40 factor @ 7% for 5 years. By interpolating, fractional interest rates can be handled as well.

Strategy

Appendix A.3 can be used to compute how large an initial deposit is needed to reach some future amount.

Estimating an item's future price

You can also use a compound rate of return table like Exhibit 14.7 or A.3 to estimate the effect of inflation. Assume Alex wants to know what inflation will do to the price of a house that currently costs $80,000. He expects annual inflation to average 5 percent. During the first year the

Exhibit 14.7

Future Value of $1 Invested Immediately and Left to Compound at Different Interest Rates

| Investment period (years) | Value of Investment When Rate of Return Is: | | | | | | | |
	5%	6%	7%	8%	9%	10%	11%	12%
1	1.05	1.06	1.07	1.08	1.09	1.10	1.11	1.12
2	1.10	1.12	1.14	1.17	1.19	1.21	1.23	1.25
3	1.16	1.19	1.23	1.26	1.30	1.33	1.37	1.40
4	1.22	1.26	1.31	1.36	1.41	1.46	1.52	1.57
5	1.28	1.34	1.40	1.47	1.54	1.61	1.69	1.76

price of the house rises to $84,000. The second year's price rise is 5 percent of that $84,000, not of the original $80,000. In other words, the math for inflationary effects is just like the math for compound interest; this means Alex can use Exhibit 14.7 or A.3 to estimate the future price of the house. The projected price of the house in 5 years is $102,400: $80,000 price × 1.28 (5% factor in Exhibit 14.7).

Compound Rate of Return Table: Equal Annual Investments

Not all investments involve a one-time deposit. In fact, we stress the importance of continued annual investments to achieve future goals. The compound rate of return table in Appendix A.4 is designed to handle this situation. Again the $1 was used to make the table flexible. We assume that $1 will be invested every year. Our second assumption is that the $1 is deposted at the *end* of each year. Third, all interest is reinvested and continues to earn additional interest. As before, the amounts are approximate, since factors are rounded to two decimal points.

Appendix A.4 covers interest rates from 1 to 18 percent—they are displayed across the top of the table. Time periods ranging from 1 to 40 years are shown down the side. Let's take a look at several uses for A.4.

Future value with annual investments

The Appendix A.4 table can be used to compute an investment's future value when there are **equal annual deposits.** For convenience, Exhibit 14.8 reproduces a section of A.4: interest rates range from 5 to 12 percent with investment periods of 1 to 5 years. Suppose we plan to invest $100 annually over the next 5 years and expect to earn 7 percent. Exhibit 14.8 or A.4 shows that $1 saved annually at 7 percent compounds to $5.75 in 5 years. Our proposed $100 would become $575; $100 annual investment × 5.75 factor @ 7% for 5 years.

Strategy

Appendix A.4 can be used to compute the future value of a series of equal annual deposits that are left to compound.

By interpolating, you can use A.4 to find the value of a fractional interest rate as well. Want some practice? What is the future value of $100

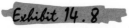

Exhibit 14.8

Future Value of $1 Invested Each Period and Left to Compound at Different Interest Rates

Investment period (years)	Value of Investment When Rate of Return Is:							
	5%	6%	7%	8%	9%	10%	11%	12%
1	1.00	1.00	1.00	1.00	1.00	1.00	1.00	1.00
2	2.05	2.06	2.07	2.08	2.09	2.10	2.11	2.12
3	3.15	3.18	3.21	3.25	3.28	3.31	3.34	3.37
4	4.31	4.38	4.44	4.51	4.57	4.64	4.71	4.78
5	5.53	5.64	5.75	5.87	5.98	6.11	6.23	6.35

deposited annually for 5 years if it earns a 7.5 percent return? Your answer should be $581:

$$\$100 \times \{5.75 + [0.5 \times (5.87 - 5.75)]\}$$

Required annual deposit to achieve a target amount

There are times when you know where you want to go—the target amount—but need to compute what it would take to get there—the required annual deposit. Suppose the target is to have $6,960 at the end of 4 years. Equal end-of-the-year deposits will be made during that time, and they will earn 10 percent. Deposit $1 per year for 4 years at 10 percent and both the A.4 table and Exhibit 14.8 show you will have $4.64. If we divide our target amount by the interest factor for the rate and time period chosen, we find that the required annual deposit is $1,500: $6,960 target/4.64 factor @ 10% for 4 years.

Strategy

Appendix A.4 can be used to compute the required annual deposit needed to achieve some future dollar goal.

INFLATION AFFECTS YOUR REAL INVESTMENT RETURN

If it has been a while since we priced an item, the price tag provides a vivid reminder of inflation's toll. Inflation also affects the return on investments, but more subtly. The money market fund that promises 6 percent on our $100 will no doubt pay that, but our **real rate of return** will not be 6 percent if inflation raises prices. Suppose that, while our account grows to $106, inflation averages 3 percent. Last year's $100 item will now cost $103. It takes $3 of our $6 return just to break even. The real return is closer to 3 percent: ($6 return − $3 inflation loss)/$100 investment. An easier approximation is:

Real return = promised return − inflation rate

For this example:

6% promised return − 3% inflation rate = 3% real return

It is not hard to imagine a real return dropping to zero or even being negative in times of high inflation such as the late 1970s and early 1980s.

Strategy

When making your investment decision, you should consider the prospects for inflation. Ignoring this factor can leave you poorer.

Annual inflation rates: A historical perspective

During the years since 1967, inflation has averaged about 6 percent. But as Exhibit 14.9 confirms, the rates have been volatile. Some years the rate has been 3 percent or less. Others have produced rates of 12 to 13 percent. As this is written, rates have been reasonably low for 3 to 5 years. There is no guarantee they will remain so. With the possibility of higher future rates, inflation will likely remain an important concern in investment decisions.

Lending Investments: Hedging against Inflation

Because the rate of return on many lending investments is fixed, their real return is sensitive to changes in the inflation rate. Several things can be done to protect such investments against inflation. First, concentrate on investments whose return is set by the supply and demand forces in the marketplace. Avoid those whose rate of return is regulated or limited. That is now much easier since most investments have been deregulated. Second, an investment's return should include an **inflation premium** to offset future inflation. If inflation rates are expected to rise, investors should seek returns that compensate. Third, during periods of rising or unsettled inflation, avoid lending investments with long maturities, since they lock in

Exhibit 14.9

Annual Percentage Increase in Consumer Prices and Purchasing Power of a 1967 Dollar

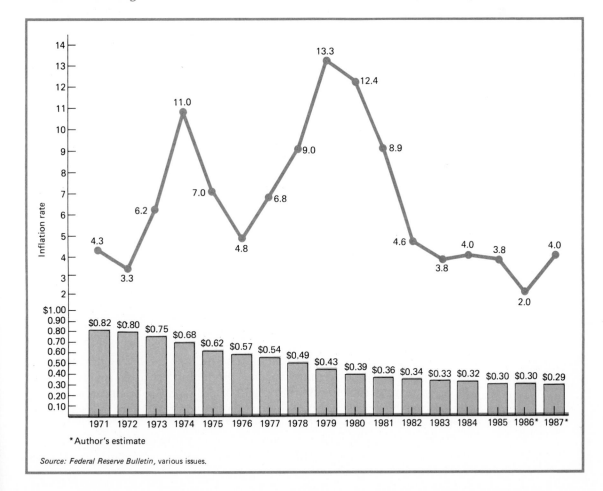

fixed rates for an extended time. Even if there is a premium, inflation may end up higher than anticipated and your real return will suffer.

Strategy

During periods when inflation is rising or the economic outlook is unsettled, limit the maturity of lending investments to 5 years or less.

Shifting to a variable return

As inflation eased after the early 1980s, lending investments with variable returns became scarcer. It may take another bout of double-digit inflation to rekindle interest. Nevertheless, a variable return is a good way to hedge against inflation. As long as the return is tied to some index that reflects conditions in the financial markets, your real rate of return is likely to remain positive. As inflation rises, the rate on a variable return instrument increases. When inflation turns down, so does the return. Your real return will probably stay positive. However, when inflation falls, your real return may not increase, as it would if you had locked in a high fixed rate.

Strategy

Lending investments with a variable rate of return offer a decided advantage when the inflation rate is volatile or increasing. Under these conditions, they protect your investment's real return.

Real returns on lending investments: A historical perspective

During periods when inflation has risen sharply, real returns have fallen. In periods of declining inflation, quite the opposite has occurred: real returns have been very positive. When figures for the periods of acceleration and the periods of deceleration are averaged, we see that the real return on most lending investments has been positive.

Fixed-rate lending investments are best when inflation is stable and low. Even high but stable inflation rates can be handled if investors demand a sufficient inflation premium to keep the real return positive. Stability is the key.

Strategy

Careful selection of fixed-return lending investments is essential when inflation rates are volatile or increasing.

Ownership Investments: Hedging against Inflation

Theoretically, ownership investments should fare far better during inflationary periods, because many income-producing ventures involve assets whose value may rise. In addition, as all prices rise, the business should be able to raise its prices. Even though expenses will rise, there still should be a residual left to enhance the owners' return.

Take a duplex apartment building as an example. First, the worth of the unit should rise as inflation pushes up prices. If prices in general double, then the unit's price should do likewise. As prices in general move up, the rents can be raised if they are not controlled. Though operating and maintenance expenses will rise, there should remain a residual to provide a return to the owners. Increases in value and earnings should allow the owners to keep a positive real return.

Has the reality of ownership investments paralleled the theory? Yes and no. Many real estate ventures and smaller businesses have fared reasonably well during inflationary periods. Real returns have generally remained positive. This has not been the case with the common stocks of larger businesses and some smaller ones. Here real returns did not hold up; some dropped to near zero, while others turned negative.

What can we conclude from this mixed picture? As a class, ownership investments are not a panacea during periods of high or volatile inflation. However, though their record is imperfect, ownership investments still deserve serious consideration. Over longer periods, often spanning a cycle of moderate to high to moderate inflation, their average real return has been positive. Second, note that timing ownership investments to avoid periods of high inflation is difficult. Often those investments have performed best during the earlier stages of a decline in inflation; if you wait to invest until a decline is well documented, you often miss the best returns. Third, ownership investments have historically provided the highest returns, albeit with considerable risk. If you seek higher returns and can accept the risks, ownership investments remain the choice. Finally, ownership investments should generally be looked upon as long-term. Selling out just because inflation may worsen can mean liquidating the investment just at the point when it begins offering a reasonable return.

CRITERIA FOR EVALUATING INVESTMENTS

We will use **six criteria to evaluate specific investments:** (1) risk exposure, (2) rate of return, (3) minimum maturity, (4) minimum dollar investment, (5) tax features, and (6) flexibility, or liquidity. These criteria can help you decide whether a particular investment is suitable. The appendix at the end of the chapter summarizes the 6 criteria for many popular investments.

Risk Exposure

Our measure of **risk exposure** is the variability of the investment's likely future returns. The more scattered those returns, the higher the risk.

Rate of Return

Calculations of an investment's annual **rate of return** should include all sources: interest, dividends, rents, capital gains, and capital losses. Some investments, such as savings or money market accounts, have a single return source: interest. Others, like common stock or rental real estate, may derive their return from several sources. Unless noted otherwise, all rates are quoted on an annual basis.

Deregulation of financial institutions

Once, regulatory agencies set the return on some investments; savings accounts and CDs were prime examples. Agencies set rate ceilings limiting the return a financial institution could pay; the institution could always pay less but never more. The ceiling was often far below prevailing market rates.

Legislation passed in the early 1980s phased out those ceilings. Investors no longer have to accept below-market rates on savings accounts, money market accounts, and CDs. Does that mean all such accounts pay competitive rates? No. That is why comparison shopping is essential. Forces of supply and demand in the market now establish the going interest rate. Financial markets establish the return on nearly all lending and ownership investments.

Minimum Maturity

The maturity of many lending investments is set when they are sold, and the borrower specifies when the investment will be redeemed at its full face value. If you want (or need) to sell before then, the borrower usually will not redeem the instrument. However, financial institutions are an exception. They will redeem the investment, often a CD, before its maturity date, but they charge a penalty for doing so. On some investments the maturity is essentially open-ended: the investor decides whether to hold them weeks, months, or years.

An investment's **minimum maturity** is the shortest time it must be held in order for the investor to receive the promised rate of return. There are several reasons for stressing minimum rather than maximum maturities:

1. The time horizon on many financial goals is 1 to 5 years. A suitable investment should often have a similar maturity.
2. Some investments are strictly temporary. The money will be used in the near future but is invested to earn a return until needed.
3. Investments with shorter maturities are subject to less interest rate risk.
4. Investments with short maturities tend to be more flexible. They can be liquidated quickly. And you can "splice" a series of them together to cover a longer period.

We group maturities into three categories: short-term is 1 year or less, intermediate-term from 1 year to 10, and long-term more than 10 years.

Minimum Dollar Investment

On many investments, a **minimum dollar amount** is specified for the initial purchase. In some cases subsequent deposits are allowed, but there may be a limit there also. For a small investor with modest capital, these limits narrow the range of available investments.

Even without a limit, the commission you pay to buy and sell can make investing small amounts unattractive. Suppose the minimum fee to purchase is $35. Invest $5,000, and the fee is manageable; it is only 0.7 percent of the initial amount: $35 fee/$5,000. On a $500 purchase, the fee becomes very burdensome; it is 7 percent of the initial amount ($35/$500); you will have to earn a 7 percent return just to break even. Furthermore, there may be a similar fee when you sell, further lowering your return.

Strategy

When you must pay a commission to buy and/or sell, consider how seriously it will affect your return.

Tax Features

Our discussion of the **tax features** of investments concentrates on federal income taxes; state income tax regulations are so diverse that they cannot be covered. The key issue is whether part, all, or none of an investment's return is subject to federal income taxes. Prior to the sweeping Tax Reform Act of 1986, the tax treatment of investments varied. Now, a more uniform treatment is law: nearly everything is subject to tax. Those investments that receive favorable tax treatment tend to be totally exempt.

The higher your marginal tax rate, the more important taxes are to your investment decision. At the highest rates, taxes can be a deciding factor.

Flexibility, or Liquidity

Flexibility (liquidity) is measured by the ease with which an investment can be converted to cash. One criterion is the time it takes to sell: if this can be accomplished quickly, that adds to flexibility. A second criterion is the cost of converting the investment to cash: if this cost is low, that adds further flexibility. Combine the two—quickly convertible at a low cost—and you have a highly liquid investment.

The precise avenue for converting investments to cash varies. For those the issuer or borrower will redeem at face value at any time, it's straightforward. All you do is ask that the investment be redeemed. Generally it's quick, and there is little or no cost. Savings accounts, money market mutual funds, and money market accounts are examples.

The issuer or borrower will redeem other investments on demand, but at less than face value. You may be charged a penalty, or your return may be reduced. While redemption is reasonably fast, a price concession is required. These investments are less flexible than the ones in the previous group. Examples include CDs from financial institutions and savings bonds.

On inflexible investments, the issuer usually will redeem the security only at its final maturity date. Sales before then have to be handled in the secondary market. Transactions in the secondary market involve investments or securities that were sold at some point in the past, and buyers such as other investors or dealers willing to purchase the security. Let's use an example—a Zug corporate bond owned by Don Swift—to show how this works. Zug will redeem the bond at its $1,000 face value in 5 years—when it matures—but not now. Don will have to sell the bond in the **secondary market.** If it's a "good" secondary market—lots of buyers and sellers of similar securities—Don can sell his bond quickly. His price, however, may not be the $1,000 face amount, particularly if the bond's interest rate is lower than the rate on comparable new bonds. Don will also pay a commission to sell the bond, and that fee reduces the flexibility of the investment. Examples of this type of investment are common stocks, corporate bonds, and many municipal bonds.

What if the secondary market is poor—few buyers and sellers? Then Don may have to cut the bond's price to attract a buyer. And the quicker he wants to sell, the larger the price concession he will have to give. Owners of highly specialized investments must often make sizable price concessions to find a buyer. Examples of this type of investment include limited partnerships and municipal bonds issued by small government units.

DEVELOPING YOUR OWN INVESTMENT STRATEGY

Early on we noted that "making a bundle" may sound nice, but it's tough to do. There is no single investment strategy that fits everyone's needs. Indeed, you should develop a strategy to meet your specific objectives. Let's look at the major steps you must take to do this.

Define the Purpose of Your Investment

A good starting point as you begin to shape your strategy is specifying in detail precisely what you want to do and why you are undertaking a particular investment. You will want to cover such things as dollar amounts, expected time horizon, consequences of not achieving the goal, and desired rates of return.

Strategy

Developing specific guidelines for what is expected from an investment can help you select a suitable one.

Decide Your Risk-Return Tolerance

More risk may increase the return, but this does not mean everyone should push way out on the risk-return trade-off line. Many will not be comfortable with high-risk investments. Decide what risk you want and can be comfortable with. As your circumstances change, reevaluate whether you can deal with more risk.

Strategy

Select a risk-return position that makes you comfortable; there is no sense losing sleep worrying about your investments.

Match an Investment to the Financial Goal

Often financial goals will have characteristics that suggest which investments would be suitable. If you have the necessary funds to do so, you may well want to select specific investments for each goal. Forcing a single investment to serve all purposes rarely is a good idea. Its maturity may not parallel the goal's, or you may find yourself settling for less flexibility than is needed.

Strategy

Selecting specific investments for each financial goal is the most effective way to match the instrument with the desired outcome.

Alter Your Strategy as Needed

Be ready to revise your investment strategy as your circumstances change. As your financial assets increase, new options may appear. You may be more tolerant of risk during some periods than at others. We are not suggesting whosesale shifts every few months, but there is no need to view your current strategy as etched in stone.

Strategy

Review your investment strategy on a regular basis to see if it should be changed.

Consider the Investment Alternatives

New investment alternatives will continue to be introduced, and if the past several years are an indication, the volume will be large. In the past, one could often settle on one or two investments and continue to use them for most needs. But the current range of options suggests you may be better served by a continuing search for suitable investments. You do not have to be on the latest investment wave; straddles, strips, butterflies, hedges, options, and other similar alternatives are best left to experts. But a continuing review of what is available is likely to be worth the effort.

Strategy

Keep current on your investment options; it takes work, but there can be financial rewards.

Summary

1. The two basic investment options are lending money to a borrower or sharing ownership in an income-producing venture.
2. Most lending investments have a fixed rate of return and a set maturity date; however, returns of some are tied (indexed) to some interest rate in the financial markets.
3. The return on an ownership investment depends on the success of the underlying venture; there is neither a lower nor an upper limit on the return.
4. Potential returns on an investment include interest income, cash dividends, income from the business, rent, and capital gains (or capital losses).
5. Risk is measured by the degree of variability in the possible future returns on an investment.
6. The more variable an investment's likely return, the higher its risk.
7. Factors that can cause an investment's future return to vary include general economic conditions, those factors unique to the investment, and changes in prevailing market interest rates.
8. When prevailing market interest rates rise, the market price of many fixed-return investments declines; the risk that this will happen is referred to as interest rate risk.
9. Most investments require a risk-return trade-off. The higher the return, the higher the risk.
10. When an investment provides a compound return, its earnings are automatically reinvested so that they can earn a return in the next period.
11. When the earnings on an investment are left to compound, the annual earnings will increase over time; earnings are significantly larger in the later years than in the early years.
12. The more frequently an investment's earnings are compounded, the higher its effective rate of return.
13. The compound interest tables in Appendix A.3 can be used to compute the future value of a single lump-sum deposit; those in Appendix A.4 can be used to compute the future value of a series of equal deposits.
14. Deducting the annual inflation rate from an investment's actual return provides an approximation of its real rate of return.
15. Historically, the real rate of return on lending

investments has often dropped to zero or become negative during periods of high inflation.

16   In theory, ownership investments should provide a better hedge against high inflation. Experience shows that some have done reasonably well, while others have fared poorly.

17   The criteria that determine the suitability of an investment include: risk exposure, rate of return, minimum maturity, minimum dollar investment, tax features, and flexibility.

18   Developing your own investment strategy entails:
   ■ Defining the purpose of the investment
   ■ Deciding your tolerance for risk
   ■ Matching the investment to your goals
   ■ Altering your strategy as needed
   ■ Considering the investment alternatives

Review your understanding of

Lending investments
Fixed return
Fixed maturity
Variable return
Ownership investments
Interest income
Dividend income
Business income
Rent
Capital gain
Capital loss
Long-term gain or loss
Short-term gain or loss
Risk
Variability of future returns
Factors affecting return
   General economic conditions
   Factors unique to investment
   Market interest rates

Interest rate risk
Risk-return trade-off
Compound rate of return
Frequency of compounding
Effective rate of return
Compound rate of return tables
   Single lump-sum deposit
   Equal annual deposits
Real rate of return
Inflation premium
Investment evaluation criteria
   Risk exposure
   Rate of return
   Minimum maturity
   Minimum dollar amount
   Tax features
   Flexibility, or liquidity
Secondary market

Discussion questions

1   Are small investors likely to find investment planning more or less challenging than they did 10 years ago? Why? In your opinion will the challenge increase or abate over the next decade?

2   List several popular investments that derive most of their return from annual interest and dividend income. List several that rely heavily on capital gains.

3   If you wanted a steady, predictable return, would lending or ownership investments be the choice? Why?

4   What measure can be used to describe risk on an investment? Sketch a risk profile like the ones in Exhibit 14.1 for a CD, a 20-year Treasury bond, and the common stock of a company that produces software for personal computers.

5   Sidney recently paid $1,000 for a Slug Corporation bond; the bond's face value is $1,000, it matures in 10 years, and it pays 10 percent interest ($100) annually. Shortly after Sidney bought the bond, market interest rates rose to 12 percent. What is likely to happen to the price of the bond? If Sidney holds it for the 10 years, what will his "stream of payments" from Slug look like?

6   Jan recently purchased 100 shares of stock in Silent Six Sedans, "motor cars for the discriminating few." List several broad factors in the economy that might affect the stock's return. Would these factors affect other common stocks? List several unique factors that might affect the stock. Will other stocks be affected by these?

7   Stan Steady and Quincy Quickbuck have been discussing where investors should be on the risk-return trade-off line in Exhibit 14.2. Quincy maintains that "thinking" investors should push far out the line. Stan counters that "rational" investors should cluster near its origin. Which of them is right? Why?

8   What is the major difference between the compound interest table in Exhibit 14.7 and its counterpart in Exhibit 14.8? Describe a situation in which the use of each might be appropriate.

9   Why is it important to determine how often an

investment's return is compounded? Why does the effective rate rise with the frequency of compounding?

10 Is an investment's real rate of return likely to be higher or lower than its promised return? What events of recent years have raised

investor awareness of the importance of real returns?

11 Which will fare better when inflation is rising: the real return on a fixed-return investment or that on an ownership investment? Why?

Problems

14.1 Fred Bear wants to accumulate an $8,000 down payment to purchase a vacation retreat in about 10 years. During that time he expects to earn 8 percent on the money.
   a If Fred deposits equal amounts at the end of each year, how large will the deposit have to be? (*Hint:* Appendix A.4 may help.)
   b If Fred does not begin deposits until 3 years before he buys the retreat, what will he have to save in each of those years?
   c Which alternative would you suggest? Why?

14.2 Chris Wing has three investment options for her $4,000 cash reserve:

	Option 1	Option 2	Option 3
Interest rate	6	6	8
Frequency of compounding	Annual	Daily	Daily

   a If the entire $4,000 is deposited immediately, how much interest will Chris earn during the next year under each of the options?
   b Which account would you recommend?
   c Which option probably has the highest risk?

14.3 Antone and Susan VanderMullen want to accumulate a $6,000 down payment for a house; the house they want currently costs $60,000. They expect to earn an 8 percent return during the 7 years it takes to save the 10 percent down payment.
   a If they make equal annual deposits, how much will they have to save each year?
   b A realtor suggested the price of houses will likely rise 5 percent each year. If a house currently costs $60,000 what will it cost in 7 years? (*Hint:* Appendix A.3 can be used here just as if this were a $60,000 investment earning 5 percent.)
   c Assuming prices do rise 5 percent a year, how much money will it take to make a 10 percent down payment in 7 years on a house that currently costs $60,000? If they make equal annual deposits, how much will they have to save each year to accumulate this new down payment? Why is this amount different from your answer for part (a)? Which is more realistic?
   d Why does the projected 5 percent price rise have such a large impact?

14.4 Shawn York is considering the two Ajax Corporation bonds detailed below:

Bond	Maturity	Price	Annual interest payment	Interest rate	Value at maturity
A	1 year	$1,000	$80	8%	$1,000
B	10 years	1,000	80	8	1,000

   a What annual dollar return will bond A pay? What will bond B pay?
   b Assume that the interest rates on new bonds comparable to the Ajax bonds increase to 10 percent. On a new 1-year bond, what annual dollar income would an investor receive? What would the annual income be on a new 10-year bond?
   c Why will the price of bond B decline more than that of bond A? [*Hint:* Compare the annual incomes over the lives of the two bonds.]

14.5 Carmine Cautious is considering three lending investments:

	Investment 1	Investment 2	Investment 3
Current rate of return	10%	9%	9%
Future return	Fixed	Fixed	Variable*
Maturity	10 years	2 years	3 years

* Interest is recomputed every 6 months; rate is based on the rate for 2-year U.S. Treasury securities

All have similar risk, require the same minimum dollar purchase, and have comparable flexibility. Carmine is concerned about future inflation.

  a If Carmine expects the inflation rate will be reasonably stable and average 4 percent over the next 10 years, what is the expected real rate of return for each investment? Which one would you advise she choose? Why?

  b If Carmine thinks the annual inflation rate will be volatile—high for several years followed by several years of moderate rates—which one would you advise she choose? Why?

14.6 Loretta Lucky recently won $20,000 in the state lottery. One of her goals is to have a $28,000 retirement fund in 20 years. How much will she have to invest immediately if the money earns 10 percent interest compounded annually?

14.7 Ned Nearterm and Len Longterm both want to accumulate retirement funds:

Saver	Time to retirement	Desired fund balance	Expected rate of return	Required annual deposit
Ned	10 years	$10,000	10%	?
Len	30 years	$30,000	10%	?

  a What annual deposit will each have to make?

  b Both Len and Ned are trying to accumulate about $10,000 every 10 years. Is their annual deposit in part (a) the same? Why or why not? (*Hint:* Carefully consider the amount of interest each will earn.)

14.8 Two banks offer the following Individual Retirement Accounts (IRAs):

Bank	Planned annual investment	Promised rate of return	Period over which investments will be made	Final IRA account balance
Small Town	$1,200	6%	20 years	?
Aggressive	1,200	12	20 years	?

  a How large a balance will each IRA account have after 20 years?

  b After 20 years, what is the total of the annual deposits? How much interest will each account earn?

  c How much would you lose by staying with the Small Town account?

14.9 If you invest $1,000 each year for 7 years and earn 8.25 percent interest, what will the investment be worth after 7 years?

Case problem

Carlos and Carla Zapata both work full-time; their combined annual salary is $33,000. Currently they have $500 in a savings account. Their only debt is an auto loan on one of their two cars. Their other assets are personal items and some furniture.

They have a number of financial goals. First, they would like to accumulate a 10 percent down payment for a $70,000 house. In addition, they would like a new travel trailer and a new boat for their trips on the lake. Of course, they would be able to use the trailer in the winter if they had some ski gear, snowmobiles, and possibly an all-terrain vehicle. They expect they would use these items next year, when Carla is considering cutting back to half time on her job.

Carlos and Carla realize they will have to save more. To do that, they guess they will just have to spend less to leave more for investments. Because their resources are limited, they think it will be essential for them to earn the highest rate of return. They have condensed everything into a single goal: accumulate a "bundle" and do it as soon as possible.

1 Would you suggest any changes in the Zapatas' investment goal? Give some examples of the goals you would suggest. What information would they need to implement your suggestions?

2 What is your opinion of their proposed "savings plan"? Do you suggest any changes?

3 Which of their goals will likely be the easiest to achieve? The most difficult?

4 Would you agree with their goal of earning the highest rate of return? If not, what changes do you suggest?

5 Should Carlos and Carla concentrate on a single investment for all of their goals? What features might differ if they used a separate investment for each goal?

6 If the Zapatas expect to buy a house in 5 years, how much would they have to save each year to have the $7,000 down payment? They expect to make equal deposits and leave the money to compound annually at 9 percent interest.

APPENDIX: SUMMARY OF MAJOR INVESTMENT ALTERNATIVES

Exhibit 14A.1 summarizes six criteria for major investment alternatives. These are the same criteria discussed in the closing sections of the chapter.

Exhibit 14A.1

Summary of Six Criteria for Major Investment Alternatives

Investment	Risk* (1)	1984–1986 Annual return (%) (2)	Minimum maturity (3)
Financial Institutions			
Savings account NOW account	None on insured account	5–7	Immediately redeemable
Money market deposit account; Super-NOW	None on insured account	5–10	Immediately redeemable
Certificate of deposit	None on insured account	6–10	Institution may set minimum
Direct Investments			
U.S. Treasury Securities	No Risk; G-1		
Bills		5–9	90 days to 1 year
Notes		6–12	2 to 10 years
Bonds		8–13	11 years and longer
Corporate notes and bonds	Low to moderate; G-1	9–13 (Aaa) 10–14 (Baa)	Notes 5 to 10 years Bonds 20 to 30 years
Municipal notes and bonds	Low to moderate; G-1	6–10 (Aaa) 7–11 (Baa)	2 to 30 years
Common stock	Moderate to high; G-2	14–15 (G-3)	No set maturity; investor decides holding period
Mutual Funds			
Money market:			
General	Low	6–11	No set maturity; redeemable
U.S. government	Very Low	5–10	by check
Corporate bonds:	G-1 and G-4;		No set maturity
Investment grade	Low	9–13	
Aggressive	Moderate to high	10–14	
Common stock	Moderate to high, depending on fund's objective; G-2	16–17 (G-5)	No set maturity
Municipal bonds,	G-1 and G-4		No set maturity
Investment grade	Low	7–11	
Aggressive	Moderate	8–12	

*General Comments:
G-1 Price will change as market interest rates change.
G-2 Market price subject to wide swings due to changes in the stock market.
G-3 10-year average for broad sample of common stocks. "1986 Mutual Fund Ratings," *Forbes*, Sept. 8, 1986.
G-4 Low if fund buys high-quality bonds [rated A or better]; higher if fund buys lower quality bonds [rated Baa or lower].
G-5 10-year average for broad sample of mutual funds. "1986 Mutual Fund Ratings." *Forbes*, Sept. 8, 1986.

Investment	Typical minimum investment (4)	Tax feature† (5)	Flexibility (6)
Financial Institutions			
Savings account NOW account	No minimum	T-1	Highly flexible; no fees or penalties on withdrawals
Money market deposit account; Super-NOW	Institution can set limit	T-1	Highly flexible, rate may drop on smaller balance
Certificate of deposit	Institution can set limit	T-1	Limited flexibility; interest is reduced as penalty, but institution will redeem
Direct Investments			
U.S. Treasury Securities			
Bills	$10,000	T-2	Can be sold in strong secondary market; commission on sale
Notes	$1,000 or $5,000		
Bonds	$1,000		
Corporate notes and bonds	$5,000	T-1	Can be sold prior to maturity; secondary markets range from strong to weak; commission on sale
Municipal notes and bonds	$5,000	T-3	Can be sold prior to maturity; secondary markets range from moderate to weak; commission on sale
Common stock	$1,000; broker's fee can be prohibitive on small amounts	T-1	Readily salable in good secondary market; commission on all sales
Mutual Funds			
Money market:			Highly flexible; can be redeemed by check
General	$1,000	T-1	at any time; investor decides
U.S. Government	$1,000	T-1	
Corporate bonds:			
Investment grade	$1,000	T-1	Highly flexible; redeemable at any time;
Aggressive	$1,000	T-1	investor decides holding period; no-load fund has no fee; load fund has fee
Common stock	$1,000	T-1	Highly flexible; redeemable at any time; investor decides holding period; no-load fund has no fee; load fund has fee
Municipal bonds		T-3	Highly flexible; redeemable at any time;
Investment grade	$1,000		investor decides holding period; no-load
Aggressive	$1,000		fund has no fee; load fund has no fee

†Tax Features:
T-1 Income is fully taxable for federal and state income tax purposes.
T-2 Income fully taxable for federal income taxes but exempt from state taxes.
T-3 Income is exempt from federal income taxes and from some state income taxes.

CHAPTER 15

Fixed - income investments

AFTER COMPLETING THIS CHAPTER YOU WILL HAVE LEARNED

- Why deregulation has changed how financial institutions set interest rates
- The major investment attributes of savings, share, and money market accounts
- The advantages and disadvantages of savings, share, and money market accounts as investments
- The major investment attributes of a certificate of deposit (CD)
- The advantages and disadvantages of a CD
- The major investment attributes of EE savings bonds
- How a savings bond's variable interest rate operates
- The advantages and disadvantages of a savings bond as an investment
- The major investment attributes of Treasury bills, notes, and bonds
- How selling a Treasury security before maturity can raise or lower its promised return
- The advantages and disadvantages of Treasury securities as investments
- The major investment attributes of corporate bonds
- The advantages and disadvantages of corporate notes and bonds as investments
- The major investment attributes of municipal bonds
- How to decide whether municipal bonds are for you
- The advantages and disadvantages of municipal notes and bonds as investments

*T*he fixed and variable return investments discussed in this chapter share these features:

- You agree to lend a specified sum of money.
- The borrower promises to repay that amount on some date.
- You earn a return on the money that can either be (1) constant (rate fixed at the time of the loan) or (2) variable (return is indexed to some rate in the financial markets).
- The borrower pays interest at regular intervals.

These terms are set when you make the investment.

There are several reasons for making the effort to understand lending investments. First, they appeal to many investors because they carry less risk than ownership. Second, the variety of lending choices is extensive, and a good money manager needs to know what is available. As choices increase, you must tailor your investment to your goal. Finally, your financial plan is likely to involve selecting and managing lending investments. You have to understand the character of lending investments if you wish to make an informed investment choice.

We will concentrate on investments suitable for someone with $500 to $5,000 to invest. Risk will be kept low. Barring a total catastrophe in the financial system, most will provide a stable return.

We will use the six criteria introduced in Chapter 14 to assess the merits and special features of each investment. Then we will evaluate major strengths and weaknesses.

LENDING INVESTMENTS FROM FINANCIAL INSTITUTIONS

Banks, S&Ls, savings banks, and credit unions offer several investment options. Exhibit 15.1 illustrates the process of how they gather funds and loan that money out. The institution gathers funds from investors (on the right). The investors are offered savings accounts, share accounts, money market accounts, or certificates of deposit (CDs) in exchange for their money. The investor receives a return—interest—on that money. The institution's repayment promise backs each savings account, CD, or money market account.

The financial institutions re-lend the money (left side of Exhibit 15.1) and charge interest on the loans. By setting the rates it charges to the borrowers higher than the rates it pays to the investors, the institution earns a return for its services. To understand how rates are set, let's look at rates before deregulation (B.D.) and after deregulation (A.D).

Interest Rates before Deregulation

Prior to 1986, upper limits were set on the rates financial institutions could offer. Under these "interest ceilings," the institutions could pay less interest but not more. In addition, some accounts had dollar minimums, and specific penalties were prescribed for redeeming an investment before maturity. The Depository Institutions Deregulation and Monetary Control

Act of 1980 began to remove these restrictions, and by early 1986 interest rates had been decontrolled.

Interest Rates after Deregulation

Critics predicted that **deregulation** would have dire consequences. Some claimed hordes of investors would descend on institutions and strip them of their deposits. Others claimed that cutthroat competition would drive interest rates sky high. Larger institutions supposedly enjoyed economies of scale which would let them steal investors from smaller institutions. None of the predictions has come true thus far. Financial institutions operate much the same A.D. as they did B.D.

The major reason for deregulation was to let market forces of supply and demand set interest rates. But those supply and demand forces vary, because banks, credit unions, and S&Ls are regional or local, not national. In one area, a bank may experience heavy loan demand, while those in another market have few borrowers. Likewise, some institutions might attract plentiful funds while others are scrambling to meet their needs. Since investors generally want the highest rate of return for a given level of risk, it is vital that they compare competing options.

Strategy

Since interest rates can differ, compare the returns offered by competing financial institutions.

Basis points

Rather than talking in fractional percentages, we will use **basis points** to compare interest rates: 1 percentage point divides into 100 basis points. If a bank offers 0.5 or 1 percent more than a competitor, we say it pays 50 or 100 basis points more.

Exhibit 15.1

Role of Financial Institutions in the Lending and Borrowing Process

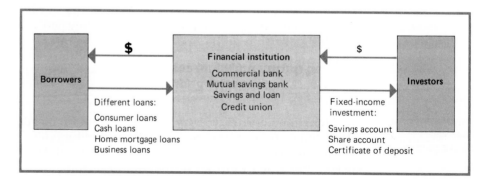

Savings or Share Accounts and Money Market Accounts

Most depository financial institutions offer savings or share accounts, and many offer money market accounts. Traditional savings and share accounts are designed for people with limited funds, while money market accounts were created for individuals with more funds. The two differ in their minimum initial deposit requirements and their withdrawal options.

Savings and share accounts

Nearly all banks, S&Ls, and savings banks offer **savings accounts.** And most credit unions offer **share accounts.** Traditionally, these have been the choice of small investors. An initial deposit of $100 or less will open an account, but if the balance falls below the institution's minimum, there generally is a maintenance fee.

Savings accounts were not deregulated until 1986, so experience with deregulated rates is limited. Since the amount needed to open an account is small, rates are likely to be among the lowest offered to investors.

At credit unions, the basic account is the share account. Rather than interest, you earn dividends on a share account. These accounts have been deregulated for some time, so there is more rate experience. Share accounts frequently offer higher returns than savings accounts, though rates are still low in comparison to other investment options.

Money market accounts

Money market accounts were created during the move to deregulation. But there were government restrictions. You had to have $2,500 to open an account, and if the balance dropped below that, your interest rate was slashed. You could write up to three checks per month against your account without a penalty. The new feature was that money market accounts had no interest ceilings.

Now federal restrictions are gone. Still, some financial institutions have their own restrictions. Most require $1,000 or more to open an account. Some have tiered interest rates: above the minimum balance you receive one rate, but below it you receive the savings account rate. Some even raise the rate as your balance rises; at $5,000 a higher rate starts, at $10,000 a still higher rate. Many still limit you to three checks per month, but you often can make unlimited withdrawals in person.

Strategy

Review a money market account's restrictions and limits to see if they seriously reduce its usefulness or appeal.

Major Investment Attributes: Savings, Share, and Money Market Accounts

To assist you in deciding between savings, share, and money market accounts, Exhibit 15.2 summarizes five of the investment attributes that were introduced in the last chapter. We'll have some additional comments on both rate of return and risk exposure. The sixth attribute, flexibility, is not shown in the exhibit, because it does not lend itself as well as the others to summary in table form. However, we'll comment on it in a separate section below.

Rate of return   In the post-deregulation era, investors need to take an active role in managing lending accounts. They should compare rates to make certain the selected one is competitive. Once an account is established, they must monitor its return, since this can change. Savings accounts require special care; institutions know that many people do not compare returns, and some offer substandard returns.

What is a competitive return? The *Wall Street Journal*, *Barron's*, and *Money* publish lists showing what rate the top institutions in the country are paying (lists appear weekly in the first two and monthly in the last). Consider opening an account with one of these, or use the list to determine current competitive rates.

Strategy

When selecting a savings, share, or money market account, compare returns.

Risk exposure   Risk is minimal when an account is **insured** by one of the federally sponsored programs: (1) the **Federal Deposit Insurance Corporation (FDIC)** for commercial and savings banks, (2) the **Federal Savings and Loan Insurance Corporation (FSLIC)** for savings and loan associations, or (3) the **National Credit Union Agency (NCUA)** for credit unions. If the institution cannot redeem its accounts, the insurance repays up to a maximum for each account: currently $100,000. If you use different ownership combinations ("Mary E. Bass" for one account and "Mary E. Bass joint with Sam T. Bass" for another), each is covered for $100,000. Nearly all institutions have federal insurance, so accept nothing less.

Flexibility   Flexibility is a major strength of savings accounts, share accounts, and money market accounts. The issuer will redeem all or part of your account whenever you ask. Many pay interest right to the day of withdrawal. Even a limit of three checks per month on a money market account is not seri-

Exhibit 15.2

Major Investment Attributes: Savings, Share, and Money Market Accounts

Investment	Rate of return	Risk exposure	Minimum maturity	Minimum* investment	Tax feature
Savings account	Set by market supply and demand.	Zero if insured.	No set minimum.	$ 100	Interest fully taxable.
Money market account	Set by market supply and demand.	Zero if insured.	No set minimum.	2,500	Interest fully taxable.
Share account	Set by market supply and demand.	Zero if insured.	No set minimum.	25	Dividends fully taxable.

* Typical minimum investment; each institution sets its own level.

ous, because you can usually withdraw the needed money in person (assuming it is nearby).

Special Features of These Accounts

Most savings, share, and money market accounts have similar basic features, but in the quest for customers, some institutions have added extra features. These are intended to make the basic account more attractive. Depending on your needs, you may find one or more of these extras attractive.

How is the interest paid?

A good savings, share, or money market account pays interest **from the day the money is deposited until the day it is withdrawn.** Since an account's balance fluctuates as you add and draw funds, you want one that pays interest on your daily balance. Some institutions use the lowest balance for the month or quarter to compute interest. Others base interest on the daily average in your account. All such variations are unacceptable.

In today's competitive environment, look for an account that pays daily interest. Accounts that pay frequent interest *and* add it to your account give you compound interest. The more frequent the compounding, the higher the effective rate. At a minimum, interest should be added every 3 months for quarterly compounding.

Strategy

When comparing accounts, ask the effective annual return after compounding of interest.

Deposit and transfer options

Many institutions will accept deposits by mail; some even pay the postage, which is an advantage if the institution is not close or its hours are inconvenient.

Some institutions let you transfer funds from savings to checking with a phone call. Many will transfer a given amount from your checking account to your savings account each month at your request.

Automatic teller machines (ATMs)

Convenience is the major advantage of being able to access your account through **Automatic Teller Machines (ATMs)** which accept deposits, withdrawals, and transfers 24 hours a day. As ATMs become common, an account from an institution miles away may become as easy and quick to use as a local one.

Advantages and Disadvantages: Savings, Share, and Money Market Accounts

The very features which make savings, share, and money market accounts attractive—flexibility and small initial deposit—contribute to their major shortcoming: low returns. You pay for low risk and flexibility with a low return. Money market accounts require a larger initial deposit, but their rate is often higher.

Strategy

An investor with limited funds (several hundred dollars or less) should consider a savings or share account, but those who have more funds will usually find a money market account a better choice.

Suitable Financial Goals: Savings, Share, and Money Market Accounts

Savings, share, and money market accounts are excellent when flexibility and low risk are required. They are a good place for the emergency cash reserve discussed in Chapter 3. Money for a goal you expect to implement very soon might also be invested here. They can also provide a temporary investment for funds while you decide on a longer-term investment.

Strategy

Savings, share, or money market accounts are best for those who need low risk and high flexibility.

CERTIFICATES OF DEPOSIT

The distinguishing feature of **certificates of deposit (CDs)**—which are provided by the same institutions that offer savings, share, and money market accounts—is their fixed maturity. When you buy a CD, you promise to leave the money on deposit for a set period, from as little as a few days to more than 10 years. You lose flexibility but receive a higher return. As you lengthen the maturity, the return usually rises.

CDs in the A.D. Environment

CDs have been deregulated since about 1983, so there is considerable experience. There can be significant differences in the return offered by different institutions: spreads of 200 or more basis points among similar CDs are not unknown. Picking up an extra 1 or 2 percent interest justifies a search for a competitive rate.

Earlier regulations limited the maturities of CDs, and some institutions never threw away the rules. You can buy a 24-month CD, or a 36-month . . . but 33 months! Are you trying to make our job difficult? Others seized the opportunity and now offer any maturity from 1 to 101 months.

Look.. I don't mind promising to leave the money in the Certificate of Deposit until it matures... ..but can we dispense with "Cross your heart and hope to die"?

Major Investment Attributes: Certificates of Deposit

Exhibit 15.3 summarizes five of the six investment attributes for CDs; the table can help you decide whether a CD is appropriate for your circumstances. Of the five, rate of return and risk exposure require further comment. Prior to deregulation, return on most CDs was uniform; now that institutions have greater freedom to set the rates, investors have to be more selective. We'll also discuss the sixth attribute, flexibility.

Rate of return

Investor choice was easy in the B.D. environment. Because they had no interest flexibility, institutions had to find other means to attract customers: an electric blanket or cookware gave you a choice between a warm bed and a warm dinner. Now institutions can set their rates, but few offer the investor a handout. Still, a careful study of competing rates can give you a payoff of 50 to 200 basis points. Some guidelines follow.

Developing a "benchmark" rate. You can determine a "fair" return for a CD in several ways. To establish your **benchmark rate,** call institutions in your area and check rates. Or check the rate on a Treasury security with the same maturity as your desired CD; they should pay about the same rate. (Rates on Treasury securities are published in the *Federal Reserve Bulletin,* the *Wall Street Journal,* or *Barron's,* and they are available in most libraries.)

You can also check the listings of "top" CD rates in the *Wall Street Journal, Barron's,* and *Money.* Each highlights the better returns paid on CDs for a sample of maturities. The institution and sometimes its phone number are provided. Such a list serves two purposes. It tells you whether the CD rate Old Lost Hope Bank is offering is competitive. And it allows you to contact one of the listed institutions to see if it accepts out-of-state customers.

Strategy

A benchmark interest rate helps you determine whether a CD's return is competitive.

Effective return is a good comparative measure. Suppose one CD's interest rate is 8.5 percent, but a competing one offers 8.85 percent. Which is better? No, it's not a "Who's buried in Grant's tomb?" question. If interest on the first CD is compounded daily, its **effective return** is 8.87 percent. If the other CD compounds annually, its effective return is 8.85 percent.

Exhibit 15.3

Major Investment Attributes: Certificates of Deposit

Rate of return	Risk exposure	Minimum maturity	Minimum investment	Tax feature
Set by market supply and demand	No risk if insured	30 days	$500	Fully taxable

The 8.5 percent CD is better. This confirms our earlier point: compare returns by using the effective annual return after all compounding. If the institution cannot or will not tell you what that rate is, look elsewhere.

Strategy

Use the effective return after compounding as the standard of comparison for CDs.

Variable rate CDs. One drawback of a fixed-rate CD is that rising interest rates can leave you earning a substandard return, particularly if the maturity is long. Many investors ended up in this position during the high inflation of the late 1970s and early 1980s. Once they had learned the disadvantage of fixed rates, investors shied away from the offerings. Financial institutions introduced **variable rate CDs** in response.

When inflation abated, so did variable rate CD offerings. That is unfortunate, since they fill a real need when interest rates are rising or highly volatile. Tying returns to some interest rate in the financial markets keeps investors from being "locked in."

An example will illustrate. Suppose Barb buys a 3-year fixed-rate CD offering 8 percent. Fran buys a variable rate 3-year CD that starts at 8 percent but will have its rate reset monthly. If interest rates rise to 9 percent the next month, so will Fran's CD, but Barb will be stuck at 8 percent. When interest jumps to 10 percent a month later, Fran will see her return rise, but Barb will be stuck. Barb is hardly going to feel that a fixed-interest CD is a bargain. But what if rates dip to 7 percent the first month and 6 percent the second? Fran's CD is going to head down as quickly as it went up, and now Fran will doubt her choice.

When can a variable rate CD be a good choice? First, when interest rates are rising or unusually volatile. Second, when the maturity is long, say longer than 5 years. Third, when you do not want to be locked into some rate.

Strategy

Consider a variable rate CD if interest rates are rising or are exceptionally volatile, or if you want a rate that tracks the market.

Risk exposure   CDs purchased from an institution insured by the FDIC, FSLIC, or NCUA carry negligible risk. Coverage is limited to $100,000, but that is rarely a problem. Insist on an insured CD; the insurance costs you nothing, and most institutions carry it.

Flexibility   Two features make a CD flexible. First, the institution that issued the CD will redeem it prior to its maturity date. Second, there is no fee or commission to redeem. But there is usually an interest penalty for early redemption.

Caution: interest penalty ahead. Institutions charge a penalty—specified as a number of days' or months' interest—**if you redeem a CD before maturity.** Usually, the longer the CD's maturity, the more severe the penalty.

Before deregulation, there was a standard penalty for each maturity; an institution could charge more but not less. Those set minimums have been abolished: institutions can charge what they want.

An example will illustrate how an early redemption penalty can reduce return, even cause a loss. Take a sample $1,000 CD that has an 18-month maturity and promises a 12 percent return. The penalty for early redemption is 3 months' interest. Assume the CD is redeemed after 10 months; earned interest will be $100: $1,000 investment × 12% rate × (10 months/12 months). But the penalty is $30: $1,000 investment × 12% rate × (3 months/12 months). After the penalty, only $70 of interest remains. Actual return is only 8.4 percent [$70/$1,000 investment × (12 months/10 months)], not the promised 12 percent.

If the CD were redeemed after only 2 months, you would actually lose money. Interest earned would be $20: $1,000 × 12% rate × (2 months/12 months). But the penalty would be $30. The investor would receive $990 of the original $1,000 back. Mark that an experience!

Avoiding early redemption

You can avoid interest penalties with good planning. Do not select a maturity longer than the period for which you expect to hold the CD. Selecting a 5-year CD when you expect to need the money in 3 years is poor planning. Always check a CD's penalty *before* you buy. A 30-day penalty is about the minimum, 90 days is severe but probably acceptable, 6 months is unacceptable.

Strategy

Choose a CD with a maturity you can accept, or invest in a money market account. If there is a possibility you might have to redeem early, look for a minimum penalty.

But suppose the unexpected happens and you must redeem your CD before its maturity. Do you have an option? Yes. You can borrow the money you need until the CD matures. Some institutions will use the CD as collateral for a loan so you do not have to redeem it. Borrowing is often the best choice if the CD has 12 months or less to maturity.

To decide whether to borrow or to redeem the CD, you need two figures. First, compute your net interest (interest earned minus the penalty) if you redeem. We computed this in the last section, so let's continue with the 18-month, 12 percent, $1,000 CD example. When we redeemed the CD after 10 months, the net interest was $70. Now compute how much interest you would receive if you did not redeem the CD but borrowed the money. Over 18 months our sample CD will earn $180, ignoring compounding. Under this option you will not redeem the CD, so you will have to borrow $1,000.

If the loan carries a 14 percent rate and you repay in a lump sum at the end (you repay the loan using the money from the maturing CD), your finance charge for the 8 months will be $93.33: $1,000 loan × 14% finance charge × (8 months/12 months). After paying the charge, $86.67 of the CD's interest remains: $180 interest − $93.33 finance charge. Borrowing is better than redeeming the CD early and receiving only $70 of interest.

Strategy

Borrowing is best when your net return (CD interest minus loan finance charge) exceeds the after-penalty interest by redeeming the CD early.

Special Points to Consider

There are several special points that you should consider when purchasing a certificate of deposit.

Consider an out-of-state institution

In the B.D. environment, comparison shopping for CDs yielded better cookware but little more. Looking to invest outside the immediate area offered little benefit, since financial institutions did little recruiting of non-local customers. The CD market was essentially regional.

Deregulation changed that. Now aggressive institutions seek customers by advertising in major newspapers. Many have toll-free numbers. The lists of CD rates in the *Wall Street Journal, Barron's,* and *Money* have also encouraged investors to broaden their horizons. The CD market is becoming national. Most CDs are still purchased locally, but it is now much easier to look outside an area.

Should you consider an out-of-state CD? Yes, if it offers more. CDs require little ongoing management. If you buy one and hold to maturity, you hardly need an office nearby. If you have questions, you can call (it's a toll-free number, in many cases). Since buying a CD often means investing a sizable amount for an extended period, an extra 50, 100, or 150 basis points on the return can be significant.

Look for an institution with FDIC, FSLIC, or NCUA insurance. You should also compare the effective annual rate after compounding; it should be higher than local rates. Finally, a toll-free number is a plus.

Renewal of the CD when it matures

Several weeks before a CD matures most institutions send a notice asking what you want done. Do nothing, and the CD will probably renew for a similar term to maturity, with the new interest rate based on what the institution is currently offering. If the CD is renewed, you may have 7 to 10 days during which you can cancel without penalty, but after that you pay an interest penalty to redeem it.

If you decide to renew a CD, make sure its interest rate is competitive. If it is not, you may want to shift to a different institution.

Strategy

Monitor your maturing CDs to avoid an automatic renewal for an inappropriate maturity or at a substandard rate.

Advantages and Disadvantages: Certificates of Deposit

Exhibit 15.4 lists advantages and disadvantages of CDs. Most entries are self-explanatory, but the rate of return deserves a comment. The return on a good CD is competitive with rates on other low-risk investments and probably almost matches the return on a Treasury security with a similar maturity. Interest ceilings no longer prevent institutions from offering competitive returns, but they often fail to do so. Careful selection of a CD ensures a competitive return, reasonable compounding, reasonable penalties, and a workable initial investment.

Suitable Financial Goals: Certificates of Deposit

With their wide range of maturities, CDs can match the time horizon of most financial goals, but they are especially useful for goals that will be implemented in 1 to 5 years. A little searching should uncover a CD whose minimum dollar amount is not unduly large, and many investors find their very low risk appealing.

U.S. SAVINGS BONDS

Series EE savings bonds are sold to individuals by the Treasury. They are designed for small investors: minimum investment is $25. The Treasury also offers a specialized savings bond called Series HH, but when we say *savings bond*, we mean Series EE.

Major Investment Attributes: U.S. Savings Bonds

Exhibit 15.5 summarizes five of the six investment attributes which were introduced in the last chapter for savings bonds. Of these, rate of return and risk exposure require some additional comments. The sixth attribute, flexibility, requires a more detailed discussion. The combination of all six

Exhibit 15.4

Advantages and Disadvantages: Certificates of Deposit

Advantages	Disadvantages
Widely available.	Interest penalty if redeemed early.
Initial deposit is small for most.	Sizable minimum investment required for some.
Risk is near zero if insured.	
Variable rates offered on some.	
Interest rates set by forces in the financial markets.	

Exhibit 15.5

Major Investment Attributes: Series EE Savings Bonds

Rate of return	Risk exposure	Minimum maturity	Minimum investment	Income tax features
Variable with a 6% floor.	None.	At least 5 years to earn promised rate of return.	$25	Fully taxable at federal level; tax can be deferred. Exempt from state and local income taxes.

should help you compare the merits of savings bonds with those of competing investments.

Rate of return   Instead of paying interest directly, savings bonds are sold at a discount. The difference between the purchase price and a bond's face value is the return. Purchase price is presently one-half the bond's face value: a $100 bond costs $50, a $500 bond costs $250, etc. In about 12 years a bond is worth its face value.

The interest rate on savings bonds is variable: 85 percent of the return on a 5-year Treasury security. Because the rate is reset to the average Treasury return every 6 months, the return varies. The return on savings bonds responds to the same market forces of supply and demand that affect the underlying Treasury securities. To provide investors some rate assurance, the bonds guarantee a 6 percent return—there is an interest "floor."

Let's use Phil Patriotic's $100 savings bond as an example to demonstrate how the floor works. Suppose 5-year Treasury securities currently offer 8 percent. Since 85 percent of that is 6.8 percent (exceeding the 6 percent floor), that is Phil's rate. If the 5-year rate dropped to 7 percent, 85 percent of it would be only 5.95 percent, Phil's rate would be the 6 percent minimum.

To receive the promised return, Phil has to hold the bond at least 5 years. If he redeems it early, he receives less than 6 percent. The shorter his "hold," the lower his interest rate.

Risk exposure   Savings bonds are backed by the full faith and credit of the U.S. government, so risk exposure is negligible.

Tax features   Interest on savings bonds is exempt from all state and local income taxes but is fully taxable for federal income tax purposes. But you have two options for reporting the interest:

1   Include part of it in income each year and pay taxes on it.
2   Defer the interest until you redeem the bond. Then the entire return is included as income that year, and you pay tax on it; this method is widely used.

The second option's main attraction is that it defers the income until a time when your marginal tax rate will possibly be lower. It has a disadvantage, too: the income is concentrated into a lump sum. If the earnings are large enough, they can boost your tax rate.

Flexibility   Savings bonds can be redeemed through banks, S&Ls, credit unions, savings banks, and Federal Reserve banks. There is no secondary market where they are traded, but there is no fee for redeeming them.

Savings bonds are reasonably flexible. But there are several drawbacks. You cannot redeem a bond unless you have had it 6 months. Furthermore, if you redeem before 5 years, the penalty cuts your return significantly; the bond's minimum maturity has to be considered 5 years. They are not short-term investments.

Strategy

Plan to keep your series EE bonds at least 5 years. If you expect to redeem before that, consider another investment.

Advantages and Disadvantages: U.S. Savings Bonds

Exhibit 15.6 summarizes the major advantages and disadvantages of savings bonds. Most of the table entries are self-explanatory, but rate of return and the tax deferral feature deserve comment. While the indexing of the return on savings bonds is an attractive feature, we need to provide some additional guidelines so you can judge just how attractive it is. Likewise, the tax deferral feature is frequently touted as a major advantage. Yet it may be oversold at times. Our discussion will show why.

Rate of return

Savings bonds would be more attractive if their rate were indexed at 100 percent, rather than 85 percent, of the 5-year Treasury return. An insured CD carries no more risk than a savings bond, but may offer a better return. And the maturity can be much less than 5 years.

Strategy

Before purchasing a series EE bond, compare its return to what a comparable, insured CD offers; the CD may be better.

We have fewer reservations about savings bonds if interest rates are rising or volatile. Then the savings bond's variable rate is an advantage. It may be worth sacrificing some return for a rate that will track market interest rates.

Strategy

A savings bond is at its best when interest rates are rising or highly volatile.

Option to defer income taxes

Taking the option to defer federal income taxes on the bond's interest can be advantageous. The key is whether your marginal tax will be lower when you must declare the interest income. If it will be, deferral is attrac-

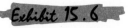

Exhibit 15.6

Advantages and Disadvantages: Savings Bonds

Advantages	Disadvantages
Virtually risk-free.	Limited rate of return.
Available in small denominations.	Rate may not be competitive with rate on comparable CD.
Maturity is automatically extended; interest payments continue.	Sizable interest penalty for early redemption.
Tax on interest can be deferred.	
Variable interest rate can be attractive, at times.	

tive. But take Yvonne Yuppie, whose career and earnings are rising nicely and are likely to continue doing so. Deferring postpones the tax pain. But in a few years Yvonne's tax rate will be higher, not lower. A municipal bond may be a better investment than savings bonds: more on this later.

<table>
<tr><td>Suitable Financial Goals: U.S. Savings Bonds</td><td>The lengthy maturity of savings bonds makes them suitable for long-term financial goals. They work best if the goal will not be implemented for 6 or more years. But even for long-term goals, CDs are often a good substitute for savings bonds. Risk is no higher, and they may provide a higher return. Also, you can obtain maturities far shorter than the effective 5-year minimum for savings bonds.</td></tr>
</table>

Suitable Financial Goals: U.S. Savings Bonds

The lengthy maturity of savings bonds makes them suitable for long-term financial goals. They work best if the goal will not be implemented for 6 or more years. But even for long-term goals, CDs are often a good substitute for savings bonds. Risk is no higher, and they may provide a higher return. Also, you can obtain maturities far shorter than the effective 5-year minimum for savings bonds.

U.S. TREASURY SECURITIES

There are three major types of fixed-income **U.S. Treasury securities:** bills, notes, and bonds. They are targeted to investors with more funds, carrying denominations from $1,000 to $10,000. All three securities are readily marketable. The Treasury will not purchase a bill, note, or bond before maturity, but you can sell it to another investor through the well-developed secondary market for these instruments.

Treasury Bills

Treasury bills have maturities of 91, 182, and 364 days. The minimum purchase is $10,000, but the Treasury will readily accept *much* more. These are discount instruments, so you pay less than face value. As with savings bonds, the difference between what you pay and the face amount constitutes your return. The 91- and 182-day bills are sold weekly; 364-day bills are sold monthly.

Treasury Notes

Treasury notes have maturities of 2 to 10 years, beginning where bills stop. Minimum purchase is $1,000 if the note's maturity exceeds 4 years and $5,000 if it is less. Notes pay interest every 6 months, so when you purchase a new note your cost is about the face value. The shorter maturities are offered more frequently than the longer ones.

Treasury Bonds

Treasury bonds have maturities longer than 10 years; 20- and 30-year bonds are common. Minimum purchase is $1,000, and the bonds pay interest twice yearly. Presently legislation limits the issuance of bonds, so new bonds are sold less frequently than new notes.

Major Investment Attributes: Treasury Securities

Exhibit 15.7 summarizes five of the major investment attributes introduced in the last chapter for Treasury bills, notes, and bonds. Of these five, rate of return and risk exposure require additional comment. Since both return and risk are affected by a shift in market rates, the impact of such a shift needs to be discussed. The sixth attribute, flexibility, is also discussed.

Rate of return

Treasury bills, notes, and bonds are sold in the open financial market, so their interest rates are set by supply and demand. If the supply of new securities is large and the demand by investors limited, interest rates rise to attract buyers. If there are numerous prospective investors but a limited supply of new securities, the Treasury can lower the interest rate.

Shifts in supply and demand can cause large swings in interest rates. Exhibit 15.8 plots the interest rate on 3-year notes from late 1985 through 1986. The spread between the highest and lowest rate during the period approaches 3 percent. Rates changed direction a total of four times. Recently, interest rates on Treasury securities have been volatile.

Generally speaking, the longer the maturity, the higher the interest rate. Sometimes, however, the relationship is negative. Some question the logic of maturities beyond 10 years if the return is only slightly higher. As the section on risk stresses, long maturities subject you to considerable interest rate risk.

Strategy

Maturities beyond 10 years should only be considered if you expect interest rates to be stable or drop, you have a definite need for a long maturity, and the added return for accepting extended maturity is at least 150 to 300 basis points.

Risk exposure   Treasury securities are backed by the full faith and credit of the federal government, so the default risk on bills, notes, and bonds is near zero. But securities with longer maturities carry interest rate risk.

Recall that **interest rate risk** arises because changes in market rates cause a security's price to move the opposite way. That is beneficial when rates drop, since your securities rise in value. But if rates rise, the securities are worth less. And the longer the maturity, the larger the security's price drop. The investor who sells when rates are climbing will suffer a loss unless the security is held to term. Hold to maturity, and you avoid the direct loss, but even then you have a loss because you received a return that was less than prevailing market rates.

Strategy

By choosing instruments with maturities in the 2- to 5-year range, you can reduce interest rate risk.

Exhibit 15.7

Major Investment Attributes: Treasury Bills, Notes, and Bonds

Rate of return	Risk exposure	Minimum maturity	Minimum investment	Income tax features
Rate set by market forces of supply and demand.	No risk of default; there is interest rate risk.	Bills: 91 days. Notes: 2 years. Bonds: 11 years.	$10,000 $1,000/$5,000 $1,000	Fully taxable at federal level; exempt from state and local taxes.

Flexibility   You can quickly sell a Treasury bill, note, or bond in the secondary market. But the brokerage firm or bank that handles the sale will charge a fee. If interest rates have been stable since you bought it, the sale price should be the same as what you paid for the security. If they have risen, you get less. If they have dropped, you may be able to get more.

**Special Points
to Consider**   There are several points about Treasury securities that need to be reviewed. In particular, the purchase procedure for new Treasury securities is somewhat different from that for any of the other investments we'll discuss in this chapter.

Exhibit 15.8

Interest Rates on 3-Year U.S. Treasury Notes, October 1985 to December 1986

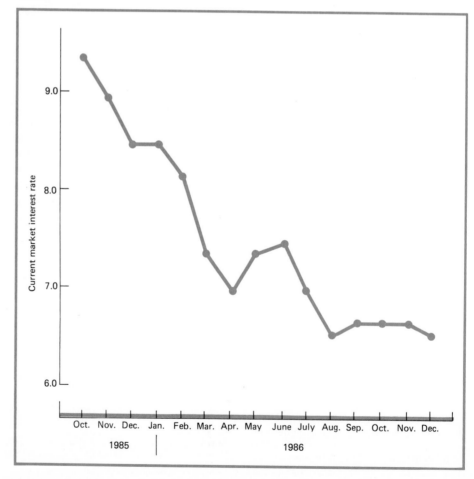

Purchasing in the primary market

The Treasury sells its new bills, notes, and bonds at auction. The auction is announced 1 to 2 weeks before it takes place; during that time you can submit a bid through any Federal Reserve bank or branch. The *Wall Street Journal* and the financial sections of many metropolitan newspapers carry announcements of forthcoming **Treasury auctions.** Rather than submit a bid with a specific interest rate, most individuals submit noncompetitive bids: you offer to accept the average interest rate on all accepted competitive bids. This is the easiest route for novice investors. If you write your nearest Federal Reserve bank, they will send a booklet explaining how to bid.

Purchasing in the secondary market

Up to now we have portrayed the **secondary market** as a place to sell a security, but you can also buy there. You can only buy through a bank or broker, so there is a commission.

Comparable securities carry about the same interest rates in the secondary and primary markets. There is no added return. You can, however, buy immediately, without waiting for a Treasury auction. And the selection is wider, since it includes most Treasury securities that have not matured.

Redemption of treasury securities

Treasury bills are redeemed automatically at maturity; the investor receives a check directly from the Treasury. For notes and bonds, the investor must send the security to the nearest Federal Reserve bank shortly before it matures. Send it by certified mail so there is a receipt.

Strategy

Treasury notes and bonds pay no interest beyond the maturity date, so submitting them several weeks before maturity is important.

Advantages and Disadvantages: Treasury Securities

Exhibit 15.9 shows the principal advantages and disadvantages of Treasury securities. The exemption from state and local income taxes deserves comment. Individuals with a high marginal state or local income tax rate may find the tax exemption raises their return above what a fully taxable CD delivers.

Exhibit 15.9

Advantages and Disadvantages: Treasury Bills, Notes, and Bonds

Advantages	Disadvantages
Interest is exempt from state income tax.	Sizable minimum purchase.
Risk is essentially zero.	Considerable interest rate risk on longer maturities.
Rate of return is set by market supply and demand.	Interest rates can fluctuate widely.
No fee to submit a noncompetitive bid.	New issues are offered only at specific auction times.
Strong secondary market allows sale before security matures.	Fees lower return on small purchases in the secondary market.
	Investor effort to buy and redeem is moderately high.

Suitable Financial Goals: Treasury Securities

Several features make Treasury securities ideal for financial goals that will be implemented in 1 to 10 years. Given their low risk, your actual return will equal the promised return unless you sell before maturity. Their wide range of maturities means they can be used to meet most goals. Last, the strong secondary market for Treasuries ensures the investor a quick sale if necessary, though at the prevailing market price.

There are also several hurdles. Minimum dollar amounts are high. Infrequent auctions mean following announcements to find the security you want. Commissions to buy and sell in the secondary market can markedly reduce returns on small investments.

Strategy

Treasury securities work best for investors who have (1) sizable amounts to invest, (2) high marginal state or local income tax rates, (3) time to monitor forthcoming auctions, and (4) the need for a low-risk investment.

CORPORATE BONDS

Regardless of what product or service corporations provide, most borrow money to finance their operations. Selling **corporate notes and bonds** is a common way they do this. By selling to many investors—who become the lenders—the firm can raise sizable amounts of money, even if each investor buys just a few bonds. Buyers range from individuals who buy a few thousand dollars worth to pension funds that buy millions.

Convention defines *a note as an instrument that matures in 10 years or less, a bond as one that matures in more than 10*. The interest rate is generally fixed and set in advance as is the specific day, month, and year when the note or bond matures. A few corporate bonds have carried variable rates, but this is not usual. Standard practice is to pay interest twice a year. At maturity, the corporation promises to redeem the bond at its face amount, usually $1,000.

What can a bondholder do if the interest or face amount is not paid promptly? Even if the corporation is unprofitable, it must pay, and bondholders can take legal action to force payment. In a worst-case scenario, the firm could be forced into bankruptcy; its assets would be sold to repay its debts. Bondholders and creditors have to be fully repaid before the firm's common stock owners receive anything. Such defaults rarely happen. The majority of firms pay the interest on time and redeem their debt instruments at maturity. Concentrate on quality bonds to assure timely repayment.

Major Investment Attributes: Corporate Bonds

Exhibit 15.10 lists five of the six investment attributes of corporate notes and bonds (we use *bond* for both notes and bonds) introduced in the last chapter. Rate of return needs further comment because both the quality of the note and its maturity can have a significant effect. Risk exposure requires further review to explain how the ratings issued by the major rating services can be used to judge the quality of a note or bond. Flexibility, the sixth attribute, is also discussed.

Rate of return   Interest rates on corporate bonds are established by supply and demand. Bonds compete not only with other corporate bonds but with other lending investments as well. Bond interest rates depend heavily upon the bonds' maturity and perceived quality (risk). The greater the perceived risk, i.e. the lower the quality, the higher the return. Generally, the longer the bond's maturity, the higher its return.

Risk exposure   Risk on corporate bonds ranges from low to moderately high. On a high-quality bond, the range of possible future returns will cluster about the promised return. You might receive slightly less than promised. On medium-quality bonds, the range of possible returns is larger, and your actual return is more likely to vary from the one promised. For lower-quality issues, the range of possible outcomes is even more variable, and there is a possibility that actual returns will differ from the promised ones.

A corporate bond's actual return depends heavily on the success of the corporation. To judge a bond's quality, you have to analyze the factors that can affect the firm's success, and that's difficult, time-consuming, technical, and sometimes uninteresting. There is good news: bond-rating agencies have done the work for you.

Bond-rating services. Moody's and Standard & Poor's (S&P) are two highly regarded agencies that grade the quality of bonds. They review the issuing firm's strengths and weaknesses, what is happening in its industrial sector, how it compares to the competitors, and other factors.

The two rating systems are not identical, though they are quite similar; the **quality grades assigned by Moody's** differ somewhat from the **quality grades assigned by Standard & Poor's.** Exhibit 15.11 summarizes the top six quality grades used by each of the services. Investors willing to assume some risk might select bonds in any of the top four grades, but those who are averse to risk should limit themselves to the top two grades. As expected, returns fall as quality rises. Investors who can tolerate moderate to high risk might concentrate on the fourth and lower grades, where returns are higher.

Exhibit 15.10

Major Investment Attributes: Corporate Notes and Bonds

Rate of return	Risk exposure	Minimum maturity	Minimum investment	Income tax features
Rate set by market supply and demand forces.	Low to moderate; rating agencies provide quality grades.	3–5 years	$5,000	Interest and capital gains fully taxable.

Diversify your holdings to lower risk. Few corporations encounter serious financial difficulty, but it can and does happen. When it does, the firm's bondholders can suffer consequences ranging from a minor drop in return to losing most of their initial investment. As a protection against such experiences, investment professionals suggest **diversification—** splitting investments among 5 to 10 different bond issues. Then if one of the corporations encounters financial adversity, you have some protection against severe losses. You are applying the old adage: Don't put all of your eggs in one basket. Diversification becomes more important as quality drops, since low-rated bonds are more likely to be subject to financial difficulty.

But diversification has its costs. Buying a number of issues at $5,000 a crack adds up to *big* bucks quickly. Adding more bond issues means more work to select, purchase, and track the investment. Finally, diversifying is often more effective if you select industries with different economic cycles; that means more work to select suitable issues.

Flexibility

The corporate bonds of large firms generally have a good secondary market. You pay a commission to sell, but you can sell prior to maturity. The price will, of course, be determined by conditions in the financial markets. If interest rates are now higher than the bond's coupon rate, the price will be less than face value. When current rates are less than what the bond offers, the investor may sell for a profit. Sales commissions and swings in market value limit the flexibility of corporate bonds.

Bonds from smaller corporations have a less active secondary market. Selling may take some effort. And the bond's price may be less than in a strong market. For very small companies, the secondary market can be nearly nonexistent. The less robust the secondary market, the less flexible the bond. Not only are there sales commissions and lower prices, the lack of investor interest may depress prices even further.

Exhibit 15.11

Summary of Quality Grades Assigned by Major Bond-Rating Services

Moody's		Standard and Poor's	
Rating	*Description*	*Rating*	*Description*
Aaa	Best quality	AAA	Highest grade
Aa	High quality	AA	High grade
A	High medium grade	A	Upper medium grade
Baa	Lower medium grade	BBB	Medium grade
Ba	Possessing speculative elements	BB	Lower medium grade
B*	Generally lacking characteristics for desirable investment	B*	Speculative

* Both agencies have grades lower than B. They are not shown here because only an aggressive investor should consider such low-quality bonds.

Strategy

Flexibility of corporate bond investments is reduced by selling fees, swings in market price, and weak secondary markets; plan to hold bonds to maturity.

Advantages and Disadvantages: Corporate Bonds

Exhibit 15.12 outlines the principal advantages and disadvantages of corporate bonds. Most entries in the table are self-explanatory, but the "investor effort" requires further comment. All of the investments discussed thus far have had very low risk. With corporate bonds you have to decide your risk tolerance. Having done that, you still have to decide which bond you will buy; and with a $5,000 minimum purchase the number will be small. You must continually monitor the bond's quality rating for possible downgrading.

Suitable Financial Goals: Corporate Bonds

Given the range of quality, there should be a corporate bond that parallels your risk preference. Furthermore, the return rises with the level of risk, important for someone seeking a higher return. With a $5,000 minimum purchase, corporate bonds are only suitable when the dollar amount for the underlying financial goal is large.

Individual corporate bonds are investments for a select group. The minimum dollar amount and the need to diversify mean that the buyer must be someone with considerable resources. The work of selecting and monitoring bonds demands a fairly sophisticated investor who has the time and energy for background and detail work. Many investors do not fit this profile. If corporate bonds attract them, they may be better served by a corporate bond mutual fund; more on this in Chapter 17.

Strategy

Individual corporate bonds are best for a moderately sophisticated investor with a fair amount to invest.

Exhibit 15.12

Advantages and Disadvantages: Corporate Notes and Bonds

Advantages	Disadvantages
Investors can select from a range of risk levels.	Minimum purchase is typically $5,000.
Bonds and notes are assigned a quality grade by rating agency.	Lower-quality issues carry significant risk.
Most notes and bonds are rated by Moody's or S&P's.	Adequate diversification requires $25,000 to $50,000.
Larger issues have good secondary market where bond can be sold.	Fee to purchase or sell issue can reduce the promised return.
	Investor effort to buy and redeem is moderately high.

MUNICIPAL BONDS	**Municipal bonds and notes** are issued by municipalities, states, housing authorities, airports, and other governmental agencies. The securities generally have a fixed interest rate, which is set at the time they are issued, as are their maturities, which range from a few months to 30 years. *Remember, notes have a maturity under 10 years, and bonds over 10.*

General Obligation Securities

Municipalities, states, and other agencies that have authority to assess and collect taxes issue **general-obligation securities.** Money collected from taxes is used to pay the interest and redeem the securities at maturity. The authority to levy taxes backs the securities; most are rated as medium- to high-quality.

Revenue Securities

Revenue securities are issued by an agency that uses the money to build and operate some special project or facility. Revenues from the project or facility pay the interest and redeem the security at maturity. For example, a municipality might issue a sewage revenue bond to build a new disposal plant. Users of the plant pay fees, and the fees are used to pay interest and redeem the bonds.

However, if the user fees prove insufficient, the municipality probably will *not* levy a tax to pay off the bonds. Payment of the interest on a revenue bond and the bond's redemption at maturity depend on the ability of the underlying project to generate revenues. The quality of these securities is directly related to the prospects of the project or facility they finance.

Major Investment Attributes: Municipal Bonds

Exhibit 15.13 summarizes five of the six major investment attributes introduced in the last chapter for municipal securities. Of these five, three need additional comment. First, we need to examine how supply and demand factors affect the return on municipal securities. Second, we need to outline the steps you can take to judge the quality of a municipal security. Finally, the special tax features of municipal bonds need further explanation. The sixth attribute, flexibility, is also discussed.

Rate of return

Municipal securities compete in the financial markets with other lending investments; therefore the interest rate is set by demand and supply. That means interest rates are subject to significant swings. Because municipal securities are exempt from federal income taxes (more on this

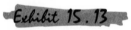

Exhibit 15.13

Major Investment Attributes: Municipal Notes and Bonds

Rate of return	Risk exposure	Minimum maturity	Minimum investment	Income tax features
Rate set by market supply and demand forces.	Low to moderate; agencies provide quality grades.	1–3 years	$5,000	Interest exempt from federal tax and possibly state tax; capital gains fully taxable.

later), the rate is less than what a comparable, fully taxable security would offer.

Risk exposure   Returns on municipal securities are variable. If everything goes as planned, and it does most of the time, your actual return will equal the promised one, but that is not guaranteed. If the issuing municipality, state, or agency encounters financial difficulty, your return can be less. The risk on municipal notes and bonds ranges from low to moderately high. General obligation issues usually have the lowest risk, while revenue issues are often more chancy.

To judge a particular risk, you need a detailed financial analysis of the issuer. But you are spared that task because Moody's and Standard and Poor's rate many municipal bonds. While the criteria differ, the quality grades are identical to those in Exhibit 15.11. Bonds graded AAA to A are suitable for investors unwilling to assume much risk. Risk-averse investors should concentrate on the top two grades. More aggressive investors can select bonds in the fourth grade and below . . . if they are willing and able to tolerate risk.

Diversification can help lower risk. Diversifying your holdings can help reduce risk. A bond or note in financial difficulty has less impact if it is only one part of your holdings. Diversification becomes more important when you buy lower-quality securities. As the likelihood of the borrower running into financial difficulty increases, it becomes more and more necessary for the investor to lessen the potential effect of the problem bond.

But diversification carries the same costs we noted in our discussion of corporate bonds. It requires a large investment, and you must spend considerable time managing and tracking your holdings.

Tax features   **Tax-exempt interest** is the main attraction of municipal securities. Most issues sold before 1987 are exempt from federal taxes. Since then a

very few taxable issues have appeared. Some states also exempt the interest from their income tax if the issuer is located in the state. The federal tax exemption and the possible state exemption can make returns on municipal securities attractive to investors with high marginal tax rates.

Capital gains and losses on municipal securities receive no special tax treatment; gains are fully taxable and losses fully deductible. If you pay $950 for a municipal note and later redeem it for $1,000, the $50 gain will be fully taxable.

Flexibility

For securities issued by larger municipalities there is a reasonable secondary market. You pay a sales commission, and the prices are determined by market conditions. If interest rates have risen since you purchased the security, the selling price will likely be less than you paid. A drop in rates can push the price above what you paid.

As long as there is a reasonable secondary market, flexibility is fair to good. But the secondary market for securities issued by small municipalities is far less developed. The lack of an active secondary market for a note or bond can mean a lower market price for that issue than for one that's more heavily traded. For a small issue, there may be little or no secondary market. For moderate to small issues, the flexibility is weak to nonexistent.

Advantages and Disadvantages: Municipal Bonds

Exhibit 15.14 summarizes the major advantages and disadvantages of municipal notes and bonds as an investment. Most of the entries are self-explanatory, but the tax-exempt feature needs further review. Since this feature is one of the security's major benefits, a complete understanding of it is essential. The list of points in Exhibit 15.14 should help you decide whether a municipal security is appropriate for you.

How valuable is the tax exemption?

Investors with the highest marginal tax rates clearly gain by having interest exempt from income taxes. Does that mean this particular tax exemption is good for everyone? No. Municipal securities pay a lower return. Suppose Lew Lowrate—15 percent marginal tax rate—and Maude Midrate—35 percent marginal tax rate—are discussing investment

Exhibit 15.14

Advantages and Disadvantages: Municipal Notes and Bonds

Advantages	Disadvantages
Interest is exempt from federal and possibly state income taxes.	Lower-quality issues have moderately high risk levels.
Investors can choose from a range of risk levels and associated returns.	Considerable investor effort required to select and manage.
Quality grades assigned by well-regarded rating agencies.	Adequate diversification requires $25,000 to $50,000.
Bonds and notes from larger issuers are rated by Moody's or S&P's.	Fee to purchase or sell can reduce return on small transactions.
Larger issues have reasonable secondary market.	

options. They have narrowed their choices to a corporate note paying a fully taxable 8 percent return and a comparable quality municipal note paying a tax-exempt 6.5 percent. Because it is exempt, the second provides a 6.5 percent after-tax return. After-tax return on the corporate note will be 6.8 percent for Lew [8% return − (8% return × 15% marginal tax)] and 5.2 percent for Maude [8% return − (8% return × 35% marginal tax)]. Lew should pick the corporate note; even taxed, its return is better. Maude will want the municipal note; her higher tax rate makes the (tax-exempt) feature worthwhile.

Strategy

Compare the after-tax return on comparable taxable and tax-exempt investments, and select whichever has the higher return.

Suitable Financial Goals: Municipal Bonds

Municipal notes and bonds have some features that limit their appeal. Given the $5,000 minimum purchase, they are suitable only for goals that involve sizable amounts. Only investors with considerable resources can buy them. The $25,000 to $50,000 needed for a diversified position also limits the number of investors who can enter the market. Second, because of the sales commissions and possibly limited secondary market, you should only purchase them if you expect to hold to maturity. Third, the investor has to devote considerable effort to selecting suitable issues; then their performance has to be monitored to see that it matches original expectations. Last, the whole selection and management process requires an investor of some sophistication.

For these reasons, the purchase of individual municipal notes and bonds is best left to investors who can and want to get involved. What if municipal securities look attractive but you want to lessen your involvement? Then a mutual fund that specializes in municipal securities may be best; more on this in Chapter 17.

Summary

1 Fixed-return investments promise to pay a set return at prescribed intervals over the investment's specified maturity. The rate paid on a variable return investment is indexed to a rate in the financial markets.

2 Since deregulation was completed in 1986, financial institutions can set their interest rates at whatever level they wish.

3 Federally sponsored insurance programs— FDIC, FSLIC, and NCUA—reduce the risk on savings, share, and money market accounts to near zero.

4 Savings, share, and money market accounts are highly flexible, but their returns are among the lowest for fixed-return investments.

5 Certificates of deposit (CDs) have a fixed maturity; generally, the longer the maturity, the higher the interest rate.

6 The *Wall Street Journal, Barron's,* and *Money* publish lists of institutions currently offering high rates on selected CD maturities.

7 When a CD is redeemed before maturity, there is an interest penalty; institutions set their own penalties.

8 Savings bonds are sold at a discount; the difference between the purchase price and redemption value is the investor's interest.

9 The interest rate on a Series EE savings bond is the higher of
  ▪ 85 percent of the return on 5-year Treasury securities
  ▪ 6 percent
10 The variable return on a savings bond should track interest rates in the financial markets.
11 Interest on a savings bond is fully taxable at the federal level, but the investor can defer recognizing that interest until the bond is redeemed.
12 A savings bond cannot be redeemed for 6 months after purchase and must be held 5 years for the investor to receive the promised return.
13 Maturities of Treasury securities range from short-term (bills), through intermediate-term (notes), to long-term (bonds).
14 New Treasury securities are sold at an auction; an investor can submit a noncompetitive bid for about a week following the announcement.
15 There is a very active secondary market for Treasury securities, where existing issues can be bought or sold.
16 Corporate notes and bonds are backed by the firm's promise to pay the interest and redeem the security at its face amount.
17 Risk on corporate notes and bonds ranges from low to moderately high, depending on the quality of the issue.
18 Two major rating agencies assign quality grades to most corporate notes and bonds.
19 Diversification can help lower the risk faced by the investor in bond issues.
20 Individual corporate notes and bonds are best for investors who have both sufficient funds for these investments and the time to select and manage them.
21 General obligation and revenue issues are the two major types of municipal securities.
22 Interest on most municipal securities is exempt from federal income taxes; it may be exempt from state tax if the issuer is located in that state.

Review your understanding of

Deregulation
Basis points
Savings account
Share account
Money market account
FDIC, FSLIC, NCUA insurance
Day of deposit to day of withdrawal
ATM
Certificate of deposit (CD)
  Benchmark CD rate
  Effective return
  Variable rate CD
  Early redemption penalty
Series EE savings bonds
U.S. Treasury securities
  Treasury bill

Treasury note
Treasury bond
Treasury auction
Interest rate risk
Secondary market
Corporate note
Corporate bond
Quality grades: Moody's
Quality grades: Standard & Poor's
Diversification
Municipal note
Municipal bond
General obligation security
Revenue security
Tax exemption

Discussion questions

1 How do money market and savings accounts differ? Does a money market account have any advantages? Disadvantages?
2 Why should you consider only insured financial institutions? Does the insurance cost you anything?
3 What types of goals would be served by a savings, share, or money market account? Why are these accounts not suitable for all goals?
4 Has deregulation increased or decreased an investor's responsibility when selecting such things as money market accounts and CDs? Once the investment is selected, is active management still necessary?

5 How does the penalty for redeeming a CD early operate? Can it be avoided? How would you decide if borrowing the needed money is best?
6 How would you establish a "benchmark" rate to help you decide if the rate a CD offers is competitive? What are the advantages and disadvantages of purchasing a CD from an institution outside the immediate area?
7 Would a CD be a good vehicle for accumulating funds for a financial goal that will be implemented in 2 to 6 years? Are there shortcomings?
8 Give an example of a situation in which a variable rate CD would be a good choice. A poor

choice? Are variable rate CDs becoming more or less prevalent?

9 A public service announcement extolling the virtues of savings bonds has convinced Patricia Patriotic they would be a good "universal" investment. Before Patricia enrolls, do you have any advice for her?

10 Are there any differences between a Treasury note and a savings bond? Do notes have any advantages? Disadvantages?

11 What is the difference between Treasury securities sold in the primary and the secondary market? On which one could you make a noncompetitive bid? Does bidding this way offer any advantages?

12 Is a detailed, in-depth review of the issuing corporation or municipality needed to judge the quality of a corporate or municipal bond? Why?

What is meant by an investment "grade"? Are there advantages to investing in a less than investment grade bond? Disadvantages?

13 What does it mean to diversify your corporate or municipal bond holdings? Are there advantages to doing this? Disadvantages?

14 Why are individual corporate and municipal notes and bonds unsuitable for many investors? Profile an investor who would find such purchases advantageous.

15 Why do people buy municipal securities when their interest rates are 100 to 300 basis points less than those of comparable quality corporate securities? Some who would like to redistribute wealth claim the exemption on municipal bonds should be dropped to "tax the idle rich." Why single out these securities?

Problems

15.1 Ralph may have to redeem the 30-month, 9 percent CD he bought for $1,000 9 months ago. Penalty for early redemption is 3 months interest. (*Note:* Ignore interest compounding in your answers.)

  a How much interest will Ralph receive if he redeems now?

  b Based on the interest in part (a), what is his approximate rate of return? (*Hint:* Ralph earned that interest in 9 months.)

  c When he bought this CD, Ralph could have bought a 3-month CD offering 6.5 percent. Assuming he could have continued to reinvest at that 6.5 percent rate, would a series of 3-month CDs have worked out better?

15.2 Last National Bank will loan Mary Swift $1,000 if she uses her $1,000, 24-month CD as security. The CD carries a 12 percent interest rate and has a 3-month penalty for early redemption. The loan's APR is 15 percent with payment due when the CD matures in 6 months. (*Note:* Ignore interest compounding.)

  a For how long will Mary need the loan? How will she repay it?

  b What will the finance charge on the loan be?

  c After paying that finance charge, how much interest will Mary have?

  d Should she take the loan or redeem early? Why?

15.3 Becky and Fred Bear are considering alternatives for a short-term investment:

| | Investment Option | | |
Feature	Traditional savings account	Money market deposit account	Share account
Current rate of return	5.5%	9%	7%
Minimum investment	$100	$2,500*	$200
Insured	Yes	Yes	Yes

* Interest rate drops to 5% if balance is less than $2,500.

The Bears are also looking for a place to put the $3,000 they currently have in their emergency fund. They wonder which of these accounts would be most suitable for their emergency fund and for use as a short-term investment.

  a Becky and Fred expect to leave the $3,000 in the account they choose for 3 years. What would the balance in each of the accounts be at the end of that time if interest were compounded annually? (*Hint:* Appendix A.3 may be of interest.)

  b Are these accounts suitable for either the Bears' emergency fund or their short-term investment? Why?

    c Fred wonders about the risk involved in concentrating a large sum in the money market deposit account. Should he?

    d Which account would you recommend?

    e What special features or restrictions should the Bears consider when evaluating the accounts?

15.4 Orville Overwhelmed has been bombarded by advertisements for money market accounts. He admires the marketing effort that went into their clever names, but he presumes that they are all about the same. He has details on three accounts:

Feature	Money stacker	Money reaper	Money grower
Current interest rate	8%	9%	9.25%
Compounding	Daily	Daily	Annually
Insured	Yes	Yes	Yes
Minimum initial deposit	$1,000	$2,000	$5,000
Withdrawals	Unlimited	Unlimited	Unlimited
Provision for checks to be drawn on account	Yes (3 checks monthly)	Yes (3 checks monthly)	No

    a What are each account's strengths? Are they all equally suitable?

    b What is the effective rate of return on each account? (*Hint:* Exhibit 14.6 may be helpful.)

    c Should Orville switch from his current savings account?

15.5 Marie Bowman has narrowed her choice to two CDs. Ignore compounding of interest as you review her alternatives and answer the questions:

Feature	Last ditch	Best bet
Maturity	3½ years	3½ years
Current interest rate	9%	9%
Insured	Yes	Yes
Interest rate variability	Fixed over life of CD	Variable; equals return on 3-year Treasury notes; reset each month
Redemption penalty	30 days' interest	3 months' interest

    a What are the major differences between the two CDs?

    b If the return on 3-year Treasury notes for the next 11 months turns out to be:

Feb.	Mar.	Apr.	May	June	July	Aug.	Sept.	Oct.	Nov.	Dec.
10%	11%	12%	13%	11%	10%	9%	8%	10%	10%	12%

       What return would the CD from Last Ditch provide? The CD from Best Bet?

    c In what type of interest rate environment is the variable rate CD the best choice? When is it the poorest choice?

Case problem

Anne Jones is reviewing her investment program for possible changes. Her current teaching job pays $24,500 annually. From that she plans to save $1,500 during the year. Her present investments include $1,500 in a savings account and $500 in savings bonds.

    Her financial goals for the next 7 years include the following:

Financial goal	Expected completion	Cost
Attend graduate school in summer	9 months	$1,000
European trip	2 years	3,500
Replace present car	5 years	5,500
10% down payment on a condominium	7 years	4,500

Anne expects to split her monthly savings, with $100 going to the savings account and $50 to savings bonds.

Anne plans to concentrate on fixed-return investments for now. She wants to avoid the risk of common stocks and is unclear how mutual funds operate. Interest on her present savings account—3 percent compounded annually—has her concerned. Her list of possible investment options includes:

Investment	Financial institution	Insured	Minimum balance	Effective return
Savings account	S&L	Yes	$ 100	5.61%
Money market account	S&L	Yes	2,500	8.50
CD (6-month maturity)	Bank	Yes	200	9.00
CD (3-year maturity)	S&L	Yes	500	10.00
Share account	Credit union	No	50	7.00
Savings bonds-EE	Treasury	No	25	6.00*

* If held to maturity, return is higher of (1) 85% of 5-year Treasury note or (2) 6%.

Anne has developed the worksheet that is shown below to support her investment plan. To develop that worksheet, she assumed a 10 percent rate of interest. She has broken down the annual interest earnings into two portions. First, she receives a full year's interest on the balance she has at the start of the year. But she only receives about one-half year's interest on the $1,500 she expects to deposit during the year. That is because she will be depositing it monthly throughout the year; deposits made late in the year will earn little interest. Anne has worked out the first 3 years of the worksheet.

			Year				
Sample Investment Worksheet	1	2	3	4	5	6	7
1. Investment balance: start of year	$2,000	$2,775	$1,128				
2. Add: annual deposit	1,500	1,500	1,500				
3. Interest on beginning balance	200 (1)	278 (3)	113 (4)				
4. Interest on annual deposit	75 (2)	75 (2)	75 (2)				
5. Amount available: line 1 + line 2 + line 3 + line 4	$3,775	$4,628	$2,816				
6. Less: amount withdrawn for current year's goal	1,000	3,500	—				
7. Investment balance: end of year	$2,775	$1,128	$2,816				

Note: $interest = \dfrac{investment}{balance} \times \dfrac{interest}{rate} \times \dfrac{time}{period}$

(1) $200 = \$2,000 \times 10\% \times 1$ year
(2) $ 75 = 1,500 \times 10 \times ½$ year
(3) $278* = 2,775 \times 10 \times 1$ year
(4) $113* = 1,128 \times 10 \times 1$ year
* Rounded to nearest dollar

1   At her present savings rate, can Anne achieve the financial goals she has listed? (*Hint:* It will help if you complete her worksheet for all 7 years.)
2   What are the strengths and weaknesses of Anne's present investments?
3   What investments would you suggest as substitutes? Why?
4   Would you suggest a different investment for each goal, or can one serve all the goals? Why?
5   How would you implement the investment plan you suggested in parts (3) and (4)?
6   Is Anne's assumed 10 percent return realistic? What rate of return would your suggested investments provide?

CHAPTER 16

Common stocks: A variable income investment

AFTER COMPLETING THIS CHAPTER YOU WILL HAVE LEARNED

- The nature of common stock ownership
- That your return as a common stock shareholder consists of dividends and changes in the stock's market price
- How to value a stock dividend or a stock split
- How inflation affects a common stock's return
- How to interpret a secondary market listing for a common stock
- When a full-service broker is best and when a discount broker is best
- How dollar-cost averaging operates
- Whether you should purchase common stocks
- The strengths and weaknesses of diversification

Almost every how-to-invest-and-make-a-million-bucks book begins something like this: "Had your parents invested $1,000 in the common stock of Resorts International (which owned the first gambling casino in Atlantic City, New Jersey) in 1975, it would have been worth approximately $55,000 in 1979." That stock provided an average annual compound return of 172 percent, an impressive performance for an investment!

Suppose your parents had invested $1,000 in Chrysler Corporation in 1981 instead; the investment would have been worth $13,800 by the end of 1985, an average annual return of 93 percent. Such enticements are too good to resist, aren't they? But before you call a stockbroker with a buy order, here are a few more impressive performance stories.

If your parents had invested $1,000 in Apple Computer in mid-1983, their stock would have been worth $450 by the end of 1985, an annual loss of 27 percent; now *that's* performance.

Maybe they would have selected Avon Corporation—many professional investors who follow the market on a regular basis did—for a $1,000 investment in 1972. By mid-1979, that investment would have recorded an annual loss of 14 percent for the 7 years.

Worse yet, your parents might have invested in Chrysler Corporation too early. Had they invested $1,000 in 1976, their stock's value would have fallen to $370 in 3 years: an annual return of *minus* 17 percent.

These stories illustrate investment performance, too, but hardly the sort to make you think of making your first million by trading common stock.

The books that lead off with great success stories rarely complete the picture with examples of stocks that lose money for their owners. There are big winners and losers of course, but most successful investors will tell you that common stocks are doing their best when they provide satisfying, reasonably stable returns.

In our discussion, we will offer a balanced survey of the stock market. We do not want you to come away thinking common stocks are the greatest thing since Jello wrestling, nor do we want to suggest that they are akin to Dr. Swift's All-Purpose Spring Elixir.

Fortunes have been made in the stock market, but it is totally unrealistic to invest in common stocks with that expectation. On the other hand, the stock market is not so illogical that you should think of your success or failure as a result of a roll of the dice. Some work digging up facts, some reasonable judgments, a dollop of common sense, maybe a little luck, and you can effectively invest in the market, averaging 10 to 15 percent annually from your stock investments.

COMMON STOCK: OWNERSHIP IN A CORPORATION

Corporations have several appealing features. The common stock of a corporation conveys ownership to the holder; when you own shares, you are part owner. A corporation is a separate entity that transacts business and borrows money in its own name. The promise to repay debts comes from the corporation. If it cannot, the lenders cannot legally pursue the common stock owners; therefore, your liability for the corporation's debts is limited to what you paid for its stock.

Owners of common stock have certain **shareholder rights.** They can sell their shares to other investors without affecting the corporation, so an ownership change does not require dissolution of the corporation. Corporations can have one owner or tens of thousands of owners. What fraction of the corporation you own depends on what share of the total common stock you own. A person who holds 10 percent of the stock owns 10 percent of the firm. Usually, the number of shares of common stock is very large, and most shareholders own a very small fraction.

Ownership

As an owner, you have a voice in how the firm is managed. However, ownership is usually separated from control. Shareholders' management role is limited to electing a board of directors who control the company; they set its long-term goals and policies. The board selects the management team that implements policy and goals on a day-to-day basis.

Corporate earnings

Common stock shareholders are entitled to the corporation's earnings. The firm's earnings may be paid as cash dividends or retained to finance its continued growth. Rapidly expanding corporations need large amounts of money for expansion, and pay few dividends. Corporations whose expansion is slower have smaller reinvestment needs and pay out a higher proportion of earnings as dividends.

Shareholders benefit either way. A cash dividend provides money to stock owners. But retained earnings also come back to shareholders eventually: they purchase machines, buildings, and other facilities that generate future earnings and profits.

It's one of the side benefits of owning stock in the Montrose Flypaper Company.

The board of directors decides how the corporation's earnings should be allocated, basing its judgment on the firm's needs and history of dividend payments. Most firms believe it is important to pay regular dividends to stockholders. Once they begin paying a certain dividend, they attempt to continue the dividend every year, even if the firm's earnings fluctuate.

Closing down and liquidating the corporation. If a corporation terminates its operations and **liquidates,** all debts, loans, and bonds must first be repaid. The shareholders get what is left. When corporations liquidate because of financial problems, there is generally little left for the shareholders.

Time horizon

Like most ownership investments, common stock has no set maturity period. Common stocks can be sold to other investors until the corporation ceases operations. The firm usually does not redeem its shares.

Shareholder Return

Your return on common stock comes from the dividends it pays and any change in the stock's market price. All cash dividends on common stocks are taxed at the regular rate. All capital gains, whether long- or short-term, are fully taxable. Most capital losses are deductible.

Cash dividend

Cash dividends are usually quoted as a dollar amount per common stock share. Dividends are ordinarily distributed in four equal, quarterly payments, although a few companies pay unequal amounts each quarter. When earnings are unusually good, a firm may declare a special year-end dividend on top of its regular dividends. Thus, a nonrecurring $1 per share year-end payment might supplement a company's regular $2.00 dividend.

The annual return on a stock is calculated by dividing the dividend by the market price. If XQ Corporation's current market price is $40, the yield from its annual $2 dividend payment is 5 percent: $2/$40.

Exhibit 16.1 shows the average annual **dividend yield** for a large sample of common stocks. Only the return from cash dividends is shown; increases or decreases in the stock's market price are not included. The annual rate of return for common stocks has varied considerably during the past 10 years, but most of that variance has been caused by changes in market prices; dividends have remained relatively constant.

Market price change

The market price of any common stock depends on its corporation's prospective earnings. When the outlook is good, a stock's market price will increase. When the outlook is poor, its price will fall. Of course other factors can cause a **change in market price;** whatever the cause, the change affects your total rate of return.

Let's go back to XQ Corporation and its $2 cash dividend. If the price of XQ's common stock goes from $40 to $42 during the year, the potential return from the increase is 5 percent: ($42 − $40)/$40. The return is "potential" because you only receive it if you sell the shares.

Returns generated by market price change can vary tremendously. Price appreciation is your major source of return on stocks that pay little or nothing in dividends.

Total return = cash dividend + market price change

To calculate your total return on a common stock, you add its annual cash dividend to any market price change. Total return for XQ Corporation is 10 percent: 5% dividend return + 5% return from price change. However, don't forget that the price change figure can be negative. If XQ's price per share had fallen to $36, the total return would have been −5 percent: 5% dividend return added to the −10% price change.

Stock dividend

Some corporations also use common stock as a dividend for shareholders. Usually, a **stock dividend** is quoted as a percentage of total shares outstanding: for example, if Fred Bear owns 15 shares of XQ Corporation and it declares a 10 percent stock dividend, Fred receives 1.5 shares. If the firm does not issue fractional shares (many do not), Fred can either take the cash equivalent of the half share at its current market price, or he can pay for half a share and receive 2 full shares.

Some investors think stock dividends provide a return on their total investment. But do they? Suppose ZAP Corporation had 100 common stock shares owned evenly by 10 shareholders. If the firm pays a 10 percent stock dividend, each shareholder now has 11 shares. Have shareholders gained from the dividend? Initially, each shareholder owned 10 percent of ZAP, and therefore was entitled to 10 percent of its earnings. After the dividend, ZAP has 110 shares, and each shareholder owns 11 shares, still 10 percent of ZAP!

Is the corporation worth more because it is divided into 110 shares rather than 100? Of course not. The net effect of a stock dividend is to create more shares, but each share is smaller. Since the firm's earnings are divided into 110 pieces, the price per share will be less than before the

Exhibit 16.1

Annual Dividend Yield on a Representative Sample of Common Stocks

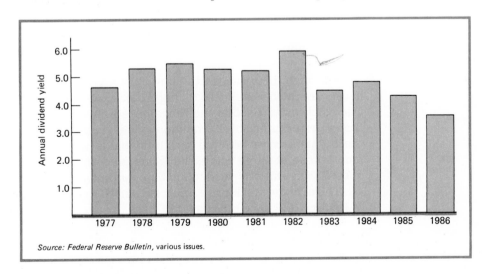

Source: *Federal Reserve Bulletin,* various issues.

dividend. After a stock dividend, the total value of your stock holding will probably remain unchanged.

Stock split

Like a stock dividend, a **stock split** creates more shares. When fewer than 25 percent more shares are created, we speak of a stock dividend; if more than 25 percent, a stock split. A stock split might produce (1) two new shares for each existing share (a 100 percent increase in the number of shares), (2) three new shares for one old share (a 200 percent increase), or (3) three new shares for two existing shares (a 50 percent increase). A stock split has the same effect as a stock dividend. The value of your common stock holdings remains basically unchanged.

Often a corporation declares a stock split to reduce its stock's price to make it more attractive and affordable. Thus, management may want the market price of XQ stock in the $20 to $30 range; it is currently $50. Declaring a 2 for 1 stock split should drop the stock's price to the $20 to $30 range.

Historical Investor Total Rate of Return

Over the 39 years between 1926 and 1965, investor returns on common stocks averaged 9.3 percent per year.[1] But, individual year returns varied tremendously, from massive losses following the 1929 market crash to large, positive returns during the 1950s. How much of this historical experience will be repeated over the next few years? Stock prices will probably fluctuate in a smaller range than they did between 1926 and 1965, and the dividend yield is likely to be more stable over the next 10 years. Together, the two trends should dampen the swings in total investor return over the next 10 years. However, an investor's total return can exceed 25 percent when stock prices are recovering from a sharp decline, or fall equally in a falling market.

Common Stocks and Inflation

Common stocks are often considered a hedge against inflation. As noted earlier, some ownership investments have fared well during inflationary periods. Inflation usually increases a firm's selling prices and costs at the same rate, but it also raises earnings. The firm's assets should rise in value with inflation. The net effect should be larger dividends and a rise in share prices.

Although theory suggests common stocks should be a good inflationary hedge, are they? Exhibit 16.2 charts stock prices from 1920 through 1986. The stock index used is the Dow Jones Industrial Average (DJIA), which traces performance of 30 common stocks. Price declines and increases on these 30 stocks are believed to reflect what is happening overall to the common stocks of large industrial firms, and the DJIA is the most widely quoted price statistic used to indicate market changes.

The average stock price index is charted in "current dollars" at the top of Exhibit 16.2. The index simply gives the average price of the stock each

---

[1] L. Fisher and J. H. Lorie, "Rates of Return on Investments in Common Stock: The Year-by-Year Record, 1926–65," *Journal of Business*, July 1968, pp. 291–316.

Exhibit 16.2

Inflation and Common Stock Prices: Dow Jones Industrial Average in Current and Constant Dollars

THE 'CONSTANT - DOLLAR' DOW

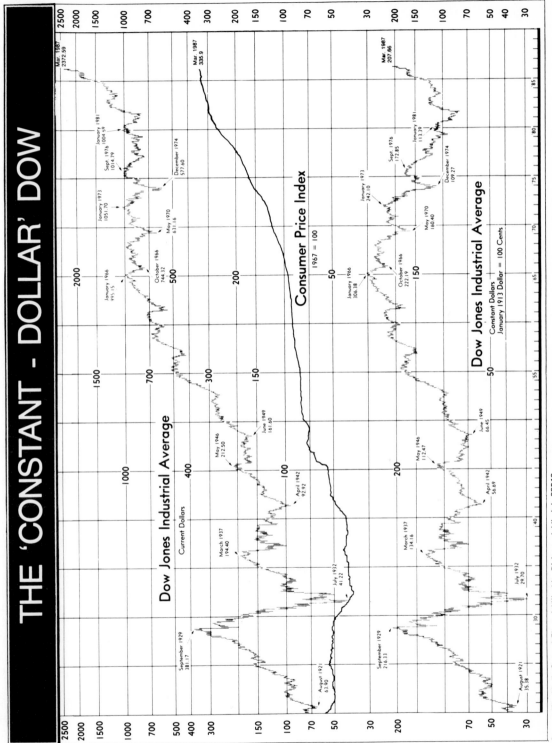

Source: The Media General Financial Weekly, Richmond, Virginia 23219.

year—it tells us nothing about the price of the stock with respect to inflation. In the middle of the exhibit is a line representing the consumer price index, one measure of inflation. The index at the bottom shows the average stock price in "constant dollars," with the base figure set at $1 in 1913. Taken together, the three sections let us follow quoted prices, inflation rates, and stock prices in inflation-adjusted dollars.

Several observations can be drawn from Exhibit 16.2.

First, during recent years, the constant dollar index declined most sharply when the consumer price index rose most rapidly. The price index generally performed best when consumer prices were rising only moderately. Clearly, common stock prices did not provide a good hedge against the sharp price increases of the late 1960s and 1970s.

Second, although there have been several sharp advances in common stock prices during the past 25 years, most of those increases have been offset by inflation.

And third, the overall pattern of stock price changes during the 1970s was not encouraging. Investors who bought common stocks during the late 1960s or early 1970s and held them have seen the price of those shares eroded by inflation. An exception are investors who were wise enough—or lucky enough—to buy at the lows of 1970 and 1974. But even professional investors rarely can tell when prices are lowest and ready to rise.

Real investor return

Over the 20 years from the late 1950s to the late 1970s, an investor's annual real return (cash dividends, plus market price change, less inflation) was approximately 2.2 percent.[2] That is less than the 4 to 4.5 percent real return we feel a high-quality common stock should provide. During the 9 years between 1969 and 1978, when inflation was high, the real return was a negative 3.51 percent (a loss!).[3]

Common stocks seem to provide a hedge against low inflation rates (not more than 5 percent inflation per year), but they offer no protection when inflation hits 10 percent or more.

Stock Valuation

Let's review two measures that are used to describe a particular common stock: earnings per share and the price-earnings ratio.

Earnings per share

A stock's **earnings per share (EPS)** is computed by dividing the corporation's after-tax annual earnings by the number of shares of common stock the corporation has. If Zug Products' annual earnings (after payment of taxes) are $1,500,000 and it has 300,000 shares of common stock, the EPS figure is $5: $1,500,000 earnings/300,000 shares. Our EPS computation was based on Zug's historical earnings—what Zug did last year. Annual earnings for a future year can also be used to compute a projected EPS.

Price-earnings ratio

A stock's **price-earnings (P/E) ratio** is computed by dividing its market price per share by its earnings per share. The P/E ratio shows the relation-

---

[2] Roger G. Ibbotson and Rex A. Sinquefield, "Stocks, Bonds, Bills and Inflation: Update," *Financial Analysts Journal*, July–August 1979, p. 41.
[3] *Ibid.*

ship between market price and annual earnings. A stock that currently sells for $10 and has EPS of $1 has a P/E ratio of 10. The stock sells for 10 times its earnings. Some stocks sell at 30 to 50 times earnings while others sell at 3 to 5 times earnings. Why the difference? It is caused by such things as future earnings' prospects, a highly respected company management, a glamorous product line, or even better publicity.

Common Stock Categories

Common stocks are often grouped into categories. The most widely used groupings are blue chip, growth, and speculative stocks.

Blue chip stock

A **blue chip stock** is issued by a large, well-regarded corporation. Most of these stocks have a history of consistent earnings and steady dividends. The growth rate of their earnings is generally not spectacular. The financial community sees these firms as well-managed and financially strong. Blue chip stocks ordinarily present the lowest risk of all common stocks.

Growth stock

A **growth stock** is usually defined as one issued by a corporation whose earnings have grown at above average rates. A true growth stock must offer the prospect of above average growth in the future. Merely increasing sales is not enough; the firm must also increase its earnings. Being a growth stock is a temporary condition. A firm growing at 15 percent annually would double in size every 5 years, and such rapid expansion cannot continue for long periods.

Most growth firms pay low dividends, to allow their earnings to be used for further expansion. P/E ratios on growth stocks, especially of highly respected firms, tend to be well above the market average. The prices of growth stocks can be volatile, dropping sharply when the market declines and rushing up when the market advances.

Many investors continually search for "undiscovered" growth stocks. They hope to purchase the shares before their price reflects the firm's potential. Once a stock is recognized as a growth stock, its price rises sharply and early investors profit. But finding an "undiscovered" growth stock is no small task. The "promise" of many candidates turns out to be the work of the accountant's creative pen, management's financial maneuvers, or wonderful public relations.

Speculative stock

A **speculative stock** is usually issued by a company that has a poor, or no, track record. Investors buy the stock on the prospect of the firm's future earnings rather than its past accomplishments. Sometimes the company has a product that could revolutionize its industry. Sometimes the firm has been highly successful but is currently experiencing difficulty; if its problems could be solved, it could prosper again. But investors in a speculative stock have little assurance that earnings will increase or that their shares will rise sharply. For every stock that succeeds, dozens that look equally promising do not.

THE STOCK MARKETS

Common stocks can be purchased in the primary market or in the secondary market. As we'll see, most of what people ordinarily think of as stock trading takes place in the secondary market.

Primary Market

New issues of common stock are sold in the **primary market.** The actual sale is handled by specialized underwriters; the corporation receives the sale proceeds minus a commission. A new company might sell common stock to obtain funds to begin operation. An existing company might sell a new issue to finance a major expansion. Since most firms obtain the money they need by retaining earnings, the number of new issues is small.

Secondary Market

The **secondary market** is the one where most investors buy and sell stock and is what most people mean when they say "the stock market." Stocks traded in this market are currently held by some other investor. Secondary market transactions involve a shareholder who wishes to sell shares and an investor who wants to buy that stock. The corporation that issued the stock has no role in the transaction, and does not receive proceeds from the sale. A stock's price reflects the supply of and demand for the stock at that precise moment. If many shareholders want to sell but only a few investors are interested in buying, the price will decline. Conversely, a heavy demand by new investors coupled with limited supply will cause the price to rise.

Reading a secondary market list

Exhibit 16.3 shows a fictional secondary market listing of common stocks. While the actual lists in the *Wall Street Journal* and other major newspapers may differ in format, their content is similar. A company's common stock may be listed on one or more stock exchanges, including (1) the New York Stock Exchange; (2) the American Stock Exchange; (3) regional exchanges—Midwest, Pacific, Boston, and so on; and (4) the over-the-counter market.

Let's examine the listing by reviewing the entry for Atwood Chemical near the middle of Exhibit 16.3. Columns 1 and 2 show the stock's highest and lowest prices for the previous 12 months. Atwood's stock ranged from 26⅜ ($26.375) to 18⅞ ($18.875). The amount following the stock's name (0.95) is its annual dividend. Under "Sales 100's" is the number of shares traded that day in 100's: 7,800 shares of Atwood stock were traded on October 14. Next comes the stock's current dividend yield, which is 4.1%: $0.95 dividend/$23 market price. The next column shows the stock's P/E

Exhibit 16.3

Hypothetical Secondary Market Listing of Common Stocks Traded on October 14, 1987

1987							Price			
High	Low	Stock	Dividend	Sales 100's	Dividend yield	P/E ratio	High	Low	Close	Change
24⅛	21⅞	Algoma Products	1.00	13	4.3	10	23¼	23⅛	23⅛	−⅛
19⅜	18¼	American Power	2.50	3	13.5	6	18	18½	18½	—
26⅜	18⅞	Atwood Chemical	0.95	78	4.1	11	23⅜	22½	23	¼
9⅜	9	Azoor Finance	0.04	17	0.4	12	9⅛	9	9	−⅛
75¾	70⅛	Baker Foods	2.75	6	3.9	5	71¼	71⅛	71¼	½
78⅛	45¼	Beeker Oil	0.10	33	0.2	45	47½	47⅜	47⅜	−⅜

ratio; it is calculated from the current closing price and the most recent EPS. High, low, and closing prices for the day follow. Net price change from the previous to the current day's closing price is last.

Stock Market Indexes

Stock market indexes attempt to show the current state and recent performance of the total market. Each stock index is based on a sample of selected stocks, but the sample varies. Some indexes sample principally industrial stocks: e.g., the Dow Jones Industrial Average (30 industrial firms) and Standard & Poor's 425 Industrials (425 industrial firms). Others, such as the Standard & Poor's 500 Index, New York Stock Exchange Index, and American Stock Exchange Index, cover a broader cross section of stocks.

Danger! Here Come the Bulls and Bears

When stock prices are rising, we say that the market is a "bull market"; when they're declining, it's a "bear market." When these terms are applied to investors, a **bear** is a pessimist who expects stock prices to decline, and a **bull** is an optimist who expects stock prices to rise. So when someone discusses whether the current market is bullish or bearish, you can either pass the bull back or bear it.

SELECTING A COMMON STOCK

Techniques for evaluating and selecting common stocks generally fall into two categories: technical analysis and fundamental analysis. Each group of analysts would argue that its technique is "best" for selecting common stocks. We might raise the question: Is *either* technique "best"? Can an investor operating in an efficient market (more on this theory later) select common stocks, using technical or fundamental analysis, with sufficient consistency to provide above average returns?

I'll tell you one thing, Mildred,.. considering our differing opinions, I think investing in the stock market was a foolish decision.

Technical
Analysis

Supporters of **technical analysis** believe that the price of a common stock moves according to a series of definite patterns. They argue that by identifying these patterns, people can predict the future direction of a stock's price. That prediction becomes the basis for buying and selling stocks. Advocates of technical analysis (who refer to themselves as "technicians") believe that certain patterns of stock prices will repeat themselves in the market: by recording, or "charting," the price trend and volume of trading in a particular stock, they believe they can identify the potential for gain.

Fundamental
Analysis

Proponents of **fundamental analysis** identify promising common stocks by analyzing the underlying factors that give a particular stock its value: product, competition, profitability, financing and others. These analysts maintain that an investor can determine the **intrinsic value** of a particular stock. The only concern of the "fundamentalists" (the title they take) regarding the current market price is its relationship to this "intrinsic" value. If the price is less than the stock's underlying value, the stock is a purchase candidate, and if the price exceeds the estimated value, the stock should be sold.

Fundamentalists argue that market price and intrinsic value will converge as other market participants recognize the true worth of a stock. If an investor can spot a gap between the two before other buyers or sellers do, it is possible to make a profit.

Fundamentalists begin by estimating the prospects for the industrial sector of which the firm is part: they consider operating costs, competition within the industry, import competition, future tax regulations, and other factors. Then they assess specifics for the company: future sales, strengths of the firm's present products, outlook for future products, and how profitable future sales may be. A detailed fundamental analysis requires much data and many estimates. The outcome will not always show the stock as overvalued or undervalued. It may show it is correctly valued in the market—so the effort is sometimes unproductive.

Efficient market theory

Supporters of the **efficient market theory** argue that a stock's market price already reflects all published information about that stock. Therefore, no one can consistently glean enough tidbits of new information to allow a "superior projection" of a stock's future price. Efficient market theorists maintain that even a diligent search, coupled with good analysis (no matter what kind) will not identify common stocks which will earn consistently higher rates of return. True, the price of some selected common stocks will rise, but backers of the efficient market theory argue that the price of other selected stocks will decline and investors will earn an average return overall when the winners and losers are combined.

Even new information on a particular common stock will not improve the investor's chance for success. Supporters of the theory say that as soon as the new information becomes known (and they argue that this happens rapidly), a stock's market price will adjust.

Suppose the stock market is highly efficient. What are the implications of an efficient market for an investor seeking to select winning common stocks?

For one thing, the theory suggests we could be as successful by merely putting a stock listing on a board and throwing a dart to select a stock as by doing an elaborate analysis. In fact, the dart method requires more skill: we have to hit the target! If success or failure depends entirely on chance, it is impossible to be an informed investor. The efficient market theory raises the question of whether the time spent searching for undervalued or undiscovered stocks is really worthwhile. A random selection technique might do as well.

The dismal performance of some investment organizations (pension funds, bank trust departments, mutual funds) that invest heavily in common stocks provides support for the efficient market theory. Despite their claim of professional expertise, few have consistently outperformed the average return for the stock market.

Information Sources

A number of publications and newsletters cover the stock market. Exhibit 16.4 lists some of them. Usually, the major sources review recent performance, current status, and future prospects for the industry. In addition, many industries have trade journals that discuss current developments and topics of special interest to the industry. Exhibit 16.5 provides a select list of journals that provide data on individual corporations within each industry. Most of these sources can be found in your public library.

BUYING COMMON STOCKS

To buy or sell a common stock in the secondary market you must have a stockbroker's assistance. The broker brings together the buyer and the seller. Some operate as full-service brokers, others are discount brokers.

Exhibit 16.4

Information Sources for Data on Specific Industries

Title	Publisher	Type of publication
Industry Surveys	Standard & Poor's Corporation	Analyzes, in detail, major industries' operating statistics. Updated by quarterly supplements. Completely revised every 1 to 3 years.
Value Line Investment Survey	Arnold Bernhard & Co., Inc.	Analyzes the current state and future prospects of four to six industries. Published weekly.
The Outlook	Standard & Poor's Corporation	Highlights several industries in each week's issue.
United Business & Investment Report	United Business Service	Analyzes current business trends and specific industry factors. Published every 2 weeks.
Business Week	McGraw-Hill, Inc.	Summarizes recent performance data on major industries on a recurring basis.
Forbes	Forbes, Inc.	Analyzes the past and prospective performance of major industries in one issue each year.

Full-Service Brokers

Full-service brokers can represent a national company that has offices throughout the United States or a regional firm with just a few offices (maybe only one). Most full-service brokers provide a range of customer services. Many publish their own newsletters, discussing the general state of the stock market and reviewing common stocks they consider good investments. Often, they prepare research (purchase) reports, which analyze a company and provide buy or sell advice.

Discount Brokers

Discount brokers have appeared on the scene more recently; most firms are only 10 to 15 years old. Like full-service brokers, they can be local, regional, or national. They do not provide investment advice, newsletters, or analyses. They have one function: to execute your buy or sell order. Since they offer fewer services, they can charge considerably lower commissions.

Brokerage Commissions

Exhibit 16.6 shows that many large brokers charge similar commissions. Its lower section illustrates the sizable savings discount commissions provide.

 **Exhibit 16.5**

Information Sources for Individual Corporations Within Different Industries

Title	Publisher	Comment
Stock Reports	Standard & Poor's Corporation	Detailed data on corporations listed on the New York and American stock exchanges, plus major issues from the over-the-counter market. Updated regularly.
Moody's Manuals	Moody's Investor Services, Inc.	In-depth historical sketch together with current data on all major corporations. Updated regularly.
Corporation Records	Standard & Poor's Corporation	In-depth historical sketch and recent operating data on major firms. Updated frequently.
Value Line Investment Survey	Arnold Bernhard & Co., Inc.	Comparative analysis of large firms within major industries. Each industry's review is updated every 13 weeks.
The Outlook	Standard & Poor's Corporation	Reviews major current events that affect an industry or specific stock. Also comparative analysis of a major industry and its firms.
United Business & Investment Report	United Business Service	Typically reviews individual companies within a selected industry or specialized area. Published every 2 weeks.
Forbes	Forbes, Inc.	The industry analysis issue, appearing early each year, covers the major firms within each industry. In addition, each issue discusses a number of companies.
Business Week	McGraw-Hill, Inc.	Summarizes the current performance and future prospects of several major firms each week.

Exhibit 16.6 can be used to compute what the commission was as a percentage for four sample transactions (we use the average commission of full-service brokers for these sample transactions):

Number of shares (1)	Market price per share (2)	Total purchase price: col. 1 × col. 2 (3)	Commission charged on purchase (4)	Commission as a percentage of the purchase price: col. 4 × col. 3 (5)
50	$30	$1,500	$42	2.8%
50	50	2,500	58	2.3
100	30	3,000	67	2.2
100	50	5,000	85	1.7

Since a common stock investment always involves both a purchase and a sale, you pay twice; the round-trip commission cost is double those shown. Purchase a $30 stock from a full-service broker, and its price will have to rise 4 to 6 percent or it will have to pay a 4 to 6 percent dividend before your commissions are covered. For a $50 stock you'll need a dividend or a price increase of 3 to 5 percent to cover transaction costs. Commissions on small transactions can sharply reduce your return, especially if you trade frequently.

Which Broker? Since both full-service and discount brokers can execute a buy or sell order, base your decision on the services you need.

If you know what you want to buy or sell, a discount broker will serve.

Exhibit 16.6

Commission to Trade 50 to 100 Shares at a Full-Service Brokerage House and a Discount Brokerage

Brokerage firm	50 Shares		100 Shares	
	$30 stock	$50 stock	$30 stock	$50 stock
Full-service broker*				
Highest commission	$43	$60	$68	$90
Average commission	42	58	67	85
Lowest commission	42	56	66	81
Discount broker†				
Highest commission	$32	$40	$44	$60
Average commission	27	31	34	41
Lowest commission	25	25	25	25

* Based on commission data from three large brokers.
† Based on commission data from five discount brokers.
Source: Unpublished study by Larry R. Lang.

And if you trade actively (make frequent purchases and sales), the lower commission can mean the difference between a profit and breaking even.

If, however, you require investment advice, or if you need and use research reports, a full-service broker should be your choice. But be sure you receive some services for the higher commissions. If the firm's research report is nothing but a data summary—rather than a true analysis of a stock's strengths and weaknesses—you're not getting what you're paying for. Also analyze the broker's recommendations to see whether they provide solid information and justification for each selection rather than broad, sweeping generalizations that suggest little research.

Timing of Stock Investments

Because common stock has no set maturity, investors must decide when to buy and sell. The old Wall Street axiom "buy low and sell high" offers no guidance: who decides what is "low," and at what point is "high" reached?

Buy and hold

Under the **buy-and-hold strategy,** common stock is held as long as it continues to provide a return commensurate with its risk. If an investor finds a stock that has more potential, it should replace the currently held shares. For the majority of small investors, buy-and-hold is probably the best strategy.

Short-term trading

When an investor engages in **short-term trading,** the objective is quite different. The time horizon is hours, days, or weeks rather than years, and the investor's profit depends on a small change in a stock's price. Short-term trading requires heavy investor involvement: identifying potential profit opportunities is time-consuming, and there is little time to react to changes.

Dollar-cost averaging

The investor who was uses the technique called **dollar-cost averaging** forces himself or herself to skirt the question: Is the price right? Rather than invest a single large amount, the investor implements a continuing plan, purchasing shares at regular intervals. If the plan is followed, the investor's money buys more shares when the price is down and fewer shares when it is high.

An example will illustrate. Rather than invest $2400 at one time, Wilma Swift decides to invest $600 in XQ Corporation every 3 months. Exhibit 16.7 shows that if Wilma had purchased 24 shares each quarter at the prevailing price, her average cost for each of 96 shares would have been $22.50. Instead, by investing a set dollar amount each quarter, she bought 114 shares at an average cost per share of $21.05.

Dollar-cost averaging forces an investor to buy when prices are low. For most of us, buying stock when the market is declining is far more difficult than buying when it is rising. Remember, if a stock is a good buy at $30 per share, it should be a great buy at $20, and one whale of a buy at $15. Of course, if a stock's prospects have reversed, the investment should be discontinued.

Strategy

To make dollar-cost averaging work, stick to your investment schedule, no matter whether the market is rising or falling.

Reaction to a declining market

Watching the value of your stocks decline in a falling market is no fun, but it can be costly to panic and sell when the whole market is dropping. Before you sell your stock to switch to different shares, consider the commissions. If your stock recovers, you may have similar costs to repurchase your holding. Switching to a new stock in the hope it will do better may have little effect except to cost you commissions.

COMMON STOCKS: ARE THEY FOR YOU?

Common stocks are not for everyone. Their price volatility is just too high for some investors to tolerate. But the price fluctuations and associated risk are not the only factors that should cause some people to screen themselves out of the pool of potential stock market investors. The sections that follow should help you decide whether common stock investments should be part of your financial plan.

How Do You Measure Up?

Some people are better suited than others to be stock investors. Exhibit 16.8 has a checklist to help you determine your ''stock fitness.'' The questions stress qualitative and psychological aspects of stock investment rather than financial points.

Most of your answers should be yes ones before you seriously consider common stock. If sharp swings in your return will cause you sleepless nights or ulcers, stick to fixed-income investments. If you want to invest in common stocks, yet want to avoid managing them, consider a mutual fund (discussed in Chapter 17).

Risk

Risk on a common stock can range from moderate to very high, depending on the company. Common stocks generally rank near the top of the scale for risk. Returns on a common stock are often very volatile: much more so than returns from other investments.

Variability in a common stock's future return is caused by many factors. Anything that affects the firm's fortunes will likely be reflected in the stock's return. General factors such as declines and expansions in the

Exhibit 16.7

Example of Dollar-Cost Averaging: $600 Invested Each Quarter in the Same Common Stock

Quarter (1)	Share price (2)	Amount invested (3)	Shares purchased (4)	Total shares (5)	Cumulative investment (6)	Average purchase cost* col. 6 ÷ col. 5 (7)
First	$25.00	$600	24	24	$ 600	$25.00
Second	30.00	600	20	44	1,200	27.27
Third	15.00	600	40	84	1,800	21.43
Fourth	20.00	600	30	114	2,400	21.05
Average†	$22.50					

* Cumulative investment divided by total shares.
† Simple average of the price for four quarters.

overall economy affect a stock's price. And so do the factors that affect the industry that also forms part of the "environment" in which the particular company operates.

Diversifying Your Stock Holdings

Diversification means splitting your investments among several stocks; it is one of the principal ways to reduce your risk. Diversification helps the investor reduce the high variability that characterizes returns on individual common stocks.

Selecting stocks to provide good diversification is a complicated process that requires considerable expertise. The actual process is sufficiently involved that we will not cover it here. But a simplified description will illustrate the central goal of diversification.

First, when you diversify, you invest in several companies. This lessens the possibility that you'll lose everything because of a single firm's cri-

---

Exhibit 16.8

Questions to Help You Judge Your "Stock Fitness Score"

	Yes	No
Time Commitment		
Will you spend:		
1. 10 to 15 hours weekly reviewing current business developments?	( )	( )
2. 10 to 40 hours to thoroughly evaluate a stock?	( )	( )
3. 1 to 2 hours each month to review your present stocks?	( )	( )
Investor Interest		
Will you:		
1. Find financial data and brokerage research reports interesting?	( )	( )
2. Have the confidence to question a research report that offers unsupported conclusions?	( )	( )
3. Find the prospect of picking a winner exciting?	( )	( )
4. Be interested in thoroughly analyzing a stock?	( )	( )
Stock Selection		
Do you think:		
1. That you can pick successful stocks?	( )	( )
2. That good investment opportunities may exist in unglamorous industries?	( )	( )
3. That you could buy a stock which appears to have good potential if it is not a current favorite?	( )	( )
4. That a thorough analysis is a better basis for picking a stock than a hot tip?	( )	( )
Anticipated Rate of Return		
Can you:		
1. Accept a 10 to 14 percent average annual return?	( )	( )
2. Understand that a 20 to 30 percent annual return is unrealistic?	( )	( )
3. Accept a price decline of 20 to 50 percent?	( )	( )
4. Sleep nights knowing this year's return may be either plus or minus 20 percent?	( )	( )

sis; it is unlikely that all the companies you invest in will simultaneously encounter financial difficulty.

Second, by selecting companies from different industries, you cut your dependence on the fortunes of a single industry. If you select industries that have different expansion and contraction cycles, your overall return will be more stable: when sales in one industry are contracting and earnings are shrinking, another industry may be expanding and enjoying rising earnings.

Diversification presents several hurdles, however. To diversify adequately, an investor has to buy 10 to 15 different stocks. Investors with limited resources may not be able to purchase enough stocks to diversify. And while spreading the investment among many issues may stabilize returns, it may also mean accepting an "average" market return. For some, this may offset the benefits of diversification.

Summary

1 Common stock represents ownership in a corporation. As owners, common stock shareholders are entitled to the corporation's earnings.
2 A stock's cash dividend and any change in its market price provide returns to the shareholder. Total shareholder return includes both.
3 The real return—current return less the rate of inflation—on common stock has been highest during periods of moderate inflation and lowest during periods of high inflation.
4 During periods of high inflation, common stocks have not been a good hedge against inflation.
5 Earnings per share (EPS) and the price-earnings (P/E) ratio are frequently used in valuing a common stock.
6 Most people buy and sell common stocks in the secondary market; these shares have been previously owned.
7 The widely publicized market indexes—the Dow Jones Industrial Average, Standard & Poor's 500, and the New York Stock Exchange Index—show the current condition and the

recent performance of a sample of common stocks; the samples are usually considered representative of the overall stock market.
8 Techniques for analyzing and selecting common stocks can be divided into two categories: those that rely on technical analysis and those that rely on fundamental analysis.
9 There is considerable evidence that stock prices fully reflect current public information. Thus, even a professional investor cannot predict future changes in price with sufficient accuracy to earn a better than average return.
10 Discount brokerage firms limit their services to buying and selling shares; therefore, they can charge lower fees than firms which provide a broader range of services.
11 When you use dollar-cost averaging, you invest a specific amount of money at regular intervals in a particular common stock.
12 By diversifying their investments in common stocks, investors can reduce the variability of future returns and their risk.

Review your understanding of

Shareholders' rights
Corporate earnings
Liquidating a corporation
Cash dividend
Dividend yield
Market price change
Stock dividend

Stock split
Earnings per share (EPS)
Price-earnings (P/E) ratio
Blue chip stock
Growth stock
Speculative stock
Primary market

Secondary market
Stock market indexes
Bulls and bears
Technical analysis
Fundamental analysis
Intrinsic value
Efficient market theory

Full-service broker
Discount broker
Buy-and-hold strategy
Short-term trading
Dollar-cost averaging
Diversification

Discussion questions

1 If the general public were asked what annual rate of return a common stock investment should yield, do you think the most frequent answer would be:
   a Less than 10 percent?
   b Between 10 and 20 percent?
   c More than 20 percent?
   Do you think this expectation is realistic? Why?
2 What specific advantages does the corporate form of business organization offer its common stock shareholders?
3 Does a shareholder benefit when a company retains part of its earnings? In the future, will the shareholder benefit? What form will these benefits take?
4 Who is entitled to a corporation's earnings? Who decides what part of the earnings is paid as dividends? What factors affect the decision to pay out dividends?
5 During the past 5 years, XQ Plastics has grown so rapidly that it paid no cash dividends. It paid a 10 percent stock dividend each year, and there was a 2 for 1 stock split 3 years ago. How do these actions affect the shareholder? Has the shareholder's dividend return been 10 percent? Why does a company declare a stock dividend or split?
6 Why might a common stock theoretically be a better hedge during an inflationary period than a fixed-income investment? Has recent experience supported this theory?
7 How does a blue chip stock differ from a growth stock? Which investors should concentrate on blue chip stocks? On growth stocks?
8 Assume the evening newscast reports that the Dow Jones Industrial Average rose 5 points that day. What does that mean? How could you use this information? What is the purpose of the Dow Jones Industrial Average?
9 What is meant by the statement: The market price of a common stock already reflects currently available information. What should happen to a stock's price if favorable information about the company appears in today's newspaper? Can an investor earn above average returns by reviewing and analyzing existing, widely distributed data about common stock? What implications does this have for stock selection techniques?
10 How do full-service brokerage firms differ from discount brokers? What type of investor would be best served by each type?
11 What are the advantages of dollar-cost averaging? Are there disadvantages? What sort of investors should use it?
12 What are the advantages of diversifying your stock investments? Are there disadvantages and constraints?

Problems

19.1 Sandra Carmine paid $30 per share for 50 shares of Glug Petroleum Products 2 years ago. Glug has been highly profitable, so its shares currently sell for $36. It paid quarterly dividends of $0.15 per share during those 2 years. Sandra has decided she wants to sell her shares.
   a What was Sandra's annual dividend yield?
   b What was her approximate annual percentage return from the rise in Glug's market price? (Ignore any compounding.)
   c What was Sandra's overall rate of return for each of those years? (Ignore selling commissions and compounding.)
19.2 Arvin Absent temporarily mislaid shares in Speciality Plastics Corporation when he moved. Arvin knows he purchased 100 shares 3 years ago. Furthermore, he remembers that Speciality has declared the following stock dividends and splits:

Date declared	Dividend or split
End of first year	20 percent stock dividend
End of second year	10 percent stock dividend
End of third year	2 for 1 split

When Arvin originally purchased his shares, Speciality Plastics Corporation had 10,000 shares of common stock outstanding.

a How many shares does Arvin currently own?

b What fraction of the company does he now own?

c Has that fraction of ownership changed over the 3 years? Why?

d How many shares of stock does Speciality Plastics currently have outstanding?

19.3 Leonard Longshot recently received a hot tip. The tipster told him that Big Roller, Inc. common stock is where the action is. The company hopes to franchise a series of gambling casinos (much like fast food restaurants) throughout the United States. Leonard's newspaper's financial section showed the following stock market listing for Big Roller.

Price range		Company	Div	Sales 100's	Div yield	P/E ratio	High	Low	Close	Change
High	Low									
85½	1¼	Big Roller, Inc.	$0.01	400	.02%	106	55¼	50½	53	−5

As a newcomer to the stock market, Leonard is unsure what all this means.

a On the basis of the listings, what has been happening to the market price of the firm's stock?

b Does this stock provide a good dividend? If an investor is going to receive a reasonable overall return on this stock, where will it have to come from? Why?

19.4 Chantile De Brode owns 50 shares of Zug Corporation; their current price is $60 per share. She plans to sell her shares in the near future. She will likely use one of two brokerage firms:

Firm	Commission	Customer services
Fast Phil's Full-Line Brokerage House	2.3 percent of the sales proceeds.	Offers advice and recommendations; executes buy and sell orders.
Boris's Bargain Brokerage House	$15 flat fee and 18 cents per share.	Executes buy and sell orders.

a What commission will each firm charge?

b Which one would you recommend? Why?

c Assume Chantile's combined rate of return on the stock is 10 percent before commissions. What will her net return be after commissions if she uses Fast Phil? If she sells through Boris? (*Hint:* Compute what percentage of the sale Boris's commission is.)

Case problem

Bill and Jan Stein plan to invest $2,000 from their savings account in common stocks. They earn $40,000 annually, but save only $750 each year. Much of their income is used for the rent on their luxury apartment, for their extensive travel, and for a new car each year (they currently own two cars). Bill and Jan have heard that common stocks are for those who want to get ahead. They feel the breathtaking returns on common stocks will encourage them to save more. They have three investment goals:

1 A short-term emergency cash fund of $500

2 A $2,000 fund for Jan to complete a graduate degree beginning 2 years from now

3 A down payment of $6,000 to purchase a house in 4 years

They plan to use their common stock investment to reach their goals. Given their limited savings, they feel a 25 to 30 percent annual return is needed. On the basis of that return, they have estimated the following 4-year savings plan:

		Year		
	1	*2*	*3*	*4*
Beginning balance	$2,000	$3,250	$2,813	$4,266
Earnings on balance (25%)	500	813	703	1,067
Total	$2,500	$4,063	$3,516	$5,333
Add: new savings for year	750	750	750	750
Less: withdrawals	0	2,000	0	6,000
Ending balance	$3,250	$2,813	$4,266	$83

The Steins have seen a number of advertisements extolling the "buy" recommendations large brokers provide. They expect to rely heavily on the broker for buying and selling advice. They are interested in undiscovered, undervalued growth stocks that will double in a few months. They have not selected a brokerage firm.

The Steins cannot decide what type of stock they should select. Bill favors conservative, blue chip stocks, but Jan believes they should aim for the highest returns on speculative stocks. Their list of stocks includes (all hot tips):

Stock	Price range over past 3 years	Current Performance (per Share)			Business activity
		Price	*Earnings*	*Dividend*	
1	$15–25	$20	$3.33	$2.00	Gas and electric utility
2	5–42	40	1.00	—	Manufacturer of slot machines for gambling casinos; in business 2 years
3	50–85	75	3.75	2.25	Soft-drink manufacturer
4	30–90	50	3.33	2.50	Auto manufacturer
5	0.25–1.35	1	None	—	Gold mining

1   What are the strengths and weaknesses of the Steins' plan for this foray into the stock market?
2   Is their savings plan a good one? Would you recommend any changes? How would your recommendations affect the Steins' present goals?
3   Do you have any general comments about their list of stocks? Where can they find information on those five companies?
4   Do you think a brokerage firm can deliver what the Steins expect? What type of firm do the Steins need?
5   Overall, do you feel that the Steins are ready for the stock market? Do you have suggestions or recommendations for additional preparation?

CHAPTER 17

Mutual funds, annuities, and other managed investments

AFTER COMPLETING THIS CHAPTER YOU WILL HAVE LEARNED

- How mutual funds operate
- How to compute the net asset value (NAV) of mutual fund shares
- The difference between no-load, low-load, front-load, and back-load mutual funds
- The three major sources of return when you own a mutual fund
- The investment objectives of popular mutual funds, and the major investment vehicles they use
- Similarities and differences between the major types of money market mutual funds, note and bond mutual funds, and common stock mutual funds
- How to assess the risk of a common stock mutual fund
- The major advantages that mutual funds offer individual investors
- Major sources of information on mutual funds
- Guidelines for selecting a money market mutual fund
- Guidelines for selecting a suitable bond mutual fund
- Guidelines for choosing a common stock mutual fund
- How a deferred annuity operates and what savings its tax deferral provides
- The three steps you can take to judge the adequacy of the return on a variable annuity
- How a unit investment trust operates and who should consider one
- What a limited partnership offers and who should consider one

utual funds that invest in common stocks have been around for more than 50 years. Their early years coincided with the Great Depression; growth was *not* spectacular. During the 1950s and 1960s, however, the number and size of these funds soared. Mutual funds that invest in notes and bonds have a shorter history; their most dramatic growth has been in the past 3 to 6 years. Money market mutual funds were introduced in the 1970s. Their growth in recent years has slowed markedly from its early pace.

The increase in the number and variety of mutual funds has altered their role in the management of personal finances. Prior to the mid-1970s few people included mutual funds in their financial plans. Those who did usually had sizable investments. As mutual funds became more common, individual investors began to recognize the advantage and versatility of mutual funds. Common stocks were no longer the sole investment vehicle; mutual funds could also deliver current income through lending investments. Now, mutual funds are common elements in well-developed financial plans.

The goal of this chapter is to provide the background you need to determine what mutual funds can offer your financial plan, how to select them, and what their weaknesses are. Its second intent is to review the merits of annuities. Since the Tax Reform Act of 1986 left their tax deferral feature intact, while it curtailed some other options, annuities are now being actively promoted.

The chapter closes with a brief review of two other professionally managed investment options: (1) unit investment trusts and (2) limited partnerships.

WHAT ARE MUTUAL FUNDS?

Mutual funds use the money of many investors to purchase a group, or "portfolio," of investments. Investors rely on the mutual fund's managers to select and purchase the investments and to manage them.

Exhibit 17.1 illustrates how a mutual fund operates. Alice Average decides to invest $500 in Last Ditch mutual fund. For her $500, Alice receives shares in the fund. The right side of the exhibit illustrates.

The managers of Last Ditch pool Alice's money with that of other investors and purchase major investments—common stocks, corporate bonds, municipal notes, or other instruments. Based on the fund's investment objectives, the fund manager decides what to buy, when to buy it, and when to sell it. The left side of Exhibit 17.1 illustrates these steps.

What if Alice wants her money back? Can she get it? Yes. The flows in Exhibit 17.1 reverse. Now Alice redeems her shares; Last Ditch sends her a check. Where does Last Ditch obtain the cash? It could sell some of its investments, but that is rarely necessary. On the day Alice redeems shares, someone else probably invested in the fund. That money can repay Alice.

Open-End Mutual Fund

Exhibit 17.1 illustrates how an **open-end mutual fund** works, and this type of fund will be our exclusive focus. *Open-end* means the fund will sell shares to all investors who want to buy. The open-end fund also stands ready to redeem the shares of its investors. A highly successful fund will attract an influx of new investors, and the number of shares may expand sharply. An unattractive fund might lose investors and be forced to disband.

Net Asset Value per Share

At the close of each business day a mutual fund computes the **net asset value (NAV)** of its shares. To determine NAV:

- **Total** the current market value of the fund's investments
- **Deduct** the fund's liabilities
- **Divide** the net value by the total number of fund shares

Last Ditch mutual fund in Exhibit 17.1 will illustrate. We will compute the NAV as of Friday the thirteenth. At the end of the day, the fund values all of its investments at their current price: $1,020,000. Its liabilities, what it owes to others, total $20,000. The net value of its holdings is therefore $1,000,000: $1,020,000 total investments − $20,000 liabilities. Since Last Ditch currently has 100,000 shares, its NAV is $10: $1,000,000 net value/100,000 shares. Last Ditch's NAV on the twelfth was probably different, and it may be different at the close of the next business day.

Sale of new shares

Suppose Alice Average invested $500 in Last Ditch on Friday the thirteenth. With a $10 NAV, her $500 buys 50 shares. Let's see if both Alice and Last Ditch's existing shareholders were treated fairly. With Alice's $500 added, the net value of the fund's investments rises from $1,000,000 to $1,000,500, and the number of shares increases from 100,000 to 100,050. After the transaction, the shares are still worth $10: $1,000,500 net value/100,050 shares. Alice received fair value because her 50 shares

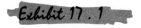

Exhibit 17.1

Investing Indirectly through a Mutual Fund

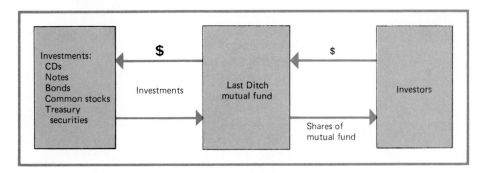

are worth $500. Existing shareholders were fairly treated because their shares were worth $10 and still are.

Strategy

A fund's NAV is a "fair" price for new shares. The new investor receives full value, and the existing shareholders neither gain nor lose.

Redemption of existing shares

Let's now assume that Alice bought 50 shares of Last Ditch sometime *before* the thirteenth. On Friday the thirteenth, she decides to redeem 30 of those shares. With an NAV of $10, she receives a check for $300. Was she treated fairly? Yes. The shares were worth $10 each, and that is what she received. How about the shareholders that remained? After it pays the $300, the net value of Last Ditch's investments drops from $1,000,000 to $999,700; but total shares go from 100,000 to 99,970. The remaining shareholders were treated fairly because the NAV remains at $10: $999,700 net value/99,970 shares.

Strategy

A fund's NAV is the "fair" price at which to redeem existing shares. The redeeming shareholder receives the proper amount, and the remaining shareholders are neither better nor worse off.

Sale of Mutual Fund Shares: Direct or through a Sales Force

A mutual fund may sell shares directly to investors, or it may market them through a sales force. Exhibit 17.2 illustrates both: direct sales by Best Bet mutual fund on the left, sales of Sure Thing mutual fund by a salesperson on the right. Suppose that Earl Swift plans to invest $1,000 in one of these, and that the NAV is $10 for all transactions.

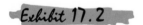

Exhibit 17.2

Comparison of No-Load and Load Mutual Funds

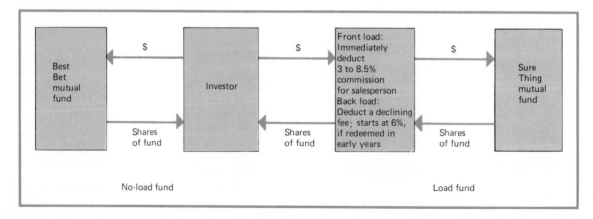

Direct sale:
No-load
mutual fund

If Earl decides to invest in Best Bet, he purchases shares directly from the fund. **No-load funds** sell shares without a sales commission or fee, but purchases require some work on the part of the investor. Earl will have to (1) identify the fund, (2) request information from it (many have toll-free telephone numbers), (3) decide if the investment is appropriate, and (4) if it is, mail in the application with his money. Because there are no commissions, Earl's $1,000 buys 100 shares: $1,000/$10 NAV.

To redeem shares in a true no-load fund, one just reverses the process; there are no fees or commissions. Redeeming 100 shares when the NAV is $10 gives the investor back $1,000.

Direct sale:
Low-load
mutual fund

Some mutual funds that were previously no-load have added a fee. Sales are still direct, and the investor still does the investigative work. But the **low-load fund** deducts from 0.5 to 3 percent from the investment. If the mutual fund had a 1 percent load, Earl would pay a $10 fee on his $1,000 investment. Only $990 remains, so he actually purchases 99 shares: $990 net investment/$10 NAV.

Most low-load funds charge no fee for redeeming shares. But a few do assess a fee of from 0.5 to 1 percent on redemption to discourage frequent shifting in and out of a fund.

Sales organi-
zation: Front-
load mutual
fund

Let's look at the load fund on the right side of Exhibit 17.2. A salesperson—it could be a broker, a financial planner, or an insurance agent—singles out the fund, provides information, and suggests it is appropriate to Earl's needs. Earl has considerably less work to do, but there is a cost. A commission ranging from 3 to 8.5 percent is deducted immediately; hence the term **front-load fund.** If Sure Thing carries an 8.5 percent front

LOAD, NO-LOAD? FRONT-END LOADS.. OPEN-END? WHAT AM I BUYING HERE.. ..AN INVESTMENT PACKAGE OR A DUMP TRUCK?

load, Earl pays an $85 commission ($1,000 $\times$ 8.5%) on his $1,000. Earl's investment buys only 91.5 shares: $915 net investment/$10 NAV. Who gets the $85 commission? The person who sold the shares receives most of it. With most front-load funds you pay a commission each time you invest money. Generally there is no fee when you redeem shares.

Sales force: Back-load mutual fund

To blunt investor criticism of the front load and obscure the fee, **some mutual funds switched to a back load,** a "contingent sales fee." If you redeem the shares before a prescribed period—usually 4 to 6 years—you pay a fee. The back load might start at 6 percent and declines 1 percent for each year you hold the fund: after 1 year, it's 5 percent; after 2, it's 4 percent; and so on. A salesperson selects the fund, provides information, and decides if it's appropriate for the investor. For this work, he or she receives a commission.

We'll use the example of Earl Swift's $1,000 investment to show how this works. The back load starts at 6 percent and declines 1 percent annually. Initially Earl receives 100 shares for his $1,000: $1,000/$10 NAV. He would pay a $60 fee ($1,000 $\times$ 6%) to redeem the first year; by year 6 the fee would be $10. Back loads discourage investors from redeeming shares after making the investment.

Price Quotes on Mutual Funds

The *Wall Street Journal, Barron's,* and the financial sections of major newspapers carry price data on mutual funds. Exhibit 17.3 shows the three prices a typical list gives:

NAV. *Computed by dividing the net value of the fund's investment by the total number of shares. No-load funds and back-load funds sell and redeem shares at NAV. Front-load funds redeem shares at NAV.*

Offering price. *Equals the NAV plus the commission for the salesperson. Front-load and low-load funds sell shares at this price. No-load funds often have "NL" shown here.*

Change in NAV. *Shows the change in the fund's NAV from yesterday or the previous week.*

 **Exhibit 17.3**

Representative Newspaper Price Quotation for Mutual Funds

	NAV	Offer price	NAV change
Allied Growth	10.20	NL*	+.08
American Income	30.00	31.25	−.02
Bet-a-Buck	5.20	NL*	+.09
Go for Broke	18.30	20.00	+.11
Shoo-In	6.35	NL*	−.01

* NL = no-load fund.

Which funds in Exhibit 17.3 are load, and which are no-load? Allied Growth, Bet-a-Buck, and Shoo-In are no-load; they have "NL" in the "Offer price" column. American Income and Go for Broke are front-loads or low-loads; their offering price exceeds the fund's NAV. Since the NAV of three of the five funds increased, market prices probably rose from the previous day.

Sources of Return on a Mutual Fund

A mutual fund can provide three different kinds of return. It may pay a dividend on its shares. It may distribute the gains earned on investments. Or the fund's investments may rise in value, boosting the NAV of your shares. Let's look at each possible source of return.

Dividend distributions

When a mutual fund collects dividends or interest on its investments, it passes these to investors. **Dividend distributions** to the fund's shareholders—top part of Exhibit 17.4—can be made monthly, quarterly, or annually. Regardless of frequency, the dividend is set as a dollar amount per fund share. The more shares you own, the bigger your distribution.

Distribution of capital gains

When a mutual fund sells an investment for more than it paid, it has a capital gain which is then distributed to its shareholders. Most funds accumulate their gains for the year to make one distribution as a set amount per share. The more shares owned, the larger your **capital gains distribution.**

What if the fund suffers a loss? Losses offset gains, lowering (even eliminating) distributions. The lower part of Exhibit 17.4 illustrates. Historically, funds have distributed short-term gains—investments held 6 months or less—separately from those on investments held more than 6 months. That is less significant now since both gains are fully taxable.

Mutual Fund Distributions

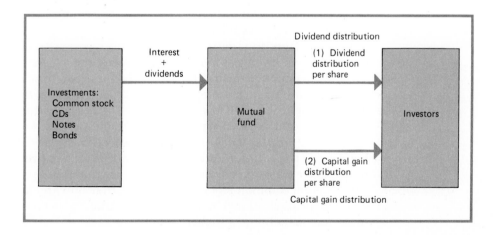

Changes in the NAV of the fund's shares

The NAV of a fund's shares parallels the market value of the fund's investments. If the number of shares is constant, the NAV will rise as the market value increases and drop as it declines. If a fund holds a common stock that continues to rise in price, it may decide to hold those shares rather than sell. Do the fund's shareholders participate in the price rise? Definitely. As the stock rises, so will the fund's NAV.

Some might argue these are only paper gains. True, but that has a decided tax advantage. Suppose you bought 100 shares when a fund's NAV was $10. If the fund's NAV rises to $20, your investment is worth $2,000 (100 shares × $20 NAV). You have a $1,000 paper gain, but none of it has to be recognized until you redeem the shares; you defer income taxes until then.

Can a fund's NAV decline? And if it does, won't that reduce the mutual fund's return? Yes, on both counts. A drop in market value—a not uncommon happening for some funds—reduces the fund's NAV. That could cause you a loss. But it confirms that a change in NAV affects your return.

Total investor return on a mutual fund

An example will show how all three elements combine to give the total return. On January 2, Rachel Risktaker invested in Best Bet, a no-load mutual fund. Its NAV was $10, so she purchased 100 shares with her $1,000 investment. During the next 12 months the fund distributed a dividend of $0.50 per share: Rachel received $50 (100 shares × $0.50). It also distributed $0.40 per share as a capital gain: Rachel received $40: (100 shares × $0.40). Last, by year-end the rise in the market value of Best Bet's investments boosted its NAV to $10.20. Rachel's 100 shares are now worth $1,020 (100 shares × $10.20). The $50 dividend, $40 capital gain, and $20 rise in market value give a $110 total gain. On her initial $1,000 investment, that is a respectable 11 percent return: $110 return/$1,000 initial investment.

Operating expenses

For simplicity, we have ignored the costs of operating the mutual fund. But the fund has major **operating expenses.** First, the fund has to pay for record keeping, preparing financial reports, sending out account statements, promotional expenses, telephone fees and other administrative costs. Second, the fund has to pay the professional manager who selects investments, reviews holdings, and decides what needs to be sold.

All investors in a mutual fund pay these costs. Part of the return the fund earns on its investments is used to pay these expenses. How much? The typical **expense ratio** (total fund expenses/total fund assets) can range from less than 0.5 percent to more than 2 percent. That lowers your return by the same fraction. If the fund earned 14 percent, the net return to its investors might be 13.5 percent, 12 percent, or less. Several things can contribute to differences in the expense ratio. Small funds often have higher expense ratios. Funds that concentrate on fixed-return investments tend to have lower expense ratios than those that invest in common stocks. Even among common stock funds, those that buy and sell stocks aggressively may have higher expense ratios. Last, some professional money managers just charge a higher fee.

Does that mean the "best" mutual fund has the lowest expense ratio? Not necessarily; it depends on the fund's performance. Suppose High Dollar fund delivered a 15 percent return to its shareholders *after* paying operating expenses of 2 percent. Mediocre Performance fund held its operating expenses to only 1 percent but earned only 13 percent *after* expenses for its shareholders. High Dollar's superior return justifies its higher expense ratio.

When a publication lists a mutual fund's return, it is calculated *after* deducting all expenses. And that is, after all, the return you are interested in.

Strategy

A fund's expense ratio is a concern, but a higher ratio may be justified if the fund's net return is higher.

Caution: 12b-1 expenses ahead

The original intent of the **12b-1 fee**—named for the Securities and Exchange Commission rule that authorized it—was to cover marketing and promotional expenses. Small funds were supposed to use it to attract additional assets which would help them lower the expense ratio to all shareholders, and some did that. But some large funds use it to pay commissions. They replace an obvious front load with a more subtle back load, then add an annual 12b-1 fee.

The fee can range from 0.25 percent to 1.5 percent and provides the money to pay the commissions of the sales force. While that may not seem like much, remember it reduces your return by the same amount and is assessed every year. A fund with a 1.25 percent fee would charge you a total of 12.5 percent over 10 years! Makes the old, obvious 4 to 8.5 percent front load seem small-time.

Some mutual funds include the fee in their expense ratio (there is currently some discussion of requiring this), and others state it separately. Either way it becomes a "hidden load" that reduces your return. How should you handle the fee? Compare the historical returns among funds with and without fees. Unless the fund with the 12b-1 fee truly delivers a higher net return *after* all fees and expenses, avoid it, especially if 12b-1 fees are 1 percent or more.

Strategy

Unless a fund delivers superior performance for its 12b-1 fee, avoid it. You are merely paying a hidden load—a payment that goes on and on and on.

TYPES OF MUTUAL FUNDS: INVESTMENT OBJECTIVES

Mutual funds must supply potential investors with a statement of their **investment objectives.** They will specify whether the fund is seeking income, growth of capital, price stability, or other results. It is not enough to say "to make a bundle any way we can." Common objectives are to earn current income, to stress long-term growth of capital, or to earn tax-free income. Depending on the objective, risk can range from moderate to very high. A second part of the statement specifies what investment the fund expects to use to achieve its goals.

Mutual funds print a **prospectus** that explains objectives, goals, and minimum investment amounts, states rules and procedures for making investments or redemptions, gives a summary of the fund's historical returns, and provides an address and telephone number for contacting the fund. Funds must provide a copy to all prospective investors.

Strategy

Reviewing a fund's prospectus is an essential step in the investment process.

Mutual funds can be grouped into broad categories. Exhibit 17.5 summarizes the investment objectives and major investment vehicles for 12 such categories. Each of those categories falls into one of three overall types: (1) money market funds, (2) bond funds, and (3) common stock funds.

Money Market Mutual Funds

Money market funds concentrate on low-risk investments with very short maturities: 30 to 90 days. Risk ranges from low to very low. Because of the short maturity, the fund's investments have a stable market value. This allows the fund to fix the NAV at $1.

Interest earned on the fund's investments is your sole return. The short maturity means the fund continually purchases new investments. As interest rates rise or fall, the fund's return follows. With a slight lag, the fund's return tracks interest rates in the financial markets.

General-purpose money market funds

General-purpose money market funds invest in commercial paper, bankers acceptances, jumbo CDs, and other financial instruments. Most have very low risk, a short maturity, and require a large ($1,000 is typical) minimum investment. By pooling funds from many investors the fund can hold a diversified group of these investments.

Government money market fund

Government money market funds invest exclusively in securities backed by the U.S. government. While its investments are guaranteed, the mutual fund itself is not insured or guaranteed by the government. Risk is even less than for a general-purpose fund, but return is 25 to 125 basis points (recall that's 0.25 to 1.25 percent) lower.

Tax-exempt money market fund

Tax-exempt money market funds invest in short-term municipal securities. Because interest on those securities is exempt from federal income tax, dividend distributions from the fund are exempt. Risk levels are similar to a general purpose fund's, but your return is only 65 to 75 percent of what you would receive elsewhere due to the tax-exempt feature. Even with the lower return, investors with high marginal tax rates find these funds attractive.

Bond Mutual Funds

Bond mutual funds invest in notes and bonds that provide a fixed return. Some funds concentrate on corporate securities, some on municipals, and

Exhibit 17.5

Chief Types of Mutual Funds, with Investment Objectives, Major Investments, Minimums, and Risk Exposure

Mutual fund	Investment objective	Major investments	Typical minimum investment	Risk exposure
Money Market Funds				
General money market	Income	Commercial paper, CDs, bankers' acceptances	$1,000	Low
Government	Income	Treasury and federal agency securities	1,000	Very low
Tax-exempt	Tax-free income	Short-term municipal securities	2,500	Low
Bond Funds				
Investment grade: corporate bond	Income	High-quality corporate notes and bonds	1,000	Low
Aggressive: corporate bond	Income	Lower-quality corporate notes and bonds	1,000	Moderately high
Government	Income	Treasury and federal agency securities	1,000	Very low
Investment grade: municipal bond	Tax-free income	High-quality municipal notes and bonds	2,500	Low
Aggressive: municipal bond	Tax-free income	Lower-quality municipal notes and bonds	2,500	Moderately high
Common Stock Funds				
Aggressive growth	Maximum capital growth	Common stocks with very good growth potential	1,000	Very high
Growth	Long-term growth; income is a secondary objective	Common stocks with good growth potential	1,000	High
Growth and income	Long-term growth and income	Common stocks that pay dividends and have growth potential	1,000	Moderately high
Income	Income with some potential for growth	Common stock and fixed-return investments that provide high current income	1,000	Moderate
Specialized	Growth, income, or some combination	Common stocks concentrated in one industry or outside the U.S.	1,500	Extremely high

some on government securities. The usual investment objective is to receive high current income with some safety of principal. Risk can range from very low on government bond mutual funds to moderately high on aggressive corporate and municipal bond mutual funds.

Maturities of the underlying investments can range from 2 or 3 years to 20 years and more. NAV on these funds is *not* fixed. As an earlier chapter noted, prices of fixed-return securities move inversely with market interest rates: the longer the maturity, the larger the price change. When interest rates rise, a fund's NAV can drop significantly. Your return will do likewise.

An example will illustrate. When Tricia Timid bought 100 shares of Steady Rock, a no-load bond fund, its NAV was $10. A short time later, market interest rates began rising. The market value of Steady Rock's bond investments did the opposite; the value of Tricia's 100 shares followed suit. She will only receive the current NAV, so she may suffer a loss. If interest rates had fallen, Tricia would have had a gain.

Returns on a bond mutual fund come primarily from its dividend distributions. Capital gains distributions are likely to be less significant: when interest rates are stable, the fund's investments will neither rise nor fall in value, so the potential for gains is limited. When rates are volatile, chances of major gains or losses increase. Returns from the third source, changes in the fund's NAV, can range from limited to substantial.

Strategy

When interest rates are volatile, be prepared for swings in a bond mutual fund's NAV; the longer the maturity, the larger the swing. It could mean significant gains or losses.

Corporate bond funds: Investment grade

Investment grade corporate bond funds concentrate on high-quality corporate bonds and notes. By only accepting notes and bonds with the top three Moody's or S&P's quality grades, these funds keep risk low. A typical investment objective is high current income with safety.

Some bond funds limit investment maturities to less than 4 years. While not constant, NAV for these short-term bond funds is reasonably stable. Interest rate risk is low. Other funds concentrate on investments with long maturities, often in excess of 20 years. NAV for these funds can be much less stable. A rise in market interest rates can drop the fund's NAV sharply; interest rate risk is significant.

As this is written, few funds concentrate on maturities in the 10- to 12-year intermediate range.

Strategy

Decide whether the higher return of a fund that invests in bonds with longer maturities justifies its more volatile NAV. If interest rates are volatile, shorter maturities are advised.

Corporate bond fund: Aggressive

Aggressive corporate bond funds concentrate on lower-quality corporate bonds and notes, often with the objective of receiving very high income. Many concentrate on securities rated BBB or Baa and lower. As a consequence, risk is moderately high. But the trade-off is a return 200 to 500 basis points higher than return from an investment grade fund. Most of these funds concentrate on long maturities, so interest rate risk is high.

Government bond fund

Government bond funds invest in Treasury securities, federal agency securities, and some mortgage-backed securities. The funds are not guaranteed by the government, but their investments usually are. Risk is rated as low. A common investment objective is current income with a high degree of safety. Maturities on the underlying investments range from 10 to more than 20 years. When interest rates are steady, that is fine. But as rates change, the fund's NAV moves the opposite way. Rising rates can send the NAV plummeting. Interest rate risk, especially on the longer maturities, is significant.

Since income from many government securities is exempt from state income taxes, what about returns on these funds? They are probably not exempt. Before you invest, check the fund's prospectus, call the mutual fund, or contact your state tax office.

Municipal bond fund: Investment grade

Investment grade municipal bond funds concentrate on tax-exempt securities rated in one of the top three quality grades by Moody's or S&P's. Risk is therefore low. Fund dividends are exempt from federal income taxes, and a portion may be exempt from state income taxes. A typical investment objective is tax-free current income with safety.

Maturities range from short to very long. Short-term funds concentrate on maturities of 4 years or less; the NAV for these funds is reasonably stable. Intermediate-term funds invest in securities with maturities of 6 to 12 years; changes in interest rates can produce a volatile NAV. Long-term funds, choosing investments with maturities of 20 years or more, are most sensitive to changes in market interest rates. Rising or falling interest rates can drop or boost NAV sharply. The trade-off is that return rises with maturity.

Strategy

Decide if the higher return on a longer-maturity fund justifies its more volatile NAV. When rates are volatile, shorter maturities are advised.

Municipal bond fund: Aggressive

Aggressive municipal bond funds invest in lower-quality municipal securities, mostly those rated BBB or Baa and below. Risk will be moderately high, but returns will be better. Dividend distributions from these funds are usually exempt from federal income taxes and sometimes from state income taxes. A typical investment objective is high, tax-free current income.

Most aggressive municipal bond funds concentrate on long maturities—20 years and up—so NAVs will be affected by interest rate changes.

Common Stock Mutual Funds

Mutual funds that invest in common stocks launched the industry in the 1920s. There are some good reasons why they have endured and expanded. First, selecting common stocks is a technical, time-consuming task. Second, a common stock's return depends heavily on the success of the underlying business venture, so well-informed decisions are crucial. Third, once purchased, a common stock must be monitored, since a firm's prospects can change quickly and dramatically. Fourth, good diversification is essential, but achieving it takes skill and a large, rectangular pile of money. Individuals faced with these challenges increasingly turn to the professional management of a common stock mutual fund.

Investment objectives for common stock mutual funds cover a far broader spectrum than those of either bond or money market funds. At the conservative end, some funds emphasize current income with limited capital growth. In the middle range, the emphasis shifts: current income and long-term growth of capital receive equal billing. With more aggressive funds, income becomes secondary and long-term capital growth is primary.

A mutual fund's investment objective largely determines its sources of return. If the fund emphasizes current income, dividend distributions predominate. The importance of these dividends drops as the emphasis shifts to long-term capital growth, and appreciation of the fund's underlying common stock investments takes on added importance. Major sources of return include capital gains distributions from the fund and appreciation of its NAV due to the rise in the price of the fund's investments. For aggressive funds, returns are almost exclusively from capital gains and appreciation in the fund's NAV.

Beta: A measure of a common stock mutual fund's risk

Beta is widely used as a measure of a common stock mutual fund's risk. Beta measures how volatile the fund's return is relative to the overall stock market. A beta of 1.0 indicates that the fund has the same volatility as the overall market. A beta of 0.5 suggests the fund is one-half as volatile as the market. A beta of 1.5 suggests the fund is 1½ times as volatile as the overall market. Mutual fund betas generally fall into the 0.3 to 1.9 range, with the higher betas indicating higher risk.

Suppose we have two mutual funds: (1) High Flyer, with a beta of 1.5, and (2) Steady Rock, with a beta of 0.5 (incidentally, you generally do not have to compute your own betas; a number of mutual fund publications do it for you). What would happen if the overall stock market rose 10 percent? (Realistic this figure may not be; easy to work with, it is.) High Flyer would advance 15 percent (1.5 beta × 10% market change), while Steady Rock would rise 5 percent (0.5 beta × 10% market change). In a rising market, high-beta funds should outperform their lower-beta counterparts.

But what if the market sinks 15 percent? Now Steady Rock, true to its name, comes through: it drops 7.5 percent (0.5 beta × 15%), but that is far short of High Flyer's 22.5 percent plunge (1.5 beta × 15%). Steady Rock, or any low-beta fund, will suffer far less in a market decline.

Which is best overall, high beta or low? It depends. Risk-averse investors will want to stay in the low-beta range. Investors willing and able to accept risk should consider funds with moderate to higher betas.

Generally, the more conservative a fund's investment objective, the lower its beta. Funds that emphasize current income often have low betas. Funds that emphasize long-term capital growth have higher betas. Let's examine risk and other features of the funds whose characteristics we've outlined in Exibit 17.5.

Aggressive growth funds

The investment objective of **aggressive growth funds** is maximum capital gains, not current income. These funds often invest in companies that are out of the mainstream: recently formed firms, firms whose product or service has good but uncertain future prospects, firms emerging from serious financial difficulty, or small, less well known firms. Risk on these funds is high.

Betas for this group of funds are among the highest; many are well above 1.0. NAVs for this group are quite volatile. A market upturn can bring large rewards, but a downturn may mean major declines. Potential returns are high but far from assured. Actual returns are sometimes disappointingly low.

Growth funds

Growth funds concentrate on the long-term appreciation of invested capital. Dividends provide some return, but capital gains are likely to be the major component. Growth funds often invest in companies that have a solid record of growth that is expected to continue. These firms have a longer history and may pay a small dividend, but their names are not likely to be household words. Risk is usually high.

Betas in the growth group are below those of the aggressive group, ranging between 0.9 and 1.1. The NAVs in this group can experience sizable swings. A market upturn can propel them up quickly, but a downturn can do considerable damage. Because of the risk, potential returns are high. Still, many growth funds have delivered no better return than others with significantly less risk.

Growth and income funds

Growth and income funds generally have a balanced investment objective: long-term capital growth with current income. Dividend distributions and capital gains are important sources of returns. The funds often concentrate on firms with a solid record of paying dividends and steady growth. Because these firms often have a longer history, the risk is considered only moderately high.

Betas for growth and income funds are generally lower than for straight growth funds, perhaps 0.7 to 0.9. NAVs for this group are less sensitive to swings in the overall stock market. You may miss the breathtaking appreciation when the market rises, but during a decline they drop far less.

Income funds

Income funds are often a hybrid of the common stock fund and the bond fund. The typical investment objective is current income with some capital appreciation. Dividend distributions are a major source of returns, and capital gains normally constitute a smaller return component. Income funds generally invest in well-established firms with a history of paying dividends and promise of continuing to do so. Many also invest in corporate bonds. Risk is moderate to moderately high.

Betas for income funds are generally the lowest for any group of common stock funds, ranging from 0.5 to 0.7. Their NAVs follow the market but are less sensitive than those of the other fund groups and far less prone to wide swings.

Specialized funds

A **specialized mutual fund** concentrates on a narrow range of investments. During the past several years, their numbers have gone up sharply.

Precious metals funds. Precious metals funds invest in the common stocks of national and international firms that deal in gold and other precious metals. Frequently these funds include mining companies. And many funds have the option of also purchasing the precious metal itself; to date, not many have used this extensively. The success or failure of the mutual fund depends on the fortunes of the metal and its related industry. Returns have ranged from breathtaking to abysmal, and they can swing through that range quickly! Risk is very high.

Sector funds. A sector fund targets a specific industry—health care, banking, insurance, chemicals, defense—for all its investments. It ignores all the rules of diversification. The right industry at the right time produces excellent returns. The wrong one or wrong time constitutes a disaster. Risk is extremely high.

Strategy

Only the sophisticated and risk-tolerant should consider highly speculative funds. Sector funds are for the pros, soothsayers, and psychics.

International funds. International funds invest in the common stocks of companies outside the United States. Most do, however, diversify their holdings over a number of different industries in the foreign location. All the standard economic, industry-specific, and competition-related factors still apply, but with international investments you add fluctuations in currency exchange rates and foreign controls. Risk takes on a whole new dimension with this fund group. Beta measurements are less meaningful for international funds, since their stocks are driven by completely different forces.

Despite all these warnings, note that international funds can be useful in an investment program, since they let you diversify investments beyond U.S. borders.

Strategy

For those wanting to diversify their investments outside the United States, an international mutual fund can be an excellent vehicle.

ADVANTAGES OF MUTUAL FUNDS

Mutual funds can provide significant benefits to investors. Some of these flow from their professional money management, some from their systematic records, and the rest from their ability to pool small amounts to achieve economies of scale when investing. Exhibit 17.6 summarizes the major benefits.

Diversification across Investments

Purchase a money market, bond, or common stock mutual fund, and you have instant diversification. Depending on the size and type, mutual funds own from twenty to several hundred different investments. With their pooled funds from many small investors, they can purchase a widely diversified portfolio of investments, rather than putting all their eggs in one basket. Commissions have less effect on returns because of the large purchases.

Poor performance by an individual investment has less impact on a mutual fund's overall results, though a winning investment will not boost returns by as much either. Diversification does not eliminate risk, but it reduces it. And the higher the risk on the underlying investment, the more important it is to be diversified.

"Diversification" of Money Management

Mutual funds also allow you to "diversify" your money managers. You can spread your investment across several mutual funds, "hiring" several managers. In fact it is generally a good idea to do so. That way your investment results do not depend solely on one manager's expertise.

Exhibit 17.6

Summary of Advantages of Mutual Fund Investments

Advantage	Benefit to individual investor
Diversification of investments	Investor spreads risk by holding a portfolio of investments.
Diversification of management	By opening several accounts, investor gets access to expertise of several professional money managers.
Wide choice of investments	Investor has access to many investment options through different funds.
Professional management	Investor does not have the responsibility of selecting, buying, monitoring, and possibly selling investments.
Dollar-cost averaging	Allows moderate-sized, recurring deposits to a mutual fund account.
Simplified record keeping	Periodic reports summarize activity in investor's account.
Automatic reinvestment	Investor can have dividend and/or capital gains distributions reinvested in additional shares.
Systematic withdrawal	Systematic withdrawal plan allows investor to make regular withdrawals from an existing mutual fund account.
Check writing	Check-writing feature permits immediate access to an account via a check.
Family of mutual funds	Provides investor with a choice of mutual funds with widely differing investment objectives.
Telephone transfer or switching	Money can be shifted between accounts within a family of mutual funds.

But for mutual funds, as elsewhere, there are limits to how much you can diversify. You have to meet the minimum investment requirement to open an account. And you do not want so many accounts that you cannot track them. Purchasing several funds is more important with common stock funds, corporate bond funds, and municipal bond funds.

Access to a Wide Choice of Investments

Mutual funds can be used to invest in a wide variety of different investments. In some cases the minimum demanded for direct investment is too large for private investors: $100,000 and up. Even the $5,000 minimum for most corporate and municipal bonds makes buying them questionable except through a mutual fund, especially if you want diversification. Last, some investments require such extensive technical analysis that many investors simply lack the background needed to invest directly; again the professional management of a mutual fund can be the answer.

Professional Money Management

Numerous studies and rating services have raised the question: How do professional money managers do relative to the overall market? The answer: Much worse than many investors would like. Even those that better the market may not be able to do so consistently. Many nearly match the market. And the remainder earn returns that are considerably below the market.

Does that mean you pay a fee for mediocrity? No. A good manager still has much to offer:

- You are relieved of all buy and sell decisions.
- You do not have to monitor individual investments.
- You are less likely to get caught up in today's cat's meow—often tomorrow's dog.
- You no longer have the worry of managing your investment portfolio.

For most people, these benefits justify paying a management fee. If the manager can outperform the market part of the time, so much the better.

Dollar-Cost Averaging

When you use the technique known as **dollar-cost averaging,** you invest a fixed amount at regular intervals. That way you have a series of investments, not one concentrated foray into the market. Dollar-cost averaging can help you avoid purchasing an investment when it might be at an all-time high price or when its return is very low. A mutual fund can be an ideal vehicle because most will accept small, regular investments.

Exhibit 17.7 illustrates averaging in a common-stock mutual fund during a declining and a rising market. Dollar-cost averaging produces an average cost of $5.93; that is less than the $6.75 average price during this declining market. Likewise, the $10.67 average cost under dollar-cost averaging was less than the $11 average price during the rising market period.

A dollar-cost averaging plan requires self-discipline and conviction. It is easy to be enthusiastic in a bull market as prices rise, but it takes courage to invest as the bear market slides ever downward. Yet some of the most rewarding investments are made during the declining phases.

Simplified Record Keeping

Record keeping for mutual funds is easier than tracking individual securities. First, the number of investments is smaller; 1 to 5 funds rather than 10 to 15 securities. Second, mutual funds send statements, like the one in

Exhibit 17.7

Dollar-Cost Averaging in a Declining and a Rising Stock Market.

| Amount invested | Declining Market | | | Rising Market | | |
	Price per share	Number of shares purchased		Price per share	Number of shares purchased
$120	$10	12		$ 8	15
120	8	15		10	12
120	5	24		12	10
120	4	30		15	8
$480 (Total)	$ 6.75 (Average price)	81 (Total)		$11 (Average price)	45 (Total)

$$\text{Average cost (\$5.93)} = \frac{\$480 \text{ invested}}{81 \text{ shares}}$$

$$\text{Average cost (\$10.67)} = \frac{\$480 \text{ invested}}{45 \text{ shares}}$$

Exhibit 17.8, summarizing shares held, dates and prices of any purchases or sales, dividends and capital gains distributions. A year-end report summarizes dividends and capital gains for tax purposes.

Automatic Reinvestment

Automatic reinvestment is an option offered by most mutual funds. Investors can choose to have both dividends and capital gains reinvested, one reinvested, or neither. Even if the amount is small, most funds will reinvest it, and reinvesting uses dollar-cost averaging to purchase more shares. Better yet, most front-load funds do not charge fees for reinvesting.

Exhibit 17.8

Mutual Fund Monthly Statement

CONFIRMATION STATEMENT AND INVEST-BY-MAIL FORM
To add to your account please make check payable to:

Fidelity Group

FIDELITY EQUITY-INCOME FUND, INC.   PAGE 1

Return this portion with your check to: Fidelity Service Co. P.O. Box 2656 Boston, Ma. 02208

Mckenzie Woodrow
954 Cliffview Drive
Elm Grove, MI   75620

Amount of Investment

$

FUND NO   23
ACCOUNT NO   101202303
IDENT. OR SOC. SEC. NO.   222-33-4444

23 0101202303   45   911

SEE REVERSE SIDE FOR COMPLETE INSTRUCTIONS ON HOW
TO MAKE ADDITIONAL INVESTMENTS TO YOUR ACCOUNT.

PLEASE KEEP THIS PORTION FOR YOUR RECORDS   02/16/87

ALPHA CODE	ACCOUNT NO.	FUND NO.			FIDELITY EQUITY-INCOME FUND, INC.
Woodrow-Mckenzie	101202303	23			

Confirm Date	Trade Date	Transaction		Dollar Amount	Share Price	Shares This Transaction
		BEGINNING BALANCE				246.493
01/07	11/16	INCOME REINVEST	.650	160.22	20.12	7.963
03/16	03/01	INCOME REINVEST	.330	83.97	17.98	4.670
03/16	03/01	SHORT TERM C G	.660	167.94	17.98	9.340
03/16	03/01	CAP GAIN REINV	.830	211.20	17.98	11.746
06/21	06/01	INCOME REINVEST	.350	98.07	18.51	5.298
06/11	06/11	IMMEDIATE PURCHASE		250.00	18.46	13.543
09/20	08/16	INCOME REINVEST	.350	104.67	17.71	5.910
01/03	11/22	INCOME REINVEST	.650	198.23	22.58	8.779
02/17	02/17	DUPLICATE CONFIRM				

355371

Your payment option is		Certificate shares held by you +	Shares on deposit	=	Total shares owned
Income dividends	Capital gains				
SHARES	SHARES	0	313.742		313.742

BOX 3 QUALIFIES FOR DIV. EXCLUSION

0000

Tax I.D. No.	(1) Distributions This Year	(2) Income This Year	(3)	(4) Capital Gains This Year (4)
04-6133142	826.07	614.87		211.20

WHEN THIS STATEMENT IS MARKED 1099 THE INFORMATION ABOVE
WILL BE FILED WITH THE INTERNAL REVENUE SERVICE PURSUANT
TO FEDERAL LAW.

IF YOU NEED ADDITIONAL INFORMATION ON THIS ACCOUNT, WRITE:
FIDELITY SERVICE CO. P.O. BOX 193, BOSTON, MA 02101
OR CALL (800) 225-6270—IN MASSACHUSETTS CALL COLLECT (617) 227-1888

Strategy

Request automatic reinvestment if you have no immediate need for dividend or capital gains distributions and want to buy more shares.

Systematic Withdrawal Plan

Mutual funds offer **systematic withdrawal plans;** the investor is sent a set amount each month. If the amount is no greater than dividend and capital gains distributions, the number of shares will remain steady. If withdrawals are larger than distributions, shares are sold. As the number of shares drops, the distributions also fall, since they are based on the number of shares owned. That could mean selling even more shares to maintain the distribution.

Most funds allow you to change the amount withdrawn at any time. Such programs can provide a steady retirement income, as we will see later.

Check-Writing Privilege

Most money market mutual funds permit you to **write checks against your account.** Some corporate and municipal bond funds—mostly those with short maturities—also offer checking. The usual minimum check amount is $500. Blank checks are free, and there is no service fee. Most businesses and financial institutions readily accept the checks, so you have ready access to your money.

Families of Mutual Funds

Larger mutual fund organizations offer a whole **"family" of funds,** ranging from money market accounts through bond funds to common stock funds. Within each group there may be several funds. The investor in these fund families gets increased flexibility, since you can meet a wide range of investment needs but stay within the same general fund. Some front-load fund families allow transfers within the family with no added load, which improves flexibility.

Telephone Transfers

Firms offering a family of funds may permit **telephone transfers** from one fund to another. Many offer toll-free numbers which you use to transfer between accounts or to establish an account in a new fund using money from an existing one. But there are limitations. Both funds must be in the same family, and both must be registered in the same name: a fund is not about to let Sid Swindle transfer money from Ann Weber's account to his name.

Suppose you wanted to use $1,200 from your money market account to make a $100 transfer to another fund in each of the next 12 months. Or suppose you wanted to shift from a high-beta aggressive stock fund to a growth and income fund. Or maybe you want to leave stocks for the safety and stability of a money market mutual fund. A single call each month would suffice.

Telephone transfer is useful, but some ads oversell its worth. They picture Brenda Bold adroitly maneuvering among the shoals of the investment world with the aid of her telephone transfer. At 10:00 A.M., she deftly switches from her high-beta common stock fund; the market plunges minutes later. She only stays in her new bond fund account several hours because she switches just before market interest rates soar. Sensing a recovery, she's back to the stock fund by 2:00 P.M. Wanting to make sure she sleeps well, she's back in a money market fund before day's end. We doubt many investors have the skills or savvy to do this—or should even consider it. In fact, some funds limit the number of transfers to prevent such shuffling.

SPECIAL USES OF MUTUAL FUNDS

Mutual fund accounts can be established for minors and as tax-deferred retirement plans. Establishing an account for either of these specialized purposes is easy because the mutual fund has already taken the needed legal and administrative steps. Let's look at why they can work well for both purposes.

Accounts for Minors

Mutual funds will usually open an account in a minor's name under the Uniform Gift to Minors Act. In effect, the adult makes a gift to the minor: an adult can give $10,000 annually to a minor with no gift tax consequences; a couple can give $20,000 tax-free. The minor owns the account, and it carries his or her Social Security number. All dividend and capital gains distributions are reported on the minor's tax return. But an adult, the custodian, retains control until the minor comes of age at either age 18 or age 21.

There can be advantages. The child's tax rate is often lower, so less tax is paid. To age 14, the first $500 is not taxed, and the next $500 is taxed at the child's rate (currently 15 percent); amounts beyond that are taxed at the parent's rate. At age 14 and above, everything beyond $500 up to about $17,000 is taxed at the child's rate. The adult's creditors cannot attach the account, since it is the child's.

But there are also disadvantages. Once made, the gift cannot be reversed. Second, there are restrictions on how money in the account can be used if a parent made the gift: use it for the child's "normal" support and the account's earnings may have to be included on the parent's tax return. Once the child reaches majority, he or she can do whatever he or she wishes with the money.

Retirement Plans: IRA and Keogh

Most mutual fund groups accept both Individual Retirement Accounts (IRAs) and Keogh accounts (both were introduced in Chapter 5; Chapter 18 provides more detail). The mutual fund handles the administrative details on these accounts, saving you work. Since most fund families offer these accounts, you have many investment choices. And while many funds charge a fee, it's small enough to have little effect on your return. Finally, these accounts have the legally required restrictions that allow the dividend, capital gains, and price appreciation to accumulate without immediate tax consequences.

INFORMA-TION ON MUTUAL FUNDS

Publications that track mutual funds have grown almost as fast as the funds themselves. Exhibit 17.9 summarizes the major sources of information on mutual funds. The information these publications provide can be divided into three broad categories.

The most basic is background information on different funds: investment objective, minimum investment, size of fund, how long it has operated, special accounts offered, address and telephone number.

Higher-level publications provide performance data on mutual funds, such as historical returns for various periods, beta measures of risk, estimates of what a $1,000 investment might have grown to, dividend and capital gains data, comparative returns for similar funds, and returns for some "market" stock or bond index.

Finally, some publications offer "judgmental" information: performance ratings, a "suggested fund buy-and-sell list," risk analyses, and recommended investment strategies.

Using the Information Sources

Of those listed in Exhibit 17.9, is there one "best" source? Probably not. A lot depends on what role you want to play in selecting a mutual fund. An investor who is making a detailed analysis of funds needs both background

Exhibit 17.9

Major Publications Providing Information on Mutual Funds

Publication	How often published	Information provided
Investor's Directory of the No-Load Mutual Fund Assoc.	Annually	1, 2, 3, 5, 6, 7
Wiesenberger Investment Company Services	Monthly, quarterly, and annually	1, 2, 3, 4, 5, 6, 7, 8, 9, 10, 11, 12, 13, 14
United Mutual Fund Selector	Biweekly	1, 2, 3, 4, 5, 6, 8, 9, 12, 13, 14, 15
Barron's	Quarterly	2, 6, 8, 9, 10, 14
Business Week	Annually	1, 2, 4, 6, 8, 9, 12, 13, 15, 17
Changing Times	Annually	8, 9, 15
Forbes	Annually	4, 6, 8, 9, 12, 13, 16
Money	Annually	1, 2, 4, 8, 9, 15

Key:
1 Fund address and telephone number
2 Investment objective
3 Minimum investment
4 Front load or initial sales charge
5 Date fund was established
6 Total assets of fund at some recent date
7 Special investor services
8 Return for past 1 to 12 months
9 Return in past 3 to 10 years

10 Value of assumed $10,000 investment
11 Summary of fund's major holdings
12 Comparative returns for funds and market
13 Expense ratio as percentage of assets
14 Dividend and capital gains distributions
15 Risk exposure rating
16 Fund rating in "bull" and "bear" markets
17 Rating of risk-adjusted performance

and performance data. Another may want general background, performance "info," and some judgment calls. Investors who do not desire significant involvement need detailed recommendations: the more specific the better.

Strategy

Decide your role in selecting and managing mutual fund investments; then you will be better able to determine which information sources best meet your needs.

Most Information Is Historical

There are risks involved in using historical data as your sole guide when selecting mutual funds. Studies suggest that mutual funds which perform very well in one period may not in the next: yesterday's winner becomes tomorrow's also-ran.

Does that mean historical data has little worth? Not at all. Some funds compile solid 3- to 5-year performance records. They may not be in the top 10 or 20 in any one year, but they have consistently good records most years. Though a repeat is not guaranteed, the fund has demonstrated it can do some things right. Following the same line of reasoning, avoid funds with a lengthy and consistent history of poor performance. Past history can help you identify funds that expose their investors to high risk but never deliver any added return. Past history can show whether a fund is consistent; if it soars for 6 or 12 months and then shows months of dismal results, it is no find. Finally, some funds' managements just seem to be more adept at avoiding or minimizing investment pitfalls.

Historical information offers no certainty, but it makes more sense to put money in a fund that has avoided major blunders rather than hoping some losing manager's lucky number has to come up some time!

SHOULD YOU OWN A MUTUAL FUND?

Imagine you have accumulated money and are reviewing investment options. Common stocks look interesting, but you wonder whether buying individual shares or a mutual fund makes more sense. Or you are undecided between buying a municipal bond versus a municipal bond mutual fund. Your choice centers on (1) how much money you have to invest, (2) the level of involvement you want, and (3) your special needs or constraints.

Exhibit 17.10 can help you decide between investing directly or through a mutual fund. Mutual funds deserve a hard look if most of your responses to the checklist questions are negative. My experience suggests mutual funds are best for many people, particularly those who lack the time, dedication, dollars, expertise, data sources, and training to pursue individual investments.

PURCHASING A MONEY MARKET FUND

Purchasing a money-market fund is reasonably simple. Since there are many to choose from, you are likely to find one that meets your needs. While each fund determines its own practices and procedures, their terms, features, and services are often similar. If several funds offer a service, competition forces most others to follow.

Match the Fund to Your Risk-Return Preference

Set your risk-return preference, then select the money market fund that matches it. For highly risk-averse investors, sacrificing 25 to 100 basis points for the lower risk of a government money market fund is justified. Investors willing to tolerate higher risk may want a general-purpose fund.

Does Your Tax Bracket Justify a Tax-Exempt Fund?

Should you choose a tax-exempt money market fund? Receiving tax-free income may be nice, but it only makes sense if it provides more money after taxes. Compare the after-tax return on a general-purpose fund to what the tax-exempt fund offers. Only take the tax-exempt fund if its return is higher.

Concentrate on Large Funds

While the risk on the investments that general-purpose funds buy is low, diversification is still desirable. Large funds can do that easily. And they have a bigger asset base over which to spread their operating expenses, which holds down your costs.

Check Writing Is Essential

Insist on a fund with a check-writing privilege; it makes the fund more flexible. Best are funds that allow checks for less than $500.

Exhibit 17.10

Checklist: Should You Choose a Mutual Fund?

	Yes	No
1. Do you have enough money to diversify your investments?	____	____
2. If you do not diversify, can you accept the added risk?	____	____
3. Will you have $1,000 or more each time you want to make an investment?	____	____
4. Are you well enough trained in economics, finance, and accounting to analyze individual investments?	____	____
5. Do you have time to make a detailed analysis of individual investments?	____	____
6. Will you monitor your investment once you have made it?	____	____
7. Do you enjoy managing your investments?	____	____
8. Will you keep the records necessary to track individual investments?	____	____

Telephone Exchange, or Switching	Telephone switching means little unless you have investments in several funds within a family. The feature lets you use money in the money market to purchase shares in a different mutual fund. Or you can quickly redeem the shares you presently have in another mutual fund and transfer the money to the money market fund.
Historical Rates of Return	Several of the publications listed in Exhibit 17.9 compile extensive statistics on the past performance of money market funds. Though differences between funds within each broad category are small, a review of the manager's past record is recommended.
INVESTING IN A BOND FUND	Since the number of bond funds has increased sharply, you now have a far wider choice than you would have in the past. You are likely to find one with an investment objective that parallels your needs. But the proliferation has made your selection more challenging.
Concentrate on No-Load Funds	Most studies confirm that no-load and front-load funds perform equally . . . if we ignore the load. Factor it in and the load funds lose. Front loads can sharply lower returns in the early years. Back-load funds limit flexibility by setting a stiff penalty for early redemption.
Concentrate on Funds with Large Total Assets	Diversification is an important factor to consider when choosing both corporate and municipal bond funds. Large funds have greater resources for monitoring their holdings, and they can take advantage of economies of scale when selling and purchasing bonds and notes. They have the money to buy many different issues. Finally, the large fund's asset base can hold down the fund's expense ratio. That can improve the investor's net return.
Match the Investment Objective to Your Risk-Return Preference	Before you start a search for the "ideal" bond fund, decide your risk-return preference. Your willingness to accept risk will determine what funds you should consider. If you are uncomfortable with risk, it is often better to accept a lower return as a trade-off for security. If your financial situation and tolerance permit more risk, consider more aggressive funds.
Consider Funds with Short to Intermediate Maturities	Limits on the maturity of investments can reduce the swings in a fund's NAV. With this in mind, some funds operate in the short range—generally less than 4 years—or the intermediate range—generally less than 12 years. When rates are rising or highly volatile, a short or intermediate maturity makes sense. These funds are also the best choice if you plan to redeem the shares in the next 6 to 12 months. As this is written, choices of maturities in the municipal area are good, but only fair in the corporate and government areas.
Does a Tax-Exempt Bond Fund Make Sense?	Avoiding taxes on a fund's dividend distributions is an attractive concept, but is a tax-exempt fund the best? The key is the after-tax return. Select a tax-exempt fund if its return is higher than that on a taxable fund after you pay the income taxes. If the taxable fund's return is larger even after taxes, take it and pay the tax.

Historical Rates of Return	Several of the sources listed in Exhibit 17.9 provided detailed performance data for bond mutual funds. A comparison of returns across a number of funds with similar investment objectives can highlight the differences between them. Though there is not that much difference between low-risk funds, returns from aggressive funds can vary tremendously. Some of the very funds that relied on aggressive financial instruments to enhance return have had the opposite happen: their returns plunged. They had returns far below those of less aggressive funds. A careful review of past results is time well spent.
SELECTING A COMMON STOCK FUND	Selecting a common stock mutual fund is a *major* challenge. First, the number of funds is already sizable (currently more than 600), and it is growing (up 75 percent in the past 5 years).[1] Second, there is considerable diversity within each of the five investment objective categories. Differences between funds in different categories can be even greater. Third, individual funds are not above portraying themselves in the "best" light, so a common stock mutual fund's performance must be reviewed under several economic scenarios. Finally, common stocks are complex and so are the mutual funds that purchase them.
Match the Investment Objective to Your Risk-Return Preference	First decide your risk "comfort level." High-risk investment can be exciting: the panorama from atop the highs can be breathtaking, but so can peering up from the cavernous lows. Your high-risk venture can make for good social conversation. It often means higher returns. But are you comfortable with that risk? It is not worth constant anxiety, sleeplessness, or worry.
	We are not trying to steer everyone to a federally insured CD; it's tough to lose sleep with a CD, but the returns show why. Rather, take time to decide what amount of risk *you* want.
	Once you set the risk level, you can decide whether aggressive, growth, growth and income, or income should be your choice. Single out your objective, and the field of 600 funds should shrink quickly.
Concentrate on No-Load Funds	For many, no-load funds should be the first and often sole choice. Load funds are best reserved for someone who needs and wants the guidance of the salesperson; you sacrifice return to pay for it. Even if you want the help, you should have reservations. Some salespeople provide excellent guidance, but the guidance the investor receives can also be worthless or even harmful. To protect yourself, you need to understand the basics yourself. And if you have come that far, why not push a bit further and select your own no-load funds?
	What about back-load funds? Better than front-loads—that is faint praise—but still no match for no-loads. You are locked in during those

---

[1] *Investment Company Institute 1986 Mutual Fund Fact Book*, Investment Company Institute, Washington D.C., 1986, p. 19.

early years; and there may be hefty 12b-1 fees to boot. Suppose the fund is a loser, or the economic environment suggests it's time to switch funds: you could face a costly back-load fee to get out. And you still need background to judge the quality of the salesperson's advice.

Well, how about low-load funds? Our rule is simple. Ask yourself: Is the low-load fund delivering something for its fee? If yes, go ahead. If not, then do some more searching in the no-load ranks.

Strategy

No-load funds are by far the best choice for many. Second choice is low-load funds. Third are back-load funds. And a distant fourth are front-load funds.

Common Stock Mutual Funds Are Long-Term Investments

Common stock mutual funds should be considered long-term investments. It simply takes time for the ownership investments that underlie common stocks to produce results; likewise for the mutual funds that buy them. Furthermore, as the last chapter noted, stock prices can be highly volatile; the NAV of common stock mutual funds can, too. If there is a sharp price drop, you will want to hold a mutual fund for possible price recovery. You cannot do that if you have an immediate need for the money.

As a general guide, plan to keep a common stock mutual fund for at least 2 years, possibly 5 years or more. Common stock mutual funds are

no place for next month's rent money, the down payment on a house, or your emergency cash reserve.

Invest on a Regular Basis

Investor enthusiasm seems to peak when the stock market is about to drop through the floor. Then it seems nearly a "sure thing" that you'll make money. But that can be, and often is, the worst time to jump into the market. Yet that same group of investors often deserts the market just when it is poised for a solid advance. You can often avoid the turmoil and prevent being whipsawed by investing on a regular basis.

Strategy

Set a regular monthly investment amount and then use it to make dollar-cost averaging work for you.

Buy More Than One Mutual Fund

There are literally dozens of professional mutual fund managers out there waiting to serve you. In my opinion, you ought to give several a chance. It would be nice if some publication could single out the "best" manager for the next several years, but no such crystal ball exists. Rather than bet all of your money on a single manager, why not hire a team of managers?

It usually costs no more to place $1,000 in two funds than to invest the entire $2,000 in one, but with two funds you have the expertise of two managers. Some managers just do better in certain economic environments; if you have several, you improve your chances of "hiring" an effective one. Good diversification principles tell you not to concentrate on a single investment, so why concentrate on a single mutual fund manager? Diversifying your fund holdings takes work, but not much more than wisely choosing a single fund. Any analysis of mutual funds will reveal a number of promising candidates. Rather than struggle to select the "best," settle for several good ones.

Strategy

Diversify across mutual funds; you gain the expertise and experience of several managers. Diversification may not guarantee a winner, but it lessens risk.

ANNUITIES

Annuities are managed investment vehicles that many life insurance companies sell. Traditional annuities offered one investment choice: a fixed, guaranteed return. You had to choose the insurance company, but there were plenty of salespeople to convince you they could "help." All that has changed: now annuities can be had with fixed or variable returns. The return on the variable rate annuity is based on the performance of an underlying pool of investments, and you can choose different types of pools. There are pools that invest in fixed-return bonds and notes of varying maturity and risk. Others invest in variable return options, including common stocks and real estate.

Payout of Benefits

Annuities promise a fixed-dollar payment that continues for a set period, generally someone's lifetime. That is why some people claim annuities provide an income you cannot outlive. The person who receives the payments is the **annuitant. Immediate annuities** begin making payments shortly after they are purchased and are often used in retirement planning (see Chapter 18). But we will spend our time on **deferred annuities,** on which payments are delayed, often for years. During the delay, earnings accumulate for future payment. One attraction is that no income tax has to be paid on the earnings while they accumulate.

Payment of Premiums

You make a one-time payment to purchase a **single-premium annuity.** The minimum can be $5,000 or more. Purchasers make a series of premium deposits to buy an **installment annuity;** smaller amounts are accepted since the premium payments continue for an extended period. Some companies sell annuities that combine features of both: they require a large initial premium, but buyers can make subsequent deposits.

Special Tax Advantages

Assume that Fred Bear pays $5,000 for a single-premium annuity. He will *not* be able to deduct any part of that on his tax return, so he is investing after-tax dollars. Once the annuity is purchased, the income taxes on interest, dividends, or capital gains are deferred as long as these earnings remain in the annuity. All the money is reinvested to earn additional amounts in the future. This tax deferral feature is touted as a major advantage. While a deferred annuity can provide a tax-deferred investment vehicle, there are disadvantages.

Tax penalty on early withdrawals

If you draw earnings from an annuity, you pay regular income taxes on them. You pay no tax on your premium payments, of course, since you have already paid taxes on that money. The IRS assumes that the first money you withdraw will be earnings, so those dollars are taxable. Unless you are over 59½ or disabled, you may have to pay a 10 percent penalty on the amount drawn. For someone with a 30 percent marginal tax rate, taxes and a penalty can take quite a bite: on a $1,000 withdrawal, there would be $300 in taxes ($1,000 draw × 30% tax rate) and a $100 penalty ($1,000 draw × 10% penalty). To top it off, the insurance company may extract its own penalty.

Strategy

An annuity should be considered a long-term investment. The combination of taxes plus penalty can significantly reduce your final return if you take the money out early.

Fees to Purchase and Maintain an Annuity

Traditional annuities carried a 3 to 9 percent front-load fee that was deducted from the initial payment; $30 to $90 on a $1,000 premium went for that fee. Much of it went to pay the agent's commission for selling the annuity. Now many companies have switched to a **back-load fee** that declines over time. Withdrawing your money from these annuities subjects you to a fee as high as 9 percent in the first year. Fees usually decrease each year you own the annuity. After 10 years or so, the fee for cashing in the annuity disappears. In effect, that fee helps ensure the buyer will hold the annuity for some minimum period. Some insurance companies also charge a flat fee of several hundred dollars or more when the annuity is purchased.

Strategy

A back-load fee substantially reduces your flexibility. Paying a 9 percent back load, the required income taxes, and a 10 percent penalty can decimate your return.

Even if you make no withdrawals, you still pay an annual fee on an annuity. Part is for administrative costs, part for the mortality charge for the insurance, and the rest for managing the investments. Altogether, you may pay 2 to 3 percent of the annuity's balance annually. While that may not seem like much, consider: if the annuity's investments earn 8 percent, the annual fee might take a quarter or more of it, bringing your net return to 6 percent! Some insurance companies advertise only their *gross* return before the annual fee . . . another glowing example of "What the large print giveth, the small print taketh away."

Strategy

*The annual maintenance fees on an annuity lower the actual return. Consider their effect **before** you buy.*

Choosing an Annuity: Investment Options

You should consider investment performance when you purchase an annuity. Remember, a deferred annuity is primarily an investment vehicle. If its rate of return is poor, it fails in its major purpose. Good tax deferral cannot overcome dismal performance. Second, the combination of penalties, taxes, and fees locks you into an annuity for a long time. Why be stuck in a consistently poor performer? Finally, the annuity must perform well if it is to overcome the burden of the annual fees.

Let's look at three broad investment options for annuities: fixed return, variable return using a fixed-income vehicle, and variable return using common stocks.

Fixed-return annuity

A **fixed-return annuity** offers a specific return for a set period. The initial return might be guaranteed for as little as 6 months or as long as 5 years, and then the rate of return is reset. Most annuities provide a minimum guaranteed rate, but it's typically only 3 to 4 percent.

There are dangers when the rate is reset. Suppose Last Ditch Annuity offers a "teaser" rate of 10 percent when rates in the financial markets are considerably less. Mesmerized, Barney pays $5,000 for a single-premium annuity but fails to note that the 10 percent is guaranteed for only

6 months. Five months later, the company notifies him that 7 percent is the new rate—less than the going rate in the financial markets. Barney faces two choices. He can withdraw the money and face a 10 percent IRS penalty plus a 9 percent back load—an immediate $950 loss—or he can take the sub-par rate of return.

An escape clause is essential. Some annuities include an **escape clause** that allows you to redeem the annuity with no back load if your rate drops precipitously; most will let you out if the new rate is 1 or 1.5 percent less than the initial rate. You still face the IRS penalty, though you may avoid it by exchanging the existing annuity for another. If you decide to exchange for another annuity, you need competent tax advice to make certain it qualifies under the tax rules.

Strategy

An escape clause is essential, especially if the annuity levies a sizable back-load charge and its current interest rate seems too good to be true.

Variable return annuity with fixed-income investments as base

The investment **return on some variable return annuities is based on the performance of a pooled fund of fixed-income investments.** As with a mutual fund, premiums from a large number of annuities are used to purchase the investments. Some annuities offer several different investment pools. One might concentrate on money market investments. Another might invest in long-term, investment grade corporate bonds. And for the risk takers, there may be a fund that invests in lower-quality bonds. The promised return rises with the more aggressive investments, but so does the risk. There is no "set" return. The annuity does as well as its pool of investments.

Judging the annuity's performance. Most annuities provide a quarterly or annual summary of the underlying investment pool's performance. You have to judge the adequacy of the pool's return to decide how well your investment has done. As the first part of the chapter confirmed, judging mutual funds is reasonably easy. A number of publications provide comparative returns for mutual funds and data on different types of funds. It is not as easy with annuities. Few publications follow the performance of the investment pools that underlie annuities. That means developing your own comparison. You can use the following three-step procedure:

- Classify your annuity's investment objective using the same guides and categories as for fixed-return mutual funds.
- Use the "average return" given in the published mutual fund data for funds with an investment objective similar to your annuity as a "benchmark" rate.
- Compare your annuity's net return (after fees are deducted) to this benchmark.

If the annuity betters or equals the average, give it a passing grade. Did it fall below the average? If it was very poor, it may be time to switch; but consider the possible fees and penalties.

Strategy

A good annuity's return should at least equal the average return for mutual funds with similar investment objectives.

Variable return annuities using a common stock vehicle

Some variable return annuities offer the option of investing your premiums in a pool of common stocks. The performance of the common stocks in that pool determines your return. In a good year, that return may impress you. But down-year earnings are more likely to depress you! Within this group, you may have several choices, ranging from a fund that concentrates on blue-chip issues to one that stresses small, little known, high-tech firms, the latter with *lots* of risk. Generally, variable annuities that offer you investment options carry a higher degree of risk than those that do not.

Judging the annuity's return. While annual or quarterly performance summaries for the underlying investment pool may describe the fund's results in glowing terms, an immediate question is: How good is it? We suggest that to evaluate you use the same three-step procedure used when the pool invests in fixed-return securities. Classify the pool by investment objective. This can be a challenge, but it needs to be done to develop a ''benchmark'' from the mutual fund data for use in judging performance. You have a good fund if its return topped or matched the average rate for mutual funds with similar investment objectives. If return failed to meet this test, you might want to consider switching to another annuity (observing caution on penalties and back loads), especially if the pool has a string of losing years. Even the expense of switching can be better than holding a loser for years, waiting for your paltry annuity balance to confirm the bad choice.

Strategy

A good annuity should match or exceed the average return on mutual funds that have a similar investment objective.

Strengths and Weaknesses of Annuities

Exhibit 17.11 summarizes the major strengths and weaknesses of annuities as an investment. Most entries are self-explanatory, but tax deferral, risk, and flexibility need further comment.

Tax deferral is touted as an annuity's major advantage, but whether you can take advantage of it depends on your circumstances. First, tax deferral carries the price of sharply reduced flexibility: if you have to withdraw the money within a few years of purchase, various penalties may eliminate any advantage of deferral. Second, your marginal tax rate also affects the value of deferral: the lower it is, the less valuable deferral is. Finally, deferral provides the greatest dollar benefits when you buy a large annuity. Someone with limited funds gains less.

All annuities have at least one risk component: the financial strength of the issuing insurance company. Our advice here is straightforward: concentrate on insurance companies that are rated A or A+ by Best and Company (we discussed these ratings back in Chapter 10). A reference librarian at a larger library can help you find ratings on different insurance companies. Or call the commissioner of insurance in your state for the rating on a specific company.

The risk exposure on the underlying pool of investments adds a second possible risk component for variable return annuities. The amount of risk shifts according to the underlying investment chosen. Risk on an investment grade bond fund is probably low. Shift to a fund that concentrates on lower-grade securities and risk rises. Choose a common stock fund that concentrates on small, high-tech firms, and risk soars. Investing through an annuity does not remove this second risk component. If you are uncomfortable with an investment to begin with, avoid it here also.

Strategy

On a variable return annuity, select the investment option whose risk matches your tolerance.

Exhibit 17.11

Strengths and Weaknesses of Annuities

Strengths
1. Income taxes on the earnings are deferred.
2. Risk is low on fixed-return annuities purchased from life insurance companies that are rated A or A+ by Best and Company.
3. Variable return annuities offer the purchaser a reasonably broad range of investment options.
4. There is no dollar limit on the amount you invest in an annuity.

Weaknesses
1. Unless you are disabled, money withdrawn before age 59½ is subject to both:
   a. Full income taxes
   b. A 10 percent penalty on the amount drawn
2. The annual management and administrative fees to maintain some annuities are so high that their net returns may not be competitive.
3. Back-load fees can sharply reduce the proceeds if an annuity is redeemed after only a few years, making it senseless to switch to another annuity.
4. The combination of high administrative fees, sales commissions, and lackluster performance of the underlying pool of investments reduces the net return on some variable return annuities below what comparable investment options offer.
5. A stiff back-load fee coupled with a 10 percent IRS penalty can make an annuity even less flexible than an IRA.
6. Risk on variable return annuities can range from low to high, depending on the underlying investment vehicle.

The combination of taxes and the IRS penalty, plus possible back-load fees, seriously reduce flexibility. Once purchased, an annuity is a long-term commitment; only a dire emergency or a complete performance disaster justifies early withdrawal. Drop annuities from your list of possible investment options if you might need early access to the money.

Strategy

Depending on your marginal tax bracket, a no-load municipal bond mutual fund may be a better choice than an annuity. The income is tax-free and the fund gives you far more flexibility.

Even if you expect to hold the annuity for an extended period, there may be better choices. An IRA—we discuss the particulars in the next chapter—carries the same 10 percent penalty but may provide several advantages. You can choose from a tremendous range of investments, many with lower fees. Furthermore, many charge no front- or back-load fee.

Strategy

An IRA provides some of the same tax deferral features and the IRS penalty for early withdrawal is no larger, yet the annual administrative fees may be less, and most IRAs carry no front-load or back-load fee.

UNIT INVEST-MENT TRUSTS

A **unit investment trust** is a pool of investments that are being held in trust for a group of investors. When you buy a unit, you purchase an interest in the trust. The typical price of a unit is $1,000; the minimum purchase for some trusts is five units. Most trusts concentrate on notes and bonds, but some common stock unit trusts have been introduced. For those investors willing to accept some risk, a corporate bond trust may be the choice. Municipal bond trusts are for investors seeking tax-exempt income. And government trusts are for those seeking low risk.

Usually, a sponsoring organization puts together the pool of notes or bonds and then proceeds to sell units to investors. For example, the trust might own municipal securities totaling $6,000,000; at $1,000 per unit, there will be 6,000 units for sale: $6,000,000 total/$1,000 unit. Once these are sold, there will be no additional units. The securities in the trust are not actively managed; new securities are not added, and existing securities are rarely sold. The trust continues to exist until all the securities mature.

What Does Each Unit Offer?

For their payment, investors receive a proportional interest in the trust. You buy the units from a salesperson for $1,000 plus a front-load fee that averages 3 to 4 percent. Since the trust is large, it will hold a diversified portfolio of notes and bonds.

Interest earned on the bonds and notes is paid to each investor, typically monthly. If that interest is from municipal securities, it is exempt from federal income tax. Expenses of operating the trust will generally average 0.25 to .5 percent of the trust's assets annually; these are deducted from your interest payments.

Most trusts will *not* repurchase your units. Instead, they have to be sold in the secondary market. Often the sponsoring group or the brokerage firm that sold the units maintains such a market. While there is no direct fee, the quoted price may be less than the unit's current value. This discount provides a commission when the unit is sold to the next investor.

Major Advantages and Disadvantages

Let's start with the good news. Because its operating expenses are lower, a unit investment trust may provide a somewhat higher return than a comparable mutual fund. The trust has a definite life span; at some future point the securities mature and you get your money back, assuming no one defaults on repayment. Returns on the trust are highly predictable; once the securities are purchased, your return is fixed. Last, a moderate investment buys a diversified portfolio of notes and bonds.

Now for the not so good news. The return is somewhat higher than from a no-load mutual fund, but you pay a fee to obtain it. It will likely take years to recoup the front load from those fractionally higher returns. There may be times when the portfolio of securities would benefit from some management, but the trust does not do that. Selling the units before maturity can significantly lower the return, so the lower operating costs can disappear quickly. Your range of choices is more limited; most trusts do not invest in lower-grade securities. The minimum purchase and high unit cost simply exceed the means of many investors. Finally, you cannot acquire units by making a series of deposits; you have to pay the entire amount immediately. That concentrates your investment at a single point in time.

Who Should Consider One?

Potential investors for unit investment trusts should:

- Currently have a sizable pool of money to invest
- Require a highly predictable stream of interest payments
- Expect to hold the units until the trust matures—perhaps as long as 30 years
- Have investment objectives that will not change over an extended period

How many people fit this profile? Probably not too many. For the great majority of investors the shortcomings of unit trusts simply outweigh the advantages.

Strategy

Before buying a unit investment trust, make certain it meets your needs; a no-load bond mutual fund may be a better choice.

LIMITED PARTNERSHIPS

Limited partnerships are specialized organizations for conducting business. Usually there are a number of limited partners plus a general partner. Both limited and general partners share in the profits or losses of the business; the precise breakdown is set forth in the partnership agreement. Management is usually left to the general partner. The general partner has unlimited liability for the partnership's debts and other obligations. All of the general partner's personal assets can be seized to satisfy the partnership's debts—a high-risk position. The liability of limited partners is confined to the amount they invested in the business.

Limited liability is a major attraction of this type of partnership. As a limited partner you can participate in the successes of the business while only risking your initial investment. For a typical investment of $5,000 you become part owner of the business. If it loses money initially, you may be able to include that loss on your tax return. In fact, potential tax advantages were one of the major factors that encouraged the early growth of limited partnerships, but the Tax Reform Act of 1986 sharply curtailed that advantage.

What Do You Receive for Your Money?

You usually buy a proportional interest in a partnership. Most partnerships are sold by salespeople who receive a commission that ranges from 8 percent upward. As a limited partner, you participate in the earnings and losses of the business; you may not be able to deduct all of the business's losses under present tax regulations. Your liability for the business's debts is limited to your initial investment.

A "good" partnership in the right business, in the right location, and at the right time can provide an excellent return. Let one or two of those pieces be missing, and your return can be mediocre or you can suffer a sizable loss. Judging the merits of a partnership is a technical, involved, and challenging task. Even with the best analysis, success is far from assured.

Who Should Consider One?

Necessarily our analysis has provided only a brief introduction to the complex world of limited partnerships. But what we've said is sufficient to let us profile the attributes of a suitable investor:

- A sizable net worth is essential; this is a nondiversified investment.
- The investment's horizon has to be long; selling a partnership interest is difficult, and the price may be only a fraction of the initial investment.
- A thorough understanding of the risks is important; these are complex investments.
- Competent tax advice is crucial; the new tax regulations have made this a treacherous area.
- Willingness and ability to accept high risk are necessary.
- To make an informed choice, the investor needs to understand the underlying business venture.

How many investors fit the profile? Not many. Limited partnerships are probably best left to sophisticated investors who have the knowledge and resources to ride out a few "experiences" along the way.

1   Mutual funds pool money from many small investors to purchase investments such as money market instruments, notes, bonds, and common stock.

2   When you invest in a mutual fund, you buy shares and own part of the fund.

3   Mutual funds compute the net asset value (NAV) of their shares at the close of each business day. The computation is:

$$\text{NAV} = \frac{\begin{array}{c}\text{current market} \\ \text{value of mutual} \\ \text{fund's investment}\end{array} - \begin{array}{c}\text{liabilities of} \\ \text{mutual fund}\end{array}}{\text{number of mutual fund shares}}$$

4   NAV is used to compute the number of shares a given amount of money purchases. It is also used to compute the proceeds when you redeem existing shares.

5   Investors purchase no-load and low-load shares directly from the mutual fund.

6   Shares in front-load and back-load mutual funds are sold by salespeople. Front-load funds deduct the salesperson's commission immediately from the investor's deposit; back-loads often recoup it by charging investors a series of 12b-1 fees while they own the shares.

7   The *Wall Street Journal, Barron's,* and the financial section of most metropolitan newspapers carry price quotations for mutual fund shares.

8   An investor's return on a mutual fund comes from a combination of:
   ■ Dividend distributions
   ■ Capital gains distributions
   ■ Changes in the NAV of the fund's shares

9   All mutual funds have operating expenses; these are frequently quoted as an expense ratio: expenses/total fund assets. Some funds add an additional 12b-1 fee to cover marketing and promotional expenses.

10 A mutual fund must supply every prospective investor with a prospectus that explains its investment objective, features, and operating procedures.

11 The three broad categories of mutual funds are
   ■ Money market funds
   ■ Note and bond funds
   ■ Common stock funds
   Investment objectives for the funds within a group can range from conservative to very aggressive.

12 Beta is a widely used measure that describes the volatility of a common stock mutual fund relative to the overall stock market. Funds with a beta greater than 1.0 are more volatile than the market; a beta of 1.0 indicates the fund parallels the market; a beta below 1.0 indicates the fund is less volatile. The higher a fund's beta, the higher its risk.

13 Mutual funds give a small investor:
   ■ Access to a wide range of investments
   ■ Diversification within an investment group
   ■ A choice of professionals to manage those investments

14 Mutual fund groups that offer a "family" of funds provide a range of different investment objectives; it may be possible to meet different needs within the family. Many allow telephone switching between their funds.

15 Mutual funds can be used to establish accounts for minors and as retirement accounts.

16 A number of publications compile data on mutual funds. The information ranges from basic background, through performance and operating statistics, to the "judgmental" information that certain publications provide.

17 Key checkpoints when selecting a money market mutual fund include:
   ■ Setting your risk-return preference
   ■ Deciding if tax-exempt income is warranted
   ■ Concentrating on large funds
   ■ Seeking the check-writing option

18 When selecting a bond fund, you should:
   ■ Decide your risk-return preference
   ■ Concentrate on large funds
   ■ Focus on no-load funds unless you need the salesperson's guidance
   ■ Decide if tax-exempt income is best

19 The key factors to consider when selecting a common stock mutual fund include:
   ■ Matching the fund's investment objective to your risk-return preference
   ■ Concentrating on no-load funds
   ■ Limiting the use of funds to long-term goals
   ■ Considering dividing your investment between two or more funds

20 Federal income taxes are deferred on the earnings that accumulate in annuities. The higher your marginal tax rate, the more valuable that deferral.

21 Unless you are disabled, withdrawals from an annuity before age 59½ are fully taxable and there is a 10 percent penalty on the amount drawn.

22 The back-load fee on many annuities—it can range up to 9 percent—significantly reduces flexibility; in most cases, the fee drops by 1 percent for each year you hold the annuity.

23 The return on a variable return annuity is based on the performance of the underlying pool of investments. Risk ranges from low to high, depending on the type of investment.

24 You can judge the adequacy of the return on a variable return annuity by comparing it to the "average return" on mutual funds with comparable investment objectives.

25 Unit investment trusts sell proportional interests (called units) in a pool of investments that will not be actively managed by the trust.

26 Limited partnerships allow the limited partners (the investors) to participate in the underlying business venture's income and losses while risking only their initial investment.

Review your understanding of

Mutual fund
Open-end fund
Net asset value (NAV)
No-load fund
Low-load fund
Front-load fund
Back-load fund
Dividend distribution
Capital gains distribution
Operating expense
Expense ratio
12b-1 fee
Investment objective
Prospectus
Money market mutual fund
    General purpose
    Government
    Tax exempt
Bond mutual fund
    Corporate bond: investment grade
    Corporate bond: aggressive
    Government bond
    Municipal bond: investment grade
    Municipal bond: aggressive

Common stock mutual fund
    Aggressive growth
    Growth
    Growth and income
    Income
    Specialized
Dollar cost averaging
Automatic reinvestment
Systematic withdrawal
Check writing
Family of mutual funds
Telephone transfers
Annuitant
Immediate annuity
Deferred annuity
Single-premium annuity
Installment annuity
Back-load fee
Fixed-return annuity
Escape clause
Variable return annuity
Unit investment trust
Limited partnership
Limited liability

Discussion questions

1 How does investing in a mutual fund differ from directly purchasing common stocks or bonds and notes? Which group of investors, those with limited resources or those with extensive resources, is likely to be attracted to mutual funds? Why?

2 Why does a mutual fund compute its NAV at the end of the business day? How does it do that and how is this statistic used?

3 Connie Concerned has narrowed her choice of common stock mutual funds to two:
   ■ *Low Cost Fund.* Operating expense ratio is 0.95% of total assets.
   ■ *Big Cost Fund.* Operating expense ratio is 2.01% of total assets.
   Should Connie dismiss Big Cost Fund because of its higher expense ratio?

4 Sidney Smidley's local paper had the following mutual fund price quotations:

Fund	NAV	Offer price	NAV change
Fine Deal	10.50	10.71	+.10
Low Cost	6.50	6.50	+.06
Sure Thing	8.00	8.75	+.09
Zero Sum	24.32	24.32	−.03

   a Is Fine Deal likely to be a no-load, low-load, or front-load fund? What about Low Cost? Sure Thing? Zero Sum?
   b What does the "NAV change" column suggest?

5   When Donna Salestype—she works at a brokerage firm—suggests mutual funds to a customer, will her list of funds include all types or only selected ones? Why?

6   Assume you recently purchased shares in Sure Thing mutual fund. What are your sources of potential return? Explain how each source would be treated on your tax return.

7   What are the three major categories of mutual funds? What does each invest in? Which type likely has the lowest risk? The highest?

8   Name several publications from which you could obtain information on a mutual fund's investment objective. What source might tell you more about the fund's features and operating points?

9   Boris Befuddled has only a small amount to invest, doesn't want to manage the investments (balancing his checkbook is tough), and would like to set up an ongoing plan. Is Boris a candidate for mutual funds?

10 How do the three major types of money market mutual funds differ? Name several ways that one might use them to manage one's finances. How do they differ from the money market accounts discussed in the last chapter?

11 Would you expect the return on a municipal bond fund to exceed or be less than the return on a comparable quality corporate bond fund? Why? How would you decide if you should buy shares in the municipal bond fund?

12 Grazelda Swartz is considering two common stock mutual funds: Quick Growth (beta is 1.2) and Stable Times (beta is 0.6). How should each fund perform if the stock market rises 8

percent? If it falls 10 percent? What type of investor would likely be most satisfied with each?

13 Since a back-load mutual fund does not deduct a fee from the investor's money when the shares are purchased, does that mean the investor never pays a sales commission? Assume the fund has an annual 1.25 percent 12b-1 fee. Do investors pay a commission? For how long?

14 Should investors limit themselves to a single mutual fund within each investment objective, or consider several within each category? Why? Is there an added cost for buying shares in more than one?

15 Barney recently paid $5,000 for a single-premium annuity that "guarantees" a 10 percent return. Other annuities were only offering 8 to 9 percent, so that seemed attractive. In fact, Barney never bothered to read the fine print in the contract. Does he have a bargain? What points should he check?

16 Wanda has narrowed the investment options on her variable return annuity to two:
   ■ Fund 1 is an aggressive income vehicle that invests in corporate bonds rated BB or below.
   ■ Fund 2 is an aggressive growth common stock fund that concentrates on firms in the biotech field.
   Wanda checked, and the insurance company offering the annuity is rated A by Best and Company. Is this a low-risk investment? Does the risk carried by the two funds differ?

17 What are the similarities and differences between the four funds below?

Fund	Major investment	Quality	Maturity
1	Corporate notes	Rated A or better	Less than 4 years
2	Corporate bonds	Rated BBB or below	More than 20 years
3	Municipal bonds	Rated A or better	More than 20 years
4	Municipal notes	Rated A or better	Ranges from 4 to 10 years

Problems

17.1 The managers of Big Growth Mutual Fund want to compute its net asset value (NAV) per share on April 1; they have the following information:
   Market value of fund's investments on April 1. $50,100,000.
   Original purchase price of fund's investments. $50,200,000.
   Fund's total liabilities on April 1. $20,000.
   Number of current Big Growth shares. 1,000,000.
   Number of Big Growth shares when fund was established 10 years ago. 100,000.
   What is the NAV of Big Growth's shares?

17.2 Howard Hopeful plans to invest $1,000 in a common stock mutual fund. One alternative is Technology Fund, a no-load fund with an NAV of $10 per share. Worldwide Fund is Howard's second choice. It is a load fund (8.5 percent commission on each purchase) whose NAV is also $10.
   a How many Technology Mutual Fund shares will Howard's $1,000 buy?
   b How many Worldwide Fund shares will Howard's $1,000 buy?

     c   Assume that neither fund is expected to distribute a dividend or capital gain for the next year. To earn a 10 percent rate of return on the original $1,000 investment over the next year, what will Technology Fund's NAV per share have to be? What must Worldwide Fund's NAV per share be?

     d   Based on your answer to part (c), which mutual fund must have the superior performance?

17.3   Rhonda Regular has invested $240 in New High Fund (a no-load fund) every 3 months this past year. Details on those investments include:

Amount invested	Date invested	Fund's NAV on date invested	Shares purchased
$240	March	$12	———
240	June	8	———
240	September	6	———
240	December	4	———

As this table all too clearly shows, a stellar performer New High Fund has not been.

     a   How many shares did Rhonda buy during the year?

     b   What was her average price per share?

     c   Assume that rather than investing $240 each quarter, Rhonda had bought 32 shares each quarter. What would Rhonda's total investment have been under that plan? Her average price per share?

     d   If New High's present NAV per share is $5, what is Rhonda's profit or loss under the $240 per month investment plan? What is it under the 32 shares per quarter plan?

17.4   During the past 12 months, Steady Return Mutual Fund had the following returns on its investments: The fund earned $250,000 in interest and dividends.

The long-term capital gains earned on investments Steady Return Mutual Fund sold during the year totaled $100,000.

Steady Return will deduct $50,000 in management and operating expenses from the dividend and interest amounts. The balance will be distributed to the holders of the 400,000 shares that Steady Return currently has outstanding.

     a   What is the dividend distribution on each Steady Return share?

     b   How large a capital gain will Steady Return distribute on each share?

     c   Assume Sam Smalldollar owns 100 Steady Return shares. What dollar distribution will Sam receive? How should Sam treat this distribution on his tax return?

17.5   Ron and Linda Swartz are considering establishing a mutual fund for their daughter, Rachel, through the Uniform Gift to Minors Act. The Swartzes plan to purchase 50 shares of Winner Mutual Fund for Rachel's account. Based on Winner's prior year's performance, the Swartzes expect it to distribute $1.70 per share as dividends and $1.40 per share as long-term capital gains this year. Rachel currently has no other sources of income.

     a   What returns will Rachel's account likely pay?

     b   Assuming that the returns you estimated in part (a) were paid, how would those items appear on Rachel's tax return? Is she likely to owe any income taxes? (*Hint:* Chapter 5 will help you answer this question.)

     c   If Ron and Linda's marginal tax rate is 28 percent, how much will they save in taxes by placing the account in Rachel's name?

17.6   During her 2 years of ownership, Cindy's single-premium annuity has earned $1,000; that has raised its value from the $5,000 she paid to $6,000. She is currently considering redeeming the entire annuity to use the money for a condominium down payment. The annuity originally carried an 8 percent back load, but that is now 7 percent. Her marginal tax rate is 28 percent.

     a   What fees or penalties will she have to pay if she redeems?

     b   After paying any and all costs you computed in part (a), what amount will she have left?

     c   Has it been a good investment?

Case problem

Karen and Carl Wilbur want to develop a detailed investment plan. Their two careers provide a substantial income; their marginal tax rate for federal and state income taxes is 35 percent. The Wilburs expect to invest about $400 each month.

Since graduation, they have repaid most of their education loans. Their other liabilities include a $6,000 balance on an auto loan and $1,200 on various credit cards. The auto loan will be repaid over the next 24 months, while the credit card balance will be repaid in 4 months.

The Wilburs do not own a house. As one part of their investment plan, they want a component that will shelter part of their income from taxes. Karen is self-employed, so she has no employment benefits. Because she is self-employed, she pays high Social Security taxes.

Both Carl and Karen are sufficiently busy that they do not want to purchase individual bonds or common stocks. They are just beginning their search for a mutual fund, so they have not singled out a specific one. Presently they have $3,000 in a savings account plus a $500 balance in their NOW account.

Carl and Karen have the following financial goals:

Financial goal	Target date	Amount	Rationale for goal
Keogh plan	Retirement	$200 each month	Provide for Karen's retirement; use this account's tax-deferral feature.
Down payment	4 years	$8,000 total	Purchase a condominium.
Education fund	14 years	$50 each month	Accumulate an education fund for their 5-year-old child.
Emergency fund	Immediately	$3,000	They use the balance in their 4.5% savings account for this.

1   What type(s) of mutual fund might be suitable for the Keogh account? Develop a rationale to support your recommendations.
2   What tax advantages does a Keogh plan offer? With such an account, are dividend distributions, capital gains distributions, and appreciation in the fund's NAV treated differently for tax purposes?
3   What monthly amount will they have to contribute to accumulate the $8,000 down payment? Does your estimate factor in inflation?
4   What type(s) of mutual funds would you suggest they consider for their down payment goal? Does their high marginal tax rate influence your recommendations? Why?
5   What should Carl and Karen do with the dividend and capital gains distributions from the mutual funds you suggested in part (4)?
6   Develop several strategies for their education fund. Outline the major strengths and weaknesses of each option. What type of mutual fund might be suitable for each option?
7   What mutual fund, if any, would you suggest for the emergency fund? What features should the Wilburs stress when searching for the fund you have recommended?
8   How should Carl and Karen decide whether funds that sell direct (no-load and low-load) or funds that sell through a sales force (front-load and back-load) would be best for them? Which group likely involves the least work? Are there disadvantages to this group?
9   Would you suggest the Wilburs read several publications on mutual funds before beginning their search? Which ones?

CHAPTER 18

Planning your retirement years

AFTER COMPLETING THIS CHAPTER YOU WILL HAVE LEARNED

- Why early retirement planning is important
- What the four principal sources of retirement income are
- When and how you become "vested" in a pension plan
- How defined-benefit pension plans differ from defined-contribution plans
- Why tax-deferred retirement accounts are good for accumulating retirement funds
- Who qualifies for the common tax-deferred retirement accounts
- How to estimate the retirement income you will need
- How to estimate the amount of your Social Security retirement benefit
- Why advance planning is necessary if you wish to retire before age 65
- How to estimate the dollar amount each source of retirement income will provide
- How to compensate for inflation in a retirement plan
- How an annuity provides retirement benefits you cannot outlive
- How to develop a payout plan for your retirement accounts

For those just starting a career, retirement planning will seem a distant concern. Yet there are good reasons to begin retirement planning now. Planning is easy to postpone until it is too late. Most people switch careers several times during their working life. With each new employer comes a qualifying period for the pension plan. Even if you fulfill the qualifying period for each employer, drawing benefits from several plans curtails your total benefit. The principal reason for the lower benefit is that the salaries used in computing benefits will be the lower salary levels you earn early in your employment. More important, people are living longer: most of us will have a lengthy retirement. Planning can help ensure that we will be secure and comfortable.

Some might say: I don't have to plan because I qualify for an employer-provided pension plan. But many employers are reducing pension plan benefits; future pension benefits may be even less generous. Others will note that Social Security (even the name suggests strength) provides retirement benefits. Still, the system never was meant to sustain you in retirement, and benefits are *not* likely to rise.

To anticipate and compensate for these changes, you need an ongoing retirement plan. The outcome of a secure, comfortable retirement cannot be left to chance. You need to provide for your own welfare.

RETIREMENT PLANNING: WHY START NOW?

To ensure success, a retirement plan should be initiated between ages 25 and 40—the earlier the better. To maintain the standard of living you enjoy while working, you need considerable income. Accumulating the investments to generate that income takes time. The earlier you start, the more manageable the monthly or annual amount needed to achieve your goal. Furthermore, the earlier the money is deposited, the more it earns. The rule of 72 (divide 72 by the interest rate to estimate how long for the money to double) confirms that early deposits have the best chance to double and possibly double several times. Finally, long-term plans provide the flexibility that allows you to consider options—investments with longer maturities and higher risks. The greater returns such a strategy provides can increase your retirement fund.

Federal income tax regulations are designed to encourage you to save for retirement. While the sweeping revisions of 1986 limited some choices, especially IRAs, benefits remain. Some retirement plans provide immediate tax savings on the money you contribute. Nearly all allow you to defer taxes on the interest, dividends, and capital gains that the funds in the plan earn until the time when the money is withdrawn. These tax savings increase your earnings and can help you reach your investment goal.

BUILDING RETIREMENT INCOME

Retirement income generally comes from four sources: (1) Social Security benefits, (2) private pension plans, (3) withdrawals from a tax-deferred retirement account, and (4) general investments. There are limits to what you can do to enhance your position in terms of the first two, but you can and should manage the last two.

Social Security Retirement Benefits

The original intent of the **Social Security retirement benefit** was to "supplement" other sources of retirement income. Social Security benefits were never intended as anyone's sole retirement income. People were expected to have "other" income sources such as employer-provided pension plans or investments. For those not covered by a pension—nearly one-half of those working in private industry—accumulating a personal retirement fund is essential.

Qualifying for benefits

All who have worked steadily since their mid-twenties will almost certainly qualify for Social Security. Nearly all occupations are covered by Social Security; the taxes you pay into the plan will earn you the quarters of credit which qualify you for benefits. Switch positions and your credits will follow you.

If your work record has some breaks—years you didn't work or had minimal earnings—you are still likely to qualify, but your payments may be smaller since they are based on "average" earnings.

Benefits for retired workers

Full Social Security retirement benefits start at age 65. If you **retire earlier,** your payment is reduced. For example, at age 63½ you receive only 90 percent of the age-65 benefit. At age 62 (the earliest you can receive retirement benefits) the payment drops to 80 percent. Retire late and benefits increase 3 percent for each year after 65.

Benefits for your spouse

Partners of retired workers also receive a **spousal retirement benefit;** they can select the higher of two benefit options. First, they can qualify for retirement benefits based on their own work record. Those who have an extensive work history may want to choose this plan. The standard rules apply: full benefits at 65, reduced benefits for an early start, and higher benefits for retiring after 65.

A spouse may also qualify for benefits under a partner's work record. Retiring at age 65, the spouse receives 50 percent of the worker's benefit. This declines to 37.5 percent when the spouse retires at age 62.

Computation of retirement benefits

Social Security benefits generally rise with income, but not proportionately. Someone earning $20,000 might qualify for a $650 monthly retirement benefit. Double those earnings, and the benefit might only rise to $900, a mere 38 percent! Why? As income rises, Social Security replaces less of each income dollar; it replaces 90 percent at first, but replacement eventually drops to 15 percent. It replaces *no* income above the maximum wage subject to Social Security taxes ($43,800 in 1987).

Strategy

*As income rises, **you** must provide a larger share of retirement income because Social Security benefits do not rise proportionately.*

Employer-Sponsored Pension Plans

Many employers provide pension plans for their employees. While these plans are common among public-sector employers, fewer than half of private-sector employers offer them. Employers do not have to offer a plan, but if they do it must comply with the standards and rules set forth in the **Employee Retirement Income Security Act (ERISA).** The rules cover such things as rights of plan participants, vesting requirements (more on this later), disclosure minimums that must be provided to employees, and limits on the type and dollar amount of investments used to fund the plan. Employers decide what benefits the plan will provide. Since there is no mandated minimum benefit, your payment could range from generous to inadequate. The mere existence of a pension plan does not ensure a secure, comfortable retirement.

Vesting: will you take it with you?

Vesting is the term used to indicate when certain pension rights become legally yours. Until they do, the benefits you have accumulated remain the property of the employer. If you leave an employer, you retain your vested rights. When you retire, the employer will pay a pension benefit based on your salary during the years you worked for the firm, the number of years you were with the firm, and the degree to which you are vested in the plan. Switch jobs and you might receive limited pension benefits from several employers.

Vesting takes three forms:

- *Immediate.* You are fully vested when you begin work. You immediately start accruing pension benefits. Immediate vesting is not widespread.
- *Graduated.* A fraction of your benefits is vested each year you're employed. A plan might vest 20 percent after 3 years, and 20 percent every following year. Leave before you've worked 3 years, and you receive nothing. After 7 years you are fully vested. Current rules allow a plan to vest more rapidly, but the total time cannot exceed 7 years.
- *Cliff.* During the first 4-plus years of employment, you vest nothing. At the end of the fifth year, you are 100 percent vested. Stay 5 years and you get it *all.* Leave before you've worked 5 years, and you get *nothing.* The 5-year period is the maximum; the plan can vest more quickly.

What if you leave when you are 60 percent vested? At retirement, you receive 60 percent of your full benefit. If Ben's salary and years of service would have provided a $120 monthly benefit (Ben only worked 5 years for the employer, so it's small) with full vesting, he would receive $72 monthly: $120 full benefit × 60% vesting.

Understand the vesting schedule. Vesting is an important criterion for assessing the adequacy of a pension plan. When considering a new position, request information on how the employer's vesting operates. Current rules (they were revised in 1986) require more rapid vesting than in the past.

Thinking of changing positions? Carefully review your current vesting position, especially if your plan has "cliff" vesting. If you leave just months before that critical, all-or-nothing point, you may sacrifice sizable pension

*Defined-benefit
pension plans*

benefits. The new position should have some attractive incentives to justify such a sacrifice.

Under a **defined-benefit pension plan** your likely pension benefit is specified using a formula. Two widely used methods of computing the benefit are on a flat-dollar basis and on a percent of salary basis.

Flat dollar amount. If you are in a flat-dollar plan, your benefit is based on your years of service multiplied by a set dollar amount. For example, the plan might pay $10 per month for each year of service. If you worked for the employer for 20 years, your monthly benefit would be $200. Work 30 years, and the benefit rises to $300. Your final salary is *not* a factor in such plans; all workers with the same seniority receive the same benefit.

Percent of salary. Percent of salary plans base benefits on (1) a percentage replacement factor, (2) years of service with the employer, and (3) some average of the employee's salary over the final years of employment. Generally, the benefit computation is:

$$\frac{\text{Pension}}{\text{benefit}} = \frac{\text{replacement}}{\text{percentage}} \times \frac{\text{years of}}{\text{service}} \times \frac{\text{average}}{\text{salary}}$$

Replacement percentages range from 1 to 1.8; the higher the percentage, the more generous the benefit.

Years of service usually span the period from when you begin with the employer until retirement, though most plans do not count time on leave. If there is an extended period when you do not work, some employers restart the clock at zero.

The way the average salary used in the computations is arrived at varies widely. Some plans include only a few years in the "average." A plan might average your salary for your highest 3 years, often the years just before retirement. Others use more years, averaging the 5 highest years during your last 10 years of work. Still others average salaries from *all* the years with the employer. Plans with short averaging periods offer several advantages. The low salaries of early years are not counted. If your salary has reflected inflation, the salary figures from more recent years match current purchasing power.

Strategy

Pension plans that average your salary from only the highest 3 to 5 years are often the most attractive.

An example will illustrate. Ben has accumulated 22 years of service with his employer. For each year of service, the plan replaces 1.3 percent of the $19,000 that is the average of his 5 highest years of salary in the past 10 years. Ben's pension benefit will be $5,434 annually: 1.3% replacement × 22 years service × $19,000 average salary.

Traditionally, defined-benefit plans have been the most common. But there has been a recent shift to defined-contribution plans.

Defined-contribution pension plans

Under a **defined-contribution pension plan** the employer contributes a set amount of money (perhaps 10 percent of your salary annually) to your retirement account. And it is the final balance in your account that determines your retirement benefit. If Jan's retirement account has been swollen by employer contributions and earnings on the account's balance, she can draw a generous benefit. If the account grows moderately, she will have to settle for less. If her account does miserably, Jan has a problem at retirement. As long as her employer contributed the required amount, the resulting balance and investment results along the way are her responsibility.

Estimating future pension benefits Estimating the probable pension benefit of a defined-contribution plan is not easy. An example illustrates the challenges. Tricia's employer will contribute 10 percent of her annual salary to her pension account during each of the 20 years she expects to work. First challenge: What rate of return will it earn? Second challenge: How fast will her salary grow? Tricia's $22,000 salary is likely to rise with inflation, so next year's contribution will exceed $2,200. Third challenge: Project the future value of each contribution. No matter how large their number, they will be "inflated" dollars. Fourth challenge: How do we adjust for inflation so we can judge their real value? We need adjusted dollars to estimate what standard of living the annual retirement benefit will provide. Fifth challenge: How long will Tricia be retired, and what return will her account earn during that time? Estimating a defined-contribution plan's actual retirement benefit requires much work and many assumptions.

Reviewing pension plan provisions

Judging the adequacy of an employer-provided pension plan is part of sound financial planning. Most employers help in this effort by providing a booklet summarizing the features of their plan and the way it operates. It should be required reading, preferably *before* hiring on. Unfortunately, many people delay analyzing their pension plan until it is too late to take corrective action; they could end up with inadequate pension benefits.

The character and quality of a prospective employer's pension plan should be one of the factors you consider in accepting a position. You don't have to turn down a job simply because its pension benefits are poor, but there should be offsetting factors. Even if you are already employed, a review of your employer's pension plan is in order. Exhibit 18.1 outlines some points to consider in your review.

Once you are in a plan, your employer has to provide an annual statement summarizing your benefits on request. Many employers do so voluntarily, but some require that an employee ask for the information.

Strategy

Ask for an annual statement of your pension benefits if it is not provided automatically. If you have questions, ask your employer.

**Tax-Deferred
Retirement
Accounts**

Tax-deferred retirement accounts are the most effective way to accumulate money for retirement. They are called tax-deferred because you do not eliminate income taxes but postpone them. By not having to pay the taxes now, you reap a distinct advantage; the entire amount is available to be invested in the account. Furthermore, all of the account's earnings can be reinvested, because taxes on *this* income do not have to be paid now. Later, when you withdraw the money, you will have to pay taxes, but by then your tax rate may be lower.

To illustrate the advantage of tax deferral, let's use Sidney Secure's Individual Retirement Account (IRA) as an example. We'll assume that Sidney can deduct the full deposit to the IRA. Exhibit 18.2 will compare an IRA account (middle column) and a general investment account (far right). Sidney's marginal tax rate (federal plus state) is 30 percent. He expects to earn a 10 percent return on each account.

Guidelines for Evaluating an Employer-Provided Pension Plan

Area of concern	Recommendations
1. When do you become vested in the plan?	The best plan vests immediately; graduated vesting over a period of years is second best; cliff vesting at the end of 5 years is poorest.
2. Do employees have to contribute to the plan?	Plans where the employer makes the entire contribution are best; plans where the employee's contribution is low are acceptable.
3. What happens if you have a break in service due to layoff or leave?	A good plan allows you to "pick up" your previous years of service if the break is fairly brief.
4. Can you retire before age 65?	A good plan allows retirement at partial benefits as early as age 55; plans that tie early retirement to years of service are acceptable.
5. How much are benefits reduced for early retirement?	A typical plan reduces benefits about 5 percent for each year you retire before age 65.
6. Is the plan defined-benefit or defined-contribution?	Estimating retirement benefits is easier for defined-benefit plans; it is much more difficult for a defined-contribution plan.
7. If a defined-benefit plan, what "average wage" is the benefit based on?	Good plans use earnings figures from the most recent 3 to 5 years to compute pension benefits; less desirable are those that use your entire wage history.
8. Are pension benefits reduced by Social Security benefits?	A good plan has no reduction; many plans have moderate reductions, so you may not be able to avoid this; large benefit reductions are unacceptable.
9. Does the plan provide several payout options?	A good plan offers options that continue payments to a surviving spouse; a range of from 50% to 100% of the original benefit is usual.
10. Do benefits continue to rise if you work past age 65?	Potential retirement benefit should continue to rise after age 65.

Sidney begins by contributing $1,000 of his income to each account. There are no income taxes on his IRA deposit, so $1,000 is deposited. Sidney is **investing before-tax dollars** because he deferred taxes. The case is far different with the general investment account which appears on the far right. Only $700 of Sidney's $1,000 ends up in the account: the other $300 is paid in taxes. Here, Sidney is investing after-tax dollars. Clearly an investment made with before-tax dollars begins with a decided advantage over its after-tax counterpart.

During the next year both accounts earn 10 percent: that is $100 for the IRA and $70 for the general account. Taxes on the IRA are deferred, so the entire $100 is reinvested. On the general investment, only $49 remains to be reinvested after a $21 tax payment ($70 × 30% marginal rate). Higher earnings and the full initial investment continue to boost the IRA above the general account. After 20 years of $1,000 annual deposits, the IRA will have a balance of $57,275. The same contribution to the general investment account produces $28,697.

Of course withdrawals from the IRA are fully taxable; no tax was paid on the deposits or earnings. Not so with the general account; all taxes were paid along the way. But even if Sidney's rate remained at 30 percent on all withdrawals, he would have $40,093.50 after paying $17,182.50 in taxes: $57,275 IRA balance × 30% marginal rate. That is still far better than the general account's $28,697.

Are there disadvantages?

All tax-deferred retirement accounts have highly restrictive withdrawal provisions. They must be considered long-term commitments due to the tax penalties. Once you are age 59½, you can generally withdraw the money without penalty. You will, however, have to pay income taxes on the amount drawn. If you die or are disabled, there is no penalty but standard taxes apply. Any other withdrawals carry a 10 percent penalty in addition to all regular income taxes. Those two could easily take 30 to 40 percent of the withdrawal!

Exhibit 18.2

Comparison of a Tax-Deferred Retirement Account and General Investment Account

		Investment Account	
		IRA retirement	General investment
Initial Deposit		$1,000	$1,000
Less: Taxes on initial deposit: 30% marginal tax rate		0	300
Net investment		$1,000	$ 700
Return for first year: 10%	$100		$70
Less: Taxes on return: 30% tax rate	0		21
Net after-tax earnings		100	49
Balance after 1 year		$1,100	$ 749

Strategy

*Tax-advantaged retirement options are long-term commitments
because penalties and taxes make early withdrawal very costly.*

Available tax-deferred retirement options

There are four widely available tax-deferred retirement options: (1)
Keogh plans, (2) IRAs, (3) salary reduction plans for employees of educational and some nonprofit organizations (also called 403(b) plans), and (4)
salary reduction plans for employees in private industry (also called 401(k)
plans). Exhibit 18.3 summarizes the major points of each plan. Note that
these accounts have been and likely will continue to be altered by new tax
legislation. Before proceeding, you will want to consult a tax reference book
for possible recent changes.

Keogh plan. Individuals with self-employment income can establish a
Keogh (or HR-10) plan. That income does not have to be your sole support,
but contributions can only be made on self-employment income. Assume
that in addition to working full time for an accounting firm, Phil prepares
tax returns for his own clients on the side. He can make a Keogh contribution on the $2,000 he earned from preparing returns but not on his regular salary.

On your tax return, Keogh contributions are deducted as an adjustment
to gross income; you pay no income taxes on the contributions.

Exhibit 18.3

Summary of Common Tax-Deferred Retirement Options

Specifics	Tax-Deferred Retirement Options			
	Keogh plan	IRA plan	Salary reduction	Salary reduction
Formal name	HR-10 or Keogh	IRA	403(b)	401(k)
Who can qualify	Self-employed individuals	All paid workers	Employees of educational and some nonprofit groups	Employees of companies that offer a plan
Maximum annual contribution	20% of self-employment income; $30,000 max.	Lower of $2,000 or earned income	20% of income, but pension can lower it; $9,500 max.	25% of income, companies often have lower limits; $7,000 max.*
Earliest age to receive benefits	59½	59½	59½	59½
Preretirement withdrawal conditions (no penalty)	Death or disability	Death or disability	Death or disability	Death or disability
Available investment options	Wide choice; you decide	Wide choice; you decide	Options offered by employer	Options offered by employer

* Scheduled to rise with inflation to $9,500 maximum.

IRA plan. Everyone who earns wages can establish an **Individual Retirement Account (IRA).** The maximum contribution is the lesser of your working income or $2,000. If your spouse has no income from work, the maximum rises to $2,250.

But you may not be able to deduct the full IRA contribution as an adjustment to gross income on your tax return. The rules governing deductibility are:

- *Full.* You can deduct your full IRA contribution if you are not covered by a pension plan. Even if covered by a plan, you can still deduct the full amount if your adjusted gross income is under $25,000 (single) or $40,000 (joint).

- *Partial.* If you are covered by a plan and your adjusted gross income is over $25,000 (single) or $40,000 (joint), your deduction is reduced $200 for each $1,000 over those limits. At $35,000 (single) and $50,000 (joint), your deduction goes to zero.

- *None.* If you are covered by a pension plan and your adjusted gross income exceeds $35,000 (single) or $50,000 (joint), you cannot deduct the contribution, but you can still contribute to an IRA account with after-tax dollars. Taxes on the account's earnings are deferred regardless of whether they arose from deductible or nondeductible contributions.

Look back to the IRA column in Exhibit 18.2. We said that Sidney could deduct the "full" $1,000. Had he qualified only for a partial deduction, he would have paid taxes on part of the $1,000; once in the account there would be no taxes to pay on earnings. If his income were sufficiently high, he would have had to pay taxes—$300 in his case—on the full $1,000, but he would not pay taxes on the account's earnings.

Salary reduction: educational and some nonprofit organizations. Employees of educational and some nonprofit organizations can establish a salary reduction plan if their employer offers the option. Part of the employee's salary is directed into a qualified investment plan called a **403(b) plan.** Deposits have to be withheld from your salary before it is paid, so the employer has to agree to participate. Direct deposits by the employee are not permitted.

Contributions to a 403(b) plan are not included in the salary reported on your W-2 wage summary form; you pay no income taxes on your contribution, though you pay Social Security taxes on it. And your total salary will be counted as "income" in determining pension benefit.

Investment options are limited to those your employer offers. Nearly all employers offer annuities (more on these later) from several insurance companies. Most also offer accounts in several mutual fund families. Others allow you to select almost any investment option as long as it qualifies as a 403(b) plan.

Salary reduction: employees of private companies. Private-sector employees can also establish salary reduction plans if their employers offer an approved **401(k) plan.** All contributions have to be deducted directly from salary, since direct deposits are not permitted. Many large companies have established 401(k) plans; they are far less common at smaller firms.

Your contributions to a 401(k) plan are not paid as salary, so they are not included on your wage summary to the IRS for tax purposes. You will, however, pay Social Security taxes on the contributions. Your full salary—including 401(k) contributions—is used to compute your benefit from the employer's pension plan.

To encourage participation, some employers match part or all of the employee's contributions. An employer might contribute 1 percent of salary for each 2 percent the employee deposits. That already provides a 50 percent return, so it can raise potential earnings. Some employers set an upper limit on their matching contribution, perhaps 3 percent of salary. Others only contribute if the employee uses the money to purchase common stock in the employing company.

Investment options for 401(k) plans are rather limited. Many plans offer shares of the employer's common stock. Some add fixed-return options such as CDs, bonds, and insurance company annuities. A few offer a choice of several bond and common-stock mutual funds to supplement the employer's stock purchase alternative.

Are tax-deferred retirement options a good choice?

These options are an excellent choice for most people. You can deposit before-tax dollars. Income taxes on the account's interest, dividends, or capital gains are deferred. And that deferral continues until you withdraw the money.

Shifting income from your working years to retirement may lower your current taxes. Often your taxable income during retirement drops, so you have a lower marginal tax rate. Even if it stays the same, the tax deferral means your account grows rapidly while you are working.

Participating in one option does not preclude your using others. Wilbur Workaholic teaches at State U. and has a consulting business. He can establish a 403(b) at the university, a Keogh for his consulting income, and possibly an IRA to cap it all.

Any and all of the plans are highly visible reminders of your progress toward a retirement goal. The rising account balances can confirm your progress to that goal. Even the penalties have an advantage: they discourage drawing funds except for critical needs.

General Investment Plan

General investments you accumulate during your work career can provide retirement income. Mutual fund accounts, CDs, annuities, common stock, even sources such as the cash value in a life insurance policy or equity in a house grow during your work career. During retirement they can be drawn on for income.

A well-developed personal finance plan will (and should) include some general investments. But they are not nearly as effective for accumulating retirement funds as tax-deferred retirement accounts. First, investments are made with after-tax dollars, so you could start with only $0.60 to $0.70

of each dollar. Second, unless you invest in municipal securities or an annuity, part of each year's return is taxable; this slows the accumulation process. Finally, it is tempting to use those investments for purposes other than retirement.

There are times when general investments offer advantages over tax-deferred accounts. If your financial situation is highly unsettled, the restrictions on and penalties for withdrawing funds from tax-deferred instruments are a severe shortcoming. You may want to sacrifice the tax advantages for the added flexibility of a general investment plan. Or you may already be using your available tax-deferred retirement plan to the maximum yet still have money for investments.

PLANNING YOUR RETIREMENT

Good planning can ensure you have income to provide for yourself comfortably during a retirement that could extend for 25 years or more. Social Security is a start. Adding a pension plan helps, but it may still leave you short. And the recent trend to reduce pension benefits is hardly reassuring. What is left? Many people find they need their own personal retirement fund to complete the process.

Start by deciding how much income you need to supplement your other retirement programs. What if you later qualify for a generous pension plan? Won't the money in a personal fund be extra? At worst, you may be forced to put up with a seaside condominium rather than an economy rate three-room flat in Patuwcket, New Hampshire.

You cannot project retirement needs without using assumptions and estimates, since things will change considerably by the time you retire. But it is far better to develop a plan now and modify it along the way than to make none.

There are three key elements to formulating a retirement plan: (1) estimating what income you will need, (2) setting a tentative date for retiring, and (3) identifying where the income will come from.

I'll be the mommy and you be the daddy. I think it's time we talk about a retirement plan.

Income Needed during Retirement

Most people want to maintain a standard of living in retirement comparable to the standard of their working years. But that will not take the same income. Work-related expenses cease. Contributions to the tax-deferred retirement account and general investments will likely stop. Social Security taxes will end, and your taxes may drop.

A rule of thumb says you should plan to replace 60 to 70 percent of your working income for retirement. But the figure is a compromise. Exhibit 18.4 shows that at lower income levels the replacement amount is too low, and at upper levels too generous. Why does the replacement percentage drop as income rises? First, middle and upper income individuals save a higher proportion of their income, but savings usually cease on retirement. Second, federal and state income taxes take a higher fraction of income from those in the middle and upper ranks. The lower income of retirees lessens that burden. Finally, work-related expenses tend to be proportionately higher for those in the middle and upper ranks.

Exhibit 18.4 can help you broadly estimate your required retirement income. Ted Elgin, who is single and earns about $20,000 annually, will need about $12,200 in retirement income: $20,000 × 61% replacement. Bob and Ellen together earn $40,000—their needs should be halfway between the 60 percent for $30,000 and the 55 percent for $50,000; planning to replace about 57½ percent would prove a reasonable compromise. They will need about $23,000 to maintain their living standard: $40,000 preretirement income × 57.5%.

A more precise way to estimate future needs is to develop a retirement budget, with your present budget as a starting point. Eliminate or reduce the expenses that will change with retirement (for example, you may no longer have a mortgage payment). Next, estimate the taxes you might have to pay in retirement: Social Security taxes should drop sharply, since most

Exhibit 18.4

Retirement Income Required to Maintain Preretirement Living Standards

Before-tax preretirement income†	Required Retirement Income*			
	Single person		Married couple	
$10,000	$ 7,272	73%‡	$ 7,786	78%‡
15,000	9,941	66	10,684	71
20,000	12,282	61	13,185	66
30,000	17,391	58	18,062	60
50,000	25,675	51	27,384	55

* Assumes retiring person qualifies for Social Security.
† Assumed income for individual or couple retiring in 1980.
‡ Required retirement income as a percentage of preretirement income given in column 1.
Source: President's Commission on Pension Policy, November 1980.

sources of retirement income are exempt, and income taxes may decline because your income is lower and at least half of your Social Security retirement payment is currently exempt from federal income taxes.

In order to plan effectively, use both the replacement percentage and projected-budget methods to calculate your retirement needs.

Effect of inflation on future income needs

Without question, inflation will increase your retirement income needs. Shouldn't income estimates, whether the replacement percentages in Exhibit 18.4 or those you arrive at using the budgetary method, be adjusted upward to reflect inflation's effect? Rather than increasing our figures for defined needs, we will concentrate on adjusting the projections and computations used to estimate income sources if needed. That way retirement income will likely rise with inflation: income will grow to meet tomorrow's higher costs. Social Security benefits are already tied to the consumer price index and need no adjustment. While not adjusted directly, future pension benefits should rise as inflation pushes up your current salary. Last, the rates of return on tax-deferred retirement accounts and general investment accounts should include an inflation premium. The goal is to boost your retirement income enough to maintain your living standard.

Establishing a Proposed Retirement Date

You should project a tentative retirement date, since years of service determine benefits in many pension plans. In addition, your age not only determines eligibility for Social Security benefits, but whether they are reduced for an early start. The final balance of many tax-deferred retirement accounts depends on how long you continue deposits; the longer the money is deposited, the larger your accumulated interest and dividends.

You should also project how long your retirement will last. While not a pleasant task, this is critical to planning. A standard mortality table (see Chapter 11) will tell you how long the average man or woman lives beyond your planned retirement age. You will almost certainly want to add some years on to that, rather than face the possibility of outliving your income. A later section provides benchmarks.

The challenge of early retirement

If you plan to retire early, solid planning is needed. First, pension benefits will be less: you have fewer years of service, and many plans pay less than a 100 percent benefit if you start before 65. It is important to remember that Social Security retirement benefits will not start before age 62. Since you have fewer years to make contributions and less interest and dividends will accumulate, the balance in your tax-deferred account will be smaller.

Does that mean early retirement is impossible? No. But arranging an early retirement takes effort. More income will have to come from retirement accounts. They will have to be started early, receive regular deposits, and earn a significant return.

An early start and sustained contributions to tax-deferred retirement accounts do not guarantee early retirement. But if you develop a well thought out plan you will at least be able to see whether early retirement is possible.

Strategy

Develop retirement plans based on (1) an early retirement date, (2) a most likely retirement date, and (3) a late retirement date.

Providing the Required Retirement Income

At this point, your retirement plan covers what you want to do (your estimate of how much retirement income you will need) and when you want to do it. What remains? Now you must determine how to do it: the potential sources of income. Social Security and pension benefits will be the primary sources; they provide the foundation. Secondary sources include tax-deferred retirement accounts and general investments.

Your first step is to estimate your Social Security and pension benefits. Then you can find out what remains to be met by tax-deferred accounts and general investments.

An example is the easiest way to illustrate the process. Ann Wells's retirement plan is developed in Exhibit 18.5. Ann estimates that she needs $15,500 per year in retirement to maintain her present living standard (top line of Exhibit 18.5). She used a combination of Exhibit 18.4 and her current budget to make that estimate.

Ann's plan is to retire at age 62. She is currently 35, so she has 27 years to accumulate the needed retirement funds. While she is not fully vested in her employer's pension plan, she has 3 years of service credit. Ann plans for 30 years of retirement.

Estimating Social Security retirement benefits

You must estimate your likely Social Security retirement benefit, just as you did for survivors' and disability benefits. The Social Security administration will not provide an estimate until several years before you retire, far too late for planning purposes.

One option is to use the Social Security benefit table in Appendix A.2.

Exhibit 18.5

Planning Sources of Retirement Income

1. Total retirement income needed*	$15,500
2. Less: Social Security retirement benefit (from Appendix A.2) at age 62: $592 monthly benefit × 12 months	$ 7,104
3. Less: employer sponsored pension plan: $22,000 average income × 30 years service × 1.2% replacement fraction × 80% due to early retirement	$ 6,336
4. Retirement needs still to be covered: $15,500 total − $7,104 Social Security − $6,336 pension	$ 2,060
5. Total balance required in tax-deferred retirement account: $2,060 annual need × 30 years of retirement	$61,800
6. Less: Current balance in tax-deferred accounts	$ 5,100
7. Remaining balance that must be accumulated	$56,700
8. Annual contribution required to accumulate remainder: $56,700 remaining balance/27 years to retirement	$ 2,100

* Developed using a post-retirement budget and Exhibit 18.4.

Retirement benefits are based on your age and approximate salary; they are summarized in the far right columns. Benefits shown in A.2 are based on the assumption that a person works regularly and receives average pay raises. The dollar amounts are based on 1987 wages.

A second option is to write the Social Security Administration, Office of Public Inquiries, Baltimore, MD 21235, and ask them to estimate your likely retirement benefit. The office has indicated it might provide such estimates, and may be doing it by now.

Taking Ann Wells's $24,000 salary and her age, 35, we find a $592 monthly benefit at age 62. That is entered on line 2 of Exhibit 18.5. At this point Ann has gotten about halfway to her retirement income goal.

If you have had large gaps in your work history or sharp changes in salary, a detailed analysis based on your specific work record can provide a more accurate estimate. A worksheet like that provided in the booklet *A Guide to Social Security* can lead you through the computations (you can purchase a copy from William M. Mercer-Meidinger Inc., Social Security Division, 2600 Meidinger Tower, Louisville, KT 40202-3415).

Adjustments for inflation. Shouldn't Social Security benefits be adjusted for inflation? Recall that these benefits are indexed to the cost of living. As it rises, so should your benefit. Inflation over the next 27 years will push Ann's income needs above the $15,500 in Exhibit 18.5. As it does, Social Security benefits should follow.

Employer's pension plan

We assume that Ann Wells's employer provides a defined-benefit pension plan which offers a 1.2 percent replacement for each year of service times the average of the employee's salary for the highest 3 years. Benefits at age 62 are 80 percent of those at 65.

Ann will have 30 years of service by the time she retires. With her $22,000 average salary for the past 3 years, she has a projected benefit of $6,336: 1.2% replacement percentage × 30 years service × $22,000 average salary × 80% early retirement. This amount is entered on line 3 of Exhibit 18.5.

Adjustment for future inflation. Pension plans that average your salary during the final years generally handle inflation reasonably well up to retirement. As inflation pushes up prices, your salary should rise, and so will your pension benefit. Plans that average your entire work history are much less effective; the low salaries of the early years limit the "automatic" adjustment for inflation.

Most pension benefits are fixed once you begin drawing them, though some employers have raised benefits paid to retirees to help handle inflation. Such adjustments are rarely guaranteed, so you may want to build in a cushion when you estimate what income you will need in retirement. The "extra" income in the early years can offset the inflation-induced decline in the purchasing power of your fixed pension benefit. Ann Wells included a 10 percent contingency allowance in her $15,500 estimate for line 1 of Exhibit 18.5. Initially Ann will probably leave that extra 10 percent unused so she can save it, but as her cost of living rises while her pension benefit remains fixed, she will need the extra income.

Tax-deferred retirement accounts

Tax-deferred retirement accounts can provide income to complete your retirement plan. As noted earlier, an IRA, Keogh, 401(k), or 403(b) account provides substantial tax advantages for accumulating a retirement fund. Any of these is generally superior to general investments. The size of your required tax-deferred account depends on your retirement plan: it must rise significantly if you plan to retire early. In the same vein, the higher your income replacement goal, the higher the required balance. If your employer-supplied pension plan provides only moderate benefits, these accounts will have to supply more of the retirement income you need.

Estimating the amount you need in your tax-deferred retirement plan involves two steps. You need to calculate the amount the account must provide annually (line 4 of Exhibit 18.5). Ann Wells estimates she will need $2,060, the portion of her required $15,500 income not provided by Social Security or pension. You also need to estimate how long you expect to be retired. An annual need of $2,060 for 30 years boosts the required total for Ann's tax-deferred retirement account to $61,800 (line 5 of Exhibit 18.5). While we use the term *account*, any combination of IRA, Keogh, 401(k), and 403(b) plans could be used to meet the $61,800 target.

Accumulating the target balance. Since the total in a tax-deferred account is accumulated over time, it needs to be converted to an annual or monthly contribution. First, review your balance sheet for any balance you may already have in such an account. Ann Wells has $5,100 in a 401(k) plan with her employer; she enters that on line 6 of Exhibit 18.5. Deducting that from the total on line 5, we see that Ann still has to accumulate $56,700 (line 7).

Often the amount on line 7 of Exhibit 18.5 is significant. But a savings plan spread over years will produce the needed sizable balance. Ann has 27 years until her planned retirement in which to accumulate the $56,700 needed. To do that, she must save $2,100 annually: $57,600 remainder/ 27 years. Monthly deposits of $175 should do it: $2,100 annual/12 months.

What about inflation? Shouldn't our calculation take into account the interest the tax-deferred account earns? And shouldn't there be an adjustment for inflation? The account will earn interest and dividends while the money accumulates, and there may also be capital gains earned and reinvested. Over an extended accumulation period, earnings will be significant. And they continue during retirement while the account's balance is doled out over that extended period. All during that time, interest, dividends, and capital gains will continue to build.

Then shouldn't those earnings be accounted for somewhere in the computation? No. Instead, we assume that the earnings are needed to offset inflation. By the time Ann retires, inflation will have pushed her income needs above the $2,060 shown on line 4. But if she deposits the suggested

$2,100 annually, earnings on the account during those 27 years will boost the balance far above her $56,700 target on line 7. This larger balance is going to mean she can draw more than $2,060 annually. Those earnings will offset the ravages of inflation.

What about the account's earnings during retirement? They are needed to offset price rises *during* retirement.

In effect, we have incorporated two inflation adjustments. Returns the account earns while the money is being accumulated are expected to offset inflation during those years. Returns earned during retirement are expected to offset inflation for those years. Obviously, when we depend on earnings to deal with inflation, an account's return becomes exceedingly important.

What is an "adequate" return? The account's approximate real return (current return − expected inflation rate) is our benchmark. For our purposes that estimate is fine. You need a real return between a minimal 2 percent and a preferred 4 percent to offset inflation in most cases. Several factors affect real returns. Conditions in the financial markets can significantly alter real returns, as does your willingness to tolerate risk.

Strategy

To offset inflation, your retirement accounts need to earn a real return of between 2 and 4 percent.

General investments

General investments can and do provide a significant fraction of retirement income in some plans. They can be an important source of income. For one thing, all taxes have been paid along the way. Only current interest, dividends, and capital gains are taxed, so you can usually draw money from these investments with no tax consequences.

However, one or more tax-deferred retirement accounts make a far better vehicle for accumulating funds than general investments. Not only do you receive immediate tax relief—contributions may lower your taxable income—but the deferral of taxes on earnings provides a continuing tax shelter.

If Ann Wells's general investments were large and targeted for retirement, she would insert a line 6(b) in Exhibit 18.5. The total of her general investments would then be deducted from the required balance on line 5. If general investments are used to accumulate the target balance on line 7 of Exhibit 18.5, the computation on line 8 is similar. But it is more difficult to achieve an "adequate" real return, since part of each year's return is lost to taxes.

PAYMENTS FROM YOUR RETIREMENT PLAN

In general, you have few options as to the amount and scheduling of payments from Social Security and pension plans. Most plans pay monthly and continue as long as you live. Not so with your own retirement accounts. There you have considerable latitude on payment size and timing.

Payments from Social Security and Pension Plans

Single individuals have few decisions to make here. For most, the pattern of recurring payments that continue to their death matches their needs. The Social Security payment process for couples is automatic: upon the retired person's death, the surviving spouse can select whichever is higher: (1) the survivor's current benefit or (2) the deceased person's benefit.

Pension plans generally provide for a variety of payment plans. At one extreme, benefits cease when the covered person dies, dropping the survivor's income sharply. At the other extreme, the entire benefit continues to the survivor. The larger the fraction that continues for the survivor, the smaller the initial benefit.

Which type of payment plan is best? It depends on the survivor's need for income. If the survivor needs income badly, a significant percentage should continue to the survivor. When need is more limited, a smaller continuation percentage is acceptable. Most plans allow changes right up to the time when benefits start.

Payments during Retirement from an Annuity

Purchasing an **annuity** with the money in your tax-deferred retirement account is a conservative approach. The insurance company that sold the annuity promises to continue payments as long as you live. You cannot outlive this source of income. The insurance companies use the money from those who "die early" to continue payments to those who "die late." Your payment depends on (1) the amount you pay for the annuity, (2) your age when payments begin, (3) the rate of return paid by the insurance company on the funds, (4) the payout option you elect, and (5) when payments begin. We will spend time on the last three.

Rate of return

The rate of return the insurance company pays on the annuity has a major effect on the amount of your payment. A good annuity might pay 8 to 9 percent while a mediocre one is at 3 to 4 percent. Over an extended payment period, that significantly alters the promised payment. Careful comparison shopping is essential. Get quotes from different insurance companies based on the same inputs: dollar amount, age, starting date, and survivor rights.

Strategy

Compare the promised payments from a number of different annuities before settling on one.

Method of payment

Most annuities offer several payout options. Payments may continue until you die. Some plans guarantee payments for a set period. Or payments may continue to a designated survivor.

Straight-life option. Under the **straight-life option,** an annuity's payments continue until the annuitant (the person covered by the annuity) dies. Then payments cease, whether they have lasted a few weeks or many years. Straight life pays the highest amount per premium dollar and is particularly suited for individuals with no dependents.

Guaranteed minimum period. The **guaranteed minimum period option** assures payments for a set period, called the "certain period"; 5 or 10 years is common. If the annuitant dies during the period, payments continue to the end of the certain period. Actual payments to the beneficiary may be either a lump sum or a continuation of the monthly amounts. Once beyond the guarantee period, payments cease when the annuitant dies. Adding a guarantee period lowers the annuity's promised payment.

Joint or survivor option. When the **joint, or survivor, option** is chosen, payments cover the annuitant and a named beneficiary. If the annuitant dies, payments still continue to the beneficiary for as long as he or she lives. The beneficiary's payment can range from the annuitant's benefit to some fraction of it. Since two lives are being covered, the promised payment is less than with the straight-life option.

When payments begin: immediate or deferred

An **immediate annuity** begins making payments shortly after purchase. They are suitable for persons who have retired and need an immediate stream of income.

A **deferred annuity** postpones payments to some future time. Generally the purchaser sets the date when payments are to begin at the time the annuity is bought, but it can be changed easily. These plans are suitable for those who want to delay the start of payments.

One major advantage of a deferred annuity is that taxes on its earnings are deferred; they need not be paid until the earnings are withdrawn. Once the regular payments begin, part of each payment is taxable, since it is assumed that a portion came from tax-deferred earnings.

Annuities are purchased with after-tax dollars. You cannot reduce your taxable income by the amount invested. Consequently, a deferred annuity does not provide the immediate tax benefit of an IRA, Keogh, 401(k), or 403(b) account; these latter are a clear choice when the goal is accumulating retirement funds.

Exhibit 18.6

Advantages and Disadvantages of Annuities

Advantages	Disadvantages
1. Payments that you cannot outlive are guaranteed.	1. Few dollars are returned if annuitant dies shortly after benefits begin.
2. Income taxes on earnings accumulated in a deferred annuity are postponed.	2. There is a tax penalty on withdrawals before 59½ years of age unless disabled.
3. Guaranteed income provides peace of mind to someone concerned with adequacy of retirement savings.	3. Premiums used to purchase annuity are paid in after-tax dollars.
4. Risk is low on fixed-return annuities from insurance companies rated A or A+.	4. Returns on some annuities have been disappointingly low.
	5. Payments are fixed; annuitant cannot alter them to fit needs.

Strategy

Exhaust all tax-deferred retirement options before you consider using an annuity for accumulating a retirement fund.

Advantages and disadvantages of annuities

Exhibit 18.6 lists the major advantages and disadvantages of annuities. Two entries need further explanation. For someone whose income needs vary, an annuity's fixed payments are a decided disadvantage. When your needs exceed the annuity's payment, you will have to tap your cash reserves. When the opposite occurs, the extra income should be saved for the next shortfall. Finally, some annuities just do not offer competitive rates of return, so your resulting income can be considerably less than it might have been with another option. On balance, my opinion is that the advantages of annuities do not offset their considerable disadvantages.

Strategy

Annuities are best for someone who needs a predictable income he or she cannot outlive. Deferred annuities may be workable options if you are already contributing the maximum to tax-deferred retirement accounts, have a sizable amount to invest, and need the annuity's tax deferral.

Payments during Retirement Using Your Own Payout Plan

An ideal payout plan would have persons spending the final dollars from their retirement funds just as they permanently depart the gene pool. Save for the clairvoyant, that is hard to achieve. Nevertheless, advance planning makes it possible to structure payments so that they continue throughout

Nonliquidating payout plan

your retirement. When you devise **your own payout plan,** you may not get the certainty an annuity offers, but you do gain some other advantages.

A **nonliquidating payout plan** provides payments from the interest, dividends, and any capital gains earned by your tax-deferred accounts and general investments; the original investments remain intact. You need a large balance to produce the required income.

The left side of Exhibit 18.7 illustrates such a plan. Wanda Welloff has $100,000 in various investments; she expects to earn an 8 percent return, so she can draw $8,000 from the account annually, yet leave the $100,000 intact. If that amount is adequate for her needs, she can continue that draw indefinitely. If Wanda dies after, say, 20 years, the $100,000 will be bequeathed by her will.

Liquidating payout plan

Not everyone is as well prepared as Wanda. At retirement their invest-ments may be smaller, their needs may be greater, or both. They can design a **liquidating payout plan** under which a part of their investments is liquidated each year.

The right side of Exhibit 18.7 illustrates. Sam Shortfall has $100,000 in various investments. But he needs to draw about $10,185 annually from those investments for the planned 20 years of his retirement.

The $8,000 in dividends and interest Sam earns on that money ($100,000 at 8 percent) is not sufficient; the remaining $2,185 will have to come from liquidation of investments. If Sam continues to draw the $10,185, the entire investment will be liquidated in 20 years. As the right side of Exhibit 18.7 shows, the withdrawal in year 20 closes the account.

How large a liquidating payment an investment can provide depends on three things: (1) the investment's size, (2) the return earned during the withdrawal period, and (3) how long the payments must continue. A recent balance sheet will tell you the current market value of your investments. A review of your current investment returns will help you project likely

Exhibit 18.7

Nonliquidating and Liquidating Retirement Payout Plans for a $100,000 Investment Pool

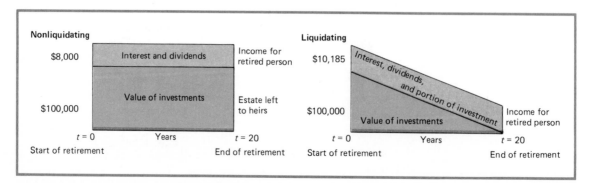

earnings. When estimating that return, consider any shifts in your investments that might raise or lower the rate. Finally, consider the likely future
direction of interest rates in the financial markets.

Once you have estimated your likely return, you can use the table in
Exhibit 18.8 to convert it to an annual dollar amount: it shows the payout
from a $1,000 investment earning different interest rates over different
periods. The table is readily usable for any multiple of $1,000. On $32,000
in investments, the payment is 32 times the amount in Exhibit 18.8; on
$132,770, the amount is 132.77 times the payment in Exhibit 18.8. The
table is set up to handle widely different assumed returns, and it covers
planned retirements of 4 to 36 years.

We'll use the example of Sam Shortfall's retirement fund to demonstrate how to use Exhibit 18.8. Sam has $100,000 at retirement and
expects it to earn 8 percent. On $1,000, he could draw $101.85 annually
for the planned 20 years. His $100,000 provides 100 times that, or
$10,185: $101.85 at 8% for 20 years × ($100,000 total/$1,000).

How long a retirement period? The **planned payout period** in an
ideal liquidating plan would match the retiree's remaining life, but that is
impossible to ensure. That leaves two conflicting imperatives. The goal of
a secure, lifelong retirement argues for a long payout period to ensure that
the investment is not exhausted too early. The goal of an adequate income
argues for a shorter period to provide the largest income for a comfortable
retirement. You must make your own trade-off. Those who emphasize
security will likely favor a longer, more conservative payout period. Shorter
payout periods would appeal to those willing to sacrifice future security for
immediate income. Our suggested payout periods would be:

- 30 to 35 years for males retiring at age 55; 34 to 39 for females
- 25 to 30 years for males retiring at age 60; 29 to 34 for females
- 20 to 26 years for males retiring at age 65; 24 to 30 for females
- 15 to 21 years for males retiring at age 70; 19 to 25 for females

Exhibit 18.8

Annual Withdrawals from $1,000 at Different Rates of Return over Various Payout Periods

Payout period (years)	Withdrawal When the Rate of Return Is:						
	4%	6%	8%	10%	12%	14%	16%
4	$275.49	$288.59	$301.92	$315.47	$329.23	$343.20	$357.38
8	148.53	161.04	174.01	187.44	201.30	215.57	230.22
12	106.55	119.28	132.70	146.76	161.44	176.67	192.41
16	85.82	98.95	112.98	127.82	143.39	159.62	176.41
20	73.58	87.18	101.85	117.46	133.88	150.99	168.67
24	65.59	79.68	94.98	111.30	128.46	146.30	164.67
28	60.01	74.59	90.49	107.45	125.24	143.66	162.55
32	55.95	71.00	87.45	104.97	123.28	142.15	161.40
36	52.89	68.39	85.34	103.34	122.06	141.26	160.77

Adequate planning cannot guarantee a long, comfortable, worry-free retirement, but it can go a long way toward resolving many of the financial concerns associated with retiring.

Summary

1 Early retirement planning provides a twofold benefit:
- Annual deposits needed to achieve a target retirement fund are smaller.
- The compounding of earnings on early deposits can double those deposits' value several times over.

2 Retirement income generally comes from four sources:
- Social Security benefits
- Employer-provided pension plan
- Withdrawals from tax-deferred retirement accounts
- General investments

3 Nearly all workers qualify for Social Security retirement benefits; spouses of workers can draw the greater of:
- 50 percent of their partner's benefit
- The benefits based on their own work record

4 Benefits from an employer-sponsored pension plan become irrevocably yours when you are vested. Vesting can be immediate, graduated so that it takes as long as 7 years to reach 100 percent, or zero until the end of 5 years of service, when you become 100 percent vested.

5 Benefits from a defined-benefit pension plan are calculated using a formula that includes years of service plus a dollar amount or a percentage of salary.

6 Under a defined-contribution plan, the employer deposits a prescribed amount in an employee's account. The account's final balance determines the retirement benefit.

7 Advantages of tax-deferred retirement accounts include:
- Deposit may be deductible for tax purposes,

or your salary may be directly reduced; you invest before-tax dollars.
- Income taxes on the account's earnings are deferred.
- Deferral of taxes continues until money is withdrawn.

8 Common tax-deferred retirement options include:
- Keogh for the self-employed
- IRA for all workers
- 403(b) salary reduction plans
- 401(k) salary reduction plans

9 Generally, you need to replace 60 to 70 percent of your preretirement income to maintain your standard of living; a more accurate method of calculating what you will need is to develop a "retirement" budget.

10 Social Security benefits and pension payments are primary sources of retirement income; tax-deferred retirement accounts and general investments are secondary sources that cover the balance of income needs.

11 By using the balance in a tax-deferred account to purchase an annuity, you obtain an income stream you cannot outlive.

12 Comparison shopping for an annuity is essential both to ensure that the annuity offers a competitive return and to make certain that the company selling it is rated A+ or A by Best and Company.

13 Individuals can develop a payout plan that distributes either income or income and principal over their planned retirement period.

14 The planned payout period for a plan should exceed the person's expected life (shown in a mortality table) so that the income is not exhausted too early.

Review your understanding of

Social Security retirement benefit
  Early retirement benefit
  Spousal benefit
Employee Retirement Income Security Act (ERISA)
Vesting
Defined-benefit pension plan
Defined-contribution pension plan
Tax-deferred retirement account
Before-tax investment dollars
Keogh plan (HR-10)
Individual Retirement Account (IRA)

Salary reduction: 403(b)
Salary reduction: 401(k)
Annuity
  Straight-life option
  Guaranteed minimum period
  Joint, or survivor, option
Immediate annuity
Deferred annuity
Personal payout plan
  Nonliquidating
  Liquidating
Planned payout period

Discussion questions

1   Why is it important to begin planning retirement early in one's working life? Are there disadvantages to doing so?

2   Stanley Secure is currently 100 percent vested in his employer's pension plan. He also expects to receive Social Security retirement benefits. Should he do any retirement planning? Why?

3   Nancy and her husband expect to retire in about 10 years at age 62. Both have lengthy work records, so they have paid considerable Social Security taxes. Will Nancy receive a Social Security benefit? What will it be based on?

4   Listed below are details on two pension plans:

Plan	Description
1	Employer contributes 5 percent of employee's salary to his or her retirement account.
2	Employer's pension retirement payment equals: 1% × average salary × years of service.

What type of plan is Plan 1? Plan 2? How is the pension benefit set for each plan? What would you need to know in order to estimate a worker's likely benefit in 20 years under each plan?

5   George recently became fully vested in his employer's pension plan. What does that mean? How long has George probably worked for the firm if it had immediate vesting? Graduated? Cliff?

6   Why is money likely to accumulate faster in a tax-deferred account than a general investment? Are contributions to tax-deferred accounts made in before-tax dollars? Explain. When are the taxes paid on these accounts?

7   Sonya teaches business courses in high school and does some accounting work for several businesses (she is not an employee of those businesses). Can she qualify for a tax-deferred retirement account? If she does, what are the limits on her contributions?

8   What are the similarities and differences between a 403(b) and 401(k) salary reduction plan? Who can qualify? Why must the employer be willing to participate?

9   The benefit formula for Jan's employer-provided pension plan is: 1.6% × average of 3 highest years' salaries × years of service. Will benefit levels be adjusted for inflation until Jan retires? How? Will that continue after Jan retires?

10   What is the justification for using a zero rate of interest when computing the required balance for a tax-deferred retirement account? Does the fact that we use a zero rate imply that the return on such an account is not important?

11   Boris is considering purchasing a single-premium, immediate annuity when he retires in 6 months. How will that annuity operate? What are its major advantages?

12   Jane Leisure has received two payment proposals on a $40,000 single-premium annuity:

Payment plan	Monthly payment	Guarantee period
1	$330	None; payments extend for Jane's lifetime.
2	$320	For 10 years at least, longer if Jane survives.

What are the strengths of each plan? What things should Jane consider when deciding between the two?

13   How are nonliquidating and liquidating payout plans similar? Different? How would you decide between the two options?

14   What factors determine the potential payment from a liquidating payout plan. What steps might an individual take when developing such a plan to ensure that the money does not run out "too soon"?

Problems

18.1   Brad Leftwich is retiring after working 20 years for Gray Products. Benefits under the company's pension plan are computed using this formula: 1.3% × average salary × years of service. Average salary is based on the highest 3 years during the employee's last 5 years of service. Brad's earnings record is:

Current year	1 year ago	2 years ago	3 years ago	4 years ago	5 years ago
$22,485	$19,500	$21,900	$18,300	$21,600	$25,500

    a What "average salary" will the firm use in the pension computation?

    b What will Brad's pension benefit be?

18.2 Maude Mobile was recently hired by Wonder Cookie. In the past, she has changed positions about every 4 to 6 years. Vesting under Wonder's pension plan proceeds as follows:

- Before 3 years of service, no vesting.
- After 3 years of service, 20 percent is vested.
- Each year thereafter, an additional 20 percent is vested.
- After 7 years of service, 100 percent vested.

    a If Maude leaves after 4 years, to what extent will she be vested? After 6 years? After 8 years?

    b Assume she leaves after 5 years. According to Wonder's pension benefit formula, her potential benefit would be:

$$\$21,000 \text{ average salary} \times 1.2\% \text{ replacement} \times 5 \text{ years of service} = \$1,260 \text{ benefit}$$

    Will she receive that entire benefit at retirement?

    c Once she leaves Wonder, will that benefit rise with inflation? Is there a disadvantage to having a string of "short service records" with a number of employers?

18.3 Mel and Morris both graduated from Olde Steady Rock in 1980 and immediately accepted employment. Their respective earnings records are:

	1987	1986	1985	1984	1983	1982	1981	1980
Mel	$23,100	$21,450	$19,800	$18,300	$16,950	$15,750	$14,550	$13,500
Morris	$23,100	$21,450	$19,800	$18,300	$16,950	$15,750	$14,550	$13,500

Benefits under Mel's pension plan are based on the average annual earnings over his entire work history. It then pays 1.3 percent of that average times years of service. Morris's plan averages the highest 3 years of his final 5 years of service. It pays 1.2 percent of that average for each year of service.

    a If both are fully vested, what is Mel's current pension benefit? Morris's?

    b Mel claims the 1.3 percent replacement makes his plan better. Do you agree?

    c During a period of high inflation and rapidly rising salaries, which plan is better? Why?

18.4 Zelda Prof (current marginal tax rate 35 percent) is developing a retirement plan. She estimates her 403(b) salary reduction plan will have to provide $2,000 annually during her 25 years of retirement. Actual retirement is about 20 years off, so she has some time to accumulate the required balance. Zelda expects to earn an 8 percent return while accumulating the money.

    a What balance does she need in her 403(b) plan at retirement?

    b What amount should she contribute each year until retirement?

    c If the account earns 8 percent, will its total balance after 20 years exceed the amount computed in part (a)? Why isn't that 8 percent included in your computation for part (a)?

18.5 Conrad Confused (he is single) needs help with his retirement plan. Thus far he has determined the following:

- Estimated Social Security benefit is $550 monthly.
- His current preretirement income is $20,000; he wants to replace 70 percent of that income.
- The pension plan from Conrad's employer will likely provide $250 each month.

    a Will Conrad have to provide any part of his retirement needs through a tax-deferred retirement account?

    b If he wants to plan for a 20-year retirement, how large a balance should he have in his tax-deferred account at retirement?

18.6 Fred Freedom's planned retirement date is about 2 months off. Presently his tax-deferred retirement account has a $40,000 balance that will be used during his planned 20-year retirement. Based on prevailing interest rates, Fred expects that account will continue to earn an 8 percent return.

    a What annual payment will a nonliquidating payout plan provide?

    b What would a liquidating plan provide each year?

    c Fred's friend (an insurance salesperson) has suggested a single-premium, immediate annuity that pays $3,860 annually on a $40,000 investment. What are its advantages?

    d Which option would you recommend? Why?

Case problem

Several recent articles on retirement planning encouraged Peg and Len Latestart to think about retirement. Both are 45, so it will be 20 years until they reach age 65. Each has an annual salary of $24,000, and their respective white-collar jobs are reasonably secure. Because their income is sizable, they have never considered planning for retirement necessary. First, both have always been covered by Social Security. Since they have paid a sizable amount into that system, they expect to receive a large retirement benefit. Second, retirement has been one of those distant goals that just did not warrant detailed planning; they always said they would start working on that goal "sometime." Third, since they are both covered by pension plans, they have always assumed that those two payments coupled with Social Security would *surely* meet all their needs.

Because both Len and Peg have changed positions and careers several times, they have never become vested in any pension plans except their current ones. Details on those two plans include:

	Covered Person	
	Len	Peg
Years of service	5 years	5 years
Current vesting	100%	100%
Benefit payment	$14 per month for each year of service	1% × "average salary" × years of service
Average salary	Not applicable	$22,000
Benefit reduction for early retirement	5% drop for each year before age 65	5% drop for each year before age 65

Peg and Len think they will likely remain with their current employers until retirement. That would give each a total of 25 years of service.

The Latestarts' combined income has pushed their marginal tax rate (state and federal) to 35 percent, so they pay considerable taxes. In fact, they claim one of the reasons they have never bothered to save for retirement is: "You lose so much of the earnings to income taxes it's hardly worth it."

Len's employer offers a 401(k) salary reduction plan in which an employee can set aside up to 6 percent of salary; maximum reduction at Len's current salary is $1,440 per year. For each 1 percent the employee contributes, the employer adds 0.5 percent; maximum employer contribution to the 401(k) is 3 percent. The plan offers a number of different investment options, ranging from fully insured CDs at 8 percent to higher-risk options that should provide a higher return.

Neither Len nor Peg currently has an IRA. They considered it, even requested a prospectus from several mutual funds, but then dismissed it. They read that the Tax Reform Act of 1986 restricted their use, so they assumed that they do not qualify, especially with their both being covered by a pension plan.

The Latestarts have developed the following guidelines for their retirement plan:
- To maintain their present standard of living, they expect they will need a $29,000 annual retirement income based on current dollars.
- They expect their retirement to extend for at least 25 years.
- They expect future inflation to continue at the current 5 percent level.
- Both want to explore the possibility of retiring at age 62; in fact, they wonder if retiring as early as age 55 may be possible.

1. What percent of their preretirement income are the Latestarts proposing to replace?
2. Approximately what Social Security retirement benefit will Len and Peg receive at age 65? At age 62? (*Hint:* Appendix A.2 may help.)
3. What pension benefit can Len and Peg expect at age 65? At age 62? (*Hint:* On the latter, reduce *both* years of service and benefits.)

4   Does Peg's pension plan make any adjustment for inflation up to the time of retirement? How about Len's? Once retired, do either of their plans continue to adjust for inflation?

5   If they retire at age 65, will Social Security and their pensions meet their needs? If not, how large a balance should they have in a retirement account? What balance is needed if they retire at age 62?

6   To accumulate the balance suggested in your answer to part (5), would you recommend general investments or tax-deferred accounts? Why?

7   Do Len and Peg qualify for any tax-deferred retirement accounts? Explain the advantages of each one.

8   What annual contribution would the Latestarts have to make to achieve your suggested account balance from part (5) at age 65? At age 62?

9   Will it be feasible for Peg and Len to retire at age 55? Develop some dollar estimates coupled with a brief discussion to support your position.

CHAPTER 19

Planning the transfer of your estate

AFTER COMPLETING THIS CHAPTER YOU WILL HAVE LEARNED

- Why you should plan for the transfer of your estate
- What a will contains and why it is important
- The role an executor plays in settling your estate
- Why anyone with minor children should name a guardian
- When to update your will
- What happens to your estate if you die without a will
- What a letter of last instruction should contain and why it is important
- How the three major types of joint ownership differ and when each is appropriate
- How a trust fund operates
- Advantages and disadvantages of the three major types of trust
- The basic structure of federal estate taxes
- How to estimate the federal estate taxes on an estate

Picture this scene in a lawyer's office. Sitting before the lawyer's walnut desk is the bereaved family of Penelope Prepared, recently deceased at age 95. The heirs quietly await the reading of the will; all expect a "remembrance." The lawyer reads the will's first paragraph: "Being of sound mind, I spent every damn cent before I died. Thanks for coming and have a nice day."

If we used such a highly practical way to dispose of our assets, exhausting them at the very moment our bodies gave out, no one would be left struggling to divide up the remains while keeping family peace. But it is not that simple. Some will die long before they reach old age. They may want to leave assets to support dependents. They may want the income from their accumulated wealth to be used for a survivor's support, with the assets ultimately distributed to someone else. Or they may have some special causes and charities to which they want to give their assets. Even if they live long, they may not plan to spend it all.

In each case, the individual has a specific wish for the distribution of his or her assets. Planning the ultimate transfer of your estate ensures your assets will be disposed in the manner you desire.

An **estate plan** has several objectives, and making one yields you a number of benefits. First, it encourages you to develop a detailed record of your assets, to ensure your worldly goods are identified if something happens to you. Second, it requires you take the legal steps needed to ensure your estate will be transferred swiftly and economically. Third, it encourages you to identify precisely to whom and when you want your estate transferred. Fourth, it reveals situations where other planning tools can help you manage your estate. Finally, it requires that you consider the financial consequences of transferring your estate—certain tax-saving and cost-saving options that will minimize the costs of transfer.

At this point some people begin to feel a bit uncomfortable. They ask why they should plan their estate. Excuses abound: "My estate is limited, so planning really shouldn't be needed." "I am single so I do not need a plan." "At my age, death is so remote, I can plan later." "Everything is held in joint ownership, so no further planning is needed." All are poor reasons for not planning the transfer of your estate.

In general, estate planning does not involve a long process, or hiring of costly experts. For most plans, the cost will be small. And the payoff of having provided a systematic and orderly transfer of your estate can far outweigh any costs if the unexpected happens.

YOUR WILL

A **will** is a legal document which provides instructions for the disposition of your estate. It need not be long; a few paragraphs may be sufficient for a simple estate. You will want to discuss your plans with your spouse and possibly your family. But once you decide what you want the will to do, writing down those wishes is straightforward.

Penelope Prepared, who opened this chapter, is far better off than many: she had a will. Most people have none. Even among those who have wills, many have not updated them to reflect dramatically altered personal circumstances or major changes in federal estate tax regulations.

Why do so few people have wills? For some it means facing their mortality. Yet writing a will may reduce stress, since the writer knows dependents have been provided for. Others believe wills are costly, though this is not the case: hiring an attorney to draft a basic will may cost as little as $50 to $200. Still others want to avoid the hard decisions: naming a guardian for minor children, naming an executor to administer the estate, selecting a firm to manage a trust. What they are reluctant to do, the courts will have to do when they die. The result can be considerable cost, delays, inconvenience, and distributions structured in a way not envisioned by the deceased.

Strategy

There are few good reasons for not having a will; the cost is moderate, and the benefits to your survivors significant. Draw up a will as the first step of your estate plan.

Major Provisions of a Will

Wills vary in length and complexity, but most have the following provisions:

- *Introductory statement.* This identifies you, states that this is your last will and testament, and revokes all previous wills.
- *Payment of debts and expenses.* This directs your estate to pay all your debts and final expenses before any distributions are made. This ensures that such items are valid deductions from your estate.
- *Appointment of an executor.* The **executor** is responsible for identifying and assembling your assets, filing necessary legal documents and tax forms, publishing notices, paying debts and expenses, and, finally, distributing assets according to the will.
- *Appointment of a guardian for minor children.* Those with minor children will want to name the adult(s) who will care for them. Appointment of a **guardian** is one of the crucial provisions in the wills of parents of minors, whether single parents or married couples. Married persons should name a guardian to cover the possibility of both husband and wife dying simultaneously.
- *List of specific gifts.* This section identifies specific items, together with the name of the person to whom you want to leave them. A detailed description is required to ensure that the correct item is singled out.
- *List of general gifts.* This section distributes gifts that come from your general assets. It usually names the recipient and some specific dollar amount.

- *Disposition of remainder of estate.* This section outlines the disposition of the elements of your estate not specifically mentioned elsewhere. It will specify the percentage of your estate that each person named in the section is to receive.

Naming an executor

The duties of executor are extensive and rather complex, particularly if the estate and bequests are complicated. The executor (1) locates your will and files it with the court, (2) identifies and inventories your assets (personal and financial), (3) administers those assets while settling the estate, (4) files insurance claims, (5) files necessary state and federal income tax and estate tax forms, (6) pays debts and expenses, (7) distributes property according to the will, and (8) provides a final accounting of all actions.

You should name an executor who is both capable of assuming these duties and willing to complete them. If you have a friend or relative who fits the profile, consider asking him or her. But do it in advance to ensure the person can and will serve. Name a substitute in case your first choice cannot do it when the need arises. If you do not know anyone able or willing to serve as your executor, many bank trust departments provide these services. Whether it be your friend or a professional executor, your estate pays a fee. Most states have specific rules as to the amount of that payment. You may want to include a statement in your will waiving a bond for the executor; that can lower costs.

Executors may be called a personal representative or an estate administrator if court appointed. Regardless of the title, their duties are similar.

Naming a guardian

If there are minor children, naming a guardian is crucial. When the will does not name a guardian, the court may select one—and not necessarily the person you would choose. If you have a spouse, a guardian should still be named to protect your children in case of your simultaneous deaths. Guardianship is a long-term responsibility, so ask the persons you wish to name and make certain they are willing. You should name a substitute, in case your first choice cannot serve when the need arises. Again, if your state allows, you may want to waive the usual bond requirement to simplify legal procedures and eliminate unnecessary cost.

Do You Need an Attorney?

Drafting a will is a technical process, and there is potential for error. A serious mistake could invalidate the entire document, allowing your survivors to face months of delays, creating unnecessary legal costs, or resulting in property distributions far at variance with your wishes. Why take the chance? For a moderate cost you can have a lawyer draft the will to ensure it conforms to all legal requirements.

Before you contact an attorney, decide what you want to do with your estate and how. Summarize your property, how title is held (more on this later), and the approximate dollar amounts. You will need to select an executor, a guardian (if there are minor children), and substitutes, and decide how you want your property distributed. Deciding the basic details in advance will reduce the attorney's time and save you money.

Strategy

Hiring an attorney to draft a will is worth the cost; the payoff comes in the form of a timely transfer of your estate at minimal costs along the lines you want.

Updating Your Will

Even the best will needs to be reviewed and updated periodically. Events that may trigger updating include (1) a change in marital status, (2) the birth of a child, (3) a move to another state, (4) death of a guardian or executor, and (5) a major change (up or down) in your net worth. Also a sweeping change in tax rules, especially when the estate is sizable, may inspire a complete review. Your attorney can provide guidance as to when updating is required.

Minor changes to a will can be made by adding a **codicil.** The codicil singles out one section of the will for change. It has to be typed, signed, and witnessed just like the original will. Major changes require a completely new will. If you have a number of codicils to an existing will, it may be time to incorporate all those items into a new will.

Strategy

Once drafted, a will needs to be reviewed and updated to match the changes in your circumstances.

Storing the Will

There are several schools of thought on storing the original copy of your will. It is secure in your safety deposit box, but there may be a delay while the box's contents are inventoried after your death. A second option is to have the attorney who prepared the will hold it, making it readily available if the attorney is still in practice. But your executor will have to contact the attorney for the will.

Regardless of where you keep your original will, always store a duplicate copy of the will in a secure place in your home. You will want to tell your executor where that copy is so he or she can obtain immediate access.

DYING WITHOUT A WILL: INTESTACY

Die without a will—**intestate**—and you miss all the trouble, hassle, and chaos of transferring your assets: your heirs suffer it all. Your worldly goods will be divided up as set forth in your state's laws. While the precise distribution varies by state, Exhibit 19.1 outlines a typical distribution schedule. The state's distribution rules may not parallel your wishes, but you will be able to do nothing to change the outcome. And there are no provisions for handling special situations. Suppose Susan's husband and minor child survive her. The laws of intestacy might distribute half her estate to the child, even though her intent was for most of it to pass to her husband.

When there are minor children, the problems multiply. A guardian will have to manage their money until they become of age: at 18 years in most states. Until that time, the guardian has to make detailed annual reports on the management of the child's money. Furthermore, a bond will have to be furnished and its cost paid from the estate. The guardian appointed by the court may not be someone you would have preferred. Once of age, all of the money immediately passes to the child; whether he or she is capable of managing it is not an issue.

Strategy

Draft a will and avoid all the problems of intestacy.

LETTER OF LAST INSTRUCTION

A **letter of last instruction** completes the documents needed for transfer of your estate. Its intent is to provide further information needed by your executor to complete the transfer. Drafting this letter does not require legal counsel, just time and motivation. Unfortunately, many people with wills probably have not completed the process by drafting a letter of instruction.

When drafting your letter, your goal should be to provide complete detail in areas where the executor will need it in order to carry out the provisions of your will. Unless your executor is better at seances than most, it will be tough to contact you for clarification. The order of instructions is not important, but detail is. The letter should give any special funeral instructions and your wishes regarding organ transplants. You need to outline the distribution of personal property such as jewelry, household goods, family heirlooms, genealogical records, and antiques. The letter should provide a detailed list of your assets, their approximate value, and their location. A copy of a recent balance sheet can help support this part. Location of such things as auto titles, property deeds, safe deposit box, insurance policies, tax returns, and canceled checks should be included here. Remember, you are trying to help the executor carry out *your* instructions. As an executor, you would appreciate detailed information: your executor deserves the same.

A copy of the final letter should be sent to your attorney and one to your executor, and you should store one in your safe deposit box. Also, a copy should be stored at home with the duplicate copy of your will.

Exhibit 19.1

Distribution of Property under Typical Laws of Intestacy

Status of deceased	Property to:
1. Married, one child	Spouse, 50%; child, 50%
2. Married, two or more children	Spouse, 33%; children, 67%
3. Married, no children, parent(s) surviving	Spouse, 75%; parent(s), 25%
4. Married, no children, parents deceased	Spouse, all
5. Unmarried, parent(s) surviving	Parent(s), all
6. Unmarried, parents deceased, surviving brother(s) and/or sister(s)	Brother(s) and/or sister(s) equally

OWNERSHIP OF PROPERTY

The way in which property is owned affects both how it can be distributed and the estate tax consequences. Let's concentrate on distribution issues here; a later section will discuss taxes. The most straightforward ownership option is to be the sole owner of assets. Generally, a sole owner is free to distribute the property in any way desired. Furthermore, the property's entire value is usually included in the owner's estate upon death.

A second option is to split ownership among several people. Let's look at the three common forms of joint ownership.

Tenants by the Entirety

Only married couples can own property as **tenants by the entirety,** and often only real estate can be held this way. When held in tenancy by the entirety, the property cannot be sold unless both husband and wife agree. Upon the death of either one, the property passes to the survivor. The transfer of the property takes place apart from the deceased person's will. Even if the will states otherwise, the property automatically passes to the survivor. While not all states have tenancy by the entirety, in those that do it is a common way for a couple to own a home.

Joint Tenants

A second form of joint ownership is **joint tenancy.** There can be more than two owners in joint tenancy. It is less restrictive than tenancy by the entirety since no special relationship is required between the owners. And it can be used to hold a wide range of assets: common stocks, mutual funds, savings and checking accounts, real estate and other goods. Any one of the joint owners can dispose of, or redeem, his or her share *without* the permission of the others, even against their wishes. That makes it

essential that you know the other owners before you decide on joint tenancy.

Upon the death of a joint owner, ownership of the property automatically passes to the surviving owners; in the case of a couple, the surviving spouse becomes the sole owner, just as with tenancy by the entirety. The deceased's will has no effect on the transfer of the property. Even if Fred's will stated his 100 shares of Zug Products should pass to his daughter, the fact that he held 200 shares jointly with his brother (100 are his, 100 belong to his brother) means the brother will own all 200 when Fred dies. Jointly owned property simply cannot be distributed through a will.

Strategy

Joint ownership of property should be reviewed to make certain you want the property to pass to the surviving owner(s). Also consider the consequences of a joint owner being able to sell his or her share at any time.

Tenancy in Common

Under **tenancy in common** there can be more than two owners, and they do not have to be related. A whole range of assets including real estate and investments (common stock, bonds, mutual funds, and savings accounts) can be held this way. As is the case with joint tenancy, any of the joint owners can sell his or her share without the permission of the remaining owners. But there is one major difference: upon death, ownership does *not* automatically pass to the surviving owner(s). Instead the deceased owner's will controls the distribution; if there was no will, then the property will be distributed according to the rules of intestacy. Had Fred, from the last example, held those 200 shares of Zug as tenant in common with his brother, then he could have distributed the 100 shares to his daughter through his will.

Because the deceased's will controls the distribution of the asset upon death, tenancy in common may be more suitable when the parties are not related, or when you want your will to control the distribution of assets. The shortcoming that owners can sell their interest at any time remains.

Community Property States

There are nine states, presently, that have community property laws: California, Idaho, Louisiana, Nevada, New Mexico, Texas, Washington, and Wisconsin. In these states, there is a fourth ownership category: community property, which usually includes everything a husband and wife earn during their marriage. There are major restrictions on granting someone other than a spouse ownership of community property; the assumption is that all community property is jointly owned by the husband and wife. This adds complexity to decisions about what types of property transfers are even possible. Competent legal assistance is needed in community property states.

USE OF TRUSTS IN ESTATE PLANNING

Trusts are used in estate planning to achieve specific goals. Despite an aura of mystery surrounding trusts, the principles behind them are straightforward. The person giving the assets, the **grantor,** deposits them with a **trustee** who holds title to them. The trustee is responsible for controlling and managing the assets, but the grantor provides management instructions in a written trust agreement. That agreement contains specific instructions on how the income earned on the assets is to be distributed to the trust's **beneficiaries.** It will also state when the trust will terminate; usually on a specific date or at the time of some event, such as a beneficiary dying or reaching a certain age. The agreement will include instructions on how the assets remaining in the trust are to be distributed.

The trustee can be an individual—a friend, relative, or business partner—or a professional trust company: many banks have trust departments. Regardless of which you choose, care is required. The trustee needs to understand the legal and tax implications of operating the trust. Second, good investment performance is needed to ensure that the trust's assets provide a reasonable income and that their value is not compromised. Finally, the trustee should be interested in managing the trust for the welfare of the beneficiaries. While beneficiaries can petition to replace the trustee, selecting a good one to begin with is much easier.

Establishing a Trust

Often a trust will be part of your will, especially when it is established to care for minor children. When the will is drafted, the attorney will also draw up the trust agreement. If the trust is established separately from the will, you will also need a lawyer to draw it up. This is not a do-it-yourself area. Cost of drafting the trust agreement can range from a low of about two hundred dollars to thousands of dollars for more complex trusts.

Reasons for Establishing a Trust

There are three common reasons for establishing a trust: (1) to conserve assets, (2) to manage property, and (3) to reduce income and/or estate taxes. Let's look at each.

Conserving assets

A trust is often used to manage assets that ultimately will pass to a minor. While in the trust, those assets will be managed for the benefit of the minor. The time when the assets will be distributed to the minor is set forth in the trust agreement. It does *not* have to be at age 18. Depending on the amount involved, those assets could be distributed at several points. For example, one-third might be distributed at age 20, another one-third at age 25, and the remainder at age 30.

Managing property

Some individuals establish trusts to eliminate for themselves the effort of managing their financial assets. Other responsibilities may keep them so busy they have little time for managing their assets. Or they may not feel sufficiently informed and skilled. Once a trust is established, the trustee assumes those duties and responsibilities.

Reducing income and estate taxes

A later section will review this point further, but trusts can be used to reduce current income taxes and possible future estate taxes. The tax savings come from shifting income to a beneficiary who is in a lower tax bracket. Reduction of estate taxes can be significant if the trust is structured to utilize the favorable sections of the estate tax legislation. However, the Tax Reform Act of 1986 has reduced the options in this area significantly.

Common Types of Trusts

We will examine three common types of trust: (1) the testamentary trust, (2) the revocable living trust, and (3) the irrevocable living trust. We will review major advantages and disadvantages plus suggest a situation where each might be used.

Testamentary trust

A **testamentary trust** is typically created by your will at the time of death. Until then, you can change any provisions of the trust or even revoke it. Since you retain control of the assets of the trust, they are part of your estate when you die. You save no estate taxes, and the assets still go through probate so there is no reduction in those costs. Because the will and the probate process are public records, any person can obtain complete details regarding the trust. Since you have not given the assets to anyone during your lifetime, such a trust creates no gift tax liability. Exhibit 19.2 summarizes major advantages and disadvantages of testamentary trusts.

A major use of a testamentary trust is to transfer management of the assets to a professional trustee. This may be desirable when there are minor children who cannot conduct their affairs or heirs who cannot manage an inheritance.

Revocable living trust

The person who contributes the assets establishes a **revocable living trust** while still alive. The assets are transferred to the trust, and it begins

Exhibit 19.2

Major Advantages and Disadvantages of Various Types of Trusts

Type of trust	Major advantages	Major disadvantages
Testamentary	1, 5	B, C, D, F
Revocable living	1, 3, 5, 6	B, D, G, H
Irrevocable living	2, 3, 4, 6, 7	A, E, G

Key to the:

Advantages	Disadvantages
1 Grantor retains control of assets and can alter or revoke the trust.	A Grantor relinquishes title and right to alter or revoke the trust.
2 Assets are not included in the estate.	B Assets are still part of the estate.
3 Eliminates probate process and its associated costs.	C No reduction in probate costs.
4 May reduce federal estate taxes.	D Does not lower federal estate taxes.
5 No gift tax to establish the trust.	E May entail a gift tax when trust is established.
6 Terms of the trust and its assets are not public information.	F Provisions of the trust and its assets become public information through the probate process.
7 Trust income may be shifted to the trust or some beneficiary.	G There are annual fees for managing the trust's assets.
	H Income produced by the trust is taxed to the grantor.

operation during the grantor's life. But the grantor retains the right to revoke the trust and recapture the assets. Full control over the trust's operation is retained: assets can be added and withdrawn, the trustee can be changed, and the provisions of the trust altered at will. Because the grantor retains control of the trust's assets, they are included in the estate at death. The trust provides no direct reduction in estate taxes, but the assets do not pass through probate. This can eliminate or reduce the costs of probate; since they can run to 3 to 5 percent of the estate's assets, the savings can be significant. The person who establishes a revocable trust eliminates the delays inherent in probate; it can take several years to probate an estate. Last, by establishing this type of trust, the grantor removes the whole process from public view; because the assets do not go through probate, there is no public record. Exhibit 19.2 outlines major advantages and disadvantages of this trust.

A revocable living trust might be used by someone who wants to transfer the daily management of a block of assets to a professional trustee. It might be used as a backup for when the grantor becomes unable or unwilling to continue to manage the assets. The grantor acts as the trustee initially, but names a successor who will take over managing the assets if the grantor is unable to.

Irrevocable living trust

The grantor establishes an **irrevocable living trust** while he or she is still living. Its major distinguishing feature is that the grantor relinquishes title to assets transferred to the trust. At the same time, the grantor gives up the right to alter or revoke the trust. That is a major disadvantage: control of the assets, control and use of the income they produce, and the right to make changes are all surrendered. Since assets are out of the grantor's control, they are not included in the estate. That may provide some savings in federal estate taxes. As with its revocable counterpart, establishment of an irrevocable trust removes the transfer of assets from probate, providing the advantage of lower costs and removing the process from public scrutiny. Since assets are being given to the trust, there can be major gift taxes to pay. The major advantages and disadvantages of this trust are summarized in Exhibit 19.2.

Such a trust might be used if the grantor no longer wishes to manage some assets: transferring them to an irrevocable living trust shifts that burden to a professional trustee. If an individual's estate is very large, the estate tax savings of this trust may provide major benefits.

FEDERAL ESTATE TAX

When your estate is transferred on your death, it may be subject to **federal estate taxes.** The "may be" is intentional, since there are a number of expenses and other items that can be deducted when computing the size of the taxable estate. Even after that is done, you can deduct certain credits against potential estate taxes. The net effect is that many estates pay little or no tax. But rather than just hope, it is far better to compute what taxes, if any, your estate might pay.

Our first task is to compute what portion of the estate is subject to tax.

Building on that, we will review the steps needed to compute the tentative estate taxes. Next we will examine the credits that can be used to reduce those taxes, possibly to zero. We will close the section with an example demonstrating how these steps fit together.

Determining Your Taxable Estate

Exhibit 19.3 summarizes the general procedure for determining your taxable estate. Federal estate taxes would be a lot simpler if all one had to do was total the estate's assets. But the list of qualifying deductions and expenses complicates the process considerably. They can reduce the estate and lower estate taxes.

Gross estate

Your **gross estate** includes all the assets you hold in your name and a portion of those you hold jointly with others. The top line of Exhibit 19.3 shows some typical items that would be included. Of those, jointly owned property requires some additional comment. You include only your interest, the portion you own, for jointly held assets. Ordinarily, that is the fraction you paid when the jointly held asset was purchased.

Outstanding debts and taxes

All of your unpaid debts and any income or property taxes you owe can be deducted from your gross estate. You total things such as the unpaid balance on your home mortgage, home equity loan, consumer loan, credit cards, property tax bills, income taxes owed, and other debts. Exhibit 19.3 shows this amount being deducted from the gross estate. All items should be included, since this deduction lowers your net estate and potential taxes.

Administrative costs and funeral expenses

All costs associated with settling your estate can also be deducted—probate fees, court costs, executor's fees, attorney's fees, accountant's fees, and appraisal costs. Your estate can also deduct the cost of your funeral. Yes, Gert, going out in style might actually lower the government's

Exhibit 19.3

Basic Structure of Federal Estate Taxes

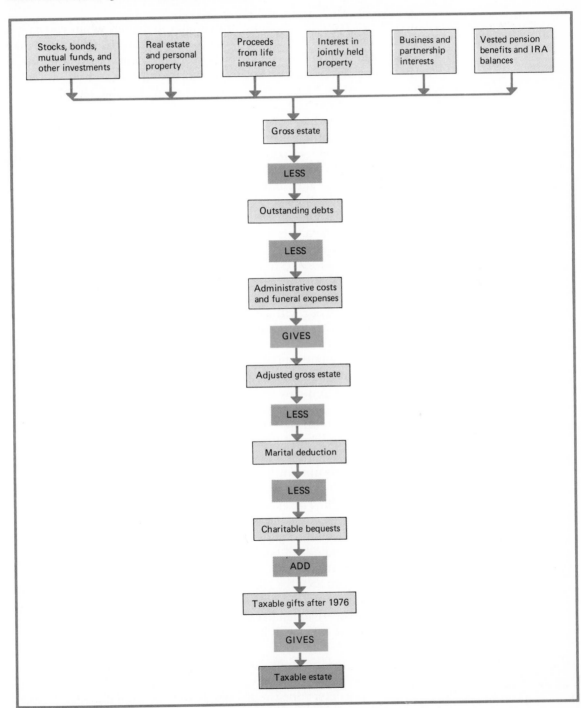

tax take! Once these items are deducted (middle section of Exhibit 19.3), you have the adjusted gross estate.

Unlimited marital deduction

Current tax regulations allow individuals to deduct whatever part of their estate they leave to their surviving spouse: this is the **unlimited marital deduction.** There is no dollar or percentage limit on the amount. In fact, the entire estate can be left to the surviving spouse and no federal estate taxes need be paid. The middle section of Exhibit 19.3 highlights this qualifying deduction. Some might ask: If married, why not leave your spouse your entire adjusted gross estate? Wouldn't that reduce the net estate to zero, and wouldn't this make your estate tax problems disappear? The answers are "yes" to point one, "possibly no" to point two. Leaving the entire amount to your spouse may just postpone the tax problem. The surviving spouse may now have a rather large estate: part of it from the deceased partner plus the spouse's own estate. When he or she dies, that combined amount would go through the estate tax computation. Since there is not likely to be a surviving spouse to leave it to, there could be considerable taxes to pay.

Charitable bequests

Assets which you leave to a qualifying charity also can be deducted from your estate. Qualifying charitable organizations include those operated for educational, literary, scientific, cultural, religious, and other approved purposes. Your will would state the amounts and to whom those charitable bequests are to be made. This reduction is shown toward the bottom of Exhibit 19.3.

Taxable gifts made after 1976

If you make very large gifts, you may have to add part of them to your estate. You can give $10,000 to any individual each year without paying any gift taxes. And you can make such a gift regardless of whether the recipient is related to you or not. A couple can join in the gift and give $10,000 each for a total $20,000 annual exclusion. The actual $20,000 can come from the husband, the wife, or both, as long as the spouse joins in. With that $10,000 annual tax-free gift allowance ($20,000 if married), you can give a sizable amount to someone over a period of years. If the gift was made after 1976 and it exceeds the allowance, it becomes a **taxable gift made after 1976.** The excess is counted as taxable and therefore has to be included in the estate. On a $40,000 gift made by a single person in one year, $30,000 would be added back. The lower section of Exhibit 19.3 shows the gifts being added back. Only individuals who make very large gifts will have any entry here.

Taxable estate

The final entry in Exhibit 19.3 is your **taxable estate.** It is the amount that remains after all qualifying deductions have been made and any large taxable gifts have been added back. Your taxable estate is the amount that your tentative estate taxes will be based on.

Determining What Estate Taxes You Owe

Exhibit 19.4 outlines the steps used to compute the estate taxes you owe. The starting point is the taxable estate we calculated in the previous section. Our goal is to determine the net estate tax that remains after deducting all allowed credits.

Tentative federal estate taxes

Exhibit 19.5 is used to estimate the tentative estate tax. The first two columns show a series of income brackets, since the estate tax rates are progressive: the higher the estate's value, the larger the percentage taken for taxes. Our table starts at $60,000 and runs up through $1,000,000; actual tables from the Internal Revenue Service cover a wider range. The next three columns summarize the taxes that have to be paid. An example will illustrate. Suppose the taxable estate totaled $225,000. That places the estate in the bracket from $200,000 to $250,000. Tentative taxes would be $62,800: $54,800 base tax + [32% × ($225,000 − $200,000)].

Exhibit 19.4

Steps Used to Compute the Net Federal Estate Tax Due

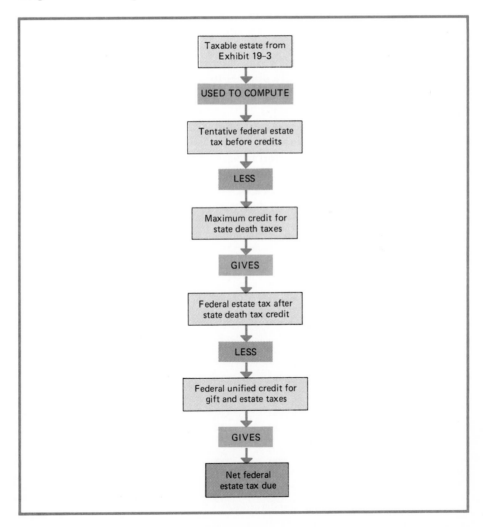

Maximum state death tax credit

You can deduct a **state death tax credit** from federal estate taxes for any state death taxes paid. The maximum allowed credit is based on your taxable estate. As the estate's value rises, so does the percentage allowed for the credit. The last three columns of Exhibit 19.5 summarize the maximum credit for the different income brackets. Our previous example will illustrate. Maximum credit on this taxable estate of $225,000 is $1,800: $1,200 base credit + [2.4% × ($225,000 − $200,000)].

Federal unified credit for gift and estate taxes

All individuals are entitled to deduct a **federal unified estate tax credit** against their tentative estate taxes. For 1987 that credit is $192,800. Because the credit is so large, it eliminates the need to pay federal estate taxes on most estates. In effect, your taxable estate can total $600,000 without your having to pay any estate taxes once the federal credit is deducted. Current estimates suggest that less than 1 percent of estates will have to pay any taxes.

Net federal estate tax due

The final entry in Exhibit 19.4 is the net federal estate tax you must pay. For most, this amount will be small or zero. If your calculations show significant taxes are going to be due, you need to explore some estate-planning strategies that can reduce taxes. Since that is a rather specialized topic that only applies to a limited number of estates, we will not cover it here. A tax lawyer or accountant should be consulted.

Computation of Net Federal Estate Taxes: An Example

We will use Delbert Dunsmore's case to illustrate the computation of federal estate taxes. While Delbert is alive and well, he wants to review his current situation to see if his estate might face federal estate taxes in the event of his demise. The worksheet in Exhibit 19.6 will be used to conduct Delbert's tax review. While our major concern is the net tax on line 14 of that exhibit, we will review all the steps taken to arrive there.

 *Exhibit 19.5*

Table of Federal Estate Tax Rates

If Taxable Estate Is:		Tentative Federal Estate Tax Is:			Maximum State Death Tax Credit Is:		
More than	*But less than*	*This amount*	*Plus this percentage*	*Of the amount over*	*This amount*	*Plus this percentage*	*Of the amount over*
$ 60,000	$ 80,000	$ 13,000	26%	$ 60,000	—	—	—
80,000	100,000	18,200	28	80,000	—	—	—
100,000	150,000	23,800	30	100,000	—	.8%	$100,000
150,000	200,000	38,800	32	150,000	$ 400	1.6	150,000
200,000	250,000	54,800	32	200,000	1,200	2.4	200,000
250,000	300,000	70,800	34	250,000	2,400	2.4	250,000
300,000	500,000	87,800	34	300,000	3,600	3.2	300,000
500,000	700,000	155,800	37	500,000	10,000	4.0	500,000
700,000	750,000	229,800	37	700,000	18,000	4.8	700,000
750,000	900,000	248,300	39	750,000	20,400	4.8	750,000
900,000	1,000,000	306,800	39	900,000	27,600	5.6	900,000

To estimate his gross estate, Delbert has combined his personal property, condominium, his mutual fund accounts, his other financial assets, the vested balance in his pension plan, his IRA accounts, and his life insurance. The combined total is the $281,000 entered on line 1 of Exhibit 19.6. Delbert's assets are quite large for several reasons. His condominium is in a good location so it has appreciated significantly since he purchased it. Second, his employer-provided, defined contribution pension fund presently has a sizable balance. His lengthy work history with that employer has provided a steady inflow of annual deposits and he is fully vested. Finally, the death benefit from his employer-provided life insurance also boosts his gross estate.

Delbert's debts include balances on his mortgage and auto loan, several small credit card debts, and the current year's real estate taxes. Those items total $40,500 (line 2 of Exhibit 19.6). Delbert estimates it would cost about $12,000—probate and court costs, plus fees for the attorney, executor, and accountant—to settle his estate; he enters this amount on line 3 of the worksheet. In addition, his estate would pay an estimated $2,500 for funeral costs; line 4 of Exhibit 19.6 shows this amount. Once the deductions shown on lines 2 through 4 are subtracted, Delbert's adjusted gross estate equals $226,000 (line 5).

Delbert is single so he has no entry for the marital deduction (line 6). A married individual would enter that portion of the estate that is going to his or her spouse on this line and deduct it from the adjusted gross estate to lower potential taxes. Delbert has, however, decided to leave $1,000 to his

Exhibit 19.6

Worksheet for Computing Net Federal Estate Taxes

Line	Description	Amount
1	Gross estate	$281,000
2	Minus: Total debts and taxes	40,500
3	Estate administrative costs	12,000
4	Funeral expenses	2,500
5	Adjusted gross estate	$226,000
6	Minus: Marital deductions	—
7	Charitable bequests	1,000
8	Add: Taxable gifts made after 1976	—
9	Taxable estate	$225,000
10	Tentative federal estate tax*	$ 62,800
11	Minus: State death tax credit†	1,800
12	Net federal estate tax after death tax credit	$ 61,800
13	Minus: Unified federal gift and estate tax credit	192,800
14	Net federal estate tax due	—

* Federal estate tax computed using Exhibit 19.5: $54,800 base tax + 32%($225,000 − $200,000) = $62,800.
† State death tax credit computed using Exhibit 19.5: $1,200 base tax + 2.4%($225,000 − $200,000) = $1,800.

alma mater; his will provides the details of this bequest. It qualifies as a charitable deduction, so it is entered on line 7 of Exhibit 19.6. Delbert has not gifted more than $10,000 to any one person within a single year, so he has no taxable gifts. Had he done so, the taxable gifts would be entered on line 8 and added back to his estate. Delbert's taxable estate on line 9 of Exhibit 19.6 totals $225,000 after all deductions.

The tentative estate tax on a $225,000 taxable estate like Delbert's in Exhibit 19.6 is the $62,800 shown on line 10. It was computed using Exhibit 19.5; the footnote to Exhibit 19.6 explains the computation. Similarly, for the $225,000 estate, he would be entitled to a maximum state death tax credit of $1,800 shown on line 11. The second footnote to Exhibit 19.6 shows how that was computed using Exhibit 19.5. After deducting the state death tax credit, Delbert's net estate tax is $61,000; this is shown on line 12.

Delbert qualifies for a $192,800 unified estate tax credit, so this is entered on line 13 of Exhibit 19.6. That more than offsets the $61,000 tax liability on line 12, so his estate would owe no tax. Sorry, but you cannot "claim" a refund for the unused portion of the unified credit; Delbert receives no benefit from the unused $131,800 portion. Now if Delbert receives that promotion, hits it lucky in the sweepstakes, picks the winner in the fifth race, or is left a bundle by Aunt Lucy (or a little of all four), he may well need that credit as his estate continues to grow.

Summary

1 An estate plan gives you the opportunity to distribute your assets according to your wishes, without undue delays, and at a reasonable cost.

2 While people find a plethora of excuses for *not* planning the transfer of their estate, the benefits can far outweigh the time and cost of preparation that go into a plan.

3 A will is the legal document that contains your written instructions for disposing of your assets, names the executor who is to supervise that process, and outlines any trusts that are to be established should you die.

4 The typical will contains a number of major provisions. In general, a will:
   - Includes an opening section that identifies you
   - Directs payment of your debts and expenses
   - Appoints an executor
   - Names a guardian if there are minor children
   - Provides a list of specific gifts
   - Contains a list of general gifts
   - Provides for the disposition of the balance of the estate

5 An executor's duties include locating your assets, filing insurance claims, filing state and federal estate tax plus income tax forms, paying the estate's debts and expenses, distributing property according to the will, and providing a final accounting of all actions.

6 The cost to have an attorney draft a basic will is usually moderate. Drafting of a will is a rather technical process, so hiring an attorney is money well spent.

7 Updating your will to reflect changed circumstances is critical if the will is to accomplish its objective. Minor changes can be handled through codicils attached to the will. Major changes require a completely new will.

8 The original copy of a will can be stored in your safe deposit box or at your attorney's office. A duplicate should be kept with your financial records at home.

9 If you die without a will, the laws of intestacy in your state determine how your assets are distributed. That distribution is fixed and allows no consideration of special circumstances or needs.

10 A letter of last instruction is an informal statement that outlines any special requests and can help the executor settle your estate; a copy should be stored at home where it can be found easily.

11 Generally only married couples can hold

property as tenants by the entirety; a home is often held that way. To sell the asset, both parties have to agree. When one dies, the survivor becomes the sole owner.

12 Two people or more, related or not, can hold property as joint tenants. Any owner can sell *without* the permission of the others. Upon death, the surviving owners take over the deceased's share.

13 The form of joint ownership known as tenancy in common allows several people to own an asset. Any owner can sell without the permission of the others. Upon death, the deceased's share is distributed according to his or her will.

14 The grantor transfers assets to a trust so that they will be professionally managed by the appointed trustee. Instructions in the trust document specify how the income is to be distributed, when the trust's assets are to be distributed, and to whom.

15 Major reasons for establishing a trust include:
   ■ Conserving the assets for a minor or an heir who is incapable of managing the bequest

■ Having the assets professionally managed
■ Possible savings in federal estate taxes or income taxes

16 The major types of trusts are a testamentary, a revocable living, and an irrevocable living trust.

17 The taxable estate on which federal taxes are based is computed as:

Gross estate
− debts and taxes
− administrative costs and
   funeral expenses
− marital deduction
− charitable bequests
   Taxable estate

18 The owner of an estate can deduct a state death tax credit and the unified estate tax credit from the tentative estate tax liability to determine the net estate tax due.

19 Many estates pay no estate taxes because the unified estate tax credit covers the tax liability when the estate is $600,000 or less.

Review your understanding of

Estate planning
Will
Executor
Guardian
Codicil
Intestacy
Letter of last instruction
Tenants by the entirety
Joint tenants
Tenancy in common
Trust
Grantor

Trustee
Beneficiary
Testamentary trust
Revocable living trust
Irrevocable living trust
Federal estate tax
   Gross estate
   Unlimited marital deduction
   Taxable gifts made after 1976
   Taxable estate
   State death tax credit
Federal unified estate tax credit

Discussion questions

1 Fred and Francine Fasttrack have not done any estate planning. With no dependents and a combined income that is substantial, they question the need. Can you suggest several benefits an estate plan might provide?

2 Do most people have a will? What are the benefits of having one? Why do you think those who do not have one are avoiding drafting one?

3 Why is it critical that you ask your proposed executor whether he or she is willing to serve before placing the name in your will? What are the principal duties of the executor? Given those duties, what attributes would you want the executor to have?

4 What is the purpose of naming a guardian? Are single parents the only ones who have to name one? Why?

5 List several situations that might suggest the

need to revise a will. Which ones might be handled with a codicil? Which ones suggest a complete new will?

6 What happens if you die without having made a valid will? What determines the disposition of your assets? List several problems that might arise when someone dies without a will.

7 What is the major purpose of a letter of last instruction? How can a letter complement a will? Does the letter have to be drafted by your attorney?

8 In what ways are the three forms of joint ownership—tenancy by the entirety, joint tenancy, and tenancy in common—similar? Different? Outline a situation in which each type would be appropriate.

9 Fred and Tom own the condominium they share as joint tenants. Fred's will states that the

money from the sale of the condominium upon his death is to be left to his mother. When he dies, will that request be followed? Why? Would another type of joint ownership have been more suitable? Why?

10 The *Daily Nowhere* recently announced that Barney Bungled's estate was being probated. In his will, Barney called for the establishment of a trust upon his death; assets in the trust are for support of his minor children. What kind of trust is this? What major things would the trust agreement likely specify?

11 Wilbur Welloff is considering establishing a revocable living trust. Give several reasons Wilbur might want to do this. What are its advantages? Any disadvantages?

12 What types of things have to be included in a person's gross estate? Would the person's taxable estate equal the gross amount? Why?

13 What is the single largest factor limiting the number of estates that must pay federal estate taxes? How large an estate can Sandra leave without facing any estate taxes?

Problems

19.1 Stephanie Sidetrack has summarized the following data for use in developing an estimate of her estate taxes:

Life insurance. $90,000 face amount; her son is the beneficiary.
Lakeside condominium. Current value is $85,000; she owns it jointly with her two sisters; each paid $20,000 of the unit's $60,000 purchase price.
Retirement account. Current balance is $8,500; she is 100 percent vested.
Personal property. Current estimated value is $15,000; original purchase prices totaled $24,500.
Mutual fund accounts. Current balances total $11,400; her original investments totaled $9,700.
  a. What is her gross estate?
  b What other data will Stephanie have to develop to compute her net estate?

19.2 Ralph Prettygood estimates that his gross estate is about $315,000 for federal estate tax purposes. Having made it this far, he is unclear how to proceed. He has developed the following estimates:
Gifts. $50 gift for niece's graduation, $1,000 for mom's cruise.
Donations. $50 to Bilgestate University last year; his will calls for a $100 gift upon his death.
Debts. Mortgage balance is $46,700; car loan ($11,600 originally) is now $6,400; credit cards, $560; property taxes, $2,300.
Final expenses. Estimated cost to settle estate, $18,500; projected funeral costs, $4,000.
  a What is Ralph's net taxable estate?
  b Based on your answer in part (a), what is the likelihood his estate will have to pay any federal estate taxes? Why?

19.3 Bosworth Bundle estimates his current gross estate is about $510,000 for federal estate tax purposes. After deducting his debts, taxes, costs to settle his estate, and other qualifying deductions, he estimates his taxable estate would be about $400,000.
  a What is the tentative federal estate tax?
  b What is the maximum state death tax credit the estate would qualify for?
  c If Bosworth qualifies for the current standard unified federal estate tax credit of $192,800, will his estate owe any taxes?

19.4 Sidney and Barb are reviewing the options for dividing up their estate should something happen to one or both of them. After a detailed review, they estimate each would have an adjusted gross estate of about $500,000. To start the process, they are reviewing the options if Sidney were to die first. They have identified two options:

Option 1. Sidney's entire estate would be left to Barb. That $500,000 could be deducted as a marital deduction. Barb's estate would then rise to $1,000,000.
Option 2. Sidney's estate could be placed in a testamentary trust. Barb receives the income from the trust, but its assets will be distributed to someone else when she dies. Because Barb does not receive the trust's assets directly, they are not counted as part of her estate when she dies. She will, however, still have her present $500,000 estate.
To simplify the computations, assume neither will make a charitable bequest or have a taxable gift. Likewise, you may ignore the state death tax credit each estate might qualify for. Assume both estates qualify for a $192,800 unified tax credit against federal estate taxes.
  a What estate tax will Sidney's estate pay under Option 1? How much tax will Barb's estate pay when she dies?
  b Under Option 2, what estate tax will Sidney's estate have to pay? What tax will Barb's estate pay when she dies?
  c How does the total tax for both estates compare for Option 1 and Option 2? Which would you suggest? Why does your choice entail less total tax?

Case problem

Harvey and Carol Postpone have always been too busy to do any estate planning, or to write a will. Both have been quite successful in their respective careers. Harvey, age 39, works as a customer representative for a large corporation. That work takes him on the road several days a week to troubleshoot problems at customers' plants. Carol, age 38, commutes each day to her position in the city. She also finds she spends considerable time on the road driving to various school events for their children aged 12 and 10.

Currently Harvey and Carol earn a combined salary of about $55,000. That salary, along with several other factors, has made their financial situation moderately complex. First, Harvey has always considered himself a bit of an investment mogul; he presently has a number of small to moderate-sized investments. Since he transfers money among those investments frequently, he never bothers to keep detailed records. Carol's employment changes during the past several years have added further complexity. She has become partially vested in the employer's pension plan each time she has moved. To ensure an adequate retirement, she has always left her balance in each plan. In addition, both she and Harvey have participated in their employer's 401(k) plan whenever one was offered. Also both have used an IRA account to accumulate retirement funds. A fourth factor has been their frequent, but small, purchases of life insurance. Over the years they have bought different policies to ''help'' their friends who were insurance salespeople. Last, in addition to their house, they own interests in several time-sharing vacation resorts.

Presently Harvey and Carol hold the house as tenants by the entirety. Many of their investments are held as joint tenants. But they do have some individually owned items, since Carol prefers lower-risk investments while Harvey goes for the more aggressive ones. Some of Harvey's investments were inherited from his aunt; should something happen to him, Harvey would like to have those provide an education fund for the children.

Carol expects that one of her sisters would raise the children if something happened to both her and Harvey. Harvey also expects one of his relatives might step forward and offer to care for the children if the need arose. While they have not written any of these plans out, they expect the relatives would settle the details. Likewise, they expect someone would take care of the financial details of their estate.

1. What are the strengths and weaknesses of Carol and Harvey's present estate plan?
2. If, by some unfortunate circumstance, both Harvey and Carol died simultaneously in an accident, what would likely happen to their estate, given their present plans? What would happen to their children? What would likely happen when the children reach age 18 and are no longer minors?
3. What specific details do Harvey and Carol need to pay attention to if they are going to strengthen their present plan? What steps should they take? What reasons would you offer to justify your suggested changes?
4. Should Harvey and Carol have a will, given their present situation? If so, what points should it address? Why?
5. Is there any reason they might need a letter of last instruction? What should it contain if you think it is needed?
6. What advantages might there be if Harvey and Carol were to transfer their assets to a trust for the children in the unlikely, but possible, event of their both dying? What type of trust might be appropriate?

Appendixes

Monthly Payments on a $1,000 Loan

Maturity of the Loan		Annual Percentage Rate (APR)							
Years	Months	5%	6%	7%	8%	9%	10%	11%	12%
	6	$169.11	$169.60	$170.09	$170.58	$171.07	$171.56	$172.05	$172.55
	12	85.61	86.07	86.53	86.99	87.45	87.92	88.38	88.85
	18	57.78	58.23	58.68	59.14	59.60	60.06	60.52	60.98
	24	43.87	44.32	44.77	45.23	45.68	46.14	46.61	47.07
	30	35.53	35.98	36.43	36.89	37.35	37.81	38.28	38.75
	36	29.97	30.42	30.88	31.34	31.80	32.27	32.74	33.21
	42	26.00	26.46	26.91	27.38	27.84	28.32	28.79	29.28
	48	23.03	23.49	23.95	24.41	24.89	25.36	25.85	26.33
	54	20.72	21.18	21.64	22.11	22.59	23.07	23.56	24.06
	60	18.87	19.33	19.80	20.28	20.76	21.25	21.74	22.24
	66	17.36	17.83	18.30	18.78	19.27	19.76	20.26	20.77
	72	16.10	16.57	17.05	17.53	18.03	18.53	19.03	19.55
	78	15.04	15.51	15.99	16.48	16.98	17.49	18.00	18.52
	84	14.13	14.61	15.09	15.59	16.09	16.60	17.12	17.65
8		12.66	13.14	13.63	14.14	14.65	15.17	15.71	16.25
9		11.52	12.01	12.51	13.02	13.54	14.08	14.63	15.18
10		10.61	11.10	11.61	12.13	12.67	13.22	13.78	14.35
11		9.86	10.37	10.88	11.42	11.96	12.52	13.09	13.68
12		9.25	9.76	10.28	10.82	11.38	11.95	12.54	13.13
13		8.73	9.25	9.78	10.33	10.90	11.48	12.08	12.69
14		8.29	8.81	9.35	9.91	10.49	11.08	11.69	12.31
15		7.91	8.44	8.99	9.56	10.14	10.75	11.37	12.00
16		7.58	8.11	8.67	9.25	9.85	10.46	11.09	11.74
17		7.29	7.83	8.40	8.98	9.59	10.21	10.85	11.51
18		7.03	7.58	8.16	8.75	9.36	10.00	10.65	11.32
19		6.80	7.36	7.94	8.55	9.17	9.81	10.47	11.15
20		6.60	7.16	7.75	8.36	9.00	9.65	10.32	11.01
21		6.42	6.99	7.58	8.20	8.85	9.51	10.19	10.89
22		6.25	6.83	7.43	8.06	8.71	9.38	10.07	10.78
23		6.10	6.69	7.30	7.93	8.59	9.27	9.97	10.69
24		5.97	6.56	7.18	7.82	8.49	9.17	9.88	10.60
25		5.85	6.44	7.07	7.72	8.39	9.09	9.80	10.53
26		5.73	6.34	6.97	7.63	8.31	9.01	9.73	10.47
28		5.54	6.15	6.80	7.47	8.16	8.88	9.61	10.37
30		5.37	6.00	6.65	7.34	8.05	8.78	9.52	10.29
32		5.23	5.86	6.53	7.23	7.95	8.69	9.45	10.22
34		5.10	5.75	6.43	7.14	7.87	8.63	9.39	10.18
36		5.00	5.66	6.35	7.07	7.81	8.57	9.35	10.14
38		4.90	5.57	6.28	7.01	7.76	8.53	9.31	10.11
40		4.82	5.50	6.21	6.95	7.71	8.49	9.28	10.08

Annual Percentage Rate (APR)

13%	14%	15%	16%	17%	18%	20%	22%	24%	26%
$173.04	$173.54	$174.03	$174.53	$175.03	$175.53	$176.52	$177.52	$178.53	$179.53
89.32	89.79	90.26	90.73	91.20	91.68	92.63	93.59	94.56	95.53
61.45	61.92	62.38	62.86	63.33	63.81	64.76	65.73	66.70	67.68
47.54	48.01	48.49	48.96	49.44	49.92	50.90	51.88	52.87	53.87
39.22	39.70	40.18	40.66	41.15	41.64	42.63	43.63	44.65	45.68
33.69	34.18	34.67	35.16	35.65	36.15	37.16	38.19	39.23	40.29
29.76	30.25	30.75	31.25	31.75	32.26	33.30	34.35	35.42	36.50
26.83	27.33	27.83	28.34	28.86	29.37	30.43	31.51	32.60	33.72
24.56	25.06	25.58	26.10	26.62	27.15	28.23	29.33	30.45	31.60
22.75	23.27	23.79	24.32	24.85	25.39	26.49	27.62	28.77	29.94
21.29	21.81	22.34	22.88	23.42	23.97	25.10	26.25	27.42	28.62
20.07	20.61	21.15	21.69	22.25	22.81	23.95	25.13	26.33	27.55
19.06	19.60	20.14	20.70	21.26	21.84	23.00	24.20	25.43	26.68
18.19	18.74	19.30	19.86	20.44	21.02	22.21	23.43	24.68	25.95
16.81	17.37	17.95	18.53	19.12	19.72	20.95	22.22	23.51	24.84
15.75	16.33	16.92	17.53	18.14	18.76	20.03	21.33	22.67	24.04
14.93	15.53	16.13	16.75	17.38	18.02	19.33	20.67	22.05	23.46
14.28	14.89	15.51	16.14	16.79	17.44	18.79	20.17	21.58	23.03
13.75	14.37	15.01	15.66	16.32	16.99	18.37	19.78	21.23	22.70
13.31	13.95	14.60	15.27	15.94	16.63	18.04	19.48	20.95	22.46
12.95	13.60	14.27	14.95	15.64	16.34	17.77	19.24	20.74	22.27
12.65	13.32	14.00	14.69	15.39	16.10	17.56	19.06	20.58	22.13
12.40	13.08	13.77	14.47	15.19	15.91	17.39	18.91	20.46	22.03
12.19	12.87	13.58	14.29	15.02	15.76	17.26	18.80	20.36	21.94
12.00	12.70	13.42	14.14	14.88	15.63	17.15	18.70	20.28	21.88
11.85	12.56	13.28	14.02	14.76	15.52	17.06	18.63	20.22	21.83
11.72	12.44	13.17	13.91	14.67	15.43	16.99	18.57	20.17	21.79
11.60	12.33	13.07	13.82	14.59	15.36	16.93	18.52	20.14	21.76
11.50	12.24	12.99	13.75	14.52	15.30	16.88	18.49	20.11	21.74
11.42	12.16	12.92	13.69	14.46	15.25	16.84	18.46	20.08	21.73
11.34	12.10	12.86	13.63	14.42	15.21	16.81	18.43	20.07	21.71
11.28	12.04	12.81	13.59	14.38	15.17	16.78	18.41	20.05	21.70
11.22	11.99	12.76	13.55	14.34	15.15	16.76	18.40	20.04	21.69
11.13	11.91	12.70	13.49	14.29	15.10	16.73	18.37	20.03	21.68
11.06	11.85	12.64	13.45	14.26	15.07	16.71	18.36	20.02	21.68
11.01	11.80	12.61	13.42	14.23	15.05	16.70	18.35	20.01	21.67
10.97	11.77	12.58	13.39	14.21	15.03	16.69	18.34	20.01	21.67
10.94	11.74	12.56	13.38	14.20	15.02	16.68	18.34	20.00	21.67
10.91	11.73	12.54	13.37	14.19	15.02	16.68	18.34	20.00	21.67
10.90	11.71	12.53	13.36	14.18	15.01	16.67	18.34	20.00	21.67

Appendix A.2

Estimated Monthly Benefit from Social Security for Survivors' Benefit, for Disability, and for Retirement

| Your age in 1987 | Present annual income | Monthly Benefit for Your Survivors | | | | Benefit if Disabled | | Monthly Benefit at Retirement | | | |
		Only 1 child	Spouse & child or 2 children	Spouse & 2 children or more than 2 children	Spouse at 60	Your benefit	Your benefit with children	Your Benefit at: Age 62	Age 65	Spouse's Benefit at: Age 62	Age 65
25	$12,000	$356	$ 712	$ 808	$339	$473	$ 709	$349	$433	$162	$208
	17,000	448	896	1,105	427	595	892	442	548	205	263
	24,000	578	1,156	1,348	551	767	1,150	557	690	259	332
	33,000	658	1,316	1,535	627	875	1,312	636	788	295	378
	44,000 & up	752	1,504	1,754	717	998	1,497	730	905	339	435
30	12,000	354	708	803	338	470	705	361	449	168	218
	17,000	446	892	1,102	425	592	888	458	569	213	276
	24,000	575	1,150	1,341	548	762	1,143	577	717	268	348
	33,000	656	1,312	1,530	625	872	1,308	659	818	306	397
	44,000 & up	748	1,496	1,745	713	976	1,464	756	940	352	456
35	12,000	352	704	795	336	470	705	371	462	173	227
	17,000	443	886	1,096	422	592	888	470	585	219	287
	24,000	570	1,140	1,331	544	760	1,140	594	740	277	363
	33,000	653	1,306	1,523	622	866	1,299	678	843	316	414
	44,000 & up	726	1,452	1,693	692	936	1,404	777	967	362	475
40	12,000	352	704	795	336	470	705	368	458	171	225
	17,000	442	884	1,095	421	590	885	465	579	217	284
	24,000	569	1,138	1,327	542	760	1,140	591	736	276	361
	33,000	645	1,290	1,506	615	852	1,278	672	837	313	411
	44,000 & up	690	1,380	1,611	658	904	1,356	762	948	356	465
45	12,000	352	704	795	336	470	705	368	459	172	226
	17,000	442	884	1,095	421	590	885	465	580	217	285
	24,000	569	1,138	1,327	542	758	1,137	594	741	277	365
	33,000	629	1,258	1,467	599	836	1,254	671	836	313	411
	44,000 & up	661	1,322	1,542	630	876	1,314	746	929	348	458
50	12,000	352	704	795	336	470	705	385	482	180	241
	17,000	442	884	1,095	421	590	885	486	608	228	304
	24,000	564	1,128	1,317	538	754	1,131	624	780	292	390
	33,000	615	1,230	1,436	587	822	1,233	691	864	324	432
	44,000 & up	641	1,282	1,495	611	856	1,284	756	946	354	473
55	12,000	352	704	795	336	470	705	382	478	179	239
	17,000	442	884	1,095	421	590	885	481	602	225	301
	24,000	558	1,116	1,303	532	746	1,119	616	770	288	385
	33,000	605	1,210	1,411	577	808	1,212	673	842	315	421
	44,000 & up	626	1,252	1,460	597	836	1,254	723	904	339	452

Note: Benefit amounts are based on the assumption that you have worked steadily and that your pay raises were of average size. For the retirement benefit, we also assume that your current salary level will continue unchanged, and that the overall salary levels will not rise. A more detailed estimate, with a worksheet, is explained in the booklet *1987 Guide to Social Security;* a copy can be purchased from William M. Mercer-Meidinger, Inc., 2600 Meidinger Tower, Louisville, KT 40202-3415.

Source: Detlefs, Dale R., *1987 Guide to Social Security,* William M. Mercer-Meidinger, Louisville, 1986.

Value of $1 Invested at Interest Rates from 1 to 18 Percent Compounded Annually

Rate of Interest or Inflation

Investment period in years	1%	2%	3%	4%	5%	6%	7%	8%	9%	10%	11%	12%	13%	14%	15%	16%	17%	18%
1	1.01	1.02	1.03	1.04	1.05	1.06	1.07	1.08	1.09	1.10	1.11	1.12	1.13	1.14	1.15	1.16	1.17	1.18
2	1.02	1.04	1.06	1.08	1.10	1.12	1.14	1.17	1.19	1.21	1.23	1.25	1.28	1.30	1.32	1.35	1.37	1.39
3	1.03	1.06	1.09	1.12	1.16	1.19	1.23	1.26	1.30	1.33	1.37	1.40	1.44	1.48	1.52	1.56	1.60	1.64
4	1.04	1.08	1.13	1.17	1.22	1.26	1.31	1.36	1.41	1.46	1.52	1.57	1.63	1.69	1.75	1.81	1.87	1.94
5	1.05	1.10	1.16	1.22	1.28	1.34	1.40	1.47	1.54	1.61	1.69	1.76	1.84	1.93	2.01	2.10	2.19	2.29
6	1.06	1.13	1.19	1.27	1.34	1.42	1.50	1.59	1.68	1.77	1.87	1.97	2.08	2.19	2.31	2.44	2.57	2.70
7	1.07	1.15	1.23	1.32	1.41	1.50	1.61	1.71	1.83	1.95	2.08	2.21	2.35	2.50	2.66	2.83	3.00	3.19
8	1.08	1.17	1.27	1.37	1.48	1.59	1.72	1.85	1.99	2.14	2.30	2.48	2.66	2.85	3.06	3.28	3.51	3.76
9	1.09	1.20	1.30	1.42	1.55	1.69	1.84	2.00	2.17	2.36	2.56	2.77	3.00	3.25	3.52	3.80	4.11	4.44
10	1.10	1.22	1.34	1.48	1.63	1.79	1.97	2.16	2.37	2.59	2.84	3.11	3.39	3.71	4.05	4.41	4.81	5.23
11	1.12	1.24	1.38	1.54	1.71	1.90	2.10	2.33	2.58	2.85	3.15	3.48	3.84	4.23	4.65	5.12	5.62	6.18
12	1.13	1.27	1.43	1.60	1.80	2.01	2.25	2.52	2.81	3.14	3.50	3.90	4.33	4.82	5.35	5.94	6.58	7.29
13	1.14	1.29	1.47	1.67	1.89	2.13	2.41	2.72	3.07	3.45	3.88	4.36	4.90	5.49	6.15	6.89	7.70	8.60
14	1.15	1.32	1.51	1.73	1.98	2.26	2.58	2.94	3.34	3.80	4.31	4.89	5.53	6.26	7.08	7.99	9.01	10.15
15	1.16	1.35	1.56	1.80	2.08	2.40	2.76	3.17	3.64	4.18	4.78	5.47	6.25	7.14	8.14	9.27	10.54	11.97
16	1.17	1.37	1.60	1.87	2.18	2.54	2.95	3.43	3.97	4.59	5.31	6.13	7.07	8.14	9.36	10.75	12.33	14.13
17	1.18	1.40	1.65	1.95	2.29	2.69	3.16	3.70	4.33	5.05	5.90	6.87	7.99	9.28	10.76	12.47	14.43	16.67
18	1.20	1.43	1.70	2.03	2.41	2.85	3.38	4.00	4.72	5.56	6.54	7.69	9.02	10.58	12.38	14.46	16.88	19.67
19	1.21	1.46	1.75	2.11	2.53	3.03	3.62	4.32	5.14	6.12	7.26	8.61	10.20	12.06	14.23	16.78	19.75	23.21
20	1.22	1.49	1.81	2.19	2.65	3.21	3.87	4.66	5.60	6.73	8.06	9.65	11.52	13.74	16.37	19.46	23.11	27.39
21	1.23	1.52	1.86	2.28	2.79	3.40	4.14	5.03	6.11	7.40	8.95	10.80	13.02	15.67	18.82	22.57	27.03	32.32
22	1.24	1.55	1.92	2.37	2.93	3.60	4.43	5.44	6.66	8.14	9.93	12.10	14.71	17.86	21.64	26.19	31.63	38.14
23	1.26	1.58	1.97	2.46	3.07	3.82	4.74	5.87	7.26	8.95	11.03	13.55	16.63	20.36	24.89	30.38	37.01	45.01
24	1.27	1.61	2.03	2.56	3.23	4.05	5.07	6.34	7.91	9.85	12.24	15.18	18.79	23.21	28.63	35.24	43.30	53.11
25	1.28	1.64	2.09	2.67	3.39	4.29	5.43	6.85	8.62	10.83	13.59	17.00	21.23	26.46	32.92	40.87	50.66	62.67
26	1.30	1.67	2.16	2.77	3.56	4.55	5.81	7.40	9.40	11.92	15.08	19.04	23.99	30.17	37.86	47.41	59.27	73.95
27	1.31	1.71	2.22	2.88	3.73	4.82	6.21	7.99	10.25	13.11	16.74	21.32	27.11	34.39	43.54	55.00	69.35	87.26
28	1.32	1.74	2.29	3.00	3.92	5.11	6.65	8.63	11.17	14.42	18.58	23.88	30.63	39.20	50.07	63.80	81.13	102.97
29	1.33	1.78	2.36	3.12	4.12	5.42	7.11	9.32	12.17	15.86	20.62	26.75	34.62	44.69	57.58	74.01	94.93	121.50
30	1.35	1.81	2.43	3.24	4.32	5.74	7.61	10.06	13.27	17.45	22.89	29.96	39.12	50.95	66.21	85.85	111.06	143.37
31	1.36	1.85	2.50	3.37	4.54	6.09	8.15	10.87	14.46	19.19	25.41	33.56	44.20	58.08	76.14	99.59	129.95	169.18
32	1.37	1.88	2.58	3.51	4.76	6.45	8.72	11.74	15.76	21.11	28.21	37.58	49.95	66.21	87.57	115.52	152.04	199.63
33	1.39	1.92	2.65	3.65	5.00	6.84	9.33	12.68	17.18	23.23	31.31	42.09	56.44	75.48	100.70	134.00	177.88	235.56
34	1.40	1.96	2.73	3.79	5.25	7.25	9.98	13.69	18.73	25.55	34.75	47.14	63.78	86.05	115.80	155.44	208.12	277.96
35	1.42	2.00	2.81	3.95	5.52	7.69	10.68	14.79	20.41	28.10	38.57	52.80	72.07	98.10	133.18	180.31	243.50	328.00
36	1.43	2.04	2.90	4.10	5.79	8.15	11.42	15.97	22.25	30.91	42.82	59.14	81.44	111.83	153.15	209.16	284.90	387.04
37	1.45	2.08	2.99	4.27	6.08	8.64	12.22	17.25	24.25	34.00	47.53	66.23	92.02	127.49	176.12	242.63	333.33	456.70
38	1.46	2.12	3.07	4.44	6.39	9.15	13.08	18.63	26.44	37.40	52.76	74.18	103.99	145.36	202.54	281.45	390.00	538.91
39	1.47	2.16	3.17	4.62	6.70	9.70	13.99	20.12	28.82	41.14	58.56	83.08	117.51	165.69	232.92	326.48	456.30	635.91
40	1.49	2.21	3.26	4.80	7.04	10.29	14.97	21.72	31.41	45.26	65.00	93.05	132.78	188.88	267.87	378.72	533.87	750.38

Appendix A.4

Future Value of $1 Invested at the End of Each Year at 1 to 18 Percent Interest

Period in years	1%	2%	3%	4%	5%	6%	7%	8%	9%
1	1.00	1.00	1.00	1.00	1.00	1.00	1.00	1.00	1.00
2	2.01	2.02	2.03	2.04	2.05	2.06	2.07	2.08	2.09
3	3.03	3.06	3.09	3.12	3.15	3.18	3.21	3.25	3.28
4	4.06	4.12	4.18	4.25	4.31	4.37	4.44	4.51	4.57
5	5.10	5.20	5.31	5.42	5.53	5.64	5.75	5.87	5.98
6	6.15	6.31	6.47	6.63	6.80	6.98	7.15	7.34	7.52
7	7.21	7.43	7.66	7.90	8.14	8.39	8.65	8.92	9.20
8	8.29	8.58	8.89	9.21	9.55	9.90	10.26	10.64	11.03
9	9.37	9.75	10.16	10.58	11.03	11.49	11.98	12.49	13.02
10	10.46	10.95	11.46	12.01	12.58	13.18	13.82	14.49	15.19
11	11.57	12.17	12.81	13.49	14.21	14.97	15.78	16.65	17.56
12	12.68	13.41	14.19	15.03	15.92	16.87	17.89	18.98	20.14
13	13.81	14.68	15.62	16.63	17.71	18.88	20.14	21.50	22.95
14	14.95	15.97	17.09	18.29	19.60	21.02	22.55	24.22	26.02
15	16.10	17.29	18.60	20.02	21.58	23.28	25.13	27.15	29.36
16	17.26	18.64	20.16	21.83	23.66	25.67	27.89	30.32	33.00
17	18.43	20.01	21.76	23.70	25.84	28.21	30.84	33.75	36.97
18	19.62	21.41	23.41	25.65	28.13	30.91	34.00	37.45	41.30
19	20.81	22.84	25.12	27.67	30.54	33.76	37.38	41.45	46.02
20	22.02	24.30	26.87	29.78	33.07	36.79	41.00	45.76	51.16
21	23.24	25.78	28.68	31.97	35.72	39.90	44.87	50.42	56.77
22	24.47	27.30	30.54	34.25	38.51	43.39	49.00	55.46	62.87
23	25.72	28.85	32.45	36.62	41.43	47.00	53.44	60.89	69.53
24	26.97	30.42	34.43	39.08	44.50	50.82	58.18	66.77	76.79
25	28.24	32.03	36.46	41.65	47.73	54.87	63.25	73.11	84.70
26	29.53	33.67	38.55	44.31	51.11	59.16	68.68	79.95	93.32
27	30.82	35.34	40.71	47.08	51.67	63.71	74.48	87.35	102.72
28	32.13	37.05	42.93	49.97	58.40	68.53	80.70	95.34	112.97
29	33.45	38.79	45.22	52.97	62.32	73.64	87.35	103.97	124.14
30	34.79	40.57	47.58	56.09	66.44	79.06	94.46	113.28	136.31
31	36.13	42.38	50.00	59.33	70.76	84.80	102.07	123.35	149.58
32	37.49	44.23	52.50	62.70	75.30	90.89	110.22	134.21	164.04
33	38.87	46.11	55.08	66.21	80.06	97.34	118.93	145.95	179.80
34	40.26	48.03	57.73	69.86	85.07	104.18	128.26	158.63	196.98
35	41.66	49.99	60.46	73.65	90.32	111.43	138.24	172.32	215.71
36	43.08	51.99	63.28	77.60	95.84	119.12	148.91	187.10	236.12
37	44.51	54.03	66.17	81.70	101.63	127.27	160.34	203.07	258.38
38	45.95	56.11	69.16	85.97	107.71	135.90	172.56	220.32	282.63
39	47.41	58.24	72.23	90.41	114.10	145.06	185.64	238.94	309.07
40	48.89	60.40	75.40	95.03	120.80	154.76	199.64	259.06	337.88

Period in years	Rate of Interest								
	10%	11%	12%	13%	14%	15%	16%	17%	18%
1	1.00	1.00	1.00	1.00	1.00	1.00	1.00	1.00	1.00
2	2.10	2.11	2.12	2.13	2.14	2.15	2.16	2.17	2.18
3	3.31	3.34	3.37	3.41	3.44	3.47	3.51	3.54	3.57
4	4.64	4.71	4.78	4.85	4.92	4.99	5.07	5.14	5.22
5	6.11	6.23	6.35	6.48	6.61	6.74	6.88	7.01	7.15
6	7.72	7.91	8.12	8.32	8.54	8.75	8.98	9.21	9.44
7	9.49	9.78	10.09	10.40	10.73	11.07	11.41	11.77	12.14
8	11.44	11.86	12.30	12.76	13.23	13.73	14.24	14.77	15.33
9	13.58	14.16	14.78	15.42	16.09	16.79	17.52	18.28	19.09
10	15.94	16.72	17.55	18.42	19.34	20.30	21.32	22.39	23.52
11	18.53	19.56	20.66	21.81	23.05	24.35	25.73	27.20	28.76
12	1.38	22.71	24.13	25.65	27.27	29.00	30.85	32.82	34.93
13	24.52	26.21	28.03	29.98	32.09	34.35	36.79	39.40	42.22
14	27.98	30.09	32.39	34.88	37.58	40.51	43.67	47.10	50.82
15	31.77	34.41	37.28	40.42	43.84	47.58	51.66	56.11	60.97
16	35.95	39.19	42.75	46.67	50.98	55.72	60.93	66.65	72.94
17	40.55	44.50	48.88	53.74	59.12	65.08	71.67	78.98	87.07
18	45.60	50.40	55.75	61.73	68.39	75.84	84.14	93.41	103.74
19	51.16	56.94	63.44	70.75	78.97	88.21	98.60	110.28	123.41
20	57.28	64.20	72.05	80.95	91.03	102.44	115.38	130.03	146.63
21	64.00	72.27	81.70	92.47	104.77	118.81	134.84	153.14	174.02
22	71.40	81.21	92.50	105.49	120.44	137.63	157.41	180.17	206.34
23	79.54	91.15	104.60	120.20	138.30	159.28	183.60	211.80	244.49
24	88.50	102.17	118.16	136.83	158.66	184.17	213.98	248.81	289.49
25	98.35	114.41	133.33	155.62	181.87	212.79	249.21	292.10	342.60
26	109.18	128.00	150.33	176.85	208.33	245.71	290.09	342.76	405.27
27	121.10	143.08	169.37	200.84	238.50	283.57	337.50	402.03	479.22
28	134.21	159.82	190.70	227.95	272.89	327.10	392.50	471.38	566.48
29	148.63	178.40	214.58	258.58	312.09	377.17	456.30	552.51	669.45
30	164.49	199.02	241.33	293.20	356.79	434.75	530.31	647.44	790.95
31	181.94	221.91	271.29	332.32	407.74	500.96	616.16	758.50	934.32
32	201.14	247.32	304.85	376.52	465.82	577.10	715.75	888.45	1103.50
33	222.25	275.53	342.43	426.46	532.04	664.67	831.27	1040.49	1303.13
34	245.48	306.84	384.52	482.90	607.52	765.37	965.27	1218.37	1538.69
35	271.02	341.59	431.66	546.68	693.57	881.17	1120.71	1426.49	1816.65
36	299.13	380.16	484.46	618.75	791.67	1014.35	1301.03	1669.99	2144.65
37	330.04	422.98	543.60	700.19	903.51	1167.50	1510.19	1954.89	2531.69
38	364.04	470.51	609.83	792.21	1031.00	1343.62	1752.82	2288.23	2988.39
39	401.45	523.27	684.01	896.20	1176.34	1546.17	2034.27	2678.22	3527.30
40	442.59	581.83	767.09	1013.70	1342.03	1779.09	2360.76	3134.52	4163.21

Appendix A.5

Recommended Readings

CHAPTER 1

Business Week:

"Testing the Cushion under Your Nest Egg," April 8, 1985, pp. 117–118.

Changing Times:

"Is Your Adviser As Sharp As You Think?" February 1987, pp. 37–42.

"Chart Your Course," January 1986, pp. 42–45.

"Computerized Financial Plans: How Good?" October 1985, pp. 47–53.

Consumer Reports:

"Financial Planners: What Are They Really Selling?" January 1986, pp. 37–44.

Money:

"Financial Planner," December 1986, pp. 196–200.

"How to Get Peerless Financial Advice," December 1986, pp. 192–194.

"How to Make Yourself Financially Secure," October 1983, pp. 66–69.

"How to Get Your Finances Together," October 1982, pp. 60–63.

"Seven Serious Mistakes with Your Money," November 1981, pp. 101–106.

Ms:

"Expert Advice: What a Financial Planner Can & Can't Do for You," October 1986, pp. 40–43.

The Wall Street Journal:

"Your Money Matters." This daily column covers a wide range of topics related to personal finance; it currently appears on the first page of the paper's second section.

Working Woman:

"Money: The Best Guides," June 1984, pp. 36–41.

Booklets:

Your Financial Plan and *Your Savings and Investment Dollar*, Money Management Institute, Household Financial Services, 2700 Sanders Road, Prospect Heights, Ill. 60070.

CHAPTER 2

Changing Times:

"Ready . . . Set . . . Go! Get Organized," January 1987, pp. 63–65.

"Figure Where You Stand," January 1985, pp. 32–38.

Consumer Reports:

"Where Does All of the Money Go?" September 1986, pp. 581–592.

Money:

"The Simple Science of Keeping Records," March 1987, pp. 197–204.

U.S. News & World Report:

"Sizing Up Your Finances," June 8, 1987, pp. 52–55.

"Let a Home Computer Handle Your Money?" November 11, 1985, p. 92.

CHAPTER 3

Changing Times:

"Make Your Pay Go All the Way," February 1986, p. 58.

"How to Manage All That Money," March 1981, pp. 29–33.

Consumer Reports:

"Where Does All the Money Go?" September 1986, pp. 581–592.

Money:

"Great Places to Put Your Rainy-Day Cash," March 1986, pp. 113–124.

"Creating a Budget," October 1983, pp. 71–76.

Booklets:

Your Financial Plan, Money Management Institute, Household Financial Services, 2700 Sanders Road, Prospect Heights, Ill. 60070.

CHAPTER 4

Changing Times:

"Banking 101," February 1986, p. 56.

"All-In-One Accounts," June 1986, pp. 35–37.

Consumer Reports:

"Credit Unions: Are They Better Than Banks?" February 1986, pp. 108–111.

"You and the Banks," September 1985, pp. 508–516.

"When Is It Your Money?" November 1984, pp. 648–649.

Money:

"How to Save on Checking," September 1985, pp. 83–88.

CHAPTER 5

Business Week:

"A Program That Speeds Your 1040," March 9, 1987, p. 122.

Consumer Reports:

"Your Taxes: Up or Down?" March 1987, pp. 164–171.

"Tax Audit: Improving Your Odds," March 1987, pp. 155–158.

The CPA Journal:

"Changes to Tax on Individuals—TRA 1986," December 1986, pp. 16–26.

Money:

"How to Avoid a Tax Audit," February 1987, pp. 119–126.

"Investments That Can Save You Taxes," February 1987, pp. 135–154.

"Top Tax Practitioners," December 1986, pp. 204–206.

The National Public Accountant:

"Making Your Way through the Tax Reform Maze," April 1987, pp. 33–38.

"Choosing Between Separate & Joint Filing," March 1987, pp. 34–36.

Sylvia Porter's Personal Finance:

"Preparing to Meet Your Tax-Preparer," February 1987, p. 40.

Booklets:

Your Federal Income Tax, Internal Revenue Service, Washington, D.C. This and other booklets that explain various tax issues can be obtained from your local IRS office or by calling their toll-free telephone number: 1 (800) 442-1040.

CHAPTER 6

Changing Times:

"What the Credit Bureau Is Saying about You," July 1983, pp. 56–59.

"The New Rules about Bankruptcy," May 1979, pp. 31–32.

"What Credit Counselors Do for People in Debt," March 1978, pp. 45–47.

Consumer Reports:

"What Makes a Good Credit Risk?" May 1983, pp. 254–259.

Money:

"Getting on Top of Your Debt," April 1987, pp. 95–108.

"How Lenders Size You Up," April 1987, pp. 145–154.

"A Fire Sale on Cash," September 1985, pp. 93–96.

"Sure Ways to Score with Lenders," September 1984, pp. 121–126.

U.S. News & World Report:

"Thinking of Your House as a Cash Cow," June 8, 1987, pp. 56–57.

"Turning Your House into a Credit Card," March 9, 1987, pp. 49–50.

"Wiping Clean the Slate of Debt," April 21, 1986, p. 58.

Working Woman:

"Haunted by Your Credit History?", October 1984, pp. 50–56.

Booklets:

Managing Your Credit, Money Management Institute, Household Financial Services, 2700 Sanders Road, Prospect Heights, Ill. 60070.

CHAPTER 7

Changing Times:

"Sizing Up Home-Equity Deals," February 1987, pp. 31–35.

"How to Find the Best Loans Now," February 1987, pp. 22–29.

"Credit Life Insurance: Oversold and Overpriced," March 1986, pp. 62–64.

Consumer Reports:

"The Hidden Power of Plastic," February 1987, pp. 119–122.

"Should You Hock Your Home?" November 1986, pp. 739–743.

"Credit Insurance: The Quiet Overcharge," July 1979, pp. 415–417.

Money:

"Domesticating the Home-Equity Loan," December 1986, pp. 129–136.

"Extracting Cash from Your House," April 1986, pp. 97–100.

"Puttin' On the Ritz," March 1986, pp. 185–190.

"The New Perils of Debt," December 1985, pp. 187–193.

CHAPTER 8

Business Week:

"Autos—Leasing vs. Buying: How the Numbers Add Up," March 9, 1987, pp. 120–121.

Changing Times:

"Car Values down the Road," February 1987, pp. 87–89.

"Things They Must Tell You When You Lease Something," March 1977, pp. 41–42.

Consumer Reports:

Annual Auto Issue. Entire April issue is devoted to purchasing and other automobile related topics.

Sylvia Porter's Personal Finance:

"Saving Money on Major Purchases," March 1987, pp. 65–68.

Books:

Complete Guide to Used Cars, Consumer Guide, Publications International, Ltd., Skokie, Ill.

Consumer Reports Books Guide to Appliances, Consumers Union, Mount Vernon, N.Y.

1987 Buying Guide Issue, Consumers Union, Mount Vernon, N.Y.

1987 Cars, Consumer Guide, Publications International, Ltd., Skokie, Ill.

1987 Consumer Buying Guide, Consumer Guide, Publications International, Ltd., Skokie, Ill.

Booklets:

Your Automobile Dollar and *Your Equipment Dollar*, Money Management Institute, Household Financial Services, 2700 Sanders Road, Prospect Heights, Ill. 60070.

198X Gas Mileage Guide. Contains fuel economy estimates along with size classifications for most current models. Published by the U.S. Department of Energy each year. Available from auto dealers or request a copy from: Fuel Economy, Consumer Information Center, Pueblo, Colo. 81009.

CHAPTER 9

Business Week:

"It Pays to Let a Pro Check Out That New House," April 27, 1987, p. 131.

Changing Times:

"Bargain for That House Like a Pro," May 1987, pp. 45–50.

"The New Bottom Line," January 1987, pp. 121–124.

"Protection You Get from a Home Inspection," July 1983, pp. 64–67.

"Legal Ways to Break That Lease," May 1983, pp. 52–54.

"Buying a Home Today: Is a Mobile Home for You?" May 1982, pp. 61–65.

"The Condo Option," April 1982, pp. 33–36.

Consumer Reports:

"Time to Refinance Your Mortgage?" October 1986, pp. 646–649.

"Should You Buy or Rent?" July 1981, pp. 393–397.

"What About a Condo or Co-Op?" July 1981, pp. 398–399.

Money:

"Starter Home: Your First Step Is the Biggest," June 1987, pp. 72–82.

"How to Get the Right Mortgage," July 1986, pp. 105–110.

"Buy a House That Needs Paint," April 1986, pp. 66–74.

"Honing in on Your Town's Hot Blocks," April 1986, pp. 60–62.

"Investing in Condominia," May 1981, pp. 59–62.

"Dealing and Wheeling in Mobile Homes," March 1980, pp. 54–56.

"Ins and Outs of Inspecting a House," July 1973, pp. 20–27.

Sylvia Porter's Personal Finance:

"Real Estate under Reform," February 1987, pp. 53–58.

Booklets:

Your Housing Dollar, Money Management Institute, Household Financial Services, 2700 Sanders Road, Prospect Heights, Ill. 60070.

CHAPTER 10

Changing Times:

"Is Your Coverage up to Date?" January 1985, pp. 57–60.

Money:

"Insurance Agent," December 1986, pp. 200–202.

"Weave Your Own Safety Net," November 1986, pp. 95–98.

"How to Save $500 a Year on Insurance," September 1986, pp. 85–92.

"Insuring against the Unkindest Cuts," October 1983, pp. 95–98.

CHAPTER 11
Consumers Digest:
"Protection or Investment?" September 1986, pp. 31–34.

Consumer Reports:
"Universal Life Insurance," August 1986, pp. 515–530.

"Whole Life Insurance," July 1986, pp. 447–470.

"How Much Life Insurance Do You Need?" June 1986, pp. 372–377.

"What Will Social Security Pay?" June 1986, pp. 377–378.

"Term Insurance: Why Plain Vanilla Is Best," June 1986, pp. 379–402.

Money:
"Your Life as a Tax Shelter," March 1987, pp. 153–165.

"It's Still Life Insurance, After All," March 1987, pp. 167–178.

"Those Wicked New Spins on the Old Sales Pitches," March 1987, pp. 191–194.

CHAPTER 12
Changing Times:
"Second Thoughts on HMOs," May 1987, pp. 33–38.

"What to Know Before You Go HMO," November 1984, pp. 59–62.

"Health Insurance When You're Not in a Group," March 1983, pp. 21–23.

"Disability Insurance: Are You Covered If You Can't Work?" April 1982, pp. 58–60.

"Insurance That Covers the Dentist Bills," May 1977, pp. 43–44.

Consumer Reports:
Disability Insurance," March 1983, pp. 122–126 and 154.

Money:
"When a Nursing Home Becomes Your Poorhouse," March 1986, pp. 175–182.

"Checking Your Medical Policy's Health," September 1982, pp. 72–74.

Ms.:
"Health Insurance: All You Need to Know . . ." May 1985, pp. 14–22.

Sylvia Porter's Personal Finance:
"The Changing Picture of Health," February 1987, pp. 46–52.

U.S. News & World Report:
"The Financial Agony of Long-Term Illness," February 9, 1987, pp. 53–55.

CHAPTER 13
Changing Times:
"Car Insurance: Cut the Cost of Your Coverage," May 1987, pp. 59–62.

"After the Smoke Clears," February 1987, pp. 65–70.

"How Forgiving Is Your Auto Insurance?" November 1984, pp. 42–44.

Consumer Reports:
"Homeowners Insurance," August 1985, pp. 473–482.

"Auto Insurance: How It Works," September 1984, pp. 501–505.

"Auto Insurance: Which Companies Are Best?" September 1984, pp. 506–510.

"Auto Insurance: What Ever Happened to No-Fault?" September 1984, pp. 511–513.

Money:
"A Precrash Course in No-Fault Insurance," June 1974, pp. 31–32.

Sylvia Porter's Personal Finance:
"To Claim or Not to Claim . . ." March 1987, pp. 87–92.

U.S. News & World Report:
"The Right Way to Cut Insurance Costs," September 1, 1986, pp. 53–54.

CHAPTER 14
Business Week:
December Issue. The December issue generally contains a series of articles on possible investments for the forthcoming year.

Changing Times:
"Taking the Plunge: How to Start Investing," April 1987, pp. 22–28.

"Will the Real Yield Please Stand Up," January 1987, pp. 125–132.

"Investment Formulas That Cut Your Risk," July 1983, pp. 35–37.

Financial World:
"Risk vs. Reward," January 20, 1987, pp. 118–119.

Money:

"New Strategies for a New Era," June 1986, pp. 56–60.

"Managing Your Portfolio Like a Pro," May 1986, pp. 152–156.

"The Only Economic Indicators You Need," January 1985, pp. 73–78.

"The Quest for Investment Safety," July 1984, pp. 46–53.

"Securites and Their Uses," September 1983, pp. 55–58.

"What to Do When It's Time to Invest," October 1982, pp. 82–86.

U.S. News & World Report:

"A Dozen Painless Ways to Help a Nest Egg Grow," June 8, 1987, pp. 58–60.

"Would You Panic If Your Stock Took a Dive?" June 8, 1987, pp. 60–61.

"The Global Money Game," May 11, 1987, pp. 49–57.

"Money: Making More & Keeping More," November 24, 1986, pp. 56–65.

"How to Make Your Money Grow," June 9, 1986, pp. 53–66.

Booklets:

Your Savings and Investment Dollar, Money Management Institute, Household Financial Services, 2700 Sanders Road, Prospect Heights, Ill. 60070.

CHAPTER 15

Business Week:

"In the CD Wars, the Customers Are Winning," June 8, 1987, p. 151.

Changing Times:

"A Saver's Guide to the New CDs," February 1984, p. 10.

"Savings Bonds Are a Better Deal Now," June 1983, pp. 55–57.

Consumer Reports:

"Money Market Investing: Bank or Funds?" September 1983, pp. 453–454.

Fortune:

"Municipal Bonds without the Hassle," May 14, 1984, pp. 196–198.

The Journal of Portfolio Management:

"Bonds versus Stocks: Another Look," Winter 1987, pp. 33–38.

The National Public Accountant:

"Buying U.S. Treasury Securities," January 1987, pp. 36–37.

Money:

"Lower Taxes Promise a Bond-anza for Income Investors," October 1986, pp. 149–160.

"Treasuries/Agencies," August 1983, pp. 58–59.

"Corporate Bonds," August 1983, pp. 60–62.

"Tax-Exempt Bonds," August, 1983, pp. 62–64.

CHAPTER 16

Business Week:

"It Can Pay to Buy Stock a Bit at a Time," May 18, 1987, pp. 156–157.

"Reading between the Lines of an Annual Report," March 23, 1987, pp. 164–165.

"What a Discount Broker Can Do for You," August 29, 1983, pp. 77–78.

Changing Times:

"How to Say No (or Yes) to Your Broker," March 1987, pp. 77–81.

"Cheap Ways to Buy More Stock," January 1986, pp. 81–84.

"Stock Market Basics for Beginners," June 1981, pp. 41–46.

Consumers Research:

"How to Invest in the Stock Market," May 1986, pp. 15–19.

Money:

"The Right Time to Sell Your Stocks," February 1986, pp. 123–128.

"The Perils of Margin Investing," February 1986, pp. 141–146.

"Stock Analysis Checklist," September 1983, p. 69.

"Finding a Broker to Suit Your Taste," September 1983, pp. 72–74.

CHAPTER 17

Business Week:

"Getting the Most from Mutual Funds," February 23, 1987, pp. 64–67.

Late February Issue. This issue typically contains a detailed listing of performance data on mutual funds.

"Picking an Equity Mutual Fund," August 15, 1983, pp. 120–122.

Changing Times:

"Annuities: Shelters' Last Stand," June 1987, pp. 80–86.

"A Plan for All Seasons," April 1987, pp. 31–32.

"How to Figure Your Real Return," April 1987, pp. 69–70.

"Meeting the Demand of the Financial Future: The Growing Role of Mutual Funds," November 1986, pp. 57–64.

"Find a Fund to Match Your Goals," September 1986, pp. 63–67.

"Should You Still Be in a Money Market Fund?" January 1983, pp. 47–52.

Consumers Digest:

"Mastering Mutual Funds," September 1986, pp. 27–30.

Consumer Reports:

"A Guide to Mutual Funds," July 1985, pp. 390–397.

"Bond Funds," October 1984, pp. 593–597.

"How to Judge Money Market Funds," January 1983, pp. 30–34.

Forbes:

Late August or Early September Issue. This issue is devoted to a series of articles on mutual funds and other investments.

Money:

"Best Way to Buy Foreign Stocks," May 1987, pp. 75–86.

"At Last a Way to Compare Loads and Fees," May 1987, p. 37.

"Braving the Bold New World of Income Funds," May 1986, pp. 93–108.

"Figuring Your Own Fund's Performance," May 1986, p. 113.

"When a Load Becomes a Burden," July 1985, pp. 135–138.

"Keeping It Simple with Mutual Funds," December 1984, pp. 71–74.

"Moving Around in the Best of Families," April 1983, pp. 62–72.

U.S. News & World Report:

"Choosing a Fund: A Survival Guide for Small Investors," February 16, 1987, pp. 56–58.

Booklets:

Investors Guide and Mutual Fund Directory. Published by the No Load Mutual Fund Association; a copy can be purchased from the Association's headquarters at 11 Penn Plaza, Suite 2204, New York, N.Y. 10001.

CHAPTER 18

Changing Times:

"Make Your Payout Pay Off," April 1987, pp. 51–55.

"Nurture Your Nest Egg," January 1985, pp. 68–72.

"Your Pension Plan; Will It Be There When You Need It," May 1983, pp. 26–30.

"Know the Pension Plan Before You Start the Job," January 1981, pp. 47–50.

Consumer Reports:

"Your IRA: Still a Good Deal?" January 1987, pp. 12–15.

"Will You Ever Collect a Pension," March 1982, pp. 124–130.

The CPA Journal:

"Retirement Plan Alternatives," July 1986, pp. 48–59.

Money:

"The IRA Lives! New Moves for a New Era," March 1987, pp. 58–64.

"Your Benefits May Never Be the Same," March 1987, pp. 87–100.

"Add Up the Assets You Can Rely On," November 1986, pp. 76–77.

"Invest to Build Wealth You Can Live On," November 1986, pp. 81–84.

"Size Up Any Retirement Offer," November 1986, pp. 88–92.

"Company Benefits Reel from the Zeal of Reform," October 1986, pp. 109–116.

"The Compelling Case for Keoghs," December 1985, pp. 171–180.

"Making Hay with Your 401(k)," January 1985, pp. 103–108.

"How Safe Is Your Pension?" July 1982, pp. 105–110.

The National Public Accountant:

"What's Happened to the IRA?" April 1987, pp. 22–25.

U.S. News & World Report:

"Want to Quit Early? It'll Take a Bundle," June 8, 1987, pp. 63–64.

"Does an IRA Still Make Sense?" October 27, 1986, p. 49.

CHAPTER 19

Business Week:

"Protect Your Beneficiaries with 'Post Mortem' Tax Planning," May 16, 1983, pp. 127–128.

"Estate Tax Law Is Changing Again," May 7, 1984, pp. 156–160.

Changing Times:

"Take Care of Your Heirs," September 1986, pp. 32–38.

"A Will Isn't the Only Way," January 1985, pp. 73–77.

"Beating the High Cost of Probating a Will," May 1981, pp. 45–48.

"Pluses and Minuses of Joint Ownership," October 1979, pp. 15–18.

Consumer Reports:

"Yours, Mine, and Ours," January 1986, pp. 48–50.

"What You Should Know about Wills," July 1980, pp. 434–439.

Money:

"How to Keep It All in the Family," December 1985, pp. 46–51.

"How to Avoid Estate Taxes," December 1985, pp. 60–66.

"If There's a Will, There's a Way," December 1985, pp. 70–74.

"How to Be an Executor without Coming to Grief," September 1982, pp. 104–110.

"No Way without a Will," August 1981, pp. 94–100.

U.S. News & World Report:

"Smart Ways to Plan Your Estate," June 2, 1986, pp. 46–47.

"ABC's of Making a Will," May 7, 1984, pp. 67–70.

Index